SELLING

Building Partnerships

SELLING

Building Partnerships

Stephen B. Castleberry
University of Minnesota Duluth

John F. Tanner, Jr.
Baylor University

8

McGraw-Hill Irwin

McGraw-Hill
Irwin

SELLING: BUILDING PARTNERSHIPS
Published by McGraw-Hill/Irwin, a business unit of The McGraw-Hill Companies, Inc., 1221
Avenue of the Americas, New York, NY, 10020. Copyright © 2011, 2009, 2007, 2004, 2001,
1998, 1995, 1992 by The McGraw-Hill Companies, Inc. All rights reserved. No part of this
publication may be reproduced or distributed in any form or by any means, or stored in a
database or retrieval system, without the prior written consent of The McGraw-Hill Companies,
Inc., including, but not limited to, in any network or other electronic storage or transmission, or
broadcast for distance learning.

Some ancillaries, including electronic and print components, may not be available to customers
outside the United States.

This book is printed on acid-free paper.

1 2 3 4 5 6 7 8 9 0 QDB/QDB 1 0 9 8 7 6 5 4 3 2 1 0

ISBN   978-0-07-353001-7
MHID   0-07-353001-8

Vice president and editor-in-chief: *Brent Gordon*
Publisher: *Paul Ducham*
Managing development editor: *Laura Hurst Spell*
Director of development: *Ann Torbert*
Editorial coordinator: *Jonathan Thornton*
Vice president and director of marketing: *Robin J. Zwettler*
Associate marketing manager: *Jaime Halteman*
Vice president of editing, design, and production: *Sesha Bolisetty*
Managing editor: *Lori Koetters*
Senior buyer: *Michael R. McCormick*
Design coordinator: *Joanne Mennemeier*
Senior photo research coordinator: *Jeremy Cheshareck*
Photo researcher: *Ira C. Roberts*
Senior media project manager : *Susan Lombardi*
Media project manager: *Suresh Babu, Hurix Systems Pvt. Ltd.*
Cover design: *Joanne Mennemeier*
Cover image: © *Rob Melnychuk/Getty Images*
Typeface: *10/12 Sabon*
Compositor: *Laserwords Private Limited*
Printer: *Quad/Graphics*

Library of Congress Cataloging-in-Publication Data
Castleberry, Stephen Bryon.
  Selling : building partnerships/Stephen B. Castleberry, John F. Tanner, Jr.—8th ed.
    p. cm.
  Includes index.
  ISBN-13: 978-0-07-353001-7 (alk. paper)
  ISBN-10: 0-07-353001-8 (alk. paper)
  1. Selling. I. Tanner, John F. II. Title.
  HF5438.25.W2933 2011
  658.85—dc22

                                      2010025662

www.mhhe.com

To Susie—you're still my best friend, my trusted confidant, and my partner in all things. And to my Creator, Redeemer, and Friend, without whom I would be nothing.

—Steve Castleberry

To Karen—you make all the hard work worthwhile.

—Jeff Tanner

PREFACE

To start the preface of the last edition, we wrote, "The selling profession is at a critical time. For that past two years, Manpower, the placement agency, has reported that sales is the most difficult job to fill. Never in our 20 years of teaching sales have we seen the demand for professional salespeople to be so great, which presents you with a great opportunity. You have an opportunity to participate in a period of rapid change for the sales profession as you prepare young people for a career." Then the economic tsunami hit, and things changed rapidly. You know that even good salespeople were affected by the economic tsunami of 2008 and 2009. But some aspects haven't changed. Finding good salespeople is still difficult for most companies. And our sales students are still in high demand. At the same time, more college-educated sales professionals are now in the field than ever before, and they demand excellence from our students. Salespeople are being asked to do more because they are a critical element in the value chain. Partnering skills, internal and external, are more important than they've ever been.

As a result, we've remained faithful to the premises that caused us to write the first edition almost 20 years ago:

- Partnering skills are critical skills for all businesspeople.
- Adaptive communication skills—probing, listening, and presentation—are important in all areas of life, but especially for salespeople.
- Students need to practice these skills through role playing.
- Helping people make the right decisions is not only the most ethical sales strategy but also the most effective strategy for long-term success.

At the same time, we've recognized that several factors are changing the face of selling:

- Increased use of multichannel go-to-market strategies, including inside sales.
- Changing roles for both technology and salespeople.

- Rapid economic change and the impact of the recession.
- Changing trends in how organizations buy—specifically continue increased use of technology, self-service, and supplier relationship management.

As we've revised the text, faithful adopters will see that we've held to the principles that made this book unique when it was launched and kept it in a leadership position. While others may have tried to copy role playing, partnering, or technology, none have truly captured the essence that makes this book the leading text.

WHAT'S NEW IN THE EIGHTH EDITION

- **"Selling Yourself"**—a new feature at the end of each chapter that relates the material in the chapter to the student's life *right now*. It's more than just the student's job search process, however. Selling Yourself helps students see the connections among the chapter material and all aspects of their lives, such as how a student can sell an organization to new members, how to work with apartment managers to resolve issues, how to improve interactions with friends and family members, how to add value as a group member in a class team project, and so forth.
- **Original examples** written specifically for this book, provided by current sales programs and salespeople, many of whom took the class and used this book.
- New chapter-opening **profiles**—all chapters open with a real salesperson or sales manager's perspective on the chapter. Each profile is new and original to this edition, and we've also integrated the profiles into each chapter as a running example to increase this feature's functionality.
- All new **"Building Partnerships"**—boxed features that provide more detailed examples of chapter material and present chapter material in a slightly different light.

- New **"Sales Technology"**—boxed features in each chapter, many new to this edition, that illustrate how technology is used. The result is a much better understanding of what professionals are calling Sales 2.0 or Sales in the Cloud (cloud computing). You'll find many types of technology, including knowledge management technology, CRM technology, and even GPS technology used in routing sales calls.

- All new **"From the Buyer's Seat"**—this feature was introduced in the last edition, and the feedback was overwhelmingly positive. Buyers, though, are no more stationary than salespeople, so we've created all new features for this edition, integrating the best of the last edition into the text.

- **Feature questions**—embedded in the end-of-chapter material are discussion questions that direct students back to the profiles, "Building Partnerships," "From the Buyer's Seat," and "Sales Technology" features so these features are read and used more fully.

- New **NetSuite role plays**—we've written a new set of role plays featuring NetSuite, the software used in the National Collegiate Sales Competition. NetSuite is a hosted application, and its Web site has role-based demonstrations so students can learn what the product does for different people in the sales organization. At the end of most chapters you will find a role play using NetSuite, and additionally there are 10 prospect scenarios (with two buyer information sheets each in the Instructor's Manual) at the end of the book.

IMPORTANT FEATURES OF SELLING: BUILDING PARTNERSHIPS

The importance of partnering to business and partnering skills to students has changed the way sales is done and taught. Moreover, partnering changes the way buyers buy. Several unique features place this book at the cutting edge of sales technology and partnering research:

1. A continued emphasis on the partnering process, with recognition that multiple sales models may be appropriate in a company's total go-to-market strategy. We focus on the partnering process as the highest level of selling because the other models of transaction—focus, problem solver, and relational partner—still need to be learned as a foundation to partnering.

2. A thorough description of the partnering and buying processes used by business firms and the changes occurring in these processes. A number of important

trends affecting buyers, such as supplier relationship management (SRM), also affect sellers.

3. A discussion of methods of internal and external partnering so that the supply chain delivers the right value, in recognition of the salesperson's role in relationship management and value creation. This emphasis also broadens the applicability of the course for students who may not be interested in a sales career.

4. An emphasis throughout the text on the need for salespeople to be flexible—to adapt their strategies to customer needs, buyer social styles, and relationship needs and strategies.

5. A complete discussion of how effective selling and career growth are achieved through planning and continual learning.

6. An emphasis on the growing need for salespeople in organizations to carry the voice of the customer to all parts of the organization and beyond to suppliers and facilitators. This role is reflected in new product development, supply chain management, and many other functions in a customer-centric organization.

These unique content emphases are presented in a highly readable format, supported by the following:

- **Ethics questions**—at least two questions at the end of each chapter relate the chapter material to ethics.

- **Four-color exhibits and photographs** to support the examples highlighted in the book. Students find this book to be easy to read and use.

- **"Thinking It Through"**—these features embed discussion questions into the text itself; for this edition, we've also offered teaching suggestions to integrate this feature more fully. There are several of these features in each chapter.

- **Minicases**—two small cases are available at the end of each chapter. These are useful for in-class exercises or discussion or as homework.

- **Ethics icon**—because we've emphasized ethical partnering since the inception of this book, we highlight the integration of ethics by noting any ethics discussion with an icon in the margin. You'll find ethics discussed in every chapter.

- **Key terms**—each key term defined in a chapter is listed at the end of the chapter, along with the page number on which the term is discussed. Key terms reflect current usage of sales jargon in the field, as well as academic terms.

- **Glossary**—key terms are also defined in a glossary at the end of the book.

FOR FACULTY

- Instructor's manuals are available with any text, but the quality often varies. Because we teach the course to undergraduates, as well as presenting and participating in sales seminars in industry, we believe that we have created an Instructor's Manual (available at the Online Learning Center, www.mhhe.com/castleberry8e) that can significantly assist the teacher. We've also asked instructors what they would like to see in a manual. In addition to suggested course outlines, chapter outlines, lecture suggestions, and answers to questions and cases, we include helpful suggestions for how to use the video segments. On that site, you'll also find the slides, which are integrated into our teaching notes.

- **Slides** are available in PowerPoint, but given feedback from users (and our own experience), we've simplified their presentation. They are easily adapted to your own needs, and you can add material as you see fit.

- **NEW video clips** are on the Instructor's DVD. Several companies have graciously offered video segments, plus we've recorded and produced our own in conjunction with companies. As we continue to get new segments, adopters will find these available from our Web site (www.sellingbuildingpartnerships.com) so you can either download them or simply access the Web site during class if your classroom is Web-enabled. Use these videos to illustrate individual techniques of selling quickly and easily.

- We also include many of the **in-class exercises** we have developed over the years. These have been subjected to student critique, and we are confident you will find them useful. You will also find a number of **additional role play scenarios.**

- Students need to practice their selling skills in a selling environment, and they need to do it in a way that is helpful. **Small group practice exercises, including role playing,** complete with instructions for student evaluations, are provided in the Instructor's Manual. These sessions can be held as part of class but are also designed for out-of-class time for teachers who want to save class time for full-length role plays.

- The **Test Bank** has been carefully and completely rewritten. Questions are directly tied to the learning goals presented at the beginning of each chapter and the material covered in the questions and problems. In addition, key terms are covered in the test questions. Application questions are available so students can demonstrate their understanding of the key concepts by applying those selling principles.

- The **Web site,** www.sellingbuildingpartnerships.com, is your Web site. This Web site is a place for faculty to share materials, as well as a place where it is easy for us to quickly bring you up-to-date materials. Here you will find short slide decks (three to five slides) about current sales and sales management research that is template-free so you can integrate it into existing presentations as you see fit. You will also find new videos, presentation slide decks from other faculty and sales professionals, job announcements for students, and other materials designed to support your teaching. Short cases from previous editions are also posted there if you would like to include these as essay questions on exams or in-class exercises. We hope you will also contribute to the site. Instructor materials are password-protected so students do not have access to them.

- **New chapters**—at www.sellingbuildingpartnerships.com you'll find several new chapters that students can access, such as Writing Proposals, Account Management, and others. We use these chapters ourselves in advanced selling classes, but you may find these necessary in your introductory sales course or in a sales management course. Students can access and download these chapters at no cost.

PARTNERING: FROM THE FIELD TO THE CLASSROOM

Faculty who use our book have reviewed it and offered suggestions, and we have taken their comments seriously. What is different is that sales executives and field salespeople who are locked in the daily struggle of adapting to the new realities of selling also reviewed *Selling: Building Partnerships*. They have told us what the field is like now, where it is going, and what students must do to be prepared for the challenges that will face them.

Students have also reviewed chapters. They are, after all, the ones who must learn from the book. We asked for their input prior to and during the revision process. And judging by their comments and suggestions, this book is effectively delivering the content. There are, however, several places where their comments have enabled us to clarify material and improve on its presentation.

As you can see in "About the Authors," we have spent considerable time in the field in a variety of sales positions. We continue to spend time in the field engaging in personal selling ourselves, as well as observing and serving professional salespeople. We believe the book has benefited greatly because of such a never-ending development process.

Acknowledgments

Staying current with the rapidly changing field of professional selling is a challenge. Our work has been blessed with the excellent support of reviewers, users, editors, salespeople, and students. Reviewers include the following:

Jim Boles, Georgia State University
Leff Bonney, Florida State University
Brad Cox, Midlands Technical College
Edward Friz, Middle Tennessee State University
Dana Hale, Georgia Southern University
Doug Hughes, Michigan State University
Tará Lopez, Southeastern Louisiana University
Christine Seiler, Bowling Green State University
Karl Sooder, University of Central Florida

Readers will become familiar with many of the salespeople who contributed to the development of the eighth edition through various selling scenarios or profiles. But other salespeople, sales executives, buyers, and sales professors contributed in less obvious, but no less important, ways. For providing video material, reviewing chapters, updating cases, providing material for selling scenarios, and other support, we'd like to thank the following:

Sean Anderson, Grainger
Matt Arneson, Buildings Xchange
Ronald N. Borrieci, COB Embry-Riddle Aeronautical University
Ken Bluedorn, Lake Superior Bottle Shop
Ashley Braine, Dell
Tracey Brill, Abbott Labs
Becky Burton, Automation Xchange
Heather Carr, Career Professionals
Caitlin Christoff, Process Technology Xchange
Susan Denny, Cisco
Dr. Greg DiNovis, College of St. Catherine
Mike Donley, Opus Medical
Professor Susan Emens, Kent State University
Chris Evers, Swisher International
Gina Garuso, Meat Processing Xchange
Graham Gedmestad, Automation Xchange
Tom Gottschald, Team Goodyear Tire and Gemini Service Center
Amanda Gonzales, NetworkIP
Matt Haberle, Maximum Impact
Scott Hanna, University of Minnesota Duluth
Dr. David Henard, North Carolina State University
Barbara Kellgren, Lutron Electronics
Michael Krause, Sales Sense Solutions, Inc.

Danielle Lord, U.S. Foodservice
Jeff Lynn, Hartford Insurance Group
Angie Main, Midwest Communications
Dave Moore, ADP
Eddy Patterson, Stubb's Bar-B-Q
Terry Perrella, Sammy's United
Dr. Jim Prost, University of San Francisco
Neil Rackham, Huthwaite, Inc.
Jen Rennelt, Career Professionals
Dr. Rick Ridnour, Northern Illinois University
Leif Ringstad, Samsung Telecommunications
Layne Skoyen, Process Technology Xchange
Professor Karl Sooder, University of Central Florida
Chad Stinchfield, Hospira
Dr. Jeff Strieter, State University of New York College–Brockport
Dan Termunde, Hilti
Mike Thomas, Jersey City
Dr. Brian Tietje, California Polytechnic State University
Michael Wendinger, University of Minnesota Duluth
Dr. Vicki West, Texas State University
Kristy Wilke, Buildings Xchange

In addition to the support of these individuals, many companies also provided us with material. We'd like to express our sincere gratitude for their support.

The McGraw-Hill team, as is the usual, was wonderful to work with. Laura Spell is our sponsoring editor, and we're happy to welcome her to the project. Jonathan Thornton is our editorial coordinator and is blessedly dogged in staying on top of things. Jaime Halteman is our intrepid marketing manager and started working with us on the previous edition—we look forward to more innovations such as the webinars and other activities. We're glad to have Lori Koetters as our capable and easy-to-work-with project manager, and Michael McCormick served as production supervisor. We really like the design of this and the previous edition—thanks to Joanne Mennemeier's contribution as designer. Jeremy Cheshareck was another one who is both capable and easy to work with. Suresh Babu is the media project manager, and we hope to lean on his talents to continue to provide you with excellent media resources.

Several people assisted in research and manuscript preparation, and we gratefully appreciate their help: Jeannie Castleberry and W.T. Tanner. Students who made helpful comments and reviewed for us include Joanna Browne and John R. Tanner. Many other students and teachers have made comments that have helped us strengthen the overall package. They deserve our thanks, as do others who prefer to remain anonymous.

—Steve Castleberry

—Jeff Tanner

ABOUT THE AUTHORS

STEPHEN B. CASTLEBERRY

Dr. Castleberry received his PhD from the University of Alabama in 1983. He taught at the University of Georgia for six years and for three years was UARCO Professor of Sales and Marketing at Northern Illinois University. Currently he is a professor of marketing at the University of Minnesota Duluth. He has received seven awards for teaching excellence, including the highest recognition by the University of Minnesota system of its most distinguished scholar teachers. His commitment to teaching has resulted in a number of cases, as well as articles in the *Journal of Marketing Education, Business Case Journal,* and *Marketing Education Review,* that describe his teaching style and methods.

Dr. Castleberry's research has been published in many journals, including the *Journal of Personal Selling and Sales Management, Industrial Marketing Management, Journal of Selling and Major Account Management, Journal of Business and Industrial Marketing, Journal of Business to Business Marketing, Journal of Marketing Management, Journal of Consumer Marketing, Journal of Business Research, Journal of the Academy of Marketing Science,* and *International Journal of Research in Marketing.* He has also presented his work at the National Conference in Sales Management, as well as other national and regional conferences. He is past marketing editor of the *Journal of Applied Business Research* and serves on several journal editorial boards. He has received research grants and support from entities such as the London Business School, Gillette, Quaker Oats, Kimberly Clark, Proctor & Gamble, Coca-Cola Foods Division, and the Alexander Group/JPSSM.

Dr. Castleberry appeared as an academic expert in eight segments of *The Sales Connection,* a 26-segment video production shown on national PBS TV stations. He also appeared as the special guest on several broadcasts of *Sales Talk,* a nationally broadcast call-in talk show on the Business Radio Network.

Dr. Castleberry has held various sales assignments with Burroughs Corporation (now Unisys), Nabisco, and G.C. Murphy's and has worked as a consultant and sales trainer for numerous firms and groups. His interests outside academic life include outdoor activities (canoeing, hiking, bicycling, snowshoeing, skiing, and so on) and everything related to living on his 100-acre farm in northern Wisconsin. He is an elder in his church and a volunteer firefighter and first responder in the small township he lives in. He and his wife currently own and operate a publishing company, marketing and distributing popular press books internationally.

Stephen B. Castleberry

scastleb@d.umn.edu
www.d.umn.edu/~scastleb

JOHN F. TANNER, JR.

Dr. Tanner is the research director of Baylor University's Center for Professional Selling and associate dean of research and faculty development. He earned his PhD from the University of Georgia. Prior to entering academia, Dr. Tanner spent eight years in industry with Rockwell International and Xerox Corporation as both salesperson and marketing manager.

Dr. Tanner has received several awards for teaching effectiveness and research. His sales teaching efforts have been recognized by student organizations, *Sales & Marketing Management,* and the *Dallas Morning News.* Dr. Tanner has authored or coauthored 13 books, including *Business Marketing: Connecting Strategy, Relationships, and Learning* with Bob Dwyer, and *The Hard Truth about Soft Selling* with George Dudley.

Research grants from the Center for Exhibition Industry Research, the Institute for the Study of Business Markets, the University Research Council, the Texas Department of

Health, and others have supported his research efforts. Dr. Tanner has published over 65 articles in the *Journal of Marketing, Journal of Business Research, Journal of Personal Selling and Sales Management*, international journals, and others. He serves on the review boards of several journals, including *Marketing Education Review, Journal of Personal Selling and Sales Management*, and *Industrial Marketing Management*.

Dr. Tanner writes a weekly blog, TannerismsonTuesday, about sales and sales management topics. An internationally recognized speaker and author on issues regarding customer relationships, Dr. Tanner has presented seminars at international conventions of several trade organizations, including the International Exhibitor's Association and the Canadian Association of Exposition Managers. Since 2006 he has taught executive and graduate programs in India, Australia, Trinidad, Colombia, Canada, France, the United Kingdom, and Mexico, primarily as part of the CRM at the Speed of Light executive certification program.

Jeff_Tanner@BAYLOR.EDU
hsb.baylor.edu/html/tanner

Walkthrough

Selling: Building Partnerships was the first text to bring a partnership/relationship approach into the selling course, offering a solid framework on which to hang plenty of practice and real-world application. The eighth edition of this popular text builds on that foundation with updated content, improved hands-on exercises, and powerful technology that's sure to make the material more engaging for professors and students alike.

The **chapter opening profiles** in this edition are the product of strong selling partnerships. Faculty from around the country introduced Steve Castleberry and Jeff Tanner to their former students who had gone on to careers in sales. The results are exciting new profiles from sales professionals who were students with an earlier edition and understand the philosophy of this book. Students can easily relate to these young professionals who have benefited from wonderful faculty and *Selling: Building Partnerships.*

PROFILE

"Buyers will object when they think you are DUMB, which means that the salesperson Doesn't Understand My Business."

Rachel Gober

PROFILE My name is Rachel Gober, and I graduated from Texas State University in December 2008 with a bachelor's degree in marketing. I was honored to participate at the National Collegiate Sales Competition in 2007, where our sales team was privileged to be led by the one and only Mrs. Vicki West.

The National Collegiate Sales Competition is actually where I was recruited by Standard Register, a company that specializes in document management systems and services for the health care, industrial manufacturing, financial services, government, retail, and transportation industries.

During my experience here so far, I have found three keys to helpfully respond to objections: (1) anticipate objections and prepare your response, (2) reduce objections from the beginning by helping the buyer to trust you, and (3) ask questions and listen to the answers.

In sales, you are going to get objections from prospects at every stage in the sales cycle, so you might as well be ready for them. When I first started making cold calls, I had a list of typical objections that our reps hear, and wrote out responses to each of them. I kept this sheet in front of me every day when I was on the phone until I felt comfortable with them. It may sound corny, but some buyers use objections just to make you nervous or to get you off the phone or out of their office, so it is better to be prepared than to be left stuttering and mumbling. For example, this is typical: Prospect's objection: "What are you trying to sell me?" My response: "At this point I'm not trying to sell anything. I don't know enough about your current process to recommend a solution, so right now I would just like to set an appointment with you to learn more about it."

Once I set the appointment, I try to find ways to help the buyer trust me. This often reduces objections. For example, buyers will object when they think you are DUMB, which means that the salesperson Doesn't Understand My Business. Many times, at my initial meetings with prospects, I will explain to them the DUMB acronym, and ask them questions about their business so they know I am not trying to sell them something; rather I am trying to learn more about them so that I can put together a custom solution that best fits their needs.

It is important to let buyers know that you are on their side, and you understand where they are coming from. For example, a common objection is "We are happy the way we are currently doing things." By asking simple questions like "How's that working for you?" or "That's great, I'm glad you have a system that works for you, but what could make it better?" you will typically uncover areas for improvement that your product or service might be able to help with.

I think of objections as an opportunity to build relationships with my customers, gain knowledge about their business, and learn how to sell to them.

Visit our Web site at www.standardregister.com.

Professional sales **ethics** have always been the hallmark of this text, and the new edition integrates ethics throughout each chapter, as well as in discussion questions devoted to this topic. Each chapter has separate ethics discussion questions, some of which were suggested by former students' experiences or current events.

If you want to sell a part such as a belt for a John Deere harvester made in Ottumwa, Iowa, then you must be able to sell and service this plant in Arc-les-Gray, France, too.

manuf
that gl
plexity
key fa

DERIV

Salesp
vidual
require
ers. Sa
rather
chases
deman
sumers
for tou
by San
screen:

HOV

Current and continued emphasis on selling examples from Canada, Mexico, and all around the globe reflects the reality of the global nature of selling.

Many technologies, including the sales cloud (or Sales 2.0 technology), PDAs, GPS, the Internet, and CRM software, have changed how salespeople operate. The eighth edition includes all new illustrations with its feature **"Sales Technology,"** which discusses how selling and technology interact within the context of each chapter.

"Thinking It Through" boxes (two per chapter) are engaging exercises that can inspire classroom dialogue or serve as a short-essay exam question to help students experience concepts as they read.

thinking **it** through

Review the stages in the decision-making process described earlier in the chapter. Do you go through those stages when making an important purchase? How does the Internet affect the way you buy products and services? What effect does it have on each stage of the process?

"From the Buyer's Seat" is an all-new original feature that provides students with a buyer's inside perspective. **"Building Partnerships"** boxes examine how successful salespeople build relationships. All are original to the book—many using examples provided by former students and other sales professionals.

From the BUYER'S SEAT

4.1

KEEP OPEN LINES OF COMMUNICATION, PLEASE

By James Hill, Cliffs

I'm a senior buyer for Cliffs, a large U.S. mining company. Some of my salespeople are truly outstanding, and I enjoy doing business with them. For example, I buy $4.5 million worth of motors each year. I partner with my motor suppliers, and they are excellent at communicating with me and keeping me informed.

I also need to know "good news" as well. One of my suppliers from Japan was shipping in several large motors, each of which weighed over four tons. Well, the supplier shipped them earlier than he had informed me. They arrived early, and I didn't have a crane available to unload them. Communicating with me that they were shipping early could have avoided many headaches when the trucks arrived!

BUILDING Partnerships

3.1

DEVELOPING A DIVERSE SUPPLIER BASE

For many years, increasing supplier diversity has been an objective for businesses. According to Sherri Macko, manager of supplier diversity at American Airlines, her company believes that success comes from diversity. "The value in supplier diversity lies in the way these suppliers sometimes offer a different approach to meeting our needs and their flexibility to do whatever it takes to get the job done," she says.

Diversity in purchasing means buying from vendors owned by minorities, women, and disabled veterans.

commitment to supplier diversity has been unwavering, through all economic climates, because it's built on tangible economic benefits."

Companies that seek greater diversity in their supplier base must work at it. Since most minority-, veteran-, disabled-, or women-owned businesses are small, they often need help simply finding the opportunities. That's why Delta Airlines recently launched a new Web site specifically for helping these smaller companies find opportunities to sell to Delta.

CASE PROBLEMS

CASE PROBLEMS

case **1.1**

Tropical
Landscaping, Inc.

Jenna Jones has been the owner and general manager of Tropical Landscaping for the last five years, having bought the business from the entrepreneur and landscape architect who started it 25 years earlier. Tropical is a full-service lawn care company that caters to the business sector, not the consumer sector. They are experts in designing, irrigation, and maintenance of landscapes and have a strong reputation for fast, efficient, and reasonably priced services.

When Jenna purchased the company there were three full-time salespeople who called on businesses in the region. One quit right after she arrived, and Floyd, a knowledgeable landscaper with good connections in the business community, was hired as a replacement. Floyd has been a real asset to the firm, building business in the commercial landscape design area.

Jenna thought everything was going smoothly until yesterday, when Chad, another salesperson, dropped a bombshell. He turned in his notice. Chad indicated he was going to work for a local competitor who was paying him about 25 percent more than Jenna.

Jenna sat in her office, mulling over the situation and half-heartedly working on the job description for Chad's position, when one of her most trusted administrative assistants, Katie, walked in. After they chatted for a few minutes, the following conversation ensued:

Class-tested **minicases** at the end of each chapter work well as daily assignments and as frameworks for lectures, discussion, or small group practice. Each chapter includes at least one new minicase. The cases encourage students to apply theories and skills learned in the text to solve sales situations.

ROLE PLAY CASE

In this chapter's role play interaction, you are still meeting with the same person you did for Chapter 3. (If you did not do the role play at the end of Chapter 3, you will need to review that information now.) That person is telling you about the business. Feel free to ask questions, but your main objective is to listen and understand all you can about the business environment in which he or she operates. Practice active listening skills; after the role play, identify which listening techniques you used. Further, identify the three most important elements about the person's business that you need to understand. Interpret the buyer's body language. Finally, any time you hear jargon, write the word or phrase down.

Note: For background information about these role plays, please see page 27.

To the instructor: Additional information needed to complete the role play is available in the Instructor's Manual.

Students can practice their partnering skills in brand new **role play exercises** that encourage personal growth and experiential learning. Each role play features NetSuite, the software used in national collegiate sales competition. Also, comprehensive role plays are available at the end of the book, with additional role plays included in the Instructor's Manual.

Supplements

The **Video Library** features new video segments customized for the text (including video examples of sales openings, objections with responses, and closings; dealing with a preoccupied buyer, real world examples of telemarketing sales calls, a real world example of using WebX to give a presentation) in addition to material from Achieve Global's Professional Selling Skills Seminar (PSS).

The **Online Learning Center** www.mhhe.com/castleberry8e houses the Instructor's Manual, PowerPoint slides, test bank, and a link to McGraw-Hill's course management system, PageOut for the Instructor. It also includes study outlines, quizzes, key terms, career information, video clips, and online resources for the student.

CONTENTS IN BRIEF

CONTENTS

SELLING

Building Partnerships

chapter 1

SELLING AND SALESPEOPLE

SOME QUESTIONS ANSWERED IN THIS CHAPTER ARE

- What is selling?
- Why should you learn about selling even if you do not plan to be a salesperson?
- What is the role of personal selling in a firm?
- What are the different types of salespeople?
- What are the rewards of a selling career?

PROFILE

PROFILE I have always been a people person and someone that enjoys a challenge. My name is Lauren Bearden, and I am a 2009 graduate of the Northern Illinois University Sales Program. I began my college career at Northern not knowing what field of study I wanted to pursue, but after meeting with the career services team, it became apparent that my true fit would be the college of business. From that point it was an easy decision that marketing should be my field of study—I'm outgoing and love working with people and learning about new products.

In my first marketing class I learned about the Professional Selling Program at Northern. It is a selective entry program and one of the top sales programs in the country. My parents had always said I would be good in sales, so I thought I would give it a shot. Also, as a competitive person, the idea of getting into a top program posed a task that I was up to.

In order to enter the program, I had to not only interview, but also conduct a role play trying to sell a textbook to the head of our sales program, Dr. Dan Weilbaker. Sitting in front of Dr. Weilbaker was my first experience selling ever, and I have to admit I was so nervous I let out a string of "word vomit" (as Dr. Weilbaker calls it) during my presentation. I was on my agenda and didn't give my "client" the opportunity to tell me the key information I needed to hear to get the sale. While I couldn't close the deal in that role play, getting through it was my first step in learning how to get in front of customers and ask the right questions—and not do all of the talking!

Throughout college I worked as an intern at the Career Services office, where I learned the importance of networking and put the skills I learned to use with the recruiters who came through our doors. While I was fortunate to be surrounded by career information and job search skills on a daily basis throughout college, it was really my extracurricular activities that gave me an edge when it came time to interview. Completing internships and being actively involved in several organizations and professional groups demonstrated the leadership, organization skills, and drive it would take to be a successful team player in a sales organization. Differentiating yourself—whether in an interview, or a cold call, is what gets you noticed and gets your foot in the door. Doing your research, staying up to date on your clients' industries, and going the extra mile amounts to big payoffs.

By job searching and reaching out to recruiters and contacts I had built in my years working at the career services office, I earned a position at AT&T, the largest telecommunications provider in the country and a *Fortune* 10 company, where I was placed in an extensive six-month mobility training program.

As an account executive in the AT&T Business Sales Leadership Program, I learned the ins and outs of the products I would be selling, how to sell strategically, and what it would take to close business. It was an intense program, but having a strong knowledge of the products and services I would be selling made it easier to show value to my customers in the field.

After training I transitioned into the acquisition segment of the AT&T Premier Client Group. This segment focuses on gaining new business, and required momentum right out of the gates. I was attracted to the opportunity that the position presented because it focuses on hunting for new business. This means active prospecting and meeting with new potential customers. Without a doubt, establishing a career in sales takes a great amount of time, energy, and long days, but the hard work and activity are what lays the foundation for future sales and success—and let's not forget about the money!

In my new role as a corporate account executive, I meet with businesses, learn the business processes, and find ways mobility can improve those processes. Building trust is the key to earning the right to act as a consultant to clients, which brings value and differentiates a salesperson among the competition.

Because I sell to all different market verticals, I am able to meet and work with a variety of people every day. One day I could be conducting a meeting in a high-power executive office, and the next I could be out in a hard hat touring the manufacturing plant of a company. The change and diversity of each day make me excited about my career and keep me challenged. Being able to meet with so many new people is my favorite part of selling—it sure beats being behind a desk and computer all day! The relationships and contacts you make selling will carry into your professional life no matter what route you take with your career.

Without a doubt, sales offers the freedom, recognition, and financial benefits that few other roles can offer. I hope you find sales as rewarding as I do.

See our Web site at:
www.att.com

WHY LEARN ABOUT PERSONAL SELLING?

What's the first thing that pops into your mind when you hear the phrase "personal selling"? Do you conjure up images of fast-talking, nonlistening, pushy guys who won't take no for an answer? Does the cartoon in Exhibit 1.1 resonate with your idea of a seller? Maybe your definition would be something like this: "Personal selling is the craft of persuading people to buy what they do not want and do not need for more than it is worth."[1] If so, it's not all that surprising because that is exactly how television and the movies have represented salespeople for over 100 years.

If that is your view of selling, we encourage you to read and study this book carefully. You're going to learn things about selling that you never knew before.

Exhibit 1.1

"People like sincerity - learn to fake that and you've got it made."

© Business Cartoons by UK Cartoonist Morris/Visual Humour

Let's start with a more accurate definition of a professional salesperson, which is quite different from the one just mentioned. **Personal selling** is a person-to-person business activity in which a salesperson uncovers and satisfies the needs of a buyer to the mutual, long-term benefit of both parties. This definition stresses that selling is more than making a sale and getting an order. Selling involves helping customers identify problems, offering information about potential solutions, and providing after-sale service to ensure long-term satisfaction. The phrase often used to describe this is **customer-centric,** which means making the customer the center of everything the salesperson does.[2] Quite a bit different from the image of the seller in the cartoon, isn't it?

The days of salespeople dragging around briefcases overstuffed with brochures and knocking on every door they can find to drum up interest in their companies' products are waning. Buyers simply don't tolerate such salespeople. Buying firms today compete in global markets, using sophisticated communication, transportation, and management information systems. And these sophisticated buyers are demanding **24/7 service** (which means they expect a selling firm to be available for them 24 hours a day, 7 days a week). Today's professional salespeople coordinate the resources of their companies to help customers solve complex problems. They use e-mail and Web conferencing to communicate with customers and support staff around the world; exchange information from their firms' computers with their own laptop computers so they can know more about their prospects and customers; and develop client-specific multimedia presentations to illustrate the benefits of their firms' products and services. In all of this, the seller's goal is to add **value,** which is the total benefit that the seller's products and services provide to the buyer. When describing this to prospects, the seller often refers to the collection of buyer-specific benefits as the **customer value proposition.**[3] Jeff Lehman, author of *The Sales Manager's Mentor,* would suggest that the nucleus of the salesperson's life is the value proposition, because without the value proposition, there is no real and meaningful presentation.[4] As you can read in "From the Buyer's Seat 1.1," buyers want long-term relationships that result in increased value for their firms. Customer value propositions are discussed more fully in Chapter 9.

EVERYONE SELLS

This text discusses personal selling as a business activity undertaken by salespeople. But keep in mind that the principles of selling are useful to everyone, not just people with the title of salesperson. Developing mutually beneficial, long-term relationships is vital to all of us. In fact, the author team has taught the principles in this book to many groups of nonsalespeople. Let's look at some examples of how nonsalespeople sell ideas.

As a college student, you might use selling techniques when asking another student to go out on a date or to ask a professor to let you enroll in a course that is closed out. When you near graduation, you will certainly confront a very important sales job: selling yourself to an employer.

To get a job after graduation, you will go through the same steps used in the sales process (discussed in Part 2, Chapters 6 through 14). First you will identify some potential employers (customers). On the basis of an analysis of each employer's needs, you will develop a presentation (as well as answers to questions you might encounter) to demonstrate your ability to satisfy those needs. During the interview you will listen to what the recruiter says, ask and answer questions, and perhaps alter your presentation based on the new information you receive

From the BUYER'S SEAT

WHAT I WISH SALESPEOPLE WHO CALLED ON ME KNEW

By Lt. N.C. McCahill, U.S. Navy

I'm a procurement officer for the U.S. Navy. What's my wish list of things I'd tell new salespeople? Here we go.

Almost on a daily basis I have salespeople who ask me the frustrating, and almost illegal, question, "So, how does our bid look compared to others you've gotten?" Don't ask. Just bid the best you can and don't worry about the others.

I want to establish a long-term agreement and honest relationship with my suppliers. But the first meeting with some sellers is almost like a first date. They're trying to put their best face forward. Don't. I need honest answers and I need to know what you can and can't do. I'll find out eventually anyway, so why play the game of trying to impress me beyond what you can deliver?

I don't like sellers who just stop by to say, "Hi!" I'm guessing they are doing so just so they can count my call on their call sheets and impress their managers. It doesn't impress me. If you don't have a reason to stop by, then don't! My time is valuable.

Salespeople need to have patience. I'm not going to change the way I do things overnight. If something is working, I'm not looking to change. If I do change, it's going to take me a long time. Accept that.

Low price does not equal low cost. There's generally a reason for a higher price, which is higher quality, and I'm willing to pay for it. Don't try to sell me your cheapest model.

I am a professional buyer and know exactly what salespeople are trained to do and to say. I know all the "tricks" they might try to use on me, and I get pretty upset when I see them playing games with me, as though I was too dumb to catch on to their game.

One thing that really burns me up is the way suppliers try to take all of my money. What do I mean? We're in the public sector and everything is budget driven. When I tell a salesperson the budget we have to work with, they usually spend it all. For example, I had to procure services to have a new parking garage built. I told the various sellers that our budget was $10 million. You guessed it, all the bids came in at that amount. They knew what our budget was, and decided to bid for all of the money we had. It's not a lot different from a used car salesman, who knows you have $6,000 to spend and makes sure to take all of your $6,000.

One thing I love is when a seller tells me, "Sorry, I don't have what you need. But my competitor does. Here's their contact information..." That impresses the socks off of me! It builds trust and a long-term relationship. I really get tired of salespeople who stop by and say, "Let me buy you lunch." I'm not allowed to accept meals, and even if I was, I don't want to be beholden to buy from you just because you bought me a $25 meal one day. I know you want to sell deeper to me, but I don't like to get too comfortable with one supplier. I keep my eyes open in the market and test to see if other companies have a better product. I actually like to have several suppliers working for me: approved suppliers are those who can make what we need, and preferred suppliers are those we prefer to give most of our business to. That way, if my preferred supplier can't handle an order, I already have a relationship with other approved suppliers. So don't be surprised if I don't give you 100% of my business.

Don't tell me how bad your competition is. I've had sales reps ask who we were currently using and then proceed to tell me how bad that supplier was. I don't want to hear what your competitor can or can't do, I want to hear what you can do. Besides, it's an insult to my intelligence to point that out. I may already be aware of the problems, and that is part of the reason I am willing to talk to you.

Source: Lt. N.C. McCahill, U.S. Navy, personal correspondence; names changed to protect confidentiality; used with permission.

during the interview. At some point you might negotiate with the employer over starting salary or other issues. Eventually you will try to secure a commitment from the employer to hire you. This process is selling at a very personal level. Chapter 17 reviews the steps you need to undertake to get a sales job.

Nonsalespeople in business use selling principles all the time. Engineers convince managers to support their R&D projects; industrial relations executives use selling approaches when negotiating with unions; and aspiring management trainees sell themselves to associates, superiors, and subordinates to get raises and promotions.

It's not just businesspeople who practice the art of selling. Presidents encourage politicians in Congress to support certain programs; charities solicit contributions and volunteers to run organizations; scientists try to convince foundations and government agencies to fund research; and doctors try to get their patients to adopt more healthful lifestyles. People skilled at selling value, influencing others, and developing long-term relationships are usually leaders in our society.

CREATING VALUE: THE ROLE OF SALESPEOPLE IN BUSINESS

Firms exist only when their products and services are sold. And salespeople sell by creating value for their customers. It takes skill for salespeople to uncover exactly what a customer is looking for and how a potential product or service could add such value. Because this is so critical, this topic is covered in great detail in many chapters in this book.

Firms have many options in how they can approach customers as they add value, and the various methods are sometimes called **go-to-market strategies.** Strategies include selling through the Internet, field sales representatives, business partners, resellers, manufacturer agents, franchises, telemarketers, and others. Selling firms determine which strategy to use for each customer based on such factors as the estimated value of the customer over the lifetime of the relationship, often called **customer lifetime value.**[5] (Because this concept is so important, it is more fully discussed in Chapter 14.) Organizations whose go-to-market strategies rely heavily on salespeople are called **sales force–intensive organizations.** Naturally some firms use several strategies at the same time, and this is called **multichannel strategy.** For example, Motorola uses the Internet for very small customers, telemarketers for midsized customers, and a field sales force for large, important customers.

Another way to view the role of salespeople in business is to realize that they are one element in the firms' marketing communications program, as Exhibit 1.2

Exhibit 1.2
Communication Methods

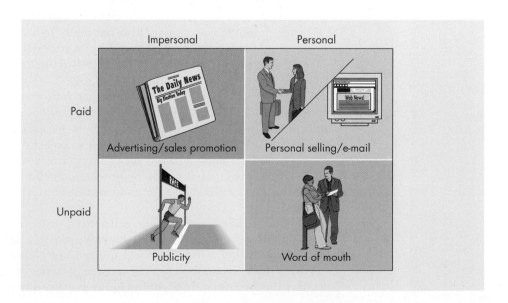

indicates.[6] Advertising uses impersonal mass media such as newspapers and TV to give information to customers, while sales promotions offer incentives to customers to purchase products during a specific period. Salespeople provide paid personal communication to customers, whereas publicity is communication through significant unpaid presentations about the firm (usually a news story). Finally, communication also occurs at no cost through word of mouth (communication among buyers about the selling firm).

Each of the communication methods in Exhibit 1.2 has strengths and weaknesses. For example, firms have more control when using paid versus unpaid methods. However, because publicity and word of mouth are communicated by independent sources, their information is usually perceived as more credible than information from paid communication sources. When using advertising, Internet sites, and sales promotions, companies can determine the message's exact content and the time of its delivery. They have less control over the communication delivered by salespeople and have very little control over the content or timing of publicity and word-of-mouth communication. Personal selling comes out on top in flexibility because salespeople can talk with each customer, discover the customer's specific needs, and develop unique presentations for that customer. Not surprisingly, personal selling is the most costly method of communication. The average cost of a sales call can be 10,000 times more expensive than exposing that single customer to a newspaper, radio, or TV ad.

Because each communication vehicle in Exhibit 1.2 has strengths and weaknesses, firms often use **integrated marketing communications,** which are communication programs that coordinate the use of various vehicles to maximize the total impact of the programs on customers.

For example, when Stouffer's introduced its new Spa Cuisine Classics, dinners that were inspired by chefs from wellness spas across the country, it used integrated marketing communications. Salespeople called on supermarkets and wholesale clubs. Advertising was created to generate awareness in consumers' minds. Coupons were offered to consumers to create interest and spur more rapid sales. Taste tests in stores were offered to build excitement and word of mouth. Publicity was generated that focused on the dinners' balance of great taste combined with the nutrition of whole grains. Although using salespeople in this example was an expensive part of the communication mix, it was important to do so to ensure that customers' precise needs were met.

Many students think—incorrectly—that advertising is the most important part of a firm's promotion program. However, many industrial companies place far more emphasis on personal selling than on advertising. Even in consumer product firms such as Procter & Gamble, which spends more than $8 billion annually on advertising, personal selling plays a critical role.

Students sometimes also have the mistaken notion that the growing world of e-commerce and the Web as a source of information are causing the demise of salespeople. This simply is not true. However, it is critical that the salesperson actually add value in this new reality. As one expert notes, "Companies are no longer relying on a salesperson to get them information . . . if you aren't directly helping the person in front of you by providing intelligence and insight that they can't get anywhere else, having a good relationship isn't going to get you sales anymore."[7]

Let's look at this from another perspective—your own life. Have you purchased anything from the Internet? Probably every student has—travel, music, clothing, books, and more. Have you noticed that, other than Internet services, everything you purchased on the Web existed in some form before the Web? Why, then, has the Web become such a ubiquitous place for commerce? Simple. The

Internet makes products and services available the way the consumer wants to buy them. Those who sell via the Web gain competitive advantage by selling the way the buyers (or at least some buyers in some situations) want to buy.

The reality for salespeople is that if they want to sell effectively, they have to recognize that the buyer has needs that are met not only by the product but also by the selling process itself. These needs include time, shopping costs such as gas if they drive around, and others. Part of the salesperson's responsibility is to sell the way the buyer wants to buy.

In general, sellers sell to make a profit. Why do buyers buy? Typically a student will say, "To satisfy a need or a want," and that is a good basic answer. More helpful is to recognize that buyers also buy to make a profit. But they calculate profit differently. A seller's profit is selling price minus cost of goods sold and selling costs. A buyer's profit, or value, is the benefit received minus the selling price and costs and hassles of buying, or time and effort as noted in this equation:

$$\text{Value} = \text{Benefits received} - (\text{Selling price} + \text{Time and effort to purchase})$$

For example, when someone buys a product from a salesperson, the buyer's profit may be higher than that obtained by buying on the Internet due to the benefits received (expert knowledge in determining the appropriate product to purchase, assistance with installation, resolution of concerns, creation of new offerings based on the buyer's specific needs, and so forth).

WHAT DO SALESPEOPLE DO?

The activities of salespeople depend on the type of selling job they choose. The responsibilities of salespeople selling financial services for General Electric differ greatly from those of salespeople selling pharmaceuticals for Merck or paper products for James River. Salespeople often have multiple roles to play, including client relationship manager, account team manager, vendor and channel manager, and information provider for their firms.[8] Studies have shown that when a salesperson's role encompasses more than simply the selling function, the seller's firm has more overall value.[9]

Sales reps help with installations to ensure proper use.

CLIENT RELATIONSHIP MANAGER

Sales jobs involve prospecting for new customers, making sales presentations, demonstrating products, negotiating price and delivery terms, writing orders, and increasing sales to existing customers. But these sales-generating activities (discussed in Chapters 6 through 14) are only part of the job. Although the numbers would vary greatly depending on the type of sales job, one study found that salespeople spend less than 35 percent of their time on-site in face-to-face meetings with customers and prospects (for world-class firms that percentage rises to 40 percent, whereas for poorly performing firms the percentage drops to just 20 percent).[10] The rest of salespeople's time is spent in meetings, working with support people in their companies (internal selling), traveling, waiting for a sales interview, doing paperwork, and servicing customers.

Rather than buying from the lowest-cost suppliers, many buyers now are building competitive advantages by developing and maintaining close, cooperative relationships with a select set of suppliers, and salespeople play a key role in these relationships.[11] When salespeople fail in maintaining these relationships, the results are catastrophic. Research indicates that buyers worldwide are deserting firms they used to do business with in record numbers when their expectations are not met. For example, two-thirds of consumers surveyed cited poor service as the reason they left a provider in the last 12 months.[12]

The salesperson's job does not end when the customer places an order. Sales representatives must make sure customers get the benefits they expect from the product. Thus salespeople work with other company employees to ensure that deliveries are made on time, equipment is properly installed, operators are trained to use the equipment, and questions or complaints are resolved quickly. Progressive selling firms like Standard Register and Johnson & Johnson's Ortho-Clinical Diagnostics are beginning to implement **six sigma selling programs,** which are designed to reduce errors introduced by the selling system to practically zero. Chapter 14 provides more insights on developing ongoing relationships through customer service.

ACCOUNT TEAM MANAGER

Salespeople also coordinate the activities within their firms to solve customer problems.[13] Many sales situations call for team selling, and at least one study shows that salespeople who attempt to go it alone (sometimes called being "lone wolves") perform poorly, have lower job satisfaction, and have higher turnover intentions.[14] An example of team selling occurred when Dick Holder, president of Reynolds Metal Company, spent five years "selling" Campbell Soup Company on using aluminum cans for its tomato juice products. He coordinated a team of graphic designers, marketing people, and engineers that educated and convinced Campbell to use a packaging material it had never used before. Approaches for improving efficiency by working closely with other functional units in the firm are fully discussed in Chapter 16.

VENDOR AND CHANNEL MANAGER

Sometimes it is necessary to interact with other partners and vendors to meet a customer's needs, and salespeople are often the key managers of these many relationships. For example, if a customer buys a new jet from Boeing, with features that will be added by a third-party vendor, the salesperson will need to coordinate the efforts of the vendor with Boeing. Glenn Price, who sells life and disability insurance with Northwestern Mutual, realizes the importance of working with channel partners. "Today the financial services industry is very complex, as are the needs of my clients, and I can't be all things to all people. I can, however, create a team of specialists. For areas outside of my expertise, all I have to do is identify which specialists are needed and bring them in. This approach allows me to operate at maximum efficiency while providing the highest level of expertise and service to my clients."[15] "Sales Technology 1.1" describes how one company uses technology to keep all members in the channel well informed.

INFORMATION PROVIDER TO THEIR FIRM

Salespeople are the eyes and ears of the company in the marketplace. For example, when Bob Meyer, a salesperson at Ballard Medical Products, was demonstrating a medical device, a surgeon commented that he could not tell whether the device was working properly because the tube was opaque. Meyer relayed this information to the vice president of engineering, and the product was redesigned, substituting a clear tube for the opaque tube.

To truly have effective impact on their organization, salespeople need to be skillful at disseminating the knowledge they have acquired from customers to other

SALES Technology

MAKE IT EASY FOR YOUR CUSTOMERS TO TRACK INFORMATION

Enterprise is one of the largest and most successful rental car companies in the world. It has achieved that status due to hard work and creative use of technology to keep all of its customers in the loop. Although some readers may have rented a car from Enterprise and witnessed firsthand how Enterprise uses the Web and e-mail to keep consumers updated, some may not know how Enterprise works with corporate customers.

Enterprise has strong ties with insurance companies and works hard to ensure the absolute best level of service possible in the industry. It has created a Web-based application called ARMS that allows insurance companies to easily keep track of car rentals. The ARMS automotive application connects thousands of body shops all across the United States to the Enterprise software system. With these systems, Enterprise can quickly and easily discover the status of customer repairs and can even have updates sent electronically to the business customer (in this case, the insurance company that is providing a rental car while a consumer's damaged car is being repaired). The result is no more telephone tag, trying to find out the status of the repairs and whether the rental car is going to be needed longer. This helps the insurance company as well as the consumer who is getting the car repairs. For example, if the repair is taking longer than was anticipated, ARMS can automatically notify the insurance company requesting a longer rental period for the consumer. Not surprisingly, insurance companies love this system, and the new technology has helped Enterprise get a bigger piece of the rental business for car repairs.

Sources: Enterprise.com; Kirk Kazanjian, *Exceeding Customer Expectations* (New York: Current Doubleday Books, 2007).

Salespeople share important market information with their boss and others in the firm.

people in their companies.[16] In their reporting activities, salespeople provide information to their firms about expenses, calls made, future calls scheduled, sales forecasts, competitor activities, business conditions, and unsatisfied customer needs. It's not surprising, therefore, that the vice presidents of finance and manufacturing in most firms, for example, care greatly about the work and information provided by salespeople. Much of this information is now transmitted electronically to the company, its salespeople, and its customers and is contained in a **customer relationship management (CRM)** system.[17] For example, each night salespeople at Curtin Matheson Scientific, a distributor of clinical and laboratory supplies in Baton Rouge, Louisiana, enter call report information and download all the ordering and shipping information for their customers from the company mainframe to their laptop computers. Chapter 16 discusses the relationship between salespeople and their companies in great detail.[18]

TYPES OF SALESPEOPLE

Almost everyone is familiar with people who sell products and services to consumers in retail outlets. Behind these retail salespeople is an army of salespeople working for commercial firms. Consider an iPod or MP3 player you might purchase in a store. To make the player, the manufacturer bought processed material, such as plastic and electronic components, from various salespeople. In addition, it purchased capital equipment from other salespeople to mold the plastic, assemble the components, and test the player. Finally, the player manufacturer bought services such as an employment agency to hire people and an accounting firm to audit the company's financial statements. The manufacturer's salespeople then sold the players to a wholesaler. The wholesaler purchased transportation services and warehouse space from other salespeople. Then the wholesaler's salespeople sold the players to a retailer.

SELLING AND DISTRIBUTION CHANNELS

As the MP3 player example shows, salespeople work for different types of firms and call on different types of customers. These differences in sales positions come from the many roles salespeople play in a firm's distribution channel. A **distribution channel** is a set of people and organizations responsible for the flow of products and services from the producer to the ultimate user. Exhibit 1.3 shows the principal types of distribution channels used for business-to-business and consumer products and the varied roles salespeople play.

Business-to-Business Channels

The two main channels for producers and providers of business-to-business, or industrial, products and services are (1) direct sales to a business customer and (2) sales through distributors. In the direct channel, salespeople working for the manufacturer call directly on other manufacturers. For example, Nucor salespeople sell steel directly to automobile manufacturers, Dow Chemical salespeople sell plastics directly to toy manufacturers, and Nielsen salespeople sell marketing research services directly to business customers.

In the distributor channel the manufacturer employs salespeople to sell to distributors. These salespeople are referred to as **trade salespeople** because they sell to firms that resell the products (that is, they sell to the trade) rather than using them within the firm. Distributor salespeople sell products made by a number of manufacturers to businesses. For example, some Intel salespeople sell microprocessors to distributors such as Arrow Electronics, and Arrow salespeople then resell the microprocessors and other electronic components to customers such as HP.

Many firms use more than one channel of distribution and thus employ several types of salespeople. For example, Dow Chemical has trade salespeople who call on distributors as well as direct salespeople who call on large companies.

Sales Jobs and the Distribution Channel

In the second business-to-business channel (see Exhibit 1.3), a missionary salesperson is employed. **Missionary salespeople** work for a manufacturer and promote the manufacturer's products to other firms. However, those firms buy the products from distributors or other manufacturers, not directly from the salesperson's firm. For example, sales representatives at Driltech, a manufacturer of mining equipment, call on mine owners to promote their products. The mines, however, place orders for drills with the local Driltech distributor rather than with Driltech directly. Normally missionary and local distributor salespeople work together to build relationships with customers.

Frequently missionary salespeople call on people who influence a buying decision but do not actually place the order. For example, Du Pont sales representatives call on Liz Claiborne and other clothing designers to encourage them to design garments made with Teflon, and Merck sales representatives call on physicians to encourage them to prescribe Merck pharmaceutical products.

Consumer Channels

The remaining channels shown in Exhibit 1.3 are used by producers and providers of consumer products and services. The third channel shows a firm,

Exhibit 1.3
Sales Jobs and the
Distribution Channel

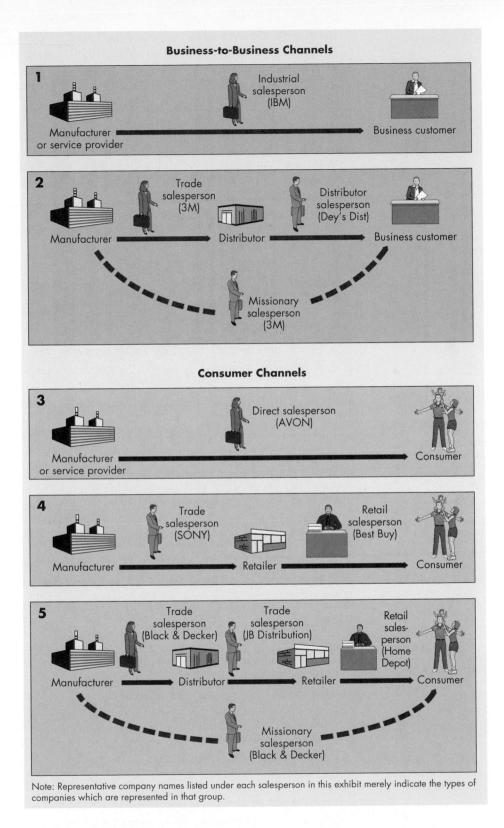

Business-to-Business Channels

1 Manufacturer or service provider → Industrial salesperson (IBM) → Business customer

2 Manufacturer → Trade salesperson (3M) → Distributor → Distributor salesperson (Dey's Dist) → Business customer
Missionary salesperson (3M)

Consumer Channels

3 Manufacturer or service provider → Direct salesperson (AVON) → Consumer

4 Manufacturer → Trade salesperson (SONY) → Retailer → Retail salesperson (Best Buy) → Consumer

5 Manufacturer → Trade salesperson (Black & Decker) → Distributor → Trade salesperson (JB Distribution) → Retailer → Retail salesperson (Home Depot) → Consumer
Missionary salesperson (Black & Decker)

Note: Representative company names listed under each salesperson in this exhibit merely indicate the types of companies which are represented in that group.

such as State Farm Insurance, whose salespeople sell insurance directly to consumers. The fourth and fifth channels show manufacturers that employ trade salespeople to sell to either retailers or distributors. For example, Revlon uses the fourth channel when its salespeople sell directly to Walmart. However, Revlon uses the fifth channel to sell to small, owner-operated stores through distributors. Missionary salespeople are also used in consumer channels. For example, a Black & Decker missionary salesperson may go to a Home Depot store to meet customers there and see how well Home Depot is serving its customers.

Some of the salespeople shown in Exhibit 1.3 may be manufacturers' agents. **Manufacturers' agents** are independent businesspeople who are paid a commission by a manufacturer for all products or services sold. Unlike distributors and retailers, agents never own the products. They simply perform the selling activities and then transmit the orders to the manufacturers.

DESCRIBING SALES JOBS

Descriptions of sales jobs often focus on six factors:

1. The stage of the buyer–seller relationship.
2. The salesperson's role.
3. The importance of the customer's purchase decision.
4. The location of salesperson–customer contact.
5. The nature of the offering sold by the salesperson.
6. The salesperson's role in securing customer commitment.

Stage of Buyer–Seller Relationship: New or Continuing

Some sales jobs emphasize finding and selling to new customers. Selling to prospects requires different skills than does selling to existing customers. To convince prospects to purchase a product they have never used before, salespeople need to be especially self-confident and must be able to deal with the inevitable rejections that occur when making initial contacts. On the other hand, salespeople responsible for existing customers place more emphasis on building relationships and servicing customers. For example, Lou Pritchett of Procter & Gamble, in a continuing relationship with Walmart, increased sales to Walmart from $400 million a year to over $6 billion a year by being creative and building partnerships. And the more important the buyer, the larger the group of sellers engaged in selling to that buyer. Hormel has a team of 50 who sell to Walmart in Bentonville, Arkansas.

Salesperson's Role: Taking Orders or Creating New Solutions

Some sales jobs focus primarily on taking orders. For example, most Frito-Lay salespeople go to grocery stores, check the stock, and prepare an order for the store manager to sign. However, some Frito-Lay salespeople sell only to buyers in the headquarters of supermarket chains. Headquarters selling requires a much higher level of skill and creativity. These salespeople work with buyers to develop new systems and methods, and sometimes even new products, to increase the retailer's sales and profits. Sometimes while creating solutions, a salesperson will need to be bold in helping buyers understand how a product or service can meet their needs, as "Building Partnerships 1.1" illustrates.

Importance of the Purchase to the Customer

Consumers and businesses make many purchase decisions each year. Some decisions are important to them, such as purchasing a building or a business telephone system. Others are less crucial, such as buying candy or cleaning supplies. Sales

I'M SORRY BUT I DISAGREE; YOU SHOULD HIRE THIS PERSON...

I work for a company that matches jobs with entry-level job candidates. A big part of my job consists of soliciting businesses that might have job openings, and then once I actually gain that account I retain it and become their main point of contact for job candidates. Obviously we build strong relationships with companies, and they really feel comfortable trusting us and our opinions on candidates.

A difficulty arises when I need to push a company to make a move on a candidate that they may not feel would be a good fit for their organization, but in my opinion the candidate is a great fit. Recently I was working with this corporate account, and I have a wonderful friendship and strong working relationship with the hiring manager. She decided she was going to pass on (not hire) one of our top candidates. I thought the candidate was a great fit, and obviously I wanted to place the candidate and make the money. But how could I encourage the hiring manager to see that she was making the wrong decision without being pushy and overbearing? How could I show her the value in the candidate and explain why she should reconsider hiring her? What would you do?

I do a number of things in this kind of situation. First, I ask questions about their needs to make sure we're on the same page, and then ask the hiring manager why she thinks the candidate doesn't meet those needs. Sometimes I ask the hiring manager to give my candidate another job interview. Maybe it was just a bad day for the job candidate or the hiring manager. Finally, I occasionally ask the hiring manager to test the candidate out: Put them through the paces of the actual job itself, if possible. For example, put the candidate on the phone to see if he can in fact make cold calls. Testing the actual skills can often show that a candidate does have the needed qualifications, even though she didn't interview well.

Above all, I maintain the relationship and realize that all of my candidates won't get hired. But I do try my best to create a win–win–win situation where the hiring manager, the candidate, and my company all win in the end.

Source: Personal correspondence with Heather Carr, Career Professionals; used with permission.

---

jobs involving important decisions for customers differ greatly from sales jobs involving minor decisions. Consider a company that needs a computer-controlled drill press. Buying the drill press is a big decision. The drill press sales representative needs to be knowledgeable about the customer's needs and the features of drill presses. The salesperson will have to interact with a number of people involved in the purchase decision.

Even though many sales jobs do not involve building long-term partnerships, we stress the concept of developing partnering relationships throughout this textbook because the roles of salespeople in many companies are evolving toward a partnering orientation. As you'll see in Chapter 16, partnering orientations are important within one's own organization as well as with customers. Further, salespeople are called on to build partnerships with some accounts and other types of relationships with other accounts. The partnering orientation does not prevent salespeople from developing other types of relationships; rather, people who are good partners are likely to also be good at other types of relationships. Understanding partnerships is critical to understanding the professional selling process, as will become apparent as the book unfolds.

Location of Salesperson–Customer Contact: Field or Inside Sales

Field salespeople spend considerable time in the customer's place of business, communicating with the customer face-to-face. **Inside salespeople** work at their

Field salespeople go directly to the customer's place of business.

employer's location and typically communicate with customers by telephone or letter.

Field selling typically is more demanding than inside selling because the former entails more intense interactions with customers. Field salespeople are more involved in problem solving with customers, whereas inside salespeople often respond to customer-initiated requests.

Which do you think you would prefer, an inside sales job or a field sales job? What makes one more attractive to you than the other?

The Nature of the Offering Sold by the Salesperson: Products or Services

The type of benefits provided by products and services affects the nature of the sales job. Products such as chemicals and trucks typically have tangible benefits: Customers can objectively measure a chemical's purity and a truck's payload. The benefits of services, such as business insurance or investment opportunities, are more intangible: Customers cannot easily see how the insurance company handles claims or objectively measure the riskiness of an investment.

Intangible benefits are harder to sell than tangible benefits because it is difficult to demonstrate intangible benefits to customers. It is much easier to show a customer the payload of a truck than the benefits of carrying insurance.

The Salesperson's Role in Securing Customer Commitment: Information or Placing an Order

Sales jobs differ by the types of commitments sought and the manner in which they are obtained. For example, the Du Pont missionary salesperson might encourage a clothing designer to use Du Pont Teflon fibers. The salesperson might ask the designer to consider using the fiber but does not undertake the more difficult task of asking the designer to place an order. If the designer decides to use Teflon fabric in a dress, the actual order for nylon will be secured by the fabric manufacturer salesperson, not the Du Pont salesperson.

THE SALES JOBS CONTINUUM

Exhibit 1.4 uses the factors just discussed to illustrate the continuum of sales jobs in terms of creativity. Sales jobs described by the responses in the far right column require salespeople to go into the field, call on new customers who make important buying decisions, promote products or services with intangible benefits, and seek purchase commitments. These types of sales jobs require the most creativity and skill and, consequently, offer the highest pay.

The next section examines the responsibilities of specific types of salespeople in more detail.

EXAMPLES OF SALES JOBS

The following are brief examples of several of the thousands of sales jobs that exist today. As you read each example, notice the vast differences in the type of compensation, the number of accounts, the length of an average sales call, the length of the order cycle, the need to prospect, and so forth. All are based on real

Exhibit 1.4
Creativity Level of
Sales Jobs

Factors in Sales Jobs	Lower Creativity	Higher Creativity
1. Stage of the customer-firm relationship	Existing customer	New customer
2. The salesperson's role	Order taking	Creating new solutions
3. Importance of the customer's purchase decision	Low	High
4. Location of salesperson-customer contact	Inside company	Field customer
5. Nature of the offering sold by the salesperson	Products	Services
6. Salesperson's role in securing customer commitment	Limited role	Significant role

salespeople and the sales jobs they got when they first graduated from college. As you read the examples, think about which would be more attractive to you personally.

Chris is a salesperson for IBM Large Systems, selling mainframe computers to organizations. She has five clients, provided to her by her company, and does no prospecting for new accounts. She is paid a straight salary and travels by plane three to five days each week. Each visit to an account is roughly three hours long. For the first three years she had no sales. In her third year she made the largest sale in the company's history.

Lauree works for Standard Register selling business forms and document management solutions. She has 200 clients and does a good bit of searching for new accounts. She is paid salary plus commission and gets orders essentially every single day, with no overnight travel. Each visit lasts about 45 minutes.

Scott works for Pfizer, a pharmaceutical company, calling on 100 doctors to tell them about his company's drugs. He is paid a salary plus a year-end bonus, and as a missionary salesperson never gets an actual order from a doctor (the patients buy the Pfizer drugs). He does no overnight travel and never searches for new accounts, and each call is about five minutes long.

Jim sells Makita power tools and serves 75 dealers. He is paid a salary plus commission and does very limited searching for new accounts. He gets orders every day and has little overnight travel. Each call is about 30 minutes long.

Jeff works for Hormel, selling refrigerated meat products as well as pantry products like canned chili, and has about 100 accounts. He does no searching for new accounts and is paid a salary plus a year-end bonus. Each call lasts about 10 minutes, and he has no overnight travel.

Niki works for MetLife, selling life, auto, homeowners, long-term care, and disability insurance as well as investments (IRAs, mutual funds, annuities, and so forth). She has 250 clients, has no overnight travel, and is paid straight salary. She does a good bit of searching for new accounts, and here average first in-person sales call to a new account lasts about 30 minutes.

The next section reviews some of the skills required to be effective in the sales positions just discussed.

CHARACTERISTICS OF SUCCESSFUL SALESPEOPLE

The market is full of books and articles discussing why some people are successful in selling and others are not.[19] Yet no one has identified the profile of the "perfect" salesperson because sales jobs are so different, as the examples just provided illustrated. In addition, each customer is unique. However, the following traits are generally associated with successful salespeople.

SELF-MOTIVATED

Most salespeople work in the field without direct supervision. Under these conditions they may be tempted to get up late, take long lunch breaks, and stop work early. But successful salespeople are self-starters who do not need the fear inspired by a glaring supervisor to get them going in the morning or to keep them working hard all day. Furthermore, successful salespeople are motivated to learn, and they work at improving their skills by analyzing their performance and using their mistakes as learning opportunities.

DEPENDABILITY AND TRUSTWORTHINESS

This book focuses on business-to-business selling situations in which the customer and salesperson often have a continuing relationship. Such salespeople are interested not only in what the customers will buy this time but also in getting orders in the years to come. Customers develop long-term relationships only with salespeople who are dependable and trustworthy.[20] When salespeople say the equipment will perform in a certain way, they had better make sure the equipment performs that way! If it doesn't, the customer will not rely on them again. And dependability and trustworthiness can't just be a false front: Salespeople who are genuine and come across as authentic are better-performing salespeople.

thinking **it** through

Take a minute and think about yourself. How dependable are you right now? Can people count on you to do what you say you will do? Or do they have to look you up and remind you of your promises? You don't start developing dependability when you graduate from college; it is something you should be working on right now. What can you do to start improving your dependability?

ETHICAL SALES BEHAVIOR

Honesty and integrity are critical for developing effective relationships. Over the long run, customers will find out who can be trusted and who cannot. Good ethics are good business.[21] Ethical sales behavior is such an important topic that much of Chapter 2 is devoted to it.

CUSTOMER AND PRODUCT KNOWLEDGE

Effective salespeople need to know how businesses make purchase decisions and how individuals evaluate product alternatives. In addition, effective salespeople need product knowledge—how their products work and how the products' features are related to the benefits customers are seeking. Chapter 3 reviews the buying process, and Chapter 5 discusses product knowledge.

ANALYTICAL SKILLS AND THE ABILITY TO USE INFORMATION TECHNOLOGY

Salespeople need to know how to analyze data and situations and use the Internet, databases, and software to effectively sell in today's marketplace.[22] Information technology will be discussed in every chapter in this book, and the use of analytical tools will be covered in Chapter 9 and other chapters.

COMMUNICATION SKILLS

The key to building strong long-term relationships is to be responsive to a customer's needs. To do that, the salesperson needs to be a good communicator. But talking is not enough; the salesperson must also listen to what the customer says, ask questions that uncover problems and needs, and pay attention to the responses.

To compete in world markets, salespeople need to learn how to communicate in international markets. For example, business is conducted differently in Europe than in the United States. In the United States business transactions generally proceed at a rapid pace, whereas Europeans take more time reaching decisions. European customers place more emphasis on the rapport developed with a salesperson, whereas U.S. firms look more at the size and reputation of the salesperson's company. Because Europeans want to do business with salespeople they like and trust, the latter devote a lot of time to building close personal relationships with customers. Chapter 4 is devoted to developing communication skills, with considerable emphasis on communicating in other cultures.

FLEXIBILITY AND AGILITY

The successful salesperson realizes that the same sales approach does not work with all customers; it must be adapted to each selling situation. The salesperson must be sensitive to what is happening, and agile enough to make those adaptations during the sales presentation. Again, it is this flexibility that causes companies to spend so much money on personal selling instead of just advertising, which can't be tailored as easily or quickly to each individual.

CREATIVITY

Creativity is the trait of having imagination and inventiveness and using them to come up with new solutions and ideas. Sometimes it takes creativity to get an appointment with a prospect. It takes creativity to develop presentation that the buyer will long remember. It takes creativity to solve a sticky installation problem after the product is sold.

CONFIDENCE AND OPTIMISM

Successful salespeople tend to be confident about themselves, their company, and their products. They optimistically believe that their efforts will lead to success. Don't confuse confidence, however, with wishful thinking. According to research, truly confident people are willing to work hard to achieve their goals. They are open to criticism, seek advice from others, and learn from their mistakes. They expect good things to happen, but they take personal responsibility for their fate. People who lack confidence, according to these same studies, are not honest about their own limits, react defensively when criticized, and set unrealistic goals.

Salespeople need emotional intelligence to be able to recognize customers' emotions.

EMOTIONAL INTELLIGENCE

Emotional intelligence is the ability to effectively understand and regulate one's own emotions, and to read and respond to the emotions of others, and this is an important trait for salespeople.[23] Emotional intelligence has four aspects: (1) knowing one's own feelings and emotions as they are experienced, (2) controlling one's emotions to avoid acting impulsively, (3) recognizing customers' emotions (called *empathy*), and (4) using one's emotions to interact effectively with customers.[24] One well-known source identifies the following as evidences of emotional maturity: "the ability to deal constructively with reality, the capacity to adapt to change, a relative freedom from symptoms that are produced by tensions and anxieties, the capacity to find more satisfaction in giving than receiving, the capacity to relate to other people in a consistent manner with mutual satisfaction and helpfulness, the capacity to direct one's instinctive hostile energy into creative and constructive outlets, and the capacity to love."[25] A recent study of over 6,000 people from a wide spectrum of industries found that good decision makers consistently score high in emotional intelligence.[26] Bad decisions result from a lack of emotional intelligence, so it is not surprising that emotional immaturity plays a large role in many employee terminations. What are some good first steps in improving your emotional maturity? Learn to identify and understand your own emotions as they arise, and recognize the fact that it is often in your best interest to step away from emotional situations and become more reflective.[27] We discuss aspects of emotional intelligence as they relate to adaptive selling and effective verbal and nonverbal intelligence in Chapters 4 and 5.

ARE SALESPEOPLE BORN OR MADE?

On the basis of the preceding discussion, you can see that most of the skills required to be a successful salesperson can be learned. People can learn to work hard, plan their time, and adapt their sales approach to their customers' needs. In fact, companies show their faith in their ability to teach sales skills by spending billions of dollars each year on training programs. The next section discusses the rewards you can realize if you develop the skills required for sales success.

REWARDS IN SELLING

Personal selling offers interesting and rewarding career opportunities. More than 8 million people in the United States currently work in sales positions, and the number of sales positions is growing. In fact, based on a study of nearly 37,000 employers in 27 countries, the demand for salespeople is greater than the supply.[28] Exhibit 1.5 provides a breakdown of employment by the type of sales job.

Exhibit 1.5
Employment in Sales Positions

Type of Sales Job	Employed in 2008	Projected Employed for 2018	Average Earnings in 2008
Retail salesperson	4,500,000	+8%	$9.86/hour
Manufacturers' and wholesale sales reps	2,000,000	+7%	$70,200
Insurance sales agents	434,000	+12%	$45,430
Securities, commodities, and financial sales agents	317,200	+9%	$68,680
Real estate agents and brokers	517,800	+14%	$40,150
Sales engineers	78,000	+9%	$83,100
Advertising sales agents	166,800	+7%	$43,800
Travel agents	105,300	−1%	$30,570
Totals	8,119,100		

Source: *Occupational Outlook Handbook*, 2010–2011 edition, U.S. Department of Labor, Bureau of Labor Statistics.

INDEPENDENCE AND RESPONSIBILITY

Many people do not want to spend long hours behind a desk, doing the same thing every day. They prefer to be outside, moving around, meeting people, and working on various problems. Selling ideally suits people with these interests. The typical salesperson interacts with dozens of people daily. Most of these contacts involve challenging new experiences.

Selling also offers unusual freedom and flexibility. It is not a nine-to-five job. Most salespeople decide how to spend their time; they do not have to report in. They have the freedom to determine what they do during a day, to decide which customers to call on and when to do paperwork. Long hours may be required on some days, and other days may bring fewer demands.

Because of this freedom, salespeople are like independent entrepreneurs. They have a territory to manage and few restrictions on how to do it. They are responsible for the sales and profits the territory generates. Thus their success or failure rests largely on their own skills and efforts.

FINANCIAL REWARDS

Salespeople tend to earn more money the longer they sell, as Exhibit 1.6 clearly indicates. Occasionally the top salespeople in a firm will even earn more than the sales executives in that firm. The average amount earned by salespeople depends somewhat on the annual revenues of the firm: For firms with revenues of less than $1 million, the average salesperson earns $99,058, while for companies earning from $1 to $10 billion, the average is $199,590.[29]

The financial rewards of selling depend on the level of skill and sophistication needed to do the job. For example, salespeople who sell to businesses typically are paid more than retail salespeople. Exhibit 1.5 shows the average compensation for salespeople in various jobs.

Exhibit 1.6

Average Annual Compensation for Salespeople by Years of Sales/Marketing Experience

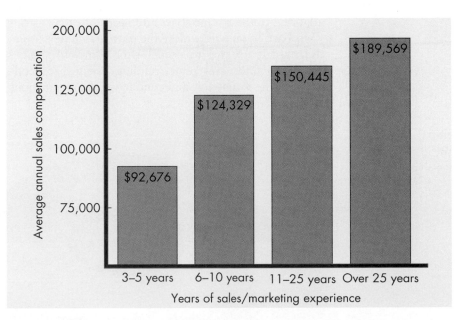

Source: Rebecca Aronauer, "Trends," *Sales and Marketing Management Magazine* 159, no. 4 (May 2007), pp. 38–39.

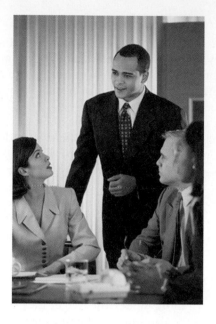

This young manager learned the ropes as a salesperson before moving into product management at his firm.

MANAGEMENT OPPORTUNITIES

Selling jobs provide a firm base for launching a business career. For example, Mark Alvarez started his sales career in the Medical Systems Division at General Electric (GE) selling diagnostic imaging equipment to hospitals in central Illinois. Over the years he held positions in the firm that included district and regional sales manager and product manager; at one point he had responsibility for all Medical Systems Division business in Latin America. Sixteen years later, he was in corporate marketing and was responsible for managing the relationships between GE's 39 divisions and key customers in the southeastern United States. These include such accounts as Federal Express, Disney, and Home Depot. Some of his businesses do more than $500 million worth of business with GE annually. His entry-level job in selling provided great experience for his current assignment. As another example, both the chairman and the CEO/president of Federated Insurance, like many of their counterparts in business, started their careers as salespeople.

THE BUILDING PARTNERSHIPS MODEL

This book is divided into three parts, as illustrated in Exhibit 1.7.

The knowledge and skills needed for successful partnerships are covered in Part 1. You will learn about the legal and ethical responsibilities of salespeople, the buying process, the principles for communicating effectively, and methods for adapting to the unique styles and needs of each customer.

In Part 2 you will explore the partnership development process and the activities needed for this to occur. After completing this section, you should have enhanced skills and understanding about prospecting, planning, discovering needs, using visual aids and conducting demonstrations effectively, responding to

Exhibit 1.7
The Building Partnerships Model

1 Knowledge and skills needed for partnerships

2 The partnership development process

3 The salesperson as a manager

Building Partnerships

objections, obtaining commitment, formally negotiating, and providing excellent after-sale service.

Finally, Part 3 discusses the role of the salesperson as a manager. You'll learn how you can improve your effectiveness as a salesperson by managing your time and territory and by managing the relationships within your own company. This section also discusses ways to manage your career.

SELLING YOURSELF ●────────────────────────

The "Selling Yourself" sections of this book are designed to help you see the connections of the chapter material with all aspects of your life right now. Of course we're all different, with different interests and activities, so some of the examples might better fit you than others. But read them all, and try to make a connection with something in your life. Selling is something you do all the time, and the ideas found in this book can help you now, not just after you graduate!

Let's say you belong to a campus club or organization that is doing a little fund-raising. You find some product or service to sell, or come up with something to raffle off. Then you set up a booth outside the bookstore and staff the booth with your friendliest and maybe most attractive club members. Sound familiar? What happens? A bunch of people won't stop at your booth, no matter how much you try to coax them. Some stop, but don't buy. Why is this happening?

Simple. You're not meeting their needs. In other words, if a student gives you cash, your club's needs are certainly getting met (you are gaining needed revenue), but the student giving the money might not be getting any of her needs met. Remember that the definition of personal selling says that both parties have their needs met, not just one party!

The solution? Discover the real wants and needs of your fellow college students (your customers, those who are going to buy from you) and then sell on that basis. Make sure the product or service or raffle is something the college students really want or need, not just something you think they might need. Do some research to find this out. If you are the one to discover that information, pass it on to your officers (that's being an information provider to your group, which is something that salespeople do, too).

And why not assign a missionary salesperson to hang around the booth? That person, who would be someone with great emotional intelligence, can approach some people who didn't stop at your booth and politely ask "Why not?" but not try to sell them anything. The missionary salesperson can also ask those who did buy "Why?" and "How is the product working out?" and pass that information back to the club's officers. Changes can be made right away to the offering or the way the offering is publicized and sold. Or it can be changed the next time your club tries to do fund-raising.

Happy selling!

SUMMARY   You should study personal selling because we all use selling techniques. If you want to work in business, you need to know about selling because salespeople play a vital role in business activities. Finally, you might become a salesperson. Selling jobs are inherently interesting because of the variety of people encountered and activities undertaken. In addition, selling offers opportunities for financial rewards and promotions.

Salespeople engage in a wide range of activities, including providing information about products and services to customers and employees within their firms.

Most of us are not aware of many of these activities because the salespeople we meet most frequently work in retail stores. However, the most exciting, rewarding, and challenging sales positions involve building partnerships: long-term, win–win relationships with customers.

The specific duties and responsibilities of salespeople depend on the type of selling position. But most salespeople engage in various tasks in addition to influencing customers. These tasks include managing customer relations, serving as the account team manager for their firm, managing the relationships with vendor and channel members, and providing information to their firm.

Sales jobs can be classified by the roles salespeople and their firms play in the channel of distribution. The nature of the selling job is affected by whom salespeople work for and whether they sell to manufacturers, distributors, or retailers. Other factors affecting the nature of selling jobs are the customer's relationship to the salesperson's firm, the salesperson's duties, the importance of the buying decision to the customer, where the selling occurs, the tangibility of the benefits considered by the customer, and the degree to which the salesperson seeks a commitment from customers.

Research on the characteristics of effective salespeople indicates that many different personality types can be successful in sales. However, successful salespeople do share some common characteristics. They are self-motivated, dependable, ethical, knowledgeable, good communicators, flexible, creative, confident, and emotionally intelligent; have good analytical skills; and aren't afraid of technology.

KEY TERMS

creativity   19
customer-centric   5
customer lifetime value (CLV)   7
customer relationship management (CRM)   11
customer value proposition   5
distribution channel   12
emotional intelligence   19
field salespeople   15
go-to-market strategies   7
inside salespeople   15

integrated marketing communications   8
manufacturers' agents   14
missionary salespeople   12
multichannel strategy   7
personal selling   5
sales force–intensive organization   7
six sigma selling programs   10
trade salespeople   12
24/7 service   5
value   5

ETHICS PROBLEMS

1. Many buyers are now demanding 24/7 response (24 hours a day, 7 days a week) from their suppliers. What impact do you think that would have on a salesperson's personal life?

2. The chapter says that selling jobs can be a great way to get your foot in the door at an employer. Let's say you really want to be in product development, not sales, yet the position that is being

offered at the company is in sales. You hope that after doing the sales job for six months to a year you'll get promoted to the product development job. Should you be honest and tell the interviewer (the sales manager) that now? Or should you act as though you want to be a career salesperson?

QUESTIONS AND PROBLEMS

1. There are many different go-to-market strategies. For which of the following products and services do you think a sales force–intensive strategy would probably not be used? Why? Make any assumptions needed, and list your assumptions in your answer.
   a. Tennis racquets.
   b. Home air conditioning maintenance service.
   c. Shredding service for sensitive documents.
   d. Solar-powered compactor garbage cans for city use on city streets (the specially designed cans actually compact the garbage that is thrown into the can four times a time, using energy from the sun, reducing the number of times the can needs to be emptied).

2. In "Building Partnerships 1.1" you read about how Ms. Carr politely disagrees with her customer if she thinks the customer is making a decision that is not in the customer's best interests.
   a. What could be some positive outcomes of such salesperson behavior?
   b. What could be some negative outcomes of such salesperson behavior?

3. Comment on each of the following statements:
   a. Salespeople rip people off.
   b. Salespeople are born, not made.
   c. Selling is just a big bag of tricks.
   d. A salesperson should never take no for an answer.
   e. A good salesperson can sell anything to anybody.

4. Fay Roberson has been working as a receptionist at her father's business for two years since graduating from college. She is considering taking a selling job with a pharmaceutical company. The job involves calling on doctors and explaining the benefits of the firm's products. What are the similarities and differences between her receptionist job and the selling job she is considering?

5. Benjamin Chapman worked his way through college by selling home theater systems at Best Buy. He has done well on the job and is one of the top salespeople in the home electronics department. Last week Safety Harness Inc. offered him a job selling seat belt kits to school bus manufacturers. Explain the differences between selling in a consumer electronics store and the Safety Harness Inc. sales job.

6. Poll at least five students who are not taking your selling course (and who, better yet, are outside the business school or program). What are their opinions about salespeople? How accurate are their opinions based on what you've read in this chapter?

7. Think about what you want in your first job out of college. Based on what you know so far from this chapter, how well does selling match your desires in a job?

8. According to the text, some sales jobs involve taking orders instead of creating new solutions. Why would anyone want a job that involves only taking orders?

9. "Sales Technology 1.1" described the use of Enterprise's ARMS system. How could having the ARMS system help an Enterprise salesperson sell to a new insurance company?

10. Assume you are a sales manager and you need to recruit someone for the following sales positions. For each position, list the qualities you would want in the recruit:
    a. Salesperson selling Web design services to small businesses.
    b. Salesperson calling on college bookstores, selling university logo backpacks.
    c. Used car salesperson.
    d. Salesperson selling janitorial services to a county courthouse.

case **1.1**

Tropical
Landscaping, Inc.

Jenna Jones has been the owner and general manager of Tropical Landscaping for the last five years, having bought the business from the entrepreneur and landscape architect who started it 25 years earlier. Tropical is a full-service lawn care company that caters to the business sector, not the consumer sector. They are experts in designing, irrigation, and maintenance of landscapes and have a strong reputation for fast, efficient, and reasonably priced services.

When Jenna purchased the company there were three full-time salespeople who called on businesses in the region. One quit right after she arrived, and Floyd, a knowledgeable landscaper with good connections in the business community, was hired as a replacement. Floyd has been a real asset to the firm, building business in the commercial landscape design area.

Jenna thought everything was going smoothly until yesterday, when Chad, another salesperson, dropped a bombshell. He turned in his notice. Chad indicated he was going to work for a local competitor who was paying him about 25 percent more than Jenna.

Jenna sat in her office, mulling over the situation and half-heartedly working on the job description for Chad's position, when one of her most trusted administrative assistants, Katie, walked in. After they chatted for a few minutes, the following conversation ensued:

> Katie: So why do you need a salesperson anyway? Why not just use advertising?
>
> Jenna: We have to have a salesperson, Katie. I mean, there's always been three salespeople in our office.
>
> Katie: But I'm asking you to think outside the dots, Jenna. Why do we need them? They cost the company a lot of money that we could save by just relying on advertising. Besides, Tropical Landscaping is already well-known in this region. There's no need for salespeople. Tropical Landscaping sells itself.

The conversation continued in this vein for a few minutes; then Katie left to work on some invoice disputes. Jenna sat there, thinking about what Katie said. Who knows? Maybe Katie had a good idea.

Questions

1. What impact would dropping one or more salespeople have on Tropical Landscaping? You might want to review the section titled "What Do Salespeople Do?" as you answer this question.

2. If you were Jenna, what would you do? Why?

case **1.2**

Mountain Valley
Spring Water

Kyle Welborn is a salesperson for Roehl Trucking. For the past three or four months he has tried to get in to see Steve Hayes, a transportation specialist at Mountain Valley Spring Water Company. Mountain Valley is an award-winning water bottler that has been in business since 1871. Its water has been served in the White House by a number of presidents, as well as in the Senate, and many celebrities have endorsed the products.

Kyle knows that Mountain Valley uses the services of a number of trucking companies, and he would like Steve to consider adding Roehl as one of its transportation suppliers. Roehl has a three-part vision statement: To be recognized by our customers as the nation's premier provider of truckload services, to be a high-energy, high-performance team, and to be the safest carrier on the road—emphasizing and expecting safe behaviors from everyone. With that vision the company has grown to be one of the largest and most profitable trucking companies in the United States.

Kyle has never actually been able to talk to Steve, not even for a few seconds. His voice mail is all he has ever gotten when making phone calls to Steve. Visits in person have resulted in Steve's secretary just taking Kyle's card and telling him that Steve will call if he is interested. Kyle is now under pressure from his sales manager because Kyle has placed Mountain Valley on his prospect list for the last three months and has nothing to show for all his efforts.

Sources: www.mountainvalleyspring.com, www.roehl.net.

Questions

1. One of the skills that salespeople should possess is creativity. Come up with three creative and totally ethical methods Kyle can use to get Steve's attention.
2. Assume Kyle does get Steve's attention with one of the methods you've described, and Steve is willing to speak with Kyle on the phone the next time he is called. What should Kyle plan on saying, assuming he has just two or three minutes of phone time?

ROLE PLAY CASE

At the end of each chapter, beginning just below this paragraph, you'll find a short role play exercise that focuses on the product NetSuite. NetSuite is a leading contact management software package. Contact management software is a form of software designed to help salespeople increase their productivity by helping them keep track of the customers they call. In addition to a calendar that tells them when to call on an account, the software can track account information concerning what has been bought, when it was bought, the decision-making process, and even personal information about each person in the account. In addition, sales managers can generate reports automatically when reps upload information to the company network. Reps don't have to type as many reports as they would otherwise, such as sales forecasts and call reports. Further, the system can tie into the company's ordering system, which helps save the salesperson paperwork time.

You can learn more about NetSuite from its Web page: www.netsuite.com.

Congratulations, you've just graduated from college! Unfortunately you focused so much on your studies that you have not interviewed for any jobs. You moved back home, but you keep in touch with the school's Career Services Center, where you saw a job posting for NetSuite. Apparently it is some sort of software for salespeople. You've not had any serious interviews, so you thought you'd sign up. Today is your interview. Be yourself; interview honestly as if you were truly talking with NetSuite. To help you prepare for this job interview role play, you may want to take some time to find out about NetSuite by visiting www.netsuite.com for more information.

To the instructor: Additional information needed to complete the role play is available in the Instructor's Manual.

ADDITIONAL REFERENCES

Batislam, Emine Persentili, Meltem Denizel, and Alpay Filiztekin. "Empirical Validation and Comparison of Models for Customer Base Analysis." *International Journal of Research in Marketing* 24, no. 3 (September 2007), pp. 201–9.

Belonax Jr., Joseph J., Stephen J. Newell, and Richard E. Plank. "The Role of Purchase Importance on Buyer Perceptions of the Trust and Expertise Components of Supplier and Salesperson Credibility in Business-to-Business Relationships." *Journal of Personal Selling & Sales Management* 27, no. 3 (Summer 2007), pp. 247–58.

Bradberry, Travis. *Emotional Intelligence* 2.0. TalentSmart: Har/Dig En edition, 2009.

"Continuous Customer Dialogues: Strategies for Growth and Loyalty in Multi-Channel Customer-Oriented Organizations." *CRM Magazine* 12, no. 6 (2008), p. S5.

Crowder, Martin, David J. Hand, and Wojtek Krzanowski. "On Optimal Intervention for Customer Lifetime Value." *European Journal of Operational Research* 183 no. 3 (December 16, 2007), pp. 1550–59.

"Customer Analytics: Becoming Customer-Centric." *CRM Magazine* 11, no. 9 (September 2007), pp. 1–3.

"Determining 'CLV' Can Lead to Making Magical Marketing Decisions: Ask the Expert" (interview). *B to B* 92, no. 6 (May 7, 2007), p. 18.

Fox, Jeffrey J. *How to Be a Fierce Competitor: What Winning Companies and Great Managers Do in Tough Times.* Jossey-Bass, 2010.

Gaffney, John. "The Myth of Customer Loyalty." *1 to 1 Magazine*, March 2007, pp. 18–22.

Grayson, Kent, Devon Johnson, and Der-Fa Robert Chen. "Is Firm Trust Essential in a Trusted Environment? How Trust in the Business Context Influences Customers." *Journal of Marketing Research* 45, no. 2 (2008).

Green Jr., Kenneth, W. R. Anthony Inman, and Gene Brown. "Just-in-Time Selling Construct: Definition and Measurement." *Industrial Marketing Management* 37, no. 2 (April 2008), pp. 131–42.

Guenzi, Paolo, and Gabriele Troilo. "The Joint Contribution of Marketing and Sales to the Creation of Superior Customer Value." *Journal of Business Research* 60, no. 2 (February 2007), pp. 98–107.

Heilman, T. "Implementing 'Extreme' Customer Service." *Evaluation Engineering* 48, no. 11 (November 2009), pp. 14–19.

Hoff, Garth. "Customer-Centric Availability Evaluations in Revenue Management Applications." *Journal of Revenue & Pricing Management* 7, no. 1 (2008), pp. 40–51.

Homburg, Christian, Ove Jensen, and Harley Krohmer. "Configurations of Marketing and Sales: A Taxonomy." *Journal of Marketing* 72, no. 2 (2008), pp. 133–54.

Hosford, Christopher. "Measuring for the Long Haul: Customer Lifetime Value Metrics Give Marketers a Long View of How to Spend." *B to B* 92, no. 6 (May 7, 2007), p. 18.

Jaramillo, Fernando, Douglas B. Grisaffe, Lawrence B. Chonko, and James A. Roberts. "Examining the Impact of Servant Leadership on Salesperson's Turnover Intention." *Journal of Personal Selling & Sales Management* 29, no. 4 (Fall 2009), pp. 351–66.

Krasnikov, Alexander, Satish Jayachandran, and V. Kumar. "The Impact of Customer Relationship Management Implementation on Cost and Profit Efficiencies: Evidence from the U.S. Commercial Banking Industry." *Journal of Marketing* 73, no. 6 (2009), pp. 61–76.

Kumar, V., and Bharath Rajan. "Nurturing the Right Customers: By Measuring and Improving Customer Lifetime Value, You'll Be Able to Grow Your Most Profitable Customers." *Strategic Finance* 91, no. 3 (2009), pp. 27–33.

Kumar, V., Rajkumar Venkatesan, and Werner Reinartz. "Performance Implications of Adopting a Customer-Focused Sales Campaign." *Journal of Marketing* 72, no. 5 (2008), pp. 50–68.

Lee, Nancy. "It's All about the Customer: Commercial Perspectives on Customer-Centric Marketing and Managing the Customer Relationship." *Social Marketing Quarterly* 3, no. 3 (September 2007), pp. 12–16.

McArdle, Kevin. "Competing on Value: How to Get Your Unique Value Recognized and Rewarded by Customers." *Precision Manufacturing*, May–June 2007, 20.

McKee, Judy. *The Sales Survival Guide: Your Powerful Interactive Guide to Sales Success and Financial Freedom.* AuthorHouse, 2009.

Miao, C. Fred, and Kenneth R. Evans. "The Impact of Salesperson Motivation on Role Perceptions and Job Performance: A Cognitive and Affective Perspective." *Journal of Personal Selling & Sales Management* 27, no. 1 (Winter 2007), pp. 89–101.

Musico, C. "They Aim to Please." *CRM Magazine* 12, no. 12 (December 2008), pp. 36–41.

Pettijohn, Charles E., Linda S. Pettijohn, and A.J. Taylor. "Does Salesperson Perception of the Importance of Sales Skills Improve Sales Performance, Customer Orientation, Job Satisfaction, and Organizational Commitment, and Reduce Turnover?" *Journal of Personal Selling & Sales Management* 27, no. 1 (Winter 2007), pp. 75–88.

Piercy, Nigel F. "Strategic Relationships between Boundary-Spanning Functions: Aligning Customer Relationship Management with Supplier Relationship Management." *Industrial Marketing Management* 38, no. 8 (November 2009), pp. 857–64.

Poujol, F. Juliet, and John F. Tanner, "The Impact of Contests on Salespeople's Customer Orientation: An Application of Tournament Theory," *Journal of Personal Selling and Sales Management* 30, no. 1 (Winter 2010), pp. 33–46.

Rich, David. "Create Your Own Upturn: A Shift from Managing Volume to Managing Relationships." *CRM Magazine* 13, no. 10 (2009), pp.14–15.

Rouzies, Dominique, et al. "Determinants of Pay Levels and Structures in Sales Organizations." *Journal of Marketing* 73, no. 6 (2009).

Rust, Roland T., Christine Moorman, and Gaurav Bhalla. "Rethinking Marketing." *Harvard Business Review* 88, no. 1 (2010), pp. 94–101.

Schieffer, Robert, and Eric Leininger. "Customers at the Core." *Marketing Management* 17, no. 1 (January–February 2008), pp. 30–37.

Schoder, Detlef. "The Flaw in Customer Lifetime Value." *Harvard Business Review* 85, no. 12 (December 2007), p. 26.

Sebor, J. "Gets Serious." *CRM Magazine* 12, no. 2 (February 2008), pp. 22–26.

Smith, J. Brock, and Mark Colgate. "Customer Value Creation: A Practical Framework." *Journal of Marketing Theory & Practice* 15, no. 1 (Winter 2007), pp. 7–23.

Taulli, T. "Three Steps to a Sound Business Model." *BusinessWeek Online* 19 (March 2, 2009).

Temkin, Bruce. "7 Keys to Customer Experience: Big-Picture Advice for How to Improve the Customer Experience over the Next Year." *CRM Magazine* 13, no. 12 (2009), p. 12.

Thomson, D. "Essential No. 2: Redefine Your Market." *BusinessWeek Online* 17 (November 16, 2009).

Thomson, D. "No. 1: The Breakthrough Value Proposition." *BusinessWeek Online* 7 (November 9, 2009).

Uncles, M. "Know Thy Changing Consumer." *Journal of Direct, Data and Digital Marketing Practice* 10, no. 1 (2008), pp. 84–85.

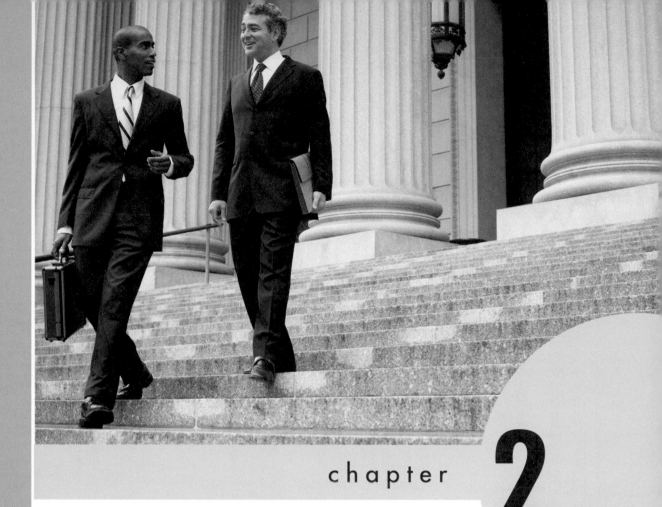

chapter **2**

ETHICAL AND LEGAL ISSUES IN SELLING

SOME QUESTIONS ANSWERED IN THIS CHAPTER ARE

- Why do salespeople need to develop their own codes of ethics?
- Which ethical responsibilities do salespeople have toward themselves, their firms, and their customers?
- Do ethics get in the way of being a successful salesperson?
- What guidelines should salespeople consider when confronting situations involving an ethical issue?
- Which laws apply to personal selling?

PROFILE

PROFILE Ethics and legal compliance are critical components of the selling process. As a leader in HP public sector sales, I'm responsible not only for developing technical solutions for our customers, but also for ensuring that we work within the required ethical and legal parameters for any given deal. Rules for public sector business can be different from those in the private sector. Further, what is considered unethical in one country may be a common custom in another. As employees of a global company working with a wide range of customers, we must always be cognizant of the rules of the business environment in which we're engaged.

At HP, we share values that include a passion for customers, trust and respect for individuals, and uncompromising integrity. These values have become inherent in our corporate culture and guide our innovation, creation, and sales and marketing behavior. As our CEO, Mark Hurd, states, "Innovation and trust are at the core of the HP brand." All employees are expected to live by these values in all business encounters.

HP employees are required to take training courses every year to keep us current on the "Standards of Business Conduct" (SBC). The corporate training and documentation cover company policies and guidelines for dealing with ethical and legal issues, such as fair competition, gifts, false claims and statements, conflicts of interest, workplace harassment, and handling of sensitive information. All HP employees who deal with public sector customers are required to take additional specialized training to help recognize the unique requirements of the U.S. public sector, and most importantly to know how to comply and, if needed, identify and contact the correct HP source for advice. A key underlying message in all communication is "Doing the right thing is not an option, but an obligation." Violation of the SBC or company policies by employees could result in disciplinary action, up to and including termination of employment.

How we conduct business impacts everyone with whom we interact, including customers, partners, coworkers, competitors, and family members. We've all heard or seen on the news those instances of individuals and organizations who are being prosecuted for unscrupulous and illegal business practices. While not all misconduct is newsworthy, any infraction can have significant impact on us individually and on our business. For example, if we provide false information or make false claims about our products or services, we could not only lose the trust of our customers and partners, but could face criminal charges. This situation could impose unnecessary litigation costs to the corporation, and could result in short- and long-term loss of revenue if customers decide to take their business elsewhere. The ramifications can also take a financial and emotional toll on our family members.

In the public sector, constituting or even creating an appearance of impropriety can be the basis for governmental inquiries or the loss of our ability to conduct government business. Violation could result in civil and or criminal fines or penalties up to and including imprisonment, termination, debarment, and severe financial damages.

One of the important parts of the sales cycle is to work the sales plan and develop/strengthen the customer relationship. While working with the U.S. public sector customer, HP employees need to be extra careful of our policy around gifts, gratuities, bribes, and kickbacks. It clearly prohibits us from offering, giving, soliciting, or receiving any gift or other thing of value in exchange for favorable treatment or advantage, or for the purpose of obtaining, or attempting to influence the award of a contract or subcontract. Some common examples of gifts are money, tickets to sporting/entertainment events, travel, lodging, training, meals/drinks (includes working lunches), and so on. Some examples of things that may not qualify as gifts include modest refreshments (certain state/local entities may consider modest refreshments), greeting cards, plaques, certificates, benefits (such as discounts) that are also available to the public or to all government employees, rewards and prizes for contests or events that are open to the public, or anything for which the government employee pays market value.

> As a hypothetical example: An HP salesperson, Mark, develops a professional relationship with Ted, a U.S. Department of Defense contracting officer who used to be in charge of a major HP contract. Although Ted is no longer directly responsible for any contracts held by HP, the two have kept in touch and grew their friendship. Mark wants to invite Ted to a major sporting event as a guest. At HP, we consider this to be an inappropriate action because although Mark and Ted may have developed a friendship over the years, Mark's interactions with Ted have been in the context of business and professional activities, and would not be seen as being "based on a personal relationship."

U.S. government agencies usually issue a request for proposal (RFP) to solicit responses/proposals from vendors. While assembling the solutioning team (HP employees, subcontractors, and partners) that will work on preparing a response to the RFP, we must ensure that there is no organizational conflict of interest (OCI) or personal conflict of interest in play. An OCI exists if a company offering to do work with a public sector entity has an unfair competitive advantage or has other interests that may impair its objectivity or ability to perform satisfactorily. At HP we must follow any applicable government requirements—plus we impose some extra requirements of our own.

The personal conflict of interest and OCI apply to HP employees, subcontractors, and partners. Violations may result in disqualification from current or future U.S. public sector business opportunities. For example, if any entity on the HP team has been hired by the government to write the specifications to be included in a competitive RFP for a computer system, HP may be precluded from bidding in the procurement.

As part of the response we usually develop a business model, technical solution, and cost/price proposal. While developing the proposal response, the HP solutioning team needs to be aware of the two chief sources of potential liability for U.S. government contractors—the False Statements Act and the False Claims Act. These statutes impose

civil or even criminal penalties on contractors who provide false or misleading information to the government in connection with a government contract.

Thus the solutioning team may never knowingly make a false statement or submit a false claim to the government. This would include the submission of inaccurate or misleading information in support of prices offered by HP to the government, the submission of improper invoices, or inaccurate or misleading representations or certifications, either to a government representative or a prime contractor when the end user is the government.

> For example, in some cases the government may request "cost or pricing data"—that is, information about the company's actual costs of doing business. Additionally, proof of certain certifications is requested to ensure compliance with various socioeconomic requirements such as equal opportunity laws. Certifications may also be used to ensure that the bidder is a responsible government contractor. (For example, HP may be asked to certify that it has not been debarred from government contracting or had a contract terminated for default.). In all these cases it is essential that this information be accurately represented to the government in order to avoid claims of "defective pricing."

If HP is selected as a finalist, the government may request a best and final offer, which initiates the contract negotiation process. The procurement integrity rules in HP's SBC ensure employee compliance with the U.S. Procurement Integrity Act. Under this act, government officials may not disclose, and HP employees may not knowingly obtain, source selection information (such as bid prices prior to public opening, evaluations, rankings, and the like) and contractor bid or proposal information (cost or pricing data, any information marked as proprietary, labor rates, and so on) in connection with a pending procurement. The Procurement Integrity Act does not apply to any information that has been publicly disclosed.

> For example, during the solutioning or contract negotiations, the HP Team may not obtain nonpublic information by illegal activities involving industrial espionage or by asking a competitor's current or former employees, partners, or contractors to violate their obligations regarding the competitor's confidential data.

Whether public or private sector, you must think about your code of ethics in any business interaction. Your best interest requires you to become familiar with the policies and processes, as well as the resources that are available to you, should you find yourself in a questionable business situation. Developing and maintaining the trust of your colleagues, customers, and partners is critical to your success as a salesperson, as well as the success of your business. By making ethical decisions, you and your organization will earn respect in the industry and consequently improve your bottom line.

Visit our Web site at www.hp.com.

ETHICS AND PERSONAL SELLING

February 16, 2010: On the front page of *The Wall Street Journal* are four articles, two of which deal with business people acting unethically and probably illegally. One article focuses on a man who sold dreams of moving to America to Dutch dairy farmers, bilking them of millions. The other article centers on a plan to convince terminally ill individuals to purchase an investment product that pays the seller on the death of the patient. In return, the patient receives an upfront fee.[1] If all you ever saw about salespeople was that front page, you'd conclude that salespeople are all crooks. The reality, though, is that most sales transactions are aboveboard and free of ethical questions. These two stories are news precisely because such behavior is rare.

Ethics are the principles governing the behavior of an individual or a group. These principles establish appropriate behavior indicating what is right and wrong. Defining the term is easy, but determining what the principles are is difficult. What one person thinks is right another may consider wrong. For example, 58 percent of sales managers in one poll report believing that sales contests between salespeople do not generate unethical behavior—such as asking customers to take unwanted orders and then returning the merchandise after the contest is over—but 42 percent do believe that unethical behaviors are a consequence of sales contests.[2] So the feelings and experiences of sales managers are mixed when it comes to a commonly accepted practice.

What is ethical can vary from country to country and from industry to industry. For example, offering bribes to overcome bureaucratic roadblocks may be an accepted practice in Middle Eastern countries but is considered unethical, and illegal, in the United States. Further, while prevailing religions may influence ethics beliefs and practices, regional differences can occur. Egypt and Turkey, for example, are both populated almost entirely by Muslims; yet in Egypt, the courteousness of the salesperson is an important indicator of ethical practices. Not so in Turkey, which is more like the United States in not placing so much emphasis on courtesy; rather, actual customer service is preferred.[3]

An ethical principle can change over time. For example, some years ago doctors and lawyers who advertised their services were considered unethical. Today such advertising is accepted as common practice. Similarly, providing free pens and other gifts to doctors was once considered standard business practice; now a growing number of doctors consider the practice unethical and have even banned some companies from their offices or medical centers.[4]

THE EVOLUTION OF SELLING

The selling function has been a part of humankind since the beginning, perhaps when one person traded meat for berries. With the arrival of the Industrial Revolution in the 1800s, companies began to make more goods more cheaply. Even so, demand outstripped supply, and for many companies, the key issue in selling was to make people aware of the product and what it could do. Forward-thinking companies such as NCR and Singer Sewing Machines hired salespeople, called

Exhibit 2.1
The Evolution of
Personal Selling

	Production	Sales	Marketing	Partnering
Time Period	Before 1930	1930 to 1960	1960 to 1990	After 1990
Objective	Making sales	Making sales	Satisfying customer needs	Building relationships
Orientation	Short-term seller needs	Short-term seller needs	Short-term customer needs	Long-term customer and seller needs
Role of Salesperson	Provider	Persuader	Problem solver	Value creator
Activities of Salespeople	Taking orders, delivering goods	Aggressively convincing buyers to buy products	Matching available offerings to buyer needs	Creating new alternatives, matching buyer needs with seller capabilities

drummers or peddlers, and sent them across the country to sell. Then the companies brought the most effective salespeople back into the company office and wrote down their sales pitches. These **canned sales pitches** were distributed to all salespeople, who were expected to follow the scripts every time without deviation.

Since that time things have changed greatly. The nature of business evolved, necessarily changing how people sell. Exhibit 2.1 illustrates how the role of the salesperson has evolved from taking orders through persuading customers to building partnerships.[5]

As Exhibit 2.1 shows, the orientations of salespeople emerged in different periods. However, all these selling orientations still exist in business today. For example, inbound telephone salespeople working for retailers like Lands' End and Spiegel are providers with a production orientation. They answer a toll-free number and simply take orders. Many outbound telephone, real estate, and insurance salespeople are persuaders with a sales orientation. Partnering-oriented selling is becoming more common as companies make strategic choices about the type of selling best suited to their situation, but recent research indicates that even within partnerships, there are times when the buyer needs to hear persuasive messages that might be scripted.[6]

Even so, the move from a production orientation to a partnering orientation has affected the ethical perspective of the sales profession. The marketing orientation has created a customer-focused perspective that increases awareness of the buyer's needs. This customer awareness naturally leads to a less selfish seller and increases the importance of ethics. Further, the partnering orientation of the current period means long-term relationships are the norm. Salespeople who are less than ethical get caught in long-term relationships. The era of the peddler who can leave town and dupe the citizens of the next town is over.

ETHICS AND PARTNERING RELATIONSHIPS

Ethical principles are particularly important in personal selling. Most businesses try to develop long-term, mutually beneficial relationships with their customers. Salespeople are the official representatives of their companies, responsible for

From the BUYER'S SEAT

THE IMPORTANCE OF ETHICS IN THE SUPPLY CHAIN: GRANITE CONSTRUCTION

By Rick Carlysle, Granite Construction

I have worked for Granite Construction for over 20 years, during which time we've grown from $300 million to about $3 billion in annual revenue. We are a civil projects construction company building major projects like airports, highways, transit systems, and the like. I started in Texas as an engineer but moved to the corporate office in California, then New York City where I am now the regional contracts administrator. I've been involved in negotiating contracts with our subcontractors for the past 14 years.

Granite established a code of ethics a long time ago. Our company has been around since 1922, and we developed that code of ethics very early on. You can find it on our Web site; we share it with our customers and our subcontractors and with our vendors. In Granite, there is no gray area—we know what the expectations are. We're one of the prime contractors, and people want to work with us because they know our ethics. It (the code of ethics) is the basis for how we work.

Dealings with other companies have been better in New York City than I thought they would be. Contractors in New York may not have the greatest image, but I've not had any under-the-table dealings and not seen anything funny. But that's likely to be as much due to our reputation; and when you have a reputation for being honest and ethical, you attract like-minded companies.

If we have four bidders for a $10m electrical package and they are all within say $1m, we talk to the low bidder so that we know we're not being low-balled. If he is missing something, we need to put in plugs to fill the gap. We don't shop the bid. We don't tell subs, "You gotta do better than that," or (wink wink), "You gotta get down to such and such number." We ask for the best bid to begin with and we work with that. Once we've won a job, I work through the negotiations with the sub on issues such as payment terms, insurance, default, retainage and bonding, and so on. During the negotiations you formulate a good relationship with the sub, and you can tell at that point if there are any questionable issues or ethics. And if there are, we address them then.

One of our projects can last from one to four years, or even longer. We have to have subs we can rely on to do the right thing. The owner of the project (the state, or airport, or other agency) has to live with us, too. Ethics and fairness really come into play regarding change orders. Envision an owner that wants to add to the project and wants a price. We have to go back to subs, ask for prices, then put it together and go back to the owner. Then it is negotiated. We need this to be a positive experience, a win–win. We are a publicly traded company, and we are open on our books with the owner. We want a fair markup and overhead. Once you've established a reputation and people believe in it and in you, then our subs know it and our customers know it, and they all want to work with us.

Our reputation is really important. Building this reputation has taken a long time, but only one mess-up can tear it down. Therefore, when it comes to ethics, we operate as if there are no second chances.

Source: Contributed by Rick Carlysle, regional contracts administrator, Granite Construction.

developing and maintaining these relationships, which are built on trust. Partnerships between buyers and sellers cannot develop when salespeople behave unethically or illegally.[7] Further, research shows that trust deteriorates rapidly even in well-established relationships if integrity becomes questionable.[8]

Legal principles guide business transactions. The issues governing buying and selling are typically straightforward when the transaction is simple and the purchase is a one-time deal. The terms and conditions can be well defined and easily written into a traditional contract. In longer-term relationships, though, legal principles cannot cover all behaviors between buyer and seller.

Ethical principles become increasingly important as firms move toward longer-term relationships. Many issues cannot be reduced to contractual terms. For example, a salesperson might make a concession for a buyer with a special problem, anticipating that the buyer will reciprocate on future orders. Yet there is no legal obligation for the buyer to do so; this type of give-and-take is exactly why trust is such an important part of relationships. Because of the high levels of investment and uncertainty, the parties in these relationships cannot accurately assess the potential benefits—the size of the pie—accruing from strategic investments in the relationships or the contributions of each party in producing those benefits. Thus the parties in a longer-term relationship have to trust one another to divide the pie fairly. Further, many business settings require that the pie be divided amongst several suppliers or subcontractors, as well as with the customer. "From the Buyer's Seat 2.1" illustrates how important ethics are in the broader supply chain.

A basic principle of ethical selling is that the customer remains free to make a choice. **Manipulation** eliminates or reduces the buyer's choice unfairly. Salespeople can persuade; but with **persuasion,** one may influence the buyer's decision, but the decision remains the buyer's. Manipulation is unethical; persuasion is not. Keep that difference in mind as you read the rest of this chapter.

Here are some examples of difficult situations that salespeople face:

- Should you give an expensive Christmas gift to your biggest customer?
- If a buyer tells you it is common practice to pay off purchasing agents to get orders in his or her country, should you do it?
- Is it acceptable to use a high-pressure sales approach when you know your product is the best for the customer's needs?
- Is it okay to *not* share information about your product that could cost you a sale?
- Should you attempt to sell a product to a customer if you know a better product exists for that application?
- If you know about the poor performance features of a competing product, should you tell the customer about them?
- How do you handle a customer who has been lied to about your product by one of your competitors?

thinking **it** through

How would you respond to the situations in the preceding list? Why? How do you think your friends and your family would respond?

FACTORS INFLUENCING THE ETHICAL BEHAVIOR OF SALESPEOPLE

Exhibit 2.2 illustrates the factors that affect the ethical behavior of salespeople. The personal needs of salespeople, the needs of their companies and customers, company policies, the values of significant others, and the salesperson's personal code of ethics affect ethical choices.[9]

Personal, Company, and Customer Needs

Exhibit 2.3 shows how the personal needs of salespeople can conflict with needs of their firms and their customers. Both the salesperson's company and its customers want to make profits. But sometimes these objectives are conflicting. For example, should a salesperson tell a customer about problems his or her firm is having with a new product? Concealing this information might help make a sale,

Exhibit 2.2

Factors Affecting Ethical Behavior of Salespeople

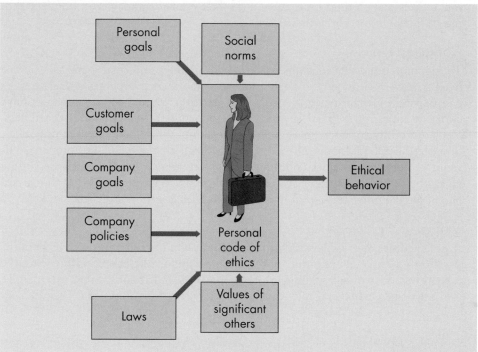

Exhibit 2.3

Conflicting Objectives

Company Objectives	Salesperson Objectives	Customer Objectives
Increase profits	Increase compensation	Increase profits
Increase sales	Receive recognition	Solve problems, satisfy needs
Reduce sales costs	Satisfy customers	Reduce costs
Build long-term customer relationships	Build long-term customer relationships	Build relationships with suppliers
Avoid legal trouble	Maintain personal code of ethics	Avoid legal trouble

increase the company's profits, and enhance the salesperson's chances of getting a promotion and a bonus; but doing so could also decrease the customer's profits when the product does not perform adequately.

Companies need to make sales, and that need can drive some unethical behavior. One salesperson was recently asked by his boss to bid on a project that required all of the work to be done locally. Yet he knew that his company planned to have some of the work done in India. The CEO's justification was that the company needed the business, and the customer was going to get a better price. The sales rep decided to not bid the job and told the CEO that he didn't. Fortunately for him, the CEO did not get upset.

Resolving serious ethical problems is difficult, but companies that resolve ethical issues well experience many benefits. Research shows that a positive ethical climate is related to job satisfaction, commitment to the organization, and intention to stay among salespeople—especially better-performing salespeople.[10] Organizations that have a positive ethical climate also have salespeople more committed to meeting the organization's goals.

Ethical conflicts often are not covered by company policies and procedures, and managers may not be available to provide advice. Thus salespeople must make decisions on their own, relying on their ethical standards and understanding of the laws governing these situations.

Company Policies

To maintain good relationships with their companies and customers, salespeople need to have a clear sense of right and wrong so their companies and customers can depend on them when questionable situations arise. Many companies have codes of ethics for their salespeople to provide guidelines in making ethical decisions. An outline of Motorola's policy appears in Exhibit 2.4. Shell's ethics policy, however, is a book some 20 pages long! Recall that Pat Gietl's company, HP, requires her and her sales colleagues to take annual training courses regarding company policies, as well as laws and regulations, to ensure that she and her colleagues make informed decisions regarding ethics issues.

Values of Significant Others

People acquire their values and attitudes about what is right and wrong from the people they interact with and observe. Some important people influencing the ethical behavior of salespeople are their relatives and friends, other salespeople, and their sales managers. Sales managers are particularly important because they

Exhibit 2.4
Ethics Policy for
Motorola Salespeople

Improper Use of Company Funds and Assets

The funds and assets of Motorola may not be used for influential gifts, illegal payments of any kind, or political contributions, whether legal or illegal.

The funds and assets of Motorola must be properly and accurately recorded on the books and records of Motorola.

Motorola shall not enter into, with dealers, distributors, agents, or consultants, any agreements that are not in compliance with U.S. laws and the laws of any other country that may be involved, or that provide for the payment of a commission or fee that is not commensurate with the services to be rendered.

Customer/Supplier/Government Relationships

Motorola will respect the confidence of its customers. Motorola will respect the laws, customs, and traditions of each country in which it operates but, in so doing, will not engage in any act or course of conduct that may violate U.S. laws or its business ethics. Employees of Motorola shall not accept payments, gifts, gratuities, or favors from customers or suppliers.

Conflict of Interest

A Motorola employee shall not be a supplier or a competitor of Motorola or be employed by a competitor, supplier, or customer of Motorola. A Motorola employee shall not engage in any activity where the skill and knowledge developed while in the employment of Motorola is transferred or applied to such activity in a way that results in a negative impact on the present or prospective business interest of Motorola.

A Motorola employee shall not have any relationship with any other business enterprise that might affect the employee's independence of judgment in transactions between Motorola and the other business enterprise.

A Motorola employee may not have any interest in any supplier or customer of Motorola that could compromise the employee's loyalty to Motorola.

Compliance with the Code of Conduct is a condition of employment. We urge you to read the complete code.

Should any questions remain, you are encouraged to consult your Motorola law department. In the world of business, your understanding and cooperation are essential. As in all things, Motorola cannot operate to the highest standards without you.

Source: Company document. Used with permission.

establish the ethical climate in their organization through the salespeople they hire, the ethical training they provide for their salespeople, and the degree to which they enforce ethical standards.[11]

Some people hesitate to pursue a sales career because they think selling will force them to compromise their principles.[12] Research, though, suggests otherwise. One series of studies finds that salespeople are less prone to unethical behaviors like exaggeration than are politicians, preachers, and even professors![13] No matter the industry, research finds that ethical behavior leads to higher customer satisfaction, trust, loyalty, and repeat purchases. As one of our former students now selling commercial real estate told us, "Unethical reps are run out of our industry." Good ethics are good business, and sales managers and salespeople know that.

Laws

In this chapter we examine ethical and legal issues in personal selling. *Laws* dictate which activities society has deemed to be clearly wrong—the activities for which salespeople and their companies will be punished. Some of these laws are reviewed later in the chapter. However, most sales situations are not covered by laws. Salespeople have to rely on their own codes of ethics and/or their firms' and industries' codes of ethics to determine the right thing to do.

A Personal Code of Ethics

Long before salespeople go to work they develop a sense of what is right and wrong—a standard of conduct—from family and friends. Although salespeople should abide by their own codes of ethics, they may be tempted to avoid difficult ethical choices by developing "logical" reasons for unethical conduct. For example, a salesperson may use the following rationalizations:

- All salespeople behave "this way" (unethically) in this situation.
- No one will be hurt by this behavior.
- This behavior is the lesser of two evils.
- This conduct is the price one has to pay for being in business.

Salespeople who use such reasoning want to avoid feeling responsible for their behavior and being bound by ethical considerations. Even though the pressure to make sales may tempt some salespeople to be unethical and act against their internal standards, maintaining an ethical self-image is important. Compromising ethical standards to achieve short-term gains can have adverse long-term effects. When salespeople violate their own principles, they lose self-respect and confidence in their abilities. They may begin to think that the only way they can make sales is to be dishonest or unethical, a downward spiral that can have significant negative effects.

Short-term compromises also make long-term customer relationships more difficult to form. As discussed earlier, customers who have been treated unethically will be reluctant to deal with those salespeople again. Also, they may relate these experiences to business associates in other companies.

Exhibit 2.5 lists some questions you can ask yourself to determine whether a sales behavior or activity is unethical. The questions emphasize that ethical behavior is determined by widely accepted views of what is right and wrong. Thus you should engage only in activities about which you would be proud to tell your family, friends, employer, and customers.

Your firm can strongly affect the ethical choices you will have to make. What if your manager asks you to engage in activity you consider unethical? There are

Exhibit 2.5
Checklist for Making
Ethical Decisions

1. Would I be embarrassed if a customer found out about this behavior?
2. Would my supervisor disapprove of this behavior?
3. Would most salespeople feel that this behavior is unusual?
4. Am I about to do this because I think I can get away with it?
5. Would I be upset if a salesperson did this to me?
6. Would my family or friends think less of me if I told them about engaging in this sales activity?
7. Am I concerned about the possible consequences of this behavior?
8. Would I be upset if this behavior or activity were publicized in a newspaper article?
9. Would society be worse off if everyone engaged in this behavior or activity?

If the answer to any of these questions is yes, the behavior or activity is probably unethical and you should not do it.

a number of choices you can make that are discussed in greater detail in Chapter 16, when we focus on relationships with your manager. From a personal perspective, however, here are three of those choices:

1. *Ignore your personal values, and do what your company asks you to do.* Self-respect suffers when you have to compromise principles to please an employer. If you take this path, you will probably feel guilty and quickly become dissatisfied with yourself and your job.
2. *Take a stand, and tell your employer what you think.* Try to influence the decisions and policies of your company and supervisors.
3. *Refuse to compromise your principles.* Taking this path may mean you will get fired or be forced to quit. Long-term benefits, though, can accrue as customers find that you are trustworthy.

You should not take a job with a company whose products, policies, and conduct conflict with your standards. Before taking a sales job, investigate the company's procedures and selling approach to see whether they conflict with your personal ethical standards. The issues concerning the relationship between salespeople and their companies are discussed in more detail in Chapter 16, and methods for evaluating companies are presented in Chapter 17.

SELLING ETHICS AND RELATIONSHIPS

The core principle at work in considering ethics in professional selling is that of fairness. The buyer has the right to make the purchase decision with equal and fair access to the information needed to make the decision; further, all competitors should have fair access to the sales opportunity. Keeping information from the customer or misrepresenting information is not fair because it does not allow the customer to make an informed decision. Kickbacks, bribes, and other unethical activities are unfair to both the customer's organization and to competitors. Those types of activities do not allow fair access to the sales opportunity. These and other situations can confront salespeople in their relationships with their customers, competitors, and colleagues (other salespeople).

RELATIONSHIPS WITH CUSTOMERS

The most common areas of ethical concern involving customers include using deception; offering gifts, bribes, and entertainment; divulging confidential information and rights to privacy; and backdoor selling.

Deception

Deliberately presenting inaccurate information, or lying, to a customer is illegal. Further, misleading customers by telling half-truths or withholding important information can also lead to legal consequences, but is more often a matter of ethics. Some salespeople believe it is the customer's responsibility to uncover potential product problems. These salespeople answer questions, perhaps incompletely, and don't offer information that might make a sale more difficult. For example, a salesperson selling life insurance may fail to mention that the policy won't pay off under certain circumstances.

Customers expect salespeople to be enthusiastic about their firm and its products and recognize that this enthusiasm can result in a certain amount of exaggeration as part of the persuasion process. Customers also expect salespeople to emphasize the positive aspects of their products and spend little time talking about the negative aspects. But practicing **deception** by withholding information or telling lies is clearly manipulative and therefore unethical. Such salespeople take advantage of the trust customers place in them. When buyers uncover these deceptions, they will be reluctant to trust such salespeople in the future. Not only that, but sophisticated buyers recognize such deceptions and assume the worst anyway.[14]

Salespeople who fail to provide customers with complete information about products lose an opportunity to develop trust. Trust is created through many actions, such as keeping all promises, especially the small promises like calling back when you say you will. In "Building Partnerships 2.1" we develop this concept of trust more completely.

Bribes, Gifts, and Entertainment

Bribes and kickbacks may be illegal. **Bribes** are payments made to buyers to influence their purchase decisions, whereas **kickbacks** are payments made to buyers based on the amount of orders placed. A purchasing agent personally benefits from bribes and kickbacks, but these payments typically have negative consequences for the purchasing agent's firm because the product's performance is not considered in buying decisions.

Entertaining clients is an accepted business practice in most industries, and this is an acceptable way to build relationships as long as the entertainment is not too lavish.

Taking customers to lunch is a commonly accepted business practice. Most salespeople take customers to lunch occasionally or frequently, and in many instances salespeople use this time to get to know the buyer better rather than pitch business. However, some companies take customers to sporting events, to play golf, or even on overnight trips to the company's plant or headquarters. In some cases these trips can become quite lavish; the pharmaceutical industry, for example, came under close governmental regulation for questionable practices regarding exotic and expensive trips for doctors who prescribe certain medications.

Determining which gifts and entertainment activities are acceptable and which are not brings up ethical issues. To avoid these issues, many U.S. companies have policies that forbid employees to accept gifts (more than pencils or coffee cups) or entertainment from suppliers. These firms require that all gifts sent to the employee's home or office be returned. IBM does not allow any gifts, even coffee cups; Walmart, the largest retailer in the world, makes no allowance for entertainment

BUILDING TRUST BUILDS PARTNERSHIPS

"Anyone working with Jessica Ni can be confident that she will overdeliver on whatever you requested, no matter how impossible the request may be," says client Jordan Levinson. "It's comforting to know there are still people out there who truly care about your brand and what you're trying to do for it. The industry at large could learn a lot from the little things Jessica does right day in and day out." With compliments like that coming from customers, it is no wonder that Jessica Ni was named Salesperson of the Year by an industry association. Jessica is a sales representative for *The Atlantic,* a monthly magazine, and works with advertisers to see that they get the most for their advertising dollars.

What Levinson is describing is a person that can be trusted. Trust, to buyers, means that the salesperson can be counted on to deliver what is needed. And when building partnerships, trust is the most important ingredient.

Randy Garutti, managing partner in charge of all purchasing for Shake Shack, a chain of hamburger restaurants in the New York City area, agrees. When asked what he looks for in a supplier, "trust" is the first word out of his mouth. Before price and before service, he wants someone he can trust. "If we run out of products,

they will put whatever we need in their car and drive it to us."

Levinson and Garutti both point out the importance of being able to count on someone to deliver. But there's also an aspect of empathy, or caring for the buyer, that seems to be important. These buyers want someone who will work for them, knowing that things don't always go as planned but that the salesperson is there to make it right. Research shows that ethical behavior builds trust. Further, buyers have difficulty separating trust in a company from trust in the salesperson, but it is clear that unethical behavior depletes trust. And without trust, there is no business opportunity—at least not with buyers like Levinson and Garutti.

Sources: The Levinson quote is from "Salesperson of the Year," *MIN Online,* http://www.minonline.com/best_sellers/Salesperson-of-the-Year-Manager-Level-Single-Title-With-Circ-Between-100K-500K-Jessica-Ni-Midwest-Integrated-Account-Manager-The-Atlantic_11207.html, accessed February 18, 2010. The Garutti quote is from Caroline Perkins, "Trust Is the Key Trait for Sales Reps, Says USHG's Garutti," *Nation's Restaurant News* 43, no. 39 (October 19, 2009), p. 18; the research cited is Mei-Fang Chen and Liang-Hung Mau, "The Impacts of Ethical Sales Behaviour on Customer Loyalty in the Life Insurance Industry," *The Service Industries Journal* 29 (2009), pp. 1–21.

because all contact between buyers and vendors can occur only at business meetings at Walmart's or the vendor's headquarters. On the other hand, many companies have no policy on receiving gifts or entertainment. Some unethical employees will accept and even solicit gifts, even though their company has a policy against such practices.

To develop a productive, long-term relationship, salespeople need to avoid embarrassing customers by asking them to engage in activities they might see as unethical. If a salesperson wants to give a gift out of friendship or invite a customer to lunch to develop a better business relationship, she or he should phrase the offer so the customer can easily refuse it. For example, a salesperson with a large industrial firm might have this conversation with a customer:

SALESPERSON: John, we have worked well together over the last five years, and I would like to give you something to show my appreciation. Would that be OK?

BUYER: That's very nice of you, but what are you thinking of giving me?

SALESPERSON: Well, I want to give you a Mont Blanc pen. I really enjoy using my pen, and I thought you might like one also. Is that OK?

BUYER: I would appreciate that gift. Thank you.

Buyers typically are sensitive about receiving expensive gifts, according to Shirley Hunter, account manager for Teradata. "It's like getting five dozen roses after a first date. It's embarrassing if anyone finds out, and you have to wonder what's the catch?"[15] Some industries used promotional items frequently; but in pharmaceutical sales, government regulations have increasingly forbidden the use of gifts because no one wants the choice of a prescription to be influenced by a salesperson's gift to a doctor. Some guidelines for gift giving are as follows:

- Check your motives for giving the gift. The gift should be given to foster a mutually beneficial, long-term relationship, not to obligate or pay off the customer for placing an order.
- Make sure the customer views the gift as a symbol of your appreciation and respect with no strings attached. Never give customers the impression that you are attempting to buy their business with a gift.
- Make sure the gift does not violate the customer's or your firm's policies.
- The safest gifts are inexpensive business items imprinted with the salesperson's company's name or logo.

Even when customers encourage and accept gifts, lavish gifts and entertainment are both unethical and bad business. Treating a customer to a three-day fishing trip is no substitute for effective selling. Sales won this way are usually short-lived. Salespeople who offer expensive gifts to get orders may be blackmailed into continually providing these gifts to obtain orders in the future. Customers who can be bribed are likely to switch their business when presented with better offers.

Special Treatment

Some customers try to take advantage of their status to get special treatment from salespeople. For example, a buyer asks a salesperson to make a weekly check on the performance of equipment even after the customer's employees have been thoroughly trained in the operation and maintenance of the equipment. Providing this extra service may upset other customers who do not get the special attention. In addition, the special service can reduce the salesperson's productivity. Salespeople should be diplomatic but careful about undertaking requests to provide unusual services.

Confidential Information

During sales calls salespeople often encounter confidential company information such as new products under development, costs, and production schedules. Offering information about a customer's competitor in exchange for an order is unethical. Many times, though, the request is not that obvious. For example, a customer asks how well your product is selling and you reply, "Great!" The customer then asks, "Well, how is it doing at HEB?" If the customer is told how many cases are sold at HEB, then HEB's right to confidentiality was violated. We discuss legal issues around privacy later in this chapter, but there are ethical issues regarding confidentiality that are not always covered by law.

Long-term relationships can develop only when customers trust salespeople to maintain confidentiality. By disclosing confidential information, a salesperson will get a reputation for being untrustworthy. Even the customer who solicited the confidential information will not trust the salesperson, who will then be denied access to information needed to make an effective sales presentation.

Backdoor Selling

Sometimes purchasing agents require that all contacts with the prospect's employees be made through them because they want to be fully informed about and control the buying process. The purchasing agent insists that salespeople get his or her approval before meeting with other people involved in the purchase decision. This policy can make it difficult for a new supplier to get business from a customer using a competitor's products.

Salespeople engage in **backdoor selling** when they ignore the purchasing agent's policy, go around his or her back, and contact other people directly involved in the purchasing decision. Backdoor selling can be risky and unethical. If the purchasing agent finds out, the salesperson may never be able to get an order. To avoid these potential problems, the salesperson needs to convince the purchasing agent of the benefits to be gained by direct contact with other people in the customer's firm.

Jason Evans, MD, wrote a letter to the pharmaceutical salespeople who called on him, and he posted it in several conspicuous places in his office building. This letter specifies his expectations for acceptable selling tactics; a few of his points are listed in Exhibit 2.6. He reports that many salespeople commented that they appreciated knowing his expectations for their behavior, and from his perspective, interactions with salespeople have improved. Yet salespeople we've interviewed find the list too restrictive. Whether fair or too restrictive, Evans's letter has caught on and can now be found in many doctors' offices.

Sneaking in the back door to sell behind the purchasing agent's back directly to a user in the buying company is considered unethical and can get a company blacklisted, unable to sell to that buyer again.

Research on buyers in general suggests additional behaviors that they think are unethical or inappropriate. Exhibit 2.7 summarizes that research. The research suggests that buyers will go out of their way to avoid salespeople who engage in these practices.[16]

RELATIONSHIPS WITH THE SALESPERSON'S COMPANY

Because salespeople's activities in the field cannot be closely monitored, their employers trust them to act in the company's best interests. Professional salespeople do not abuse this trust. They put the interests of their companies above self-interest. Taking

Exhibit 2.6
One Doctor's Request for Ethical Behavior

DO: Tell me why your drug is exceptional using the STEPS approach: *safety, tolerability, efficacy, price,* and *simplicity.*

DON'T: Say negative things about your competitors or their drugs.

DON'T: Tell me what and how much another physician in the area uses your drug.

DON'T: Invite me to dinner.

DO: Arrange for specialists to come to our office during lunch so I can pick their brains.

DON'T: Offer me pens, notepads, or any other "freebies" with your drug's name on it. The cost is in your company's budget, which raises the price you charge my patients.

Source: Adapted from Jason Evans, "Establishing Rules of the Road for Pharmaceutical Representatives," *Family Practice Management,* March 2005, pp. 10–11.

Exhibit 2.7
Buyers' View of
Unethical Sales
Behaviors

- Exaggerates benefits of product.
- Passes the blame for something he or she did to someone else.
- Lies about product availability.
- Misrepresents guarantees.
- Lies about competition.
- Sells products that people do not need.
- Makes oral promises that are not legally binding.
- Is not interested in customer needs.
- Answers questions even when he or she does not know the correct answer.
- Sells hazardous products.

Source: Adapted from William Bearden, Thomas Ingram, and Raymond LaForge, *Marketing: Principles and Perspectives* (New York: McGraw-Hill/Irwin, 2004).

this perspective may require them to make short-term sacrifices to achieve long-term benefits for their companies and themselves. Some problem areas in the salesperson–company relationship involve expense accounts, reporting work time information and activities, and switching jobs. "Sales Technology 2.1" illustrates some problems salespeople may have with use of the company computer.

Expense Accounts

Many companies provide their salespeople with cars and reimburse them for travel and entertainment expenses. Developing a reimbursement policy that prevents salespeople from cheating and still allows them the flexibility they need to cover their territories and entertain customers is almost impossible. Moreover, a lack of tight control can tempt salespeople to use their expense accounts to increase their income.

To do their jobs well, salespeople need to incur expenses. However, using their expense accounts to offset what they consider to be inadequate compensation is unethical. A salesperson who cannot live within the company compensation plan and expense policies has two ethical alternatives: (1) persuade the company to change its compensation plan or expense policy or (2) find another job. Salespeople are given expense accounts to cover legitimate expenses such as for travel. Act as though you are spending your own money; an expense account does not mean you should stay in the most luxurious hotel in town.

Reporting Work Time Information and Activities

Employers expect their salespeople to work full-time. Salespeople on salary are stealing from their employers when they waste time on coffee breaks, long lunches, or unauthorized days off. Even salespeople paid by commission cheat their companies by not working full-time. Their incomes and company profits both decrease when salespeople take time off. In "Sales Technology 2.1" we take a light-hearted look at the reality of technology and the ever-increasing ability of companies to ensure accurate reporting and full use of company time.

To monitor work activities, many companies ask their salespeople to provide daily call reports. Most salespeople dislike this clerical task. Some provide false information, including calls they never made. Giving inaccurate information or bending the truth is clearly unethical. A failure to get an appointment with a customer is not a sales call. Providing a brief glimpse of a product is not a demonstration.

THE BIG BROTHER EFFECT OF TECHNOLOGY

Orwell's frightening tale of totalitarian government control, *1984*, introduced the term "Big Brother," the notion that someone is looking over your shoulder and tracking your every movement in order to control your activities. Key to Big Brother in the Orwell novel was the use of technology, unavailable when the novel was written but maybe close to being available now.

Sneaking out to the golf course? Busted by the company-issued cell phone! GPS technology in the phone can be used to identify where a salesperson is.

Waiting until the end of the month to create your reports? Busted! The software notes when you entered the data, and the sales manager assumes the data are, at best, a little fuzzy and perhaps not all that accurate. Or at worst the manager assumes the calls weren't made, and now someone is looking for a new job.

Spending work time on Facebook? Busted! But Facebook can be a real business tool, with its IM feature used between colleagues at work, and the social network aspects used for identifying prospects (finding friends) or sending a message. Just don't put this on your wall: "Work sucks! Three more days to the weekend!"

Sending risqué photos and jokes via e-mail? Busted again! Some companies closely monitor e-mail. While stories abound of salespeople accidentally copying customers on e-mail messages that make fun of those same customers, more recently companies have cracked down on using work computers for personal activities. And it's not worth the possibility of getting fired to share jokes or pictures that some might think are funny but others think are sexual harassment.

Many salespeople complain of not being able to get away from work. Carrying a company-issued Blackberry or iPhone leads to answering e-mail and customer calls 24/7. Couple that around-the-clock availability with the facts that even though only 52 percent of salespeople reached quota last year, 85 percent of companies increased quotas further this year. and the pressure is on to stay connected. Add to that the ability to track a salesperson's activity on the Web, e-mail, or even the phone, and it can feel like Big Brother is watching every move. When every move is the right move, though, it's no problem.

Source for survey data: Jim Dickie, "Avoid the Disaster of 2009," *CRM Magazine*, February 2010, p. 10.

Switching Jobs

When salespeople decide to change jobs, they have an ethical responsibility to their employers. The company often makes a considerable investment in training salespeople and then gives them confidential information about new products and programs. Over time, salespeople use this training and information to build strong relationships with their customers.

A salesperson may have good reasons to switch jobs. However, if a salesperson goes to work for a competitor, she or he should not say negative things about the past employer. Also, disclosing confidential information about the former employer's business is improper. The ethical approach to leaving a job includes the following:

- *Give ample notice.* If you leave a job during a busy time and with inadequate notice, your employer may suffer significant lost sales opportunities. Do not be surprised, though, if you are escorted out that day. Many companies are concerned about the loss of information by, as well as lack of productivity of, someone who has turned in notice, so the policy may be that you are turned out that day.

- *Offer assistance during the transition phase.* Help your replacement learn about your customers and territory, if given the opportunity.

- *Don't burn your bridges.* Don't say things in anger that may come back to haunt you. Remember that you may want to return to the company or ask the company for a reference in the future. You may even find that the people you worked with move to a company you want to work for or sell to!
- *Don't take anything with you that belongs to the company.* That includes all your records and notes on companies you called on, even if you are going to a noncompeting company. In many states, customer records are considered **trade secrets,** or information owned by the company by which the company gains a competitive advantage. Trade secrets are protected by law, so if you take customer records with you, you could face a civil lawsuit.

RELATIONSHIPS WITH COLLEAGUES

To be effective, salespeople need to work together with other salespeople. Unethical behavior by salespeople toward their coworkers, such as engaging in sexual harassment and taking advantage of colleagues, can weaken company morale and harm the company's reputation.

Sexual Harassment

Sexual harassment includes unwelcome sexual advances, requests for sexual favors, jokes or graffiti, posting sexually explicit material on bulletin boards or cubicle walls, and physical conduct. Harassment is not confined to requests for sexual favors in exchange for job considerations such as a raise or promotion; creating a hostile work environment can be considered sexual harassment. Some actions that are considered sexual harassment are engaging in suggestive behavior, treating people differently because they are male or female, making lewd sexual comments and gestures, jokes that have sexual content shared by e-mail, showing obscene photographs, alleging that an employee got rewards by engaging in sexual acts, and spreading rumors about a person's sexual conduct.

Customers as well as coworkers can sexually harass salespeople. Salespeople are particularly vulnerable to harassment from important customers who may seek sexual favors in exchange for their business. Following are some suggestions for dealing with sexual harassment from customers:

- Don't become so dependent on one customer that you would consider compromising your principles to retain the customer's business. Develop a large base of customers and prospects to minimize the importance of one customer—a good idea for a lot of reasons.
- Tell the harasser in person or write a letter stating that the behavior is offensive, is unacceptable, and must be stopped. Clearly indicate that you are in control and will not be passive.
- Use the sexual harassment policies of your firm and your customer's firm to resolve problems. These policies typically state the procedure for filing a complaint, the person responsible for investigating the complaint, the time frame for completing the investigation, and the means by which the parties will be informed about the resolution.

Recent research indicates that sexual harassment is rare; one study found only an average of 1.3 cases per year per company in all areas of the company, not just sales.[17] That study also found that companies are much more worried about making sure their employees have a safe environment in which to work than any fear of lawsuits; in other words, executives want to make sure their people have a good environment in which to work because it is the right thing to do, not because they may get sued if they fail to do so.

Taking Advantage of Other Salespeople

Salespeople can behave unethically when they are too aggressive in pursuing their own goals at the expense of their colleagues. For example, it is unethical to steal potential customers from other salespeople. Colleagues usually discover such unethical behavior and return the lack of support. If the company has policies protecting customers or territories, such behavior can lead to immediate termination.

RELATIONSHIPS WITH COMPETITORS

Making false claims about competitors' products or sabotaging their efforts is clearly unethical and often illegal. For example, a salesperson who rearranges the display of a competitor's products in a customer's store to make it less appealing is being unethical. This type of behavior can backfire. When customers detect these practices, the reputations of the salespeople and their companies may be permanently damaged.

Another questionable tactic is criticizing a competitor's products or policies. Although you may be tempted to say negative things about a competitor, this approach usually does not work. Customers will assume you are biased toward your own company and its products and discount negative comments you make about the competition. Some customers may even be offended. If they have bought the competitor's products in the past, they may regard these comments as a criticism of their judgment.

LEGAL ISSUES

Society has determined that some activities are clearly unethical and has created a legal system to prevent people from engaging in these activities. Salespeople who violate these laws can cause serious problems for themselves and their companies—problems more serious than being considered unethical by a buyer. By engaging in illegal activities, salespeople expose themselves and their firms to costly legal fees and millions of dollars in fines.

The activities of salespeople in the United States are affected by three forms of law: statutory, administrative, and common. **Statutory law** is based on legislation passed either by state legislatures or by Congress. The main statutory laws governing salespeople are the Uniform Commercial Code and antitrust laws. **Administrative laws** are established by local, state, or federal regulatory agencies. The Federal Trade Commission is the most active agency in developing administrative laws affecting salespeople. However, the Securities and Exchange Commission regulates stockbrokers, and the Food and Drug Administration regulates pharmaceutical salespeople. Finally, **common law** grows out of court decisions. Precedents set by these decisions fill in the gaps where no laws exist.

This section discusses current laws affecting salespeople, but every year important new laws are developed and court decisions rendered. Thus you should contact your firm for advice when a potential legal issue arises.

UNIFORM COMMERCIAL CODE

The **Uniform Commercial Code (UCC)** is the legal guide to commercial practice in the United States. The UCC defines a number of terms related to salespeople.

Agency

A person who acts in place of his or her company is an **agent.** Authorized agents of a company have the authority to legally obligate their firm in a business transaction. This authorization to represent the company does not have to be in writing. Thus, as a salesperson, your statements and actions can legally bind your company and have significant financial impact.

Sale

The UCC defines a **sale** as "the transfer of title to goods by the seller to the buyer for a consideration known as price." A sale differs from a **contract to sell.** Any time a salesperson makes an offer and receives an unqualified acceptance, a contract exists. A sale is made when the contract is completed and title passes from the seller to the buyer.

The UCC also distinguishes between an offer and an invitation to negotiate. A sales presentation is usually considered to be an **invitation to negotiate.** An **offer** takes place when the salesperson quotes specific terms. The offer specifically states what the seller promises to deliver and what it expects from the buyer. If the buyer accepts these terms, the parties will have established a binding contract.

Salespeople are agents when they have the authority to make offers. However, most salespeople are not agents because they have the power only to solicit written offers from buyers. These written offers, called **orders,** become contracts when they are signed by an authorized representative in the salesperson's company. Sometimes these orders contain clauses stating that the firm is not obligated by its salesperson's statements. However, the buyer usually can have the contract nullified and may even sue for damages if salespeople make misleading statements, even though they are not official agents.

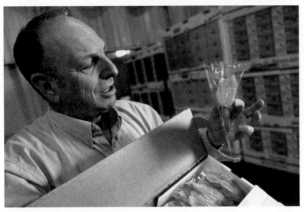

This buyer is inspecting a shipment of flowers. Because the flowers were shipped FOB destination, the buyer is not responsible for the merchandise until it shows up at the buyer's warehouse. The buyer can even turn down the sale now if the flowers are not up to standard.

Title and Risk of Loss

If the contract terms specify **free on board (FOB) destination,** the seller has title until the goods are received at the destination. In this case any loss or damage incurred during transportation is the responsibility of the seller. The buyer assumes this responsibility and risk if contract terms call for **FOB factory.** The UCC also defines when titles transfer for goods shipped cash on delivery (COD) and for goods sold on consignment. Understanding the terms of the sale and who has title can be useful in resolving complaints about damaged merchandise.

thinking **it** through

If a salesperson is not an agent, then what is the salesperson? Does not being an agent change the salesperson's obligations to the company in any way? Or to the customer?

Oral versus Written Agreements

In most cases oral agreements between a salesperson and a customer are just as binding as written agreements. Normally, written agreements are required for sales over $500. Salespeople may be the legal representatives of their firms and thus must be careful when signing written agreements.

Obligations and Performance

When the salesperson and the customer agree on the terms of a contract, both firms must perform according to those terms in "good faith," which means they have to try to fulfill the contract. In addition, both parties must perform according to commonly accepted industry practices. Even if salespeople overstate the performance of their products, their firms have to provide the stated performance and meet the terms of the contract.

Warranties

A **warranty** is an assurance by the seller that the products will perform as represented. Sometimes a warranty is called a *guarantee*. The UCC distinguishes between two types of warranties: expressed and implied. An **expressed warranty** is an oral or a written statement by the seller. An **implied warranty** is not actually stated but is still an obligation defined by law. For example, products sold using an oral or a written description (the buyer never sees the products) carry an implied warranty that the products are of average quality. However, if the buyer inspects the product before placing an order, the implied warranty applies only to any performance aspects that the inspection would not have uncovered. Typically an implied warranty also guarantees that the product can be used in the manner stated by the seller.

Problems with warranties often arise when the sale is to a reseller (a distributor or retailer). The ultimate user—the reseller's customer—may complain about a product to the reseller. The reseller, in turn, tries to shift the responsibility to the manufacturer. Salespeople often have to investigate and resolve these issues.

MISREPRESENTATION OR SALES PUFFERY

In their enthusiasm salespeople may exaggerate the performance of products and even make false statements to get an order. Over time, common and administrative laws have defined the difference between illegal misrepresentation and sales puffery. Not all statements salespeople make have legal consequences. However, misrepresentation, even if legal, can destroy a business relationship and may involve salespeople and their firms in lawsuits.

Glowing descriptions such as "Our service can't be beat" are considered to be opinions or **sales puffery**. Customers cannot reasonably rely on these statements. Following are some examples of puffery:

- This is a top-notch product.
- This product will last a lifetime.
- Our school bus chassis has been designed to provide the utmost safety and reliability for carrying the nation's most precious cargo—schoolchildren.
- The most complete line of reliable, economical gas heating appliances.

However, statements about the inherent capabilities of products or services, such as "Our system will reduce your inventory by 40 percent," may be treated as statements of fact and warranties. Here are examples of such statements found to be legally binding:

- Mechanically, this oil rig is a 9 on a scale of 10.
- Feel free to prescribe this drug to your patients, doctor. It's nonaddicting.
- This equipment will keep up with any other machine you are using and will work well with your other machines.

Rich Kraus owned a company providing document shredding services using special trucks that contain high-speed shredders. When purchasing a new truck, he looked to another small company. The salesperson was the owner's son, and his pride came through as he gave a demo and rattled off the capabilities of the equipment. Compared to Kraus's current model, this shredder was 40 percent faster and had 30 percent more capacity for storing shredded material, so he placed an order for the $250,000 truck.

Unfortunately he quickly realized the truck was capable of holding only 60 percent of the paper that the salesperson said it could. When the problem was discussed with the engineer, he admitted that the salesperson had provided incorrect information. However, he didn't want to correct the owner's son in front of a prospective customer. He added that the salesperson was a good honest person and that his enthusiasm probably just got the best of him.

Only after threatening legal action did Kraus get his money back and order a truck from his original vendor. Since then, Kraus sold his company to a larger company that purchases an average of 50 trucks per year, all from Kraus's original vendor.

As Kraus says, "Since that time we have had dozens of associates in the industry ask us about our experience with this company. It's hard to fathom how many orders it lost as a result." Risking the reputation of the company for even a single unit just wasn't worth it.[18]

The **False Claims Act,** or Lincoln Law, was passed in 1863 during the Civil War to encourage citizens to press claims against vendors that fraudulently sold to the U.S. government (all states now have their own version, too). During the war, defense contractors were selling all manner of products (including mules) that could not live up to the claims made by the salespeople. As a result, the government was losing money and the war. This law enabled a person bringing a claim of fraud to share in the proceeds if the contractor was found guilty and damages are assessed. Although this law is well over 100 years old, as you read in the opening profile, today's businesspeople like Pat Gietl at HP still have to ensure that their claims are accurate, especially when selling to the government.

U.S. salespeople need to be aware of both U.S. laws and laws in the host country when selling internationally. All countries have laws regulating marketing and selling activities. In Canada all claims and statements made in advertisements and sales presentations about comparisons with competitive products must pass the **credulous person standard.** This standard means the company and the salesperson have to pay damages if a reasonable person could misunderstand a statement. Thus a statement like "This is the strongest axle in Canada" might be considered puffery in the United States but be viewed as misleading in Canada unless the firm had absolute evidence that the axle was stronger than any other axle sold in Canada.

To avoid legal and ethical problems with misrepresentation, you should try to educate customers thoroughly before concluding a sale. You should tell the customer as much about the specific performance of the product as possible. Unless your firm has test results concerning the product's performance, you should avoid offering an opinion about the product's specific benefits for the customer's application. If you don't have the answer to a customer's question, don't guess. Say that you don't know the answer and will get back to the customer with the information.

ILLEGAL BUSINESS PRACTICES

The Sherman Antitrust Act of 1890, the Clayton Act of 1914, the Federal Trade Commission Act of 1914, and the Robinson-Patman Act of 1934 prohibit unfair business practices that may reduce competition. The courts used these laws to create common law that defines the illegal business practices discussed in this section.

Business Defamation

Business defamation occurs when a salesperson makes unfair or untrue statements to customers about a competitor, its products, or its salespeople. These statements are illegal when they damage the competitor's reputation or the reputation of its salespeople.

Following are some examples of false statements made about competitors that have been found to be illegal:

- Company X broke the law when it offered you a free case of toilet paper with every 12 cases you buy.
- Company X is going bankrupt.
- You shouldn't do business with Company X. Mr. Jones, the CEO, is really incompetent and dishonest.

You should avoid making negative comments about a competitor, its salespeople, or its products unless you have proof to support the statements.

Reciprocity

Reciprocity is a special relationship in which two companies agree to buy products from each other. For example, a manufacturer of computers agrees to use microprocessors from a component manufacturer if the component manufacturer agrees to buy its computers. Such interrelationships can lead to greater trust and cooperation between the firms. However, reciprocity agreements are illegal if one company forces another company to join the agreement. Reciprocity is legal only when both parties consent to the agreement willingly.

Tying Agreements

In a **tying agreement** a buyer is required to purchase one product in order to get another product. For example, a customer who wants to buy a copy machine is required to buy paper from the same company, or a distributor that wants to stock one product must stock the manufacturer's entire product line. Because they reduce competition, tying agreements typically are illegal. They are legal only when the seller can show that the products must be used together—that is, that one product will not function properly unless the other product is used with it.

Tying agreements are also legal when a company's reputation depends on the proper functioning of equipment. Thus a firm can be required to buy a service contract for equipment it purchases, although the customer need not buy the contract from the manufacturer.

A tying agreement, which requires someone to buy one product in order to get another, is illegal. For example, if the maker of this copier required customers to buy only its paper, that would be an illegal tying agreement.

Conspiracy and Collusion

An agreement between competitors before customers are contacted is a **conspiracy,** whereas **collusion** refers to competitors working together while the customer is making a purchase decision. For example, competitors are conspiring when they get together and divide up a territory so that only one competitor will call on each prospect. Collusion occurs when competitors agree to charge the same price for equipment that a prospect is considering. These examples of collusion and conspiracy are illegal because they reduce competition.

Interference with Competitors

Salespeople may illegally interfere with competitors by

- Trying to get a customer to break a contract with a competitor.
- Tampering with a competitor's product.
- Confusing a competitor's market research by buying merchandise from stores.

Restrictions on Resellers

Numerous laws govern the relationship between manufacturers and resellers—wholesalers and retailers. At one time it was illegal for companies to establish a minimum price below which their distributors or retailers could not resell their products. Today this practice, called **resale price maintenance,** is legal in some situations.

Manufacturers do not have to sell their products to any reseller that wants to buy them. Sellers can use their judgment to select resellers if they announce their selection criteria in advance. One sales practice considered unfair is providing special incentives to get a reseller's salespeople to push products. For example, salespeople for a cosmetics company may give a department store's cosmetics salespeople prizes based on sales of the company's product. These special incentives, called **spiffs** (or **push money**), are legal only if the reseller knows and approves of the incentive and it is offered to all the reseller's salespeople. *Spiff* stands for "special promotion incentive fund" and dates back to a time when there was more selling by retail salespeople. Even if they are legal, though, not everyone agrees that spiffs are ethical.[19]

Price Discrimination

The Robinson-Patman Act became law because independent wholesalers and retailers wanted additional protection from the aggressive marketing tactics of large chain stores. Principally, the act forbids price discrimination in interstate commerce. Robinson-Patman applies only to interstate commerce, but most states have passed similar laws to govern sales transactions between buyers and sellers within the same state.

Court decisions related to the Robinson-Patman Act define **price discrimination** as a seller giving *unjustified* special prices, discounts, or services to some customers and not to others. To justify a special price or discount, the seller must prove that it results from (1) differences in the cost of manufacture, sale, or delivery; (2) differences in the quality or nature of the product delivered; or (3) an attempt to meet prices offered by competitors in a market. Different prices can be charged, however, if the cost of doing business is different or if a customer negotiates more effectively. For example, a customer who buys in large volume can be charged a lower price if the manufacturing and shipping charges for higher-volume orders are lower than they are for smaller orders.

Using spiffs to promote one product over another, such as one brand of oven, is legal, but research shows consumers believe the practice to be unethical.

In general, firms also may not offer special allowances to one reseller unless those allowances are made available to competing resellers. Because most resellers compete in limited geographic areas, firms frequently offer allowances in specific regions of the country. However, recent Supreme Court decisions allow some leeway in offering discounts to resellers who are engaged in competitive bids. These discounts do not necessarily have to be offered uniformly to all resellers for all customers, but can be selectively offered to meet specific competitive situations. In one case a Volvo truck dealer sued Volvo, citing discounts given to other Volvo dealers in situations where the dealers were all bidding on the same customer's contract. The Supreme Court ruled that these instances did not violate the law because they were negotiated individually to meet bids from non-Volvo providers.

Privacy Laws

Privacy laws limit the amount of information that a firm can obtain about a consumer and specify how that information can be used or shared. The Gramm-Leach-Bliley Act, passed in 1999, requires written notification of customers regarding privacy policies. Note that the law does not discriminate in how the information was obtained. In other words, the law is the same for a customer who fills out a credit application or a customer who responds to questions from a salesperson. Although this law applies primarily to financial institutions, a second phase of the act became law in 2003, broadening its application. Further, any company that publishes a privacy policy is expected, by regulation of the Federal Trade Commission, to follow that policy and is liable to prosecution if it uses customer information inappropriately.

European Union law is even more stringent than U.S. law. The application of privacy applies to many more settings, and transfer of information is forbidden in nearly all circumstances. Further, the law can apply to information that could be shared among non-EU subsidiaries, which means that in some instances an account manager in Europe cannot share information with an American colleague.

Do-Not-Call Law

The federal Do-Not-Call Registry originally took effect in 2003 and was strengthened in 2007, and limits the conditions under which anyone on the registry may be telephoned at home or on a cell phone. A salesperson, for example, cannot call the number of someone on the registry if the person is not already a customer. This registry was set up by the Federal Trade Commission (FTC) under its ability to set rules for commerce, and is an administrative law. However, the FTC can levy fines against companies and individuals that violate the rules, as some companies have already learned. The rules do not apply to business phones.

INTERNATIONAL ETHICAL AND LEGAL ISSUES

Ethical and legal issues are complex for selling in international markets. Value judgments and laws vary widely across cultures and countries. Behavior that is commonly accepted as proper in one country can be completely unacceptable in another country. For example, a small payment to expedite the loading of a truck is considered a cost of doing business in some Middle Eastern countries but may be viewed as a bribe in the United States.

Many countries make a clear distinction between payments for lubrication and payments for subordination. **Lubrication** involves small sums of money or gifts, typically made to low-ranking managers or government officials, in countries where these payments are not illegal. The lubrication payments are made to get the official or manager to do the job more rapidly—to process an order more quickly or to provide a copy of a request for a proposal. For example, Halliburton, the company hired to rebuild Iraq, says, "Sometimes the company [Halliburton] may be required to make facilitating or expediting payments to a low-level government employee or employee in some other countries than the United States to expedite or secure the routine governmental action. . . . Such facilitating payments may not be illegal. . . . Accordingly, facilitating payments must be strictly controlled, and every effort must be made to eliminate or minimize such payments."[20] The policy goes on to say that any such payments must have advance authorization from the company's legal department so there will be no question whether the payment is lubrication or subordination. **Subordination** involves paying larger sums of money to higher-ranking officials to get them to do something that is illegal or to ignore an illegal act. Even in countries where bribery is common, subordination is considered unethical.[21]

RESOLVING CULTURAL DIFFERENCES

What do you do when the ethical standards in a country differ from the standards in your country? This is an old question. Cultural relativism and ethical imperialism are two extreme answers to this question. **Cultural relativism** is the view that no culture's ethics are superior. If the people in Indonesia tolerate bribery, their attitude toward bribery is no better or worse than that of people in Singapore who refuse to give or accept bribes. When in Rome, do as the Romans do. But is it right for a European pharmaceutical company to pay a Nigerian company to dispose of the pharmaceutical company's highly toxic waste near Nigerian residential neighborhoods, even though Nigeria has no rules against toxic waste disposal?

On the other hand, **ethical imperialism** is the view that ethical standards in one's home country should be applied to one's behavior across the world. This view suggests, for example, that Saudi Arabian salespeople working for a U.S. firm should go through the same sexual harassment training U.S. salespeople do, even though the strict conventions governing relationships between men and women in Saudi Arabia make the training meaningless and potentially embarrassing.

Adopting one of these extreme positions is probably not the best approach. To guide your behavior in dealing with cultural differences, you need to distinguish between what is merely a cultural difference and what is clearly wrong. You must not only respect core human values that should apply in all business situations but also respect local traditions and use the cultural background to help you decide what is right and what is wrong. For example, exchanging expensive gifts is common in Japanese business relationships, although it may be considered unethical in Western cultures. Most Western firms operating in Japan now accept this practice as an appropriate local tradition.

Research indicates that salespeople, particularly those who operate in foreign cultures, need significant corporate support and guidance in handling cultural ethical differences. Even a high level of personal morality may not prevent an individual from violating a law in a sales context, so it is imperative that companies establish specific standards of conduct, provide ethical training, and monitor behavior to enforce standards as uniformly as possible around the globe.[22]

LEGAL ISSUES

Regardless of the country in which U.S. salespeople sell, they are subject to U.S. laws that prohibit participating in unauthorized boycotts, trading with enemies of the United States, or engaging in activities that adversely affect the U.S. economy. The **Foreign Corrupt Practices Act** makes it illegal for U.S. companies to pay bribes to foreign officials; however, an amendment to the act permits small lubrication payments when they are customary in a culture. Violations of the law can result in sizable fines for company managers, employees, and agents who knowingly participate in or authorize the payment of such bribes. Recently 22 people were arrested at a conference for arms industry executives when they allegedly attempted to bribe a senior government minister in an African country. Included among those arrested was a vice president for sales with Smith & Wesson. Note that the individuals were charged with violating the law, while their companies were not indicted.[23] Siemens, a company indicted under the FCPA, paid a fine of over $1.6 billion, as well as the cost of over 100 attorneys and 1,300 forensic accountants.[24] One method companies can use to protect themselves, in the event an employee does violate the law, is to include the FCPA in the company's code of ethics. If the company takes specific steps, such as mentioning the law in company policy, the government's assumption is that the employee acted on his or her own and is individually responsible.[25]

The U.S. laws concerning bribery are much more restrictive than laws in other countries. For example, in Italy and Germany bribes made outside the countries are clearly defined as legal and tax-deductible.

SELLING YOURSELF

Most college students do not give much thought to their reputations, at least in terms of a professional reputation. Yet your actions in class and around campus add up to a professional reputation in the sense that faculty form an opinion that is shared with recruiters and others who make important decisions. For example, faculty recommendations may be necessary for scholarships, membership in prestigious organizations, and, of course, jobs. Professors and instructors base their recommendations not only on what they observe, but also on what they hear.

Carrying your weight in group projects, contributing your share in study groups, and doing your own work are actions that exhibit more than a professional work ethic; they also show your integrity. Other small things, like coming to class and leaving your cell phone silent in your backpack during class, can also contribute to a professor's estimation of a student's overall professional demeanor.

Of course, obvious actions such as claiming illness without any documentation, cheating on an exam (or even giving the appearance of cheating), or collaborating too closely with another student on an independent exercise can damage your credibility. Students may believe they can get away with such actions in classes not in their major and still get good faculty recommendations, but in reality reputation is much bigger than that. Although not every faculty member will learn a student's complete reputation, most of us learn enough from our colleagues and our students to know whom to recommend and whom to avoid.

Start working on your professional reputation now. Whether or not you decide to create one intentionally, you are building that reputation anyway.

SUMMARY

This chapter discussed the legal and ethical responsibilities of salespeople. These responsibilities are particularly important in personal selling because salespeople may face conflicts between their personal standards and the standards of their firms and customers. However, the evolution of selling has raised ethical standards and expectations; building long-term relationships with customers doesn't allow for unethical behavior.

Salespeople's ethical standards determine how they conduct relationships with their customers, employers, and competitors. Ethical issues in relations with customers involve the use of entertainment and gifts and the disclosure of confidential information. Ethical issues in relations with employers involve expenses and job changes. Finally, salespeople must be careful in how they talk about competitors and treat competitive products.

Many companies have ethical standards that describe the behavior expected of their salespeople. In evaluating potential employers, salespeople should consider these standards.

Salespeople also encounter many situations not covered by company statements and therefore must develop personal standards of right and wrong. Without personal standards, salespeople will lose their self-respect and the respect of their company and customers. Good ethics are good business. Over the long run, salespeople with a strong sense of ethics will be more successful than salespeople who compromise their own and society's ethics for short-term gain.

Statutory laws (such as the Uniform Commercial Code) and administrative laws (such as Federal Trade Commission rulings) guide the activities of salespeople in the United States. Selling in international markets is complex because of cultural differences in ethical judgments and laws that relate to sales activities in various countries.

KEY TERMS

administrative law   48
agent   48
backdoor selling   44
bribes   41
business defamation   52
canned sales pitch   34
collusion   52
common law   48
conspiracy   52
contract to sell   49
credulous person standard   51
cultural relativism   55
deception   41
ethical imperialism   55
ethics   33
expressed warranty   50
False Claims Act   51
free on board (FOB) destination   49
FOB factory   49
Foreign Corrupt Practices Act   56
implied warranty   50

invitation to negotiate   49
kickbacks   41
lubrication   54
manipulation   36
offer   49
orders   49
persuasion   36
price discrimination   53
privacy laws   54
reciprocity   52
resale price maintenance   53
sale   49
sales puffery   50
sexual harassment   47
spiffs (push money)   53
statutory law   48
subordination   55
trade secrets   47
tying agreement   52
Uniform Commercial Code (UCC)   48
warranty   50

QUESTIONS AND PROBLEMS

1. There are certainly many ethical and legal issues in selling, as this chapter demonstrates. Do you think there are more ethical and legal issues in selling than other jobs, such as accounting, finance, retail store management, or the like? Which issues raised in the chapter are likely to be present, no matter the job, and which are likely to be specific to sales jobs?

2. Rick Carlysle of Granite Construction says he doesn't run into ethical challenges when dealing with salespeople. What is it about Granite that would prevent a seller from acting unethically? How important is reputation in his business? Whose reputation is more important in influencing ethical behavior?

3. For centuries the guideline for business transactions was the Latin term *caveat emptor* (let the buyer beware). This principle suggests that the seller is not responsible for the buyer's welfare. Is this principle still appropriate in modern business transactions? Why or why not? How has the evolution of selling influenced ethics in professional selling?

4. You are calling on an account when the customer asks how the lawsuit is going. "What lawsuit?" you reply. Your competitor, it seems, has been saying that you are within a week of declaring bankruptcy because a former customer is suing. How do you respond to the customer? What other action should you take?

5. Some professors believe that ethics cannot be taught; only laws need to be taught. Do you agree? Why or why not? What do you think Pat Gietl's (in the opening profile) answer would be to this question? Why? Would her answer differ from that of someone who sells to other businesses?

6. Your customer asks you what you think of a competitor's product. You know from experience with other customers that it is unreliable and breaks down frequently. Further, given this particular customer's needs, you expect that this issue would be an even bigger problem if the customer chose this product. How do you respond? Be specific about what you would say.

7. Your company has a contact management software system in which you enter all the information you can about your customers. The company wants to partner with another firm in marketing products. Your company wants to give your database to the other firm so the other firm can create marketing pieces and e-mail them to your clients. Is this legal? Is it ethical? Why or why not?

8. Review Dr. Evans's list of requests for salespeople (Exhibit 2.6).
   a. What principle seems to underlie all his requests?
   b. He requests that salespeople not ask what he prescribes or why—he feels that this is collecting marketing information and debating his choices. In addition, he requests that salespeople not ask him to prescribe their drug—he'll make that decision on a case-by-case basis when appropriate. These are two standard practices in selling: finding out what customers' current products are and asking for the order. Why would he consider these bothersome practices? Should his request be honored in all situations with all customers? Why or why not?

9. For each of the following situations, evaluate the salesperson's action and indicate what you think the appropriate action would be:
   a. In an electronics store, salespeople are offered an extra $50 for each sale of HDTV models that are being closed out. The manufacturer is offering the extra spiff, and management is fully aware of it. Salespeople, though, are encouraged to not mention either the spiff or the fact that these are closeout models.
   b. A customer asks if you can remove a safety feature because it slows down the operators of the equipment.
   c. The custom of the trade is that competitive firms submit bids based on specifications provided by the buyer; then the buyer places an order with the firm offering the lowest bid. After a salesperson submits a bid, the purchasing agent calls him and indicates that the bid is too high; the lowest bid so far is almost 8 percent lower than that. The buyer asks the salesperson to submit another bid at a price at least 10 percent lower.
   d. A few months after joining a company, you learn about a credit card that gives you a 20 percent cash refund on meals at certain restaurants. You get the card and start taking

clients to restaurants offering the rebate, pocketing the rebate.

e. A customer gives a salesperson a suggestion for a new service. The salesperson does not turn in the idea to her company, even though the company's policy manual states that all customer ideas should be submitted with the monthly expense report. Instead the salesperson quits her job and starts her own business using the customer's suggestion.

CASE PROBLEMS

case **2.1**

E-Town

Marty Selig was looking over his financial statement for E-Town, his small chain of electronics stores. Marty's company sells electronics such as HDTVs, but where he really distinguishes his company from big box discounters like Best Buy and Walmart is in service. His best opportunities to provide value and make money are for services such as installing home theaters. But a tight economy has buyers either downsizing their purchases or not buying at all, and Marty is worried about whether his business will make it.

A knock at the door interrupted his thoughts. "Hey, Marty!" exclaimed Amanda Duron as she entered his office and sat down. "We've just come out with a limited offer, something that we have very few units for, and we're targeting value-added resellers like E-Town." Amanda represented a lesser-known Korean brand of televisions and other electronics. "What we'd like to do is consolidate all of our remaining inventory on this year's models into stores like yours, then offer a 30% rebate to you. You can use it as a spiff for your reps, a sales price for customers, or a combination of the two. And we won't consolidate these models into any store here in San Antonio except E-Towns. What do you say?"

"Why the big rebate? Are these closeouts?" he asked.

"Yes, they are. With this big rebate, I can't help you with advertising costs, but you can offset advertising costs by charging full price and keeping the rebate. Or, as I said, offer your sales staff a spiff."

"How many do I have to take?"

"I worked out a plan that is 50 units per store, and based on your past sales with us, I've already got a matrix for allocating the various models to each store. Can I count on you for this promotion? I'd rather it be E-Town than Circuit Country!" she said, mentioning one of Marty's toughest competitors.

Marty considered her offer. The brand she represented had good picture quality but was known, at least among dealers, for needing more service. The cost for installation was also a bit higher in home theater applications because of the way the cabling had to be done, but more service and higher installation costs would mean more revenue for Marty.

Marty decided to take Amanda up on her offer. He marked the TVs down 10 percent, offered the salespeople a 10 percent spiff (ranging from $50 to $350), and applied the final 10 percent to local advertising costs. As he walked through one of his stores, he overheard a salesperson say about one of Amanda's TVs, "This TV is every bit as good as that one (pointing to a different brand), but this sale price makes it the best choice for you."

Questions

1. If you were Marty, how would you have spent the 30 percent rebate? Are there any ethical issues in the choices he made?
2. Should Marty step in and clarify what the salesperson is talking about? Or let the rep handle the customer?
3. Many retail store clerks work on straight commission and may get spiffs for selling certain products. Should this information be publicly available—perhaps posted somewhere in the store? Why or why not?

DuBois Polymers manufactures and distributes chemicals in the northwest United States and western Canada. Usually the company sells to a distributor, which sells to the customer that uses the chemicals. Mitch Thompson is Betsy Briles's biggest customer. His business, which distributes chemicals in British Columbia and Washington State, represents nearly 15 percent of Betsy's annual sales. Recently Betsy acquired a new account in the same area, Crago Chemicals, which has the potential to be just as large. Her most recent meeting with Mitch, though, went like this:

"Look, Crago Chemicals underbid us on the Canuck contract by 10 percent. You must be offering them a better price than us, and I want to know why," said Mitch.

Betsy knew that Crago bid that job with no profit in order to expand into Vancouver and that the price she quoted them was actually 5 percent more than Mitch's. "Mitch, I'm not giving them a better price—they don't buy as much as you do from us, so I can't."

"Huh. You'll have to do better than that. You know that the Farley contract is coming up, and it is going to be big. I want to know what they intend to do about it."

"Mitch, if I told you their pricing strategy, as if I knew it, why would you ever trust me with your information?"

"C'mon. I'm your biggest customer. We have to stick together."

"Well, I don't know their strategy."

"Try to find out. And while you're at it, I think I can get the Hudson Pulp and Paper account away from National if you'll give me just a 5 percent discount on those products."

Betsy knew she was as low as she could go pricing-wise. But if she gave him a few barrels a month free and marked it down as a sample, then she would effectively lower the price and get away with it. And National was not one of her accounts—if Mitch won the Hudson account, she would see another $100,000 in revenue per month.

Questions

1. What should she do about the Farley situation? Should she try to find out if Canuck plans to bid on the Farley contract and, if so, what its strategy is?
2. What should she do about the Hudson account?
3. Describe her relationship with Mitch. Where should she go with this account in the future?

ROLE PLAY CASE

(Note: If you've not completed the Role Play Case in Chapter 1, you should review it before starting this role play.) Weaver Medical is a national distributor of medical equipment. You are calling on Ms. Weaver, and everything seems to be going well. M&F has 48 salespeople, managed by six sales managers who report to Ms. Weaver. Currently they e-mail sales call reports to their managers at the end of each week, and sales are forecast for the following week. Weaver uses these forecasts to manage inventory, but always orders less than forecast because salespeople are overly optimistic. Sales are also lower than she would prefer, and she thinks with better knowledge of what is happening in each account, she could help salespeople perform better.

It's time to ask for the order. You should summarize how NetSuite lets the manager summarize the sales team's activities daily. Salespeople no longer have to e-mail their reports; they simply have to log into NetSuite and enter the day's activities. Not only will NetSuite give the managers a forecast daily, but it will also summarize each rep's performance by level of the sales process. The manager can then use that information to pinpoint how to improve each rep's performance. Once you've summarized, ask for an order of 55 units. Each buyer will be given a sheet with information about how to respond.

ADDITIONAL REFERENCES

Bellizi, Joseph A. "Honoring Accounts of Top Sales Performers and Poor Sales Performers Who Have Engaged in Unethical Selling Behavior." *Journal of Global Business Issues* 2, no. 2, pp. 207–15.

Bristow, Dennis N., Rajesh Gulati, Douglas Amyx, and Jennifer Slack. "An Empirical Look at Professional Selling from a Student Perspective." *Journal of Education for Business* 81, no. 5 (2006), pp. 242–49.

Cadogan, John Nick Lee, Anssi Tarkiainen, and Sanna Sundqvist. "Sales Manager and Sales Team Determinants of Salesperson Ethical Behavior." *European Journal of Marketing* 43, no. 7/8 (2009), pp. 907–22.

Calderaro, Fabio, and Anne T. Coughlan. "Spiffed-Up Channels: The Role of Spiffs in Hierarchical Selling Organizations." *Marketing Science* 26, no. 1 (2007), pp. 31–52.

Hansen, John D., and Robert J. Riggle. "Ethical Salesperson Behavior in Sales Relationships." *Journal of Personal Selling & Sales Management* 29, no. 2 (2009), pp. 151–66.

Hoivik, Heidi von Weltzien. "East Meets West: Tacit Messages about Business Ethics in Stories Told by Chinese Managers." Journal of Business Ethics 74, no. 4 (2007), pp. 457–69.

Mantel, Susan P. "Choice or Perception: How Affect Influences Ethical Choices among Salespeople." *Journal of Personal Selling & Sales Management* 25, no. 1 (2005), pp. 43–57.

Nevins, Jennifer L., William O. Bearden, and Bruce Money. "Ethical Values and Long-Term Orientation." *Journal of Business Ethics* 71, no. 3 (2007), pp. 261–74.

Pettijohn, Charles, Linda Pettijohn, and A.J. Taylor. "Salesperson Perceptions of Ethical Behaviors: Their Influence on Job Satisfaction and Turnover Intentions." *Journal of Business Ethics* 78, no. 4 (2008), pp. 547–57.

Román, Sergio, and José Luis Munuera. "Determinants and Consequences of Ethical Behaviour: An Empirical Study of Salespeople." *European Journal of Marketing* 39, no. 5–6 (2005), pp. 473–496.

Sangtani, Vinita, and John Andy Wood. "The Impact of Stigma: Negative Stereotypes of Salespeople." *Journal of Selling and Major Account Management* 7, no. 4, pp. 38–52.

Schwepker Jr., Charles H., and David J. Good. "Sales Management's Influence on Employment and Training in Developing an Ethical Sales Force." *Journal of Personal Selling & Sales Management* 27, no. 4 (2007), pp. 325–39.

Schwepker Jr., Charles H., and Michael D. Hartline. "Managing the Ethical Climate of Customer-Contact Service Employees." *Journal of Service Research* 7, no. 4 (2007), pp. 377–97.

Valentine, Sean, and Tim Barnett. "Perceived Organizational Ethics and the Ethical Decisions of Sales and Marketing Personnel." *Journal of Personal Selling & Sales Management* 27, no. 4 (2007), pp. 373–389.

Weeks, William A., Terry W. Loe, Lawrence B. Chonko, Carlos Ruy Martinez, and Kirk Wakefield. "Cognitive Moral Development and the Impact of Perceived Ethical Climate on the Search for Sales Force Excellence: A Cross-Cultural Study." *Journal of Personal Selling & Sales Management* 26 (Summer 2006), pp. 205–24.

Zhuang, Guijun, and Alex Tsang. "A Study of Ethically Problematic Selling: Methods in China with a Broader Concept of Gray Marketing." *Journal of Business Ethics* 79, no. 1–2 (2008), pp. 85–101.

chapter **3**

BUYING BEHAVIOR AND THE BUYING PROCESS

SOME QUESTIONS ANSWERED IN THIS CHAPTER ARE

- What are the different types of customers?
- How do organizations make purchase decisions?
- Which factors do organizations consider when they evaluate products and services?
- Who is involved in the buying decision?
- What should salespeople do in the different types of buying situations?
- Which changes are occurring in organizational buying, and how will these changes affect salespeople?

"I look at the buying process it takes, the many buying decisions involved, and I'm fascinated. First, the process is quite complex. . . . Second, the buying process is multifaceted. . . . It is important to understand your buyers in order to execute a successful plan."

Jenna Weber, Hormel

PROFILE

I started my career with Hormel Foods as a meat products marketing intern for a summer. As an intern, I learned about the marketing side of the business. Most importantly, I got a taste of how our product managers run multiple projects simultaneously while interacting with almost every department in our company, from accounting to logistics to the sales field. Not only are marketing managers responsible for creating products that the end consumer will like, but they need to keep in mind the retailers (Walmart, Kroger, SUPERVALU, and so on). After the conclusion of my internship, I finished my last semester and received my marketing degree from the University of Wisconsin–Eau Claire. From there, I trained as a sales representative at our Kansas City location. This role taught me about the consumer products industry, Hormel Foods, and our competitors at the store level. In seven months, I gained a brief understanding of consumers at the retail level and how promotions are executed. After training, I was promoted to an account in the East.

My understanding of how a product got from raw materials to the grocery store, and from my cart to my house, was very limited prior to working at Hormel Foods. I had never really thought about it. Now, I look at the process it takes, the many buying decisions involved, and I'm fascinated. First, the process is quite complex. Raw materials are manufactured in a plant to create pepperoni. That pepperoni is sent from a Hormel warehouse to a warehouse for a grocery chain. The pepperoni then gets sent on a truck from the warehouse to the retail store where it is placed on the shelf and ready for sale. Second, the buying process is multifaceted—which I didn't expect. There are multiple decisions that are made between the plant and your home. The corporate buyer from a grocery chain decides to purchase our pepperoni, and then the manager of the pepperoni category at the store level decides where to carry it. Now, you (the consumer) walk into the store, stand in front of the pepperoni set, and decide which brand to take home. The corporate buyer and category manager are just as important as the end consumer. If the corporate buyer or the category manager doesn't purchase HORMEL® pepperoni, then customers of that store don't even have the option to buy our brand. My role is to give the consumer every opportunity to purchase Hormel products by getting the products on the shelf and supporting the products through promotions.

I currently work with a regional retail customer that has over 100 stores in the Northeast. Pepperoni is just one category out of 23 that I manage at my retail account. I must sell products, promotions, and strategies for each one of my categories. However, the most difficult part of my job is dealing with different buyers. Some categories have the same buyer. For example, HORMEL® chili, DINTY MOORE® beef stew, and SPAM® are all purchased by the same grocery buyer. But there are five different buyers overall, and each buyer has a different style. For example, my meat buyer is very relationship oriented and appreciates that I bring him donuts and coffee. We talk about his children, his plans for the weekend, and of course the business. He doesn't like long presentations with data-filled pages. He just wants to know, "Will this item sell?" He is easy to deal with, especially on promotions that are run annually (such as hams during the holidays).

Another buyer is the complete opposite. He wants to know every detail of the item, including pages of analytical data that support the success of the product. He takes longer to make a decision and needs data to prove his choice. This can be good and bad. For example, we were running a bacon promotion, and I argued with my meat buyer that one truckload wasn't enough. It didn't matter to him that I had past history of similar promotions that proved he needed more; he simply refused. Conversely, for a large promotion in grocery, I used multiple analytical tools to prove the volume my grocery buyer needed. By showing him the facts, I successfully sold him three truckloads of displays. As you can see, it's important to understand your buyer's personality and the most effective way to connect with him or her.

The end consumer is also very important in the buying process. While I do not sell to consumers directly, they play a key role in my decision making. When planning a promotion, does it make the most sense to present a deal at 2/$4 or at $1.99? In making that choice, I have to decide which price point seems like the best deal to my end user. For an item that a customer may already buy multiples of, such as CHI-CHI'S® salsa, 2/$4 makes the most sense. However, most people won't purchase more than one 38-ounce DINTY MOORE® beef stew, so that item is better left at a single price point. Along with deciding price, I also have to choose which products are items that should be displayed. Most of Hormel's products are impulse items, but it is up to the retailer if they are worthy of an end-cap or aisle display. My job is to ensure that Hormel products are highly visible to our end user, thus encouraging increased sales.

Whether it is the corporate buyer or the end consumer, the purchasing process is very complex. It is important to understand your buyers and your consumers in order to execute a successful plan. Hormel is committed to helping all of its employees understand these processes and providing them with the tools to be successful.

Visit our Web site at www.hormelfoods.com.

TYPES OF CUSTOMERS

Business is full of a wide variety of customers, including producers, resellers, government agencies, institutions, and consumers. Each of these customer types has different needs and uses a different process to buy products and services. In many situations salespeople will have only one type of customer, but in other territories they may have many different types of customers. Thus salespeople may need to use different approaches when selling to different types of customers.

PRODUCERS

Producers buy products and services to manufacture and sell their products and services to customers. Buyers working for producers are involved in two types of buying situations: buying products that will be included in the products the company is manufacturing or buying products and services to support the manufacturing operation.

OEM PURCHASERS

Buyers for **original equipment manufacturers (OEMs)** purchase goods (components, subassemblies, raw and processed materials) to use in making their products. For example, when one of Jenna Weber's (profiled at the start of this chapter) distributors sells pizza toppings to a restaurant, that it is an OEM purchase. The pizza topping is a processed material used in making the restaurant's product, pizza. Another example of an OEM buyer would be Dell. Dell is an OEM purchaser. It may use Intel processors in its computers, but Dell is the OEM. Sometimes, though, Dell sells computers to other OEM manufacturers. For example, when you use a kiosk at the airport to print your boarding pass, the computer inside it is a Dell, but the kiosk is put together and sold by someone else.

Salespeople selling OEM products need to demonstrate that their products help their customers produce products that will offer superior value. For example, Tim Pavlovich, OEM salesperson for Dell, says that one reason why Dell gets contracts like the kiosk contract is because Dell has a nationwide service team already in place and can fix the computers anywhere in the world.

Most OEM products are bought in large quantities on an annual contract. The purchasing department negotiates the contract with the supplier; however, engineering and production departments play a major role in the purchase decision. Engineers evaluate the products and may prepare specifications for a custom design. The production department works with the supplier to make sure the OEM products are delivered "just in time."

OEM customers are building long-term relationships with a limited number of OEM suppliers. Thus relationship building with more than one department in a customer firm is particularly important when selling OEM products.

END USERS

When producers buy goods and services to support their own production and operations, they are acting as **end users.** End-user buying situations include the purchase of capital equipment; maintenance, repair, and overhaul (MRO) supplies; and services. **Capital equipment** items are major purchases, such as mainframe computers and machine tools that the producer uses for a number of years. **MRO supplies** include paper towels and replacement parts for machinery. **Services** include Internet and telephone connections, employment agencies, consultants, and transportation.

Because capital equipment purchases typically require major financial commitments, capital equipment salespeople need to work with a number of people involved in the purchase decision, including high-level corporate executives. These salespeople need to demonstrate the reliability of their products and their support services because an equipment failure can shut down the producer's operation. Capital equipment buying often focuses on lifetime operating cost rather than the initial purchase price because the equipment is used over a long period. Thus capital equipment salespeople need to present the financial implications as well as the operating features and benefits of their products.

MRO supplies and services are typically a minor expense and therefore are usually less important to businesses than are many other items. Purchasing agents typically oversee MRO buying decisions. Because they often do not want to spend the time to evaluate all suppliers, they tend to purchase from vendors who have performed well in the past, creating functional relationships.

Although the cost of MRO supplies is typically low, availability can be critical. For example, the failure of a $10 motor in an industrial robot can shut down an entire assembly line. Some professional services, such as accounting, advertising, and consulting, also are important to the company and may be purchased in a manner similar to capital equipment purchases.

RESELLERS

Resellers buy finished products or services with the intention to resell them to businesses and consumers. Hormel sells precooked meats, such as pepperoni for pizza toppings, to resellers—distributors who then sell to restaurants. Other examples of resellers include McKesson Corporation, a wholesaler that buys health care products from manufacturers and resells those products to drugstores; Brazos Valley Equipment, a dealer for John Deere, selling tractors, harvesters, combines, and other agricultural implements to farmers; and Dealer's Electric, selling lighting, conduit, and other electrical components to electricians and contractors. All these are resellers, and they buy for similar reasons.

Resellers consider three elements when making decisions about which products to sell: profit margin, turnover, and effort. Resellers want to maximize their return on investment (ROI), which is a function of **profit margin** or how much they make on each sale, **turnover** or how quickly a product will sell, and how much effort it takes to sell the product. Buyers for resellers often simplify their decisions by a focus on either profit margin or turnover, but all resellers are interested in putting together an assortment of products that will yield the greatest overall ROI.

Salespeople work with resellers to help them build their ROI. Not only do salespeople help resellers choose which products to sell, but they also train resellers on how to sell and service products, build point-of-purchase displays and promotions, and may also help resellers with developing advertising and marketing campaigns to boost sales. For example, with increasing competition between grocery chains, retailers are asking suppliers to create excitement and generate traffic in stores.

"Retailers' expectations for our products' performance continue to escalate. Price is important but not the only thing retailers are demanding," Eddy Patterson, of Stubb's Legendary Kitchen, said. "We need to look at innovative ways that not only help sell our products and create brand awareness but also ways to contribute to the success of our customers, the retailers who sell our products." For example, Stubb's Bar-B-Q has sold its line of barbecue sauces and marinades in supermarkets and has created a loyal following. Stubb's recently entered a license agreement for Stubb's All Natural Charcoal Briquettes and a Stubb's cookbook. By entering a licensing agreement with third-party manufacturers, Stubb's created complementary items to build its brand awareness. Stubb's has developed not only another revenue source for the company but also exposure for the brand in areas beyond current supermarket retailers. This creates a win for the retailers, a win for Stubb's Bar-B-Q, and a win for the licensing manufacturers.[1]

Patterson then took the cross-licensed products and created in-store promotions to help retailers sell the products. "We also gained incredible merchandising opportunities within our core stores by cross-promoting the newly developed items. Many of our supermarket retailers bought the Stubb's cookbooks and had stands next to the sauce displaying both items. We expect our charcoal to have the same effect from our retailers by creating lobby displays promoting the sauce and charcoal as a nice tie-in."

Stubb's partners with grocers to cross-promote the full line of Stubb's products with in-store displays, building sales for both Stubb's and the retailer.

Note that the same customer can act as an OEM manufacturer, an end user, and a reseller. For example, Dell Computer makes OEM buying decisions when it purchases microprocessors for its computers, acts as an end user when it buys materials handling equipment for its warehouse, and functions as a reseller when it buys software to resell to its computer customers when they place orders.

GOVERNMENT AGENCIES

The largest customers for goods and services in the United States are federal, state, and local governments, which collectively purchase goods and services valued at more than $1 trillion annually. Not counting defense spending, the federal government purchases the equivalent of 14 percent of the country's entire gross domestic product, making it the largest customer in the world.[2] Government buyers typically develop detailed specifications for a product and then invite qualified suppliers to submit bids. A contract is awarded to the lowest bidder. The government has also developed procedures for small purchases without a bid, streamlining the process and reducing costs.

Effective selling to government agencies requires a thorough knowledge of their unique procurement procedures and rules. Salespeople also need to know about projected needs so they can influence the development of the buying specifications. For example, Harris Corporation worked for six years with the Federal Aviation Administration and finally won a $1.7 billion contract to modernize air traffic communication systems.

Some resources available to salespeople working with the federal and state governments are

- Guidelines for selling to the government published by the U.S. Government Printing Office.
- The *Commerce Business Daily,* which contains all invitations for bids issued by the federal government.
- The National Association of State Purchasing Officials in Washington, D.C., which publishes information for all 50 states, including the availability of vendor guides, registration fees, and how to get on bidder lists.
- The Procurement Automated Source System (PASS), the Small Business Administration database with information about more than 900 federal purchasing agents and prime contractors working on federal contracts.
- FedBizOpps.gov, a Web site listing all business opportunities greater than $25,000. Keep in mind, though, that 90 percent of federal purchasing opportunities are less than $25,000.[3]

Many international salespeople are selling to government agencies, even though private companies may be the biggest buyers of these products and services in the United States. For example, Alcatel-Lucent, a French company that manufactures telephone equipment, sells not only to private companies such as Verizon and AT&T in the United States but also to the post, telephone, and telegraph (PTT) government agencies in many countries in Europe, Asia, and Africa.

Selling to foreign governments is challenging. The percentage of domestic product (countries may require that a certain percentage of the product be manufactured or assembled locally) and exchange rates (the values of local currencies in U.S. dollars) are as important as the characteristics of the product. Different economic and political systems, cultures, and languages also can make international selling difficult.

INSTITUTIONS

Another important customer group consists of public and private institutions such as churches, hospitals, and colleges. Often these institutions have purchasing rules and procedures that are as complex and rigid as those used by government agencies.

Packaged goods manufacturers, such as Stubbs and Hormel, sell to both resellers (supermarkets) and institutional customers (restaurants and hospitals). These customers have different needs and buying processes.

CONSUMERS

Consumers purchase products and services for use by themselves or by their families. A lot of salespeople sell insurance, automobiles, clothing, and real estate to consumers. However, college graduates often take sales jobs that involve selling to business enterprises, government agencies, or institutions. Thus the examples in this text focus on these selling situations, and this chapter discusses organizational rather than consumer buying behavior.

In the next section we contrast the buying processes of consumers and organizations. Then we describe the buying process that organizations use in more detail, including the steps in the process, who influences the decisions, and how salespeople can influence the decisions.

ORGANIZATIONAL BUYING AND SELLING ●━━━━

Salespeople who sell to consumers and salespeople who call on organizations have very different jobs. Because the organizational buying process typically is more complex than the consumer buying process, selling to organizations often requires more skills and is more challenging than selling to consumers. Relationships, too, can differ because of the size of the organizations involved.

COMPLEXITY OF THE ORGANIZATIONAL BUYING PROCESS

The typical organizational purchase is much larger and more complex than the typical consumer purchase. Organizations use highly trained, knowledgeable purchasing agents to make these decisions. Many other people in organizations are involved in purchase decisions, including engineers, production managers, business analysts, and senior executives.

Organizational buying decisions often involve extensive evaluations and negotiations over time. The average time required to complete a purchase is five months, and during that period salespeople need to make many calls to gather and provide information.

Ashley Anderson, salesperson for "The Ranch" country-western radio station in the Dallas–Fort Worth area, worked for over a year with one account before getting the sale. The account is an eye surgeon promoting his Lasik surgery practice. Ashley worked with his PR agency and him, calling at least twice a month on one or both. "I think three factors finally won him over," says Ashley. "First, over the course of the year, I built a strong relationship with him and he began to trust me. Second, I was able to show him that advertising with us would reach a market no one else was going after. And third, I leveraged a free month of advertising to create an urgency to make a decision." Two years later he still advertises with "The Ranch."

The complexity of organizational purchase decisions means salespeople must be able to work effectively with a wide range of people working for their customer and their company. For example, when selling a new additive to a food processor such as Nabisco, an International Flavors and Fragrances salesperson may interact with advertising, product development, legal, production, quality control, and customer service people at Nabisco. The salesperson needs to know the technical and economic benefits of the additive to Nabisco and the benefits to consumers.

In addition, the salesperson coordinates all areas of his or her own firm to assist in making the sale. The salesperson works with research and development to provide data on consumer taste tests, with production to meet the customer's delivery requirements, and with finance to set the purchasing terms. (Working effectively within the salesperson's organization is discussed in more detail in Chapter 16.)

The complexity of organizational selling is increasing as more customers become global businesses. For example, Deere and Company has a special unit to coordinate worldwide purchases. The unit evaluates potential suppliers across the globe for each of its product lines and manufacturing facilities. Further, the company wants to standardize products made in different plants. A harvester made in Ottumwa, Iowa, should have the same belt as the same model harvester made at Arc-les-Gray, France. Thus a salesperson selling belts to Deere must work with the special corporate buying unit as well as with the employees at each

If you want to sell a part such as a belt for a John Deere harvester made in Ottumwa, Iowa, then you must be able to sell and service this plant in Arc-les-Gray, France, too.

manufacturing location around the world.[4] There's no doubt that global competitiveness is a key factor increasing the complexity of organizational buying, but global sourcing is also a key factor for achieving a sustainable competitive advantage.[5]

DERIVED VERSUS DIRECT DEMAND

Salespeople selling to consumers typically can focus on individual consumer or family needs. Organizational selling often requires salespeople to know about the customer's customers. Sales to OEMs and resellers are based on derived demand rather than direct demand. **Derived demand** means that purchases made by these customers ultimately depend on the demand for their products—either other organizations or consumers. For example, Apple's iPad has not only increased sales for touch screens made by Wintek and computer chips made by Samsung; the demand for the equipment that makes touch screens and computer chips has also been affected.[6]

HOW DO ORGANIZATIONS MAKE BUYING DECISIONS?

To effectively sell to organizations, salespeople need to understand how organizations make buying decisions. This section discusses the steps in the organizational buying process, the different types of buying decisions, and the people involved in making the decisions.[7]

STEPS IN THE BUYING PROCESS

Exhibit 3.1 shows the eight steps in an organizational buying process.

Exhibit 3.1
Steps in the Organizational Buying Process

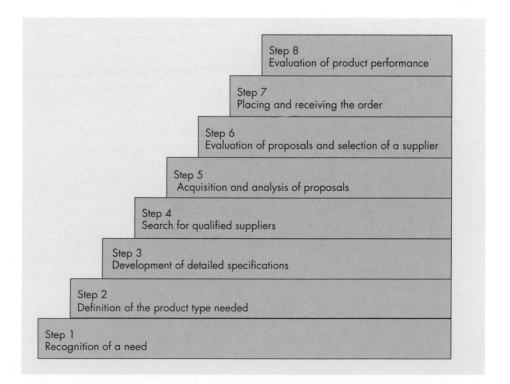

Step 8
Evaluation of product performance

Step 7
Placing and receiving the order

Step 6
Evaluation of proposals and selection of a supplier

Step 5
Acquisition and analysis of proposals

Step 4
Search for qualified suppliers

Step 3
Development of detailed specifications

Step 2
Definition of the product type needed

Step 1
Recognition of a need

Recognizing a Need or a Problem (Step 1)

The buying process starts when someone realizes a problem exists. Employees in the customer's firm or outside salespeople can trigger this recognition. For example, a supermarket cashier might discover that the optical scanner is making mistakes in reading bar code labels. Salespeople often trigger the buying process by demonstrating how their products can improve the efficiency of the customer's operation.

Defining the Type of Product Needed (Step 2)

After identifying a problem, organization members develop a general approach to solving it. For example, a production manager who concludes that the factory is not running efficiently recognizes a problem, but this insight may not lead to a purchase decision. The manager may think the inefficiency is caused by poor supervision or unskilled workers.

However, a production equipment salesperson might work with the manager to analyze the situation and show how efficiency could be improved by purchasing some automated assembly equipment. Thus the problem solution is defined in terms of purchasing a product or service—the automated assembly equipment needed—and the buying process moves to step 3. If the decision to continue requires senior management participation, research suggests that these executives will approve the manager's request to consider the purchase, then leave it up the manager to cover the next few steps before stepping back in when a final decision is made.[8]

Developing Product Specifications (Step 3)

In step 3 the specifications for the product needed to solve the problem are prepared. Potential suppliers will use these specifications to develop proposals. The buyers will use them to objectively evaluate the proposals.

Steps 2 and 3 offer great opportunities for salespeople to influence the outcome of the buying process. Using their knowledge of their firm's products and the customer's needs, salespeople can help develop specifications that favor their particular product. For example, a Hyster forklift might have superior performance in terms of a small turning radius. Knowing this advantage and the customer's small, tightly packed warehouse, the Hyster salesperson might influence the customer to specify a very small turning radius for forklifts—a turning radius that only Hyster forklifts can provide. Competing salespeople, who first become aware of this procurement after the specifications are written, will be at a severe disadvantage.

Searching for Qualified Suppliers (Step 4)

After the specifications have been written, the customer looks for potential suppliers. The customer may simply contact previous suppliers or go through an extensive search procedure: calling salespeople, asking for a list of customers, and checking with the customers on each supplier's financial stability and performance. Many purchasing agents now use the Internet to find suppliers.

Acquiring and Analyzing Proposals (Step 5)

In step 5 qualified suppliers are asked to submit proposals. Salespeople work with people in their company to develop their proposal.

Evaluating Proposals and Selecting a Supplier (Step 6)

Next the customer evaluates the proposals. After a preferred supplier is selected, further negotiations may occur concerning price, delivery, or specific performance features. The appendix to this chapter shows a model used in evaluating proposals.

Placing an Order and Receiving the Product (Step 7)

In step 7 an order is placed with the selected supplier. The order goes to the supplier, who acknowledges receipt and commits to a delivery date. After the product is shipped, the buying firm inspects the received goods and then pays the supplier for the product. During this step salespeople need to make sure the paperwork is correct and their firm knows what has to be done to satisfy the customer's requirements.

Evaluating Product Performance (Step 8)

In the final step of the purchasing process, the product's performance is evaluated. The evaluation may be a formal or informal assessment made by people involved in the buying process.

Salespeople play an important role in this step. They need to work with the users to make sure the product performs well. In addition, salespeople need to work with purchasing agents to ensure that they are satisfied with the communications and delivery.

This after-sale support ensures that the salesperson's product will get a positive evaluation and that he or she will be considered a qualified supplier in future procurement. This step is critical to establishing successful long-term relationships. (Building relationships through after-sale support is discussed in more detail in Chapter 14.)

CREEPING COMMITMENT

Creeping commitment means a customer becomes increasingly committed to a particular course of action while going through the steps in the buying process. As decisions are made at each step, the range of alternatives narrows; the customer becomes more and more committed to a specific course of action and even to a specific vendor. Thus it is vital that salespeople be involved in the initial steps so they will have an opportunity to participate in the final steps.

In instances involving purchasing components or materials as part of new product development, buyers are more interested in early involvement by possible vendors than when buying other types of products. Called *early procurement involvement* or *early supplier involvement,* this strategy has potential suppliers participate in the actual design process for a new product. BASF, the giant German chemical company, engages in early vendor involvement to ensure that the proper levels and quality of supply are available.[9] Other companies use supplier involvement to aid in designing a more effective new product.[10] Whatever the reason, each design decision represents a creeping commitment to a final set of decisions that are difficult to undo.

thinking **it** through

What steps did you go through in making the choice to attend this university? How can you relate your decision-making process to the eight steps in the organizational buying process? Did any decisions you made early in the process affect decisions you made later in the process? What roles did your family and friends play in the decision process?

TYPES OF ORGANIZATIONAL BUYING DECISIONS

Many purchase decisions are made without going through all the steps just described. For example, a Frito-Lay salesperson may check the supply of his or her products in a supermarket, write a purchase order to restock the shelves, and present it to the store manager. After recognizing the problem of low stock, the manager simply signs the order (step 6) without going through any of the other steps. However, if the Frito-Lay salesperson wanted the manager to devote more shelf space to Frito-Lay snacks, the manager might go through all eight steps in making and evaluating this decision.

Exhibit 3.2 describes three types of buying decisions—new tasks, modified rebuys, and straight rebuys[11]—along with the strategies salespeople need to use in each situation. In this exhibit the "in" company is the seller that has provided the product or service to the company in the past, and the "out" company is the seller that is not or has not been a supplier to the customer.

NEW TASKS

When a customer purchases a product or service for the first time, a **new-task** situation occurs. Most purchase decisions involving capital equipment or the initial purchase of OEM products are new tasks.

Because the customer has not made the purchase decision recently, the company's knowledge is limited, and it goes through all eight steps of the buying

Exhibit 3.2
Types of Organizational Buying Decisions

	New Task	Modified Rebuy	Straight Rebuy
Customer Needs			
Information and risk reduction	Information about causes and solutions for a new problem; reduce high risk in making a decision with limited knowledge	Information and solutions to increase efficiency and/or reduce costs.	Needs are generally satisfied.
Nature of Buying Process			
Number of people involved in process	Many	Few	One
Time to make a decision	Months or years	Month	Day
Key steps in the buying process (Exhibit 3.1)	1, 2, 3, 8	3, 4, 5, 6, 8	5, 6, 7, 8
Key decision makers	Executives and engineers	Production and purchasing managers	Purchasing agent
Selling Strategy			
For in-supplier	Monitor changes in customer needs; respond quickly when problems and new needs arise; provide technical information.	Act immediately when problems arise with customers; make sure all of customer's needs are satisfied.	Reinforce relationship.
For out-supplier	Suggest new approach for solving problems; provide technical advice.	Respond more quickly than present supplier when problem arises; encourage customer to consider an alternative; present information about how new alternative will increase efficiency.	Convince customer of potential benefits from reexamining choice of supplier; secure recognition and approval as an alternative supplier.

process. In these situations customers face considerable risk. Thus they typically seek information from salespeople and welcome their knowledge. One study found organizational buyers rate salespeople as a more important information source than the Internet, particularly when the success of the purchase is likely to be difficult to achieve and to evaluate.[12]

From the salesperson's perspective, the initial buying process steps are critical in new-task situations. During these steps the alert salesperson can help the customer define the characteristics of the needed product and develop the purchase specifications. By working with the customer in these initial steps, the salesperson can take advantage of creeping commitment and gain a significant advantage over the competition. The final step, postpurchase evaluation, is also vital. Buyers making a new purchase decision are especially interested in evaluating results and will use this information in making similar purchase decisions in the future.

STRAIGHT REBUYS

In a **straight rebuy** situation, the customer buys the same product from the same source it used when the need arose previously. Because customers have purchased the product or service a number of times, they have considerable knowledge about their requirements and the potential vendors. MRO supplies and services and reorders of OEM components often are straight rebuy situations.

Typically a straight rebuy is triggered by an internal event, such as a low inventory level. Because needs are easily recognized, specifications have been developed, and potential suppliers have been identified, the latter steps of the buying process assume greater importance.

Some straight rebuys are computerized. For example, many hospitals use an automatic reorder system developed by Baxter, a manufacturer and distributor of medical supplies. When the inventory control system recognizes that levels of supplies such as tape, surgical sponges, or IV kits have dropped to prespecified levels, a purchase order is automatically generated and transmitted electronically to the nearest Baxter distribution center.

When a company is satisfied and has developed a long-term supplier relationship, it continues to order from the same company it has used in the past. Salespeople at in-companies want to maintain the strong relationship; they do not want the customer to consider new suppliers. Thus these salespeople must make sure that orders are delivered on time and that the products continue to get favorable evaluations.

Salespeople trying to break into a straight rebuy situation—those representing an out-supplier—face a tough sales problem. Often they need to persuade a customer to change suppliers, even though the present supplier is performing satisfactorily. In such situations the salesperson hopes the present supplier will make a significant mistake, causing the customer to reevaluate suppliers. To break into a straight rebuy situation, salespeople need to provide compelling information to motivate the customer to treat the purchase as a modified rebuy.

MODIFIED REBUYS

In a **modified rebuy** situation, the customer has purchased the product or a similar product in the past but is interested in obtaining new information. This situation typically occurs when the in-supplier performs unsatisfactorily, a new product becomes available, or the buying needs change. In such situations sales representatives of the in-suppliers need to convince customers to maintain the relationship and continue their present buying pattern. In-suppliers with strong customer relationships are the first to find out when requirements change. In this case customers give the supplier's salespeople information to help them respond to the new requirements.

Salespeople with out-suppliers want customers to reevaluate the situation and to actively consider switching vendors. The successful sales rep from an out-supplier will need to influence all the people taking part in the buying decision.

WHO MAKES THE BUYING DECISION?

As we discussed previously, a number of people are involved in new-task and modified rebuy decisions. This group of people is called the **buying center,** an informal, cross-department group of people involved in a purchase decision. People in the customer's organization become involved in a buying center because they have formal responsibilities for purchasing or they are important sources of information. In some cases the buying center includes experts who are not full-time employees. For example, consultants usually specify the air conditioning equipment that will be used in a factory undergoing remodeling. Thus the buying center defines the set of people who make or influence the purchase decision.[13]

Salespeople need to know the names and responsibilities of all people in the buying center for a purchase decision, and sometimes they need to make sure the right people are participating. For example, Ron Swift, vice president for Teradata, a maker of data warehousing equipment and software, was called in by the marketing director of a cell phone services provider to discuss the problem of customer churn (customers leaving for a competitor). The marketing director believed better customer information would solve the revenue loss problem, so he wanted to consider a data warehouse, a significant investment in information systems, in which to store that information. The process began without anyone from the information systems department! Fortunately, with Ron's experience, the Teradata team was able to involve the chief information officer and the right people from his area, as well as the financial people needed to understand the budgeting implications. With the correct buying team in place, the right system was designed, resulting in a churn reduction of 20 percent and additional revenues of nearly $50 million in only a few years.[14]

USERS

Users, such as the manufacturing personnel for OEM products and capital equipment, typically do not make the ultimate purchase decision. However, they often have considerable influence in the early and late steps of the buying process—need recognition, product definition, and postpurchase evaluation. Thus users are particularly important in new-task and modified rebuy situations. Salespeople often attempt to convert a straight rebuy to a modified rebuy by demonstrating superior product performance or a new benefit to users.

INITIATORS

Another role in the buying process is that of **initiator,** or the person who starts the buying process. A user can play the role of the initiator, as in, "This machine is broken; we need a new one." In fact, often it is users' dissatisfaction with a product used by the organization that initiates the purchase process.[15] In some instances, though, such as in OEM product decisions, the initiator could be an executive making a decision such as introducing a new product, which starts the buying process.

INFLUENCERS

People inside or outside the organization who directly or indirectly provide information during the buying process are **influencers.** These members of the buying

The buying center for radiology equipment includes (clockwise from lower left) the technicians operating the equipment (users), the radiologists (gatekeepers and influencers), and the hospital administrator (the decision maker).

center may seek to influence issues regarding product specifications, criteria for evaluating proposals, or information about potential suppliers. For example, the marketing department can influence a purchase decision by indicating that the company's products would sell better if they included a particular supplier's components. Architects can play a critical role in the purchase of construction material by specifying suppliers, even though the ultimate purchase orders will be placed by the contractor responsible for constructing the building. Influence can be technical, such as in product specifications, but can also involve finances and how a decision is made.

Miller and Heiman, two noted sales consultants, assert that there are four types of influencers. One is the **economic influencer,** or person who is concerned about the financial aspects of the decision. Another is the user, which we will discuss later. A third is the **technical influencer,** a person who makes sure the technical requirements (including logistics, terms and conditions, quality measurements, or other specifications) are met. Miller and Heiman state that these people usually have the authority only to say no (meaning the salesperson did not meet the specifications, so the proposal is rejected), so they play a gatekeeping role (discussed more in a moment). The fourth role or type of influencer is the coach. The **coach** is someone in a buying organization who can advise and direct you, the salesperson, in maneuvering through the buying process in an effective fashion, leading to a sale. In addition, this person may advocate for you in private conversations among members of the buying center. As you can imagine, finding a coach is an important factor when decision processes are complex and involve a lot of people.[16]

GATEKEEPERS

Gatekeepers control the flow of information and may limit the alternatives considered. For example, the quality control and service departments may determine which potential suppliers are qualified sources.

Purchasing agents often play a gatekeeping role by determining which potential suppliers are to be notified about the purchase situation and are to have access to relevant information. In some companies all contacts must be made through purchasing agents. They arrange meetings with other gatekeepers, influencers, and users. Such gatekeeping activity is not a power play; rather, it ensures that purchases are consolidated under one contract, thus reducing costs and increasing quality. These single contracts are growing in popularity as a way to reduce costs globally.[17] When dealing with such companies, salespeople may not be allowed to contact members of the buying center directly. When purchasing agents restrict access to important information, salespeople are tempted to bypass the purchasing agents and make direct contact. This backdoor selling approach can upset purchasing agents so much that they may disqualify the salesperson's company from the purchase situation. In Chapter 7 we discuss ethical strategies that salespeople can use to deal with this issue.

DECIDERS

In any buying center one or more members of the group, **deciders,** make the final choice. Determining who actually makes the purchase decision for an organization is often difficult. For straight rebuys the purchasing agent usually selects the vendor and places the order. However, for new tasks many people influence the decision, and several people must approve the decision and sign the purchase order.

In general, senior executives get more involved in important purchase decisions that have a greater effect on the performance of the organization. For example, the chief executive officer (CEO) and chief financial officer (CFO) play an important role in purchasing a telephone system because this network has a significant impact on the firm's day-to-day operations.

To sell effectively to organizations, salespeople need to know the people in the buying center and their involvement at different steps of the buying process. Consider the following situation. Salespeople selling expensive intensive care monitoring equipment know that a hospital buying center for the type of equipment they sell typically consists of physicians, nurses, hospital administrators, engineers, and purchasing agents. Through experience, these salespeople also know the relative importance of the buying center members in various stages of the purchasing process (see Exhibit 3.3). With this information the intensive care equipment salespeople know to concentrate on physicians throughout the process, nurses and engineers in the middle of the process, and hospital administrators and purchasing agents at the end of the process.

SUPPLIER EVALUATION AND CHOICE

At various steps in the buying process, members of the buying center evaluate alternative methods for solving a problem (step 2), the qualifications of potential suppliers (step 4), proposals submitted by potential suppliers (step 5), and

Exhibit 3.3

Importance of Hospital Buying Center Members in the Buying Process for Intensive Care Monitoring Equipment

Step in Buying Process	Physicians	Nurses	Hospital Administrators	Purchasing Engineers	Agents
Need recognition (step 1)	High	Moderate	Low	Low	Low
Definition of product type (step 2)	High	High	Moderate	Moderate	Low
Analysis of proposal (step 5)	High	Moderate	Moderate	High	Low
Proposal evaluation and supplier selection (step 6)	High	Low	High	Low	Moderate

Exhibit 3.4
Factors Influencing
Organizational Buying
Decisions

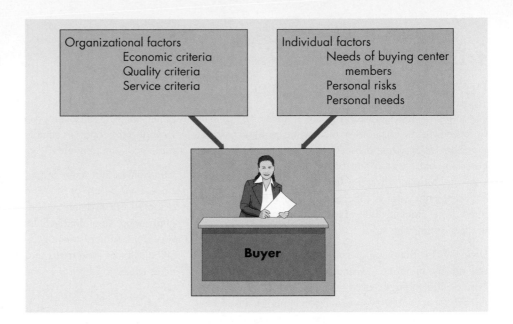

the performance of products purchased (step 8). Using these evaluations, buyers select potential suppliers and eventually choose a specific vendor.

The needs of both the organization and the individuals making the decisions affect the evaluation and selection of products and suppliers (see Exhibit 3.4). Often these organizational and personal needs are classified into two categories: rational needs and emotional needs. **Rational needs** are directly related to the performance of the product. Thus the organizational needs discussed in the next section are examples of rational needs. **Emotional needs** are associated with the personal rewards and gratification of the person buying the product. Thus the personal needs of buying center members often are considered emotional needs.

ORGANIZATIONAL NEEDS AND CRITERIA

Organizations consider a number of factors when they make buying decisions, including economic factors such as price, product quality, and supplier service. In addition, organizations also consider strategic objectives, such as sustainability (choosing vendors and products that are good for the planet) and social diversity. Learn more about supplier diversity in "Building Partnerships 3.1."

Economic Criteria

The objective of businesses is to make a profit. Thus businesses are very concerned about buying products and services at the lowest cost. Organizational buyers are now taking a more sophisticated approach to evaluating the cost of equipment. Rather than simply focusing on the purchase price, they consider installation costs, the costs of needed accessories, freight charges, estimated maintenance costs, and operating costs, including forecasts of energy costs.

Life-cycle costing, also referred to as the total cost of ownership, is a method for determining the cost of equipment or supplies over their useful lives. Using this approach, salespeople can demonstrate that a product with a higher initial cost will have a lower overall cost. An example of life-cycle costing appears in Exhibit 3.5. (Approaches salespeople can use to demonstrate the value of their products to customers are discussed in more detail in Chapter 9.)

DEVELOPING A DIVERSE SUPPLIER BASE

For many years, increasing supplier diversity has been an objective for businesses. According to Sherri Macko, manager of supplier diversity at American Airlines, her company believes that success comes from diversity. "The value in supplier diversity lies in the way these suppliers sometimes offer a different approach to meeting our needs and their flexibility to do whatever it takes to get the job done," she says.

Diversity in purchasing means buying from vendors owned by minorities, women, and disabled veterans. Part of the strength of diversity purchasing programs is that such vendors represent segments of the market, and as such, are able to help their customer, the buyer, understand and realize opportunities in those diverse segments. For example, Proctor & Gamble recently set a goal of spending at least 16% of its marketing budget with minority- and women-owned businesses. These marketing suppliers will bring a perspective that may be difficult for traditional vendors.

AT&T, which spends over $6 billion annually with diverse suppliers, believes that sound business benefits result from its supplier diversity program, which was recently given several awards. Margaret Rawls, executive director of AT&T, notes, "For 41 years, AT&T's commitment to supplier diversity has been unwavering, through all economic climates, because it's built on tangible economic benefits."

Companies that seek greater diversity in their supplier base must work at it. Since most minority-, veteran-, disabled-, or women-owned businesses are small, they often need help simply finding the opportunities. That's why Delta Airlines recently launched a new Web site specifically for helping these smaller companies find opportunities to sell to Delta.

Companies like P&G, AT&T, and Delta also provide workshops to help these smaller companies operate more profitably. Such workshops deliver benefits to the bigger companies because when suppliers are more efficient, lower prices and other benefits accrue to the buyers too. As Macko says, "Overall, supplier diversity is a good business decision."

Sources: Sherri Macko, personal correspondence, used with permission; "Delta Air Lines Uses New Web site to Expand Outreach to Diverse Business Suppliers," *Airline Industry Information,* January 12, 2010; "AT&T Leads in Diversity of Businesses in Supply Chain," *RBOC Update* 21, no. 1 (January 2010), pp. 1–3; Andre McMains, "P&G Reaffirms Need for Supplier Diversity," *Adweek* 50, no. 42 (November 30, 2009), p. 6.

Quality Criteria

Many firms recognize that the quality and reliability of their products are as important to their customers as price. Firms expect their suppliers to support their efforts to provide quality products. A recent study in Japan indicates that suppliers are evaluated on both the quality of their service and the quality of their products because both impact the quality that the buyer can deliver to its customer.[18] Salespeople often need to describe how their firms will support the customer's quality objectives.

To satisfy customer quality needs, salespeople need to know what organizational buyers are looking for. For example, Lionel Dace, of Dace and Dace, was calling on an engineer who was trying to source metal containers. His company had designed a new milkshake machine, and this container was supposed to hold milk inside a milkshake machine. The engineer was beating up Dace over price, and showed him another container from a competitor at a lower price. Dace saw that it was cheaply made using a completely different process than the one he had to offer. The lower-priced version might hold up under moderate use, but Dace thought it didn't look as good as the machine the engineer and his team had designed. However, Dace had been calling on this buyer for three years and

Exhibit 3.5
Life-Cycle Costing

	Product A	Product B
Initial cost	$35,000	$30,000
Life of machine	10 years	10 years
Power consumption per year	150 MWh*	180 MWh*
Power cost at $30/MWh	$45,000	$54,000
Estimated operating and maintenance cost over 10 years	$25,000	$30,000
Life-cycle cost	$105,000	$114,000

Note: A more thorough analysis would calculate the net present value of the cash flow associated with each product's purchase and use.

*MWh = megawatt-hour

had heard nothing but price, price, price. Out of exasperation, Dace looked at the engineer and said, "Is this really what you want it to look like? Can you be proud of that?" Dace says the buyer was immediately transformed; although he had focused on low price, he really wanted something that looked as sleek as the machine he had designed. Dace got the sale, but perhaps more importantly, the nature of their relationship changed for the better.[19]

Service Criteria

Organizational buyers want more than products that are low-cost, perform reliably, and are aesthetically pleasing. They also want suppliers that will work with them to solve their problems. One primary reason firms are interested in developing long-term relationships with suppliers is so they can learn about each other's needs and capabilities and use this information to enhance their products' performance. **Value analysis** is an example of a program in which suppliers and customers work together to reduce costs and still provide the required level of performance.[20]

Representatives from the supplier and the purchasing department and technical experts from engineering, production, or quality control usually form a team to undertake the analysis. The team begins by examining the product's function. Then members brainstorm to see whether changes can be made in the design, materials, construction, or production process to reduce the product's costs but keep its performance high. Some questions addressed in this phase are the following:

- Can a part in the product be eliminated?
- If the part is not standard, can a standard (and presumably less expensive) part be used?
- Does the part have greater performance than this application needs?
- Are unnecessary machining or fine finishes specified?

Salespeople can use value analysis to get customers to consider a new product. This approach is particularly useful for the out-supplier in a straight rebuy situation. David Lenling, a sales representative for Hormel, used value analysis to sell pepperoni to a 35-unit group of pizzerias in the Cincinnati area. The owner had been using the same pepperoni and bacon topping for over 15 years and was reluctant to switch. Lenling showed how the Hormel pepperoni product cost $5 per case more but offered 1,200 more slices in a case with the same weight, which equated to an additional $12 of pepperoni or a $7 per case net savings, enough to make about 35 more pizzas per case. The owner of the chain was unaware of these differences until Lenling actually weighed his current product. Through value analysis, Lenling was able to interrupt a straight rebuy. Further, Lenling's buyer agreed that the Hormel product tasted better and was less greasy, resulting in a better-looking and tastier pizza, which might result in customers coming back more often. Because Hormel products are of high quality and sell at a premium price, Lenling and other sales representatives have to prove that the products are worth the extra money. They use value analysis to help purchasing agents determine how much it costs to use the product, rather than how much the product costs. That's why Lenling was able to win that large pizza chain's business.[21]

INDIVIDUAL NEEDS OF BUYING CENTER MEMBERS

In the preceding section we discussed criteria used to determine whether a product satisfies the needs of the organization. However, buying center members are people. Their evaluations and choices are affected by their personal needs as well as the organization's needs.

Types of Needs

Buying center members, like all people, have personal goals and aspirations. They want to get a raise, be promoted to a high-level position, have their managers recognize their accomplishments, and feel they have done something for their company or demonstrated their skills as a buyer or engineer.

Salespeople can influence members of the buying center by developing strategies to satisfy individual needs. For example, demonstrating how a new product will reduce costs and increase the purchasing agents' bonus would satisfy the purchasing agents' financial security needs. Encouraging an engineer to recommend a product employing the latest technology might satisfy the engineer's need for self-esteem and recognition by his or her engineering peers.

Risk Reduction

In many situations, members of the buying center tend to be more concerned about losing benefits they have now than about increasing their benefits. They place a lot of emphasis on avoiding risks that may result in poor decisions, decisions that can adversely affect their personal reputations and rewards as well as their organization's performance. Buyers first assess the potential for risk and then develop a risk reduction strategy.[22] To reduce risk, buying center members may collect additional information, develop a loyalty to present suppliers, or spread the risk by placing orders with several vendors.

Because they know suppliers try to promote their own products, customers tend to question information received from vendors. Customers usually view information from independent sources such as trade publications, colleagues, and outside consultants as more credible than information provided by salespeople and company advertising and sales literature. Therefore, they will search for such information to reduce risk when a purchase is important.

Advertising, the Internet, and sales literature tend to be used more in the early steps of the buying process. Word-of-mouth information from friends and colleagues is important in the proposal evaluation and supplier selection steps. Word-of-mouth information is especially important for risky decisions that will have a significant impact on the organization or the buying center member. "Sales Technology 3.1" illustrates the importance of the Internet for word-of-mouth information.

WEB-ENABLED WORD OF MOUTH

Facebook, Google Buzz, Twitter. Only a few years ago, none of these brands existed. Now they are dominant ways for people to access the Internet and each other. What does this mean for buyers?

Web reviews are one implication. When a buyer wants to evaluate a potential supplier, not only are there articles about how good (or bad) the supplier is, there are also blogs, tweets, and postings on review sites such as Epinions. Most consumers, especially those under 40, use these to find information for important purchases, and business buyers are no different. In fact, one survey finds 87 percent of business buyers turning to the Internet for information about almost every purchase.

What's interesting is that the buyers are in control of much of the content that is on the Web. Make someone mad and it shows up in a blog that reaches several thousand peers. Think a couple of thousand buyers don't matter? In a B2B market, you may have only a couple thousand buyers total.

Dell, in fact, has a staff of 45 people who monitor blogs, tweets, and other social media posts by buyers. When a complaint is registered, these staff members respond directly to the individual who complained. But they also use the information to create new services that might make Dell's offerings more attractive.

Customers also want to be able to offer input into new product development and use the Web to do so. Microsoft created an advertising campaign about Windows 7, presenting stories of individuals who claim responsibility for coming up with the ideas that became new features. Whether or not customers actually created those ideas is another story, but the campaign played to the desire customers have to offer input into new product development. IdeaStorm is a Web site that Dell operates specifically to allow users to post new product or feature ideas (see www.ideastorm.com). These ideas are then sorted by Dell personnel, and the better ones are sent to engineers to make their way into products.

Buyers use the Web as an information source. But they also use it as a place to register their complaints, voice their wants and desires, and talk to each other about which vendors are the best to do business with. Smart companies dynamically participate with these Web-active buyers.

Sources: "Brands Using Twitter," *Revolution*, December 2009, p. 17; Richard Bush, "The Changing Face of B2B," *Marketing*, January 14, 2009, p. 5; David Gelles, "The New Corporate Firefighters," *Financial Times*, January 22, 2009, p. 12.

Another way to reduce uncertainty and risk is to display **vendor loyalty** to suppliers—that is, to continue buying from suppliers that proved satisfactory in the past. Converting buying decisions into straight rebuys makes the decisions routine, minimizing the chances of a poor decision. One name for this is **lost for good;** for all the out-suppliers, this account can be considered lost for good because the in-supplier has cemented this relationship for a long time. Organizations tend to develop vendor loyalty for unimportant purchase decisions, though they will often look to vendors who have proved trustworthy when beginning to search in a risky situation. In these situations the potential benefits from new suppliers do not compensate for the costs of evaluating these suppliers.

The consequences of choosing a poor supplier can be reduced by using more than one vendor. Rather than placing all orders for an OEM component with one supplier, for example, a firm might elect to purchase 75 percent of its needs from one supplier and 25 percent from another. Thus if a problem occurs with one supplier, another will be available to fill the firm's needs. If the product is proprietary—available from only one supplier—the buyer might insist that the supplier develop a second source for the component. Such a strategy is called **always a share,** which means the buyer will always allocate only a share to each vendor.

These risk reduction approaches present a major problem for salespeople working for out-suppliers. To break this loyalty barrier, these salespeople need to develop trusting relationships with customers. They can build trust by offering performance guarantees or consistently meeting personal commitments. Another approach is to encourage buyers to place a small trial order so the salesperson's company can demonstrate the product's capabilities. On the other hand, the salesperson for the in-supplier wants to discourage buyers from considering new sources, even on a trial basis.

PROFESSIONAL PURCHASING'S GROWING IMPORTANCE

The purchasing profession is undergoing dramatic changes. Companies have recognized the impact that effective purchasing can make on the bottom line. For example, if a company can save $5,000 on a purchase, $5,000 is added to net income. If sales go up $5,000, of which most is additional costs, only $500 may be added to net income. Most large firms have elevated their directors of purchasing to the level of senior vice president to reflect the increasing importance of this function. As Russ Boyd, senior procurement specialist for Perot Systems, notes, "More CEOs are bringing purchasing (departments) to the table, asking where can you help us." Phil Krotz, of Rockwell Collins, agrees, meeting regularly with his company's CEO to help create initiatives that generate significant financial returns to the company.[23] Combine recognition of the power of purchasing with technology, and you can see why trends in professional purchasing are changing the business environment. The overall strategy is called supply chain management.

SUPPLY CHAIN MANAGEMENT

Supply chain management (SCM) began as a set of programs undertaken to increase the efficiency of the distribution channel that moves products from the producer's facilities to the end user. More recently, however, supply chain management has become more than just logistics; it is now a strategy of managing inventory while containing costs. Supply chain management includes logistics systems such as just-in-time inventory control, as well as supplier evaluation processes such as supplier relationship management systems.

The **just-in-time (JIT) inventory control** system is an example of a logistics supply chain management system used by a producer to minimize its inventory by having frequent deliveries, sometimes daily, just in time for assembly into the final product. In theory each product delivered by a supplier must conform to the manufacturer's specifications every time. It must be delivered when needed, not earlier or later, and it must arrive in the exact quantity needed, not more or less. The ultimate goal is to eventually eliminate all inventory except products in production and transit.

To develop the close coordination needed for JIT systems, manufacturers tend to rely on one supplier. The selection criterion is not the lowest cost, but the ability of the supplier to be flexible. As these relationships develop, employees of the supplier have offices at the customer's site and participate in value analysis meetings with the supplier. The salesperson becomes a facilitator, coordinator, and even marriage counselor in developing a selling team that works effectively with the customer's buying center. Resellers are also interested in managing their inventories more efficiently. Retailers and distributors work closely with their suppliers to minimize inventory investments and still satisfy the needs of customers. These JIT inventory systems are referred to as **quick-response** or **efficient consumer response (ECR)** systems in a consumer product distribution channel.

(Partnering relationships involving these systems are discussed in more detail in Chapter 14.)

Automatic replenishment (AR) is a form of JIT where the supplier manages inventory levels for the customer. The materials are provided on consignment, meaning the buyer doesn't pay for them until they are actually used. These types of arrangements are used in industrial settings, where the product being consumed is a supply item used in a manufacturing process, as well as in retail settings. Efficient consumer response systems use automatic replenishment technology through **electronic data interchange (EDI),** or computer systems that share data across companies. Exhibit 3.6 illustrates the communications associated with placing orders and receiving products that are transmitted electronically through EDI. Recent research has indicated that adopting systems involving both EDI and quick response or JIT delivers a number of benefits to the firm, in addition to lower costs. These benefits include greater flexibility in manufacturing, improved stability of supply, and other operating benefits. Though EDI has been around a long time, read Sean Gardner's perspective on implementing global EDI for Nestlé in "From the Buyer's Seat 3.1."

Material requirements planning (MRP) systems are an important element in JIT programs. These systems are used to forecast sales, develop a production schedule, and then order parts and raw materials with delivery dates that minimize the amount of inventory needed, thereby reducing costs. Effective JIT requires that customers inform suppliers well in advance about production schedules and needs.

SUPPLIER RELATIONSHIP MANAGEMENT

Supplier relationship management (SRM) is a strategy by which organizational buyers evaluate the relative importance of suppliers and use that information

Exhibit 3.6
EDI Transactions

From the BUYER'S SEAT

3.1

GLOBAL EDI AT NESTLÉ

Featuring Sean Gardner, B2B Strategies

EDI, or electronic data interchange, has been around for more than three decades. Originally created to enable electronic buying, EDI was offered by vendors such as American Hospital Supply and Xerox as a way to gain competitive advantage. By offering to manage their customers' inventories automatically through EDI, including reordering supplies automatically, these companies offered EDI to their customers as a way for their customers to cut ordering costs.

Now, 30 years later, you might expect EDI to be ubiquitous. But while the basic advantages of EDI haven't changed (assured supply and lower operating costs due to automatic ordering and inventory management), global supply chain management systems have added so many layers of complexity that global EDI systems simply don't exist. At least, not yet.

Working on a global EDI system for Nestlé, Sean Gardner, Cadre Director of B2B Strategies, explains the challenges. "One size doesn't fit all. Not when you have so many markets and so many countries, each with their own computer network systems and their own preferred ways of doing things, some of which work very efficiently and some of which are not so efficient."

One tremendous challenge is the need for collaboration between Nestlé and its customers. "How we collaborate with our customers in Israel is different than it is in the United States." The EDI system has to have flexibility to account for such collaboration across customers and across markets. "It's not just our salespeople who have to collaborate, but all of the areas of the business that drive customer service," notes Gardner.

Nor is it just collaboration with customers. "Any EDI system has to also account for collaboration up the supply chain. Our vendors, including transport, banking, and others, have to be able to collaborate with us and our customers through our EDI system."

Globalizing EDI is more than globalizing a software platform. Some markets might be paying 20 times what they would pay on a global contract made possible through global EDI, whereas some markets may only be paying 5 times. That may sound like great savings are possible for everyone; but in reality, some markets operate so efficiently that there is resistance to any new system. And existing relationships may be replaced with new suppliers or customers when a global EDI system is implemented. Not everyone wants to lose those existing relationships. "Any change that changes how people operate is not easy."

When you process millions of transactions a month, the lure of global technology solutions is tempting. But realizing the benefits can take years. Gardner estimates it may take as long as four years to fully implement an EDI system throughout all of Nestlé. "If you want to compete in an environment where your customers want to work with fewer suppliers, you have to do what they want. And that includes trimming costs all throughout the supply chain," states Gardner. Global EDI is one way to do that.

to determine with whom they want to develop partnerships. The first step is to identify the **annual spend,** or amount that is spent with each vendor and for what products. One outcome is the ability to consolidate purchases and negotiate better terms. After the relative importance is identified, organizational buyers frequently use a formal method, called **vendor analysis,** to summarize the benefits and needs satisfied by a supplier. When using this procedure, the buyer rates the supplier and its products on a number of criteria such as price, quality, performance, and on-time delivery.[24] Note that the ratings of suppliers can be affected by the perceptions and personal needs of the buyers. Then the ratings are weighted by the importance of the characteristics, and an overall score or evaluation of the vendor is developed. Exhibit 3.7 shows a vendor evaluation form used by Chrysler Corporation. The appendix to this chapter describes

Kingfisher plc, a European firm that owns and operates retail stores such as Castorama, uses supplier relationship management software from SAS Institute to track supplier performance.

the multiattribute model, which is useful in analyzing how members of the buying center evaluate and select products. The model also suggests strategies salespeople can use to influence these evaluations.

SRM software is being used by companies like Kingfisher plc, a company with some 1,400 stores across 17 countries and leading European retail brands such as Castorama and BUT. The company's Asia sourcing office in Hong Kong buys over 8,000 products from more than 150 suppliers. SRM software enables the company to identify problems, such as a delivery problem with one vendor in particular. Caterpillar, the construction and agriculture equipment manufacturer, instituted SRM software and training for all employees involved in purchasing. The training, created by Accenture, was more than just about the software; it was also about the strategy so the company could maximize its return on the software investment.[25]

SRM isn't always about improving profits. Sustainability, for example, is an important trend in purchasing and means making purchasing decisions that do not damage the environment. Bell Inc., a Sioux Falls, South Dakota, manufacturer of packaging products, worked with the U.S. Postal Service (USPS) to develop sustainable packaging products. The project required Bell to work with its suppliers, but the important element that allowed the project to flourish was the trust already built by actively managing relationships with suppliers. As Ben Graham, vice president for sales and supply chain, notes, "The project required us to work with a third-party accrediting agency that went back to our supply chain to understand the impact of the components of our packaging on the waste stream. It's a huge process, and it's not easy to go back to a supplier asking it to share its recipes. That takes confidentiality, trust, and understanding." Key for suppliers, Graham says, is to recognize the direction Bell's business is taking, the company's goals in the marketplace, and how they as suppliers fit in that strategy. "Once they understand that and see the opportunity they get very excited," he says. "Suppliers take part in our success."[26]

THE INTERNET AND BUSINESS-TO-BUSINESS SELLING

Companies like Amazon.com and eBay that sell products to consumers over the Internet are well known, but the number of business-to-business transactions over the Internet is many times greater than the number of business-to-consumer transactions.

How does the Internet affect salespeople? Most businesses view their Web sites on the Internet as a tool for supporting salespeople rather than replacing them. Buyers go to supplier Web sites to get information about product specifications and availability, place orders, and check on the status of orders. Thus salespeople will be able to spend less time on transactions and more time building relationships.

Exhibit 3.7
Sample Vendor Analysis Form

Supplier Name: _____ Type of Product: _____

Shipping Location: _____ Annual Sales Dollars: _____

	5 Excellent	4 Good	3 Satisfactory	2 Fair	1 Poor	0 N/A
Quality (45%)						
Defect rates	___	___	___	___	___	___
Quality of sample	___	___	___	___	___	___
Conformance with quality program	___	___	___	___	___	___
Responsiveness to quality problems	___	___	___	___	___	___
Overall quality	___	___	___	___	___	___
Delivery (25%)						
Avoidance of late shipments	___	___	___	___	___	___
Ability to expand production capacity	___	___	___	___	___	___
Performance in sample delivery	___	___	___	___	___	___
Response to changes in order size	___	___	___	___	___	___
Overall delivery	___	___	___	___	___	___
Price (20%)						
Price competitiveness	___	___	___	___	___	___
Payment terms	___	___	___	___	___	___
Absorption of costs	___	___	___	___	___	___
Submission of cost savings plans	___	___	___	___	___	___
Overall price	___	___	___	___	___	___
Technology (10%)						
State-of-the-art components	___	___	___	___	___	___
Sharing research & development capability	___	___	___	___	___	___
Ability and willingness to help with design	___	___	___	___	___	___
Responsiveness to engineering problems	___	___	___	___	___	___
Overall technology	___	___	___	___	___	___

Buyer: _____ Date: _____

Comments: _____

Source: Chrysler Corporation.

In some instances, though, buyers do use the Web instead of buying through salespeople. Reverse auctions are one mechanism that buyers use on the Web. A **reverse auction** is an auction, but instead of a seller offering a product and buyers bidding, a buyer offers a contract and sellers bid. Also, instead of prices rising, they fall as sellers compete to win the sale. Reverse auctions work best when the product being purchased can be specified completely and clearly, when the purchase is large enough to attract multiple suppliers and they are competitive, and when the buying company has the infrastructure to support a reverse auction.[27] Buyers are finding that you can't just stick a product description on the Web and have a reverse auction; it takes planning, accessibility of personnel to answer sellers' questions, and other resources. When it works, though, it can save both money and time. Tata Motors, the India-based auto manufacturer and owner of the Jaguar and Land Rover brands, used reverse auctions to save over $100 million per year. Now 40 percent of Tata purchases are made through reverse auctions.[28] Heinz had a similar experience, using reverse auctions thousands of times and reducing costs by over $60 million. Heinz found that being completely open and honest with suppliers about what was needed made the auctions work more effectively, leading to greater savings and satisfaction because it gave suppliers some flexibility in what they could offer. Their experience has been supported in research showing that reverse auctions can save buyers a great deal of money when buyers know exactly what they need.[29]

Reverse auctions are just one way to use the Internet. In "Sales Technology 3.1" we discuss how buyers use the Internet and the possible effect on salespeople.

thinking it through

Review the stages in the decision-making process described earlier in the chapter. Do you go through those stages when making an important purchase? How does the Internet affect the way you buy products and services? What effect does it have on each stage of the process?

SELLING YOURSELF

When you are selling your ideas or selling yourself in a job search, recognize that there is a buying center. Although a sales manager may make the final decision on whether you are hired, chances are that you'll interview with at least four people before the job offer will come. Similarly, once you have the job and you have an idea for a new program or product, you will have to sell that idea to management. That decision will likely include someone from finance, someone from operations, and so on, creating a buying center. Each member of the center will take on different roles and may be present for only part of the decision. Each member may also have different criteria.

Further, you need to understand the process by which the decision is made. In a job search, the decision to hire someone has been made before anyone talks to you. At that point your concern is making it from the large pool of college students they've interviewed at six different campuses to the group they bring into the office, to the final selection of new employees. Similarly, management approval of your idea is likely to follow a process not unlike that of any organizational purchase. Keep in mind that your idea is competing against other ideas from other people, just as your candidacy for a sales job is compared to other college students from your school and others.

SUMMARY

Salespeople sell to many different types of customers, including consumers, business enterprises, government agencies, and institutions. This text focuses on selling to organizations rather than to consumers. Selling to organizations differs from selling to consumers because organizations are more concentrated, demand is derived, and the buying process is more complex.

The organizational buying process consists of eight steps, beginning with the recognition of a need and ending with the evaluation of the product's performance. Each step involves several decisions. As organizations progress through these steps, decisions made at previous steps affect subsequent steps, leading to a creeping commitment. Thus salespeople need to be involved in the buying process as early as possible.

The length of the buying process and the role of various participants depend on the customer's past experiences. When customers have had considerable experience in buying a product, the decision becomes routine—a straight rebuy. Few people are involved, and the process is short. However, when customers have little experience in buying a product—a new task—many people are involved, and the process can be lengthy.

The people involved in the buying process are referred to as the buying center. The buying center is composed of people who are initiators, users, influencers, gatekeepers, and deciders. Salespeople need to understand the roles buying center members play to effectively influence their decisions.

Individuals in the buying center are concerned about satisfying the economic, quality, and service needs of their organization. In addition, these people have personal needs they want to satisfy.

Organizations face an increasingly dynamic and competitive environment. Purchasing is becoming a strategic weapon with the development of supply chain management and supplier relationship management strategies.

The Internet is playing a much more important role in business-to-business transactions than it plays in the widely publicized business-to-consumer e-businesses. Business-to-business applications of the Internet are designed to support salespeople's ability to build relationships with major customers.

KEY TERMS

always a share   81
annual spend   84
automatic replenishment (AR)   83
buying center   74
capital equipment   65
coach   75
creeping commitment   71
deciders   76
derived demand   69
economic influencer   75
efficient consumer response (ECR)   82
electronic data interchange (EDI)   83
emotional needs   77
end users   65
gatekeepers   75
influencers   74
initiators   74
just-in-time (JIT) inventory control   82
life-cycle costing   77
lost for good   81
material requirements planning (MRP)   83

modified rebuy   73
MRO supplies   65
new task   72
original equipment manufacturer (OEM)   64
producers   64
profit margin   65
quick-response system   82
rational needs   77
resellers   65
reverse auction   86
services   65
straight rebuy   73
supplier relationship management (SRM)   83
supply chain management (SCM)   82
technical influencer   75
turnover   65
users   74
value analysis   79
vendor analysis   84
vendor loyalty   81

ETHICS PROBLEMS

1. You know that American Airlines and Delta Airlines both have goals for purchasing from women- and minority-owned businesses (see "Building Partnerships 3.1"). You have a product that is innovative and patented, and it will save airlines like American and Delta over 30 percent in fuel costs. But your business does not qualify as woman- or minority-owned because you are a white male, so you are thinking of bringing a partner into the business—your sister. Is this appropriate? Or would it be better to license the product to an already certified minority-owned business?

2. You are talking about this class to someone who isn't familiar with business. When you mention you are studying how people make buying decisions and that this information will help you become a better salesperson, your friend says you are just trying to learn how to manipulate people more effectively. How do you respond?

QUESTIONS AND PROBLEMS

1. In the opening profile, Jenna Weber describes the personalities of two different buyers. Are these two personalities the only two types you would expect to see? She says one is easy to get along with, yet this one didn't buy her bacon promotion. Why, in your opinion, is that? What could she have done better?

2. Michelle Obama, as First Lady, has made childhood obesity an important issue. Suppose her goals include reducing sugar content in children's cereals, making vegetables more palatable, and reducing fat in the overall diet. Identify three product categories (not including vegetables) for which derived demand would influence manufacturers and producers of consumer packaged goods (foods sold to be cooked or eaten at home). Include at least one product affected positively and one affected negatively.

3. Assume you work for a division of 3M that makes medical monitoring systems. How would the purchasing decision process differ in the following situations? Which situation is a new task? A modified rebuy? A straight rebuy? How likely is the buyer to get other people in the organization involved? Which types of people are likely to get involved in each decision? Which situation is likely to produce the slowest decision?
   a. The organization is purchasing a custom-designed machine to be used in the manufacturing of metal racks that house multiple monitoring systems.
   b. An organization reorders plastic shields that it uses in making medical monitoring equipment from a regular supplier, a supplier that it has bought from in the past.
   c. The organization is designing a new line of medical monitoring equipment and wants an improved and updated microprocessor. It is considering its past suppliers as well as some suppliers that it has not bought from before.

4. Review each purchase in question 3. What information would you need to conduct a value analysis for each? Note: You will need some different and some similar information in each situation.

5. A chain of restaurants wants to purchase a new order entry computer system tied into an accounting system that manages food inventory and automatically replenishes food items. Which criteria for evaluating supplier proposals might be used by (a) the purchasing agent, (b) the information systems department, (c) a store manager, and (d) the head of the legal department? How would this purchase differ from a purchase of the same products by a company that resells store fixtures and equipment to small restaurants?

6. Dub Oliver runs the maintenance department at the paper mill, and he buys lots of hardware to fix equipment. Right now, he orders most of it through a Web site at NCH. If you work for Home Depot, how would you try to make a sale to Oliver? Assume you have a Web site he can order through, too.

7. When is vendor loyalty important? Find at least one example in the chapter (there are several) where vendor loyalty would prove to be important, and discuss why it was important in that particular instance. What can buyers do to improve vendor loyalty? When might vendor loyalty be inefficient or wasteful?

8. Does EDI result in greater loyalty? If so, how? Reread What are the challenges in creating and implementing a global EDI system? Why might some members of a company resist the adoption of a global EDI system?

9. Mitchell's Metal Shop is considering the purchase of a new press, a machine that bends sheet metal. The cost is $10,000, which is about 25 percent of the firm's profit for the quarter. Ford Motor Company is also considering buying new presses—30 of them. Discuss how risk is different for Frank Mitchell, owner of Mitchell's Metal Shop, and Ford.

10. How are the buying criteria for an OEM the same as a reseller? Why? How are the criteria likely to be different, and why? What type of buyer is likely to have criteria that are very different? Why are these criteria so different?

CASE PROBLEMS

case 3.1

Going Out through the Backdoor

Travis Bruns is a sales representative for Crown Lift Services in Houston, Texas. In his own words, he describes an ethics issue with a buyer.

Last year I was in a real cutthroat bidding war for a $300,000-plus sales opportunity. Over the course of two months the competitive field had been narrowed down to two organizations, mine and the incumbent organization. The customer had set up a set of strict guidelines for the bidding process. One of those was that they had designated a "point of contact" (POC) that was to be the liaison through which all bids and proposals were to channel through to the VP. My organization and I had truly put our best foot forward on pricing and proposed service after the sale, and although the negotiations had been rough, we were able to sell the value of our solution, retain a fair amount of profit, and were told we had the deal: a true win–win. On the final day that the bid was open, I received a call from the point of contact asking me to lower my price. I was confused. I inquired about the previous discussions that had taken place in which we had mutually agreed that the price of our proposal was fair and good. I could hear some level of discomfort if not embarrassment in the POC's voice, so I came right out and asked him, "I get the sense that you are not comfortable with what is happening here either. What happened?"

He replied, "Well, Travis, [your competitor] called one of the other managers in the office and was able to find out the pricing in your proposal. He then went around me and called the VP directly and offered a much lower price. The VP then called me and asked me to get you to lower your price or the other company will get the business."

I was dumbfounded. I asked the customer, "If I cannot lower my price, are you telling me this deal is over for me?"

"I think so," he replied.

Source: Travis Bruns. Used with permission.

Questions

1. What would you do? Do you lower your price or walk away? Why? Write out specifically what you would say next.

2. Do buyers have to follow the same ethics principles as sellers? For example, sellers have to fully disclose all information. Do buyers? Why or why not? What ethical principle violation occurred here?

Shirley Parker, CEO of her family's pet food manufacturing company, called some of the employees together to discuss employee benefits. Mark, the human resources director, asked her to call the meeting because the company needed to hire new workers, but he was finding it difficult because there were few benefits.

"We need a health plan for our employees. The plan must have doctors who are close to where our employees work, not close to the plant," says Fred, the plant manager.

Rachael, the production supervisor, added, "I'm concerned about retirement benefits, too. This is a private company, so we can't build a pension through a stock option plan. But I'd like something for retirement."

Chuck, the CFO, said, "Yeah, but you're talking about adding costs. Where's the benefit to the company? What budget will this come out of?"

They talked some more about the situation, and Shirley closed the meeting by saying, "Look, Chuck, I'd like you to head up a committee to gather some ideas from some different companies. Mark, you should be on this committee, too. Once you guys have narrowed things down a bit, let's get together and you can show me what you found."

Questions

1. What is the likely makeup of the buying center?
2. List the roles in the buying center, based on material in the chapter. Are all of the roles filled with someone?
3. What type of purchase situation is this? What implications will that have if you are a salesperson selling employee benefit plans?

ROLE PLAY CASE

During much of the rest of the semester, you will be calling on one of three accounts. The accounts are listed here with some information. Information that you gain on each call can be used in subsequent calls as you practice the skills and apply the concepts introduced in each chapter.

Spear One: Spear One is a company that creates special marketing events for clients all across the country. For example, when a PGA golf tournament is in town, Spear One may produce a special event for a client that involves the tournament, some of the players, the client's customers, and so forth. Think party planner for a business.

McLane Properties: McLane Properties is a commercial real estate company located in a major metropolitan town. While McLane has a lot of industrial space available, its primary focus is retail development and management. It leases out about 30 percent of the city's retail space and is the largest retail property management firm in town. Clients include stores like Old Navy, Gap, Academy, Radio Shack, and others.

Dart Paper Products: Dart makes paper products like cups, plates, napkins, and other products that are sold through distributors to restaurants, caterers, and institutional cafeterias (such as at universities or prisons) or directly to government agencies. Dart is the second largest paper products maker in North America, with operations also in Europe and Asia.

Today you want to find out what you can about who is involved in the decision process. You have an appointment arranged with a sales manager, thanks to a lead from an American Marketing Association workshop where you presented a session on sales productivity and software. Start from the beginning: Introduce yourself and your company, thanking the buyer for today's meeting, and then tell the buyer you'd like to ask some questions. Ask questions about the buying process, based on what you know from this chapter. After the role play, see if you can chart the buyer's organizational structure and the buying center.

APPENDIX MULTIATTRIBUTE MODEL OF PRODUCT EVALUATION AND CHOICE

The multiattribute model is a useful approach for understanding the factors individual members of a buying center consider in evaluating products and making choices. The multiattribute model is one approach that companies can take to making purchases and is most often used in complex decisions involving several vendors.[30] Many business decisions are straight rebuys, but the original vendor selection decision may have involved a multiattribute approach. The vendor analysis form used by Chrysler (see Exhibit 3.7) illustrates the use of this model in selecting vendors. The model also provides a framework for developing sales strategies.

The multiattribute model is based on the idea that people view a product as a collection of characteristics or attributes. Buyers evaluate a product by considering how each characteristic satisfies the firm's needs and perhaps their individual needs. The following example examines a firm's decision to buy laptop computers for its sales force. The computers will be used by salespeople to track information about customers and provide call reports to sales managers. At the end of each day, salespeople will call headquarters and upload their call reports.

PERFORMANCE EVALUATION OF CHARACTERISTICS

Assume the company narrows its choice to three hypothetical brands: Apex, Bell, and Deltos. Exhibit A.1 shows information the company has collected about each brand. Note that the information goes beyond the physical characteristics of the product to include services provided by the potential suppliers.

Each buying center member, or the group as a whole in a meeting, might process this objective information and evaluate the laptop computers on each characteristic. These evaluations appear in Exhibit A.2 as ratings on a 10-point scale, with 10 being the highest rating and 1 the lowest.

How do members of the buying center use these evaluations to select a laptop computer? The final decision depends on the relationship between the performance evaluations and the company's needs. The buying center members must consider the degree to which they are willing to sacrifice poor performance on

Exhibit A.1
Information about Laptop Computers

Characteristic/Brand	Apex	Bell	Deltos
Reliability rating	Very good	Very good	Excellent
Weight (pounds)	3.0	4.5	7.5
Display size (inches)	15.0	13	10.1
Display visibility	Good	Very good	Excellent
Speed (clock rate in gigahertz)	2.4	3.0	2.4
RAM (memory in gigabytes)	2	2	4
Number of U.S. service centers	140	60	20

Characteristic/Brand Rating	Apex	Bell	Deltos
Reliability	5	5	8
Weight	8	5	2
Display size	8	6	4
Display visibility	2	4	6
Speed	4	8	4
RAM	3	3	8
Service availability	7	5	3

one attribute for superior performance on another. The members of the buying center must make some trade-offs.

No single product will perform best on all characteristics. For example, Apex excels on size, weight, and availability of convenient service; Bell has superior speed; and Deltos provides the best reliability and internal memory.

IMPORTANCE WEIGHTS

In making an overall evaluation, buying center members need to consider the importance of each characteristic. These importance weights may differ from member to member. Consider two members of the buying center: the national sales manager and the director of management information systems (MIS). The national sales manager is particularly concerned about motivating his salespeople to use the laptop computers. He believes the laptops must be small and lightweight and have good screen visibility. On the other hand, the MIS director foresees using the laptop computers to transmit orders and customer inventory information to corporation headquarters. She believes expanded memory and processing speed will be critical for these future applications.

Exhibit A.3 shows the importance these two buying center members place on each characteristic using a 10-point scale, with 10 representing very important and 1 representing very unimportant. In this illustration the national sales manager and the MIS director differ in the importance they place on characteristics;

Exhibit A.3
Information Used
to Form an Overall
Evaluation

Characteristic	Importance Weights		Brand Ratings		
	Sales Manager	MIS Director	Apex	Bell	Deltos
Reliability	4	4	5	5	8
Weight	6	2	8	5	2
Display size	7	3	8	6	4
Display visibility	8	5	2	4	6
Speed	1	7	4	8	4
RAM	1	6	3	3	8
Service availability	3	3	7	5	3
Overall evaluation					
Sales manager's			168	150	141
MIS director's			137	157	163

however, both have the same evaluations of the brands' performance on the characteristics. In some cases people may differ on both importance weights and performance ratings.

OVERALL EVALUATION

A person's overall evaluation of a product can be quantified by multiplying the sum of the performance ratings by the importance weights. Thus the sales manager's overall evaluation of Apex would be as follows:

$$
\begin{aligned}
4 \times 5 &= 20 \\
6 \times 8 &= 48 \\
7 \times 8 &= 56 \\
1 \times 4 &= 4 \\
1 \times 3 &= 3 \\
8 \times 2 &= 16 \\
3 \times 7 &= \underline{21} \\
&\ 168
\end{aligned}
$$

Using the national sales manager's and MIS director's importance weights, the overall evaluations, or scores, for the three laptop computer brands appear at the bottom of Exhibit A.3. The scores indicate the benefit levels the brands provide as seen by these two buying center members.

VALUE OFFERED

The cost of the computers also needs to be considered in making the purchase decision. One approach for incorporating cost calculates the value—the benefits divided by the cost—for each laptop. The prices for the computers and their values are shown in Exhibit A.4. The sales manager believes Apex provides more value. He would probably buy this brand if he were the only person involved in the buying decision. On the other hand, the MIS director believes that Bell and Deltos offer the best value.

SUPPLIER SELECTION

In this situation the sales manager might be the key decision maker, and the MIS director might be a gatekeeper. Rather than using the MIS director's overall evaluation, the buying center might simply ask her to serve as a gatekeeper and

Exhibit A.4
Value Offered by Each Brand

| | Overall Evaluation (Benefits Points) | Assigned Value | |
		Computer Cost	Benefit/Cost
Sales manager			
Apex	167	$1,600	$0.10
Bell	152	1,800	0.08
Deltos	143	1,800	0.08
MIS director			
Apex	130	$1,600	0.08
Bell	169	1,800	0.09
Deltos	177	1,800	0.10

determine whether these computers meet her minimum acceptable performance standards on speed and memory. All three laptops pass the minimum levels she established of a 2-gigahertz clock rate and a 3-gigabyte internal memory. Thus the company would rely on the sales manager's evaluation and purchase Apex laptops for the sales force.

Even if a buying center or individual members do not go through the calculations described here, the multiattribute model is a good representation of their product evaluations and can be used to predict product choices. Purchase decisions are often made as though a formal multiattribute model were used.

thinking **it** through

If you were selling the Bell computer to the national sales manager and MIS director depicted in the text and in Exhibits A.3 and A.4, how would you try to get them to believe that your computer provides more value than Apex or Deltos does? What numbers would you try to change?

IMPLICATIONS FOR SALESPEOPLE

How can salespeople use the multiattribute model to influence their customers' purchase decisions? First, the model describes the information customers use in making their evaluations and purchase decisions. Thus salespeople need to know the following information to develop a sales strategy:

1. The suppliers or brands the customer is considering.
2. The product characteristics being used in the evaluation.
3. The customer's rating of each product's performance on each dimension.
4. The weights the customer attaches to each dimension.

With this knowledge salespeople can use several strategies to influence purchase decisions. First, salespeople must be sure their product is among the brands being considered. Then they can try to change the customer's perception of their product's value. Some approaches for changing perceived value are

1. Increase the performance rating for your product.
2. Decrease the rating for a competitive product.
3. Increase or decrease an importance weight.
4. Add a new dimension.
5. Decrease the price of your product.

Assume you are selling the Bell computer and you want to influence the sales manager so he believes your computer provides more value than the Apex computer. Approach 1 involves altering the sales manager's belief about your product's performance. To raise his evaluation, you would try to have the sales manager perceive your computer as small and lightweight. You might show him how easy it is to carry—how well it satisfies his need for portability. The objective of this demonstration is to increase your rating on weight from 5 to 7 and your rating on size from 6 to 8.

You should focus on these two characteristics because they are the most important to the sales manager. A small change in a performance evaluation on these characteristics will have a large impact on the overall evaluation. You would not want to spend much time influencing his performance evaluations of speed or memory because these characteristics are not important to him. Of course your objectives when selling to the MIS director would be different because she places more importance on speed and memory.

This example illustrates a key principle in selling. In general, salespeople should focus primarily on product characteristics that are important to the customer—characteristics that satisfy the customer's needs. Salespeople should not focus on the areas of superior performance (such as speed in this example) that are not important to the customer.

Approach 2 involves decreasing the performance rating of Apex. This strategy can be dangerous. Customers prefer dealing with salespeople who say good things about their products, not bad things about competitive products.

In approach 3 you try to change the sales manager's importance weights. You want to increase the importance he places on a characteristic on which your product excels, such as speed, or decrease the importance of a characteristic on which your product performs poorly, such as display visibility. For example, you might try to convince the sales manager that a fast computer will decrease the time salespeople need to spend developing and transmitting reports.

Approach 4 encourages the sales manager to consider a new characteristic, one on which your product has superior performance. For example, suppose the sales manager and MIS director have not considered the availability of software. To add a new dimension, you might demonstrate a program specially developed for sales call reports and usable only with your computer.

Approach 5 is the simplest to implement: Simply drop your price. Typically firms use this strategy as a last resort because cutting prices decreases profits.

These strategies illustrate how salespeople can adapt their selling approach to the needs of their customers. Using the multiattribute model, salespeople decide how to alter the content of their presentation—the benefits to be discussed—based on customer beliefs and needs. (Chapter 4 describes adaptive selling in more detail and illustrates it in terms of the form of the presentation—the communication style the salesperson uses.)

ADDITIONAL REFERENCES

Andersson, Svante, and Per Servais. "Combining Industrial Buyer and Seller Strategies for International Supply and Marketing Management." *European Business Review* 22 (2010), pp. 64–82.

Autry, Chad W., and Susan L. Golicic. "Evaluating Buyer–Supplier Relationship–Performance Spirals: A Longitudinal Study." *Journal of Operations Management* 28 (March 2010), pp. 87–104.

Briggs, Ellen. and Douglas Grisaffe, "Service Performance–Loyalty Intentions Link in a Business-to-Business Context: The Role of Relational Exchange Outcomes and Customer Characteristics." *Journal of Service Research* 13 (2010), pp. 37–52.

Brinkmann, Jorg. "An Analysis of Buying Center Decisions through the Salesforce." *Industrial Marketing Management* 36, no. 7 (2007), pp. 998–1012.

Glynn, Mark S. , Judy Motion, and Roderick J. Brodie. "Sources of Brand Benefits in Manufacturer–Reseller B2B Relationships." *Journal of Business & Industrial Marketing* 22, no. 6 (2007), pp. 400–13.

Gonzalez-Padronn, Tracy, G. Tomas Hult, and Roger Calantone. "Exploiting Innovative Opportunities in Global Purchasing: An Assessment of Ethical Climate and Relationship Performance." *Industrial Marketing Management* 37, no. 1 (2008), pp. 69–79.

Howard, Paul, and Declan Doyle. "An Examination of Buying Centres in Irish Biotechnology Companies and Its Marketing Implications." *The Journal of Business & Industrial Marketing* 21, no. 5 (2006), pp. 266–76.

Kotabe, Masaaki, Michael J. Mol, and Janet Y. Murray. "Outsourcing, Performance, and the Role of E-Commerce: A Dynamic Perspective." *Industrial Marketing Management* 37, no. 1 (2008), pp. 37–49.

Leach, Mark. "Examining Exchange Relationships among High-Tech Firms in the Evolving Global Economy." *Journal of Business & Industrial Marketing* 24 (2009), pp. 78–94.

Lindgreen, Adam, Balazs Revesz, and Mark Glynn. "Purchasing Orientation." *Journal of Business & Industrial Marketing* 24 (2009), pp. 148–72.

Lucero, Carrete. "A Relationship Model between Key Problems of International Purchasing and the Post-Purchase Behavior of Industrial Firms." *Journal of Business & Industrial Marketing* 23 (2008), pp. 332–47.

Lynch, Joanne, and Leslie de Chernatony. "Winning Hearts and Minds: Business-to-Business Branding and the Role of the Salesperson." *Journal of Marketing Management* 23, no. 1–2 (2007), pp. 123–36.

Marshall, Roger, Peter Alan Reday, Na Woonbong , and Shashank Shekhar Agrawal. "Response Time Measurement of Group Purchasing–Decision Power Structures." *Journal of Business Research* 60, no. 7 (2007), pp. 711–24.

Moon, Mark A. , and Leff Bonney. "An Application of the Investment Model to Buyer–Seller Relationships: A Dyadic Perspective." *Journal of Marketing Theory and Practice* 15, no. 4 (2007), pp. 335–47.

Paulraj, Antony, and Injazz J. Chen. "Strategic Buyer–Supplier Relationships, Information Technology, and External Logistics Integration." *Journal of Supply Chain Management* 43, no. 2 (2007), pp. 2–14.

Paulssen, Marcel, and Matthias M. Birk. "Satisfaction and Repurchase Behavior in a Business-to-Business Setting: Investigating the Moderating Effect of Manufacturer, Company, and Demographic Characteristics." *Industrial Marketing Management* 36, no. 7 (2007), pp. 983–97.

Pels, Jaqueline, Kristian Moller, and Michael Saren. "Do We Really Understand Business Marketing?" Getting beyond the RM and BM Matrimony." *Journal of Business & Industrial Marketing* 24 (2009), pp. 322–49.

Piercy, Nigel F., and Nikala Lane. "Ethical and Moral Dilemmas Associated with Strategic Relationships between Business-to-Business Buyers and Sellers." *Journal of Business Ethics* 72, no. 1 (2007), pp. 87–99.

Ritter, Thomas. "A Framework for Analyzing Relationship Governance." *The Journal of Business & Industrial Marketing* 22, no. 3 (2007), pp. 196–209.

Roy, Subroto, and Kiva Sivakumar. "The Role of Information Technology Adoption in the Globalization of Business Buying Behavior: A Conceptual Model and Research Propositions." *Journal of Business & Industrial Marketing* 22, no. 4 (2007), pp. 220–34.

Sashi, C.M., "Buyer Behavior in Business Markets: A Review and Integrative Model," *Journal of Global Issues* 3 (Summer 2009), pp. 129–38.

Skarmeas, Dionysis, Constantine S. Katsikeas, Stavroula Pyropoulou, and Esmail Salehi-Sangari. "Market and Supplier Characteristics Driving Distributor Relationship Quality in International Marketing Channels of Industrial Products." *Industrial Marketing Management* 27, no. 1 (2008), pp. 23–29.

Svahn, Senja and Mika Westerlund. "Purchasing Strategies in Supply Relationships." *Journal of Business & Industrial Marketing* 24 (2009), pp. 173–89.

Tomas, G., M. Hult, David J. Ketchen Jr., and Brian R. Chabowski. "Leadership, the Buying Center, and Supply Chain Performance: A Study of Linked Users, Buyers, and Suppliers." *Industrial Marketing Management* 36, no. 3 (2007), pp. 393–406.

chapter **4**

USING COMMUNICATION PRINCIPLES TO BUILD RELATIONSHIPS

SOME QUESTIONS ANSWERED IN THIS CHAPTER ARE

- What are the basic elements in the communication process?
- Why are listening and questioning skills important?
- How can salespeople develop listening skills to collect information about customers?
- How do people communicate without using words?
- What are some things to remember when communicating via technology like phones, e-mail, and social networking?
- How does a salesperson adjust for cultural differences?

PROFILE

PROFILE My name is Azure Barbeau, and I graduated from the College of St. Catherine in 2004 with a bachelor of science degree in health care sales. One of the major courses I took for this degree was "sales force leadership" with Professor Gregory Di Novis. Since graduation I have carried two roles in the business selling marketplace. My first role was with a copier/printer company selling to small to midsize companies, and I'm currently working with a leading medical device company selling in the orthopedic marketplace. One very important concept that I embrace every day is to communicate better with my customers.

Customer relationships are the cornerstone to successful sales transactions. Relationships are built off your communication with your customer. As a sales representative, I communicate every day through my language, both verbal and nonverbal communication, through conversations, e-mails, cell phones, and my digital pager. The most important thing to remember when trying to communicate with your customers is to understand your own verbal and nonverbal communication styles. Do you typically smile? Cross your arms when you talk with someone? Make proper eye contact? Do you have good posture when you are listening to someone talk? Do you have the urge to talk over people? All of these verbal and nonverbal cues can make or break your effectiveness in delivering a message about you.

Effective communication with your customers fulfills many purposes. The goal of communicating clearly is the sharing of information that meets their needs as well as yours. In the health care sales industry, identifying a customer's needs is extremely important, especially because it directly affects patients. Identifying the way your customer best communicates is another tool to use to be most effective. Although e-mail and text messaging are very popular, these may not be the best way to communicate with some older generations.

E-mail can be a great way to express detailed messaging, although your personal touch is easily lost or misinterpreted. Delivering information in person is one of the most beneficial and powerful ways of communicating. I personally like this method because you can read their nonverbal cues while you are delivering or listening to your customer. There are many things you can learn just by observing their actions. Do they act engaged or interested in what you have to offer? Or do they cut you off short or look the other way? Simple things like this can tell you much more about how you are portraying a message.

Communicating in the health care sales marketplace has taught me to be versatile in my communication styles. I adapt my verbal and nonverbal styles based on whom I am talking with. If I am communicating with a doctor about a new product I will adapt my style to his or her needs. Often you are given a very limited amount of time in which you as the salesperson must best communicate a message in the most effective manner in the shortest period of time. Understanding their time sensitively will allow you to respect their circumstances, which will, in turn, increase their respect for you. Adapting to your audience will help you to keep your messages clear, concise, and audience-appropriate.

BUILDING RELATIONSHIPS THROUGH TWO-WAY COMMUNICATION •

As we will discuss further in Chapter 13, open and honest communication is a key to building trust and developing successful relationships. To develop a good understanding of each other's needs, buyers and sellers must effectively communicate with each other by actively talking and listening.

THE COMMUNICATION PROCESS

Exhibit 4.1 illustrates the **two-way communication** process. The process begins when the sender, either the salesperson or the customer, wants to communicate some thoughts or ideas. Because the receiver cannot read the sender's mind, the sender must translate these ideas into words. The translation of thoughts into words is called **encoding.** Then the receiver must decode the message and try to understand what the sender intended to communicate. **Decoding** involves interpreting the meaning of the received message.

Consider a salesperson who is describing a complex product to a customer. At one point, a perplexed look flits across the customer's face. The salesperson receives this nonverbal message and asks the customer what part of the presentation needs further explanation. This **feedback** from the customer's expression tells the salesperson that the message is not being received. The customer then sends verbal messages to the salesperson in the form of questions concerning the operation and benefits of the product.

COMMUNICATION BREAKDOWNS

Communication breakdowns can be caused by encoding and decoding problems and the environment in which the communications occur. The following sales interaction between a copier salesperson and a prospect illustrates problems that can arise in encoding and decoding messages:

What the salesperson means to say: We have an entire line of Toshiba copiers. But I think the Model 900 is ideally suited for your needs because it provides the basic copying functions at a low price.

What the salesperson actually says (encodes): The Model 900 is our best-selling copier, and it's designed to economically meet the copying needs of small businesses like yours.

Exhibit 4.1
Two-Way Flow of Information

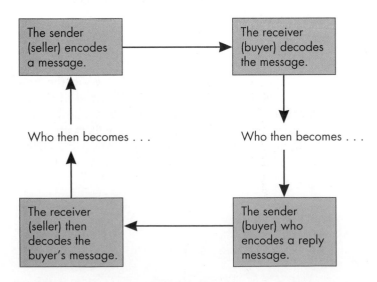

Background noise from traffic can hinder effective communication. The salesperson should attempt to move the discussion to a quieter location so the noise will not distract the customer.

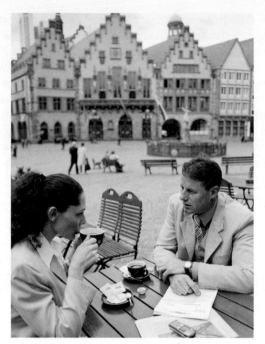

What the customer hears: The Model 900 is a low-priced copier for small businesses.

What the customer thinks (decodes): This company makes cheap copiers with limited features, probably for businesses that don't have much money. But I need a copier with more features. I think I'd better look elsewhere for a better copier.

What the customer actually says: I don't think I'm interested in buying a copier now.

In this situation the salesperson assumed that price was very important to the prospect, and the prospect thought (incorrectly) that the salesperson's company made only low-priced, low-performance copiers.

Communication can also be inhibited by the environment in which the communication process occurs. For example, noises can distract the salesperson and the customer. **Noises** are sounds unrelated to messages being exchanged by the salesperson and the customer, such as ringing telephones or other conversations nearby. To improve communication, the salesperson should attempt to minimize noises in the environment by closing a door to the room or suggesting that the meeting move to a quieter place.

Other environmental issues must be dealt with before effective communication can occur. For example, people communicate most effectively when they are physically comfortable. If the room is too hot or too cold, the salesperson should suggest changing the temperature controls or moving to another room. These types of environmental issues and possible solutions are discussed in Chapters 7 and 8. For now, realize that effective communication can't occur without the proper environment.

Finally, it is important to note that buyers do not always follow this communication model perfectly.[1] Some buyers, and sellers for that matter, have agendas that do not always result in honest, straightforward attempts to reveal truth. Rather, they may at times use communication as a tool to mask their true motives and intentions. You have probably done this yourself—when caught doing something wrong, and wishing to avoid detection or punishment, you masked the truth or said things you hoped would be interpreted in ways that were favorable to you.

thinking **it** through

Think of a big disagreement you had with someone recently (perhaps with a boyfriend, girlfriend, professor, or parents). Did any miscommunication occur? Why was the communication poor? Was it due to noise, poor feedback, poor encoding, poor decoding, or what?

SENDING VERBAL MESSAGES EFFECTIVELY

CHOICE OF WORDS

As Quintilion, the famous Roman orator, said, "Choice of words is the origin of eloquence." Salespeople don't have to be eloquent, but most could use some pointers to develop their skills in word choice. Use short words and phrases to demonstrate strength and force (like *accelerated* and *intervened*) or to provide charm and grace (like *crystal clear* and *crisp copies*). Avoid trite words such as *nice* and *good* and phrases that make you sound like an overeager salesperson such as *a great deal*, *I guarantee you will . . .*, and *No problem!* Also avoid using off-color language, slang, and foul language, even with established customers.

Every salesperson should be able to draw on a set of words to best help present the features of a product or service. The words might form a simile, such as *This battery backup is like a spare tire;* a metaphor such as *This machine is a real workhorse;* or a phrase drawing on sensory appeal, such as *smooth as silk* or *strong as steel*. To find the best way to use words, it often helps to listen to the way your customer talks.

One source says the five most powerful words today are *consequences, impact, reliability, mission,* and *commitment*.[2] However, even though using certain words may make you feel like you're "cutting edge," be careful about using words that have become so common in business conversations as to be almost meaningless. Words like *core competence, value added, enterprisewide, fault-tolerant,* and *mission-critical* are often cited as examples. Avoid them because they can make you come across as phony.

Words have different meanings in different cultures and even in different subcultures of the United States. In England the hood of a car is called the *bonnet* and the trunk is called the *boot*. In Boston a milkshake is simply syrup mixed with milk, whereas a frappe is ice cream, syrup, and milk mixed together. Studies show that about half of blacks over the age of 40 prefer the designation "black," whereas those 18–39 years old prefer "African American."[3]

VOICE CHARACTERISTICS

A salesperson's delivery of words affects how the customer will understand and evaluate his or her presentation. Poor voice and speech habits make it difficult for customers to understand a salesperson's message. **Voice characteristics** include rate of speech, loudness, inflection, and articulation.

Customers tend to question the expertise of salespeople who talk slower or faster than the normal rate of 140 words per minute. Salespeople should vary their rate of speech depending on the nature of the message and the environment in which the communication occurs. Simple messages can be delivered at faster rates, and more difficult concepts should be presented at slower rates.

Loudness should be tailored to the communication situation. To avoid monotony, salespeople should learn to vary the loudness of their speech. Loudness can also be used to emphasize certain parts of the sales presentation, indicating to the customer that these parts are more important.

Inflection is the tone or pitch of speech. At the end of a sentence, the tone should drop, indicating the completion of a thought. When the tone goes up at the end of a sentence, listeners often sense uncertainty in the speaker. Use inflection to reduce monotony. If you speak with enthusiasm, it will help your customer connect emotionally.[4] However, don't forget to be yourself. The buyer can be turned off if you're obviously just trying to copy the successful communication traits of someone else.

Articulation refers to the production of recognizable sounds. Articulation is best when the speaker opens his or her mouth properly; then the movements of the lips and tongue are unimpeded. When the lips are too close together, the enunciation of certain vowels and consonants suffers.

STORIES

While they are entertaining, stories can also make points most effectively. Great stories often include conflicts, trials, and crises and help the listener think through

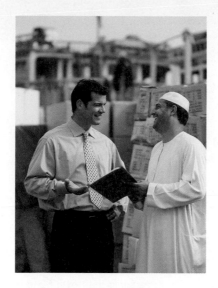

In order for the salesperson to communicate with this buyer, he must use words and stories that are meaningful and interesting to the buyer.

choices and outcomes of those decisions. Of course salespeople cannot assume all customers are familiar with trade jargon, and thus they need to check with their customers continually to determine whether they are interpreting sales messages and stories properly.

Salespeople can paint word pictures to help customers understand the benefits or features of a product. A **word picture** is a graphic or vivid story designed to help the buyer easily visualize a point. To use a word picture effectively, the salesperson needs to paint as accurate and reliable a picture as possible. Exhibit 4.2 provides an example of a word picture that a Toyota Highlander salesperson might use when calling on the owner of a real estate firm.

Effective stories often include an **analogy,** which is when the speaker attempts to draw a parallel between one thing and another. For example, to explain how a new machine controller is always monitoring and is ready to respond instantly, the seller could say this:

> It's kind of like a broadband Internet connection. It's always on. This controller never goes to sleep, never hangs up. It's not like a dial-up connection, where you have to dial a number every time you want to get your e-mail or surf the Web. This controller is sitting there, 24 hours a day, 7 days a week, 365 days a year, watching for the smallest malfunction and then taking immediate action to resolve the problem.

KEEP OPEN LINES OF COMMUNICATION

Although this might seem obvious, sometimes the obvious needs to be stated: As a salesperson you must always keep the lines of verbal communication with the buyer open. That means you must contact buyers often, keep them fully informed,

Exhibit 4.2
Example of a Word Picture

Situation
A Toyota salesperson is calling on Jill, the owner of a commercial real estate firm. The goal of the word picture is to demonstrate the value of the four-wheel-drive option.

Word Picture
Jill, picture for a moment the following situation. You have this really hot prospect—let's call him Steve—for a remote resort development. You're in your current car, a Cadillac STS. You've been trying to get Steve up to the property for months, and today is his only free day for several weeks. The property, up in the northern Georgia mountains, is accessible only by an old logging road. The day is bright and sunny, and Steve is in a good mood. When you reach the foot of the mountains, the weather turns cloudy and windy. As you wind up the old, bumpy road, a light rain begins. You've just crossed a small bridge when a downpour starts; the rain is pelting your windshield. Steve looks a little worried. Suddenly your car's tires start spinning. You're stuck in the mud.

Now let's replay the story, assuming that you buy the Toyota Highlander we've been talking about. [Salesperson quickly repeats the first paragraph of this story, substituting "Toyota Highlander" for "Cadillac STS."] Suddenly your car tires start spinning. You're stuck in the mud. Calmly you reach down and shift into four-wheel drive. The Toyota pulls out easily, and you reach the destination in about five minutes. Although it's raining, the prospect looks at the land and sees great potential. On the way back down the mountain, you discuss how Steve should go about making an offer on the property. Jill, I hope I've made a point. Can you see why the four-wheel-drive option is important for you, even though it does add to the base price of the car?

From the BUYER'S SEAT

KEEP OPEN LINES OF COMMUNICATION, PLEASE

By James Hill, Cliffs

I'm a senior buyer for Cliffs, a large U.S. mining company. Some of my salespeople are truly outstanding, and I enjoy doing business with them. For example, I buy $4.5 million worth of motors each year. I partner with my motor suppliers, and they are excellent at communicating with me and keeping me informed.

Unfortunately some of my salespeople just aren't good at keeping the lines of communication open. I need to know, at all times, what's going on with my order and delivery. I tell my suppliers, "Tell me as soon as you know if something goes wrong at your plant." For example, I had a supplier who was making custom pipe for my company. My company, in anticipation of the coming pipe, had crews and equipment ordered and standing by to start installing the pipe in early May. The pipe was supposed to come from my supplier by the end of April. April came and went, and no pipe was delivered. Turns out there was a problem in the supplier's plant. But the seller never told me about it, afraid it would make him or his company look bad. My phone call to him was not pretty. My message? "Tell me if you're having troubles, so my company can redeploy its resources effectively!"

I also need to know "good news" as well. One of my suppliers from Japan was shipping in several large motors, each of which weighed over four tons. Well, the supplier shipped them earlier than he had informed me. They arrived early, and I didn't have a crane available to unload them. Communicating with me that they were shipping early could have avoided many headaches when the trucks arrived!

Sometimes my suppliers have suggestions on how to make our business run more efficiently. That's great. But they always need to communicate that to me, not just take matters into their own hands. We buy cases of belt dressing, which is used to keep the belts from slipping. Those belts are used to load ships and must work effectively. My salesperson, Dave, decided to save me some money, without telling me. Instead of shipping the $2.99/can brand of belt dressing we had always used, which worked great, he shipped some cases of $1.99/can brand. My guys at the dock assumed they were supposed to use this cheaper dressing, so they did. The result? It took us 12 hours to load the ore boat instead of the usual 8 hours. That cost us $50,000 extra. Needless to say, I was less than impressed! And Dave heard about it, too.

Source: James Hill, Cliffs, personal correspondence; used with permission; names changed to protect anonymity.

and make sure you are accessible for their contact. "From the Buyer's Seat 4.1" gives examples of when sellers failed to do so—and the consequences.

ACTIVE LISTENING

Many people believe effective communication is achieved by talking a lot.[5] Inexperienced salespeople often go into a selling situation thinking they have to out-talk the prospect. They are enthusiastic about their product and company, and they want to tell the prospect all they know. However, salespeople who monopolize conversations cannot find out what customers need. One authority suggests an **80–20 listening rule:** Salespeople should listen 80 percent of the time and talk no more than 20 percent of the time.[6]

People can speak at a rate of only 120 to 160 words per minute, but they can listen to more than 800 words per minute. This difference is referred to as the **speaking–listening differential.** Because of this differential, salespeople often become lazy listeners. They do not pay attention and often remember only 50 percent of what is said immediately after they hear it.

Effective listening is not a passive activity. Salespeople who practice **active listening** project themselves into the mind of the speaker and attempt to feel the way the speaker feels. Firms are spending millions of dollars on speech analytics technology for their call centers so they can discover the customer's emotions during a phone conversation.[7] Salespeople should be able to do that more effectively because they are face-to-face with the customer. If a customer says she needs a small microphone, a Sony salesperson needs to listen carefully to find out what the term *small* means to this particular customer—how small the microphone has to be, why she needs a small microphone, and what she will be willing to sacrifice to get a small microphone. Active listening enables the salesperson to recommend a type of microphone that will meet the customer's specific needs.

Active listeners think while they listen. They think about the conclusions toward which the speaker is building, evaluate the evidence being presented, and sort out important facts from irrelevant ones. Active listening also means the listener attempts to draw out as much information as possible. Gestures can motivate a person to continue talking. Head nodding, eye contact, and an occasional *I see, Tell me more,* or *That's interesting* all demonstrate an interest in and understanding of what is being said.[8] Take a moment to complete the questionnaire in Exhibit 4.3 to rate your active listening skills.

Exhibit 4.3
Test Your Active
Listening Skills

	My performance could be improved substantially			My performance needs no improvement	
During a typical conversation:					
1. I project an impression that I sincerely care about what the person is saying.	1	2	3	4	5
2. I don't interrupt the person.	1	2	3	4	5
3. I don't jump to conclusions.	1	2	3	4	5
4. I ask probing questions.	1	2	3	4	5
5. I ask continuing questions like "Could you tell me more?"	1	2	3	4	5
6. I maintain eye contact with the person.	1	2	3	4	5
7. I nod to show the person that I agree or understand.	1	2	3	4	5
8. I read the person's nonverbal communications.	1	2	3	4	5
9. I wait for the person to finish speaking before evaluating what has been said.	1	2	3	4	5
10. I ask clarifying questions like "I'm not sure I know what you mean."	1	2	3	4	5
11. I restate what the person has stated or asked.	1	2	3	4	5
12. I summarize what the person has said.	1	2	3	4	5
13. I make an effort to understand the person's point of view.	1	2	3	4	5
14. I try to find things I have in common with the person.	1	2	3	4	5

Scoring: 60–70 = Outstanding; 50–59 = Good; 40–49 = Could use some improvement; 30–39 = Could definitely use some improvement; Under 30 = Are you listening?

Source: An adaptation of the ILPS scale, Stephen B. Castleberry, C. David Shepherd, and Rick E. Ridnour, "Effective Interpersonal Listening in the Personal Selling Environment: Conceptualization, Measurement, and Nomological Validity," *Journal of Marketing Theory and Practice,* Winter 1999, pp. 30–38.

Suggestions for active listening include (1) repeating information, (2) restating or rephrasing information, (3) clarifying information, (4) summarizing the conversation, (5) tolerating silences, and (6) concentrating on the ideas being communicated.[9]

REPEATING INFORMATION

During a sales interaction the salesperson should verify the information she or he is collecting from the customer. A useful way to verify information is to repeat, word for word, what has been said. This technique minimizes the chance of misunderstandings:

CUSTOMER: I'll take 20 cases of Nestlé milk chocolate hot cocoa and 12 cases of the rich chocolate.

SALESPERSON: Sure, Mr. Johnson, 20 cases of milk chocolate and 12 cases of rich chocolate.

CUSTOMER: Wait a minute. I got that backward. The rich chocolate is what sells the best here. I want 20 cases of the rich chocolate and 12 cases of the milk chocolate.

SALESPERSON: Fine. Twelve milk chocolate, 20 rich chocolate. Is that right?

CUSTOMER: Yes. That's what I want.

Salespeople need to be careful when using this technique, however. Customers can get irritated with salespeople who echo everything.

RESTATING OR REPHRASING INFORMATION

To verify a customer's intent, salespeople should restate the customer's comment in his or her own words.[10] This step ensures that the salesperson and customer understand each other:

CUSTOMER: Your service isn't what I had expected it would be.

SALESPERSON: I see, you're a bit dissatisfied with the financial advisor services I've been giving you.

CUSTOMER: Oh, no. As a matter of fact, I've been getting better service than I thought I would.

CLARIFYING INFORMATION

Another way to verify a customer's meaning is to ask questions designed to obtain additional information.[11] These can give a more complete understanding of the customer's concerns:

To be an effective listener, the salesperson demonstrates an interest in what the customer is saying and actively thinks about questions for drawing out more information.

CUSTOMER: Listen, I've tried everything. I just can't get this drill press to work properly.

SALESPERSON: Just what is it that the drill press doesn't do?

CUSTOMER: Well, the rivets keep jamming inside the machine. Sometimes one rivet is inserted on top of the other.

SALESPERSON: Would you describe for me the way you load the rivets onto the tray?

> CUSTOMER: Well, first I push down the release lever and take out the tray. Then I push that little button and put in the rivets. Next, I push the lever again, put the tray in the machine, and push the lever.
>
> SALESPERSON: When you put the tray in, which side is up?
>
> CUSTOMER: Does that make a difference?

This exchange shows how a sequence of questions can clarify a problem and help the salesperson determine its cause.

SUMMARIZING THE CONVERSATION

An important element of active listening is to mentally summarize points that have been made. At critical spots in the sales presentation, the salesperson should present his or her mentally prepared summary. Summarizing provides both salesperson and customer with a quick overview of what has taken place and lets them focus on the issues that have been discussed:

> CUSTOMER: So I told him I wasn't interested.
>
> SALESPERSON: Let me see whether I have this straight. A salesperson called on you today and asked whether you were interested in reducing your costs. He also said he could save you about $125 a month. But when you pursued the matter, you found out the dollar savings in costs were offset by reduced service.
>
> CUSTOMER: That's right.
>
> SALESPERSON: Well, I have your account records right here. Assuming you're interested in getting more for your company's dollar with regard to cell service costs, I think there's a way we can help you—without having to worry about any decrease in the quality of service.
>
> CUSTOMER: Tell me more.

TOLERATING SILENCES

This technique could more appropriately be titled "Bite your tongue." At times during a sales presentation, a customer needs time to think. This need can be triggered by a tough question or an issue the customer wants to avoid. While the customer is thinking, periods of silence occur. Salespeople may be uncomfortable during these silences and feel they need to say something. However, the customer cannot think when the salesperson is talking. The following conversation about setting a second appointment demonstrates the benefits of tolerating silence:

> SALESPERSON: What day would you like me to return with the samples and give that demonstration to you and your team?
>
> CUSTOMER: [*obviously thinking*]
>
> SALESPERSON: [*silence*]
>
> CUSTOMER: OK, let's make it on Monday, the 22nd.

CONCENTRATING ON THE IDEAS BEING COMMUNICATED

Frequently what customers say and how they say it can distract salespeople from the ideas the customers are actually trying to communicate. For example, salespeople may react strongly when customers use emotion-laden phrases such as *bad service* or *lousy product*. Rather than getting angry, the salesperson should

BUILDING Partnerships

COMMUNICATION IS KEY IN MY BUSINESS

As a sales representative for ArthroCare Sports Medicine, my job takes me directly into the operating room, where I help hospital staff and surgeons use my products. Good communication is the cornerstone to my sales success. I need to be able to communicate to many different people, and my sales presentations need to have the message adapted to the audience.

I believe that my most effective sales calls have been when the customer is talking more than me. Some buyers are closed and not willing to share information. An attentive salesperson will learn to pay very close attention to verbal and nonverbal cues from a buyer. Some buyers like to start each meeting by talking about personal issues ("How are your kids?"). Other buyers only want to talk business, and will stop talking when personal issues are brought up. By effectively listening to their responses and reading their body language, I can determine which discussion road the buyer wants to proceed on.

Almost as importantly, I need to be able to effectively communicate within my firm. My sales manager is responsible for many different salespeople and territories, and it's important to let him know when I am working on a big sale or making an important presentation. Many of my sales managers have been successful salespeople in their careers, and they like to talk sales strategy or learn what has been effective in my territory. Communication with other marketing people in my company is also very important. In medical companies, marketing departments are in charge of developing new products and improving existing ones. It is critical for me to advise them of issues I have encountered with their products and let them know any ideas to help improve or design new products.

Source: Mike Donley, ArthoCare Sports Medicine, personal correspondence; used with permission.

try to find out what upset the customer so much. Salespeople should listen to the words from the customer's viewpoint instead of reacting from their own viewpoint.[12] And as "Building Partnerships 4.1" describes, salespeople need to improve their communication skills within their firms, not just with their customers.

READING NONVERBAL MESSAGES FROM CUSTOMERS

In addition to asking questions and listening, salespeople can learn a lot from their customers' nonverbal behaviors.[13] John Napier, author of the book *Hands*, put it this way: "If language was given to men to conceal their thoughts, then gestures' purpose was to disclose them. Experts on nonverbal behavior say we literally leak our true or masked feelings through our body language and movements."[14] When two people communicate with each other, spoken words play a surprisingly small part in the communication process. Words are responsible for only 40 percent of the information people acquire in face-to-face communication. Voice characteristics account for 10 percent of the message received, and the remaining 50 percent comes from nonverbal communications.[15] In this section we discuss how salespeople can collect information by observing their customers' **body language.** Later in the chapter we examine how salespeople can use the three forms of **nonverbal communication**—body language, space, and appearance—to convey messages to their customers. Note that experts don't always agree on what nonverbal cues mean. The examples provided in this chapter are those commonly accepted by sales trainers.

The customer in the upper panel is giving negative nonverbal signals of arms crossed and no smile. Both buyers and the seller in the lower panel are giving positive, nonverbal signals.

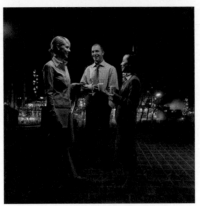

BODY ANGLE

Back-and-forth motions indicate a positive outlook, whereas side-to-side movements suggest insecurity and doubt. Body movements directed toward a person indicate positive regard; in contrast, leaning back or away suggests boredom, apprehension, or possibly anger. Changes in position may indicate that a customer wants to end the interview, strongly agrees or disagrees with what has been said, or wants to place an order.

FACE

The face has many small muscles capable of communicating innumerable messages. Customers can use these muscles to indicate interest, expectation, concern, disapproval, or approval. The eyes are the most important area of the face. The pupils of interested or excited people tend to enlarge. Thus by looking at a customer's eyes, salespeople can often determine when their presentations have made an impression. For this reason many Chinese jade buyers wear dark glasses so they can conceal their interest in specific items and bargain more effectively. Even the rate at which someone blinks can tell a lot about a person. The average blink rate for a relaxed person is 10 to 20 blinks per minute (bmp). During normal conversation, it increases to about 25 bmp. A bmp rate over 50, and particularly over 70, indicates high stress levels.

Eye position can indicate a customer's thought process. Eyes focused straight ahead mean a customer is passively receiving information but devoting little effort to analyzing the meaning and not really concentrating on the presentation. Intense eye contact for more than three seconds generally indicates customer displeasure. Staring indicates coldness, anger, or dislike.

Customers look away from the salesperson while they actively consider information in the sales presentation. When the customer's eyes are positioned to the left or right, the salesperson has succeeded in getting the customer involved in the presentation. A gaze to the right suggests the customer is considering the logic and facts in the presentation, and gazing to the left suggests more intense concentration based on an emotional consideration. Eyes cast down offer the strongest signal of concentration. However, when customers cast their eyes down, they may be thinking, *How can I get my boss to buy this product?* or *How can I get out of this conversation?* When customers look away for an extended period, they probably want to end the meeting.

Skin color and skin tautness are other facial cues. A customer whose face reddens is signaling that something is wrong. That blush can indicate either anger or embarrassment. Tension and anger show in a tightness around the cheeks, jawline, or neck.

ARMS

A key factor in interpreting arm movements is intensity. Customers will use more arm movement when they are conveying an opinion. Broader and more vigorous movement indicates the customer is more emphatic about the point being

The open hands on the left are a positive signal by a salesperson. The intertwined fingers in the middle indicate that the salesperson is expressing his power and authority. On the right the salesperson is playing with his hands, indicating underlying tension.

communicated verbally. Always remember cultural differences. For example, it's rude to cross your arms in Turkey.

HANDS

Hand gestures are very expressive. For example, open and relaxed hands are a positive signal, especially with palms facing up. Self-touching gestures typically indicate tension. Involuntary gestures, such as tightening of a fist, are good indicators of true feelings. The meanings of hand gestures differ from one culture to another.[16] For example, the thumbs-up gesture is considered offensive in the Middle East, rude in Australia, and a sign of OK in France. In Japan the OK sign made by holding the thumb and forefinger in a circle symbolizes money, but in France it indicates that something is worthless.

LEGS

When customers have uncrossed legs in an open position, they send a message of cooperation, confidence, and friendly interest. Legs crossed away from a salesperson suggest that the sales call is not going well. Note that crossing your feet and showing the bottoms of your shoes are insulting in Japan.

BODY LANGUAGE PATTERNS

Exhibit 4.4 illustrates the patterns of signals that generally indicate the customer is reacting positively or negatively to a salesperson's presentation. However, no

Exhibit 4.4
Patterns of Nonverbal
Reactions to Presentation

Positive Signals	Negative Signals
Uncrossed arms and legs	Crossed arms or legs
Leaning forward	Leaning backward or turned away from you
Smiling or otherwise pleasant expression	Furrowed brow, pursed lips, frowning
Nodding	Shaking head
Contemplative posture	Fidgeting, distracted
Eye contact	No eye contact
Animated, excited reaction	Little change in expression, lifeless

single gesture or position defines a specific emotion or attitude. To interpret a customer's feelings, salespeople need to consider the pattern of the signals via a number of channels. For example, many men are comfortable in informal conversations with their arms crossed. It doesn't necessarily mean they're against you or what you're saying.

In business and social situations, buyers often use nonverbal cues to try to be polite. As a result salespeople often have difficulty knowing what a customer is really thinking. For example, smiling is the most common way to conceal a strong emotion. Salespeople need to know whether a customer's smile is real or just a polite mask. The muscles around the eyes reveal whether a smile is real or polite. When a customer is truly impressed, the muscles around the eyes contract, the skin above the eyes comes down a little, and the eyelids are slightly closed.

Here are some other signals that customers may be hiding their true feelings:

- *Contradictions and verbal mistakes.* People often forget what they said previously. They may leak their true feelings through a slip of the tongue or a lapse in memory.
- *Differences in two parts of a conversation.* In the first part of a conversation, a customer may display some nervousness when asked about the performance of a competitor's product and then respond by outlining the competitor's product's faults. Later in the conversation, the evaluation of the competitor's product may be much more positive.
- *Contradictions between verbal and nonverbal messages.* For example, a facial expression may not match the enthusiasm indicated by verbal comments. Also, a decrease in nonverbal signals may indicate that the customer is making a cautious response.
- *Nonverbal signals.* Voice tone going up at the end of a sentence, hesitation in the voice, small shrugs, increased self-touching, and stiffer body posture suggest that the customer has concerns.

When customers disguise their true feelings, they are often trying to be polite, not deceptive. To uncover the customer's true feelings and build a relationship, the salesperson needs to encourage the customer to be frank by emphasizing that she or he will benefit from an open exchange of information. Here are some comments a salesperson can make to encourage forthright discussion:

- Perhaps there is some reason you cannot share the information with me.
- Are you worried about how I might react to what you are telling me?
- I have a sense that there is really more to the story than what you are telling me. Let's put the cards on the table so we can put this issue to rest.

SENDING MESSAGES WITH NONVERBAL COMMUNICATION

The preceding section described how salespeople can develop a better understanding of their customers by observing their body language. Salespeople can also use their own body language, spacing, and appearance to send messages to their customers. This section explores that aspect of body language.

USING BODY LANGUAGE

During a 30-minute sales call around 800 nonverbal signals are exchanged.[17] Astute salespeople use these signals to communicate more effectively with customers. For example, salespeople should strive to use the positive signals shown in Exhibit 4.4. Cooperative cues indicate to customers that the salesperson sincerely wants to help them satisfy their needs. Obviously salespeople should avoid using negative cues.

Remember this word of warning: The most effective gestures are natural ones, not those you are forcing yourself to perform. A buyer can spot nongenuine nonverbals. Use as much of this information as you can, but don't become so engrossed in following all the rules that you can't be yourself.

Facial Muscles

Nonverbal communication is difficult to manage. Facial reactions are often involuntary, especially during stressful situations. Lips tense, foreheads wrinkle, and eyes glare without salespeople realizing they are disclosing their feelings to a customer. Salespeople will be able to control their facial reactions only with practice.[18]

As with muscles anywhere else in the body, the coordination of facial muscles requires exercise. Actors realize this need and attend facial exercise classes to learn to control their reactions. Salespeople are also performers to some extent and need to learn how to use their faces to communicate emotions.

Nothing creates rapport like a smile. The smile should appear natural and comfortable, not a smirk or an exaggerated, clownlike grin. To achieve the right smile, stand before a mirror or a video camera and put your lips in various smiling positions until you find a position that feels natural and comfortable. Then practice the smile until it becomes almost second nature.

Eye Contact

Appropriate eye contact varies from situation to situation.[19] People should use direct eye contact when talking in front of a group to indicate sincerity, credibility, and trustworthiness. Glancing from face to face rapidly or staring at a wall has the opposite effect. However, staring can overpower customers and make them uncomfortable.

Gestures and Handshaking

Gestures can have a dramatic impact.[20] For example, by exposing the palm of the hand, a salesperson indicates openness and receptivity. Slicing hand movements and pointing a finger are very strong signals and should be used to reinforce only the most important points. In most cases pointing a finger should be avoided. This gesture will remind customers of a parent scolding a child. When salespeople make presentations to a group, they often use too few hand gestures. Gestures should be used to drive home a point. But if a salesperson uses too many gestures, acting like an orchestra conductor, people will begin to watch the hands and miss the words.

The location of your hands during gestures can have a huge impact on the message received.[21] For example, imagine a salesperson standing and giving a presentation to a small group of businesspeople. If she drops her hands down by her sides while presenting and keeps them there, she will come across as passive and lacking enthusiasm. Hand gestures presented at about the height of her navel help the salesperson come across as truthful. Gestures at chest level suggest she has real passion about a topic, while those above the head are interpreted as great passion. Try each of these locations of gestures in front of a mirror while saying "I love you" to see what impact the location of gestures has on the interpretation of the spoken words.

In terms of shaking hands, salespeople should not automatically extend their hands to prospects, particularly if a prospect is seated.[22] Shaking hands should be the prospect's choice. If the prospect offers a hand, the salesperson should respond with a firm but not overpowering handshake while maintaining good eye contact. Chances are that you have experienced both a limpid handshake—a hand with little or no grip—and a bone-crunching grip. Either impression is often lasting and negative. Also, if you tend to have sweaty hands, carry a handkerchief.

Women should shake hands in the same manner men do. They should avoid offering their hand for a social handshake (palm facing down and level with the ground, with fingers drooping and pointing to the ground). Likewise, a man should not force a social handshake from a woman in a business setting.

The salesperson selling in an international context needs to carefully consider cultural norms regarding the appropriateness of handshaking, bowing, and other forms of greeting.[23] For example, the Chinese prefer no more than a slight bow in their greeting, whereas an Arab businessperson may not only shake hands vigorously but also keep holding your hand for several seconds. A hug in Mexico communicates a trusting relationship, but in Germany such a gesture would be offensive because it suggests an inappropriate level of intimacy. Germans tend to pump the hand only once during a handshake. Seventy-four percent of British adults admit they no longer reach out a hand to greet friends or colleagues.[24] Some African cultures snap their fingers after shaking hands, but other Africans would see this act as tasteless. And some Eastern cultures use the left hand for hygienic purposes, so offering a left hand to them would insult them.

Posture and Body Movements

Shuffling one's feet and slumping give an impression of a lack of both self-confidence and self-discipline. On the other hand, an overly erect posture, like that of a military cadet, suggests rigidity. Salespeople should let comfort be their guide when searching for the right posture.

To get an idea of what looks good and feels good, stand in front of a mirror and shift your weight until tension in your back and neck is at a minimum. Then gently pull your shoulders up and back and elevate your head. Practice walking by taking a few steps. Keep the pace deliberate, not halting; deliberate, controlled movements indicate confidence and empathy. Note cultural differences like the fact that Japanese people value the ability to sit quietly, and can view a fidgety American as uncontrolled.

THE ROLE OF SPACE AND PHYSICAL CONTACT

The physical space between a customer and a salesperson can affect the customer's reaction to a sales presentation. Exhibit 4.5 shows the four distance zones people use when interacting in business and social situations. The **intimate zone** is reserved primarily for a person's closest relationships; the **personal zone** for close friends and those who share special interests; the **social zone** for business transactions and other impersonal relationships; and the **public zone** for speeches, teachers in classrooms, and passersby. The exact sizes of the intimate and personal zones depend on age, gender, culture, and race. For example, the social zone for Latinos is much closer than that for North Americans. Latinos tend to conduct business transactions so close together that North Americans feel uncomfortable.

Customers may react negatively when they believe salespeople are invading their intimate or personal space. To show the negative reaction, customers may assume a defensive posture by moving back or folding their arms. Although approaching too close can generate a

This buyer and seller are in the intimate zone.

Exhibit 4.5
Distance Zones for Interaction

Intimate zone:
0–2 feet

Social zone:
4–12 feet

Personal zone:
2–4 feet

Public zone:
beyond
12 feet

negative reaction, standing too far away can create an image of aloofness, conceit, or unsociability.

In general, salespeople should begin customer interactions at the social zone and not move closer until an initial rapport has been established. If the buyer indicates that a friendlier relationship has developed, the salesperson should move closer.[25]

In terms of touching, buyers fall into two touching groups: contact and noncontact. Contact people usually see noncontact people as cold and unfriendly. On the other hand, noncontact people view contact people as overly friendly and obtrusive. People who like to be touched tend to respond to touch with increased persuasion and liking for the salesperson. Although some customers may accept a hand on their backs or a touch on their shoulders, salespeople should generally limit touching to a handshake. Touching clearly enters a customer's intimate space and may be considered rude and threatening—an invasion.

APPEARANCE

Physical appearance, specifically dress style, is an aspect of nonverbal communication that affects the customer's evaluation of the salesperson. Two priorities in dressing for business are (1) getting customers to notice you in a positive way and (2) getting customers to trust you. If salespeople overdress, their clothing may distract from their sales presentation. Proper attire and grooming, however, can give salespeople additional poise and confidence. One salesperson for Smith & Nephew, a medical equipment company, says he always dresses like a chameleon. "Dress like your doctor," is his motto. If the doctor is in suit and tie, he wears a suit and tie; if the doctor prefers casual dress, the seller does likewise.

At one time dressing for work was simple: You just reached in the closet and picked from your wardrobe of blue, gray, and pinstripe suits. Today things are not that simple. With casual days and dress-down Fridays, styles and dress codes vary considerably from office to office. Salespeople should learn the norms for dress in their field and follow them closely.[26]

During a given day a salesperson may have to visit his or her company's and customers' offices, each of which may have a different dress code. And sometimes the buyer will have dress codes that even visiting salespeople must follow. For example, Target has dress codes that apply to salespeople who want to make presentations at its company offices.

Vicki West has developed five timeless principles for a salesperson wanting to dress for success.[27] We describe these here.

Principle 1: Consider the Geography

The temperature: Clothing choices are obviously influenced by temperature trends and variations. San Francisco is different from Minneapolis, which differs Austin, Texas, in humidity, temperature, and weather patterns. These factors dictate the fiber and type of clothing worn. Although linen and cotton are cool, warm-weather fabrics suitable almost the entire year in the southern part of the United States, they would be appropriate only in the late spring and summer in other locales.

The local cultural norms: Some cities are formal, and others are known for their casual culture. The economic and business sectors of a community often play a pivotal role in the local cultural norms for clothing choices. An example of a cultural norm difference within the short distance of 200 miles is that between Dallas and Austin, Texas. Dallas is more formal than Austin in most industry sectors. Dallas is known as a "headquarters" town with large regional and national businesses represented. Austin has a large segment of population employed in education, high technology, and the music industry, all of which typically have a younger, more casual workforce.

Principle 2: Consider Your Customers

Their appearance: Customers wear many different types of clothing, which are often dictated by the demands of their profession. Farmers, bankers, high-technology workers, and educators all dress differently depending on the functional demands of their daily work. A salesperson's appearance is certainly impacted by the customers' industry.

Their expectations for your appearance, however, generally reflect their impression of your industry. Salespeople representing the banking industry would be expected to dress differently from salespeople in the music recording industry.

Principle 3: Consider Your Corporate Culture

Norms for your industry should dictate the general parameters for appearance choices. It is obvious that corporate cultures change from time to time. Recently the trend has been to dress more casually in the hot-weather months, even in conservative industries such as banking and finance. However, the consensus of many industry groups is that it is important to wear professional business attire regularly, with some exceptions based on geography and a salesperson's customer base.

Principle 4: Consider Your Aspirations

Top levels of your organization generally set the tone for an entire organization. If you aspire to reach a high level in the organization, it's important to note what expectations your organization might have for your general appearance.

An old rule is to dress *one level above your position.* Watch your immediate superior, who will decide whom to promote. If you want a promotion to the next level in the organization, dress as if you already have the position; then you will be perceived as a good fit for the job.

Principle 5: Consider Your Own Personal Style

Wait until you have the halo effect before making a personal style statement. The "halo effect" refers to the tendency to generalize one positive aspect of your behavior to all aspects of your behavior. This phenomenon can work to your benefit. No one wants to look like a corporate drone with no individual style, but the first week on the job may not be the best time to make your personal appearance statement. Wait until you have proved your professional skills, no matter what the industry, before wearing clothing that may be deemed inappropriate to your particular industry.

Be reasonable in your wardrobe choices. Being individualist and memorable can be a positive decision, depending on the range of choices that are acceptable to a specific industry group. But choosing outrageous or completely unsuitable clothing is probably not in the best interests of your personal career development. And like it or not, large jewelry, piercings, tattoos, heavy perfumes and colognes, short skirts, shorts, revealing blouses or shirts, pink or turquoise hair, and so forth are simply considered inappropriate in most sales situations.

COMMUNICATING VIA TECHNOLOGY

In addition to face-to-face interactions, salespeople communicate with customers by using the telephone, fax, e-mail, and voice mail. As shown in Exhibit 4.6, these methods vary in the interactivity of the communications, the ability to use verbal and nonverbal communication channels, and the quantity of information that can be conveyed. **Response time** is the time between sending a message and getting a response to it.

TELEPHONE AND VOICE MAIL COMMUNICATIONS

Salespeople need to use the phone correctly and effectively. All of us have used telephones since childhood; many of us have developed bad habits that reduce our effectiveness when talking over the phone. Perfect your phone style by practicing alone before making any calls. Make sure you know what you want to say before placing the call. Many would argue that it is a polite gesture to start by asking, "Is this a good time to talk?" Don't be too rushed to be nice; it is never acceptable to be rude. And don't forget to smile as you talk. Even though the prospect won't see it, she or he will hear it in your enthusiastic tone of voice.

Active listening is as important when conversing over the phone as when conversing in person. Take notes and restate the message or any action you have agreed to undertake. In addition, you will need to encourage two-way communication. If you have ever talked with two-year-olds over the phone, you know that if you ask them a yes-or-no question, they tend to shake their heads yes

Exhibit 4.6
Comparison of Various Methods of Salesperson Communications*

	Face-to-Face	Telephone	Voice Mail	Fax	E-Mail
Response time	Fast	Fast	Slow	Slow	Slow
Salesperson can use verbal communications	Yes	Yes	Yes	No	No
Salesperson can hear buyer's verbal communications	Yes	Yes	No	No	No
Salesperson can read buyer's nonverbal communications	Yes	No	No	No	No
Quantity of information seller can send	Highest	Average	Lowest	Varies	Varies
Quantity of information buyer can send	Highest	Average	None	None	None

*Ratings can vary greatly given the situation.

or no rather than verbalize a response. Similarly, you cannot nod your head to encourage someone to continue talking on the phone. Instead you must encourage conversations with verbal cues such as *Uh-huh, I see,* or *That's interesting.* Finally, just as in face-to-face conversation, you must be able to tolerate silences so customers have an opportunity to ask questions, agree or disagree, or relate a point to their circumstances.

It is important to set objectives for your phone call and strategize what you're going to say and why. Here is an example of using the phone to make an appointment:

1. [*State customer's name.*] Hello, Mr. Peterson? (*Pause.*)

2. [*Introduce yourself and show preparation.*] This is Amanda Lowden with Cisco Systems. I was talking to your director of operations, Marvin Schepp, and he suggested I talk with you.

3. [*Politely check time.*] I hope I didn't catch you in the middle of something urgent or pressing? (*Pause.*)

4. [*State purpose and build credibility.*] I'm calling to let you know about our new carrier routing system. I've shown it to several other systems engineers in town, and they found its self-healing and self-defending operating system to be something they wanted to explore further.

5. [*Commitment to action.*] I'd like to meet with you and share some feedback from your business associates. Could you put me on your calendar for 30 minutes next Monday or Tuesday?

6. [*Show appreciation and restate time, or keep door open.*] Thank you, Mr. Peterson. I'll be at your office at 9 a.m. on Tuesday. [*or*] I appreciate your frankness, Mr. Peterson. I'd like to get back to you in a couple of months. Would that be all right?

Use proper techniques and etiquette when leaving voice mail messages:[28]

- If making a cold call to set up an appointment, don't leave a message. Just call back later.
- Leave a clear, concise message that includes a suggested time for a return call (so you can be prepared for that call).
- Speak slowly and distinctly.
- A little casual conversation up front is acceptable, but don't waste the prospect's time.
- Ask for a callback.
- Slowly repeat your name and phone number at the end of your message.

For your own voice mail system, use a fresh greeting on your system each day. Tell callers if a time limit exists for your voice mail, and if possible, offer the option to talk to someone immediately.

E-MAIL COMMUNICATIONS

Technology makes the transfer of information fast and easy.[29] But it also holds the salesperson at arm's length and makes it difficult to develop rapport. High tech doesn't replace face-to-face interactions; it merely supplements and enhances personal exchanges. Following are some suggestions for salespeople with regard to e-mail communication:

Developments in technology enable salespeople to improve their communications with customers.

- Don't be lulled into thinking that immediacy (fast) means the same thing as intimacy (close, friendly relationship) in communication. Buyers generally prefer face-to-face communications over other media types. When asked, 90 percent of buyers said face-to-face communication builds high trust, 81 percent said it reduces confusion and misunderstanding, and 76 percent said it is easier to understand.[30] And sometimes snail mail still works the best.[31]

- For the subject line, use important information to avoid having the e-mail deleted unread (for example, don't use "hello" as your subject line). And make it sound easy to deal with (such as "Two Short Questions").

- Make sure the first few lines of the e-mail are important. Many people read only the first few lines before deleting a message. Use a heading and bullets to help the reader follow a longer e-mail message.

- It is hard for buyers to read your nonverbal messages in e-mail because they can't see them (and you can't read theirs).[32] Studies show that many users do not grasp the tone or intent of e-mail, and using smiley faces or other emoticons just makes it more confusing.

- Learn the customer's preferences for e-mail. Adapt the content to the customer's preferred communication style. For example, some firms have instituted "no e-mail Fridays." And never be viewed by your prospect as a spammer! See "Sales Technology 4.1" for tips on how to avoid having your e-mail messages land in the spam box.

- Avoid "techno overkill." Written communication (such as letters and printed brochures or catalogs) may be better when the customer wants to study the information at his or her leisure.

- Customers are drowning in information. Don't send long e-mail messages or large attachments unless the buyer is expecting them.[33] If you decide to send a PowerPoint presentation via e-mail, use special software that will help ensure that it gets through the virus and spam filters.

- Use speed to impress customers—especially for damage control. Exceed a customer's expectations, such as responding immediately to urgent calls via e-mail. E-mail sent to you by customers should be answered by the end of the workday.

- Don't deliver bad news via e-mail; rather, use e-mail to arrange a meeting to discuss the issue.

- If you want your e-mail read, at least according to one study, send it on Wednesdays around 11:00 a.m. The worst time to send is (not surprisingly) Saturday and Sunday.[34]

SOCIAL NETWORKING

Social networking is the use of "a variety of Web sites that allow users to share content, interact, and develop communities around similar interests."[35] Salespeople are using social networking, like blogs, LinkedIn, Twitter, and Facebook, to communicate with customers and prospects. While many of the suggestions already covered in this chapter apply to these networks, salespeople should consider other issues as well. Some suggestions for networking sites like LinkedIn and Facebook include the following[36]

- Fill out your profile completely to build trust and establish common bonds. Spend the time and money to get a great head shot photo, and include it on your site. Make sure it is appropriate for business purposes. Update your profile regularly to keep it current and interesting. Remember that many

SALES Technology

WHAT? YOU NEVER GOT MY E-MAIL?!

We've all had it happen. Someone sends us an important e-mail message, and we never get it. Then in frustration, we search through our junk mail inbox and sometimes we find it there. What happened? Why did it get junked?

This is an especially important subject for salespeople who send e-mail to clients and prospects, so let's see how filters work. First, be aware that there are many e-mail filters out there, and their rules change daily. So these tips are just some hints to get you thinking about the subject. If you want to make sure your e-mail gets through, you can hire companies to prescreen your e-mail for you.

Filters look for various words and phrases in e-mail and assign points. Get enough points, and your e-mail gets bounced into the junk mail slot. What are some phrases or other flags that will raise your points? Here are a few:

- Phrases like "once in a lifetime opportunity," "why pay more?" "call now," "money back guarantee,"

"unsubscribe" and "click here" in the body of the e-mail.
- Using too many exclamation points.
- Using Microsoft Word® to create HTML text and then inserting that into e-mail.
- Using all caps.
- Using HTML font colors of gray, red, yellow, green, blue, magenta, or "unknown to us."
- Sending just an image with no text.
- Having no subject line or a subject line of "free."
- Using font sizes that are too large.

Many sources on the Web describe how to avoid filters. Just search for "how to avoid spam filters" and follow the advice given, and you should be well on your way to getting your e-mail through.

Sources: mail chimp.com, filterbuster.com, http://www.wordbiz.com/avoidspamfilters.html.

members get updates every time someone changes his or her profile, so you're getting more exposure with every adjustment to your profile.

- Create contacts/friends lists such as "Family" and "Work Related" so you can better control the privacy of your profile and information.
- Follow all rules for the networking sites.
- Share articles and links to presentations and other information that might be helpful to prospects. Posting comments from experts will improve your credibility.
- Remember to post updates on your wall about your business. Tell about upcoming events like webinars and conferences where you will be speaking.
- Combine your Facebook/LinkedIn account with other social media sites you participate in, like Twitter.
- Respond quickly to posts and queries.
- Add your Facebook/LinkedIn URL to your e-mail signature so prospects can learn more about you.

Businesses are starting to build relationships and stay connected to their customers and prospects with micro-blogging tools like Twitter. The 140-or-less character messages are called tweets. Due to the nature of Twitter, some additional considerations apply:[37]

- Build your account and include a picture.
- Use Twitter Search to listen for your name, the name of your product, or your company.

This American salesperson needs to recognize the differences between communicating in an Arab culture and an American culture.

- Use a friendly and casual tone in messages. But make sure your tweets reflect the culture of your company.
- Make a link to things you think prospects would find interesting, like articles and Web sites. Tweets should have real value to the receiver.
- Don't create spam with Twitter.
- Share interesting things about your community and nonbusiness items to help make yourself real. Remember that you are trying to create a friendly relationship.
- Remember to listen, not just send out tweets. Respond to at least some of the replying tweets. Don't feel guilty if you don't read or respond to all tweets.

Because of the growing use of social networking, Chapters 6 and 7 will discuss ways to use these tools to prospect and learn more about new customers.

ADJUSTING FOR CULTURAL DIFFERENCES

Communication in international selling often takes place in English because English is likely to be the only language salespeople and customers have in common. To communicate effectively with customers whose native language is not English, salespeople need to be careful about the words and expressions they use. People who use English in international selling should observe the following rules:

- Use common English words that a customer would learn during the first two years of studying the language. For example, use *expense* rather than *expenditure,* or *stop* instead of *cease.*
- Use words that do not have multiple meanings. For example, *right* has many meanings, whereas *accurate* is more specific. When you use words that have several meanings, recognize that nonnative speakers will usually use the most common meaning to interpret what you are saying.
- Avoid slang expressions peculiar to American culture, such as *slice of life, struck out, wade through the figures,* and *run that by me again.*
- Use rules of grammar more strictly than you would in everyday speech. Make sure you express your thoughts in complete sentences, with a noun and a verb.
- Use action-specific verbs, as in *start the motor,* rather than action-general verbs, as in *get the motor going.*
- Never use vulgar expressions, tell off-color jokes, or make religious references.

Even if you are careful about the words you use, misunderstandings can still arise because terms have different meanings, even among people from different English-speaking countries.[38] For example, in the United States *tabling a proposal* means "delaying a decision," but in England it means "taking immediate action." In England promising to do something by the end of the day means doing it when you have finished what you are working on now, not within 24 hours. In England *bombed* means the negotiations were successful, whereas in the United States this term has the opposite meaning.

International salespeople need to understand the varying perceptions of time in general and the time it takes for business activities to occur in different countries. For example, in Latin American and Arab countries people are not strict about keeping appointments at the designated times. If you show up for an appointment on time in these cultures, you may have to wait several hours for the meeting to start. Lunch is at 3:00 p.m. in Spain, 12:00 noon in Germany, 1:00 p.m. in England, and 11:00 a.m. in Norway. In Greece no one makes telephone calls between 2:00 p.m. and 5:00 p.m. The British arrive at their desks at 9:30 a.m. but like to do paperwork and have a cup of tea before getting any calls. The French, like the Germans, like to start early in the day, frequently having working breakfasts. Restaurants close at 9:00 p.m. in Norway—just when dinner is starting in Spain. The best time to reach high-level Western European executives is after 7:00 p.m., when daily activities have slowed down and they are continuing to work for a few more hours. However, Germans start going home at 4:00 p.m.

Significant cultural differences dictate the appropriate level of eye contact between individuals.[39] In the United States salespeople look directly into their customers' eyes when speaking or listening to them. Direct eye contact is a sign of interest in what the customer is saying. In other cultures looking someone in the eye may be a sign of disrespect:

- In Japan looking directly at a subordinate indicates that the subordinate has done something wrong. When a subordinate looks directly into the eyes of his or her supervisor, the subordinate is displaying hostility.
- In Muslim countries, eye contact is not supposed to occur between men and women.
- In Korea eye contact is considered rude.
- Brazilians look at people directly even more than Americans do. Americans tend to find this direct eye contact, when held over a long period, to be disconcerting.

SELLING YOURSELF

One of the students in your class's group project has told the professor that you are hard to get along with and are just too bossy. In fact, though, your team members are slouchers and just want a C on the project; you want nothing less than an A. Your professor has asked to meet with you to discuss the situation. Good communication is important in life, but it's absolutely critical in this situation.

Make sure you are prepared and know what you want to cover by having a list of issues to address and points to make. Use excellent nonverbals, including good eye contact (so you don't seem dishonest), sit up straight (to show you are confident and sharp), and use your hands and body language to demonstrate enthusiasm for doing a good job and being a good student. Don't forget to smile! Students who feel like they are in the "hot seat" often either look like they're about to explode with anger or look like they just played hooky from school. When you smile, you demonstrate your friendly and open attitude.

It won't hurt to dress appropriately and look sharp. I'm not saying you need to wear a business suit, because you don't. But your professor is human and is affected by whether you're properly groomed and whether you look professional, instead of looking like you couldn't care less about what she or he thinks.

During the meeting, don't be afraid to ask clarifying questions if something is unclear to you or if what the professor said could be interpreted several different ways. For example, "Your peers say you are a very determined guy" can be construed as a positive or a negative statement—find out which your professor thinks it means. At the end of the meeting, summarize what was decided, and follow up with an e-mail message that same day to summarize (again) what was decided as well as thank the professor for taking the time to resolve the issue.

SUMMARY

This chapter discussed the principles of communication and how they can be used to build trust in relationships, improve selling effectiveness, and reduce misunderstandings. The communication process consists of a sender, who encodes information and transmits messages, and a receiver, who decodes the messages. A communication breakdown can occur when the sender does a poor encoding job, when the receiver has difficulty decoding, and when noise and the environment interfere with the transmission of the message.

Effective communication requires a two-way flow of information. At different times in the interaction, both parties will act as sender and receiver. This two-way process enables salespeople to adapt their sales approach to the customer's needs and communication style.

When communicating verbally with customers, salespeople must be careful to use words and expressions their customers will understand. Effective communication is facilitated through the use of word pictures and by appropriate voice characteristics like inflection, articulation, and the proper rate of speech and loudness.

Listening is a valuable communication skill that enables salespeople to adapt to various situations. To listen effectively, salespeople need to actively think about what the customer is saying and how to draw out more information. Some suggestions for actively collecting information from customers are to repeat, restate, clarify, summarize the customer's comments, and demonstrate an interest in what the customer is saying.

About 50 percent of communication is nonverbal. Nonverbal messages sent by customers are conveyed by body language. The five channels of body language communication are body angle, face, arms, hands, and legs. No single channel can be used to determine the feelings or attitudes of customers. Salespeople need to analyze the body language pattern composed of all five channels to determine how a customer feels.

Salespeople can use nonverbal communication to convey information to customers. In addition to knowing how to use the five channels of body language, salespeople need to know the appropriate distances between themselves and their customers for different types of communications and relationships. Salespeople should learn to use their physical appearance and dress to create a favorable impression on customers.

Learning how to communicate effectively with technology is critical in today's marketplace. Not only should salespeople learn how to use the phone and e-mail effectively; they should also master the use of social networking like Facebook and LinkedIn, as well as Twitter and blogs, to connect with their customers and prospects.

Finally, two-way communication increases when salespeople adjust their communication styles to the styles of their customers. In making such adjustments, salespeople need to be sensitive to cultural differences when selling internationally and in diverse subcultures.

KEY TERMS

active listening   104
analogy   103
articulation   102
body language   108
decoding   100
80–20 listening rule   104
encoding   100
feedback   100

inflection   102
intimate zone   113
loudness   102
noises   101
nonverbal communication   108
personal zone   113
public zone   113
response time   116

ETHICS PROBLEMS

1. In an effort to improve relationships and open communications, is it OK to enjoy a few beers on the golf course with your clients?[40]
2. Assume you are making a call on a person of the opposite sex in a culture where direct eye contact between the sexes is not supposed to occur. Much to your amazement, the buyer continues to look intently into your eyes. You are in an office alone with the buyer. What should you do?

QUESTIONS AND PROBLEMS

1. As a student in a college classroom, you may encounter many distractions that affect your listening ability.
   a. List five types of distractions or noise that can affect your ability to listen to your professor.
   b. What can you do to reduce each of these distractions?
2. Have a friend score you using the listening test (Exhibit 4.3) found in this chapter.
   a. Compare your friend's score with the one you gave yourself.
   b. What did this exercise teach you about your listening skills?
3. Make a chart with three columns: *Items, What I Want This Item to Communicate to Others,* and *What Others Will Think My Item Is Communicating.* In the first column list the following: *my hairstyle, the clothing I'm wearing today,* and *any jewelry or body accents* (like earrings or tattoos). In the second column describe the message you want to communicate with each item. Have someone else fill in the third column, describing what the items communicate to him or her.
4. Develop a word picture that helps explain to a 60-year-old the merits of buying a condominium instead of a house.
5. What do the following body language cues indicate?
   a. Tapping a finger or pencil on a desk.
   b. Stroking the chin and leaning forward.
   c. Leaning back in a chair with arms folded across the chest.
   d. Sitting in the middle of a bench or sofa.
   e. Assuming the same posture as the person with whom you are communicating.
6. Word choice is important. Some words, by themselves, may be perceived negatively. Come up with a better word choice that could be more positive for each of the following words: *cost, down payment, deal, objection, cheaper, appointment, commission.*
7. In "From the Buyer's Seat 4.1" you learned about a seller who substituted a cheaper belt dressing for the belt dressing the buyer usually bought. In what ways could the seller have improved communication?
8. Closely examine 10 e-mail messages you receive. Evaluate them on the basis of the suggestions offered in this chapter for the proper use of e-mail.
9. According to the chapter opening profile, although e-mail and text messaging are popular, these may not be the best way to communicate with some older people. Think about four people you know over the age of 50. What is the best way to communicate with each of the four?
10. Assume you sell college textbooks to professors who teach personal selling, and you wish to use Twitter to build relationships with professors who are customers and prospects. Create five tweets that you would post to accomplish this objective.

case **4.1**

Carriger, Esq.

Donald Molloy, a salesperson for Yellow Book USA, has just entered the office of William C. Carriger III, Esq., an attorney with an office in an impressive new building downtown. Mr. Carriger is seated behind a vast mahogany desk in a high-backed executive chair, working on some paperwork. He doesn't look up as Donald enters the room.

Donald: [walking around William's desk and extending his hand] Good morning, William! It's sure nice to finally get a chance to meet you. [laughing] I've been trying to get in here for a month of Sundays! And do you go by William or Will?

William: [not looking up from his paperwork or extending his hand as he finally responds] Please have a seat, Mr. . . . what was your name?

Donald: [dragging up a seat from the side of the room and placing it on the same side of the desk as William, then plopping down in the seat] Donald. Donald Molloy. Boy, it's sure hot out there today. Say, here's a good one I heard yesterday. A man fainted in the middle of a busy intersection, and traffic quickly piled up in all directions, so a woman rushed to help him. When she knelt down to loosen his collar, a man emerged from the crowd, pushed her aside, and said, "It's all right honey, I've had a course in first aid." The woman stood up and watched as he took the ill man's pulse and prepared to administer artificial respiration. At this point she tapped him on the shoulder and said, "When you get to the part about calling a doctor, I'm already here." Ha ha ha!

William: [not laughing, but pushing his paperwork away from him and crossing his arms] What can I do for you, Mr. Molloy?

Donald: Well, Will, I'd like to see you guys take out a bigger ad in the Yellow Pages. Can't beat the yellow pages for business, now can you?

William: [turning in his chair to look out the window, while looking at his watch] We provide professional counsel to businesses and a few nonprofit organizations, Mr. Molloy.

Donald: [taking out a pad of paper from his shirt pocket and searching his pockets for a pen] Now that's news to me, Will. I thought you guys were ambulance chasers, like all the rest. Ha ha ha!

William: [making a steeple with his hands while still looking out the office window] I would guess you would, Mr. Molloy. [swiveling in his chair to face Donald] Yes, I would guess you would. [pressing a button on his desk] Ms. Deramus . . . Mr. Molloy has completed his interview with me. Will you kindly escort him out? [looking at Donald with a smirk on his face] Have a good day, Mr. [strongly emphasizing the word Mr.] Molloy.

Questions

1. Evaluate the exchange.
2. What would you do differently if you were Donald?

case **4.2**

PWM Electronic
Price Signs

Evan Pederson is a sales rep for PWM, the world market leader in electronic price signs for gas stations. PWM offers a wide assortment of types of signs and options. The signs that Evan sells not only indicate the price of fuel sold at a gas station but also can include information about services the station offers (such as specials on food items or showers that are available). The company has been very successful over the last 20 years, with over 23,000 signs sold worldwide.

Evan, who grew up in Santa Clarita and who has been selling for PWM in California for the past three years, was just transferred to the PWM office in Mexico City.

Evan has never lived or worked in Mexico before and is thinking about what changes he might need to make as he works with gas station owners in that country.

Questions

1. Investigate the culture of Mexico in more detail by viewing Web pages and reading articles about how business salespeople can best sell there. Briefly summarize four key findings.

2. What changes should Evan consider making (compared to how he probably sold to clients in California) as he calls on prospects in Mexico? Make any assumptions necessary.

Source: www.pwm.com/pwm/pwm_lang_select.htm.

ROLE PLAY CASE

In this chapter's role play interaction, you are still meeting with the same person you did for Chapter 3. (If you did not do the role play at the end of Chapter 3, you will need to review that information now.) That person is telling you about the business. Feel free to ask questions, but your main objective is to listen and understand all you can about the business environment in which he or she operates. Practice active listening skills; after the role play, identify which listening techniques you used. Further, identify the three most important elements about the person's business that you need to understand. Interpret the buyer's body language. Finally, any time you hear jargon, write the word or phrase down.

Note: For background information about these role plays, please see page 27.

To the instructor: Additional information needed to complete the role play is available in the Instructor's Manual.

ADDITIONAL REFERENCES

Alexander, Shari. "Networking and Selling Using Body Language Secrets." *Sales & Marketing Management*, 2009, http://www.trainingmag.com/msg/content_display/sales/e3idf30b42a15c2d86a932d522a957c9d0a, accessed March 5, 2010.

Berthon, Pierre, Leyland Pitt, Jean-Paul Berthon, Colin Campbell, and Des Thwaites. "e-Relationships for e-Readiness: Culture and Corruption in International e-B2B." *Industrial Marketing Management* 37, no. 1 (January 2008), pp. 83–91.

Bowden, Mark. *Winning Body Language: Control the Conversation, Command Attention, and Convey the Right Message without Saying a Word.* New York: McGraw-Hill, 2010.

Farber, Barry. "Listen and Learn." *Entrepreneur* 35 (February 2007), p. 76.

Feigon, Josiane Chriqui, and Jill Konrath. *Smart Selling on the Phone and Online: Inside Sales That Gets Results.* AMACOM, 2009.

Gallo, Carmine. "It's Not Your Mouth That Speaks Volumes." *BusinessWeek*, February 8, 2007, p. 22.

Groves, Eric. *The Constant Contact Guide to e-Mail Marketing.* Wiley, 2009.

Hamilton, Cheryl. *Communicating for Results: A Guide for Business and the Professions.* Belmont, CA: Wadsworth, 2008.

Hartley, Gregory, and Maryann Karinch. *I Can Read You Like a Book: How to Spot the Messages and Emotions People Are Really Sending with Their Body Language.* Career Press, 2007.

Hartley, Gregory, and Maryann Karinch. *The Body Language Handbook: How to Read Everyone's Hidden Thoughts and Intentions.* Career Press, 2010.

Hollenbeck, Candice R., George M. Zinkhan, Warren French, and Ji Hee Song. "Collaborative Networks: A Case Study on the New Role of the Sales Force." *Journal of Personal Selling & Sales Management* 29, no. 2 (Spring 2009), pp. 125–36.

Marker, Scott. *Let's Get It On! Realistic Strategies for Winning the Sales Game.* MSA Publishing, 2009.

Orem, Tina. "The Silent Close." *Advisor Today* 103, no. 1 (January 2008), pp. 54–55.

Pinkard, Diane Marie. *Just Treat Me Like I Matter: The Heart of Sales.* Bonny Doon Publishing, 2008.

Raghavan, Anita. "Watch Your Body Language." *Forbes*, March 2009, p. 92.

"Take the Time to Listen." *U.S. News & World Report*, December 31, 2007, p. 61.

"What Your Eyes Say about You." *Career World* 36, no. 4 (January 2008), p. 5.

Wolvin, Andrew D. *Listening and Human Communication in the 21st Century.* Wiley-Blackwell, 2010.

Wright, Emily. "Body Language Matters." *Travel Trade Gazette UK & Ireland*, November 30, 2007, pp. 38–39.

Yeung, Rob. "Talking and Walking." *Accountancy* 140, no. 1371 (November 2007), p. 54.

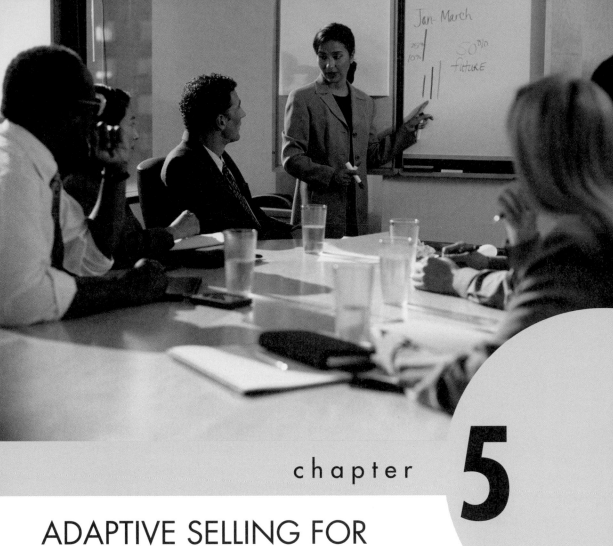

chapter **5**

ADAPTIVE SELLING FOR RELATIONSHIP BUILDING

SOME QUESTIONS ANSWERED IN THIS CHAPTER ARE

- What is adaptive selling?
- Why is it important for salespeople to practice adaptive selling?
- What kind of knowledge do salespeople need to practice adaptive selling?
- How can salespeople acquire this knowledge?
- How can salespeople adapt their sales strategies, presentations, and social styles to various situations?

PROFILE

I am Meggie Dominguez, a May 2008 graduate from Texas State University–San Marcos. I earned my BBA in management from the McCoy College of Business. I served as president of Students in Free Enterprise (SIFE) and was a Texas State representative at the National Collegiate Sales Competition, both of which were under Vicki West. Mrs. West introduced me to ADP, which is where I was hired as a district manager.

At ADP, we consider ourselves business consultants. We don't have a prescript sales pitch that is used on every call. The goal is to educate the owner on varying topics surrounding payroll to show them how a service like ADP can make them more efficient and compliant with state and federal employer laws.

Because I meet with business owners who have anywhere from 1 employee to 49 employees in every industry thinkable, the needs of the businesses are never the same. I have to customize my presentation depending on many factors. For example, a first-time restaurant owner who has 35 tipped employees will need me to explain everything we do in depth from payroll taxes and new hire reporting to FICA tip reporting. Most new business owners are not aware of all their tax liabilities and ways they can get money back from the government for having tipped employees. The owners are very appreciative that I take the time to explain all these fiduciary responsibilities and the fines they could be liable for.

On the other hand, when I meet with a longtime owner of a nonprofit company with three employees, this presentation is completely different. In this situation the owner wouldn't be interested in hearing about the "payroll 101" I was telling the new business owner. Instead he or she would want to know about payroll being directly tied to grant funding, ability to offer comprehensive benefits, and wage tracking for grant reporting. Either way, I am selling the same service but simply customizing the presentation to the buyers' needs.

When meeting with so many business owners, it is vital for me to figure out what type of social style each prospective client is. If I am meeting with someone who isn't the same style as me, I have to recognize that and change my behavior to mirror the business owner. This will set the tone for the rest of the meeting, so in order for it to be a comfortable and productive conversation, I have to be aware of what type of person I am selling to.

Being able to adapt to my prospective clients and their needs is very important! One skill that makes this easier is being knowledgeable about common concerns within certain types of businesses and confidently knowing ADP's services that will eliminate those problems. When I show the owners how seamlessly ADP can address their concerns, they trust me, which ultimately leads to them becoming a new client. With knowledge comes confidence, and confidence brings sales!

**Visit our Web site at
www.adp.com.**

Personal selling is the most effective marketing communication medium because it allows salespeople to tailor their presentations to each customer. They use their knowledge of the customer's buying process (Chapter 3) and finely tuned communication skills (Chapter 4) to learn about their customers and select effective sales strategies. Effective salespeople adapt their selling strategies and approaches to the selling situation. This chapter examines how salespeople can communicate effectively with their customers by practicing adaptive selling.

TYPES OF PRESENTATIONS

Salespeople can choose from a number of presentation types. This text examines the three most common: (1) the standard memorized presentation, (2) the outlined presentation, and (3) the customized presentation.

STANDARD MEMORIZED PRESENTATION

The **standard memorized presentation,** also called a *canned presentation,* is a completely memorized sales talk. The salesperson presents the same selling points in the same order to all customers. Some companies insist that their inside telemarketing salespeople, for example, memorize the entire presentation and deliver it word for word. Others believe that salespeople should be free to make some minor adjustments.

The standard memorized presentation ensures that the salesperson will provide complete and accurate information about the firm's products and policies. Because it includes the best techniques and methods, the standard memorized presentation can help bring new salespeople up to speed quickly and give them confidence. However, the effectiveness of the standard memorized presentation is limited because it offers no opportunity for the salesperson to tailor the presentation to the needs of the specific customer.

OUTLINED PRESENTATION

The **outlined presentation** is a prearranged presentation that usually includes a standard introduction, standard answers to common objections raised by customers, and a standard method for getting the customer to place an order. An example of an outlined presentation appears in Exhibit 5.1.

An outlined presentation can be very effective because it is well organized. It is more informal and natural than the standard memorized presentation and provides more opportunity for the customer to participate in the sales interaction. It also permits some flexibility in the approach used to present the key points.

CUSTOMIZED PRESENTATION

The **customized presentation** is a written and/or oral presentation based on a detailed analysis of the customer's needs. This type of presentation offers an opportunity to use the communication principles discussed in Chapter 4 to discover the customer's needs and problems and propose the most effective solution for satisfying those needs.[1] The customer recognizes the sales representative as a professional who is helping solve problems, not just selling products. The customized presentation lets the salesperson demonstrate empathy. Cultivating this view is an important step in developing a partnering relationship.

Each of the presentation types just discussed involves a different level of skill, cost, and flexibility. Standard memorized presentations can be delivered at a low cost by unskilled salespeople with little training. On the other hand, the customized presentation can be costly, requiring highly skilled people to analyze the customer's needs. Salespeople have the greatest opportunity to adapt their

Exhibit 5.1

Example of an Outlined
Presentation

Scenario: A Procter & Gamble Salesperson Calling on a Grocery Store Manager	
Step in Outlined Sales Presentation	**Say Something Like This**
1. Reinforce past success.	Good morning, Mr. Babcock. I was talking with one of your stockers, and he said that our Crest end-of-aisle display was very popular with customers last weekend. He said that he had to restock it three times. Looks like you made a wise decision to go with that program.
2. Reiterate customer's needs.	I know that profits and fast turns are what you are always looking for.
3. Introduce new Sure antiperspirant campaign.	We have a new campaign coming up for our Sure line.
4. Explain ad campaign and coupon drops.	We will be running a new set of commercials on all three network news programs. . . . Also, we'll be adding an insert in the Sunday coupon section with a 35-cents-off coupon.
5. Explain case allowances.	We are going to give you a $1.20 case allowance for every case of Sure you buy today.
6. Ask for end-of-aisle display and order of cases.	I propose that you erect an end-of-aisle display on aisle 7 . . . and that you order 20 cases.
7. Thank manager for order.	Thank you, and I know the results will be just as good as they were for our Crest promotion.

presentations to customer needs when using the customized presentation and the least opportunity when using the standard memorized presentation. The next section discusses the importance of adapting sales presentations.

ADAPTIVE SELLING AND SALES SUCCESS

Salespeople practice **adaptive selling** when they react to different sales situations by changing their sales behaviors. An extreme example of nonadaptive selling is using the standard memorized presentation, in which the same presentation is used for all customers. The customized presentation illustrates adaptive selling because the presentation is tailored to the specific needs of the customer.

Adaptive selling is featured in this textbook because this approach forces the salesperson to practice the marketing concept. It emphasizes the importance of satisfying customer needs. And being adaptable increases buyer trust and commitment and results in higher sales performance. It's important for salespeople to take the initiate and be adaptive.[2] The communication principles described in Chapter 4 are required to practice adaptive selling successfully. For example, a Kohler sales representative may believe that a portable generator manufacturer is interested in buying an economical, low-horsepower gasoline motor. While presenting the benefits of a low-cost motor, the sales rep discovers, by observing nonverbal behaviors, that the customer is interested in discussing overall operating costs. At this point the rep asks some questions to find out whether the customer would pay a higher price for a more efficient motor with lower operating costs. Based on the customer's response, the rep may adopt a new sales strategy: presenting a more efficient motor and demonstrating its low operating costs. Studies show that salespeople who are able to appraise the emotions of the buyer while practicing adaptive selling have higher performance.[3]

It is sometimes hard for people to realize that the world is not made up of people just like them. Many people are much older than you, while some are younger than you. They practice different religions, enjoy different foods, and shop at stores where you would never think of shopping. They have different moral beliefs and different ideas about "the perfect product" and were raised in a totally different way. Their hopes and aspirations don't match yours. Many of them would be shocked to hear what your life's dreams and goals are.

We are not just talking about differences in people in other countries. We are talking about people who live next door to you, who are sitting next to you in your classroom. Men and women often react differently to presentations. Generation Xers are different from baby boomers, who differ from the generations before them. One salesperson reported that grocery stores that cater to migrant farmers in the San Francisco area want a different product mix (such as more demand for Hormel SPAM) than a grocery store in midtown San Francisco (more demand for upscale, specialty Hormel meat products like Cure81 ham). The sooner you realize that your world is made up of diverse people, the sooner you will realize the importance of becoming adaptive. Selecting the appropriate sales strategy for a sales situation and making adjustments during the interaction are crucial to successful selling.

Salespeople should also adapt to the customer's desire for a specific type of relationship. For example, if a customer is not interested in developing a strong, long-term relationship and is more interested in maintaining a less involved relationship, the salesperson should adapt to this desire.

Practicing adaptive selling does not mean salespeople should be dishonest about their products or their personal feelings. It does mean salespeople should alter the content and form of their sales presentation so customers will be able to absorb the information easily and find it relevant to their situation. As "Building Partnerships 5.1" illustrates, sometimes a salesperson has to adapt to a difficult situation.

thinking **it** through   Do you act and talk differently to your professor than when you talk to your friends? Why do you adapt in that way?

This salesperson has acquired extensive knowledge of the customer's systems.

The advantages and disadvantages of the three types of sales presentations illustrate the benefits and drawbacks of adaptive selling. Adaptive selling gives salespeople the opportunity to use the most effective sales presentation for each customer. However, uncovering needs, designing and delivering different presentations, and making adjustments require a high level of skill. The objective of this textbook is to help you develop the skills and knowledge required to practice adaptive selling.

KNOWLEDGE MANAGEMENT

A key ingredient in effective selling is knowledge.[4] Salespeople need to know about the products they are selling, the company they work for, and the customers they will be selling to. Knowledge enables the salesperson to build self-confidence, gain the buyer's trust, satisfy customer needs, and practice adaptive selling.[5]

BUILDING Partnerships

I'M SORRY, DOCTOR, BUT I THINK YOU'RE ABOUT TO MAKE A MISTAKE

One aspect of my selling job requires me to service what I sell, and in the case of replacement joints that means going into the operating room with the surgeon and taking the role of a technical expert when it comes to the capabilities, function, and surgical technique used with my company's hardware. This scenario occurred during a total hip replacement on an 80-year-old woman. The doctor involved was a new customer, so I had brought in a wide variety of options for him to use, as I wasn't very familiar with his preferences and I wanted to be prepared for anything.

The case was going smoothly until the surgeon was deciding which component to use in the femur. There are two different types when it comes to the method of fixation of the new joint: cemented stems and press-fit stems. The stem is inserted into the intermedullary, or IM, canal, and if it is a round stem it is secured to the bone using bone cement. If it is a press-fit stem it is squared off, and you are essentially sticking a square peg into a round hole. The press-fit stem is pounded in such a manner that the four corners dig into the surrounding bone, and that provides fixation. It also leaves some open gaps in the IM canal.

The doctor decided to use a press-fit stem but decided that the bone quality wasn't what he wanted, and he didn't feel like it was secure. He told me he wanted to cement the press-fit stem in place. I knew that this was not typically done, and my training told me that it shouldn't be done in order to avoid having bone cement leak down into the IM canal, which could potentially cause a number of problems down the road. At the same time if it was done very carefully it could work without any issues. What should I do?

In this case I felt I had ethical obligations to the surgeon and the patient. I stepped out of the OR and called one of our engineers to ask him what his opinion was, and he told me that I should strongly recommend against it. I would have liked to call our regional manager, but when you have an open patient on the operating table, time is very limited. I returned to the OR and told the doctor that as a representative of our company I had to recommend against cementing that particular stem. I said this in the OR with several support staff around, providing witnesses to my recommendations. I also stated that he was the doctor and that the final decision obviously rested with him. I did not know how the doctor would respond.

The surgeon listened to my concerns and then decided to go ahead with his original decision, but did confirm that I had recommended against it. After the case was over we talked in the doctor's lounge, and he said that he was glad I had voiced my opinion but he felt it was the proper decision. I explained my position once again. He said he understood, and the business relationship did not suffer.

Source: Brendan Brooks, Smith & Nephew; used with permission.

PRODUCT AND COMPANY KNOWLEDGE

Salespeople need to have a lot of information about their products, services, and company. Purchasing agents rate product knowledge as one of the most important attributes of good salespeople. Effective salespeople need to know how products are made, what services are provided with the products, how the products relate to other products, and how the products can satisfy customers' needs. Salespeople also need to know about their competitors' products as well as their own because they are frequently asked to compare their products to competitors' offerings.

KNOWLEDGE ABOUT SALES SITUATIONS AND CUSTOMERS

Equally important with product and company knowledge is detailed information about the different types of sales situations and customers salespeople may encounter.[6] For example, Nextel salespeople need to be knowledgeable about networking and information technology and have overall expertise in how businesses operate in order to sell cell phone service to their unique customer types.

Successful sales managers give their salespeople diagnostic feedback.

By developing categories of customer types or types of sales situations, salespeople reduce the complexity of selling and free up their mental capacity to think more creatively.[7] The categories salespeople use can focus on the benefits the customer seeks, the person's role in the buying center, the stage in the buying process, or the type of buying situation. For example, a Colgate salesperson might divide buyers into several categories based on their decision-making style. When selling to emotional buyers, this salesperson might need to be more enthusiastic and engage in visual storytelling. When selling to rational buyers, this salesperson might want to stress the financial benefits of purchasing the new toothpaste.

HOW TO CREATE KNOWLEDGE

One source of knowledge would be top salespeople in the company you work for. Some firms will collect and share this information with you. For example, a telecommunications company conducted in-depth interviews with its top performers. Through these interviews, it learned about the types of situations these salespeople encountered and what strategies they used in each situation. The company developed role plays for each sales situation and used them when training new salespeople. Such role-playing enabled the new salespeople to experience the variety of situations they would actually encounter on the job. The strategies recommended by the top salespeople served as a starting point for the trainees to develop their own sales methods for handling these situations.

Salespeople also create knowledge by getting feedback from sales managers. This can be in the form of **performance feedback** ("Did you achieve the goals you set for this call?") or **diagnostic feedback** ("Let's talk about why you didn't achieve your goals"). Diagnostic feedback provides information about what you're doing right and wrong, instead of just whether you made a sale.

The following example illustrates diagnostic feedback:

SALESPERSON: Why do you think I didn't make the sale?

SALES MANAGER: You stressed the low maintenance cost, but he wasn't interested in maintenance cost. Did you see how he kept looking around while you were talking about how cheap it is to maintain the product?

SALESPERSON: What do you think I should do next time?

SALES MANAGER: You might try spending more time finding his hot button. Maintenance cost isn't it.

Other sources of knowledge include the Web, company sales manuals and newsletters, experts in the salesperson's firm, sales meetings, plant visits, and business and trade publications. Salespeople also collect information about competitors from customers, by visiting competitor displays at trade shows, and from viewing competitors' Web pages.

RETRIEVING KNOWLEDGE FROM THE KNOWLEDGE MANAGEMENT SYSTEM

Salespeople store much of their acquired knowledge in their memory, and as such, retrieval is merely accessing information in that memory. Many companies, like Isuzu Commercial Trucks, described in "Sales Technology 5.1," also have customer relationship management (CRM) systems to support their salespeople.[8] Salespeople use programs like NetSuite to store and retrieve critical knowledge

KEEPING TRACK OF THINGS—HOW ISUZU COMMERCIAL TRUCK OF AMERICA DOES IT

In this textbook we've been providing information and end-of-chapter role plays around a product called NetSuite (see the role play case at the end of Chapter 1 for more details about NetSuite). NetSuite allows salespeople to keep track of their prospects and customers and provides a number of reports and information that help salespeople and sales managers be more effective and efficient.

Isuzu Commercial Truck of America, a manufacturer of medium- and heavy-duty trucks located in Cerritos, California, found NetSuite to be just what they needed. Their old CRM system just didn't have the power the sales reps needed and was, not surprisingly, used little by the sales force. That, combined with a downturn in industrywide sales, put pressure on Isuzu to do something. The solution? NetSuite CRM.

What about salesperson reluctance to accept the new system? Often salespeople are reluctant to adopt CRM systems because they see such a system as something that helps management but doesn't help them day-to-day. "We had some old-time people who would maintain accounts on the back of an envelope, but with NetSuite's ease of use and a little internal competition, we were able to load hundreds of our most important customer contacts in the first month," says Todd Bloom, VP of marketing and fleet operations at Isuzu Commercial Truck of America.

Implementing NetSuite has helped Isuzu sales reps by reducing their time spent filling out reports and performing other administrative tasks. The result is more time to interact with key customers. "Our goal is to keep our field reps in front of the customers for the greatest amount of time," Bloom says. "Implementing NetSuite CRM will help us reduce the time we spend in meetings and doing paperwork and reports." And because the entry data and reports are standardized, reps can be evaluated on a more equitable plane.

NetSuite has also given both U.S. and Japanese management important information and insight into what salespeople are doing. And using such a cutting-edge tool has positioned the company well for further growth in its approximately 70 percent market share of the medium- to heavy-duty truck category.

Source: netsuite.com (including the customer success stories linked from that site at http://www.netsuite.com/portal/customers/main.shtml).

about accounts, products, and competitors. For example, salespeople for the Houston Aeros hockey franchise use NetSuite to store and access information about its customers. They use this knowledge when interacting with customers to develop sales strategies and purchase recommendations. Studies have shown that using a CRM system has a positive impact on being adaptive while selling.[9]

It is important for salespeople to be able to retrieve brochures and other business collateral from the knowledge management system. But perhaps more important is the ability to tap the knowledge of in-house experts. One writer calls this "genius management," which implies going beyond document management to the realm of tapping knowledge from genius within your firm.[10] Social computing tools are important in this regard.[11] Progressive firms are encouraging in-house experts, like engineers, product development specialists, and financial staff, to develop in-house blogs, wikis, and Web pages that are easily accessible and searchable by the sales force. Social networking sites like LinkedIn and Facebook can also be used to connect in-house experts with salespeople. Finally, firms are experimenting with tagging, which is including keywords with a person's name in company documents and on internal Web pages. The keywords indicate the areas of expertise for which that person can be contacted. The goal in all of this is to make it easier for salespeople to connect to experts in their own firms for ideas and assistance.

THE SOCIAL STYLE MATRIX: A TRAINING PROGRAM FOR BUILDING ADAPTIVE SELLING SKILLS

To be effective, salespeople need to use their knowledge about products and customers to adapt both the content of their sales presentations—the benefits they emphasize to customers and the needs they attempt to satisfy—and the style they use to communicate with customers. The **social style matrix** is a popular training program that companies use to help salespeople adapt their communication styles.

David Merrill and Roger Reid discovered patterns of communication behaviors, or social styles, that people use when interacting with one another.[12] Merrill and Reid found that people who recognize and adjust to these behavior patterns have better relationships with other people. The company Wilson Learning conducts training using these concepts.[13]

Here is a quick preview of what you will learn about the social style training program. As you know, the world is made up of diverse people. For example, some are fast decision makers, whereas others are slow to make just about any kind of decision; some like to talk, whereas others are quiet. To make it easier, this system divides all people into four different types or categories that are based on two dimensions. Your goal as a salesperson is to first identify which of the four types you are. Next you figure out which of the four types your customer is. Finally you adjust your behavior to mirror or match that of your customer. Now that you have a general idea of how the system works, let's look at it in more detail.

DIMENSIONS OF SOCIAL STYLES

This training program uses two critical dimensions to understand social behavior: assertiveness and responsiveness.

Assertiveness

The degree to which people have opinions about issues and publicly make their positions clear to others is called **assertiveness.** Simply having strong convictions does not make a person assertive; assertive people express their convictions publicly and attempt to influence others to accept these beliefs.

Assertive people speak out, make strong statements, and have a take-charge attitude. When under tension, they tend to confront the situation. Unassertive people rarely dominate a social situation, and they often keep their opinions to themselves. Exhibit 5.2 shows some verbal and nonverbal behavioral indicators of assertiveness.

Responsiveness

The second dimension, **responsiveness,** is based on how emotional people tend to get in social situations. Responsive people readily express joy, anger, and sorrow. They appear to be more concerned with others and are informal and casual in social situations. Less responsive people devote more effort toward controlling their emotions. They are described as cautious, intellectual, serious, formal, and businesslike. Exhibit 5.3 lists some indicators of responsiveness.

CATEGORIES OF SOCIAL STYLES

The two dimensions of social style, assertiveness and responsiveness, form the social style matrix shown in Exhibit 5.4. Each quadrant of the matrix defines a social style type.

Exhibit 5.2
Indicators of
Assertiveness

Less Assertive	More Assertive
"Ask" oriented	"Tell" oriented
Go-along attitude	Take-charge attitude
Cooperative	Competitive
Supportive	Directive
Risk avoider	Risk taker
Makes decisions slowly	Makes decisions quickly
Lets others take initiative	Takes initiative
Leans backward	Leans forward
Indirect eye contact	Direct eye contact
Speaks slowly, softly	Speaks quickly, intensely
Moves deliberately	Moves rapidly
Makes few statements	Makes many statements
Expresses moderate opinions	Expresses strong opinions

Exhibit 5.3
Indicators of
Responsiveness

Less Responsive	More Responsive
Controls emotions	Shows emotions
Cool, aloof	Warm, approachable
Talk oriented	People oriented
Uses facts	Uses opinions
Serious	Playful
Impersonal, businesslike	Personable, friendly
Moves stiffly	Moves freely
Seldom gestures	Gestures frequently
Formal dress	Informal dress
Disciplined about time	Undisciplined about time
Controlled facial expressions	Animated facial expressions
Monotone voice	Many vocal inflections

Drivers

Drivers are high on assertiveness and low on responsiveness. The slogan of drivers, who are task-oriented people, might be "Let's get it done now, and get it done my way." Drivers have learned to work with others only because they must do so to get the job done, not because they enjoy people. They have a great desire to get ahead in their companies and careers.

Drivers are swift, efficient decision makers. They focus on the present and appear to have little concern with the past or future. They generally base their decisions on facts, take risks, and want to look at several alternatives before making a decision. As compared to analyticals, who also like facts and data, drivers want to know how the facts affect results—the bottom line. They are not interested in simply technical information.

To influence a driver, salespeople need to use a direct, businesslike, organized presentation with quick action and follow-up. Proposals should emphasize the effects of a purchase decision on profits.

Exhibit 5.4
Social Style Matrix

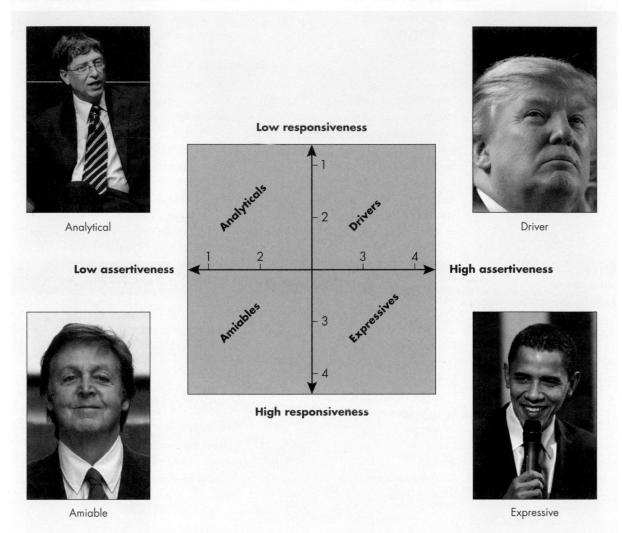

Analytical

Driver

Low responsiveness

Analyticals

Drivers

Low assertiveness   **High assertiveness**

Amiables

Expressives

High responsiveness

Amiable

Expressive

Some example of social styles (Donald Trump, Barack Obama, Paul McCartney, Bill Gates). Do you agree with where they are placed? Note that all these people may switch to a different style under certain conditions.

Expressives

Expressives are high on assertiveness and high on responsiveness. Warm, approachable, intuitive, and competitive, expressives view power and politics as important factors in their quest for personal rewards and recognition. Although expressives are interested in personal relationships, their relationships are primarily with supporters and followers recruited to assist expressives in achieving their personal goals.

People with an expressive style focus on the future, directing their time and effort toward achieving their vision. They have little concern for practical details in present situations. Expressives base their decisions on their personal opinions and the opinions of others. They act quickly, take risks, but tend to be impatient and change their minds easily.

When selling to expressives, salespeople need to demonstrate how their products will help the customer achieve personal status and recognition. Expressives prefer sales presentations with product demonstrations and creative graphics, rather than factual statements and technical details. Also, testimonials from well-known firms and people appeal to expressives' need for status and recognition. Expressives respond to sales presentations that put them in the role of innovator, the first person to use a new product.

Amiables

Amiables are low on assertiveness and high on responsiveness. Close relationships and cooperation are important to amiables. They achieve their objectives by working with people, developing an atmosphere of mutual respect rather than using power and authority. Amiables tend to make decisions slowly, building a consensus among people involved in the decision. They avoid risks and change their opinions reluctantly.

Salespeople may have difficulty detecting an amiable's true feelings. Because amiables avoid conflict, they often say things to please others despite their personal opinions. Therefore, salespeople need to build personal relationships with amiables. Amiables are particularly interested in receiving guarantees about a product's performance. They do not like salespeople who agree to undertake activities and then do not follow through on commitments. Salespeople selling to amiables should stress the product's benefits in terms of its effects on the satisfaction of employees.

Analyticals

Analyticals are low on assertiveness and low on responsiveness. They like facts, principles, and logic. Suspicious of power and personal relationships, they strive to find a way to carry out a task without resorting to these influence methods.

Because they are strongly motivated to make the right decision, analyticals make decisions slowly, in a deliberate and disciplined manner. They systematically analyze the facts, using the past as an indication of future events.

Salespeople need to use solid, tangible evidence when making presentations to analyticals. Analyticals are also influenced by sales presentations that recognize their technical expertise and emphasize long-term benefits. They tend to disregard personal opinions. Both analyticals and amiables tend to develop loyalty toward suppliers. For amiables, the loyalty is based on personal relationships; analyticals' loyalty is based on their feeling that well-reasoned decisions do not need to be reexamined.

IDENTIFYING CUSTOMERS' SOCIAL STYLES

Exhibit 5.5 lists some cues for identifying the social styles of customers or prospects.[14] Salespeople can use their communication skills to observe the customer's behavior, listen to the customer, and ask questions to classify the customer. Merrill and Reid caution that identifying social style is difficult and requires close, careful observation. Salespeople should not jump to quick conclusions based on limited information. Here are some suggestions for making accurate assessments:

- Concentrate on the customer's behavior and disregard how you feel about the behavior. Don't let your feelings about the customer or thoughts about the customer's motives cloud your judgment.

- Avoid assuming that specific jobs or functions are associated with a social style ("He must be an analytical because he is an engineer").

- Test your assessments. Look for clues and information that may suggest you have incorrectly assessed a customer's social style. If you look for only confirming cues, you will filter out important information.

Exhibit 5.5
Cues for Recognizing
Social Styles

Analytical	Driver
Technical background. Achievement awards on wall. Office is work oriented, showing much activity. Conservative dress. Likes solitary activities (e.g., reading, individual sports).	Technical background. Achievement awards on wall. No posters or slogans on office walls. Calendar prominently displayed. Furniture is placed so that contact with people is across desk. Conservative dress. Likes group activities (e.g., politics, team sports).
Amiable	**Expressive**
Liberal arts background. Office has friendly, open atmosphere. Pictures of family displayed. Personal momentos on wall. Desk placed for open contact with people. Casual or flamboyant dress. Likes solitary activities (e.g., reading, individual sports).	Liberal arts background. Motivational slogans on wall. Office has friendly, open atmosphere. Cluttered, unorganized desk. Desk placed for open contact with people. Casual or flamboyant dress. Likes group activities (e.g., politics, team sports).

SOCIAL STYLES AND SALES PRESENTATIONS

In addition to teaching trainees how to assess social style, the Merrill and Reid program also assesses the trainees' social styles. Each person is asked to have a group of his or her customers complete a questionnaire and mail it to the director of the training program. These responses are used to determine the trainee's style. Trainees frequently are surprised by the difference between their self-perceptions and the perceptions of their customers. To get a rough idea of your own social style, you can complete the assessment in Exhibit 5.6.

Interpreting self-ratings requires great caution. Self-assessments can be misleading because we usually do not see ourselves the same way others see us. When you rate yourself, you know your own feelings, but others can observe only your behaviors. They don't know your thoughts or your intentions. We also vary our behavior from situation to situation. The indicators listed in Exhibits 5.2 and 5.3 merely show a tendency to be assertive or responsive.

Is there one best social style for a salesperson? No. None is "best" for all situations; each style has its strong points and weak points. Driver salespeople are efficient, determined, and decisive, but customers may find them pushy and dominating. Expressives have enthusiasm, dramatic flair, and creativity but can also seem opinionated, undisciplined, and unstable. Analyticals are orderly, serious, and thorough, but customers may view them as cold, calculating, and stuffy. Finally, amiables are dependable, supportive, and personable but may also be perceived as undisciplined and inflexible.

The sales training program based on the social style matrix emphasizes that effective selling involves more than communicating a product's benefits. Salespeople must also recognize the customer's needs and expectations. In the sales

Exhibit 5.6
Self-Assessment of Social Styles

Assertiveness Ratings I perceive myself as:				Responsiveness Ratings I perceive myself as:			
Quiet . . . . Talkative				Open . . . . Closed			
1	2	3	4	4	3	2	1
Slow to decide . . . . Fast to decide				Impulsive . . . . Deliberate			
1	2	3	4	4	3	2	1
Going along . . . . Taking charge				Using opinions . . . . Using facts			
1	2	3	4	4	3	2	1
Supportive . . . . .Challenging				Informal . . . . Formal			
1	2	3	4	4	3	2	1
Compliant. . . . . Dominant				Emotional . . . . Unemotional			
1	2	3	4	4	3	2	1
Deliberate . . . . Fast to decide				Easy to know . . . . Hard to know			
1	2	3	4	4	3	2	1
Asking questions . . . . . . Making statements				Warm . . . . .Cool			
1	2	3	4	4	3	2	1
Cooperative . . . . .Competitive				Excitable . . . . .Calm			
1	2	3	4	4	3	2	1
Avoiding risks . . . . Taking risks				Animated . . . . Poker-faced			
1	2	3	4	4	3	2	1
Slow, studied. . . . . .Fast-paced				People-oriented . . . . Task-oriented			
1	2	3	4	4	3	2	1
Cautious . . . . Carefree				Spontaneous. . . . . Cautious			
1	2	3	4	4	3	2	1
Indulgent. Firm				Responsive . . . . Nonresponsive			
1	2	3	4	4	3	2	1
Nonassertive. . . . . Assertive				Humorous. . . . . Serious			
1	2	3	4	4	3	2	1
Mellow. . . . . Matter-of-fact				Impulsive . . . . Methodical			
1	2	3	4	4	3	2	1
Reserved. . . . . Outgoing				Lighthearted . . . . Intense			
1	2	3	4	4	3	2	1

Mark your answers above. Total the score for each side and divide each by 15. Then plot your scores on Exhibit 5.4 to see what social style you are. For fun, you may want to have several friends also score you.

Source: Based on work by David Merrill and Roger Reid, *Personal Styles and Effective Performance* (Radnor, PA: Chilton, 1981).

interaction, salespeople should conduct themselves in a manner consistent with customer expectations. Exhibit 5.7 indicates the expectations of customers with various social styles.

Although each customer type requires a different sales presentation, the salesperson's personal social style tends to determine the sales technique he or she typically uses. For example, drivers tend to use a driver technique with all customer types. When interacting with an amiable customer, driver salespeople will be efficient and businesslike, even though the amiable customer would prefer to deal with a more relationship-oriented and friendlier salesperson.

This sales training program emphasizes that to be effective with a variety of customer types, salespeople must adapt their selling presentations to customers'

Exhibit 5.7
Customer Expectations Based on Social Styles

	Customer's Social Style			
Area of Expectation	**Driver**	**Expressive**	**Amiable**	**Analytical**
Atmosphere in sales interview	Businesslike	Open, friendly	Open, honest	Businesslike
Salesperson's use of time	Effective, efficient	To develop relationship	Leisurely, to develop relationship	Thorough, accurate
Pace of interview	Quick	Quick	Deliberate	Deliberate
Information provided by salesperson	Salesperson's qualifications; value of products	What salesperson thinks; whom he/she knows	Evidence that salesperson is trustworthy, friendly	Evidence of salesperson's expertise in solving problem
Salesperson's actions to win customer acceptance	Documented evidence, stress results	Recognition and approval	Personal attention and interest	Evidence that salesperson has analyzed the situation
Presentation of benefits	What product can do	Who has used the product	Why product is best to solve problem	How product can solve the problem
Assistance to aid decision making	Explanation of options and probabilities	Testimonials	Guarantees and assurances	Evidence and offers of service

social styles. Versatility is the key to effective adaptive selling. "From the Buyer's Seat 5.1" gives a good illustration of a salesperson who didn't practice versatility—and the consequences of that behavior.

VERSATILITY

The effort people make to increase the productivity of a relationship by adjusting to the needs of the other party is known as **versatility.** Versatile salespeople—those able to adapt their social styles—are much more effective than salespeople who do not adjust their sales presentations. Here is a comparison of behaviors of more versatile and less versatile people:

How can a salesperson improve his or her versatility? Many companies have sales training programs, using tools like the social style matrix that help teach salespeople the differences in buyers. Role playing is also used extensively for managers to spot problems in salesperson versatility and to teach new ways to help improve it. For example, sales training might suggest that effective salespeople adjust their social styles to match their customers' styles. In role plays, salespeople with a driver orientation need to become more emotional and less assertive when selling to amiable customers. Analytical salespeople must increase

Less Versatile	**More Versatile**
Limited ability to adapt to others' needs	Able to adapt to others' needs
Specialist	Generalist
Well-defined interests	Broad interests
Sticks to principles	Negotiates issues
Predictable	Unpredictable
Looks at one side of an issue	Looks at many sides of an issue

SOME SALESPEOPLE JUST DON'T ADAPT TO ME, OR TO THE SITUATION

By Tracey Brill

One thing that really irritates me is when a salesperson calls on me and doesn't adapt to the situation or to my specific needs. I could tell many stories of how this works out in practice, but perhaps one example will give you a good idea.

I was in my doorway about to leave my office to meet with a vice president. I had ended a meeting in my office about three minutes early to give myself the time to get up the three flights of stairs to her (the VP's) office in time. A salesperson, whom I had never met before, stopped me in my doorway, and I explained that I was on my way to an important meeting.

The salesperson said he understood but proceeded to take my hand and shake it and introduce himself. He continued to say that he was asked to meet with me by another coworker to introduce his services. I continued to explain that I needed to go to my meeting, but I would take his card and call him later. He would not clear the doorway and continued to explain his services, which was "only going to take a minute." I explained that I really didn't have a minute, and I would call him later.

He continued to explain his services after I said I didn't have the time. I interrupted him and explained that he needed to allow me to leave my office. His disregard for my time and his desire "to only take a minute of my time" resulted in my being two minutes late for my meeting.

This salesperson works in a very competitive business. Many groups offer the same services, but I am usually interested in meeting with the different vendors to see if they have any unique feature we have not already evaluated. What did I do in this case? Instead of calling the rep back, I did my homework with the coworker who referred him to me. The project was bid to three vendors. But I didn't bid it to the salesperson that interrupted me in the doorway.

Source: Tracey Brill; used with permission.

their assertiveness and responsiveness when selling to expressive customers. Exhibit 5.8 shows some techniques for adjusting sales behaviors in terms of assertiveness and responsiveness.

THE ROLE OF KNOWLEDGE

The social style matrix illustrates the importance of knowledge, organized into categories, in determining selling effectiveness through adaptive selling. Sales training based on the social style matrix teaches salespeople the four customer categories or types (driver, expressive, amiable, and analytical). Salespeople learn the cues for identifying them. Salespeople also learn which adjustments they need to make in their communication styles to be effective with each customer type.

SYSTEMS FOR DEVELOPING ADAPTIVE SELLING SKILLS

The social style matrix developed by Merrill and Reid is one of several sales training methods based on customer classification schemes. Rather than using assertiveness and responsiveness, other classification schemes use dimensions like warm–hostile and dominant–submissive; dominance and sociability; relater, socializer, thinker, and director; logical (yellow), emotional (blue), conceptual (orange), and analytical (green); and skeptics, charismatics, thinkers, followers, and controllers.

Exhibit 5.8
Adjusting Social Styles

| Dimension | Adjustment | |
	Reduce	Increase
Assertiveness	Ask for customer's opinion. Acknowledge merits of customer's viewpoint. Listen without interruption. Be more deliberate; don't rush. Let customer direct flow of conversation.	Get to the point. Don't be vague or ambiguous. Volunteer information. Be willing to disagree. Take a stand. Initiate conversation.
Responsiveness	Become businesslike. Talk less. Restrain enthusiasm. Make decision based on facts. Stop and think.	Verbalize feelings. Express enthusiasm. Pay personal compliments. Spend time on relationships rather than business. Socialize; engage in small talk. Use nonverbal communication.

Regardless of the training system used, it is imperative that salespeople adjust to their audience. To repeat, it is also important to adjust your style when selling to diverse cultures even within your own country. For example, Hispanic salespeople may need to alter their communication style when selling to Anglo-American customers.

Expert systems have been developed to help salespeople understand their customers and develop effective sales strategies. An **expert system** is a computer program that mimics a human expert. The program contains the knowledge, rules, and decision processes employed by experts and then uses these elements to solve problems, suggest strategies, and provide advice similar to that of an expert.

Expert systems, like Insights for Sales Strategy, help salespeople understand buyers and develop effective sales strategies.

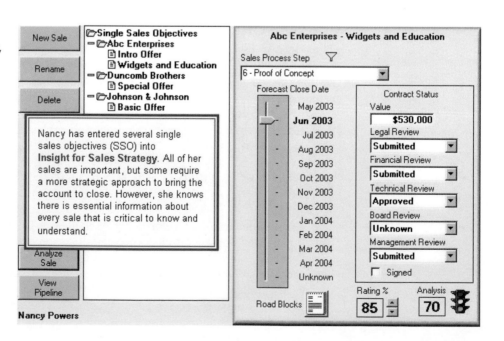

Studies show that salespeople who are willing to accept technology have higher performance.

Training methods such as the social style matrix and expert systems are simply a first step in developing knowledge for practicing adaptive selling. They emphasize the need to practice adaptive selling—to use different presentations with different customers—and stimulate salespeople to base their sales presentations on an analysis of the customer. But these methods are limited; they present only a few types of customers, and classification is based on the form of communication (the social style), not on the content of the communication (the specific features and benefits stressed in the presentation).

In addition, accurately fitting customers into the suggested categories is often difficult. Customers act differently and have different needs in different sales encounters: A buyer may be amiable in a new task buying situation and be analytical when dealing with an out-supplier's salesperson in a straight rebuy. Amiable buyers in a bad mood may act like drivers. By rigidly applying the classification rules, salespeople may actually limit their flexibility, reducing the adaptive selling behavior these training methods emphasize.

SELLING YOURSELF

Congratulations! You have an interview on campus this Thursday for an internship. You don't know a lot about the job, but you've heard other students say it's an awesome experience.

To prepare, you'll need to gain some knowledge about the internship as well as the company. You also need to learn how an interview process works and what to expect. One of the best ways to do that is to use the services of your school's outplacement office (sometimes called the career center, job center, or something like that). They are experts and have a wealth of knowledge. You want to tap that knowledge and add it to your knowledge base.

As the folks at your college's career center engage in practice interviews with you, provide constructive feedback on your résumé, or hint that perhaps your clothing or accessories might not be something you want to wear in the actual interview, accept this evaluative feedback for what it is—something to help you succeed. They're not telling you those things to hurt you or make you feel bad. The sooner you can learn not to take things personally, and accept (and even ask for) feedback on what you're doing wrong, the sooner you will start being successful. It's as simple as that. Fight feedback, and people will often stop giving it to you, making you less skilled in life.

As the meeting begins, you should start forming impressions about the social style of the interviewer. Is she an amiable or more analytical? The chapter told how you could assess this, but many of the cues you are supposed to look for won't be there because you're meeting at the school's job placement center rather than in the person's own office.

But don't give up. You can still learn a great deal from whether he wants to engage in small talk, or from whether she is taking careful written notes (or just watching you and listening to you without taking notes), or from whether he seems to have the entire interview planned out or is just adapting to your specific interview and deciding what to do next as the interview proceeds. You can also learn about her social style from how she is dressed (casually or conservatively) and from whether you are sitting across the desk from each other or next to each other. Learn from the cues that are provided and adapt your style accordingly. You'll be glad you did.

SUMMARY

Adaptive selling uses one of the unique properties of personal selling as a marketing communication tool: the ability to tailor messages to individual customers and make on-the-spot adjustments. Extensive knowledge of customer and sales situation types is a key ingredient in effective adaptive selling.

To be effective, salespeople need considerable knowledge about the products they sell, the companies for which they work, and the customers to whom they sell. Experienced salespeople organize customer knowledge into categories. Each category has cues for classifying customers or sales situations and an effective sales presentation for customers in the category.

The social style matrix, developed by Merrill and Reid, illustrates the concept of developing categorical knowledge to facilitate adaptive selling. The matrix defines four customer categories based on a customer's responsiveness and assertiveness in sales interactions. To effectively interact with a customer, a salesperson needs to identify the customer's social style and adapt a style to match. The sales training program based on the social style matrix provides cues for identifying social style as well as presentations salespeople can use to make adjustments.

The social style matrix is one example of a categorical scheme salespeople can use to improve their knowledge and adaptability. However, other schemes are used, and some have been incorporated into expert system computer programs.

KEY TERMS

adaptive selling   129
amiable   137
analytical   137
assertiveness   134
customized presentation   128
diagnostic feedback   132
driver   135
expert system   142

expressive   136
outlined presentation   128
performance feedback   132
responsiveness   134
social style matrix   134
standard memorized presentation   128
versatility   140

ETHICS PROBLEMS

1. As a salesperson, is it ethical to adjust your presentation based on social styles? Isn't that just being manipulative? Can't you just be yourself and sell?
2. You have a buyer who is a real jerk. She is in constant battles with all the salespeople who call on her, as well as with her own staff. Her business is important to you, and you don't want to lose it because you love the commissions on the sales you make. How should you adapt to her social style?[15]

QUESTIONS AND PROBLEMS

1. A salesperson stated, "I just can't stand to deal with buyers who have trouble making up their minds. I'd much rather deal with someone who shouts at me and tells me in no uncertain terms what they hate about me or my product." Based on this limited amount of information, what social style would you guess the salesperson to be? What would be your response to this salesperson?
2. In "Sales Technology 5.1" you learned how Isuzu is using NetSuite to empower its salespeople to perform more effectively and efficiently. But some salespeople, far from using the benefits of technology, were still writing

call notes on the back of envelopes. What would be your response to a salesperson who says, "I don't need all that fancy technology. My system of taking hand notes works just fine for me"?

3. A salesperson made the following comment: "I hate it when my sales manager makes calls with me. I do so much better when I'm by myself. After the call, she is always telling me what I did wrong." Based on what you learned in this chapter about knowledge systems, what would be your response to this salesperson?

4. "A good salesperson can sell any customer." Do you agree? Why or why not?

5. Would a person with an analytical social style be better at selling than a person with a driver or an expressive style? Why or why not?

6. Some people object to the social style matrix training system because they don't want to "act." Is that a valid objection? What would you say to them?

7. What social styles would you assign to the following people?
   a. Oprah Winfrey.
   b. Your favorite instructor last term.

c. The person who sits next to you in this class.
d. Your best friend.

8. The salesperson in "Building Partnerships 5.1" had to tell the surgeon that he was using a product incorrectly. Assume you are in a similar situation. You have to tell a surgeon that she is using your product incorrectly. How would you do that differently for a surgeon who is an analytical versus a driver surgeon?

9. Suppose that during a sales call, a customer says, "I'm not convinced that this new product will sell." How should you respond if this customer is a driver? An expressive?

10. Market research by a commercial cleaning company identified two types of high schools. Traditional high schools believe that teacher and staff satisfaction is based on the quality of students and that cleaning services are relatively unimportant. Private and charter high schools believe that cleaning services are important because they affect the students' and parents' perceptions of the school. What type of sales presentation would you use to sell janitorial services to each of these high school types? Which product features and benefits would you emphasize in each case?

CASE PROBLEMS

case **5.1**

Dyson Airblade

Jon TePoel is a salesperson for Dyson, Inc., in New York City, and he has been working for the company for two years. Dyson is well known for making some of the highest-quality vacuum cleaners in the world.

Recently Sir James Dyson, the owner of the company, created an air hand dryer for public restrooms, and it's one that actually works. The Dyson Airblade dries hands in only 12 seconds, uses 80 percent less energy than other air flow hand dryers, and the kills 99.9 percent of airborne bacteria with a built-in HEPA filter.

Jon is going to call on a buying team of three individuals (Marty Chuckalot, Alfred Nordstrom, and Cynthia Bergstein) for a large New York City developer. His goal is to convince them to specify Dyson Airblade hand dryers for all the public restrooms in their new construction projects. Currently the developer uses a combination of regular air dryers and paper towel dispensers.

While doing some background research, Jon has discovered a bit about his three buyers. Marty Chuckalot never arrives to a meeting without bringing his laptop, and he uses it throughout the meeting, often not seeming to pay attention to whoever is giving the presentation. Marty is quiet, never answering questions during a meeting or offering his opinions. One of his favorite phrases is, "I'm not sure if I fully understand your product. Can you tell me a bit more about it?" His personality is fairly serious, which is evident when he frequently decodes a person's message with its literal, rather than the intended, meaning. People who interact with him say they have to learn to tolerate silences and give him time to think before answering.

Alfred Nordstrom is quite a different type of buyer. Alfred seems to know everyone's first name, and everyone seems to knows him, although a few don't really like him. In conversations he often takes the lead, making his opinion well known in the group. He has been described as manipulative, but always "in a nice way." He loves to talk and can carry on a conversation about hockey for an hour if the seller will let him.

Cynthia Bergstein is the friendliest of the three buyers. She tries to make everyone feel comfortable and often softens remarks made by Alfred. She never buys from someone until she gets to know them because, as she says, "How do we know we can trust them if we don't know them well first?" She is supportive of other's decisions, even if an idea is contrary to her own point of view. She prefers to let others take the lea, and would say her strength is to be a great team player.

Questions

1. Based on the information provided in this case, identify each of the three buyers' social styles.
2. If you were Jon, what should you do to sell to this group?

case **5.2**

Cedar Point
Amusement Park

You have just been hired as a salesperson for Cedar Point Amusement Park in Sandusky, Ohio.

Cedar Point is the largest amusement ride park in the world. The park has 75 rides, including 17 roller coasters (3 of the top 10 steel roller coasters in the world are found in the park). There are other family attractions including a Planet Snoopy area for children, shows, and so forth.

Your job is to sell to corporate groups—either a single-day event or "good any day" passes that can be used by employees any day the park is open (employees don't have to attend the park together if they use good any day passes). Cedar Point offers many options for corporations, including the ability to cater meals for the event.

Questions

1. What kinds of knowledge do you need to do your job effectively?
2. How can you acquire that knowledge?
3. What type of system should you use to store that knowledge and retrieve it as needed?

Source: http://www.cedarpoint.com.

ROLE PLAY CASE

This role play requires some before-class preparation. Write a brief outline of how you would describe NetSuite to someone who has never seen it. Identify three features of NetSuite that you think would benefit your buyer, based on the information you've learned so far this semester. Then write down what you would want to say about each feature. You will take turns presenting your sales presentations to your buyer. After you give your presentation, determine what the other person's social style was. Identify the hints the buyer gave you.

If you have been using NetSuite role plays all along, you can use the same customer you have called on. If not, you will need to review the role play material at the end of Chapter 3. You can also review material about NetSuite in the role play case at the back of this book to understand NetSuite and what it does.

When you play the buyer, pick a social style different from your own. Interact with the seller in ways that give clues about your social style. Before the role play starts, think of at least five things you will do to hint at your new social style. Keep in mind that a social style includes both responsiveness and assertiveness, so make sure your hints combine both dimensions. After each role play, the salesperson should say what the other person's social style was and what clues were used to make that determination.

Note: For background information about these role plays, please see page 27.

To the instructor: Additional information needed to complete the role play is available in the Instructor's Manual.

ADDITIONAL REFERENCES

Amyx, Douglas, and Shahid Bhuian. "The Salesperson Service Performance Scale." *Journal of Personal Selling & Sales Management* 29, no. 4 (Fall 2009), pp. 367–76.

Aramo-Immonen, Heli, and Pasi Porkka. "Shared Knowledge in Project-Based Companies' Value Chain." *International Journal of Knowledge Management Studies* 6 (October 2009), p. 364.

Badrinarayanan, Vishag, and Sreedhar Madhavaram. "Workplace Spirituality and the Selling Organization: A Conceptual Framework and Research Propositions." *Journal of Personal Selling & Sales Management* 28, no. 4 (Fall 2008), pp. 421–34.

Barnes, Bradley R., Pete Naude, and Paul Michell. "Perceptual Gaps and Similarities in Buyer–Seller Dyadic Relationships." *Industrial Marketing Management* 36, no. 5 (July 2007), pp. 662–75.

Chakrabarty, Subhra, Gene Brown, and Robert E. Widing. "Closed Influence Tactics: Do Smugglers Win in the Long Run?" *Journal of Personal Selling and Sales Management* 30, no. 1 (Winter 2010), pp. 23–32.

Dickson, Peter R., Walfried M. Lassar, Gary Hunter, and Samit Chakravorti. "The Pursuit of Excellence in Process Thinking and Customer Relationship Management." *Journal of Personal Selling & Sales Management* 29, no. 2 (Spring 2009), pp. 111–24.

Dietvorst, Roeland C., et al. "A Sales Force-Specific Theory-of-Mind Scale: Tests of Its Validity by Classical Methods and Functional Magnetic Resonance Imaging." *Journal of Marketing Research* 46, no. 5 (2009), pp. 653–68.

Erickson, G. Scott, and Helen N. Rothberg. "Intellectual Capital in Business-to-Business Markets." *Industrial Marketing Management* 38, no. 2 (February 2009), pp. 159–65.

Goldsmith, Marshall, and Louis Carter. *Best Practices in Talent Management.* Pfeiffer, 2009.

Guenzi, Paolo, Laurent Georges, and Catherine Pardo. "The Impact of Strategic Account Managers' Behaviors on Relational Outcomes: An Empirical Study." *Industrial Marketing Management* 38, no. 3 (April 2009), pp. 300–11.

Hunter, Gary K., and William D. Perreault. "Making Sales Technology Effective." *Journal of Marketing* 71, no. 1 (January 2007), pp. 16–34.

Lamont, J. "Past and Future: Closing the Knowledge Loop." *KM World* 19, no. 1 (January 2010), pp. 8–19.

Liao S, Wu C. "System Perspective of Knowledge Management, Organizational Learning, and Organizational Innovation." *Expert Systems with Applications* 37, no. 2 (March 2010), pp.1096–1103.

Lohtia, Ritu, Daniel C. Bello, and Constance Elise Porter. "Building Trust in US–Japanese Business Relationships: Mediating Role of Cultural Sensitivity." *Industrial Marketing Management* 38, no. 3 (April 2009), pp. 239–52.

Powers, Thomas L., and William R. Reagan. "Factors Influencing Successful Buyer–Seller Relationships." *Journal of Business Research* 60, no. 12 (December 2007), pp. 1234–42.

Stanko, Michael A., Joseph M. Bonner, and Roger J. Calantone. "Building Commitment in Buyer–Seller Relationships: A Tie Strength Perspective." *Industrial Marketing Management* 36, no. 8 (November 2007), pp. 1094–103.

Stein, Dave. "Why Sales Process Gets the Shaft." *Sales & Marketing Management,* September/October 2008, pp. 22–24.

Van Hulse, J., and T. Khoshgoftaar. "Knowledge Discovery from Imbalanced and Noisy Data." *Data & Knowledge Engineering* 68, no. 12 (December 2009), pp.1513–42.

Wachner, Trent, Christopher R. Plouffe, and Yany Grégoire. "SOCO's Impact on Individual Sales Performance: The Integration of Selling Skills as a Missing Link." *Industrial Marketing Management* 38, no. 1 (January 2009), pp. 32–44.

Weitzel, Sloan R. *Feedback That Works: How to Build and Deliver Your Message.* Jossey-Bass, 2007.

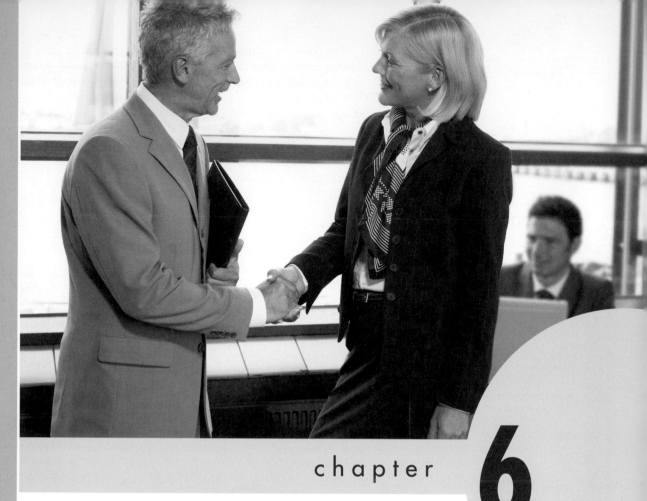

chapter **6**

PROSPECTING

SOME QUESTIONS ANSWERED IN THIS CHAPTER ARE

- Why is prospecting important for effective selling?
- Are all sales leads good prospects? What are the characteristics of a qualified prospect?
- How can prospects be identified?
- How can the organization's promotional program be used in prospecting?
- How can an effective lead qualification and management system aid a salesperson?
- How can a salesperson overcome a reluctance to prospect?

2

PART

PROFILE

PROFILE My name is Kevin Johnson, and I graduated from the University of Minnesota Duluth in 2000 with a bachelor of business administration in marketing, and took my sales class from Dr. Castleberry. I started work with Pacioli, a leader in the accounting/finance and IT marketplace, as an account executive. Our service offerings include retained search, contingency search, consulting engagements, and professional staff augmentation.

Over the last nine years, I've learned the importance of prospecting. While retaining a consistent client base is essential, so is the need for me to continue to prospect for new clients. I've found success using the following methods of prospecting: referrals from clients, industry trade magazines, trade shows, and networking. By far my most important source of prospects is satisfied customers and the referrals they offer. One important way I stay connected to my customers is through LinkedIn.

I strongly recommend that students and professionals join LinkedIn (www.linkedin .com). Yes, it's free. The best way to describe LinkedIn is that it is like Facebook and helps you stay connected with your network. Staying in contact with those people who know you do good work can really benefit you through new business opportunities and even for future employment. If you look at my LinkedIn page, you'll see that I have a number of personal recommendations right on my page. People desiring to learn more about me can see what others have said about my ability to meet their recruiting needs. I have over 41,000 network connections, either that I know personally (a direct friend of mine) or that I know through another friend (these would be friends of a friend of mine). If you take that out one level more, I have over 3,000,000 contacts in my LinkedIn network that I can contact though my friends.

Another great way to use LinkedIn is for career planning. LinkedIn has a feature that allows you to search by the titles of individuals that are a part of LinkedIn (your search capabilities grow as your number of contacts grows). You can look at roles that you would like to be in someday (for example, senior vice president of sales in the airline industry) and look at what type of experience they gained to get there. That can help you know how to structure your career and training to achieve the job of your dreams.

LinkedIn also has a good number of jobs that are posted to the site, and it can be a great resource for doing company research (for example, industry, size, number of employees). I just did a search for sales manager within the Minneapolis area and came up with four pages of results. The report also indicates if anyone in your network works in those companies.

Be consistent and thorough with prospecting, regardless of the method you use, and use careful, timely follow-up.

Visit our Web site at www.pacioli.com.

An important activity for nearly all salespeople is locating qualified prospects. In fact, the selling process generally begins with prospecting. You can be the best salesperson in the world in terms of listening, asking questions, discovering needs, giving presentations, helpfully responding to objections, and obtaining commitment. But if you are calling on the wrong person or organization, none of these skills do you any good! This chapter provides resources to help you prospect effectively and efficiently.

THE IMPORTANCE OF PROSPECTING

Prospecting, the process of locating potential customers for a product or service, is critical whether you are a new or seasoned sales professional. In fact, experts often note that prospecting is the most important activity a salesperson does.[1]

Why is it so important? Quite simply, the world is constantly changing, with a resulting estimated 15 to 20 percent annual turnover of customers. In addition, salespeople must find new customers to replace those that switch to competitors, go bankrupt, move out of the territory, merge with noncustomers, or decide to do without a product or service. A salesperson often needs to prospect even in existing accounts because of downsizing, job changes, or retirements of buyers. Sales trainer Joe Girard uses a Ferris wheel metaphor to describe the important process of adding new customers (loading new accounts onto the Ferris wheel) to replace customers you lose (people getting off the Ferris wheel). Without replacing lost accounts, your Ferris wheel will soon be running with no one on board.

Of course, prospecting is more important in some selling fields than in others. For example, the office products salesperson, stockbroker, financial advisor, or real estate sales representative with no effective prospecting plan usually doesn't last long in the business. Sales positions such as these may require 100 contacts to get 10 prospects who will listen to presentations, out of which one person will buy. Each sale, then, represents a great deal of prospecting. It is also important in these fields to prospect continually. Some sales trainers relate this process to your car's gas tank: You don't wait until the gas gauge is on empty before you fill up!

Some sales positions require less emphasis on locating new contacts. For example, a Procter & Gamble sales representative in a certain geographic area would know all the potential prospects for Crest toothpaste (all the grocery stores, drugstores, convenience stores, and so on) because they are easy to identify. For the same reason, a Du Pont sales rep selling a new line of automobile finishes to auto manufacturers and body shops in Ontario can easily identify all the main prospects. A Lockheed Martin salesperson assigned exclusively to sell the F-16 tactical fighter jet to Taiwan, South Korea, Greece, and Singapore would not spend any time trying to locate new governments to call on. For these types of sales positions, prospecting as we normally think of it (that is, looking for new leads) is not an important part of the sales process. Nevertheless, salespeople cannot ignore these obvious leads, as the next section discusses. Salespeople still have to assess whether leads are good prospects.

CHARACTERISTICS OF A GOOD PROSPECT

Prospecting actually begins with locating a **lead** (sometimes called a "suspect")— a potential prospect that may or may not have what it takes to be a true prospect.[2] Some salespeople mistakenly consider every lead a prospect without first taking the time to see whether these people really provide an opportunity to make a sale.

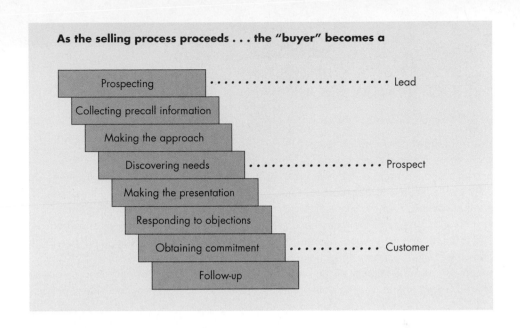

As the selling process proceeds . . . the "buyer" becomes a

Prospecting · Lead

Collecting precall information

Making the approach

Discovering needs · · · · · · · · · · · · · · · · · Prospect

Making the presentation

Responding to objections

Obtaining commitment · · · · · · · · · · · · Customer

Follow-up

To avoid that mistake, the salesperson must **qualify the lead.** Qualifying is the process of determining whether a lead is in fact a **prospect.** If the salesperson determines that the lead is a good candidate for making a sale, that person or organization is no longer considered a lead and instead is called a prospect. Note that many leads do not become prospects. Exhibit 6.1 displays the relationship between the steps in the selling process and the terminology we use to refer to the "buyer." Note that qualifying can occur during several stages: prospecting, collecting precall information, making the approach, and discovering needs.

It is important for a salesperson to understand several facts about this movement from being a lead to becoming a prospect. First, the seller should not get ahead of herself and start giving a presentation to a lead. That wouldn't be appropriate until the person has been classified as a prospect. Second, often it is the lead who turns himself or herself into a prospect, along with a creeping commitment that indicates an interest in solving his or her problem. Third, the ways in which salespeople strategically move people through the progression outlined in Exhibit 6.1 are important and will be discussed in more detail in Chapter 15.

Naturally, the amount of time spent trying to determine which leads are prospects varies in different types of selling. It depends on such factors as the type of product or service, the value of the salesperson's time, and the profit per sale. The following five questions help to qualify leads and pinpoint the good prospects:[3]

Does the lead have a want or a need that the purchase of my products or services can satisfy?

Does the lead have the ability to pay?

Does the lead have the authority to buy?

Can the lead be approached favorably?

Is the lead eligible to buy?

These questions can be asked about the person who is a lead, the lead's firm, or both. Chapter 7 discusses how to begin gathering the information needed to answer these questions, and Chapter 8 provides further instruction on how to gather the remaining needed information during actual sales calls. For now, let's look at each question a little more closely.

I'VE GOT TO HAVE YOUR HATS... NOW!

By Jeff Kramer, Christy's

We're a snowboard and ski shop called Christy's. We carry every major ski and board line. Now if you know anything about ski and board lines, you know that practically every single one also carries a line of hats. That's just the way it is. And every one of those companies gives us huge discounts on all their merchandise (including hats) due to the enormous volume of boots, boards, bindings, and so forth that we carry. In fact, we don't have enough space and demand to carry all the brands of hats that are offered, so we can be very selective and demanding.

So one day in waltzes this salesperson, Jason Neis, from KLU, a company that makes snowboard hats but not snowboards. Jason proceeds to tell us how his hats are premium, top-of-the-line products and how we should carry them for sure. My response was that all hats are about the same, and that I didn't need another line of hats. To be honest with you, I liked the hats, but just didn't see any way they would stand out from the other hats we were already selling. I thanked Jason for stopping by and said to stay in touch.

But Jason wasn't going to give up. He had done his prospecting well, and knew that we sold a lot of hats. He also knew that we were one of the top ski and board shops in the area, and he wanted his hats in our store. So he developed a plan.

First a bit of background. Our store has five snowboarders that are "team riders." That means when they're at competitions, they ride our store's logo. The Christy's logo is on their snowboards, they wear Christy's T-shirts in the lodge, and they sign in at the competitions as being sponsored by Christy's. Our riders are important center-of-influences in our snowboard community, and many younger riders look up to them as heroes.

Jason's plan was to "sign" Manny, one of our team riders, to wear KLU hats. And he did. He gave Manny a bunch of free hats, and he also gave Manny's friends all the hats they wanted. As soon as this happened, we had kids coming into our store saying, "We want to buy KLU hats, just like Manny's wearing! Where are they?"

Jason had helped create a need for his hats that I had to have met. So I called Jason on the phone and placed a huge order. Needless to say, they sold out quickly.

Source: Jeff Kramer, personal correspondence; used with permission. Names have been changed to protect confidentiality.

DOES A WANT OR NEED EXIST?

Research has supplied no infallible answers to why customers buy, but it has found many reasons. As we pointed out in Chapter 3, customers buy to satisfy practical needs as well as intangible needs, such as prestige or aesthetics.

Determining whether leads need a salesperson's products or services is not always simple. Many firms use the telephone, e-mail, or the Web to assess needs. Sometimes an exploratory interview is conducted to determine whether a lead has needs the seller's products can satisfy. Also, almost everyone has a need for some product lines; for example, practically every organization needs fax machines, computers, Internet access, copiers, paper, and a telephone system.

By using high-pressure tactics, sales may be made to those who do not need or really want a product. Such sales benefit no one. The buyer will resent making the purchase, and a potential long-term customer will be lost. The lead must want to solve his or her problem to be considered a qualified prospect. Sometimes the seller can help create a real need for the buyer, as "From the Buyer's Seat 6.1" illustrates.

DOES THE LEAD HAVE THE ABILITY TO PAY?

The ability to pay for products or services helps separate leads from prospects. For example, the commercial real estate agent usually checks the financial status of each client to determine the price range of office buildings to show. A client with annual profits of $100,000 and cash resources of $75,000 may be a genuine prospect for an office building selling in the $200,000 to $250,000 bracket. An agent would be wasting time, however, by showing this client an office building listed at $10 million. The client may have a real desire and need for the more expensive setting, but the client is still not a real prospect for the higher-priced office building if he or she doesn't have the resources to pay for it.

Ability to pay includes both cash and credit. Many companies subscribe to a credit-rating service offered by firms such as Dun & Bradstreet. Salespeople use information from these sources, often accessed directly from the salesperson's laptop, to determine the financial status and credit rating of a lead. They can also qualify leads with information obtained from local credit agencies, consumer credit agencies such as Experian, noncompetitive salespeople, and the Better Business Bureau. Salespeople are sometimes surprised at their leads' credit ratings. Some big-name firms have poor ratings.

DOES THE LEAD HAVE THE AUTHORITY TO BUY?

A lead may have a real need for a product and the ability to pay for it but lack the authority to make the purchase. Knowing who has this authority saves the salesperson time and effort and results in a higher percentage of closed sales. As discussed in Chapter 3, many people are typically involved in a purchase decision, and frequently it is unclear who has the most influence.

Because of downsizing, some firms are delegating their purchasing tasks to outside vendors. These service vendors, called **systems integrators,** have the authority to buy products and services on behalf of the delegating firm. Systems integrators usually assume complete responsibility for a project from its beginning to follow-up servicing. An example would be Lockheed Martin acting as a systems integrator for the complete mail-processing system of a new postal sorting facility in Germany. In that scenario every potential vendor would actually be selling to Lockheed Martin, not to the German government. When systems integrators are involved, salespeople need to delineate clearly who has the authority to purchase. Sometimes the overall buyer (the German government in this example) will retain veto power over potential vendors.

CAN THE LEAD BE APPROACHED FAVORABLY?

Some leads with a need, the ability to pay, and the authority to buy may still not qualify as prospects because they are not accessible to the salesperson. For example, the president of a large bank, a major executive of a large manufacturing company, or the senior partner in a well-established law firm normally would not normally be accessible to a young college graduate starting out as a financial advisor for Edward Jones. Getting an interview with these people may be so difficult and the chances of making a sale may be so small that the sales representative should eliminate them as possible prospects.

IS THE LEAD ELIGIBLE TO BUY?

Eligibility is an equally important factor in finding a genuine prospect. For example, a salesperson who works for a firm that requires a large minimum order should not call on leads that could never order in such volume. Likewise, a representative who sells exclusively to wholesalers should be certain the individuals he or she calls on are actually wholesalers, not retailers. "Building Partnerships 6.1" describes an interesting scenario in which eligibility was in question.

Another factor that may determine eligibility for a particular salesperson is the geographic location of the prospect. Most companies operate on the basis of **exclusive sales territories,** meaning that a particular salesperson can sell only to

YOU HIT A DEER?

A few years back, I was a Federated Insurance sales-person and had a large Redi-Mix Concrete contractor I was quoting. This was the second time I had quoted this account, and I had built a good relationship there. My price was $159,000 for their property and casualty insurance. I knew they paid only $150,000 the year before, but I had uncovered many coverage disadvantages and issues in their current program. I had a really great shot at selling this account. The commission rate on P&C is about 15 percent, so I would make about $23,000 if I made the sale.

The buyer said I was to stop by on Friday morning and that his current agent was coming later that afternoon with a quote. The insurance expiration day was that Saturday.

I gave my proposal, and it went very well. I gave the buyer a list of 10 things to ask the other agent in which I had coverage advantages. The buyer said he wanted to do business with me, but because his current agent was already coming in that afternoon, he felt like he should see what she had to offer and go through the issues I had pointed out.

I left and set an appointment for first thing Monday morning. On Monday at 8:00 I was there, and the owner said that I had earned the business! I was pumped! He pulled out his checkbook and gave me a check for $15,900 as a down payment. I called my underwriter to tell him the great news, and he said, "Awesome!" He asked, "When

is it effective?" I said, "As of last Saturday." He said to have them sign a form saying they had not had any claims since Saturday.

I asked the owner and he said he didn't have any claims. Then he said, "Oh, I forgot, Joe hit a deer on the way home from a job on Saturday in the company truck. It wasn't bad though, about $1,200 in damages we are guessing. Joe wasn't hurt or anything."

I was devastated! What were my options? I could call the underwriter and tell him about the claim, knowing that he most likely would tell me to give the check back and that I could not bind an account that already had a claim pending. And I'd lose $23,000 in commission. Or I could tell the owner not to worry about it, knowing that Federated would pay the claim if I pretended I didn't know about the accident and bind the account. Or I could tell the owner that I would pay for the $1,200 claim out of my pocket because I would earn a hefty $23,000 commission check.

So what did I do? I gave the owner back his check and said we couldn't do business this year. It was hard, but it was the right thing to do. He respected my decision; I ended up getting the business the following year, and he has been a satisfied client ever since!

Source: Jim Sodoma, district manager, Federated Insurance; used with permission.

---

certain prospects (such as doctors in only a three-county area) and not to other prospects. A salesperson working for such a company must consider whether the prospect is eligible, based on location or customer type, to buy from him or her.

Salespeople should also avoid targeting leads already covered by their corporate headquarters. Large customers or potential customers that are handled exclusively by corporate executives are often called **house accounts.** For example, if Marriott Hotels considers Ingersoll Rand a house account, a Marriott Hotel salesperson (who sets up events and conventions at the hotel) located in New York City should not try to solicit business from one of Ingersoll Rand's divisions located in New York City. Instead all Ingersoll Rand business would be handled by a Marriott executive at Marriott corporate headquarters.

OTHER CRITERIA

Leads that meet the five criteria are generally considered excellent prospects. Some sellers, however, add other criteria. For example, DEI Management Group instructs its salespeople to classify leads by their likelihood of buying. Salespeople may have a long list of companies that need their product, can pay for it, have authority to buy it, and are approachable and eligible. If, however, these companies have absolutely no interest in buying, the salesperson should look elsewhere.

Criteria can include many things. Some firms look at the timing of purchase to determine whether a lead is really a good prospect. Relevant questions to consider include these: When does the prospect's contract with our competitor expire? Is a purchase decision really pending? How do we know? Still other firms look at the long-term potential of developing a partnering relationship with a lead.[4] Here are some questions to ponder: What is the climate at the organization—is it looking to develop partnering relationships with suppliers? Do any of our competitors already have a partnering relationship there? Answers to these and other questions help a firm determine whether a lead is worth pursuing at this time.

HOW AND WHERE TO OBTAIN PROSPECTS

Prospecting sources and methods vary for different types of selling. A sales representative selling corrugated containers for Citation Box & Paper Company, for example, may use a system different from what banking or office products salespeople would use. Exhibit 6.2 presents an overview of some of the most common lead-generating methods. Note that there is some overlap among the methods.

Exhibit 6.2
Overview of Common Sources of Leads

Source	How Used
Satisfied customers	Current and previous customers are contacted for additional business and leads.
Endless chain	Salesperson attempts to secure at least one additional lead from each person he or she interviews.
Networking	Salesperson uses personal relationships with those who are connected and cooperative to secure leads.
Center of influence	Salesperson cultivates well-known, influential people in the territory who are willing to supply lead information.
Social media	Salesperson uses online tools like LinkedIn, Facebook, and Twitter to prospect for new customers and maintain contact with existing customers.
Other Internet uses	Salesperson uses Web sites, e-mail, listservs, bulletin boards, forums, roundtables, and newsgroups to secure leads.
Ads, direct mail, catalogs, and publicity	Salespeople use these forms of promotional activities to generate leads.
Shows, fairs, and merchandise markets	Salespeople use trade shows, conventions, fairs, and merchandise markets for lead generation.
Webinars and seminars	Salespeople use seminars and online webinars to generate leads.
Lists and directories	Salesperson uses secondary data sources, which can be free or fee-based.
Data mining and CRM systems	Salespeople use sophisticated data analysis software and the company's CRM system to generate leads.
Cold calling	Salesperson tries to generate leads by calling on totally unfamiliar organizations.
Spotters	Salesperson pays someone for lead information.
Telemarketing	Salesperson uses phone and/or telemarketing staff to generate leads.
Sales letters	Salesperson writes personal letters to potential leads.
Other sources	Salesperson uses noncompeting salespeople, people in his or her own firm, friends, and so on to secure information.

SATISFIED CUSTOMERS

Satisfied customers, particularly those who are truly partners with the seller, are the most effective sources for leads. In fact some trainers argue that successful salespeople should be getting about 75 percent of their new business through referrals from customers. Referrals of leads in the same industry are particularly useful because the salesperson already understands the unique needs of this type of organization (If you have sold to a bank already, you have a better understanding of banks' needs). Referrals in some cultures, like Japan, are even more important than they are in North America.

To maximize the usefulness of satisfied customers, salespeople should follow several logical steps. First they should make a list of potential references (customers who might provide leads) from among their most satisfied customers. This task will be much easier if the salespeople have maintained an accurate and detailed database of customers. Some current customers could be called **promoters;** these are your most loyal customers who not only keep buying from you but also urge their friends and associate to do the same.[5] Next salespeople should decide what they would like each customer to do (such as have the customer write a personal letter or e-mail message of introduction to a specific prospect, see whether the customer would be willing to take phone inquiries, have the customer directly contact prospects, or have the customer provide a generic letter of reference or write a recommendation for you on LinkedIn). Finally salespeople should ask the customer for the names of leads and for the specific type of help she or he can provide.[6]

Salespeople sometimes gather leads at **referral events,** which are gatherings designed to allow current customers to introduce prospects to the salesperson.[7] For example, a Merrill Lynch stockbroker might invite a group of current clients to a ski resort for a weekend. The skiing weekend is free for clients who bring one or more prospects. Other events that salespeople use include sporting events, theater visits, dinner at a nice restaurant, a short cruise, or golf lessons by a pro. The key is that the gathering should be fun and sociable.

Sometimes customers aren't willing to offer referrals. Why? At times it is because they know that if the salesperson somehow doesn't do a good job, they will be blamed. For this method of prospecting to work, the salesperson must continually keep the referring customer and the prospect fully satisfied. Also, asking for referrals when a new customer signs an order is probably too soon. It is usually best to wait until the new customer has had a chance to use the product and experience both the product's benefits and the level of salesperson service.

Successful salespeople keep in touch with their satisfied customers to make sure they stay satisfied. They do this by maintaining regular communication with the customer through phone calls, mailings, and personal contact. Often this includes sending the customer information that will help the customer do his or her job better. For example, a telecommunications salesperson might send a plumbing contractor information that he found about a potential new building project. Although this information has nothing to do with telecommunications, it is important and helpful for the contractor. This type of activity will be discussed further in Chapter 7.

Satisfied customers not only provide leads but also are usually prospects for additional sales. This situation is sometimes referred to as **selling deeper**

Salespeople use referral events to generate leads.

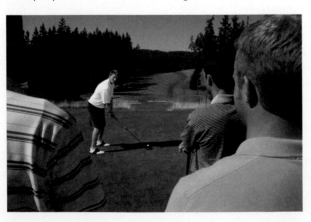

to a current customer. Salespeople should never overlook this profitable opportunity. Sales to existing customers often result in more profits than do sales to new customers. For example, if a midsized company increased its customer retention by just 5 percent, its profits would double in only 10 years. Customers that buy a lot from the selling firm at a lower service cost are sometimes affectionately referred to as "star clients."[8] Chapter 15 explores selling deeper more fully. Of course it is also possible that a customer could be the other kind of a referrer—one who tells others about how poorly you or your product performed[9] This **negative referral** is not the kind of referral a salesperson likes to get, and every effort should be made to ensure that the customer is satisfied and stays satisfied with the solution offered by the salesperson. This also will be discussed in more detail in Chapter 14.

Finally, salespeople who leave one company can bring their sales clients with them to the new company for which they work. Phil Birt did that when he was laid off from Seagate Technology during the recent recession and went to work for Bell Micro. At Bell Micro, Birt grew the revenue of one customer by $400,000 in four months and that of another customer by $100,000 in a single month.[10] Of course salespeople who change jobs must always follow the agreements signed with their first employers before transferring such business.

ENDLESS-CHAIN METHOD

In the **endless-chain method** sales representatives attempt to get at least one additional lead from each person they interview. This method works best when the source is a satisfied customer and partner; however, it may also be used even when a prospect does not buy.

Some people object to having their names used as a means of opening the door to friends or business acquaintances. Others, particularly those who trust the salesperson and are enthusiastic about the products or services, will not hesitate to provide the names of additional prospects and may even write a letter or card of introduction for the sales representative. The name of a lead provided by either a customer or a prospect, known as a **referred lead,** is generally considered the most successful type of lead. Exhibit 6.3 illustrates how a sales representative successfully used the endless-chain method.

NETWORKING

Networking is the utilization of personal relationships by connected and cooperating individuals for the purpose of achieving goals. In selling, networking simply means establishing connections to other people and then using those networks to generate leads, gather information, generate sales, and so on. Note that networking can, and often does, include satisfied customers.

Networking is crucial in many selling situations.[11] For example, trying to sell in China without successful networking, called *guanxi* in China, would be disastrous. Almost everyone can benefit by networking more actively.

Successful networkers offer a number of practical suggestions:[12]

- Call at least two people per day, and go to at least one networking event every week to increase your exposure and time with your contacts.

- Make a special effort to move outside your own comfort zone in a social setting. Learn to mingle with people you don't already know.[13] One expert calls this behavior acting like a host instead of like a guest.

- Spend most of your initial conversation with a new contact talking about his or her business, not yours, and don't forget to learn about the person's nonbusiness interests.

Exhibit 6.3
Example of the Endless-Chain Method of Prospecting

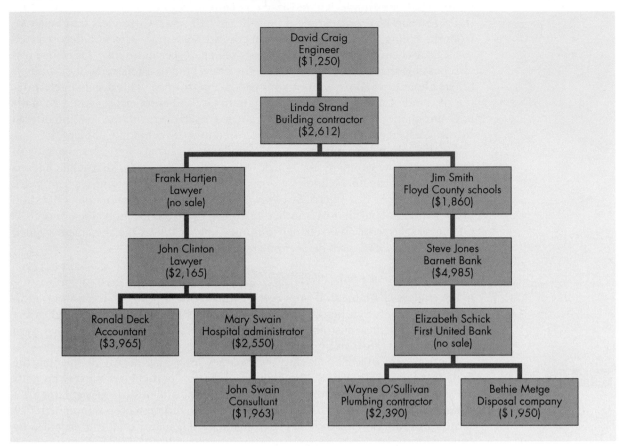

The sales representative used the endless-chain method to produce $25,690 in business (selling fax machines) within a 30-day period. All the sales resulted directly or indirectly from the first referral from an engineer to whom the sales rep had sold a mere $1,250 worth of equipment.

- Follow up with your new contact on a regular basis with cards, notes of congratulations about awards or promotions, and articles and information that might help her or him.
- Whenever you receive a lead from your contact, send a handwritten, personal note thanking the person for the information, regardless of whether the lead buys from you.
- Whenever possible, send your networking contact lead information as well. Don't make your contact feel like she or he is just being used and the only thing you care about is leads for yourself.[14]
- Make free use of your business cards. Consider having something on the back of your business card (such as humor, an inspirational quote, or an endorsement) that will encourage the person to keep it and perhaps share it with others.
- Monitor the performance of your networking to see what's working and what's not.
- Consider joining Business Network International (BNI). With over 3,600 chapters worldwide, BNI is the largest business networking organization in the world and offers members the opportunity to share ideas, contacts, and

most importantly, referrals.[15] There are thousands of other local networking organizations. For example, the Business Connection networking group meets every other Tuesday for breakfast at a local hotel in Bergen County, New Jersey.[16]

- Be prepared to introduce yourself succinctly in social settings. Some experts suggest you create a 30-second commercial (also called an "elevator speech") in which you introduce yourself and provide some pertinent information (such as education, general work history, a significant accomplishment, and a future goal).[17]

In one form of networking, the **center-of-influence method,** the salesperson cultivates a relationship with well-known, influential people in the territory who are willing to supply the names of leads. A friend of one of the authors likes to call centers of influence "bell cows" because the rest of the herd follows their lead. This method, like the endless-chain method, works best if the center of influence is already a satisfied customer of the salesperson. Here is how an industrial cleaning service salesperson used the center-of-influence method when meeting with a well-known and respected maintenance engineer:

> Now that you've had the opportunity to learn more about me and my service, I wonder if you will do me a favor? You mentioned that it was probably the best-designed package you've ever seen. I know that as an engineer you wouldn't personally need my services, but can you think of any of your business associates who could benefit from such a plan? Does one come to mind?

thinking **it** through   Who is a center of influence for you right now? How could a salesperson, who wanted to sell you something, learn who your center of influence is?

In industrial sales situations the centers of influence are frequently people in important departments not directly involved in the purchase decision, such as quality control, equipment maintenance, and receiving. The salesperson keeps in close touch with these people over an extended period, solicits their help in a straightforward manner, and keeps them informed about sales that result from their aid.

The Roper Organization, which has studied centers of influence for more than 45 years, states that they are consistent in one aspect: their degree of activity. Centers of influence tend to be those who enjoy being very socially involved in their communities. And people in the community not only trust these individuals but also seek their advice.

One true story illustrates the method's use. A Xerox representative found that decision makers from several companies would get together from time to time. These accounts formed a **buying community:** a small, informal group of people in similar positions, often from several companies, who communicate regularly, both socially and professionally. The salesperson also found that one particular decision maker in that group, or community, would share the results of any sales call with the other members of the community. Thus a call on that account had the power of seven calls. By working carefully with this center of influence, the salesperson closed nine orders from the seven accounts, with sales that totaled more than $450,000.

Centers of influence may never buy. One church furnishings representative told of a pastor who suggested that the rep call on two other churches, both of which were in the market for pews. The pastor who made the referral has not

John Deere's Web pages help solicit leads for its salespeople.

purchased pews in more than 10 years and probably will not for many more. But the salesperson continues to spend time with that pastor, who is an important center of influence in the pastoral community.

How do you find centers of influence? Try asking customers and prospects whom they consider to be the most influential person in their industry or association. Then actively cultivate a relationship with the center of influence.

SOCIAL MEDIA

As described in Chapter 4, salespeople are using social networking, like LinkedIn and Twitter, to communicate with buyers. These types of tools can also be used to prospect for new customers.

Here are some social networking tips from Mike Krause,[18] a pro on the use of social networking for salespeople, and others:[19]

- Go to the prospect's Web site. Read blogs posted there, and register yourself to receive any type of material the prospect might occasionally send out.

- Go to LinkedIn and search for the company and the person you want to call on. Try to get connected to the individual through a connection you already have.

- Once you are connected, review the prospect's LinkedIn page carefully. Look for things you have in common. See what organizations and groups your prospect belongs to or follows. Follow the same procedure for other social networking sites like Facebook, as well as specialized networking sites like CFOZone (www.cfozone.com), and make sure you tailor messages to fit the mission and tone of each specific networking site.

- Follow the prospect (both the company and the individual you will be calling on) on Twitter. Sometimes a prospect won't have a Twitter account showing on the company Web site, so you will need to do a company search on Twitter to find the prospect (search.twitter.com). Also, see whom your prospect is following on Twitter.

- Search for special interest groups that your prospect belongs to on Twitter, and read those tweets.
- If the prospect decides to follow you on Twitter, send her or him a direct message. If the prospect doesn't follow you on Twitter, you can still send a message by commenting on one of his or her tweets using Twitter's @ feature.
- Search for the prospect and the company on other networking sites like YouTube and SlideShare.
- If your company has just launched a new product or service, ask users what they think about it via Twitter. Or ask any question. Twitter is great for getting opinions from people.
- Upload your contacts from your e-mail program (like Microsoft Outlook and Gmail) to LinkedIn and Facebook to search for more connections.
- Use Find Friends in Facebook to find other people whom you might be able to add to your network.
- Look at your friends' lists of friends. Invite them to link to you.
- Use Facebook Connect to add special features to your Web site.
- Use Group in Facebook to start a group page for your product.
- Use Search to find groups and fan pages that might be related to your business.

As an example of the effectiveness of using social networking, Madeline's Catering in Rochester, New York, redesigned its Web page to fully integrate with Facebook, LinkedIn, and Twitter.[20] As a result, in only six weeks Web site traffic grew by 41 percent and phone inquiries doubled, increasing sales and profits tremendously. As another example, an employee of SoftBrands was trying to find a way to connect with the software giant SAP. The employee decided to start following the tweets of a local SAP worker, and this resulted in some small talk via tweets about sports. Eventually this moved to a face-to-face meeting with the prospect and a profitable sale.[21]

OTHER INTERNET USES

Probably the fastest-growing method of generating leads is through the Internet. Successful salespeople are using Web sites, e-mail, listservs, bulletin boards, forums, roundtables, and newsgroups to connect to individuals and companies that may be interested in their products or services. First and foremost, firms must ensure that their sites are well-developed so prospects can find information easily.

Firms also use the Web to find contact names and information. For example, John Deere, which sells construction and agriculture equipment, uses its Web site to give leads information about products, show them where the nearest dealers are located, and gather their names and addresses if they desire more information.[22] One advantage of Web-based promotions is the number of international leads that can be secured, and John Deere realizes this benefit by making its Web site available in many different languages.

Firms use the Web to solicit leads in a number of ways.[23] Most importantly, firms make sure their sites are listed on the major **search engines**—the tools individuals use to locate sites. Search engine placement can be one of the most difficult areas of marketing on the Web because many times a search engine does not have a proper category for the products a firm sells. Search engines have to be continually monitored and updated because they change their criteria regularly. Firms also use banner advertising on other Web sites, either for a fee or on a barter basis. **Banner advertising** consists of ads placed at the top, sides, or bottom of a Web page, encouraging the viewer to visit a different Web site. Another way to gather leads on the Internet is to post a message on user group sites or via e-mail, called **e-selling,** to a list the company has purchased.

Firms increasingly are taking advantage of new tools that help them use the Web more effectively in prospecting. For example, John Fales, director of inside sales of PostX (an e-mail security provider), uses Jigsaw to find decision makers in large companies, cutting his sales cycle in half.[24] Jigsaw has over 20 million contacts from across the globe, for which subscribers can download contact information (see jigsaw.com).

Personal Medicine, a start-up company that is bringing the house call back to medicine, had trouble enlisting both doctors and patients. Its solution was to use LeadShare, a Web tool offered by SlideShare. With LeadShare marketers post interesting and important information online (in the form of PowerPoint slides, PDF documents, and so forth). To review that information, the viewer must supply contact information. That information is then sent to the organization posting the information and forms the basis for sales leads.

Firms are also developing **extranets**—Internet sites that are customized for specific target markets. Extranets are usually used to build relationships with current customers, but some companies are also using these sites to generate leads. For example, Turner, a TimesWarner Company, owns TBS, TNT, Cartoon Network, Turner Classic Movies, Adult Swim, truTV, and Peachtree TV. Turner set up an extranet that is accessible only to media buyers. Buyers can access programming information, cable research data, and Turner's salespeople from the site.

ADS AND DIRECT MAIL

Firms have developed sophisticated systems to generate inquiries from leads by using advertising and direct mail. For example, Digital Juice sends out direct mail to potential customers for its royalty-free photo, film, and video library. The firm also places advertisements in trade publications. A reader of the ad can request additional information by calling a toll-free number or by returning the reader service card at the back of the magazine. On the reader service card, which is preaddressed, the interested prospect merely circles the bingo card number for Digital Juice.

Digital Juice also participates in postcard packs. A **postcard pack** is a group of postcards (usually between 15 and 50 different cards) that provides information from many firms. Each firm has one card, usually describing one product or service. One side of Digital Juice's postcard contains information about a specific product or service (such as Digital Juice's Motion Designer's Tool Kit). The other side, which is prestamped, carries Digital Juice's address. A company interested in learning more about the product simply fills in its name and address and drops the card in the mail.

Anyone who inquires about Digital Juice's products receives a cover letter, information about the advertised product, and a follow-up inquiry card. A copy of the inquiry goes to the appropriate salesperson. Based on knowledge of the territory, the salesperson decides whether a personal follow-up is appropriate. If the inquirer returns the second inquiry card (frequently called a **bounce-back card**), Digital Juice again notifies the salesperson. Then the salesperson can follow up on the lead.

SHOWS, FAIRS, AND MERCHANDISE MARKETS

Many companies display or demonstrate their products at trade shows, conventions, fairs, and merchandise markets. Sales representatives are present to demonstrate products to visitors, many of whom salespeople have not called on before. In some cases a manufacturer lives or dies by how well it does in these special selling situations. MeadWestVaco, a company that manufactures office products such as calendars, depends heavily on the annual national office products

Trade shows and fairs help salespeople discover and qualify leads.

association show. Its salespeople report that selling year-round is easier due to the impression the company makes on prospects at the show. And don't forget that one way to prospect is to simply "walk" the show and meet and learn about people who are working at other booths.

Trade shows are short (usually less than a week), temporary exhibitions of products by manufacturers and resellers. In Europe trade shows are called **trade fairs.** Once the show is over, all vendors pack up and leave. The Consumer Electronics Show showcases U.S. electronics products each year. The more than 2,500 vendors at this show are all manufacturers looking for dealers for their products; the end users of the products are not admitted. Dealers often make an entire year's worth of purchases at the show, so the show is a make-or-break situation for many manufacturers. The New York National Boat Show differs in that it has a dual audience: Vendors exhibit to end users (the boating public) as well as to resellers.

Even firms that do not use resellers may have salespeople involved in trade shows. At many trade shows all attendees are customers. For example, when the National Association of Legal Career Professionals holds its annual convention, it also invites manufacturers of office equipment and other products to exhibit wares. The trade show is an adjunct of the convention, with the audience composed entirely of end users. Progressive companies, like Thomson Reuters, create elaborate booths, develop contests and interesting takeaways, and do on-site demonstrations at trade shows. Its Camp Thomson, a whimsical summer camp-themed booth at the American Association of Law Libraries annual meeting, was very successful in generating buzz and produced over 4,000 actual demonstrations of its offerings.[25]

Merchandise markets are places where suppliers have sales offices and buyers from resellers visit to purchase merchandise. The Dallas Market Center, for example, hosts more than 50 separate markets for children's wear, western apparel, linens, and other soft goods. The sellers are the manufacturers or distributors, and they sell only to resellers, not to the public. Sellers may lease showroom space permanently or only during market weeks. Sellers who lease space permanently usually bring in buyers during off-market periods or when no markets are being held.

Buyers visit many vendors during markets, selecting the products they will carry for the next season. In some industries, almost all sales to resellers occur during markets. These industries include hardware, clothing, toys, and furniture. The major furniture markets are held in San Francisco, Toronto, and High Point, North Carolina. The biggest toy show is held annually in New York City. Major clothing markets are held for each season (such as fall and spring) in New York City, Atlanta, Paris, Dallas, and Los Angeles.

Successful salespeople practice adaptive selling (discussed in Chapter 5) when interacting with prospects who stop by their booths or markets. Thus instead of mechanically asking, Are you enjoying the show? or Can I help you with something today? sharp salespeople try to discover whether the lead has a need or a want they can meet. The seller then gives the lead helpful information and gathers information that will be used later in further qualifying the lead and preparing for a sales call. Timely follow-up of leads is critical if sales are to follow a show.

WEBINARS AND SEMINARS

Many firms use seminars and **webinars** (online seminars) to generate leads and to provide information to prospective customers.[26] For example, a local pharmaceutical representative for Bristol-Myers Squibb will set up a seminar for 8–10 oncologists and invite a nationally known research oncologist to make a presentation. The research specialist usually discusses some new technique or treatment being developed. During or after the presentation, the pharmaceutical representative for Bristol-Myers Squibb might describe how Squibb's drug Taxol helps in the treatment of ovarian and breast cancer.

What are some key things to keep in mind when planning a webinar or seminar? Make sure your seminar appeals to a specialized market and invite good prospects, especially those prospects who might not be willing to see you one-on-one. The subject should be something your attendees have a strong interest in, while your speaker must be considered an authority on the topic. Try to go as high quality as possible (remember, you're building an image) and consider serving food. Finally, you should take an active role before, during, and after the seminar.

LISTS AND DIRECTORIES

Individual sales representatives can develop prospect lists from sources such as public records, telephone directories, chamber of commerce directories, newspapers, trade publications, club membership lists, and professional or trade membership lists. Secondary sources of information from public libraries also can be useful. For example, industrial trade directories are available for all states. It is often useful to know the **standard industrial classification (SIC)** code or the **North America industry classification system (NAICS)** code, which is a uniform classification for all countries in North America, when researching using secondary sources.[27]

Salespeople can purchase a number of prospecting directories and lead-generating publications. You can purchase, by geographical area, mailing lists for all gerontologists (specialists in geriatrics), Lions clubs, T-shirt retailers, yacht owners, antique dealers, Catholic high schools, motel supply houses, multimillionaires, pump wholesalers, and thousands of other classifications. These lists can be delivered as printed mailing labels or secured directly from the Web from such sources as www.salesgenie.com.[28] Salespeople can also use such Web sources as alibaba.com, which claims to be the world's largest business-to-business marketplace, to connect with potential buyers.

Salespeople should keep in mind that lists can have several drawbacks. The lists may not be current. They may contain some inaccurate information regardless of any guarantee of accuracy. People who are on lists may be targeted by many, many firms and thus be less open to hearing from yet another salesperson. Finally, because lists are easy to obtain and use, some salespeople tend to rely on them exclusively when other methods of prospecting might result in better leads. In international selling situations, procuring lists can be much more difficult.

DATA MINING AND CRM SYSTEMS

Sophisticated firms are developing interactive **databases** that contain information about leads, prospects, and customers.[29]. For example, Pioneer, one of the country's largest producers of seed corn, has a dynamic database of 600,000 farm operators in the United States and Canada that everyone in the firm can access. The system has resulted in better sales prospecting and more tailored sales presentations.

Progressive firms are using **data mining**, which consists of artificial intelligence and statistical tools, to discover insights hidden in the volumes of data in their databases. For example, Eagle Equipment of Norton, Massachusetts, uses iMarket software to target its sales calls to the best prospects. Using the company's database, the software identifies prospects most likely to buy something and then matches that profile against a database of 12 million businesses. Chapter 15 more fully examines the use of data mining and databases.

COLD CALLING

Before learning about other prospecting methods, college students often assume salespeople spend most of their time making cold calls. In using the **cold canvass method,** or **cold calls** (by call we usually mean a personal visit, not a telemarketing call), a sales representative tries to generate leads for new business by calling on totally unfamiliar organizations. Historically, this method was used extensively. However, cold calling can waste a salesperson's time because many companies have neither a need for the product nor the ability to pay for it. This fact stresses the importance of qualifying the lead quickly in a cold call so as not to waste time. Also, today cold calling is considered rude by many purchasing agents and other professionals.

Salespeople often rate making cold calls as the part of the job they like least. Thus, as mentioned earlier, most firms now encourage their salespeople to qualify leads instead of relying on cold calls. In fact, Ameriprise banned cold calling for its 8,000 salespeople nationwide over 15 years ago. This policy forced the reps to use other methods, such as networking and referrals. But sometimes firms requires their salespeople to start making cold calls, especially in downtimes. For example, Ted Sperides, a customer service rep at Bankcard Associates, was required, as were all employees, to start making cold calls on prospects during the recent recession. He found that the key to successful cold calling was to generate attention immediately, which he did by claiming that his firm could help the buyer save money in credit card processing fees.[30]

Still, some companies use cold calling. And some companies use a selective type of cold calling they refer to as a **blitz:** A large group of salespeople attempts to call on all the prospective businesses in a given geographical territory on a specified day. For example, an office machine firm may target a specific four-block area in Guadalajara, Mexico; bring in all the salespeople from the surrounding areas; and then have them, in one day, call on every business located in that four-block area. The purpose is to generate leads for the local sales representative as well as to build camaraderie and a sense of unity among the salespeople.

SPOTTERS

Some salespeople use **spotters,** also called **bird dogs.** These individuals will, for a fee, provide leads for the salesperson. The sales rep sometimes pays the fee simply for the name of the lead but more often pays only if the lead ends up buying the product or service. Spotters are usually in a position to find out when someone is ready to make a purchase decision. For example, a janitor who works for a janitorial service company and notices that the heating system for a client is antiquated and hears people complaining about it can turn this information over to a heating contractor.

A more recent development is the use of outside paid consultants to locate and qualify leads. Small firms attempting to secure business with large organizations are most likely to use this approach. For example, Synesis Corporation, a small firm specializing in computerized training, used the services of a consultant to identify and develop leads. The result of one lead was a major contract with AT&T.

Use caution, however, when offering a cash payment to a customer for spotting. Your action may be misconstrued by the customer as exploiting the relationship. Also, some customers' firms may prohibit such behavior. Sometimes it is better to send a personal thank-you note or small gift to the customer instead.

Progressive firms use telemarketers to qualify leads before sending a salesperson on a call.

TELEMARKETING

Increasingly, firms are relying on telemarketing to perform many functions sales representatives used to perform. **Telemarketing** is a systematic and continuous program of communicating with customers and prospects via telephone. Telemarketing is not limited to consumer sales; in fact, all the examples in this section involve business-to-business companies. Telemarketing is now used to sell everything from 25-cent supplies to $10 million airplanes.

In **outbound telemarketing** telephones are used to generate and then qualify leads. These calls may be initiated directly by the salesperson, by inside sales representatives (inside sales reps were discussed in Chapter 1), or by third-party vendors. **Inbound telemarketing** uses a telephone number (usually a toll-free number) that leads and customers can call for additional information. Again, the call may be answered by several types of people: the salesperson, an inside salesperson, or a customer service representative.[31]

Firms combine outbound and inbound telemarketing to prospect effectively. For example, Motorola's Government and Enterprise Division, which sells mobile communication systems to such entities as police stations and fire departments, can use outbound telemarketing to generate and then qualify leads for its sales force. Qualified leads are turned over to field sales representatives if the order is large enough to warrant a personal visit to the company. If the prospect needs a smaller system, a separate telemarketing salesperson will handle the account. Motorola also uses inbound telemarketing by providing a toll-free number for people who want more information about a product or service Motorola offers. Because of this excellent telemarketing organization, Motorola's field reps have more time to spend with qualified prospects and more time to develop long-term customer relations.

Although the telephone is a wonderful tool that can enhance productivity, it also has some limitations. Customers often find telephone calls an annoying inconvenience, which is why up to 75 percent use voice mail to screen their calls.[32] When telephoning customers—in fact, at all times—salespeople need to respect the customers' privacy concerns and the do-not-call rules, as discussed in Chapter 2. Attracting and maintaining the customer's attention and interest is harder over the telephone than it is in person, and prospects may even continue to work or read a report or magazine. While it is true that is it much easier for a prospect to say no over the phone than in person, salespeople should often take that "no" to mean exactly what they say—no, rather than continue to try to badger the prospect into complying.

BECOMING AN EXPERT

Salespeople can prospect by becoming recognized experts in their field, resulting in prospects seeking information from them. Admittedly, that won't happen for most salespeople when they first graduate from college, but over time they can develop their expertise and seek avenues to showcase their talent.

Salespeople have many ways to demonstrate their expertise in a particular subject. Some will engage in public speaking on topics related to their expertise. Speeches at industry conventions, at luncheons and dinners hosted by prospects and industry representatives, and on college campuses provide outlets for expertise to be disseminated.

Salespeople can also demonstrate their expertise in writing. This can take many forms, including writing journal articles, publishing articles in trade publications, hosting a blog, posting on other's blogs, and so forth. One study found that

"71 percent of technology buyers regularly read white papers before making a purchase decision and 57 percent of buyers pass white papers along to colleagues."[33]

SALES LETTERS

Prospecting sales letters can be integrated into an overall prospecting plan. For example, Xerox salespeople who handle smaller businesses send prospecting sales letters every day. They follow up three days later with a telephone prospecting call and ask for an appointment for a personal visit. The telephone call begins with a question about the letter.

Because people in business receive so much mail, sales letters should be written with care. Think about the amount of junk mail and junk e-mail you receive and how much you throw away or delete without a second glance. It's not surprising that the rate of response from mailings can be as low as 2 percent. Sales letters must stand out to be successful.

One way to make sales letters stand out is to include a promotional item with the mailer. Here are some good examples:[34]

- First National Bank of Shreveport, Louisiana, targeted certified public accountants (CPAs) for one mailer. The bank timed the mailers to arrive on April 16, the day after the federal income tax filing deadline. Included in each mailer was a small bottle of wine, a glass, and cheese and crackers—a party kit designed to celebrate the end of tax season. The bank followed up with telephone calls two days later and ultimately gained 21 percent of the CPAs as new customers.

- OfficeMax sent top executives at a large bank a metal suitcase filled with piles of fake money. The box also contained an MP3 player that included videos of how OfficeMax could meet that bank's specific needs.

- Sprint sent top decision makers a personal meeting invitation housed in a specially designed attractive box with a Louisville Slugger bat enclosed. Those who agreed to meetings would receive professional baseball jerseys for their favorite baseball teams.

thinking **it** through

What would be your reaction if you received the Louisville Slugger bat just described as part of a direct mail piece? Would there be a better way to gain your attention in such a mailing? If so, how could a salesperson learn what that would be?

The salesperson must first consider the objective of any written communication (like a sales letter or e-mail message) and the audience. What action does the salesperson desire from the reader? Why would the reader want to undertake that action? Why would the reader not want to undertake the action? These questions help guide the salesperson in writing the letter.

The opening paragraph must grab the reader's attention, just as a salesperson's approach must get a prospect's attention in a face-to-face call. The opening gives the readers a reason to continue reading, drawing them into the rest of the letter. Another way to gain attention is to have a loyal client whom the prospect respects write the introduction (or even the entire letter) for the salesperson. Here's an example of an opening paragraph:

Thanks for stopping by the Datasource booth at the VON San Jose IP Communications Show. I hope you enjoyed the show and had some fun shooting hoops with us! Were you there when one highly energetic attendee shot the basketball clear over into the Mac booth and knocked the presenter's iPhone right out of his hand? You won't believe what he did next! I'll fill you in on the details in a moment, but first I'd like to invite you to something I know you're not going to want to miss.

The next paragraph or two, the body of the letter, considers why the reader would and would not want to take the desired action. Benefits of taking the action should be presented clearly, without jargon, and briefly. The best-presented benefits are tailored to the specific individual, especially when the salesperson can refer to a recent conversation with the reader. A reference such as the following example can truly personalize the letter:

> As you said during our visit at the show, you're looking for a software firm that can work with a small business like yours without making you feel like a second-class citizen. At Datasource, we've committed ourselves to working exclusively with small to midsized firms like yours.

If the salesperson and the buyer do not know each other, part of the body of the letter should be used to increase credibility. References to satisfied customers, market research data, and other independent sources can be used to improve credibility:

> You may have heard that last year we won the prestigious Youcon Achievement Award, presented by the Tennessee Small Business Development Center in recognition for outstanding service specifically to small businesses. In fact, the small businesses themselves are the voters for the award. We're proud of that award because it tangibly reflects the commitment we've shown. And we have dedicated ourselves to continue in that tradition.

The final paragraph should seek commitment to the desired course of action. Whatever the action desired, the letter must specifically ask that it take place. The writer should leave no doubt in the prospect's mind about what he or she is supposed to do. The writer should make the action for the prospect easy to accomplish, fully explain why it should be done now, and end with a positive picture. Here's an example:

> So I want to personally invite you to a free lunch seminar at Datasource. You'll hear from our partners about the very latest solutions to your technology challenges. The food promises to be great, and the information will be presented in a casual, small group setting. Please take a moment to reserve your spot at the lunch by visiting our Web site, www.datasource.com, or calling 800-343-8764. You'll be glad you did.

A postscript (or PS) can also be effective. Postscripts stand out because of their location and should be used to make an important selling point. Alternatively, they can be used to emphasize the requested action, such as pointing out a deadline.

While you are writing, remember to check your work carefully for misspelled words and grammar problems. And read it carefully, because you often don't see problems in a quick glance, as the following paragraph illustrates:[35]

> i cdnuolt blveiee taht I cluod aulaclty uesdnatnrd waht I was rdanieg. The phaonmneal pweor of the hmuan mnid, aoccdrnig to a rscheearch at Cmabrigde Uinervtisy, it dseno't mtaetr in waht oerdr the ltteres in a wrod are, the olny iproamtnt tihng is taht the frsit and lsat ltteer be in the rghit pclae. The rset can be a taotl mses and you can sitll raed it whotuit a pboerlm. Tihs is bcuseae the huamn mnid deos not raed ervey lteter by istlef, but the wrod as a wlohe.

And of course spell check won't catch everything; the following passed with flying colors:[36]

> I have a spelling checker, it came with my PC. It plainly marks four my revenue mistakes I cannot sea. I've run this poem threw it, I'm sure your pleased too no, its letter perfect in it's weigh, my checker tolled me sew.

OTHER SOURCES OF LEADS

Many salespeople find leads through personal observation. For example, by reading trade journals carefully, salespeople can learn the names of the most important leaders (and hence decision makers) in the industry. Sellers also read general business publications (such as *BusinessWeek* and *The Wall Street Journal*) and local newspapers. One salesperson even found a lead while watching a movie; he thought the restaurant featured in the film would be a good prospect for his services, and he was right.[37]

Nonsales employees within the salesperson's firm can also provide leads. Some companies strongly encourage this practice. For example, Computer Specialists Inc., a computer service firm, pays its nonsales employees a bonus of up to $1,000 for any names of prospective customers they pass along. In one year the program resulted in 75 leads and 9 new accounts.

Government agencies can also supply lead information. For example, the Commerce Department in its GLOBUS&NTDB system (www.stat-usa.gov/tradtest .nsf) identifies some of the hottest prospects for aircraft and aircraft parts, construction materials, computers and home electronics, and so forth around the world. The FedBizOpps site provides information about federal government bid opportunities and can be viewed at www.fbo.gov.

Leads can be found in many other places as well. Some prospect while doing something they enjoy, such as belonging to a cycling club.[38] Salespeople for non-competing but related products can often provide leads, as can members of trade associations. You can find leads while volunteering in your community, doing things like helping build a house for Habitat for Humanity. Good friends can also provide leads. Of course one of the best ways to learn about new business opportunities is to keep up with regional, national, and world trends from sources such as *World Watch* magazine and industry surveys (Manufacturing USA, Service USA, Standard & Poor's Industry Surveys, U.S. Industrial Outlook, and the like).

LEAD QUALIFICATION AND MANAGEMENT SYSTEMS

Salespeople need to develop a process for qualifying leads, often called a **lead qualification system.** As mentioned early in this chapter, salespeople must ensure that their leads meet the five basic criteria of a prospect. Let's look more closely at this process.

Many firms view prospecting as a funneling process in which a large number of leads are funneled (or narrowed down) into prospects and some, finally, into customers.[39] Marketing often generates these leads, but it is interesting that 80 percent of leads thus generated by marketing departments are not followed up by salespeople.[40]

Salespeople can get leads during volunteering activities.

To help salespeople use their time wisely, and to increase the number of leads that sellers actually follow up with, some firms engage in **prequalification** of leads before turning them over to the field sales force. Sometimes the prequalification process is as simple as purchasing a prequalified list. At other times a firm will use the resources of telemarketers to prequalify leads. Many lead qualification systems assign points to a prospect, rather than simply designating them as hot or cold, offering the salesperson more insight into the lead's value.[41]

LEAD SCORING HELPED ONE COMPANY ACHIEVE GREATER SUCCESS

Prosper Inc. is a highly successful company that provides services like career coaching and mentoring to entrepreneurs who wish to start businesses in such fields as e-commerce and real estate. Although the company was doing well, the business model required a continual influx of new recruits for its programs. The company had a number of lead-generating activities, but Prosper Inc.'s sales reps were losing interest in the leads they were given. Why? The leads just didn't seem to be panning out for the sales reps.

The solution? Prosper Inc. teamed up with TARGUSinfo for assistance in lead management. TARGUSinfo has a unique system of predictive analytics that scores leads by their potential to purchase across a wide range of

products and services. With the new system, Prosper sales reps were provided leads with meaningful and actionable quality scores, like the following: prime, standard, subprime, and reject.

The results? Prosper Inc. tripled its dollar revenue per lead and doubled its rate of converting leads to actual customers. Sales reps spend more time with a smaller number of leads. Prosper doesn't waste time and money with lead-generating systems that don't provide leads that turn into profits. Needless to say, Prosper is tickled with its new system.

Sources: prosperlearning.com; targusinfo.com; "Turning Prospects into Profits," Peppers & Rogers Group white paper, 2009.

Salespeople must not only qualify leads but also carefully analyze the relative value of each lead.[42] This part of the process is called a **lead management system,** which is discussed more fully in Chapter 15. Part of the decision process often includes a valuation of the prospects' expected customer lifetime value or return on investment, as well as an appraisal of what types of value the selling firm can add to the prospect. Grading prospects and establishing a priority list result in increased sales and the most efficient use of time and energy. Not doing so can cause salespeople to waste their time. Recent research shows that "at any given time, 65 percent of salespeople are pursing worthless deals."[43] There is even an association dedicated to helping companies manage their leads more effectively: the Sales Lead Management Association.[44] "Sales Technology 6.1" describes how one company tripled its revenue thanks to better lead scoring.[45]

The judicious use of technology makes lead qualification and management more efficient and effective. Most salespeople now use laptops and software packages to keep track of leads. And this is often tied into a large, complete corporate system for managing prospects and salespeople's time and territories (Chapter 15 discusses this issue more fully). For example, IBM has tied its lead generation and management system into its CRM system. The results have been better tracking and prioritization of leads and prospects.

Any good lead management system, like IBM's, should evaluate the profitability of sales resulting from various lead-generating activities instead of just counting the number of names a particular method yields. Analysis may show that the present system does not produce enough prospects or the right kinds of prospects. Salespeople may, for example, depend entirely on referred names from company advertising or from the service department. If these two sources do not supply enough names to produce the sales volume and profits desired, other prospecting methods should be considered. A salesperson should not hesitate to scrap time-honored prospecting systems even if they have been used for years in the firm or industry or even by the salesperson's own sales manager. Interestingly, a recent study found

Salespeople must learn how to overcome a reluctance to prospect.

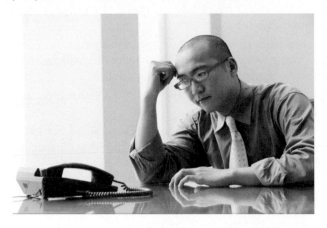

that the majority of sales organizations do not have a formal process in place for determining when to stop pursing a prospective client.[46]

OVERCOMING A RELUCTANCE TO PROSPECT

People often stereotype salespeople as bold, adventurous, and somewhat abrasive. This view that salespeople are fearless is more fiction than fact. Salespeople often struggle with a reluctance to prospect that persists no matter how well they have been trained and how much they believe in the products they sell. Many people are uncomfortable when they initially contact other people, but for salespeople reluctance to call can be a career-threatening condition.

Research shows a number of reasons for reluctance to call.[47] Reasons include worrying about worst-case scenarios; spending too much time preparing; being overly concerned with looking successful; being fearful of making group presentations, of appearing too pushy, of losing friends or losing family approval, and of using the phone for prospecting; feeling intimidated by people with prestige or power or feeling guilt at having a career in selling; and having a compulsive need to argue, make excuses, or blame others.

A recent study investigated sales call anxiety, of which sales prospecting would be one component. The authors discovered four dimensions of sales call anxiety: a negative self-evaluation by the salesperson ("I will be nervous and forget what I want to say"), imagined negative evaluations from customers ("If I don't know the answers to all her questions, she's going to think I'm stupid"), a salesperson's physiological symptoms ("I'm sweating and blushing and my hands are cold"), and a desire to perform safety-seeking behaviors (avoiding eye contact, speaking quickly, fiddling with the hands, and ultimately withdrawing from contact with the prospect).

Reluctance to call can and must be overcome to sell successfully. Several activities can help:[48]

- Start by listening to the excuses other salespeople give to justify their call reluctance behavior. Evaluate their validity. Then identify the excuses you use to avoid making calls and evaluate the validity of those excuses. You'll usually be surprised to find that most excuses really aren't valid.

- Engage in sales training and role-playing activity to improve your prospecting skills and your ability to handle questions and rejections that arise.

- Make prospecting contacts with a supporting partner or sales manager. Just their presence will often provide additional needed confidence (you won't feel so alone).

- Set specific goals for all your prospecting activity. Put them in your "to do" list. Chapter 15 will provide more direction in this activity.

- Realize the economic value of most prospecting activities.[49] For example, if you keep good records, you may discover that every phone call you make (regardless of whether that particular prospect buys) results in an average of $22 commission in the long run.

- Stop negative self-evaluations from ruling your behavior. Learn to think positively about the future instead of focusing on your past blunders.

- Remember that you are calling on prospects to solve their needs, not just so you can line your pocket with money. You are performing a vital, helpful, important service to your prospects by calling on them. (If this isn't true, maybe you should find another sales job.)
- Control your perceptions of what prospects might say about you, your company, or your products. You don't know what their reactions will be until you meet with the prospects. Leads do buy from salespeople.
- Learn and apply relaxation and stress-reducing techniques that you can implement before and during prospecting.
- Recount your own prospecting successes or those of others. Read books by people who have prospected successfully or creatively. Realize that persistence pays off in the long run.

SELLING YOURSELF

It's time to put the material in this chapter to some practical uses, like getting your first job out of college. Students often wonder how to find companies to work for. This chapter provides all the clues you need.

First, remember that for a company to be a real prospect for you (and your services as an employee) you need to meet its needs and wants in some real and meaningful way. And of course what that implies is this: If you don't have the skills or experience that a company is looking for, move on to other companies, even if it is a great company to work for and even if it pays good salaries. Otherwise you're just wasting your time.

So what are some sources of prospects for a job? As the chapter related, some of your best chances may be with companies you've worked for while in college, maybe as an intern or even as an hourly employee of some kind. They know you and what you can offer them, and if you've done a good job, then they'll likely try to hire you.

Network like crazy. Keep your ears open, and every time there is a speaker on campus from a potential employer, go to that speech and get the person's business card (and follow up after the speech with an e-mail message or letter). Also attend club meetings, and be sharp while speakers are visiting in your classes. The speakers are checking you out, whether you know it or not. As you volunteer, don't be afraid to exchange contact information with others who might be volunteering at the same time. And don't be afraid to use family and friends as part of your network. Some students hesitate to use these sources; they say they prefer to get a job on their own. But why close down a good source of leads just for pride?

Attend every job fair you can, as early in college as possible, even way before you're ready to look for a job. Use social media as described in this chapter to network and build connections. And ask to link into your professors' and the school's alumni network because there are probably some good connections there.

Don't forget the old standbys, like your college's career services center, doing Web searches, and writing letters to companies. These are still great ways to secure your first job right out of college.

SUMMARY

Locating prospective customers is the first step in the sales process. New prospects are needed to replace old customers lost for a variety of reasons and to replace contacts lost in existing customers because of plant relocations, turnover, mergers, downsizing, and other factors.

Not all sales leads qualify as good prospects. A qualified prospect has a need that can be satisfied by the salesperson's product, has the ability and authority to buy the product, can be approached by the salesperson, and is eligible to buy.

Many methods can be used to locate prospects. The best source is a satisfied customer. Salespeople can also use the endless-chain method, networking, social media, lists and directories, cold canvassing (including blitzes), spotters, and becoming known as experts via blogs, speeches, and so forth. Companies provide leads to salespeople through promotional activities such as the Internet, inquiries from advertising and direct mail, telemarketing, trade shows, merchandise markets, and webinars/seminars.

Effective prospecting requires a strong plan that hinges on developing a lead qualification and management system and overcoming reluctance to prospect.

KEY TERMS

banner advertising   161
bird dog   165
blitz   165
bounce-back card   162
buying community   159
center-of-influence method   159
cold call   165
cold canvass method   165
databases   164
data mining   164
endless-chain method   157
e-selling   162
exclusive sales territories   153
extranet   162
house accounts   154
inbound telemarketing   166
lead   150
lead management system   170
lead qualification system   169
merchandise market   163
negative referral   157

networking   157
North America industry classification system (NAICS)   164
outbound telemarketing   166
postcard pack   162
prequalification   169
promoters   156
prospect   151
prospecting   150
qualifying a lead   151
referral event   156
referred lead   157
search engines   161
selling deeper   156
spotter   165
standard industrial classification (SIC)   164
systems integrator   153
telemarketing   166
trade fair   163
trade show   163
webinars   164

ETHICS PROBLEMS

1. Suppose your sales manager says the following to you: "Look, I know how to prospect effectively! After all, I've been selling for 25 years, haven't I? And you're just starting to sell. So here's what I expect you to do. I want you to make 10 cold calls every day. That's all. Just start knocking on doors. Oh yeah, and report them on this call sheet." As you reflect on what he said, you are confused and anxious. You feel there are much better ways of prospecting than just relying on cold calling. What will you do? What, if anything, will you say to your sales manager?

2. Some people feel obligated to provide a salesperson with at least one referral when a salesperson uses the endless-chain method of prospecting, even though they don't really want to do so. Why? Because they want to be polite. What are the ethical implications of this for the salesperson asking for the referrals? What would you do if you sensed though nonverbal cues that someone was hesitant to offer any names?

QUESTIONS AND PROBLEMS

1. Describe a referral event that could be created, assuming you are a member of a club in your college. Your target market for new leads consists of students not currently members in that club.

2. Negative referrals are certainly not what a salesperson wants. Think of a time when you acted as a negative referral for a product or service or company. Why did you do it? What could the company or salesperson have done to cause you to not be a negative referral?

3. What things would concern you about prospecting? How will you deal with those concerns?

4. Assume you are a commercial printer who specializes in printing elaborate four-color books, posters, booklets, and the like. Whom might you use as paid spotters to generate leads?

5. Reluctance to prospect is a real phenomenon. What can you do now (and avoid doing now), while you're in school, to avoid being reluctant to prospect when you become a salesperson?

6. Assume you sell gasoline-powered chain saws. Locate at least one merchandise mart and one trade show or fair where you might be able to display your products.

7. How would you develop a prospect list under the following situations?
   a. You belong to a Kiwanis Club that needs to recruit new members.
   b. You sell a new software program that allows the user to fill out any standard business form online, rather than having to use a typewriter.

8. "Sales Technology 6.1" illustrated the benefits of a lead scoring system. Assume you are starting a career as a stockbroker. Develop a system for rating prospects. The system should contain several important factors for qualifying prospects and scales with which to rate the prospects on these factors. Use the system to rate five of your friends.

9. "Building Partnerships 6.1" described how one salesperson encountered an ethical dilemma: to tell the insurance company about the deer collision or not. One of his options was just to pay for the repairs to the truck out of his own pocket. Had he taken that option, he would be $21,800 richer ($23,000 in commission minus $1,200 in repair costs). Would you have taken this approach? Other than the $21,800 commission, what are some other reasons why you might want to take this approach? What are some negatives of taking this approach?

10. If you were a salesperson for the following, how would you develop a prospect list?
    a. A new line of ceiling fans that are energy-efficient.
    b. A travel agency specializing in vacations to Mexico.
    c. A manufacturer of an theft deterrent device for televisions.

CASE PROBLEMS

case **6.1**

123 Flash Chat

Most firms want employees to offer suggestions for improvement. To accomplish that, most use one of the following two methods: a suggestion box or questionnaires given out to employees. The beauty of such a system is its ease of use and the fact that it is relatively inexpensive. The disadvantage of suggestion boxes and surveys is that many employees refuse to take the time to participate. And it can often seem as though managers aren't reading the comments anyway.

Eric Reed is a salesperson for 123 Flash Chat. Flash Chat gives employees an anonymous, time-friendly way to chat with each other and managers, using an online discussion group format. The software program has many features that would be of benefit to firms, including ease of use, ease of setup and customization, password protection, complete firewall protection, no extra plug-in software needed, fully featured chat functions, moderator control features, and multilingual support.

Eric is ready to sell this program to businesses and organizations in Spokane, Washington. But first he needs prospects. He started working for Flash Chat this week, and the program hasn't been sold in this marketplace before.

Questions

1. Which prospecting methods do you think Eric should use?
2. How should Eric qualify the leads he finds? Which qualifying factors will be most important?
3. How should Eric organize his prospecting activities? How can he keep good records?

Source: 123flashchat.com.

case 6.2

Town and Country Resort and Convention Center

Located in the heart of San Diego, the Town and Country Resort and Convention Center has been in business for over 50 years and is billed as one of Mission Valley's largest and best resorts. The Town and Country is known for its luxurious accommodations, amenities that business executives cherish, and meticulous attention to the needs of meeting participants as well as convention delegates. Guests can stay in over 1,000 guest rooms either in traditional hotel towers or in cozy ranch-style garden bungalows. The resort hosts five restaurants, three swimming pools, a European health spa and fitness center, scenic gardens with 1,500 rosebushes and 2,000 palm trees, movies on the lawn in summer, an adjacent 27-hole golf course, and many exhibit halls, ballrooms, and meeting rooms. There are over 250,000 square feet of flexible meeting space. The resort is only minutes from Old Town with a trolley stop on the property. You can learn much more about the Town and Country from its Web site.

Assume you are a salesperson for the Town and Country. Your goal is to book meetings and conventions from businesses and not-for-profit organizations.

Questions

1. Provide a list of company names and addresses of five actual leads for the Town and Country. You don't have to know whether the leads already have used the Town and Country. Explain where you got the list of leads.
2. Develop the details of an appropriate referral event for the Town and Country. Provide information about the place of the event as well as what should happen during the event. Be creative. Remember that referral events should be fun for current clients as well as leads.

Source: http://www.towncountry.com/index.html.

ROLE PLAY CASE

As a NetSuite salesperson, how can you help your buyer prospect better? Think about how NetSuite might be able to help your buyer develop a comprehensive prospecting system, from lead generation to making the first appointment. One way that NetSuite can help is to automate direct mail. Using the database that salespeople create, the marketing department can send mail to every contact who meets certain criteria. For example, it can select an industry and send a letter only to prospects in that industry. Similarly, NetSuite provides reporting capabilities. Salespeople can see how effective they are at each method of prospecting and then focus their efforts on the methods that work the best. These are only some ideas—you may want to visit the Web site for more or think about how the concepts in the chapter can help your account.

Using the same account you've been selling to (Spear One, McLane Properties, Dart Paper Products), write out some questions you'd like to ask your buyer to determine how he or she prospects now and how NetSuite might help. (*Note:* If you have not done role plays before, you will need to review the information about the various role play customers that can be found at the end of Chapter 3.)

Then role-play with your buyer, trying to determine her or his needs for assistance with prospecting. Once you've identified those needs, give a short presentation about how NetSuite can help. Your professor will pass out buyer sheets.

Note: For background information about these role plays, please see page 27.

To the instructor: Additional information needed to complete the role play is available in the Instructor's Manual.

ADDITIONAL REFERENCES

Allen, Jeff F., and Gary D. McGugan. *NEEDS Selling Solutions.* Trafford Publishing, 2009.

Baber, Anne, and Lynne Waymon. *Make Your Contacts Count: Networking Know-How for Business and Career Success.* AMACOM/American Management Association, 2007.

Balfour, Frederik. "You Say Guanxi, I Say Schmoozing." *Business Week,* November 19, 2007, pp. 84–85.

Barker, Julie. "At Trade Shows, Listen Up." *Sales & Marketing Management,* November/December 2007, p. 12.

Blythe, Jim. "Trade Fairs as Communication: A New Model." *Journal of Business and Industrial Marketing* 25, no. 1 (2010), pp. 57–62.

Brogan, Chris. *Social Media 101: Tactics and Tips to Develop Your Business Online.* Wiley, 2010.

Caramanico, Dan, Marie Maguire, and Dave Kurlan. *The Optimal Salesperson: Mastering the Mindset of Sales Superstars and Overachievers.* LINX Corp., 2009.

Davies, Andrew, Tim Brady, and Michael Hobday. "Organizing for Solutions: Systems Seller vs. Systems Integrator." *Industrial Marketing Management* 36, no. 2 (February 2007), pp. 183–93.

"Delivering Quality Leads, Not Just Quantity." *CRM Magazine* 13, no. 3 (March 2009), pp. 3–6.

Dunn, Troy. "Keep It Casual and See Clients Flock to You." *Advertising Age* 79, no. 18 (2008), p. 52.

Farquharson B. "'Frigg Friday' and Other New Days." *Graphic Arts Monthly* 80, no. 1 (January 2008), p. 47.

Fitzgerald, Michael. "Let's Get Together: Making Contacts with Social Nets." *Inc.,* August 2007, pp. 54–55.

Godson, Mark. *Relationship Marketing.* Oxford University Press, 2009.

Greenberg, Kevin. "Managing Social Customers for Profit." *CRM Magazine* 13, no. 8 (August 2009), p. 1.

Gu, Flora F., Kineta Hung, and David K. Tse. "When Does Guanxi Matter? Issues of Capitalization and Its Dark Sides." *Journal of Marketing* 72, no. 4 (2008), pp. 12–28.

Hardy, Quentin. "Networking for Profit, Not Fun." *Forbes* 8 (December 2008), p. 85.

Homburg, Christian. "Customer Prioritization: Does It Pay Off, and How Should It Be Implemented?" *Journal of Marketing* 72, no. 5 (2008), pp. 110–30.

Jaffe, Joseph. *Flip the Funnel: How to Use Existing Customers to Gain New Ones.* Wiley, 2010.

Kazanjian, Kirk. *Exceeding Customer Expectations.* New York: Currency Doubleday, 2007.

Lager, M. "Looking to SCORE." *CRM Magazine* 13, no. 3 (March 2009), pp. 38–42.

Lee, Chang Hyun, and Sang Yong Kim. "Differential Effects of Determinants on Multi-Dimensions of Trade Show Performance: By Three Stages of Pre-Show, At-Show, and Post-Show Activities." *Industrial Marketing Management* 37, no. 7 (October 2008), pp. 784–96.

McCord, Paul. *Creating a Million-Dollar-a-Year Sales Income: Sales Success through Client Referrals.* Wiley, 2007.

Misner, Ivan, David Alexander, and Brian Hilliard. *Networking Like a Pro: Turning Contacts into Connections.* Entrepreneur Press, 2010.

Mrazek, Debbie. "How to Evolve beyond Networking into the 'R Zone.'" *American Salesman* 52, no. 12 (December 2007), pp. 27–30.

Obermayer, James. *Managing Sales Leads: Turning Cold Prospects into Hot Customers.* South-Western Educational Publishing, 2007.

Pugatch, Courtney Beth. "Digging for New Sales." *Response* 16, no. 1 (October 2007), pp. 50–54.

Reinders, Adrie, and Marion Freijsen. *The N Factor: How Efficient Networking Can Change the Dynamics of Your Business.* WBusiness Books, 2007.

"Salesforce.com Rolls Out Social-Networking-Like Tools: The 'Salesforce to Salesforce' On-Demand Services Are Built on Salesforce.com's Multi-Tenant Architecture and Force.com Platform." *Information Week,* December 5, 2007.

Saxon, Albert. "It's All in the Mind." *Direct* 19, no. 9 (September 1, 2007), p. 10.

Schep, Brad. *How to Find a Job on LinkedIn, Facebook, Twitter, MySpace, and Other Social Networks.* McGraw-Hill, 2009.

Schiffman, Stephan. *E-Mail Selling Techniques That Really Work!* Adams Media Corporation, 2007.

Sittig-Rolf, Andrea. *Power Referrals: The Ambassador Method for Empowering Others to Promote Your Business and Do the Selling for You.* McGraw-Hill, 2008.

Smith, Robert. *RUSH.* iUniverse, 2009.

Sneider, Mark. "A Better Way to Generate Leads." *Sales & Marketing Management,* July/August 2008, p. 9.

"Turning Prospects into Profits: Using Lead Management Innovation to Win Customers" (white paper). Peppers & Rogers Group, 2009, http://www.peppersandrogersgroup.com, accessed March 5, 2010.

Werb, Jessica. "How to Network." *BC Business* 35, no. 5 (May 2007), p. 19.

Wilson, David James. *Prospecting 101: The Ultimate Guide to Prospect Successfully to Super Grow Your Pipeline or Business.* CreateSpace, 2009.

Xu, Jun, and Mohammed Quaddus. *E-Business in the 21st Century: Realities, Challenges and Outlook.* World Scientific Publishing Company, 2010.

Zimmerman, Kevin. "Relationships at the End of Their Rope." *1to1 Magazine,* July/August 2008, pp. 33–35.

chapter

7

PLANNING THE SALES CALL

SOME QUESTIONS ANSWERED IN THIS CHAPTER ARE

- Why should salespeople plan their sales calls?
- What precall information is needed about the individual prospect and the prospect's organization?
- How can this information be obtained?
- What is involved in setting call objectives?
- Should more than one objective be set for each call?
- How can appointments be made effectively and efficiently?

2

PART

PROFILE

"The most important aspect of preparing for a sales call is ensuring that you know your audience and understand their needs."

Marcel Dalby

PROFILE My name is Marcel Dalby, and I graduated from Texas State University–San Marcos in 2005 with a bachelor's degree in business administration. Throughout my studies at Texas State the course I learned the most from was Professional Selling, led by Vicki West. This course took sales training and preparation to the next level by challenging the students with real-world scenarios through role play sales calls, interview preparation, and mock sales presentations. This hands-on training helped me to widen my sales skills, which have benefited me in my career at Waste Management where I have worked as an operations improvement manager for five years.

For an operations manager at Waste Management, you might wonder how sales skills have benefitted me in an operations role. When I first started my career with Waste Management, a 30-year veteran operations manager told me, "We are all in sales. Whether you are selling products or services directly to a potential customer or working in a manufacturing or operations role, we all have ideas we want to sell to others." He is right. The skills you learn from this text and course will help you in all aspects of your career, not just selling products or service.

Within my role as an operations manager with Waste Management, I often find myself in meetings in which I am trying to sell my ideas or process changes to coworkers. My role also requires me to participate in sales meetings with many of our larger customers or perspective customers. Regardless of the type of sale I am trying to make, the most important aspect of the meeting is ensuring that I have properly prepared for the call. There are several things to consider when preparing for a sales call.

The most important aspect of preparing for a sales call is ensuring that you know your audience and understand their needs. Prior to the sales meeting, it is critical that I have gathered as much information as possible about the prospects, their needs and desires, and any potential concerns they may have. An important part of gathering this information is knowing buyers as individuals and understanding their personalities and attitudes along with their goals and objectives. What is the customer's biggest concern: price, quality, service level guarantee? What selling style does this buyer prefer? How can I show this customer that I am best suited to meet his or her goals and objectives? Another piece of this information gathering includes reviewing my product knowledge and understanding what levels of services or equipment I can offer to the customer. This allows me to be as flexible as possible to ensure that I am offering the best solution available to meet the goals of the customer.

Another important step when planning a sales call is to set objectives. These objectives must be specific, measurable, and realistic. It is important to know if the objective of the call is to simply introduce the product, service, or idea and discuss potential concerns or if the objective is to close the sale. Often the complexity and scale of the product, service, or idea will be the determining factor when setting these objectives. For example, if I am meeting for the first time with a large school district to review their operational specifications, service levels, and overall equipment needs, it would not be reasonable to expect the customer to be positioned to finalize the sale during that meeting. On the other hand, if I am meeting with a small "mom-and-pop" restaurant to discuss these things, my objective would be to make the sale during that meeting.

Following these steps when preparing for a sales call or preparing to meet with a coworker to share ideas has helped me to be successful in my career with Waste Management.

Visit our Web site at www.wm.com.

Exhibit 7.1
A Flow Diagram of the
Planning Process

| Gathering information about the prospect and firm | Setting objectives for the call | Making an appointment |

WHY PLAN THE SALES CALL?

Successful salespeople know that advance planning of the sales interview is essential to achieve in selling. The salesperson should remember that the buyer's time is valuable. Without planning the sales call, a salesperson may cover material in which the buyer has no interest, try to obtain an order even though that is an unrealistic expectation for this sales call, or strike off into areas that veer from what the buyer needs to hear. The results are wasted time and an annoyed prospect. However, by having a clear plan for the call, the salesperson more likely will not only obtain commitment but also win the buyer's respect and confidence.

Salespeople should also remember the value of their own time. Proper planning helps them meet their call objectives efficiently and effectively. They then have more time to make additional calls, conduct research on customers, fill out company reports, and complete other necessary tasks. The result is better territory management. (See Chapter 15 for more discussion of time and territory management.)

Of course planning must fit into the salesperson's goals for the account. Some accounts have greater strategic importance and thus require more planning. (See Chapter 13 for a discussion of the types of relationships that a seller can have with a buyer and Chapter 15 about classifying accounts and prospects.) Accounts with which a firm is partnering obviously need the most planning, whereas smaller accounts may warrant less planning. Also, salespeople must not make planning an end in itself and a way to avoid actually making calls. Exhibit 7.1 shows how the concepts in this chapter are related.

OBTAINING PRECALL INFORMATION

Often the difference between making and not making a sale depends on the amount of homework the salesperson does before making a call. The more information the salesperson has about the prospect, the higher the probability of meeting the prospect's needs and developing a long-term relationship. However, the salesperson must be aware of the costs involved in collecting information. At some point, the time and effort put into collecting information become greater than the benefits obtained. And of course, for some cold calls, there will be little if any precall information collected.

Clearly a salesperson who has been calling regularly on a prospect or customer may not need to collect a lot of additional information; records and notes from prior calls may be adequate to prepare for the sales call. The same holds true for a new salesperson if the previous one kept good records. But beware! In this fast-paced world, things are changing every day. Consider the following dialogue:

SALESPERSON [*walking up to the receptionist of one of his best customers*]: Hello, Jim. I'm here

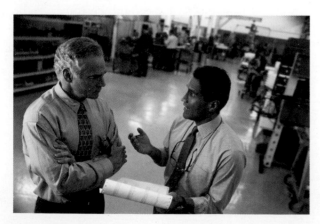

Gathering information from individuals in the prospect's firm before making a call on the prospect is often a wise investment of time.

to see Toby. I have some information I promised to share with her about our new manufacturing process. She was pretty excited about seeing it!

RECEPTIONIST [*looking tired*]: Sorry, Jeff. Toby was transferred last week to our Toronto plant. Haven't you heard about our latest reorganization? Just went into effect two weeks ago. I'm still trying to figure it out. It seems that all our engineering people are moving to the Toronto site.

The key: Don't assume that your knowledge about the account is automatically up to date.

Of course, before you make an initial call on an important prospect, you will often expend considerable effort in collecting precall information about both the individual prospect and the prospect's company. Don't expect this information gathering to be quick, easy, or cheap.

It is important to learn and maintain current knowledge about both the prospect as an individual and his or her firm. The sections that follow examine these areas more closely. Of course the salesperson should keep in mind privacy concerns, as related in Chapter 2.

THE PROSPECT/CUSTOMER AS AN INDIVIDUAL

Salespeople should attempt to learn the following types of information about a prospect or a customer:

Personal (Some of This Information Can Be Confidential)

- Name (including pronunciation).
- Family status.
- Education.
- Aspirations.
- Interests (such as hobbies) and disinterests.
- Social style (driver or another category—see Chapter 5).

Attitudes

- Toward salespeople.
- Toward your company.
- Toward your product.

Relationships

- Formal reporting relationships.
- Important reference groups and group norms.
- Bonds that the prospect has already formed with other salespeople.

Evaluation of Products/Services

- Product attributes that are important.
- Product evaluation process (see Chapter 3 for details).

THE PROSPECT'S/CUSTOMER'S ORGANIZATION

Information about the prospect's or customer's company obviously helps the salesperson understand the customer's environment. This type of information lets the salesperson identify problem areas more quickly and respond accordingly.

For example, in a modified rebuy situation, it would not be necessary to educate the prospect about general features common to the product class as a whole. Using the prospect's valuable time by covering material he or she already knows is minimized. Information like the following about the prospect's organization would be helpful:

Demographics

- Type of organization (manufacturing, wholesaling, retailing).
- Size; number of locations.
- Products and services offered.
- Financial position and its future.
- Overall culture of the organization (risk averse, highest ethical standards, forward thinking).

Prospect's Customers

- Types (consumers, retailers, wholesalers). "From the Buyer's Seat 7.1" illustrates how salespeople use this information to provide company-specific suggestions to buyers.
- Benefits they seek from the prospect's products and services.

Prospect's Competitors

- Who they are.
- How they differ in their business approaches.
- Prospect's strategic position in the industry (dominant, strong, weak).

Historical Buying Patterns

- Amount purchased in the product category.
- Sole supplier or multiple suppliers. Why?
- Reason for buying from present suppliers.
- Level of satisfaction with suppliers.
- Reasons for any dissatisfaction with suppliers or products currently purchased.

Current Buying Situation

- Type of buying process (new task, straight rebuy, or modified rebuy—see Chapter 3).
- Strengths and weaknesses of potential competitors.

People Involved in the Purchase Decision

- How they fit into the formal and informal organizational structure. Note that the number of people involved in purchasing decisions is increasing (by an average of 3.5 people in just four years).
- Their roles in this decision (gatekeeper, influencer, or the like).
- Who is most influential.
- Any **influential adversaries** (carry great influence but are opposed to us)?
- Current problems the organization faces.
- Stage in the buying cycle.

From the BUYER'S SEAT

"HONESTLY, THESE 'TWIN-TIPS' AND 'FULL TILTS' ARE JUST WHAT YOU NEED"

By Jeff Kramer, Christy's

As a buyer at a Christy's, a snowboard and ski shop, I see a lot of salespeople. Some are lousy, some are good, and then some are very good. The ones who are very good are those who really know my store and what my needs are. They plan before coming to see me and know exactly what my store needs. Let me give you a few examples.

Jeri is the sales rep for Volkl and has worked closely with our store from the day it opened seven years ago. Volkl came out with a new line of winter outerwear, and Jeri obviously wanted to get them in our store. But rather than just walk in and try to sell us the entire line of clothing, she first spent the time to carefully examine our customer base and what kinds of items we currently carry. Then, and only then, did she give her presentation, outlining for each item why she thought it would sell at Christy's. I can't tell you how much I appreciated that! She saved us a ton of time and trouble. I estimate if she hadn't done that, we would have foundered at least a year trying to figure out what items were going to sell in our store, and which ones just weren't made for our customer base. And needless to say, her new line is selling very well!

John is another one of my top sales representatives— you know, the kind that you're happy to see walk in the store, and not one that you dread talking to. John works for Atomic, and his line has traditionally done very well in our store. But in the past year, the line wasn't selling like we had hoped. What had changed? Our customer base! John realized that, due to strategic decisions we had made and the lines we were promoting heavily, our customer base had moved from a more traditional type of entry-level and intermediate skier and snowboarder, to those who demanded cutting-edge technology and style. In essence our highest-selling lines went from traditional to more freestyle. John recognized that fact and suggested we stop carrying so much inventory in traditional skis and focus more on trendy items. Specifically, he suggested we carry a wider selection of twin-tip skis and full-tilt boots. And he was dead-on. His new line sold well, and everyone was happy.

You might think that all sellers would take the approach Jeri and John did. If so, you'd be wrong.

Source: Jeff Kramer, Christy's, personal correspondence; used with permission. Names have been changed to protect confidentiality.

Policies and Procedures

- About salespeople.
- About sales visits.
- About purchasing and contracts.

thinking **it** through

It's your first week on the job as a new salesperson. Your sales manager tells you to collect a lot of information about the prospects you call on, including their preferred political party and their children's names. What would be your reaction to her request? If you didn't want to ask these personal questions, how would you approach the situation with your manager?

SOURCES OF INFORMATION

Gathering all the information listed in the preceding sections for every prospect and organization is initially impossible. The goal is to gather what is both possible and profitable. Remember, your time is valuable! Also, you don't want to fall into the trap sometimes referred to as **analysis paralysis,** which can occur if you prefer to spend practically all your time analyzing situations and finding information instead of making sales calls. Salespeople must strike a proper balance between time spent in acquiring information and time spent making calls. The Marine Corps teaches what it calls the 70 percent solution: If you've got 70 percent of the information, have done 70 percent of the analysis, and feel 70 percent confident, then act!

It is important to gather useful information—not just piles of trivial facts about a prospect. In addition, salespeople need to check the quality of any data gathered rather than assuming they are good. Salespeople must also be concerned about information overload, which can be detrimental to their jobs.

RESOURCES WITHIN YOUR COMPANY

One of the best sources of information can be the records in your own company, especially if your firm has developed a sophisticated CRM database, as described in Chapter 6.[1] The most useful databases include (in addition to standard demographic information) information about any direct inquiries made by the prospect (from direct mail inquiries, telemarketing, online requests, or the like), a sales history for the firm, whether anyone from your company has called on the prospect, and the results of any sales meetings.

Firms are devising many ways to keep the field sales force well informed. Some are using **sales portals:** online databases that include many sources of information in one place. This information can include items like account data, competitor intelligence, and news about the company, the industry, and the economy. All the salesperson has to do is use a single log-on to access all this information. For example, Continental's salespeople can log into their company's portal and quickly and easily access key insights about their business customers. Lufthansa Airlines salespeople can do the same thing, easily viewing real-time information about key customers. Rubbermaid has asked its entire sales team to record all internal communications and transaction details online. Keebler gives its sales reps an online database of trends, information, and presentation templates.

Even if your firm doesn't have such a database, you should try to gather information about your prospect. For example, wouldn't it be nice to find out before, as opposed to during, a sales call that the prospect used to be a big customer of your firm but quit for some reason?

For important sales, you may well be working with a sales team that interacts with a prospect (a topic more fully addressed in Chapter 16). This team, sometimes called a **selling center,** consists of all the people in the selling organization who participate in a selling opportunity. Members of the team may be able to provide or help you secure needed information.

THE INTERNET

A first place to look for information would be the prospect company's own Web page. It is amazing what you can find on company Web pages.

Salespeople should consider additional sources like Hoover's Web site. A salesperson could easily search by company name, ticker symbol, keywords, or a person's last name for each of the public and private organizations listed, including U.S. and international firms. For each company, there is a brief overview, a company profile, stock quotes, a list of officers, financial data, links to its Web site(s), links to press releases, and a listing of and automatic links to its major competitors. The seller could also peruse news (from Hoover's own files, plus automatic links to all major news services) or easily link to any other major Web search engine to find out more about the company, the market, or specific

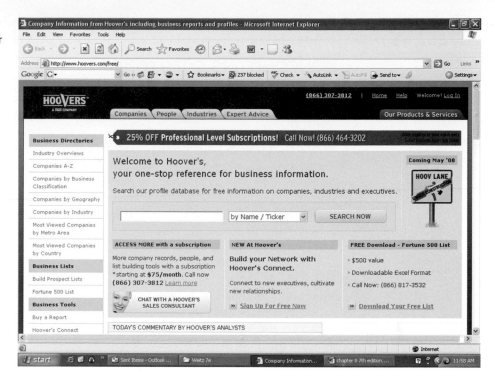

industries. News articles often include information about the firm's strategy, new product launches, plans for division changes, lawsuits, new investments, competitive challenges, and so on. To learn more about the prospect's industry, the seller can read an analysis of industry sectors, including industry snapshots, key players, trends, definitions, and links to other industry views. There are even online prospecting tools (including databases of leads, requests for proposals from firms, and industry-specific contact information).

Keep in mind that much of this information is free (for a fee you can get even more information from Hoover's, including information about over 12 million companies) and comes from just one source. Now multiply that by the thousands of online information sources that a salesperson can access, and you can see that one problem for salespeople is deciding how to manage all that information. One reason that firms are starting to build databases and sales portals is to centralize the information that's important to their field sales force.

Don't forget to use social media like LinkedIn and Facebook to learn more about prospects, as described in Chapter 6. And there are many business information providers online, like InsideView, Jigsaw, and ZoomInfo, that salespeople can use to extract information about companies and people from million of published sources.[2] Some of this information is free, and some requires payment for more exact information.

SECRETARIES AND RECEPTIONISTS

Secretaries and receptionists in the prospect's firm usually are a rich source of information. Be courteous, however, because secretaries and receptionists are accustomed to having salespeople pry for all sorts of free information. Prioritize your questions and provide justification for asking them. Above all, treat secretaries and receptionists with genuine respect. Dawn Hedges, a Zimmer salesperson who sells surgical joint replacements, has built tremendous relationships with the receptionists she calls on. For example, she knows one receptionist who doesn't let Dawn's competitors in to see the doctors. And the receptionist collects any brochures left with her by competitors and then calls Dawn and gives her the information.[3]

NONCOMPETING SALESPEOPLE

Another source for precall information is noncompeting salespeople. In fact, one of the best sources of information is the prospect's own salespeople because they empathize with your situation.

TRADITIONAL SECONDARY SOURCES

Traditional secondary data sources can also be helpful. Firms such as Standard & Poor's and Moody's publish a number of manuals and directories that are available in many public libraries. These sources can help answer questions about brand names, key contacts, historical information, the current situation and outlook for the firm and the industry, location of plants and distribution centers, market shares, and so on.

THE PROSPECT

Much information can be gleaned directly from the prospect. However, don't expect prospects to sit down and answer any and all questions you might have, especially for topics where the information is fairly easy to get (like what products the prospect makes or sells). Prospects don't have time to fill you in on all the details of their business. If you don't know the basics, many prospects will justifiably refuse to deal with you.

It is also worth mentioning that just as you are gathering information about the prospect prior to a meeting, the prospect can and often does collect information about you. Even before the sale your prospect can request price quotes via e-mail. He or she can also view your Web page, as well as your competitors' Web pages. And the prospect can easily chat with colleagues and read about you on newsgroups and blogs to learn about you and your firm. Any salesperson who doesn't understand these realities won't be prepared for the kinds of questions a prospect might ask or for comments a prospect might make.

OTHER SOURCES

Many other sources can provide information. Some information may have been gleaned at a trade show the prospect attended. Much information will be in the lists and directories from which the prospect's name came. For example, a center of influence will often be able to provide information to a Merrill Lynch financial advisor about his friends. Your current customers can often provide information about new clients. Occasionally a prospect will be important enough to warrant hiring an outside consultant to collect information, especially if you are gathering precall information for international selling. Although some information about foreign companies is available, much will not be obtainable. Salespeople in the United States are often amazed at the lack of information about foreign companies. Two good sources are the U.S. government's export portal and the U.S. Commercial Service market research library.

SETTING CALL OBJECTIVES

A most important step in planning is to set objectives for the call. Merely stating the objective "I want to make a sale" or "to tell her about my product" will not suffice. The customer's decision-making process (see Chapter 3) involves many steps, and salespeople need to undertake many activities as they guide customers through the process.

Yet, as Neil Rackham, an internationally respected sales researcher, notes, "It's astonishing how rarely salespeople set themselves call objectives of any kind—let alone effective ones. Although most books on selling emphasize the importance of clear call objectives, it's rare to see these exhortations turned into practice."[4] Why? Probably because many salespeople want to start doing something instead of "wasting time" planning. But without a plan, they actually increase their chances of wasting time.

As a first step in setting objectives, the salesperson should review what has been learned from precall information gathering. Any call objectives should be based on the results of this review. Also, the seller must keep in mind the relationship the firm wishes to have with the prospect. Not all prospects will or should become strategic partners with the seller's firm. Call objectives should not be created in a vacuum. They should be developed while taking into account the firm's goals, the sales team's goals, and the salesperson's goals. Some experts have even argued for the importance of salespeople maintaining consistency between their personal goals and selling objectives. Regardless of the type of goal you are referring to, the old adage is true: If you don't know where you're going, you may wind up somewhere else.

In their well-received sales training books about strategic selling, Miller and Heiman stress the importance of sales call planning being related to the firm's strategic goals for the account.[5] This important topic is covered in Chapter 15. For now, realize that call objectives are based on strategic decisions about the account.

CRITERIA FOR EFFECTIVE OBJECTIVES

All objectives should be specific, realistic, and measurable. A call objective that meets only one or two of these criteria will be an ineffective guide for the salesperson. We now examine each criterion in more detail.

An objective must be specific to be effective. It should state precisely what the salesperson hopes to accomplish, what the objective targets are, and any other details (suggested order quantity, suggested dates for future meetings, length of time needed for a follow-up survey, or the like). Specific objectives help the salesperson avoid "shooting from the hip" during the presentation and perhaps moving the prospect along too rapidly or too slowly.

Objectives must also be realistic. Inexperienced salespeople often have unrealistic expectations about the prospect's or customer's response in the sales call. For example, if Kia Motors currently uses Sony radios in all of its models, a Philips salesperson who expects Kia to change over to Philips radios in the first few sales calls has an unrealistic objective. It is important for sellers to plan objectives for a call that can be accomplished within the time allocated for that sales call. That doesn't mean the objectives should be easy. In reality challenging, but reachable, goals tend to lead to better performance.

For objectives to be realistic, the salesperson needs to consider factors such as cultural influences. For example, some firms have an extremely conservative corporate culture. Creating change in such a culture is time-consuming and often frustrating for the seller. The national culture is important in selling to international prospects. When selling to Arab or Japanese businesses, salespeople should plan to spend at least several meetings getting to know the other party. Developing relationships with Chinese businesspeople requires a great deal of entertaining. Selling in Russia is often slowed because of bureaucracy and incredible amounts of red tape. As these examples illustrate, culture is an important consideration in attempts to set realistic call objectives.

Finally, call objectives must be measurable so salespeople can objectively evaluate each sales call at its conclusion and determine whether the objectives were met. This suggests they should be written down. If a salesperson's stated objective is to get acquainted with the prospect or to establish rapport, how can the salesperson assess whether this goal was achieved? How can someone measure "getting acquainted"? To what extent would the salesperson have to be acquainted with the prospect to know that he or she achieved the sales call objective? A more measurable sales call objective (as well as a more specific and realistic one) is something like the following: To get acquainted with the prospect by learning which clubs or organizations she or he belongs to, which sports the prospect follows, what his or her professional background is, and how long the prospect has held the current position. With this revised call objective, a salesperson can easily determine whether the objective was reached.

A simple way to help ensure that objectives are measurable is to set objectives that require a buyer's response. For example, achievement of the following objective is easy to measure: to make a follow-up appointment with the buyer.

Successful salespeople in almost every industry have learned the importance of setting proper call objectives. Pharmaceutical salespeople for Novartis set clear objectives for each sales call they make to a physician. Then they lay out a series of objectives for subsequent calls so they know exactly what they hope to accomplish over the next several visits. One industrial products sales manager recommends that her salespeople keep their call objectives in view while they are on the sales call, helping them focus on the true goals of the sales call. Both these examples share a common theme: The salesperson needs to set specific, realistic, measurable call objectives. Exhibit 7.2 lists examples of call objectives that meet these criteria.

Some trainers use the acronym SMART to help salespeople remember how to set proper call objections. SMART suggests that call objectives should be specific, measurable, and achievable but realistic and time-based.

SETTING MORE THAN ONE CALL OBJECTIVE

Salespeople have learned the importance of setting multiple objectives for a sales call. Not only do they set a **primary call objective** (the actual goal they hope to

Exhibit 7.2
Examples of Call Objectives

Objectives Related to the Process Leading Up to the Sale

- To have the prospect agree to come to the Atlanta branch office sometime during the next two weeks for a hands-on demonstration of the copier.
- To set up another appointment for one week from now, when the buyer will allow me to do a complete survey of her printing needs.
- To inform the doctor of the revolutionary anticlotting mechanism that has been incorporated into our new drug and have her agree to read the pamphlet I will leave.
- To have the buyer agree to pass my information along to the buying committee with his endorsement of my proposal.
- To have the prospect agree to call several references that I will provide to develop further confidence and trust in my office-cleaning business.
- To have the prospect agree on the first point (of our four-point program) and schedule another meeting in two days to discuss the second point.
- To have the prospect initiate the necessary paperwork to allow us to be considered as a future vendor.

Objectives Related to Consummating the Sale

- To have the prospect sign an order for 100 pairs of Levi's jeans.
- To schedule a co-op newspaper advertising program to be implemented in the next month.
- To have the prospect agree to use our brand of computer paper for a trial period of one month.
- To have the retailer agree to allow us space for an end-of-aisle display for the summer promotion of Raid insect repellent.

Even a salesperson who fails to achieve the primary call objective will be encouraged to at least achieve the minimum call objective.

achieve) before each sales call; they also set a **minimum call objective** (the minimum they hope to achieve) because they realize the call may not go exactly as planned (the prospect may be called away or the salesperson may not have all the necessary facts).[6] On the other hand, the call may go better than the salesperson originally thought it would. Thus, although rarely achieved, an **optimistic call objective** (the most optimistic outcome the salesperson thinks could occur) is also set. The optimistic call objective will probably relate to what the salesperson hopes to accomplish for the account over the long term (that is, the account objectives—see Chapter 15).

The primary call objective, for example, of a Nestlé Foods rep might be to secure an order from a grocer for 10 cases of Nestlé Morsels for an upcoming coupon promotion. That is what the seller realistically hopes to accomplish in the call. A minimum call objective could be to sell at least 5 cases of Morsels, whereas an optimistic call objective would be to sell 20 cases, set up an end-of-aisle display, and secure a retail promotional price of $2.89.

Multiple call objectives have many benefits. First, they help take away the salesperson's fear of failure because most salespeople can achieve at least their stated minimum objective. Second, multiple objectives tend to be self-correcting. Salespeople who always reach their optimum objective realize they are probably setting their sights too low. On the other hand, if they rarely meet even their minimum objective, they probably are setting their goals too high.

It is possible to have more than one primary call objective for a single call. For example, several primary objectives a salesperson might hope to accomplish in a single meeting are to sell one unit, be introduced to one other member of the buying center, and have the prospect agree to send along a packet of information to an executive. In this example, if the salesperson genuinely hopes and expects to achieve all three objectives in the next meeting, they will all be considered primary call objectives. To aid in planning the call, some trainers suggest that the salesperson further prioritize these primary objectives into two groups: The most important primary objective is called the primary call objective, whereas the remaining ones become **secondary call objectives.** So, in this example, if selling the product is the most important thing to accomplish in the next meeting, the objectives will be as follows:

Primary call objective	Sell one unit.
Secondary call objectives	Be introduced to one other member of the buying center.
	Have the prospect agree to send along a packet of information to an executive.

SETTING OBJECTIVES FOR SEVERAL CALLS

By developing a series of specific objectives for future calls, the salesperson can develop a comprehensive strategy for the prospect or customer. This approach is especially important in a partnering relationship. To illustrate the use of multiple call objectives, Exhibit 7.3 gives a set of call objectives for visits over a period of time. The left side of the exhibit contains the long-term plan and each call objective that the Samsung salesperson developed for Johnson Electronics. Note the logical strategy for introducing the new product, the F104 DVD player. The right side of Exhibit 7.3 shows the actual call results.

The salesperson was not always 100 percent successful in achieving the call objectives. Thus several subsequent objectives needed to be modified. For

Exhibit 7.3
Multiple Call Objectives of a Samsung Salesperson Selling to Johnson Electronics

Overall Plan Developed on Oct. 1		Actual Call Results	
Expected Date of the Call	**Call Objective**	**Date of Call**	**Call Results**
Oct. 10	Secure normal repeat orders on F88 and F92. Increase normal repeat order of F100 DVD player from three to five units. Provide product information for new DVD product F104.	Oct. 10	Obtained normal order of F88. Steve decided to drop F92 (refused to give a good reason). Purchased only four F100 players. Seemed responsive to F104 but needs a point-of-purchase (POP) display.
Oct. 17	Erect a front-counter POP display for F104 and secure a trial order of two units.	Oct. 18	Steve was out. His assistant didn't like the POP (thought it was too large!). Refused to use POP. Did order one F104. Told me about several complaints with F100.
Nov. 10	Secure normal repeat orders for F88, F92, and F100. Schedule one co-op newspaper ad for the next 30 days featuring F104. Secure an order for F104s.	Nov. 8	Obtained normal orders. Steve agreed to co-op ad but bought only five F104s. Thinks the margins are too low.
Nov. 17	Secure normal repeat orders of F88, F92, and F100. Secure an order for F104s.	Nov. 18	Obtained normal order on F88, but Steve refused to reorder F100. Claimed the competitor product (Sony) is selling much better. Obtained an order of 15 units of F104.

example, because the meeting on October 10 resulted in the buyer dropping F92 DVD players, the call objectives on November 10 and November 17 need to reflect that Johnson Electronics no longer carries the F92 DVD players. The seller may also want to add a call objective for October 17: to discuss more about the situation with the F92 (because of the outcome of the October 10 meeting) and perhaps try to reintroduce it. This example illustrates the importance of keeping good records, making any necessary adjustments in the long-term call objectives, and then preparing for the next sales call. One sales vice president for a large sales force has some specific advice about setting multiple call objectives:

> The primary objective of the first session is to have another chance to visit. What this allows you to do is have your standards relatively low because you are trying to build a long-term relationship. You should be very sensitive to an opportunity to establish a second visit. What you want to do is identify aspects of the business conversation that require follow-up and make note of them. . . . The key is not the first visit . . . it is the second, the third, the twenty-second visit.[7]

Some industries typically have a long interval between when a prospect is first visited and when an actual sale is consummated. If so, this factor needs to be considered when setting up multiple call objectives and may imply that others get involved in the selling cycle. For example, the typical sale of a Kodak Image Sensor scanner (an image sensor for automated inspection applications in industrial plants) could take several years to close. After having its field sales force demonstrate the image-sensing scanner, the company can use inside sales reps (see Chapter 1 for a description of inside salespeople) to keep the prospects updated in a fashion that is consistent with the prospects' buying time frames. Kodak may also send out newsletters several times a year to prospects. It is important for salespeople to consider the company's other promotional efforts when developing multiple call objectives for a prospect.

When setting multiple call objectives, the salesperson should obviously consider whom to call on in upcoming meetings. Although it seems obvious that the decision maker (who is often a middle manager for many products and services) should be included in those calls, visiting briefly with senior-level managers may also make sense. But what information would you share with the CEO, for example? As discussed in Chapter 1, the answer is the **customer value proposition:**[8] a written statement (usually one or two sentences) that clearly states how purchasing your product or service can help solve the customer's perceived business issue ("BI"). Further, the CVP focuses on what an individual manager needs to address and resolve to be able to better contribute to overall company objectives. The customer value proposition will be more fully discussed in Chapter 9. Frequently the problem needing assistance involves a significant impediment to the firm's revenues and profits. Four common "BI's" include[9]

- Increase revenue, market share, and shareholder value.
- Increase efficiency and productivity.
- Manage costs.
- Control quality and reliability.

Appointments increase the chances of seeing the right person and having uninterrupted time with the prospect.

Often a very important consideration is the success of the individual who is your contact within the customer's firm. And there needs to be a struggle (distinct emotion) associated with it.

BUYERS ARE SETTING GOALS ALSO

Salespeople must understand that buyers may also be setting objectives for the salesperson's sales call. These objectives are based on perceptions of how the salesperson's product or service can add value, as described in Chapters 1 and 3. Salespeople's job is to discover what customers value and then find ways to improve customer value relative to their own products or services. "Building Partnerships 7.1" illustrates how one company did an excellent job of discovering the buyer's goals and then meeting those goals in a creative manner.

What are some things that buyers look for to increase value? Purchasing managers continually point to the following areas: on-time delivery, to-spec quality of products, competitive pricing, proper packaging/paperwork, technical support/service, quality of sales calls, level of technological innovation, and good emergency response. Thus sellers can expect that buyers may set goals for sales calls in these areas.

MAKING AN APPOINTMENT

After gathering precall information and setting objectives, the salesperson's next step is generally to make an appointment. Many sales managers insist that

BUILDING Partnerships

PLANNING IS CRITICAL

The company I sell for, Tek Systems, is an employment agency that connects talented information technology (IT) individuals with companies looking for their services. For example, NRC Corporation uses Tek Systems to find consultants for its IT needs, like network and PC support resources. The service the consultants supported is the corporate NRC helpdesk. There were a total of 68 consultants supporting corporate employees at NRC, with 22 of them coming from TEK Systems. NRC would often hire these consultants permanently.

Each time NRC had a need, it would contact four to five IT employment agencies, and we (along with our competitors) would bid to provide a consultant at a competitive bill rate. We provided this service one consultant at a time.

After doing business with NRC in this manner for the past 10 years, we learned from meeting with various managers in procurement that NRC was looking to buy services differently because its system was very time-consuming and costly, including the following that NRC was doing: sending out requirement information; gathering and reading résumés; scheduling and setting up interviews; performing the interviews; selecting the consultants to hire; checking references; onboarding the consultants; training the new consultants; and performance managing the new consultants.

We spent a great deal of time planning for our visit to NRC. We have learned in our business that the most creative vendor always wins, and we needed a solution that would meet the needs of NRC, Tek Systems, and the consultants themselves. We brainstormed ideas on how to accomplish this difficult task.

In the end, we chose to recommend putting a Tek Systems person permanently on site at NRC to take care of all the activities listed earlier (like interviews, screening, and training). This person would basically become the IT recruiter for NRC. Our competitors came up with vastly different solutions. However, some of their plans showed no compassion for NRC employees who might be terminated as a result of their plan.

NRC got bids from six vendors, and then narrowed it down to two. Those two went through intensive negotiations, with one vendor in one room and the other vendor in another room at NRC headquarters, at the same time. In the end we got the business. I believe it was due, in large part, to the strength of the partnership we had developed with NRC over the years, as well as our planning for the meeting.

Source: Russ Orning, Tek Systems; used with permission. Names changed to protect confidentiality of the client.

their salespeople make appointments before calling on prospects or customers. Appointments dignify the salesperson and help get the sales process off to a good start by putting the salesperson and the prospect on the same level—equal participants in a legitimate sales interview. Appointments also increase the chances of seeing the right person and having uninterrupted time with the prospect.

Experienced sales representatives use different contact methods for different customers. It's also important to point out that attitude (and the salesperson's mood) can have a tremendous impact on success in making appointments. This section describes how to see the right person at the right time and the right place, how to interact with gatekeepers, and how to gain an appointment.

THE RIGHT PERSON

Some experts emphasize the importance of going right to the top and making the first call on the highest-level decision maker. After carefully studying more than 35,000 sales calls, Neil Rackham offers a radically different view.[10] His research suggests that a salesperson should initially try to call on the **focus of receptivity**—the person who will listen receptively and give the seller needed valuable information.

Note that this person may not be the decision maker or the one who understands all of the firm's problems. In fact, this person might not even be in the buying center. (See Chapter 3 for details about various people who serve as buying center members.) But this person will talk to the salesperson and provide information.

The focus of receptivity, according to the research, will then lead the salesperson to the **focus of dissatisfaction:** the person who is most likely to perceive problems and dissatisfactions. Finally, the focus of dissatisfaction leads to the **focus of power:** the person who can approve, prevent, and/or influence action. Getting to the focus of power too quickly can lead to disaster because the seller has not yet built a relationship and does not really know the buyer's needs. In summary, Rackham notes, "There's a superstition in selling that the sooner you can get to the decision maker the better. Effective selling, so it's said, is going straight to the focus of power. That's a questionable belief."[11]

Often someone needs to introduce you to the decision maker, especially in some cultures. For example, to do business with companies in Mideast countries, it is often necessary to have introductions by trusted individuals. Former Texas Senator Phil Gramm often provides this role for UBS; Britain's former ambassador to the United Arab Emirates, Anthony Harris, assists a dozen companies, including the publisher of this textbook.[12]

Frequently in industrial selling situations, as Chapter 3 described, no single person has the sole authority to buy a product because it is a team buying decision. For example, a forklift sales representative for Clarke may have to see the safety engineer, the methods engineer, the materials-handling engineer, and the general superintendent before selling the product to a manufacturing company. In this case the salesperson should usually try to arrange a meeting with the entire group as well as with each individual.

THE RIGHT TIME

There is little agreement on the subject of the best time for a sales interview; obviously the most opportune time to call will vary by customer and type of selling.[13] The salesperson who calls on wholesale grocers, for example, may find from experience that the best times to call are from 9 a.m. to 11 a.m. and from 1:30 p.m. to 3:30 p.m. A hospital rep, on the other hand, may discover that the most productive calls on surgeons are made between 8:30 a.m. and 10 a.m. and after 4 p.m. Car washes are busiest in the winter months, with spring being the second busiest time of year. For most types of selling, the best hours of the day are from approximately 9 a.m. to 11:30 a.m. and from 1:30 p.m. to 4 p.m.

What if you are going to be one of several competitors to give a presentation? Would you want to go first or last?[14] Based on a recent study, if you're selling a lower-priced me-too product, you're better off going last because of the recency effect. If you're the market leader, you can often win the business either way, but you will probably do better if going last. And no matter what you do, avoid scheduling your presentations between those of other vendors.

THE RIGHT PLACE

Meetings can occur just about anywhere. They can even occur by video on the Internet.[15] The sales call should take place in an environment conducive to doing business. Such is not always the case, however. For example, some salespeople still take customers to topless bars. In addition to distractions, topless bars present a number of problems for the salesperson who uses them to achieve sales. For example, is it ethical to gain business by using such tactics? Also, once a buyer has purchased on the basis of this entertainment, chances are the seller will have to keep it up or lose the customer.

WEBCASTING CAN BE THE ANSWER

Steptoe & Johnson is an international law firm with more than 450 attorneys in eight offices scattered across the United States and Europe. One of the company's niches is in the area of data encryption. Standards for encryption vary from country to country, and Steptoe & Johnson maintains a complex database of what those standards are all around the globe. The firm leases that database for around $30,000 per year to corporations that need to keep abreast of such issues.

At one time the law firm sent out expert salespeople to give detailed in-person demonstrations of the capabilities of its database. Although the success rate was high for this procedure, the company needed a more cost-efficient way to use those salespeople. It still wanted to have salespeople engage in the demonstration, but without sending them around the world to do so.

The solution was virtual sales calls using WebEx. WebEx was chosen because it was easy to use and allowed interactive capabilities. Salespeople were able to give a complete demonstration of the database, and prospects were able to ask questions, in real time, via the chat feature of WebEx.

The results were overwhelming positive. The technology allowed a seamless, easy-to-follow demonstration of the encryption database to qualified prospects. Participants praised the demonstration as highly useful and even asked if Steptoe & Johnson could offer WebEx events describing other services the law firm provided.

Furthermore, with help from the WebEx team, the law firm was able to record a demonstration event and place it on the Steptoe & Johnson Web site. This generates interest and new leads for the law firm's database.

Steptoe & Johnson was so pleased with WebEx that the firm has used it for other services. As CMO John Neidecker of Steptoe & Johnson stated, "We're just thrilled that WebEx is working so well for us."

Source: www.webex.com, http://www.webex.com/who-uses-webex-and-why/other.html, accessed March 6, 2010.

Some online conferencing systems include audio streaming with slide presentations but no video. Such online providers as WebEx, ON24, and BrightTalk have gained market share in this type of presentation, and its use is growing. "Sales Technology 7.1" provides the experience of one company that used online Webcasting to its advantage.

Videoconferencing—meetings in which people are not physically present in one location but are connected via voice and video—seems to be growing in usage. In a variant on videoconferencing, called **Webcasting** or **virtual sales calls,** the meeting is broadcast over the Internet.[16] For example, due to downsizing, emWare, Inc., has only eight salespeople. According to Michael Nelson, CEO of emWare, the use of virtual sales calls is now necessary and is actually quite successful. Salespeople should learn how to plan for such meetings. One key is to carefully plan all technical elements of the presentation and to rehearse them as much as possible. (Chapter 9 provides more insight into practicing and avoiding problems.)

thinking **it** through — What would be some disadvantages of using Webcasting compared to a face-to-face sales call?

CULTIVATING RELATIONSHIPS WITH SUBORDINATES

Busy executives usually have one or more subordinates who plan and schedule interviews for them. These **screens** (or **barriers,** as salespeople sometimes call

Videoconferencing makes it easy for a U.S. salesperson to make a presentation in Germany.

Salespeople should work to achieve friendly relationships with the prospect's subordinates.

them) often make seeing the boss difficult. These screens can also take on the role of gatekeepers for the buying center (Chapter 3 discusses gatekeepers).

Sales strategists have identified several ways to interact with a screen:

- The salesperson can work "through the screen." The seller has to convince the gatekeeper that a meeting with the boss is in the boss's best interests.

- The salesperson can go "over the screen." While talking to the screen, the seller drops names of people higher up in the organization. The screen may allow the seller in to see the boss right away for fear of getting into trouble.

- The salesperson can go "under the screen" by trying to make contact with the prospect before or after the screen gets to work (or while the screen is taking a coffee break).

- The seller just bypasses the screen entirely—a strategy that can easily backfire. For example, Oracle learned, the hard way, the impact of having pushy, aggressive salespeople who constantly bypassed screens and formal committees. The result was great customer dissatisfaction.

TELEPHONING FOR APPOINTMENTS

The telephone is most often used to make an initial appointment. Salespeople can save many hours by phoning, or having others phone for them, to make appointments. Chapter 4 provided many insights on how to use the phone effectively and suggested a way to gain an appointment with a prospect.

The goal of the telephone call is to make an appointment, not to sell the product or service. Exhibit 7.4 shows appropriate responses to common objections Xerox copier salespeople encounter when making appointments. Salespeople need to anticipate objections and decide exactly how to respond, as Chapter 10 will more fully discuss.

ADDITIONAL PLANNING

A successful salesperson thinks ahead to the meeting that will occur and plans accordingly. For example, salespeople should plan how they intend to make a good first impression and build credibility during the call. It is also important to plan how to further uncover the customer's needs and strengthen the presentation. Salespeople should anticipate the questions and concerns the prospect may raise and plan to answer them helpfully. These issues are discussed in detail in the next several chapters. For now, be aware that these activities should be planned before the meeting begins.

Before making the sales call, it is important to practice. How long should a rep spend practicing? Longer than many would think. As Mark Twain wrote, "It usually takes more than three weeks to prepare a good impromptu speech." Some have even suggested that for very important presentations, the seller spend 30 minutes preparing and practicing for each minute of presentation time. While often broken, the rule does indicate the importance of planning and practicing the presentation. Of course the time spent in practicing would depend on how much time the seller has and on the goals of the presentation.

Exhibit 7.4
Responses to
Objections Concerning
Appointments

Objection from a Secretary	Response
I'm sorry, but Mr. Wilkes is busy now.	What I have to say will take only a few minutes. Should I call back in a half hour, or would you suggest I set up an appointment?
We already have a copier.	That's fine. I want to talk to Mr. Wilkes about our new paper flow system design for companies like yours.
I take care of all the copying.	That's fine, but I'm here to present what Xerox has to offer for a complete paper flow system that integrates data transmission, report generation, and copiers. I'd like to speak to Mr. Wilkes about this total service.

Objection from the Prospect	Response
Can't you mail the information to me?	Yes, I could. But everyone's situation is different, Mr. Wilkes, and our systems are individually tailored to meet the needs of each customer. Now . . . [benefit statement and repeat request for appointment].
Well, what is it you want to talk about?	It's difficult to explain the system over the telephone. In 15 minutes, I can demonstrate the savings you get from the system.
You'd just be wasting your time. I'm not interested.	The general objection is hiding a specific objection. The salesperson needs to probe for the specific objection: Do you say that because you don't copy many documents?
We had a Xerox copier once and didn't like it.	Probe for the specific reason of dissatisfaction and have a reply, but don't go too far. The objective is to get an appointment, not sell a copier.

Source: Courtesy of Xerox Corporation. Used by permission.

One other thing that some salespeople do before making the actual sales call is **seeding**—that is, sending the customer important and useful information prior to the meeting. For example, a rep can constantly search newspapers, magazines, and other sources for material that may be useful for a prospect. This material is sent to the prospect, at intervals, prior to the call, each time with a note saying something like, "Jim, I thought you would find this article useful!" The material does not include the selling firm's catalogs, brochures, pricing, and so on. Rather, it is good, useful information that will help the prospect's business. The result? The prospect views the seller as someone trying to be truly helpful and as someone who really understands the prospect's business. Seeding isn't just for prospects; it can and should occur for customers as well.

SELLING YOURSELF

You belong to a group on campus, and you're seeking some funds. Because you're taking this course, your group made you their lead spokesperson. Let's say you are a part of the campus affiliate of Habitat for Humanity, and you're trying to get some funds or merchandise (to use as a raffle item) from the local Target store to raise money for your cause. How do you plan for the meeting?

First find out what the goals and policies are of the funding source, Target. What does it want in an application to get funding? What things are the firm not willing to fund? What rules has it set for those who come personally before its review board? You'll also want to find out exactly who is on the review board, what their social styles are, and if there are any influential adversaries that are opposed to your group. And it would be nice to know if that specific review board or Target has ever approved a request from your group before (and if so, for how much and for what purposes).

How do you get all that information? Check with members of your group, Habitat for Humanity, who might have petitioned the funding source before. Also look at the minutes of your group because memories of your members might be a bit hazy or inaccurate. For details on the criteria the funding source is using, go to the Target Web page or look at printed documents you should be able to obtain fairly easily by asking. Check with the Target manager for any additional details about how best to put forth your proposal and what kinds of things to avoid (based on the manager's experience with past proposals and presenters).

Ready to meet? Not yet. First list the objectives for your group before going to the face-to-face meeting. Develop your primary goal, and also prepare a minimum goal in case things don't go as well as you hoped. For example, your primary goal might be to get $500 in cash, and your minimum goal might be to get some older merchandise (like one of last year's MP3 players that Target still has on its shelf and would donate as a raffle item). And it doesn't hurt to have an optimistic goal handy in case the review board loves your idea and wants to support it in ways you never dreamed could happen.

Finally, put together your customer value proposition. Clearly outline what your chapter of Habitat for Humanity does that is in perfect alignment with what Target is trying to achieve. With this you'll be able to show Target that by donating, it is helping achieve its own goals as well as those of your group.

SUMMARY

This chapter stressed the importance of planning the sales call. Developing a clear plan saves time for both salespeople and customers. In addition, it helps salespeople increase their confidence and reduce their stress.

As part of the planning process, salespeople need to gather as much information about the prospect as possible before the first call. They need information about both the individual prospect and the prospect's organization. Sources of this information include lists and directories, secretaries and receptionists, noncompeting salespeople, and direct inquiries made by the prospect.

To be effective, a call objective should be specific, realistic, and measurable. In situations requiring several calls, the salesperson should develop a plan with call objectives for each future call. Also, many salespeople benefit from setting multiple levels of objectives—primary, minimum, and optimum—for each call.

As a general rule, salespeople should make appointments before calling on customers. This approach enables the salesperson to talk to the right person at the customer's site.

A number of methods can be used to make appointments. Perhaps the most effective is the straightforward telephone approach.

KEY TERMS

analysis paralysis   184
barriers   194
customer value proposition   191
focus of dissatisfaction   193
focus of power   193

focus of receptivity   192
influential adversaries   182
minimum call objective   189
optimistic call objective   189
primary call objective   188

ETHICS PROBLEMS

1. Suppose that during your information-gathering phase you identify a hostile influential adversary named Mike. You know that Mike will do everything possible to see your competitor get the business. In talking about this with your sales manager, she suggests that you find some way to covertly strip Mike of his credibility and thus cause him to be a nonissue. Would you follow your manager's advice? What kinds of things would you be willing to do? What would you be uncomfortable doing?

2. During precall planning, you learn that an important prospect enjoys being treated by salespeople to visit strip clubs, of which there are several in your town. Your firm doesn't have any policy about whether you can visit one of these clubs with a client. You've never visited one with a client before. How will these facts affect your planning for your upcoming sales visit to this prospect? What will you do?

QUESTIONS AND PROBLEMS

1. Think about a job you have held. Now think about a manager who worked there. Assume that a salesperson wanted to sell your manager an important product or service. Who would be a good focus of receptivity for this salesperson? Do you think the focus of receptivity would cooperate with the salesperson?

2. In "Sales Technology 7.1" you learned how one firm uses WebEx to give presentations. Can you think of any negative aspects of using such technology for giving sales presentations to prospects?

3. This chapter listed a number of information items that a salesperson should find out about a prospect/customer as an individual. Assume you are going to sell your instructor for this course a new iPod. See how much information you can supply from the list in the text.

4. Evaluate the following objectives for a sales call:
   a. Show and demonstrate the entire line of 10 racquetball racquets.
   b. Find out more about competitors' offerings under consideration.
   c. Make the buyer trust me more.
   d. Determine which service the prospect is currently using for pest control and how much it costs.
   e. Have the buyer agree to hold our next meeting at a quieter location.
   f. Get an order for 15 charter boat cruises.
   g. Make the buyer not worry about the fact that our newspaper has been in business only three weeks.

5. Think for a moment about trying to secure a job. Assume you are going to have your second job interview next week with ADT Security Systems for a sales position. The interview will take place over the phone with the senior recruiter. You've already had one informational interview on campus. Most candidates go through a set of four interviews. List your primary objective, minimum objective, and optimistic objective for your second interview.

6. In "Building Partnerships 7.1" you learned that competing vendors were negotiating at the same time for the business of NRC. That is a stressful situation to be in because you know that your competitors are fighting for the same

business, and they want it just as much as you do. How could you find out ahead of time if NRC was planning on having both competitors at company headquarters at the same time? What additional planning would you do if you learned that was going to be the case?

7. Evaluate the following approach for getting an appointment: Ms. O'Toole, I've not got any calls to make next Thursday. Would it be OK if I stopped by for a few minutes?

8. Although there is no firm rule, list what you think to be the best time of day to call on the following individuals:

   a. A college bookstore manager (to sell backpacks).

   b. A manager at an automotive glass replacement company (to sell a new type of glue).

   c. An apartment complex manager (to sell a new mowing system).

   d. A heating contractor (to sell a new model of heating system).

9. Review the list of prospects in Question 8 and identify

   a. The worst time of day to call on each individual.

   b. The worst time of year to call on each individual.

10. Suppose you have graduated and you belong to the alumni association of your school. Your association plans to raffle off a number of donated items to raise funds for a new library. To be a success, the event will need many donated raffle prizes.

   a. Which sources will you use to identify potential sponsors?

   b. What information do you need to qualify them properly?

CASE PROBLEMS

case **7.1**

AirCharter (Part A)

Founded in 1985, AirCharter has provided charter flights to a wide array of customers, including business travelers worldwide. Thanks to AirCharter's online booking system, business travelers can secure reliable quotes and book both domestic and international flights. AirCharter has more than 3,000 aircraft, including jets (light, midsize, and large jets) and turboprops.

The company is known for its ability to cater to passengers' every desire, including gourmet meals, special beverages, entertainment while in the air, and other luxury accommodations. AirCharter also staffs a full-service VIP jet concierge program, similar to what major airlines offer. This service can help clients meet all their needs on the ground before and after the flight.

Felix Aleynykov is a salesperson for AirCharter. He is currently planning an important first visit to Abel Espinosa, a procurement officer at the AFL-CIO. The AFL-CIO is one of the largest labor federations in the United States and has three primary executive officers: president, secretary-treasurer, and executive vice president. The organization also has a large executive council that represents all the trade unions in the organization. Both the executive officers and the executive council travel across the country a great deal in their work. Felix would like to tell Abel how AirCharter can provide outstanding benefits to the AFL-CIO. Some of the special features for business travelers include the following:

• Privacy—you have the entire aircraft to yourself and can travel with passengers you know and enjoy.

• Comfort—including extra-roomy leather seats, in-flight movies, fully stocked bar, and gourmet meals that you choose.

• Ease—no time-consuming check-in process. You drive right up to the plane, and your luggage goes from your car into the plane.

• Point-to-point travel—there are no set schedules, so you fly when you want. AirCharter uses 10 times more airports than commercial airlines, so you can fly from less congested airports closer to where you live.

Questions

1. What kind of information should Felix gather about Abel before their meeting?

2. What kind of information should Felix gather about the AFL-CIO before his meeting?

3. Which sources can Felix use to gather that needed information?

Sources: http://www.aircharter.net, www.aflcio.org.

case **7.2**

Trucker's Connection

Trucker's Connection is a free magazine dedicated to truck drivers and offers information about safety, employment, and industry events. Truck drivers can pick up a free copy of this monthly magazine at over 3,200 locations, including truck stops, fuel stops, rest areas, motels, and truck parts/service shops that cater to truckers. The magazine has a 20-year history of serving the needs of truckers and has a loyal following. It has been said that the magazine is "read by more truckers in more places" than any competitive magazine.

Megan Maxwell is an advertising salesperson for *Trucker's Connection*. Her territory includes all the motel and hotel chains in the United States. In a few weeks Megan is going to be calling on Super 8, a chain of over 2,000 properties. Super 8 has a reputation of being a lower-priced motel with amenities such as a complimentary SuperStart® continental breakfast and free high-speed Internet access. Super 8 has never advertised in the *Trucker's Connection* before. Megan doesn't know if anyone from the magazine has ever called on Super 8.

Questions

1. Assume you are Megan Maxwell. List your call objectives for your first call with the marketing director for Super 8. Develop a three-call follow-up schedule, and list the objectives for each call.

2. What kind of information would you like to have before your first meeting? How could you obtain that information?

Source: *Trucker's Connection* magazine; truckersconnection.com; super8.com.

ROLE PLAY CASE

This role play continues with the same customer firm you have been selling to: Spear One, McLane Properties, or Dart Paper Products. (If you have not done role plays before, you will need to review the information about the various role play customers that can be found at the end of Chapter 3.)

Your buyer has agreed to allow you to meet with the rest of the buying center. Now it is time to plan the sales call. Write out your sales call objectives. In case you need assistance, here is some additional information from your previous calls, and feel free to ask your buyer for additional information. In addition to your call objectives, outline an agenda, or what you plan to do step-by-step.

Spear One: You are planning for a sales call with the VP of sales and marketing. You know that the company is growing about 15 percent per year. There are 45 salespeople, managed by four regional sales managers.

McLane Properties: Your sales call will be with the same person plus some of the agents who have contact management software that they bought. The ultimate decision will be made by Mr. McLane, but he is likely to buy whatever this group recommends.

Dart Paper Products: You are going to meet with the two VPs of sales. Recall that one manages a sales force of 59 salespeople and sells to distributors, while the other has institutions and government agencies as accounts, with 18 salespeople.

Once you've written your objectives, review them with your group. Make sure they meet the criteria for objectives as specified in the chapter.

Note: For background information about these role plays, please see page 27.

To the instructor: Additional information needed to complete the role play is available in the Instructor's Manual.

ADDITIONAL REFERENCES

Biba, Erin. "Webcasting Is on the Upswing: Webinar Industry Pegged at $83.3 Million in '07 and Ready to Grow More Than 28.2%." *BtoB* 93, no. 14 (2008), p. 14.

Boulton, C. "Web Conferencing Fills Void in Tight Times." *eWeek* 26, no. 1 (January 5, 2009), pp. 14–16.

Farquharson, B. "Breaking Down the Appointment." *Graphic Arts Monthly* 78, no. 2 (February 2006), p. 52.

Hawkins, Timothy G., C. Michael Wittmann, and Michael M. Beyerlein. "Antecedents and Consequences of Opportunism in Buyer–Supplier Relations: Research Synthesis and New Frontiers." *Industrial Marketing Management* 37, no. 8 (November 2008), pp. 895–909.

Ivens, Bjorn Sven, and Catherine Pardo. "Are Key Account Relationships Different? Empirical Results on Supplier Strategies and Customer Reactions." *Industrial Marketing Management* 36, no. 4 (May 2007), pp. 470–82.

Ivens, Björn Sven, Catherine Pardo, Robert Salle, and Bernard Cova. "Relationship Keyness: The Underlying Concept for Different Forms of Key Relationship Management." *Industrial Marketing Management* 38, no. 5 (July 2009), pp. 513–19.

"Just Say No to Drug Reps." *BusinessWeek*, February 4, 2008, p. 69.

Lewin, Jeffrey E., and Jeffrey K. Sager. "An Investigation of the Influence of Coping Resources in Salespersons' Emotional Exhaustion." *Industrial Marketing Management* 38, no. 7 (October 2009), pp. 798–805.

Mattson, David, and Anthony Parinello. *Five Minutes with VITO*. Pegasus Media World, 2008.

Miller, Robert B., Stephen E. Heiman, Diane Sanchez, and Tad Tuleja. *The New Conceptual Selling: The Most Effective and Proven Method for Face-to-Face Sales Planning*. New York: Warner Business, 2005.

Parinello, Anthony. *Getting to VITO (the Very Important Top Officer): Ten Steps to VITO's Office*. Hoboken, NJ: Wiley, 2005.

Shelton, Robert. "Integrating Product and Service Innovation: Industry Leaders Complement Their Product Offerings with Service Innovations to Boost Overall Customer Value." *Research-Technology Management* 52, no. 3 (2009), pp. 38–44.

chapter **8**

MAKING THE SALES CALL

SOME QUESTIONS ANSWERED IN THIS CHAPTER ARE

- How should the salesperson make the initial approach to make a good impression and gain the prospect's attention?

- How can the salesperson develop rapport and increase source credibility?

- Why is discovering the prospect's needs important, and how can a salesperson get this information?

- How can the salesperson most effectively relate the product or service features to the prospect's needs?

- Why is it important for the salesperson to make adjustments during the call?

- How does the salesperson recognize that adjustments are needed?

- How can a salesperson effectively sell to groups?

PROFILE

My name is Jennifer VanWinkle, and I graduated from the College of St. Catherine in 2007 with a degree in medical sales. While in school, I took the Fundamentals of Selling class with Dr. Greg DiNovis and obtained an internship with Ecolab, a global cleaning and sanitation company headquartered in St. Paul, Minnesota. I later accepted a full-time position with the company as a territory sales manager. Today my job takes me to restaurants, hotels, and health care facilities, where I help customers select and use products to obtain exceptional cleaning and sanitizing results.

Good communication is an extremely important aspect of the sales call process. It all starts with the initial approach. Before I contact a customer for the first time, I like to know as much as possible about his or her operation. Think of it as a job interview. You can really gain your prospect's attention and trust and build rapport quickly if you prove you've taken the time to learn about the business before your first sales call.

During your first meeting, I believe that it's important to make a good first impression. Be on time, smile, greet them by name, and be confident. This is a great opportunity to build rapport and get your main sales goals across without being pushy. A good way to build rapport is to try and relate to your customer. Look around his or her office; see if there is anything you can use to strike up a friendly conversation. Each customer will be different. You must adapt to them. Never expect them to adapt to you.

Use this first meeting to get some key information from your prospect. Find out about his or her wants, needs, and expectations. Ask a lot of questions and listen intently. For example, it's very important for me to know what my customer is looking for before I begin presenting potential product solutions. Ecolab has hundreds of solutions to choose from, and I want to make sure I give my customer exactly what he or she is looking for to solve the cleaning issue.

One way to know precisely what a customer needs is to ask open-ended questions. The more he or she talks, the more you will learn about the situation. As you will learn in this chapter, the SPIN method of questioning can be very helpful in identifying your prospect's needs. I use the SPIN method in my position at Ecolab, and it has helped me immensely. SPIN questions help differentiate the products and service I sell from Ecolab's competitors, and it's a method that my company has helped perfect within our sales teams.

One final note about the initial sales call. Make sure you are prepared for objections from your prospect and are able to quickly adjust during your presentation. In my business, I've found that there are several standard objections that customers often give. After learning the business and meeting with several customers, it has become much easier for me to prepare for those objections and respond appropriately.

Your first few sales calls might be tough, but eventually you will become a pro at responding to objections and you will know what to expect in most situations. Objections may not always be verbal, so remember to read the prospect's nonverbal reactions and adjust when necessary. If you notice something starting to go wrong, you need to change your approach so that you can ensure a close to your sale, or at least obtain another follow-up appointment.

For more information about Ecolab, visit our Web site at www.ecolab.com.

Exhibit 8.1
Essential Elements of the
Sales Call

At this point in the sales process, we assume that an appointment has been made, sufficient information about the prospect and his or her organization has been gathered, and the salesperson has developed strong objectives for the call. In this chapter we discuss how to make the actual sales call. The content of a sales call depends on the specific situation the salesperson encounters as well as the extent of the relationship the salesperson has already established with the other party.[1] Exhibit 8.1 provides an organizing framework for our discussion. We start by considering how to make a good impression and begin to develop a long-term relationship. We then examine the initial needs assessment phase of a relationship and how to relate solutions to those needs. Finally, we discuss the relationship between adaptability and successful sales calls.

There are, of course, many conceptualizations of the selling process. For example, one trainer finds value in describing the selling process as the *Four A's* (*a*cknowledge, *a*cquire, *a*dvise, and *a*ssure).[2] First the seller acknowledges the buyer by greeting/welcoming/honoring and building trust. Next the seller acquires information via needs analysis and a summary of that analysis outlining the agreement between buyer and seller about the current situation and the desired solution. Advising comes next, during which the seller narrows the possible choices to specific options, sells benefits of those options (not just features), watches for buying signals, and asks for the order. Finally, the seller assures the buyer after the sale by enhancing satisfaction with the buying decision and giving proper follow-up and referrals.

MAKING A GOOD IMPRESSION

When salespeople arrive late, make a poor entrance, fail to gain the buyer's interest, or lack rapport-building skills, it is difficult for them to secure commitment and build partnerships.[3] This section discusses how salespeople can manage the buyer's impression of them, a process termed **impression management.** Most of the information presented here assumes that the salesperson is making a first call on a prospect. However, impression management continues throughout calls.

One of the most important ways to ensure a good first impression is to be well prepared (as we discussed in Chapter 7). Some salespeople prepare a checklist of things to take to the presentation so they won't forget anything.

WAITING FOR THE PROSPECT

Being on time for a scheduled sales call is critical to avoid giving the buyer a negative impression. With the advent of cell phones, there is practically no good reason for not calling if you're going to be a few minutes late to the appointment.

Salespeople should use waiting time effectively.

Every salesperson must expect to spend a certain portion of each working day waiting for sales interviews. Successful salespeople make the best possible use of this time by working on reports, studying new product information, checking e-mail and text messages, planning and preparing for their next calls, and obtaining additional information about the prospect. (Chapter 15 covers time management more fully.)

Some trainers suggest that salespeople not wait for any prospect, under normal circumstances, more than 15 minutes after the appointment time. Why? To demonstrate that the seller's time is also important. Exceptions are necessary, of course, depending on the importance of the customer, the reason the customer is running late, and the distance the salesperson has traveled. In all cases salespeople should keep the sales call in perspective, realizing that their time is also valuable. Chapter 15 discusses just how valuable that time really is.

When the salesperson arrives, the receptionist may merely say, "I'll tell Ms. Schimpf that you are here." After the receptionist has spoken with Ms. Schimpf, the salesperson should ask approximately how long the wait will be. If the wait will be excessive or the salesperson has another appointment, it may be advisable to explain this tactfully and to ask for another appointment. Usually the secretary either will try to get the salesperson in to see the prospect more quickly or will arrange for a later appointment.

FIRST IMPRESSIONS

In the first meeting between a salesperson and a prospect or customer, the first two or three minutes can be very important. Making a favorable first impression usually results in a prospect who is willing to listen. A negative first impression, on the other hand, sets up a barrier that may never be hurdled. Note that one advantage of an existing partnering relationship is that the salesperson has already established a bond and has built a reputation based on his or her prior actions.

Salespeople may make a poor impression without realizing it. They may know their customer's needs and their own product, but overlook seemingly insignificant things that can create negative impressions. As Chapter 5 related, how you dress can affect the message you send to the buyer. Also, studies have shown that the physical attractiveness and gender of salespeople can influence purchase intentions of buyers. And don't forget that according to generation gap experts, it is often quite difficult for a Generation X (born 1965–1978) salesperson to relate to a baby boomer (born 1946–1964) buyer, and even harder to relate to a traditionalist (born 1922–1946) buyer.

So what should a seller do to create a good first impression? You should be well groomed and enter confidently (but not arrogantly) by using erect posture, lengthy stride, and a lively pace; and among the first words out of your mouth should be something like, "Thanks for seeing me." And don't forget to smile. Watch what happens when you look at someone and smile. In 99 out of 100 times, you will receive a smile in return.

But here's a caveat to the counsel just offered: Observe the prospect's state and modify your behavior as needed. When customers are in a bad mood, the last thing they want is a happy, bouncy salesperson. In fact, in such a situation, the prospect might be inattentive or even refuse to meet with such a salesperson. Adapt, and even ask if this is not a good time to meet if you perceive that the buyer is very stressed. Also, be aware that many buyers are repulsed by a salesperson who enters the room with exaggerated and false enthusiasm that her product is for sure going to solve all of the buyer's problems. It's better to be humble than to be cocky.[4]

It is also important to remember prospects' names and how to pronounce them (www.hearnames.com provides verbal pronunciation of many hard-to-say names). There are many ways to try to remember someone's name—such as giving your full attention when you hear it and then repeating the name immediately, associating it with someone else you know with the same name, associating it with the person's most prominent feature or trait, using it during the conversation, and writing it down phonetically. Whatever you do, make sure to pronounce the prospect's name correctly.

ethics

Some experts argue that the customer's name should be used in the opening statement. Dale Carnegie, a master at developing relationships, said a person's name is "the sweetest and most important sound" to that person. Using a person's name often indicates respect and a recognition of the person's unique qualities. Others disagree with this logic, claiming that using the person's name, especially more than once in any short time, sounds phony and insincere. A compromise is to use the prospect's name in the opening and then to use it occasionally during the rest of the call.

thinking it through

You walk into a prospect's office confidently. Even though you've never met her before, you aren't nervous. You've done your homework and have strong objectives for this meeting. After you introduce yourself to the prospect and sit down, you suddenly remember that you left your laptop in your car. And in that laptop is your entire presentation! Your car is several blocks away. What should you do? What would you say to the prospect?

SELECTING A SEAT

When selecting a seat, it is a good idea to look around and start to identify the prospect's social style and status (see Chapter 5). For example, in the United States important decision makers usually have large, well-appointed, private offices. But be careful. In Kuwait a high-ranking businessperson may have a small office and lots of interruptions. Don't take that environment to mean he or she is a low-ranking employee or is not interested. Walmart buyers interview salespeople in rough conditions to help instill the idea that they want the lowest prices they can get.

Asking permission to sit down is usually unnecessary. The salesperson should read the prospect's nonverbal cues to determine the right time to be seated. And note that many calls will not involve sitting down at all, such as talking to a store manager in a grocery store aisle, conversing with a supervisor in a warehouse, or asking questions of a surgeon in a post-op ward.

GETTING THE CUSTOMER'S ATTENTION

Recall from Chapter 5 that there are several types of sales presentations, including standard memorized, outlined, and customized. In this chapter we assume that the salesperson has chosen a customized presentation.

Getting the customer's attention is not a new concept. It is also the goal of many other activities you are familiar with, such as advertising, making new friends, writing an English composition, giving a speech, or writing a letter to a friend.

Time is valuable to prospects, and prospects concentrate their attention on the first few minutes with a salesperson to determine whether they will benefit from the interaction. The prospect is making a decision: Do I want to give this salesperson 15 minutes of my time? 30 minutes of my time? None of my time? This decision is made even while the salesperson is walking in the door and selecting a seat. Some claim that salespeople have less than six minutes to establish credibility with a client. The first few words the salesperson says often set the tone of the entire sales call. The **halo effect** (how and what you do in one thing changes a person's perceptions of other things you do) seems to operate in many sales calls. If the salesperson is perceived by the prospect as effective at the beginning of the call, he will be perceived as effective during the rest of the call and vice versa. There are many ways to open a presentation. An **opening** is a method designed to get the prospect's attention and interest quickly and to make a smooth transition into the next part of the presentation (which is usually to more fully discover the prospect's needs). Because each prospect and sales situation is unique, salespeople should be adaptable and be able to use any or a combination of openings. Again, keep in mind that openings are generally less important with partnering customers whom the salesperson has already met. Exhibit 8.2 provides details about a number of possible openings. But remember, many prospects won't like what

Exhibit 8.2

Openings That Salespeople Can Use to Gain Attention

Opening Method	Example	Things to Consider
Introduction opening (simply introduce yourself).	Ms. Hallgren, thank you for seeing me today. My name is Daniel Mundt, and I'm with ServiceMaster.	Simple, but may not generate interest.
Referral opening (tell about someone who referred you to the buyer).	Mr. Schaumberg, I appreciate your seeing me today. I'm here at the suggestion of Ms. Fleming of Acumen Ornamental Iron Works. She thought you would be interested in our line of wrought iron products and railings.	Always get permission. Don't stretch the truth.
Benefit opening (start by telling some benefit of the product).	Mr. Penney, I would like to tell you about a color copier that can reduce your copying costs by 15 percent.	Gets down to business right away.
Product opening (actually demonstrate a product feature and benefit as soon as you walk up to the prospect).	[Carrying a tablet PC into an office] Ms. Hemming, you spend a lot of time on the road as an investigative lawyer. Let me show you how this little handheld item can transform your car (or any place you go) into an efficient, effective office.	Uses visual and not just verbal opening; can create excitement.
Compliment opening (start by complimenting the buyer or the buyer's firm).	I was calling on one of your customers, Jackson Street Books, last week, and the owner couldn't say enough good things about your service. It sure says a lot about your operation to have a customer just start praising you out of the blue.	Must be sincere, not just flattery. **ethics**
Question opening (start the conversation with a question).	Ms. Borgelt, what is your reaction to the brochure I sent you about our new telemarketing service?	Starts two-way communication.

they deem to be "canned" approaches and will react negatively. Prospects in one study rated the following openings overwhelmingly as either negative or neutral (unsolicited small talk, 95 percent; benefit claim, 89 percent; provocative question, 84 percent).[5]

DEVELOPING RAPPORT

Rapport in selling is a close, harmonious relationship founded on mutual trust.[6] You build rapport when the prospect perceives you to be like him or her in some way. Ultimately the goal of every salesperson should be to establish rapport with each customer. Often salespeople can accomplish this with some friendly conversation early in the call. Part of this process involves identifying the prospect's social style and making necessary adjustments (see Chapter 5).

The talk about current news, hobbies, mutual friends, and the like that usually breaks the ice for the actual presentation is often referred to as **small talk.** One of the top traits of successful salespeople is the ability to be sociable. Examples include the following:[7]

I understand you went to Nebraska? I graduated from there with a BBA in 2007.

Did you see the Houston Rockets game on TV last night?

I read in the paper that you won the bass fishing tournament last weekend. I bet that was pretty exciting!

So did you have trouble getting home from work last week with that snowstorm?

Your receptionist was very helpful when I set this appointment. I never would have found this building if she hadn't told me where to park.

You don't happen to remember Marla Jones, do you? She said she went to college with you and said to say hi.

Sharing letters from satisfied customers helps a salesperson establish credibility.

Customers are more receptive to salespeople with whom they can identify—that is, with whom they have something in common. Thus salespeople will be more effective with customers with whom they establish such links as mutual friends, common hobbies, or attendance at the same schools. Successful salespeople engage in small talk more effectively by first performing **office scanning:** looking around the prospect's environment for relevant topics to talk about. "Sales Technology 8.1" describes how several salespeople use social networking sites to learn about appropriate topics of conversation.

Be careful, however, when engaging in small talk because it can be to your detriment.[8] One salesperson told of a client who asked her opinion about the economic outlook. The seller said she thought it was going down. The buyer had a different opinion, and it took months to repair the relationship. It is generally best to avoid controversial topics like politics and religion. Don't talk about your personal problems in an effort to get sympathy. Don't complain about others

SALES Technology

8.1

USE SOCIAL NETWORKING INFORMATION TO HELP GET THE CUSTOMER'S ATTENTION

If those first few minutes in a meeting are as critical as everyone claims they are, how can a salesperson use them effectively to get the prospect's attention? By using information that has been gathered about the prospect. And one good way to do that is through such social networking sites as LinkedIn, Facebook, Twitter, and MySpace.

Divya Gugnani, a venture capitalist who also runs a media company in the culinary Web site called Behind the Burner, uses LinkedIn to investigate the people she will be contacting by reviewing their profiles carefully. She then uses that information to break the ice, get the prospect's attention, and find areas of common interests and goals. For her Web site business, Divya says, "This has been a great resource for recruiting new talent, including writers, videographers, graphic designers, and interns."

When Karen Jashinsky, a recent MBA graduate, wanted to start a teen-oriented personal fitness business, she used LinkedIn to find connections with people who had similar interests. Thanks to the use of information provided by LinkedIn profiles, she is now the owner of O2 MAX, a Santa Monica, California, fitness center for teens.

Dave Brookes is the sales and marketing department of Teusner Wines. Dave uses Twitter to connect with groups of people who tweet about wine. With Twitter he gathers

feedback, builds trust with existing customers, and shares information. "There's no cost, which is fantastic for guys like us because our marketing budget is tiny," says Brookes. "And you can see that it's building. We're building relationships, and people enjoy what we're doing."

It should be noted that this social networking information gathering goes in both directions. Ken Nussbaum, a CPA, noticed that a potential client had a LinkedIn account, so he encouraged him to check out Ken's profile on LinkedIn. The man did so, and found that there would be a perfect fit between his needs and what Ken had to offer. When they met at Starbucks for coffee the first time, Ken reports that there were none of the usual worrying questions from the prospect about what Ken was able to do and what his qualifications were. As Ken stated, "LinkedIn makes it easy for potential clients to learn more about me, and having recommendations from numerous clients provides concrete examples of how I've been able to help others."

Sources: Brad and Debra Schepp, *How to Find a Job on LinkedIn, Facebook, Twitter, MySpace, and Other Social Networks* (McGraw-Hill, 2010), http://press.linkedin.com/CPANewClients, accessed March 6, 2010; http://blog.linkedin.com/2009/07/21/divya-gugnani-how-linkedin-helps-me-close-deals-and-market-myself-better, accessed March 6, 2010; http://business.twitter.com/twitter101/case_teusner, accessed March 12, 2010.

(boss, wife) or gossip about your competitors. Also, especially for first calls on prospects, you want to avoid using trite phrases like "How are you doing today?" because they don't sound sincere.

Of course salespeople should consider cultural and personality differences and adapt the extent of their nonbusiness conversation accordingly. For example, an AT&T rep would probably spend considerably less time in friendly conversation with a New York City office manager than with, say, a manager in a rural Texas town. Businesspeople in Africa place such high value on establishing friendships that the norm calls for a great deal of friendly conversation before getting down to business. Chinese customers want a lot of rapport building before they get down to business. Amiables and expressives tend to enjoy such conversations, whereas drivers and analyticals may be less receptive to spending much time in nonbusiness conversation. Studies show that salespeople who adapt and mirror their prospects are more successful in gaining desired results.[9] Also, there could be less need for small talk if the salesperson uses a question or product opening when getting the customer's attention.

At this point in the sales call, after gaining the prospect's attention and establishing some rapport, a salesperson will often share his or her goals or agenda for the meeting with the prospect. This step can help build further rapport and trust. For example:

> Just so you know, my goal today is simply to verify what your needs might be and then, as I promised in the phone call, to share with you the results of the lab test we conducted last fall.

WHEN THINGS GO WRONG

Making and maintaining a good impression is important. How nice it would be if the beginning of every call went as smoothly as we have described here. Actually, things do go wrong sometimes. The best line of defense when something goes wrong is to maintain the proper perspective and a sense of humor. It's not the first thing you have done wrong and won't be your last. A good example of a call going downhill fast is the following experience, related by a salesperson:

> I pulled my right hand out of the pocket and stuck it forward enthusiastically to shake. Unfortunately, a ball of lint, about the size of a pea, had stuck to the tip of my fingers and was now drifting slowly down onto the document he had been reading. We both watched it descend, as compelling as the ball on New Year's Eve. We shook hands anyway. I said, "Excuse me," and bent forward to blow the ball of lint off the document. As I did so, I put a dent in the front edge of his desk with my briefcase.[10]

The worst response by this salesperson would be to faint, scream, or totally lose control. A better response would include a sincere apology for the dent and an offer to pay for any repairs. Further, proper planning might have prevented this situation: If the salesperson had walked into the room with his hands out of his pockets, he would not have picked up the lint.

What if you say something that is truly embarrassing? According to Mark Twain, "Man is the only animal that blushes, or needs to." For example, one salesperson calling on an older buyer motioned to a picture of a very young lady on the buyer's desk. "Is that your daughter?" the seller asked, smiling. "That's my wife," the buyer replied, frowning. In another sales call, the salesperson saw a picture on the prospect's desk and said, "Oh wow! What a great picture! How'd you ever get a picture of yourself with John Madden, the football guy!" The buyer replied angrily, "That's not John Madden, that's my wife!"[11] Obviously both sellers made major blunders. The first thing you should do in such a situation is to apologize sincerely. Then change the subject or move on in your presentation. Try to relax and put the incident behind you. And learn this lesson: Think before you speak!

Of course you can get into trouble without even saying a word. As Chapter 4 indicated, you must be careful when using gestures in other cultures because they often take on different meanings.

IDENTIFYING THE PROSPECT'S NEEDS: THE POWER OF ASKING QUESTIONS

Once the salesperson has entered and captured the buyer's attention, it is time to identify the buyer's needs. To begin this process, a salesperson might use transition sentences like the following (assuming a product approach was used to gain attention):

> Well, I'm glad you find this little model interesting. And I want to tell you all about it. But first I need to ask you a few questions to make sure I understand what your specific needs are. Is that okay?

From the BUYER'S SEAT

WHAT MY TOP SALESPEOPLE ARE LIKE

By William Fowler, DuPont

I've been an industrial buyer for DuPont, in the textiles division, for over 15 years. I've seen some big changes over the last 15 years of buying. Sellers are getting more professional. There are still the "used car" salesman types, but most are professional now. I'm also seeing sellers get more product knowledge. The best ones have good technical skills.

I've also seen more use of team selling/team buying. I will meet with a seller, and my engineer with meet with their sales engineer. That system works great! Each of us can talk to someone at our level of expertise and knowledge. If you asked me who are my best salespeople and what makes them great, I'd have an earful for you. Let me tell you about a few.

Pete is one of the best salespeople who calls on me. He sells pipes, fittings, and valves. What impresses me is the way he takes the time to really find out my needs. Sometimes I'm not even sure what I need due to some highly technical issues related to our business. In those cases he will meet with my engineers and plant people to find out exactly what we need and then supply that product.

Dale's another great salesperson. Why? Because he really finds out what we need before telling me what he has to sell. For example, we needed an actuated valve

that had some special features. Actuated simply means that something causes the valve to open or close. I needed a valve that would open, and stay open, if the power were to shut down. Otherwise the product would back up in the furnace, get too hot, and destroy the raw material. Dale worked with my engineering staff as well as those of us in procurement and developed an "open valve" solution to the problem. His solution required him to work not only with me and my team, but also with the engineers and product developers in his firm. The result was a win–win.

I ask myself sometimes, why aren't all the other sales reps who call on me more like Pete or Dale? I'm not sure, but I would point to several reasons. Often the salespeople seem too rushed, like they have a lot of places to be and not much time. I'm sure that's partly due to their quotas and the goals their managers are requiring them to achieve. Sometimes I think they don't do a good job for me because they don't view me or my business as important. Some just seem to want to get in and get out, and not build a relationship. But if more salespeople were like Pete or Dale, my life would sure be more happy.

Source: William Fowler, DuPont, personal correspondence; used with permission. Names changed to protect confidentiality.

If the buyer gives permission, the salesperson begins to ask questions about the buyer's needs. Don't be surprised if the buyer is reluctant to provide confidential information. There are many people out there trying to steal valuable company information. The seller has to establish credibility and trust.

Occasionally a salesperson makes the mistake of starting with product information rather than with a discussion of the prospect's needs. The experienced salesperson, however, attempts to uncover the prospect's needs and problems at the start of the relationship. In reality, discovering needs is still a part of qualifying the prospect.

Research continually demonstrates the importance of needs discovery. An analysis by Huthwaite, Inc., of more than 35,000 sales calls in 23 countries over a 12-year period revealed that the distinguishing feature of successful salespeople was their ability to discover the prospect's needs.[12] Discovering needs was more important than opening the call strategically, handling objections, or using closing techniques effectively. "From the Buyer's Seat 8.1" provides additional evidence of that fact.

Exhibit 8.3
Discovering the Root Cause of the Need

Need behind the need
Our competition is gaining on us, and we need to be more responsive than they are.

More strategic "root cause of the need" (buyer ends here)

Need behind the need
We need to improve our sales performance.

Initial need expressed (buyer starts here)

Need
We need to equip our sales force with laptop computers.

There is an underlying reason for every customer need, and the salesperson must continue probing until he or she uncovers the root problem or need. This process could be called "discovering the root cause of the need" and is graphically illustrated in Exhibit 8.3.

This salesperson is discovering the prospect's needs before describing the services he offers.

As you discover needs, keep in mind that this process can be uncomfortable for the prospect. The prospect may resent your suggesting that there could be a problem or a better way to do things. When faced with direct evidence that things could be better, the prospect may express fear (fear of losing her job if things are not corrected, or of things changing and the situation getting worse than it is now). Also, remember that the time needed to discuss needs varies greatly depending on the type of industry, the nature of the product, how well the salesperson and buyer know each other, and so forth. We will come back to this issue after we examine methods of identifying needs.

Chapter 4 covered most of the important communication principles regarding how to effectively ask questions of the prospect and be a better listener. Remember to speak naturally while asking questions. You don't want to sound like a computer asking a set of rote questions. Nor do you want to appear to be following a strict word-for-word outline that you learned in your sales training classes.

We now briefly describe two of the most widely used systems of needs identification taught to salespeople today.

ASKING OPEN AND CLOSED QUESTIONS

In the first method of needs discovery, salespeople are taught to distinguish between open and closed questions and then encouraged to utilize more open questions. Many highly respected sales training organizations, such as Wilson Learning and Achieve Global, use this type of approach. **Open questions** require the prospect to go beyond a simple yes-or-no response. They encourage the prospect to open up and share a great deal of useful information. For example:

What kinds of problems have the new federal guidelines caused for your division?

What do you know about our firm?

When you think of a quality sound system, what comes to mind?

Closed questions require the prospect to simply answer yes or no or to offer a short, fill-in-the-blank type of response. Examples include the following questions:

Have you ever experienced computer downtime as a result of an electrical storm?

Is fast delivery important for your firm?

How many checks do you usually write a month?

What balance do you normally keep in your checking account?

In most cases salespeople need to ask both open and closed questions. Open questions help paint the broad strokes of the situation, whereas closed questions help zero in on specific problems and attitudes. Some trainers believe simple, closed questions are best at first. Prospects become accustomed to talking and start to open up. After a few closed questions, the salesperson moves to a series of open questions. At some point he or she may revert back to closed questions.

Angie Main, a radio advertising salesperson, likes to ask her prospects the following two open questions to discover their needs:

What misconceptions do people have about your business?

If you could tell people one thing about your business, what would you want to tell them?[13]

Notice how these questions focus on the needs of the prospect rather than the solution (how her radio station can meet those needs).

Exhibit 8.4 contains an illustrative dialogue of a bank selling a commercial checking account to a business. In this sales presentation the salesperson's questions follow a logical flow. Note that follow-up probes are often necessary to clarify the prospect's responses. At the conclusion of asking open and closed questions, the salesperson should have a good feel for the needs and wants of the prospect.

One final suggestion is to summarize the prospect's needs:

So let me see if I have this right. You write about 35 checks a month, you keep about a $5,000 balance, and you are looking for a checking account that pays interest on your unused balance and has overdraft protection. . . . Is that correct?

Summarizing helps solidify the needs in the prospect's mind and ensures that the prospect has no other hidden needs or wants.

SPIN® TECHNIQUE

The SPIN method of discovering needs was developed by Huthwaite, an international research and training organization, after analyzing thousands of actual sales calls.[14] The results indicated that successful salespeople go through a logical needs identification sequence, which Huthwaite labeled **SPIN:** situation questions,

Exhibit 8.4

Using Open and Closed
Questions to Discover
Needs

Salesperson's Probe	Prospect's Response
Have you ever done business with our bank before? [closed]	No, our firm has always used First of America Bank.
I assume, then, that your checking account is currently with First of America? [closed]	Yes.
If you could design an ideal checking account for your business, what would it look like? [open]	Well, it would pay interest on all idle money, have no service charges, and supply a good statement.
When you say "good statement" what exactly do you mean? [open]	It should come to us once a month, be easy to follow, and help us reconcile our books quickly.
Uh-huh. Anything else in an ideal checking account? [open]	No, I guess that's about it.
What things, if any, about your checking account have dissatisfied you in the past? [open]	Having to pay so much for our checks! Also, sometimes when we have a question, the bank can't answer it quickly because the computers are down. That's frustrating!
Sure! Anything else dissatisfy you? [open]	Well, I really don't like the layout of the monthly statement we get now. It doesn't list checks in order; it has them listed by the date they cleared the bank.
Normally, what balance do you have on hand in your account? What minimum balance can you maintain? [closed]	About $8,500 now. We could keep a minimum of around $5,000, I guess.
Are you earning interest in your account now? [closed]	Yes, 3 percent of the average monthly balance if we maintain at least a $5,000 balance.
What kind of service charges are you paying now? [closed] [more questions]	$25 per month, $.25 per check, $.10 per deposit.
Is there anything else that I need to know before I begin telling you about our account? [open]	No, I think that just about covers it all.

*p*roblem questions, *i*mplication questions, and *n*eed payoff questions. SPIN works for salespeople involved in a **major sale:** one that involves a long selling cycle, a large customer commitment, an ongoing relationship, and large risks for the prospect if a bad decision is made. Major sales can occur anywhere but often involve large or national accounts. For example, both Johnson Wax and Bridgestone have used SPIN for their major accounts but may use other techniques for smaller accounts.

SPIN actually helps the prospect identify unrecognized problem areas. Often, when a salesperson simply asks an open question such as, "What problems are you having?" the prospect replies, "None!" The prospect isn't lying; he or she may not realize that a problem exists. SPIN excels at helping prospects test their current opinions or perceptions of the situation. Also, SPIN questions may be asked over the course of several sales calls, especially for large or important buyers. An abbreviated needs identification dialogue appears in Exhibit 8.5; it demonstrates all components of SPIN for a salesperson selling desktop publishing programs.

Situation Questions

Early in the sales call, salespeople ask **situation questions,** which are general data-gathering questions about background and current facts. The goal of these

Exhibit 8.5
Using the SPIN
Technique to Sell
Desktop Publishing

Salesperson: Do you ever send work out for typesetting? [situation question]

Prospect: Yes, about once a month we have to send work out because we are swamped.

Salesperson: Is the cost of sending work out a burden? [problem question]

Prospect: Not really. It costs only about 5 percent more, and we just add that to the customer's bill.

Salesperson: Do you get fast turnaround? [problem question]

Prospect: Well, now that you mention it, at times the turnaround is kind of slow. You see, we aren't given very high priority because we aren't big customers for the printer. We use them only when we have to, you know.

Salesperson: What happens if you miss a deadline for your customer because the turnaround is slow? [implication question]

Prospect: That happened only once, but it was disastrous. John, the customer, really chewed me out, and we lost a lot of our credibility. As I say, it happened only once, and I wouldn't like it to happen again to John—or any of our customers, for that matter!

Salesperson: If I can show you a way to eliminate outside typesetting without having to increase your staff, would you be interested? [need payoff question]

Prospect: Sure. The more I think about it, the more I realize I have something of a time bomb here. Sooner or later, it's going to go off!

---

questions is to better understand the prospect's current situation. Because these questions are broad, successful salespeople learn to limit them; prospects quickly become bored or impatient if they hear too many of them. Inexperienced and unsuccessful salespeople tend to ask too many situation questions. In fact, many situation-type questions should be answered through precall information gathering and planning. If a salesperson asks too many situation questions, the prospect will think the salesperson is unprepared. Here are some examples of situation questions:

What's your position? How long have you been here?

How many people do you employ? Is the number growing or shrinking?

What kind of handling equipment are you using at present? How long have you had it?

Problem Questions

When salespeople ask about specific difficulties, problems, or dissatisfactions the prospect has, they are asking **problem questions.** The goal is to discover a problem. Here are some examples of problem questions:

Is your current machine difficult to repair?

Do your operators ever complain that the noise level is too high?

If a seller can't discover a problem using problem questions, then she might need to ask additional situation questions first to uncover more issues that might lead to better problem questions.

Implication Questions

Questions that logically follow one or more problem questions and are designed to help the prospect recognize the true ramifications of the problem are **implication questions.** Implication questions cannot be asked until some problem area has been identified (through problem questions). The goal of implication questions is for the prospect to see that the identified problem has some serious ramifications and implications that make the problem worthy of being resolved.

These questions attempt to motivate the prospect to search for a solution to the problem.

Implication questions relate back to some similar issues that were described in the multiattribute model in Chapter 3. In the multiattribute model, customers weigh various attributes differently in terms of importance. In the same way, some problems that are identified by problem questions have more weight (are more serious in the eyes of the buyer) than others. The goal of the salesperson is to identify problems that have high importance to the buyer.

Examples of implication questions include these:

What happens if you ship your customer a product that doesn't meet specs?

What does having to pay overtime do to your price, as compared to your competitors'?

Does the slowness of your present system create any bottlenecks in other parts of the process?

If the buyer answers these questions in a way that indicates she doesn't see serious implications of the problem identified, the seller would have to go back and ask additional implication questions, problem questions, and maybe even situation questions. The seller doesn't move ahead to need payoff questions until the prospect sees that there are serious ramifications if he does not solve the problem.

Need Payoff Questions

When salespeople ask questions about the usefulness of solving a problem, they are asking **need payoff questions.** In contrast to implication questions, which are problem-centered, need payoff questions are solution-centered:

If I can show you a way to eliminate paying overtime for your operators and therefore reduce your cost, would you be interested?

Would you like to see a reduction in the number of products that don't meet quality specifications?

Would an increase in the speed of your present system by 5 percent resolve the bottlenecks you currently experience?

If the prospect responds negatively to a need payoff question, the salesperson has not identified a problem serious enough for the prospect to take action. In that case, the salesperson should probe further by asking additional problem questions, implication questions, and then a new need payoff question.

Conclusions about SPIN

One critical advantage of SPIN is that it encourages the prospect to define the need. During the questioning phase the salesperson is focusing on problems and isn't focusing on her product. As a result, the prospect views the salesperson more as a consultant trying to help than as someone trying to push a product.

SPIN selling has been taught to thousands of salespeople. Many salespeople quickly master the technique, whereas others have more difficulty. The best advice is to practice each component and to plan implication and need payoff questions before each sales call. SPIN works well for buyers that have a real problem (like inventory piling up). It is perhaps more difficult to use when the seller is only discussing an opportunity (no real problems, but "my solution could help you make more money").

REITERATING NEEDS YOU IDENTIFIED BEFORE THE MEETING

The extent to which one has to identify needs during any call depends on the success of precall information gathering. The salesperson may fully identify the needs of the prospect before making the sales call. In that case reiterating the needs early in the sales call is advisable so that both parties agree about the problem they are trying to solve. For example:

> Mr. Reed, based on our several phone conversations, it appears that you are looking for an advertising campaign that will position your product for the rapidly growing senior citizen market, at a cost under $100,000, using humor and a well-known older personality, and delivered in less than one month. Is that an accurate summary of your needs? Has anything changed since we talked last? Is there anything else I need to know at this point?

Likewise, in multiple-call situations, going through a complete needs identification at every call is unnecessary. But it is still best to briefly reiterate the needs identified to that point:

> In my last call we pretty much agreed that your number one concern is customer satisfaction with your inventory system. Is that correct? Has anything changed since we met last time, or is there anything else I need to know?

ADDITIONAL CONSIDERATIONS

How many questions can a salesperson ask to discover needs? It depends on the situation. Generally, as the buyer's risk of making the wrong decision goes up, so does the amount of time the salesperson can spend asking the prospect questions. For example, a Boeing salesperson could address an almost unlimited number of questions to United Air Lines because the airline realizes the importance of having Boeing propose the right airplane configuration. A salesperson for Johnson Wax calling on a local grocery store, on the other hand, has little time to probe needs before discussing an upcoming promotion and requesting an end-of-aisle display. Regardless of the situation, the salesperson should carefully prepare a set of questions that maximizes the use of available time.

Occasionally the prospect will refuse to answer important questions because the information is confidential or proprietary. The salesperson can do little except emphasize the reason for asking the questions. Ultimately the prospect needs to trust the salesperson enough to divulge sensitive data. Chapters 13 and 14 discuss trust-building strategies.

At times buyers do not answer questions because they honestly don't know the answers. The salesperson should then ask whether the prospect can get the information. If the prospect cannot do so, the salesperson can often ask the buyer's permission to probe further within the prospect's firm.

On the other hand, some buyers will not only answer questions but also appear to want to talk indefinitely. In general, the advice is to let them talk, particularly in many cultures. For example, people in French-speaking countries tend to love rhetoric, the act and art of speaking; attempts to cut them off will only frustrate and anger them.

ethics

thinking it through

Prospects often provide sensitive and confidential information when they reveal facts about their situations and needs. Assume that a prospect at Allied reveals to you her firm's long-term strategy for taking business away from her number one competitor, Baker's. You are close friends with the buyer at Baker's, which is one of your biggest customers. Will you share the confidential information with the Baker's buyer?

DEVELOPING A STRATEGY FOR THE PRESENTATION

Based on the needs identified, the salesperson should develop a strategy for how best to meet those needs. This process includes sorting through the various options available to the seller to see what is best for this prospect. To do so, the salesperson usually must sort out the needs of the buyer and prioritize them. Decisions have to be made about the exact product or service to recommend, the optimal payment terms to present for consideration, service levels to suggest, product or service features to stress during the presentation, and so on. Chapter 7 also talks about developing a strategy.

Products have many, many features, and one product may possess a large number of features that are unique and exciting when compared to competitive offerings. Rather than overload the customer with all the great features, successful salespeople discuss only those that specifically address the needs of the prospect. For example, suppose that a Philips salesperson learns from SPIN questioning that a prospect is looking for a DVD recorder to use only to record new training materials. In this situation the Philips representative should not spend time discussing the DVD recorder's ability to easily record from VCRs. The buyer has no need for this feature. Talking about lots of features of little interest to the customer is a waste of time and is sometimes called **feature dumping**.[15]

OFFERING VALUE: THE SOLUTION TO THE BUYER'S NEEDS

In addition to discovering the buyer's needs, the salesperson often also learns about the decision-making process (who is involved and in what capacity—see Chapter 3 for details), the buyer's time frame for making a decision, and the money budgeted. The seller develops a strategy to effectively communicate a solution to those needs; then it is time to make a presentation that shows how they can be addressed. This step includes relating product or service features that are meaningful to the buyer, assessing the buyer's reaction to what is being said, resolving objections (covered in Chapter 10), and obtaining commitment (the topic of Chapter 11). As one best-selling author stated, "Ditch the canned 1-2-3, sometimes pushy, usually insensitive, and almost always repetitive sales strategies glamorized in the past. . . . We must be willing to learn, adapt, and listen to our customers."[16]

The salesperson usually begins offering the solution with a transition sentence, something like the following: "Now that I know what your needs are, I would like to talk to you about how our product can meet those needs." The seller's job is then to translate product features into benefits for solving the buyer's needs. To do this effectively, the salesperson must know the metrics of the prospect's decision; that is, on what criteria and in what way is the prospect evaluating possible solutions? This will be discussed more in Chapter 9 and in other chapters.

RELATING FEATURES TO BENEFITS

A **feature** is a quality or characteristic of the product or service. Every product has many features designed to help potential customers. A **benefit** is the way in which a specific feature will help a particular buyer and is tied directly to the buying motives of the prospect. A benefit helps the prospect more fully answer the question "What's in it for me?" Exhibit 8.6 shows a list of features and sample benefits for a product. The way in which a salesperson shows how a product addresses the buyer's specific needs is sometimes called the **customer benefit proposition**.[17] This concept will be described more fully in Chapter 9.

Exhibit 8.6
An Example of Features and Benefits

The salesperson usually includes a word or a phrase to make a smooth transition from features to benefits:

> This china is fired at 2,600°F, and what that means to you is that it will last longer. Because it is so sturdy, you will be able to hand this china down to your children as an heirloom, which was one of your biggest concerns.

> Our service hotline is open 24 hours a day, which means that even your third-shift operators can call if they have any questions. That should be a real help to you because you said your third-shift supervisor was inexperienced in dealing with problems.

Some trainers suggest going beyond mentioning features and benefits. One variation, **FAB,** has salespeople discussing *features*, **advantages** (why that feature would be important to anyone), and *benefits*. For example:

> This car has antilock brakes [*feature*], which help the car stop quickly [*advantage*], which provides the safety you said you were looking for [*benefit*].

In another variation, **FEBA** (*features*, *evidence*, *benefits*, *agreement*), salespeople mention the feature, provide evidence that the feature actually exists, explain the benefit (why that feature is important to the buyer), and then ask whether the buyer agrees with the value of the feature and benefit. For example:

> This car has the highest-quality antilock brakes on the market today [*feature*] as proved by this test by the federal government [*evidence*]. They will provide the safety you said you were looking for [*benefit*]; don't you agree [*agreement*]?

Buyers are not interested in facts about the product or the seller's company unless those facts help solve their wants or needs. The salesperson's job is to supply the facts and then point out what those features mean to the buyer in terms of benefits and value creation. Neil Rackham, noted sales training leader, emphasizes this theme:

> The world has changed and so has selling. Today, the primary sales job is to create value—to add problem solving and creativity, so that the customer buys the advice and expertise of the salesperson as much as they buy the product . . . [in a survey] product pitches were the number one complaint from customers, with comments such as "It's quicker, more convenient, and more objective to go to the Internet than to listen to a product pitch."[18]

Exhibit 8.7 illustrates how one trainer incorporates these concepts into a problem/solution model. The customer's needs are called "business model." The salesperson knows some, but not all, of the buyer's needs before the sales call, represented by the first three lines under "business model." However, by actively listening (see Chapter 4), the seller learns more needs during the presentation, represented by lines 4 and 5 under "Business model." Using all identified needs, the seller talks about the relevant features and benefits. While doing this, the salesperson offers proof of these assertions, based on the customer's social style (see Chapter 5). The salesperson also engages in activities to help the buyer realize the importance of meeting his or her needs sooner, providing reasons to buy now. The end result is increased sales and profits for the seller.

Buyers typically consider two or more competitive products when making a purchase decision. Thus salespeople need to know more than just the benefits their products provide. They need to know how the benefits of their products are superior or inferior to the benefits of competitive products. Of course, as you explain the benefits of your service, you must make sure the prospect is looking for those benefits.

Sometimes, when selling certain commodities, it is important to sell the features and benefits of the seller's firm instead of the product. For example, Ray Hanson of Fastenal sells fasteners such as bolts and nuts. He states, "In the fastener industry I have found that a generic product, such as a nut or bolt, doesn't have too many features and benefits. We talk to our potential customers about the features our company has and how these features could benefit them as our customers."[19]

Exhibit 8.7
The Problem/Solution Model

Features	Benefits
Important to the Final Consumer	
Organic.	You want organic products, and this product is certified organic.
Only 90 calories per serving.	You can enjoy a treat without worrying about its effect on your weight.
100% of daily need for Vitamin C in every serving.	You are getting needed nutrition from a snack.
Important to the Grocery Store	
Test marketed for two years.	Because of this research, you are assured of a successful product and effective promotion; thus your risk is greatly reduced.
$500,000 will be spent for consumer advertising in the next 18 months.	Your customers will come to your store looking for the product.
40-cent coupon with front positioning in the national Sunday insert section.	Your customers will want to take advantage of the coupon and will be looking for the product in your store.

When selling to resellers, salespeople have two sets of benefits to discuss with the prospect: what the features of the product will do for the reseller and what the product features will do for the ultimate consumer of the product. Covering both sets of features and benefits is important. Exhibit 8.8 illustrates the two sets of features.

ASSESSING REACTIONS

While making a presentation, salespeople need to continually assess the reactions of their prospects. The prospect needs to agree that the benefits described would actually help his or her company. By listening to what buyers say and observing their body language (see Chapter 4 to review how to be a better listener), salespeople can determine whether prospects are interested in the product. If buyers react favorably to the presentation and seem to grasp the benefits of the proposed solution, the salesperson will have less need to make alterations or adjustments. But if a prospect does not develop enthusiasm for the product, the salesperson will need to make some changes in the presentation.

Using Nonverbal Cues

An important aspect of making adjustments is interpreting a prospect's reactions to the sales presentation. By observing the prospect's five channels of nonverbal

Nonverbal cues help salespeople know when to make adjustments. Can you interpret the cues provided by members of this buying team (the three on the right side)?

communication, salespeople can determine how to proceed with their presentations. Chapter 4 provides more detailed information about nonverbal cues.

Verbal Probing

As salespeople move through a presentation, they must take the pulse of the situation. This process, often called a **trial close,** is more fully described in Chapter 11. For example, the salesperson should say something like the following:

> How does this sound to you?
>
> Can you see how these features help solve the problem you have?
>
> Have I clearly explained our program to you?
>
> Do you have any questions?

The use of such probing questions helps achieve several things. First, it allows the salesperson to stop talking and encourages two-way conversation. Without such probing, a salesperson can turn into a rambling talker while the buyer becomes a passive listener. Second, probing lets the salesperson see whether the buyer is listening and understanding what is being said. Third, the probe may show that the prospect is uninterested in what the salesperson is talking about. This response allows the salesperson to redirect the conversation to areas of interest to the buyer. This kind of adjustment is necessary in almost every presentation and underscores the fact that the salesperson should not simply memorize a canned presentation that unfolds in a particular sequence.

Salespeople must listen. Often we hear only what we want to hear. This behavior is called **selective perception,** and everyone is guilty of it at times. For example, read the following sentence:[20]

> Finished files are the result of years of scientific study combined with the experience of years.

Now go back and quickly count the number of f's in that sentence. Most non-native English speakers see all six f's, whereas native English speakers see only three (they don't count the f's in *of* because it is not considered an important word). The point is that once salespeople stop actively listening, they miss many things the buyer is trying to communicate.

Making Adjustments

Salespeople can alter their presentations in many ways to obtain a favorable reaction. For example, a salesperson may discover during a sales presentation that the prospect simply does not believe the seller has the appropriate product knowledge. Rather than continue with the presentation, the salesperson should redirect her or his efforts toward establishing credibility in the eyes of the prospect. Salespeople need to continually adapt to the situation at hand.

Other adjustments might require collecting additional information about the prospect, developing a new sales strategy, or altering the style of presentation. For example, a salesperson may believe a prospect is interested in buying an economical, low-cost motor. While presenting the benefits of the lowest-cost motor, the salesperson discovers the prospect is interested in the motor's operating costs. At this point the salesperson should ask some questions to find out whether the prospect would be interested in paying a higher price for a more efficient motor with lower operating costs. On the basis of the prospect's response, the salesperson can adopt a new sales strategy, one that emphasizes operating efficiency rather than the motor's initial price. In this way the sales presentation is shifted from features and benefits based on a low initial cost to features and benefits related to low operating costs.

BUILDING CREDIBILITY DURING THE CALL ●────

To develop a close and harmonious relationship, the salesperson must be perceived as having **credibility**—that is, he or she must be believable and reliable. A salesperson can take many actions during a sales call to develop such a perception.[21]

To establish credibility early in the sales call, the salesperson should clearly delineate the time she or he thinks the call will take and then stop when the time is up. How many times has a salesperson said, "This will take only 5 minutes!" and 30 minutes later you still can't get rid of him? No doubt you would have perceived the salesperson as more credible if, after 5 minutes, he or she stated, "Well, I promised to take no more than 5 minutes, and I see our time is up. How would you like to proceed from here?" One successful salesperson likes to ask for half an hour and take only 25 minutes.[22]

Another way to establish credibility is to offer concrete evidence to back up verbal statements. If a salesperson states, "It is estimated that more than 80 percent of the households in America will own handheld Web browsers by 2015," he or she should be prepared to offer proof of this assertion—for instance, hand the prospect a letter or an article from a credible source. Ways to establish credibility are discussed in greater detail in Chapter 9.

Some trainers suggest adding a **credibility statement** early in the sales call that includes features of yourself and your company. [23] The purpose of the statement is to help the buyer realize you are capable of meeting her needs. The statement can be strengthened by proving its assertions with such items as testimonials and test results (more about these in the next chapter). Here's an example of a credibility statement:

> Hank, I don't know how much you may know about Apple Valley Savings and Loan. We were founded by a Swedish immigrant back in 1932 whose stated goal was to offer the best service in the Midwest. We've now grown into the third-largest savings bank in the upper Midwest with assets exceeding $23 billion and are the only savings bank in the Midwest earning the coveted Pinnacle Award for Excellent eight years in a row. We have over 32 branches in the five-state region. I've been with the bank for the last 14 years and have spent the last 6 years working closely with higher education institutions like yours. In terms of investments, we have focused a great deal of effort on higher education. For example, we recently provided a $2.3 million loan to West Valania State University to expand its ice hockey rink.

ethics

Of course, one way to establish credibility is to avoid making statements that do not have the ring of truth to them. For example, some suggest you should avoid using a phrase like "We're the best" or "We're number one." As one skeptical buyer noted, "Just how many number ones are there in the world, anyway?" Salespeople should also remember that, in addition to damaging credibility, truth-stretching comments can come back to haunt them in the form of legal liability (see Chapter 2 for a review of legal issues).

Many salespeople have found that the most effective way to establish credibility is to make a **balanced presentation** that shows all sides of the situation—that is, to be totally honest. Thus a salesperson might mention some things about the product that make it less than perfect or may speak positively about some exclusive feature of a competitor's product. Will this approach defeat the seller's chances of a sale? No. In fact, it may increase the chances of building long-term commitment and rapport. "Building Partnerships 8.1" provides insights about one salesperson who gives balanced presentations. Salespeople can keep customers happy and dedicated by helping them form correct, realistic expectations about a product or service.

ethics

Salespeople can build credibility by recognizing cultural differences, not only in foreign markets but also in North America. How? By demonstrating sensitivity to the needs and wants of specific subcultures and avoiding biased or racist language. See Chapter 4 for more information about cultural differences.

In selling complex products, sales representatives often must demonstrate product expertise at the beginning of the sales process—for example, by telling

"I THINK YOU SHOULD USE MY COMPETITOR'S PRODUCT INSTEAD"

One aspect of my job selling replacement joints (hips, knees, and so forth) requires me to service what I sell, and in the case of replacement joints that means going into the operating room with the surgeon and taking the role of a technical expert when it comes to the capabilities, function, and surgical technique used with my company's hardware. A doctor I had worked with previously had called me to let me know that he had just seen a young man with a severe tibia fracture in the ER, and he wanted to use a set of my company's plates and screws to fix the fracture the following morning. I told him I would bring the hardware and the instruments down to the hospital that night for sterilization and that I would be there in the morning for the surgery.

Our company did not have a contract with this hospital, which means we were not allowed to keep a wide variety of equipment stocked in the hospital; rather, we were allowed to bring in only specifically requested hardware and instruments on a case-by-case basis, and then we had to remove it after the case was over. One of our competitors did have a contract, so they had basically every product they make stocked in the hospital; my company was trying to secure the same deal, which would be worth a substantial amount of money. This usually requires surgeons trying our equipment and liking the product and the service enough that they want it available at all times.

I arrived the following morning, and the surgery began on time. This type of surgery is one where the surgeon opens the area of the fracture, reduces the fracture gap, and then fixes the bone back in position with the plates and screws. Sometimes the X-rays don't provide an accurate picture of what the break will look like once the patient is open. Once this patient was opened, the fracture was somewhat more complex than the doctor had thought it would be. The doctor was examining the fracture and questioning if the plate and screw set I had brought in was going to be big enough. He said he was pretty sure he could make it work, but he wanted my opinion. I was also fairly confident that the set we had would work ,but it would probably make the surgery a little more difficult. A larger plate and screw set would work with room to spare. What should I do?

In this case I recommended that the doctor use a larger set, which meant that his only option would be the competitor's set that was stocked and sterilized in the hospital. The doctor agreed that would be the safest option, so he brought in the competitor's equipment. The competitor's rep was not available because he was in another surgery, so I stayed in the OR and helped the doctor with the case and the competitor's equipment. It meant a loss of several thousand dollars by having the doctor not use our hardware; but the doctor told me afterward that he was aware of the fact that I had sacrificed a sale by recommending he use the other equipment, but that the trust I had earned with him would guarantee that he would be using more of our equipment in the future and that he would recommend to the hospital administration that our company be given a contract. This doctor has become one of our best customers.

Source: Brendan Brooks, Smith & Nephew Inc., personal correspondence; used with permission.

---

the customer, without bragging, about their special training or education. They can also strengthen credibility with well-conceived, insightful questions or comments.

When selling complicated technical products and services, Todd Graf notes, "You have to keep it simple. Teach as you go. Make transitions slow and smooth and always ask if they understand (half the time they don't). This is key because they may have to go back and explain some of your features to the decision maker who isn't present in this meeting."[24]

Being willing to say, "I'm sorry, I was wrong on that," or "I don't know the answer to that, but I'll get it to you," will also go a long way toward establishing credibility. A seller should never use a word if he or she doesn't know the exact definition. Some buyers may even test the salesperson. Here's an example from a real salesperson who was calling on a doctor:[25]

> SALESPERSON: Because product X acts as an agonist at the kappa receptor, miosis will occur.
>
> DOCTOR: What does *miosis* mean?
>
> SALESPERSON: It means the stage of disease during which intensity of signs and symptoms diminishes.
>
> DOCTOR: No! *Miosis* means contraction of the pupils.

At this point the doctor walked out of the room, and the seller thought she had lost all credibility. Actually, he had just gone out and grabbed a dictionary. The first definition was the contraction of the pupils, and the second was the seller's definition. The salesperson's definition, not the doctor's, fit the use of the term for this medication. The doctor then shook the seller's hand and thanked her for teaching him a new definition of the word. The salesperson's credibility certainly increased.

SELLING TO GROUPS

Selling to groups can be both rewarding and frustrating. On the plus side, if you make an effective presentation, every member of the prospect group becomes your ally. On the down side, groups behave like groups, with group standards and norms and issues of status and group leadership.

When selling to groups, the salesperson must gather information about the

Selling to groups requires special skills in monitoring several individuals at once, as well as being able to respond to customers with occasionally conflicting needs.

needs and concerns of each individual who will attend. Salespeople should discover (for each prospect group member) member status within the group, authority, perceptions about the urgency of the problem, receptivity to ideas, knowledge of the subject matter, attitude toward the salesperson, major areas of interest and concern, key benefits sought, likely resistance, and ways to handle this resistance. Chapter 3 discusses many things that salespeople should consider about buying centers.

It is important to develop not only objectives for the meeting but also objectives for what the seller hopes to accomplish with each prospect present at the meeting. Planning may include the development of special visual aids for specific individuals present. The seller must expect many more objections and interruptions in a group setting compared to selling to an individual.

An informal atmosphere in which group members are encouraged to speak freely and the salesperson feels free to join the group's discussion usually works best in these situations. Thus an informal location (such as a corner of a large room as opposed to a formal conference room) is preferred. Formal presentation methods, such as speeches, that separate buyers and sellers into them-versus-us sides should be avoided. If the group members decide that the meeting is over, the salesperson should not try to hold them.

Of course most things you have learned about selling to individuals apply equally to groups. You should learn the names of group members and use them when appropriate. You should listen carefully and observe all nonverbal cues. When one member of the buying team is talking, it is especially important to observe the cues being transmitted by the other members of the buying team to see whether they are, in effect, agreeing or disagreeing with the speaker.

There are several types of group selling situations. If the group meeting is actually a negotiation session, many more things must be considered. As a result, we devote an entire chapter (Chapter 12) to the topic of formal negotiations. Also, sometimes a salesperson makes a call on a prospect as part of a selling team from his firm (for example, the team might consist of his sales manager, someone from technical support, someone from customer support, and a sales executive from the firm). These situations require coordination and teamwork. Because of the importance of the various selling team scenarios, the issue of selling teams is more fully discussed in Chapter 16.

SELLING YOURSELF

It's a fact. You're going to be selling yourself while trying to get that first job right out of college. Don't forget to use everything you've read in this chapter as you do so. Otherwise you'll look and sound like the thousands of other students who merely *hope* that the company will hire them without really keying in on what the hiring company is looking for.

Always attempt to build rapport with an interviewer. Find something you have in common with her, based on information you learned from her LinkedIn profile, from your professor, or even from the staff in the career services center at your school. Someone is bound to know something about the person. Use that information to break the ice and build a sense of "liking" between the two of you. You'll be surprised how much that simple act calms you down as you realize you really do have some things in common.

Make sure you discover interviewers' needs. What exactly are they looking for in a job candidate? If you've not already discovered it, and the information is not available on their Web site, then go ahead and ask. The interviewers won't think you're weird; they'll think you are sharp. Once you find out what those needs are, sell yourself by explicitly showing how your "features" meet their needs. For example, your résumé might state the following:

> Reading with Champions Volunteer, Birchwood Elementary School: read to elementary school students two times a week to help them gain a love for books.

You're interviewing for a sales job, not a job to read books to small children. So it's your job to convert that feature into a benefit to the interviewers with something like the following:

> You said you were looking for someone with a hard work ethic and also for someone with an ability to interact with lots of different kinds of clients. Well, my volunteer work demonstrates my work ethic because I did this activity for six months, all while I was also taking 18 credits at school. I never missed a reading at that school, either! Also, the children I interacted with at that school were not like me at all. Most came from poor backgrounds and broken families. Many had never had a book read to them before. Anyway, what all of this means to you is that I am able to interact with people who are very different from me. In fact I enjoy it. I'm sure I'll be able to adapt to the many different types of customers you say you have at your firm. Did that example help you see that I am a hard worker and that I can interact with different types of people?

Finally, establish credibility by bringing your portfolio with you to the interview. The portfolio should include copies of papers you wrote, videos of presentations you gave, and any other evidence that will demonstrate that you have the skills they are looking for.

SUMMARY

Salespeople need to make every possible effort to create a good impression during a sales call. The first few minutes with the prospect are important, and care should be taken to make an effective entrance by giving a good first impression, expressing confidence while standing and shaking hands, and selecting an appropriate seat.

The salesperson can use any of several methods to gain the prospect's attention. Salespeople should adopt the opening that is most effective for the prospect's personality style. Also critical is the development of rapport with the prospect, which can often be enhanced by engaging in friendly conversation.

Before beginning any discussion of product information, the salesperson can establish the prospect's needs by using open and closed questions. The SPIN technique is very effective for discovering needs in a major sale. In subsequent calls the salesperson should reiterate the prospect's needs.

When moving into a discussion of the proposed solution or alternatives, the salesperson translates features into benefits for the buyer. The salesperson also makes any necessary adjustments in the presentation based on feedback provided by the buyer's nonverbal cues and by verbal probing.

A close, harmonious relationship will enhance the whole selling process. The salesperson can build credibility by adhering to stated appointment lengths, backing up statements with proof, offering a balanced presentation, and establishing his or her credentials.

When selling to groups, the salesperson must gather information about the needs and concerns of each individual who will attend. The seller should also uncover the ego involvement and issue involvement of each group member. It is important to develop objectives not only for the meeting but also for what the seller hopes to accomplish with each prospect present at the meeting.

Now that you know how to start the sale, discover needs, relate features to specific benefits for the buyer, and build credibility, it is time to look more closely at how to communicate your ideas more effectively. That's the topic of the next chapter.

KEY TERMS

ETHICS PROBLEMS

1. You're an account executive for Wells Fargo Financial in Minnesota. You had an initial appointment with a customer, June, to find out what her goals were financially. The meeting went just as a typical first meeting should go, and there was a beneficial product you could create for her. However, her husband could not meet with you. After weeks of work and preparation, you have a loan that makes sense. The loan meets the goals June wanted, so you have a second appointment with her to go over exact terms . . . again without her husband. You asked when her husband could come in and sign the loan documents, and she discloses to you that her husband is not aware of the $35,000 of credit card debts the loan is going to pay off. Both the husband and wife must be present at the time of the loan. Legally you can call the husband and tell him about the loan application. What should you do?

2. You're calling on an important prospect in the paper industry, and she starts asking you how other mills are handling a specific problem. You know that this is important competitive information and that you should not provide details about a competitor. Instead you decide to give the prospect the information without specifics (like the name of the mill you're talking about). Is that OK?

Source: Erik Abrahamson, Wells Fargo Financial; used with permission.

QUESTIONS AND PROBLEMS

1. Think for a moment about trying to secure a sales job. Assume you are going to have an interview with a district manager of a consumer products firm next week for a sales position. What can you do to develop rapport and build credibility with her?

2. "I don't need to discover my prospect's needs. I sell bottled water to grocery stores and convenience stores. I know what their needs are: a high profit margin and fast turnover of products!" Comment.

3. Develop the FEBA for one of the features shown in Exhibit 8.8.

4. Assume that you are selling yard maintenance services to a homeowner. Develop a series of open and closed questions to discover the prospect's needs.

5. Assume that you represent your school's placement service. You are calling on a large business nearby that never hires graduates from your college. Generate a list of SPIN questions, making any additional assumptions necessary.

6. Prepare a list of features and benefits that could be used in a presentation to other students at your college. The objective of the presentation is to encourage them to enroll in the selling course you are taking.

7. "Sales Technology 8.1" told about the use of social networking to gain information and hence do a better job of gaining the prospect's attention. Look at the profiles of two of your friends or contacts on LinkedIn, Facebook, MySpace, or some other social networking site. Using strictly the information you find there, what are some ways you could gain that person's attention in a sales call, assuming you didn't actually know them before the call?

8. In "Building Partnerships 8.1" you read about a salesperson who told a doctor to use a competitor's product. The story has a happy ending. But what if the doctor had not become one of Brendan's best customers as a result of Brendan's actions? If Brendan knew that was going to be the outcome, should he have suggested the doctor use his product, not the competitor's product?

9. In which situations should a salesperson use a prospect's first name? When should a more formal salutation be used?

10. You're selling a new soft drink to a grocery store (choose one). Write a list of features and benefits for the grocery store, as well as a list of features and benefits for the store's customers (the shoppers who come in and buy soft drinks).

11. In "From the Buyer's Seat 8.1" you heard a buyer describe his best salespeople. The buyer said that he believes one reason more salespeople aren't great is that they are too rushed. What can a salesperson do to be less rushed and to spend the right amount of time with each customer? What can a company do to ensure that salespeople aren't too rushed?

case **8.1**

AirCharter (Part B)

Founded in 1985, AirCharter has provided charter flights to a wide array of customers, including business travelers worldwide. Thanks to AirCharter's online booking system, business travelers can secure reliable quotes and book both domestic and international flights. AirCharter has more than 3,000 aircraft, including jets (light, midsize, and large jets) and turboprops.

The company is known for its ability to cater to passengers' every desire, including gourmet meals, special beverages, entertainment while in the air, and other luxury accommodations. AirCharter also staffs a full-service VIP jet concierge program, similar to what major airlines offer. This service can help clients meet all their needs on the ground before and after the flight.

Felix Aleynykov is a salesperson for AirCharter. Today he will be making his first visit to Abel Espinosa, a procurement officer at the AFL-CIO. The AFL-CIO is one of the largest labor federations in the United States and has three primary executive officers: president, secretary-treasurer, and executive vice president. Both the executive officers and the executive council travel across the country a great deal in their work.

For more details about AirCharter and the AFL-CIO, see Case 7.1.

Questions

1. Develop a set of open and closed questions to fully discover Abel Espinosa's needs.

2. Develop a set of SPIN questions to discover Abel Espinosa's needs.

Sources: http://www.aircharter.net, www.aflcio.org.

case **8.2**

ProPlan Software

Mark Alonzo, of ProPlan, had an important appointment with a senior buyer and her assistant at a pharmaceutical company. It had taken Mark three months to get the appointment, and he was excited about the chance to finally demonstrate his company's new system planning software. As Mark was leaving his office, his sales manager learned where Mark was going and asked to come alone. Mark had no option but to say, "Sure." However, he was worried because his manager often took control of meetings and sometimes wasn't a good listener.

When the sales team got there, the buyer, Tracey, stated that she could participate for only about 30 minutes but that her assistant, Sally, would be staying for the remainder of the time. Before Mark could begin talking, Roy, his sales manager, began taking the buyers through his sales binder that had a presentation in it. It began with the history of the company.

Tracey politely interrupted and explained that she was already familiar with ProPlan, but there were certain things that she was interested in learning about their services. Tracey asked the sales team if they could produce two items for her.

Again, before Mark could answer, Roy jumped in with, "Yes, we could, and I'm going to get there in a minute." Tracey patiently waited as he continued to take her through the company history. By now almost 10 minutes had passed.

Next Roy talked about the work that ProPlan had done for other companies. This is something that many buyers are usually interested in. However, Tracey interrupted again and said they were really looking for a vendor for a couple of specific projects, and that she wanted to see what they could do for those specific situations. Roy replied, "Hang on, Tracey. I'm almost there! I promise to get there soon."

After Roy finished showing the work ProPlan did for other companies, he began to explain the benefits of working with his company because of reputation, pricing, service, and so on. Tracey asked again about the two projects, and instead of answering her questions, Roy continued to follow his canned presentation. Tracey was becoming noticeably upset and agitated, although Sally seemed quite interested.

Questions

1. You are Mark. What will you do now?
2. How can you avoid a situation like this in future calls with your manager?

Source: Tracey Brill. Used with permission.

ROLE PLAY CASE

Today we are going to start over again, "from the top" as they say in the theater. Start from the beginning of the sales call, from when you knock on the door through the needs identification stage, ending just before your presentation. All that you have learned in previous role plays about the account continues to hold true. If you've been selling to Spear One, you'll continue to do so, but you are now meeting with a different member of the buying center. The same is true for McLane Properties and Dart Paper Products. New buyer sheets will be passed out. You can have the same person play the new role or someone else in class. (*Note:* If you have not done role plays before, you will need to review the information about the various role play customers that can be found at the end of Chapter 3.)

If your class is divided into groups of three, the person who is watching should create a check sheet. Write *S, P, I,* and *N* down the left side of the paper. As the salesperson asks a question, check whether it is a situation, problem, implication, or needs payoff question. Also note if and how he or she identified or verified the decision process. *Don't forget:* At the start of the sales call, identify the type of opening used (introduction, benefit, product, curiosity, or some other form).

> *Spear One:* You will meet with the VP of sales and marketing. This is an appointment that was set up by the regional sales manager you called on earlier. You've never talked to this person before.
>
> *McLane Properties:* Mr. McLane has asked to see you. You weren't expecting this from your earlier sales calls, but you welcome the opportunity to meet the decision maker. His secretary called and made the appointment.
>
> *Dart Paper Products:* You are meeting with one of the VPs of sales. The other VP was fired, but you don't know why. The meeting was set up by the regional sales manager you called on earlier, who also told you about the firing, but she didn't know what had happened.

Note: For background information about these role plays, please see page 27.

To the instructor: Additional information needed to complete the role play is available in the Instructor's Manual.

ADDITIONAL REFERENCES

Belonax Jr., Joseph J., Stephen J. Newell, and Richard E. Plank. "The Role of Purchase Importance on Buyer Perceptions of the Trust and Expertise Components of Supplier and Salesperson Credibility in Business-to-Business Relationships." *Journal of Personal Selling & Sales Management* 27, no. 3 (Summer 2007), pp. 247–58.

Burn, Brian. *The Maverick Selling Method: Simplifying the Complex Sale.* Xlibris Corporation, 2009.

Cassell, Jeremy, and Tom Bird. *Brilliant Selling: What the Best Salespeople Know, Do, and Say.* FT Press, 2009.

Chan, Elaine, and Jaideep Sengupta. "Insincere Flattery Actually Works: A Dual Attitudes Perspective." *Journal of Marketing Research* 47, no. 1 (February 2010).

Clifford, Stephanie. "Putting the Performance in Sales Performance." *Inc.,* February 2007, pp. 87–95.

Fautsch, Leo. "Persuasion." *American Salesman* 52, no. 1 (January 2007), pp. 13–16.

Graham, John. "When the Sales Mentality Meets the Buyer Mindset." *American Salesman,* March 2007, pp. 25–30.

Griffin, Jill G., and Susan M. Broniarczyk. "The Slippery Slope: The Impact of Feature Alignability on Search and Satisfaction." *Journal of Marketing Research* 47, no. 2 (April 2010).

Johnson, Mark S., Eugene Sivadas, and Vishal Kashyap. "Response Bias in the Measurement of Salesperson Orientations: The Role of Impression Management." *Industrial Marketing Management* 38, no. 8 (November 2009), pp. 1014–24.

Keh, Hean Tat, and Yi Xie. "Corporate Reputation and Customer Behavioral Intentions: The Roles of Trust, Identification, and Commitment." *Industrial Marketing Management* 38, no. 7 (October 2009), pp. 732–42.

Laaksonen, Toni, Kalle Pajunen, and Harri I. Kulmala. "Co-evolution of Trust and Dependence in Customer–Supplier Relationships." *Industrial Marketing Management* 37, no. 8 (November 2008), pp. 910–20.

Lager, Marshall. "The Psychology of the Sale: There's a Lot Going on inside the Customer's Head, Whether You Put It There or Not. What Are Salespeople Up Against?" *CRM Magazine* 13, no. 5 (2009), pp. 34–37.

Lovas, Michael, and Pam Holloway. *Axis of Influence: How Credibility and Likeability Intersect to Drive Success.* Morgan James Publishing, 2009.

Ramani, Girish, and V. Kumar. "Interaction Orientation and Firm Performance." *Journal of Marketing* 72, no. 1 (January 2008), pp. 27–45.

Read, Nicholas A.C., and Dr. Stephen J. Bistritz. *Selling to the C-Suite: What Every Executive Wants You to Know about Successfully Selling to the Top.* McGraw-Hill, 2009.

Stoddard, James E., Stephen W. Clopton, and Ramon A. Avila. "An Analysis of the Effects of Sales Force Automation on Salesperson Perceptions of Performance." *Journal of Personal Selling & Sales Management* 27, no. 2 (Spring 2007), pp. 191–92.

Sundtoft Hald, Kim, Carlos Cordón, and Thomas E. Vollmann. "Towards an Understanding of Attraction in Buyer–Supplier Relationships." *Industrial Marketing Management* 38, no. 8 (November 2009), pp. 960–70.

Wood, John Andy, James S. Boles, and Barry J. Babin. "The Formation of Buyer's Trust of the Seller in an Initial Sales Encounter." *Journal of Marketing Theory and Practice* 16, no. 1 (Winter 2008), pp. 27–40.

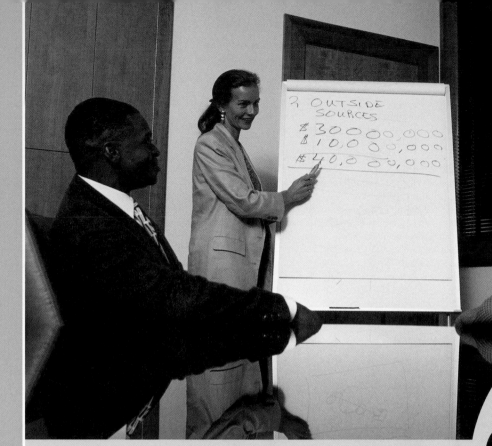

chapter **9**

STRENGTHENING THE PRESENTATION

SOME QUESTIONS ANSWERED IN THIS CHAPTER ARE

- How can salespeople use verbal tools to strengthen a presentation?
- Why do salespeople need to augment their oral communication through tools such as visual aids, samples, testimonials, and demonstrations?
- What methods are available to strengthen a presentation?
- How can salespeople use visual aids and technology most effectively?
- What are the ingredients of a good demonstration?
- Is there a way to quantify the salesperson's solution to a buyer's problem?
- How can salespeople reduce presentation jitters?

PROFILE

PROFILE A few years ago I learned to fly airplanes and earned my private pilot's license. What's the most challenging is how it demands both physical and mental capabilities at the same time. You are maneuvering the airplane and abiding by countless regulations all while communicating to the air traffic controllers in an entirely different language. It is quite the experience. Once you master the proper steps you are on your way toward safe takeoffs, landings, and accident-free flying. But only when you and your flight instructor know that everything has come together is it safe for you to take to the sky and fly solo.

The same is true when it comes to selling. When I was chosen by sales instructors Nicole Howatt-Moberg and Cyndi Gundy to be part of the team representing the University of Central Florida at the National Collegiate Sales Competition, I was eager to capitalize on the opportunity and, most importantly, make UCF proud.

The sales competition was a lot like flying. Everything had to come together with precise timing and finesse in order to achieve success. We were the number one seed going into the competition and had great expectations to live up to. Our team members were each assigned research tasks to learn about NetSuite, the product we were assigned to sell in the competition. In between practice sessions and strategy meetings we dug up every feature, benefit, and statistic that we could find. We had pages and spreadsheets full of them!

As we pulled together all our tools for the competition, our coaches, Karl Sooder and Dr. Bill Callarman, and our mentors, award-winning author Jeff Lehman and founder/CEO of SalesGravy.com Jeb Blount, continually asked us to present our value proposition. They were relentless about it! We willingly played back the list of features and benefits of NetSuite. However, it was not resonating the way we all wanted it to. Then it occurred to us that reciting a list of features and benefits was not going to make for a successful value proposition. Instead it is the succinct combination of the two that creates the attention, interest, conviction, desire, and opportunity to close the prospect.

Plainly stated, having a well-crafted value proposition is the key to capitalizing on the selling opportunity. You have to be able to state your value proposition with genuine conviction. If you own the value proposition, you will do well. We practiced ours over and over. Not until everyone on our team knew it inside out were we were ready to perform successfully at the NCSC.

When preparing for a sales presentation, try putting yourself in the shoes of the buyer. When a potential client asks you, "What does your product do and how will it help my company?" can you give them a unique and well-crafted two-sentence answer that would make sense to someone who might have only briefly heard of your company? If so, does your answer also make them want to know more? The ability to deliver on both accounts is critical to a successful career in sales. That is exactly why my coaches perpetually stressed the importance of having an effective value proposition for the competition (and my sales career). An effective value proposition was part of our core strategy back at NCSC, and is also something that I actively utilize in my sales career to this day.

My coaches (who have a significant amount of practical "seat time" at high levels inside corporate America) told me that even the largest of corporations have trouble articulating their value propositions to their sales professionals and out to their customers. Yet the value proposition is an instrumental tool that, once mastered, can pay huge dividends to the sales professional. Excellent listening skills will allow you to deliver the relative features and custom-tailored benefits to the customers while keeping it easy to understand. All too often a salesperson will resort to restating feature lists and entirely miss the key benefit to the buyers. This is a sure way to confuse them and jeopardize the sale.

At NCSC I proceeded from the initial rounds all the way to the semifinals. Along with my teammate Jessica Cernell, we earned enough points to place 7th in the nation among 50+ universities. After graduating I accepted a sales position at the industry leader in document management, IKON Office Solutions. I have since put IKON's value proposition to good use. Being able to deliver a captivating value proposition has blessed me with many sales, and I wish you the same success.

Source: Andrew Eric Gaffka © 2010; used with permission.

Visit our Web page at www.ikon.com.

CHARACTERISTICS OF A STRONG PRESENTATION

Communication tools such as visual aids, samples, testimonials, demonstrations, and the use of humor are important ingredients in most sales calls. Use of such tools focuses the buyer's attention, improves the buyer's understanding, helps the buyer remember what the salesperson said, offers concrete proof of the salesperson's statements, and creates a sense of value.

KEEPS THE BUYER'S ATTENTION

How many times has your mind wandered during classroom lectures while the instructor earnestly discussed some topic? What happened? The instructor lost your attention. In contrast, your attention probably remains more focused in a class when the instructor uses visuals and humor effectively, brings in guest speakers, and finds ways to get you actively involved in the discussion.

The same is true of buyer–seller interactions. Unless you can get the buyer actively involved in the communication process and doing more than just passively hearing you talk, the buyer's attention will probably turn to other topics. "Building Partnerships 9.1" illustrates how one salesperson regained the buyer's attention in a difficult situation.

The buyer's personality can also affect his or her attention span. For example, one would expect an amiable to listen more attentively to a long presentation than, say, a driver would. Thus an effective salesperson should consider the social style of the prospect and adapt the use of communication aids accordingly (see Chapter 5 for more about personality styles).

IMPROVES THE BUYER'S UNDERSTANDING

Many buyers have difficulty forming clear images from the written or spoken word. An old Chinese proverb says, "Tell me—I'll forget. Show me—I may remember. But involve me, and I'll understand." Appeals should be made to as many of the senses (hearing, sight, touch, taste, and smell) as possible. Studies show that appealing to more than one sense with **multiple-sense appeals** increases understanding dramatically, as Exhibit 9.1 illustrates. For example, in selling Ben & Jerry's ice cream novelties to a grocery store manager, the salesperson may describe the product's merits (an appeal to the sense of hearing) or show the product and invite the merchant to taste it (appeals to sight, touch, and taste). Appeals to the grocer's fifth sense, smell, are also possible. On the other hand, salespeople who sell machinery are limited to appeals that will affect the buyers' senses of hearing, sight, and touch.

HELPS THE BUYER REMEMBER WHAT WAS SAID

On average, people immediately forget 50 percent of what they hear; after 48 hours they have forgotten 75 percent of the message. This is unfortunate

I'VE GOT A BETTER IDEA

On December 5, 1933, the U.S. Congress passed a bill that would repeal the 18th Amendment and thus would end prohibition in this country. The implementation of prohibition had been linked to many negative social issues such as organized crime, bootlegging, and racketeering. Some historians have commented that the alcohol industry accepted stronger regulation of alcohol in the decades after repeal as a way to reduce the chance that Prohibition would return. Today the American beer industry is the most heavily regulated industry in the country, even more than the tobacco industry, and Minnesota is a leader when it comes to heavy regulation and high taxes. For example, here are the beer laws in Minnesota:

1. All retailers must be offered the same price at all times.

2. Beer distributors cannot pay for any cooperative advertising.

3. Beer distributors cannot give any product for free.

4. Beer distributors have a maximum of $300 per brand, per year, to promote the brand within the account (using things like neon lights and point-of-sale items), but this can't be in the form of price cuts for an individual retailer.

I was the sales representative for a beer distributor in Minnesota. My territory volume was trending down, and I was told by my manager that I needed to secure incremental activity to promote Miller Lite. My largest customer, Bill at Save-a-Lot Liquor, gave me an opportunity for an additional holiday ad in his weekly flyer. I knew this ad would yield a 200 percent lift in sales for the week and in turn would pay a nice commission to me.

To secure the ad, Bill was asking me to lower the price of my product by 50 cents per case to cover the cost of the ad. Bill also stated that if I decided not to participate, my competition had already committed to the ad. I believed that my competition had lowered the price in the past, and there had never been any repercussions from the authorities. What should I do? I had totally lost the interest of Bill, who would turn elsewhere to buy the bulk of his beer!

I had several options. I could write a personal check for the amount of the ad, but that would have repercussions down the road, and I was sure I'd be asked to do so again and again. I could try to see if Bill really did have the competitor's agreement to cut the price, but that could backfire on me and make the customer think I didn't trust his word. I could give all the other liquor stores in my territory the same 50 cent discount, but that would cut into our profit margins.

By law, entertainment is allowed in our industry as long as I go along for the entertainment also. In other words, I couldn't just give Bill two tickets for him and his wife to use without me being present also at the game. So, knowing he was a big football fan, I took Bill to a Vikings game. He appreciated the attention, and we did talk business as well. I had his attention again, and he went with my proposal. He's always been a good customer since, and I didn't break any laws. It was a win–win for everyone.

Source: Amir Permeh, Bernick's Beverages & Vending, personal correspondence; used with permission. Names of buyer changed to protect confidentiality.

because securing an order often requires multiple visits, and in many situations the prospect must relay to other people information learned in a sales call. In these circumstances it becomes more critical for the seller to help the buyer remember what was said.

Even selling situations involving one call or one decision maker will be more profitable if the buyer remembers what was said. Vividly communicated features create such a strong impression that the buyer remembers the seller's claims and is more likely to tell others about them.

Lasting impressions can be created in many ways. One salesperson swallows some industrial cleanser to show that it is nontoxic; another kicks the protective glass in the control panel of a piece of machinery to show that it is virtually

Exhibit 9.1
How We Learn and
Remember

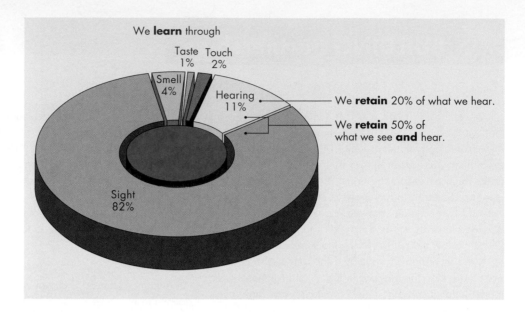

We **learn** through

Taste 1% Touch 2%

Smell 4%

Hearing 11%

Sight 82%

We **retain** 20% of what we hear.

We **retain** 50% of what we see **and** hear.

unbreakable in even the roughest conditions. Whatever the method used, the prospect is more likely to remember a sales feature if it is presented skillfully in a well-timed demonstration.

OFFERS PROOF OF THE SALESPERSON'S ASSERTIONS

Let's face it: Most people won't believe everything a salesperson tells them. Many of the communication tools we discuss in this chapter provide solid proof to back up a salesperson's claims. For example, a salesperson can easily claim that a liquid is nontoxic, but the claim is much more convincing if the salesperson drinks some of the liquid in front of the prospect.

CREATES A SENSE OF VALUE

The manner in which a product is handled suggests value. Careful handling communicates value, whereas careless handling implies that the product has little value. For example, a delicate piece of china will be perceived as more valuable if the salesperson uses appropriate props, words, and care in handling it.

HOW TO STRENGTHEN THE PRESENTATION

Salespeople should ask themselves the following questions: How can I use my imagination and creativity to make a vivid impression on my prospect or customer? How can I make my presentation a little different and a little stronger? With this frame of mind, salespeople will always try to do a better and more effective job of meeting their customers' needs. In this section we explore the many tools available to strengthen a presentation.

Before we describe the various methods, it is important to reiterate a point made in the preceding chapter. A seller should not grab a method because it sounds trendy or because it worked in a previous sales call or because it is highly entertaining. Rather, a seller should strategically select methods and media that will helpfully address the needs of the buyer. This process includes responding to the buyer's unique style (see Chapter 5 to review social styles):

- Expressives like to see strong, intense colors and lots of photos, cartoons, fancy fonts, and positive images (smiles).

- Analyticals prefer visuals that are clean and simple, a list of references, and lots of details.
- Amiables prefer visuals with people in them and a relatively slow-moving presentation.
- Drivers want crisp, professional visuals with bold lettering to highlight important points.

Strategizing also includes considering such elements as how many people will attend the presentation, which stage of the buying process they are in, what information they need, what type of situation this is (new task, modified rebuy, straight rebuy), and so on (see Chapter 3 for more buying factors to consider). In all cases, it is important to get your prospects involved and keep the focus of attention centered on them.[1]

VERBAL TOOLS
Word Pictures and Stories

The power of the spoken word can be phenomenal. To communicate effectively, the salesperson needs to remember all the hints and tools found in Chapter 4. Word pictures and stories of all types can be effective.[2] Here are some points to keep in mind when using stories:

- It is best to use stories from your own life. If you borrow one, don't act as if it is your personal story.
- Make sure you have a reason for telling the story.
- Consider using a prop, like a glove or a suitcase or something that helps tell the story and will help the prospect remember the story.
- Use the "hook" of the story to tie back directly into your presentation.
- Be accurate and vivid with the words you choose. Learn to paint a clear picture.
- Pace the story, watching your audience for cues. Use silence and pauses.
- Choose stories that fit your own style. Don't try to be someone you're not.
- Remember, stories can be short—even a few sentences.

Humor

Another way a salesperson can help keep the buyer's attention is through the use of humor. The wonderful effects of laughter will put everyone more at ease, including the salesperson. Use humorous stories from your own experience, borrowed humor, or humor adapted from another source. Here are some things to keep in mind:

- Don't oversell the joke (Here's one that'll really break you up!).
- Don't apologize before telling a joke (I wasn't ever good at telling a joke, but here goes).
- Identify any facts that are absolutely necessary for the punch line of the story to make sense (Jerry Joyner, my next-door neighbor who was always sticking his nose in other people's business,. . .).
- Use humor from your own life. Anything you got from e-mail or the Web could be circulating widely.
- Enjoy yourself by smiling and animating your voice and nonverbals.
- Practice telling the joke different ways to see which exact wording works best.
- Make sure your punch line is clear.

Beware of overdoing humor or using off-the-wall or offensive humor. Both can backfire, as one presenter found out when he used the following opening line about an overweight attendee: "Pull up two chairs and have a seat." The presenter knew right away that it was a big mistake. Always be cautious about using insider jokes, especially if you're still considered an outsider.

thinking **it** through

What humor have you seen backfire? How can you be sure the humor you are using isn't going to offend someone?

Also, understand that what is funny to one person or group may not be funny to others. For example, a foreigner from Egypt may not appreciate someone from America making fun of Egyptian culture—but someone from Egypt can tell that same joke and get plenty of laughs.

VISUAL TOOLS

A salesperson can use various visually oriented tools to strengthen a presentation. This section explores the content and use of those tools, followed by a discussion of the various media available to display the results.

Graphics and Charts

Graphics and charts help illustrate relationships and clearly communicate large amounts of information. Charts may show, for example, advertising schedules, a breakdown of typical customer profiles, details of product manufacture, profit margins at various pricing points, or the investment nature of purchasing a product.

Here are hints for developing charts and related visuals:

- Know the single point a visual should make, and then ensure that it accomplishes that point.
- Charts can easily be customized by including the name of the prospect's company in one corner or by some other form of personalization.
- Use current, accurate information.
- Don't place too much information on a visual; on text visuals, don't use more than five or six words per line or more than five lines or bullets per visual. Don't use complete sentences; the speaker should verbally provide the missing details.

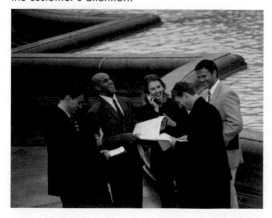

Salespeople should use humor to get and keep the customer's attention.

- Use bullets (dots or symbols before each line) to differentiate issues and to emphasize key points.
- Don't overload the buyer with numbers. Use no more than five or six columns, and drop all unnecessary zeros.
- Clearly label each visual with a title. Label all columns and rows.
- Recognize the emotional impact of colors, and choose appropriate ones. An abundance of green connected to a humorous graph might be offensive in Islamic countries because green is a religious color. In Brazil and Mexico, purple indicates death.
- If possible, use graphics (like diagrams, pie charts, and bar charts) instead of tables. Tables are often needed if

actual raw numbers are important; graphics are better for displaying trends and relationships.

- Use high-quality drawings and photographs instead of clip art if possible.
- Use consistent art styles, layouts, and scales for your collection of charts and figures. Consistency makes it easier for the buyer to follow along.
- For PowerPoint slides, use 28-point type for the titles and 24-point type for the text, using Arial or Helvetica. And use transition effects and sound clips sparingly.
- Check your visuals closely for typographical errors, misspelled words, and other errors.
- Know and obey copyright laws. You can't just grab images off the Web and use them.

Models, Samples, and Gifts

Visual selling aids such as models, samples, and gifts may be a good answer to the problem of getting and keeping buyer interest. For example, Chubb Lock salespeople carry along a miniature working model of the company's electronic door locks when calling on prison security systems buyers. The model allows the salesperson to show how the various components work together to form a fail-safe security network.

Other salespeople use cross-sectional models to communicate with the buyer. For example, salespeople for Motion Industries use a cutaway model of a power transmission friction reduction product. This model helps the buyer, usually an industrial engineer, to clearly see how the product is constructed, resulting in greater confidence that the product will perform as described. Of course for some larger products the best way to display a model is to bring the customer to the selling company's manufacturing plant, as "From the Buyer's Seat 9.1" illustrates.

Depending on the service or product, samples and gifts can make excellent sales aids and help maintain the prospect's interest after the call. In a Johnson's Wax sales campaign, salespeople called on buyers of major chains to describe the promotion. Salespeople walked into each buyer's office with a solid oak briefcase containing cans of aerosol Pledge, the product to be highlighted during the promotion. During the call the sales representative demonstrated the Pledge furniture polish on the oak briefcase. At the conclusion of the visit, the rep gave the buyer not only the cans of Pledge but also the briefcase. Of course gift giving must be done with care and not violate the rules of the buyer's company.

Catalogs and Brochures

Catalogs and brochures can help salespeople communicate information to buyers effectively. The salesperson can use them during a presentation and then leave them with the buyer as a reminder of the issues covered. Brochures often summarize key points and contain answers to the usual questions buyers pose.

Firms often spend a great deal of money to develop visually attractive brochures for salespeople. Exhibit 9.2 shows an example of a brochure used by salespeople. Creatively designed brochures usually unfold in a way that enables the salesperson to create and maintain great interest while showing them.

Photos, Illustrations, Ads, and Maps

Photos are easy to prepare, are inexpensive, and permit a realistic portrayal of a product and its benefits. Photographs of people may be particularly effective. For example, leisure made possible through savings can be communicated via

From the BUYER'S SEAT

SHOW AND TELL THAT SELLS

By Regina Conner, Kinder Morgan

I'm a buyer for Kinder Morgan, one of the largest pipeline companies in the United States and Canada. I've been at this job for five years now and have learned a lot about what separates good from not-so-good salespeople.

For one thing, I'm always impressed when salespeople invite me and others in my organization to their plant or facility. This tells me they are honest by their willingness to open up their facility. Besides, we can usually tell a lot about their capabilities by visiting their facility. I'll give an example to illustrate why this is important.

We were looking at potential suppliers for modular electrical service buildings, or what are sometimes called power distribution centers. These are usually steel-framed buildings about the size of large mobile homes—just without the wheels. Anyway, they are large and expensive. One building can run about $250,000 to $300,000. We visited three suppliers that looked good on paper. And these were suppliers we had never dealt with before. If we went solely on their proposals that they submitted, any one of

them could have done the work we needed. We were purchasing 13 of these buildings.

After visiting all three suppliers, we ruled one out right away. They were basically fabricating these buildings partly in an old warehouse, and some of the work was being done outdoors in the elements. The second supplier had clear processes and nice facilities and could definitely build what we were looking for. However, they lacked the capacity we needed. They could build one building in about six weeks and only one at a time. But we needed 13 buildings in less than six months.

The third one we visited was the one we ended up actually using. They exceeded our expectations in every regard. I should note that they weren't the low-cost supplier based on the proposals submitted. I guess the point I am trying to make is that if you are truly confident in your capabilities, show us.

Source: Regina Conner, Kinder Morgan, personal correspondence; used with permission; names changed to protect confidentiality.

Exhibit 9.2
A Brochure with Great Visual Appeal

photographs of retired people at a ranch, a mountain resort, or the seashore. Illustrations drawn, painted, or prepared in other ways also help dramatize needs or benefits. Copies of recent or upcoming ads may contribute visual appeal. Detailed maps can be easily developed, for example, to show how a magazine's circulation matches the needs of potential advertisers.

Testimonials and Test Results

Testimonials are statements written by satisfied users of a product or service. For example, company representatives who sell air travel for major airlines have found case histories helpful in communicating sales points. Air Canada recounts actual experiences of business firms, showing the variety of problems that air travel can solve.

The effectiveness of a testimonial hinges on the skill with which it is used and a careful matching of satisfied user and prospect. In some situations the testimony of a rival or a competitor of the prospective buyer would end all chance of closing the sale; in other cases this type of testimony may be a strong factor in obtaining commitment. As much as possible, the person who writes the testimonial should be above reproach, well respected by his or her peers, and perhaps a center of influence (see Chapter 6). For example, when selling to certified public accountants (CPAs), a good source for a testimonial would be the president of the state's CPA association.

Before using a testimonial, the salesperson needs to check with the person who wrote it and frequently reaffirm that he or she is still a happy, satisfied customer. One salesperson for Unisys routinely handed all prospects a testimonial from a satisfied customer of a new software package. But unknown to the salesperson, the "satisfied customer" became an unsatisfied one and actually returned the software. The salesperson kept handing out the letter until one of his prospects alerted him to the situation. He will never know how many other prospects lost interest after contacting that customer.

Salespeople should not hand out a testimonial to every prospect. Such letters should be used only if they help to address the buyer's needs or concerns. Also, be aware that prospects probably discount testimonials, thinking that the seller is presenting letters only from very satisfied customers.

Salespeople can also use test results to strengthen the presentation. Tests on the product or service may have been conducted by the seller's firm or some third-party organization (such as Consumer Reports or Underwriters Laboratories). Generally, tests conducted by independent, recognized authorities have more credibility for the prospect than tests done by the seller.

Using Media to Display Visuals

Many media are available to display the types of items just mentioned. New media, and improvements to existing media, are being introduced almost every week (like 3D interactive viewing, the use of Flash for presentations, and so forth).[3] Salespeople are encouraged to choose media that are appropriate for the exact situation and not merely choose a tool because it is new or exciting. "Sales Technology 9.1" describes the use of one advanced tool that salespeople incorporate

Most salespeople have developed a **portfolio,** which is a collection of visual aids, often placed in a binder or on a computer. Salespeople do not intend to use everything in the portfolio in a single call; rather, the portfolio should contain a broad spectrum of visual aids the salesperson can find quickly should the need arise. When showing visuals in your portfolio, make sure the portfolio is turned so the buyer can see it easily. The portfolio should not be placed, like a wall,

USE FLASH TO BUILD WOW INTO YOUR PRESENTATION

One of the most powerful tools for salespeople is Adobe's Flash. You're probably used Flash if you've ever watched a YouTube video on a PC. When compared to other video tools like Java, QuickTime, or Windows Media Player, the Flash player has a quick download time and can start being viewed much more quickly.

With Flash a user can also add animation and interactivity to the final product. You may have experienced this capability of Flash if someone has sent you a holiday greeting card online that changes as you click on various parts of the card.

The latest versions of Flash allow the user to create 3D object manipulation to animate objects at will. The output of Flash can be sent via the Web, on DVD, or even via iPhones. Examples of these types of files can be found on the Web (see www.adobeflash.com and http://silverlight.net).

Salespeople use Flash in many different ways. Some salespeople send a prospect Flash files before a sales meeting to generate interest and enthusiasm for an upcoming call. Flash files can also be left behind so the prospect can share information with others in the firm, especially in buying center situations. And given that Flash is interactive and interesting to use, some sales managers suggest

that pass-along use is greater than for a traditional brochure or handout.

Creating interactive Flash presentations can be costly and time-consuming. However, as technology progresses the creation costs will undoubtedly drop. Costs also have to be compared to gains. One gain is that salespeople can incorporate Flash into webinars and Web-based sales calls, reducing travel expense and time for salespeople.

One expert suggests that salespeople develop modular Flash presentations. That way, new modules can be inserted as products and market conditions change, rather than having to start over with a whole new Flash presentation. Modularity also allows a salesperson to practice adaptability during a call showing only the parts a buyer actually wants to see.

Microsoft Silverlight, HTML5, and other competitors are gaining market share, and it will be interesting to see what technological advances will be made in the coming years. To be sure, salespeople need to stay abreast of changes in technology and adopt whatever tools help buyers make better decisions.

Sources: http://silverlight.net; Izabella Iizuka, "Not Your Father's Presentation," *Sales & Marketing Management,* March/April 2008, pp. 33–35.

---

between you and the buyer. Remember to look at the buyer, not at your visual; maintaining eye contact is always important.

Video is another tool salespeople can use. Salespeople use video to help buyers see how quality is manufactured into a product (showing the production process at the manufacturing plant), how others use a product or service (showing a group of seniors enjoying the golf course at a retirement resort), promotional support offered with the product (showing an actual upcoming TV commercial for a product), and even testimonials from satisfied users. When using video, make sure the video is fast-paced and relatively short. Don't show more than four minutes of a video at one time.

Salespeople have adopted laptops, iPads, and other portable devices for use in sales calls. For example, Merck pharmaceutical salespeople carry laptops with a database of technical information, as well as complete copies of articles from medical journals. Progressive firms, like Aetna, are investing in **digital collateral management systems** (also called **sales asset management systems**) to archive, catalog, and retrieve digital media and text. **Collateral** is a collection of documents that are designed to generate sales, such as brochures, sales flyers and fact sheets, and short success stories. Digital collateral management systems simplify the collection and make it possible for salespeople to easily secure and adapt these selling tools for specific situations. For example, salespeople using the SAVO digital collateral management system (www.savogroup.com) can easily call up photos, videos, audio files, PowerPoint templates, Web pages, legal documents, streaming media, and just about anything else that has been digitally entered into the system.

Some salespeople use PowerPoint to give presentations. However, it is critical that salespeople not merely progress from one slide to the next. As one expert noted, "Presentations should use visuals that encourage conversation, rather than endless text that leads to the audience reading the slides."[4]

thinking **it** through

You turn the lights down for a PowerPoint computer slide presentation. A few minutes later, you start to panic when your eye catches an unusual jerking movement made by the buyer —she's falling asleep! What do you do now?

Computers not only offer excellent visuals and graphics but also allow the salesperson to perform what-if analyses. For example, when a grocery buyer asked a Procter & Gamble rep what would happen if a new product were sold for $2.69 instead of the $2.75 suggested retail price, the salesperson was able to easily change this number in the spreadsheet program. Instantly all charts and graphs were corrected to illustrate the new pricing point, and comparisons with the competitor's product were generated.

When using computers, be prepared. Have backup batteries, adapters, and copies of DVDs. Really get to know your hardware and software so you can recover if the system crashes. And make sure both you and your customer can comfortably view the output.

Images can also be displayed using other media. **Document cameras,** also called **visual presenters,** are capable of displaying any three-dimensional object without the use of a transparency. **Electronic whiteboards,** commonly referred

Examples of sales collateral for an industrial product.

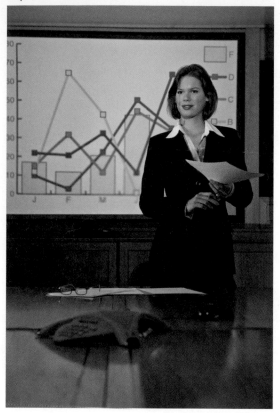

Salespeople use electronic tools to display important information.

to as SMART boards or digital easels, are used by salespeople, especially when working with customers who prefer to brainstorm an issue or problem. These are great at encouraging a group to interact with a presentation rather than merely watching it. Hewlett-Packard executives use these to make electronic presentations to remote offices in the United States and Europe with their teleconferencing system.

PRODUCT DEMONSTRATIONS

One of the most effective methods of appealing to a buyer's senses is through product demonstrations or performance tests. Customers and prospects have a natural desire to prove a product's claims for themselves. For example, orthopedic surgeons are like carpenters for human bodies: They repair damage and build new skeletons. They don't want a salesperson merely to tell them about new products; these surgeons want to touch them, feel them, and use them to see if they are good. When selling hip replacements to such doctors, sales reps demonstrate their products right in the surgery room. Because there is a definite sterile field, sales reps have to stand outside that field and use a green laser pointer to show where the surgeon should place the appliance.

One enterprising sales representative was having trouble convincing the buyer for a national retailer that the salesperson's company could provide service at all the retailer's scattered outlets. On the next trip to the buyer, the sales representative brought along a bag of darts and a map marked with the chain's hundreds of stores and service locations. The buyer was invited to throw darts at the map and then find the nearest stores. The test pointed out that the nearest location for service was always within 50 miles. This "service demonstration" helped win the representative's company a multimillion-dollar order.

Another salesperson was selling feeding tubes to a hospital. A nurse took the salesperson to a patient's bed and stated, "Here, you do it. You said it was easier to insert. Let me see you insert it."[5]

An executive briefing center.

Some products can be sold most successfully by getting the prospect into the showroom for a hands-on product demonstration. Showrooms can be quite elaborate and effective. For example, Kohler operates a marketing showroom in Kohler, Wisconsin. Prospects (architects and designers) from across the world can view and try all of Kohler's kitchen and bath fixtures. **Executive briefing centers,** which are rooms set aside to highlight a company's products and capabilities, are the ultimate presentation room.

Here are a number of helpful hints for developing and engaging in effective demonstrations:

- Be prepared. Practice your demonstration until you become an expert. Plan for everything that could possibly go wrong.

- Secure a proper place for the demonstration, one free of distractions for both you and the buyer. If the demonstration is at the buyer's office, make sure you have everything you need (power supply, lighting, and so on). Remember, it can even be an online presentation as Chapters 7 and 8 described.

- Check the equipment again to make sure it is in good working order prior to beginning the presentation. Have necessary backup parts and supplies (like paper or bulbs).

- Get the prospect involved in a meaningful way. In a group situation, plan which group members need to participate.

- Always relate product features to the buyer's unique needs.

- Make the demonstration an integral part of the overall presentation, not a separate, unrelated activity.

- Keep the demonstration simple, concise, and clear. Long, complicated demonstrations add to the possibility that the buyer will miss the point. Limit technical jargon to technically advanced buyers who you know will understand technical terms.

- Plan what you will do during any dead time—that is, time in which the machine is processing on its own. You can use these intervals to ask the buyer questions and have the buyer ask you questions.

- Find out whether the prospect has already seen a competitor's product demonstration. If so, strategically include a demonstration of features the buyer liked about the competitor's product. Also, plan to show how your product can meet the prospect's desires and do what the competitor's product will not do.

- Find out whether any buyers present at your demonstration have used your product before. Having them assist in the demonstration may be advantageous if they view your product favorably.

- Probe during and after the demonstration. Make sure buyers understand the features and see how the product can help them. Also, probe to see whether buyers are interested in securing the product.

Remember Murphy's law: What can go wrong will go wrong! And occasionally things do go wrong during a demonstration, like when Bill Gates, CEO of Microsoft, was giving the big launch demonstration of Windows 98 and his computer froze. If a demonstration "blows up" for any reason, your best strategy usually is to appeal to fate with a humorous tone of voice: Wow, have you ever seen anything get so messed up? I should run for Congress! Don't let technical glitches embarrass or frustrate you. Life is not perfect, and sometimes things just don't work out the way you plan them. If it will help, remember that prospects also are not perfect, and sometimes they mess things up as well. Maintaining a cool and level head will probably impress the prospect with your ability to deal with a difficult situation. It may even increase your chances of a sale because you are demonstrating your ability to handle stress (something that often occurs during the after-sale servicing of an account).

HANDOUTS

Handouts are written documents provided to help buyers remember what was said. A well-prepared set of handouts can be one of the best ways to increase buyer

Getting the buyer actively involved during the call is important.

retention of information, especially over longer periods. A common practice is to make a printed copy of the presentation visuals and give that to the buyers at the conclusion of the presentation.

Others would argue that your use of handouts should be more strategically focused. Thus handouts are not a last-minute thought, but rather are a tool that needs to be carefully planned while you are preparing your presentation. For example, you could draw a line on a piece of planning paper and on the left side list the things you will do and say during the presentation, while on the right side listing the items that should go into the handout. In that way the two will work together and be complementary.

What things can go into a handout? Complex charts and diagrams can be included. Because you want to keep your presentation visuals relatively simple (see the preceding hints), your handouts can supply more complete, detailed information. You may also want to include some company reports or literature. However, to avoid making the buyer wade through a lot of nonrelevant information, include only important sections. You may even want to highlight sections of the reports. Other items to include are Web addresses with a description of each site, case studies, magazine articles, and a copy of your presentation visuals themselves (with room to take notes if you're going to give the buyer your handout during the presentation). Whatever you choose, here are some tips:

- Don't forget the goal of your meeting. That should drive all your decisions about what to include in your handouts.

- Make sure the handouts look professional. Use graphics instead of text whenever possible.

- Don't cram too much information on a page. White space is fine. Try not to fill more than two-thirds of any page with information.

- Don't drown your prospect in information. Include only helpful information in your handouts.

- Handouts are even more important for foreign buyers, especially those who are nonnative English speakers. You might even consider giving them a copy of your handouts before your meeting so they can become more comfortable and familiar with concepts and phrases. Including a glossary, with definitions, will also be appreciated by foreign buyers.

WRITTEN PROPOSALS

In some industries written proposals are an important part of the selling process. Some proposals are simple adaptations of brochures developed by a corporate marketing department. But in industries that sell customized products or require competitive bidding (as many state and local governments do), a written proposal may be necessary for the buyer to organize and compare various offerings.

The RFP Process

A document issued by a prospective buyer asking for a proposal may be called a **request for proposal (RFP),** request for quote (RFQ), or request for bid (RFB). For brevity's sake, we will refer to all of these as RFPs.

The RFP should contain the customer's specifications for the desired product, including delivery schedules. RFPs are used when the customer has a firm idea of the product needed. From the salesperson's perspective, being a part of the specifying process makes sense. Using the needs identification process, the salesperson can help the customer identify needs and specify product characteristics.

Writing Proposals

Proposals include an **executive summary**—a one- or two-page summary that provides the total cost minus the total savings, a brief description of the problem to be solved, and a brief description of the proposed solution. The summary should satisfy the concerns of an executive who is too busy or unwilling to read the entire proposal. The executive summary also piques the interest of all readers by allowing a quick glance at the benefits of the purchase.

The proposal also includes a description of the current situation in relation to the proposed solution and a budget (which details costs). Some firms have even developed computer programs to automatically generate sales proposals in response to a set of questions the salesperson answers about a particular customer.[6] This is especially helpful because sometimes buyers use RFPs to keep their current suppliers in check. In such a case, a seller might want to minimize the amount of time spent responding to an RFP. (A familiar saying in sales is "You can't cash an RFP.")

When writing proposals, remember to use your most polished writing skills. And skip buzzwords, focusing on actual results that the prospect can gain from going with your proposal.[7]

Presenting the Proposal

Prospects use proposals in many different ways. Proposals can be used to convince the home office that the local office needs the product, or proposals may be used to compare the product and terms of sale with those of competitors. As we mentioned earlier, the intended use will influence the design of the proposal; it will also influence how the salesperson presents the proposal.

When the proposal is going to be sent to the home office, it is wise to secure the support of the local decision maker. Although that person is not the ultimate decision maker, the decision may rest on how much effort that person puts into getting the proposal accepted. Buying centers often use proposals to compare competitive offerings, and the salesperson is asked to present the proposal to the buying committee.

There are several options if you are going to give an oral presentation of your proposal. First, you can give the buyers a copy of the complete proposal before your presentation. During the meeting you would spend about 5 to 10 minutes summarizing the proposal and then ask for questions. Second, if you choose to give the written proposal to the buyers during the oral presentation, you may want to distribute the proposal a section at a time to avoid having them read ahead instead of listening to your oral presentation.

VALUE ANALYSIS: QUANTIFYING THE SOLUTION

To recap what we've described throughout this book, salespeople are selling value.[8] As mentioned in Chapter 3, one of the trends in buying is more sophisticated analyses by buyers. This section explores methods available to help the buyer conduct these types of analyses.

Quantifying a solution is more important in some situations than in others. Some products or services (like replacement parts or repairs) pose little risk for the prospect. These products are so necessary for the continuation of the prospect's business that little quantifying of the solution is usually needed. Other products pose moderate risk (such as expanding the production capacity of a plant for an existing successful product) or high risk (like programs designed to reduce costs or increase sales; these present higher risk because it is hard to calculate the exact magnitude of the potential savings or sales). For moderate-risk and high-risk situations, quantifying the solution becomes increasingly important. Finally, certain products pose super-high risk (brand-new products or services, which are riskier because no one can calculate costs or revenues with certainty). Attempts at quantifying the solution are imperative in super-high-risk situations. In summary, the higher the risk to the prospect, the more attention the salesperson should pay to quantifying the solution.

Salespeople can strengthen a presentation by showing the prospect that the cost of the proposal is offset by added value; this process is often called **quantifying the solution** or **value analysis.** Some of the most common ways to quantify a solution are value propositions, cost–benefit analysis, return on investment, payback period, net present value, and opportunity cost. For retail buyers, the seller usually must prove turnover and profit margins. The key is to offer information that will help buyers evaluate your offering based on their metrics. Thus if a buyer is evaluating proposals on the basis of ROI, that's the metric you should focus on in your presentation.

Customer Value Proposition

A **customer value proposition,** also called a *value proposition,* is the way in which your product will meet the prospect's needs and how that is different from the offerings of competitors, especially the next-best alternative.[9] The value bundle contained in a solid customer value proposition includes the features and benefits (financial and emotional) tailored to the prospect, the proof that those benefits actually exist, and the value of the seller and the seller's firm as the solutions provider. Simply having a superior product or delivering on your promises is no longer sufficient. Rather, what distinguishes you is how you make your customers feel while using your product. The experience is what bonds your customers to you.

As you write your customer value proposition, remember that what it contains is tailored to the individual prospect, so it needs to address three key issues: What is important to this specific prospect? How does our solution create value for this specific prospect? And how can we demonstrate our capability?

Here are some weak examples of customer value proposition statements, none of which tell how the prospect is really going to benefit, or how the seller can demonstrate that she is able to accomplish the goals for the account:

- It's the most technologically advanced system on the market today.
- We reduce training time more than any of our competitors.
- Our service was rated number one by an independent service lab.

Now here are examples of good customer value proposition statements, which include the elements discussed:[10]

- According to your CFO, dispatching multiple service vans to a customer site has been costing an estimated $20,000 a year in extra fuel costs. When you add that to the cost of unproductive personnel time and missed revenue, the loss is $850,000 per year. When you implement our Call Tracker system you will be able to reduce repeat customer service calls by 20 percent, resulting in a monthly savings of $250,000. This will require an investment of $2 million, which will be returned in only 8 months. We implemented a similar solution at Acme Transfer, which began achieving a monthly savings of

$500,000 within 90 days of installation. And I have personally overseen 15 such installations and will be there to ensure that all parties are fully trained in use of the new system.

- In this era of heightened airport security concerns, Advanced Engineering, a leading manufacturer of state-of-the-art explosives detective devices, offers a unique solution. The complete "Senso-37 Detection System" for major airports like yours requires a $200,000 investment, fully installed. Our superior system has been shown to save lives, lower human security guard costs, and decrease passenger processing time. My analysis reveals that Orlando International Airport will decrease its general security guard expenses at the major passenger screening area by $80,000/year for the next four years, giving you a payback in just 2.5 years, and also giving you and your passengers peace of mind that ALL passengers are being screened with state-of-the-art technology. When you install the system you also get an added advantage: my commitment and supervision, as one of the top salespeople in my company, that your system will be installed at Orlando International Airport on time and as promised, and that your security staff will be trained efficiently and effectively.

How do you create a customer value proposition?[11] Try brainstorming with your sales team and look for statements that truly tell your customers how your solution is going to solve their problems. Every time you write one down, keep asking, "So what difference does that make?" For example, if you write "saves time," ask, "So what does it matter if it saves time?" By doing so, you will eventually be able to reach the core value that your customer will achieve by adopting your product. Another helpful way to create a customer value proposition is by talking to your customers. They know what value you can bring to a prospect because they have experienced it firsthand and are usually willing to offer suggestions.

Cost–Benefit Analysis

Perhaps the simplest method of quantifying a solution is to list the costs to the buyer and the savings the buyer can expect from the investment, often called a **simple cost–benefit analysis.** For this analysis to be realistic and meaningful, information needed to calculate savings must be supplied by the buyer. Exhibit 9.3 shows how one salesperson used a chart to compare the costs and benefits of purchasing a two-way radio system.

In many situations the salesperson does a **comparative cost–benefit analysis** by comparing the present situation's costs with the value of the proposed solution or the seller's product with a competitor's product. For example, a company with a premium-priced product may justify the higher price on the basis of offsetting costs in other areas. If productivity is enhanced, the increased productivity has economic value.

Return on Investment

The **return on investment (ROI)** is simply the net profits (or savings) expected from a given investment, expressed as a percentage of the investment:

$$\text{ROI} = \text{Net profits (or savings)} \div \text{Investment}$$

Thus if a new product costs $4,000 but saves the firm $5,000, the ROI is 125 percent ($5,000 \div $4,000 = 1.25). Many firms set a minimum ROI for any new products, services, or cost-saving programs. Salespeople need to discover the firm's minimum ROI or ROI expectations and then show that the proposal's ROI

Exhibit 9.3
Cost–Benefit Analysis
for a Mobile Radio

Monthly Cost

Monthly equipment payment (five-year lease/purchase)*	$1,555.18
Monthly service agreement	339.00
Monthly broadcast fee	+ 533.60
Total monthly cost for entire fleet	$2,427.78

Monthly Savings

Cost savings (per truck) by eliminating backtracking, unnecessary trips (based on $.36/mile × 20 miles × 22 days/month)	$158.40
Labor cost savings (per driver) by eliminating wasted time in backtracking, etc. ($8.00/hour × 25 minutes/day × 22 days/month)	+ 73.33
Total cost savings per vehicle	231.73
Times number of vehicles	× 32
Total monthly cost savings for entire fleet	$7,415.36

	Years 1–5	Year 6+
Monthly savings	$7,415.36	$7,415.36
Less: monthly cost	− 2,427.78	− 872.85
Monthly benefit	4,987.58	6,542.51
Times months per year	× 12	× 12
Annual benefit	$59,850.96	$78,510.12

*Payment reflects ongoing cost of service agreement and broadcast fees.

meets or exceeds those requirements. For an ROI analysis to be accurate, it is important for the seller to collect meaningful data about costs and savings that the buyer can expect.

Payback Period

The **payback period** is the length of time it takes for the investment cash outflow to be returned in the form of cash inflows or savings. To calculate the payback period, you simply add up estimated future cash inflows and divide them into the investment cost. If expressed in years, the formula is

$$\text{Payback period} = \text{Investment} \div \text{Savings (or profits) per year}$$

Of course the payback period could be expressed in days, weeks, months, or any other period.

As an example, suppose a new machine costs $865,000 but will save the firm $120,000 per year in labor costs. The payback period is 7.2 years ($865,000 ÷ $120,000 per year = 7.2 years).

Thus, for the buyer, the payback period indicates how quickly the investment money will come back to him or her and can be a good measure of personal risk. When a buyer makes a decision, his or her neck is "on the line," so to speak, until the investment money is at least recovered. Hence it's not surprising that buyers like to see short payback periods.

For large capital outlays, the prospect usually needs to see the return on investment, payback period, and/or net present value.

We have kept the discussion simple to help you understand the concept. In reality the calculation of the payback period would take into account many other factors, such as investment tax credits and depreciation.

Net Present Value

As you may have learned in finance courses, money left idle loses value over time (a dollar today is worth more than a dollar next week) because of inflation and the firm's cost of capital. Thus firms calculate the value of future cash inflows in today's dollars (this process is called *discounting the cash flows*). One tool to assess the validity of an opportunity is to calculate the **net present value (NPV),** which is simply the net value today of future cash inflows (discounted back to their present value today at the firm's cost of capital) minus the investment. The actual method of calculating NPV is beyond the scope of this book, but many computer programs and calculators can calculate NPV quickly and easily.

$$\text{Net present value} = \text{Future cash inflows discounted into today's}$$
$$\text{dollars} - \text{Investment}$$

As an example of the preceding formula, let's assume that a $50 million investment will provide annual cash inflows over the next five years of $15 million per year. The cash inflows are discounted (at the firm's cost of capital), and the result is that they are actually worth $59 million in today's dollars. The NPV is thus $9 million ($59 million − $50 million).

As with ROI and payback period, many firms set a minimum NPV. In no case should the NPV be less than $0. Again, we have kept this discussion simple to help you understand the basic concept.

Opportunity Cost

The **opportunity cost** is the return a buyer would have earned from a different use of the same investment capital. Thus a buyer could spend $100 million to buy any of the following: a new computer system, a new production machine, or a controlling interest in another firm.

Successful salespeople identify other realistic investment opportunities and then help the prospect compare the returns of the various options. These comparisons can be made by using any of the techniques we have already discussed (cost–benefit analysis, ROI, payback period, NPV). For example, a salesperson might help the buyer determine the following information about the options identified:

	NPV	Payback Period
Buying a new telecommunications system	$1.6 million	3.6 years
Upgrading the current telecommunications system	0.4 million	4.0 years

Salespeople should never forget that prospects have a multitude of ways to invest their money.

Selling Value to Resellers

When resellers purchase a product for resale, they are primarily concerned with whether their customers will buy the product and how much they will make on each sale. For example, when an Xbox salesperson meets with Walmart to sell video games, he is armed with data showing how much profit is made every time Walmart sells a game and how fast the games sell. The Walmart buyer uses this information to compare the performance of Xbox video games with objectives and with other products sold in the same category, such as Sony's PlayStation.

PROFIT MARGIN Profit margin is the net profit the reseller makes, expressed as a percentage of sales. It is calculated, and thus influenced, by many factors. For example, if Linz Jewelers bought 100 rings for $1,000 each ($100,000), spent $45,000 in expenses (for advertising, salesperson commission, store rent, and other items), and sold them all at an average price of $3,000 ($300,000 in revenue), the profit would be $155,000, with a profit margin of 52 percent ($155,000 ÷ $300,000 = .52).

INVENTORY TURNOVER Inventory turnover is typically calculated by dividing the annual sales by the average retail price of the inventory on hand. Thus it measures how fast a product sells relative to how much inventory has to be carried—how efficiently a reseller manages its inventory. The reseller would like to have in the store only the amount needed for that day's sales because inventory represents an investment. Thus large retailers such as Cub Foods receive daily delivery of some products. If the reseller is able to reduce its inventory level, it can invest this savings in stores or warehouses or in the stock market.

For example, if Linz Jewelers usually kept eight rings in stock, inventory turnover would be calculated by dividing total sales in units (100 rings) by average inventory (8 rings). Thus inventory turnover would be 100 ÷ 8, or 12.5 times. The answer represents the number of times that Linz sold the average inventory level. Another way to calculate this is to divide total sales ($300,000 in the Linz example) by the average price of inventory (8 units at $3,000, or $24,000). The answer is the same: 12.5 times.

A reseller does not necessarily want to increase inventory turnover by reducing the amount of inventory carried. Several negative consequences can result. For example, sales may fall because stockouts occur more frequently and products are not available when customers want to buy them. Expenses can increase because the reseller has to order more frequently. Finally, the cost of goods sold may increase because the reseller pays higher shipping charges and does not get as big a quantity discount.

Sellers provide resellers with information to prove that inventory turnover can be improved by buying from them. They describe their **efficient consumer response (ECR), quick response (QR), automatic replenishment (AR),** and just-in-time (JIT) inventory management systems designed to reduce the reseller's average inventory and transportation expenses but still make sure products are available when end users want them. Chapter 3 described the use of these information systems in depth.

As an example, the September 11, 2001, tragedy created an outpouring of patriotic feelings among Americans. Within 24 hours there was a shortage of American flags, and there is only one major American flag manufacturer. The company had 80,000 flags in inventory on September 11. By the close of business September 12, both Target and Walmart had completely sold out of flags—over 150,000 each. When the stores opened September 13, Walmart had 80,000 more flags, whereas Target had none. How? Walmart's QR system was updated every five minutes, whereas Target didn't update its inventory system until the stores were closed in the evening. Walmart had an order placed with expedited shipping before the stores closed and before Target knew it was out of flags! Similar situations occurred in other product categories, such as flashlights, batteries, battery-powered radios, bottled water, guns, ammunition, and other products that frightened Americans wanted. As you can see, EDI and ECR systems can give resellers significant competitive advantage.

Electronic data interchange (EDI) is a computer-to-computer transmission of data from a reseller, such as Walmart, to vendors (such as American Flag Company) and back. Resellers and vendors that have ECR or QR relationships use EDI to transmit purchase orders and shipping information.

RETURN ON SPACE A key investment that resellers make is in space—retail store space and warehouse space. A measure that retailers use to assess the return on their space investment is sales per square foot or sales per shelf foot. In a grocery store or a department store, shelf or display space is a finite asset that is used to capacity. Products therefore must be evaluated on how well they use the space allocated to them. For example, if a retailer generates $200 per square foot in sales with Tommy Hilfiger merchandise and only $150 selling Ralph Lauren merchandise, it may increase the space allocated to Tommy Hilfiger and reduce the space allocated to Ralph Lauren.

DEALING WITH THE JITTERS

Let's face it. For many people giving a presentation is a frightening experience. Even seasoned salespeople can get the jitters when the presentation is for a very important client or when the prospect has been rude in an earlier meeting. It all comes down to fear: the fear of being embarrassed or failing, the fear of exposing our lack of knowledge in some area, the fear of losing our train of thought. The reasons don't even have to be valid. If you have the jitters, you need to help resolve them.

Here are some tips from the experts on how to reduce presentation jitters:

- Know your audience well.
- Know what you're talking about. Keep up to date.
- Prepare professional, helpful visuals. These not only help your audience understand the presentation, but also can help you remember important points.
- Be yourself. Don't try to present like someone else.
- Get a good night's sleep.
- For presentations to groups, feed off the energy and enthusiasm of several friendly, happy-looking people in your audience. (Note: That's what professors often do!)
- Recognize the effect of fear on your body and reduce the accompanying stress manifestations by stretching, taking deep breaths to relax breathing, and so on.
- Visualize your audience as your friends—people who are interested and eager to hear what you have to say.
- Psych yourself up for the presentation. Think of the successes you have had in your life (previous presentations that went well or other things you have done well).
- Realize that everyone gets nervous before a presentation at times. It is natural. In fact, it can help you keep from being cocky.
- *Practice, practice, practice!* And finally, practice.

SELLING YOURSELF

You're a member of another team project for a class. Your team is going to have to give a class presentation on the findings of your research. How can the ideas found in this chapter help?

For one thing, you now realize that giving a presentation is more than merely standing up and talking. Your team is going to have to find ways to keep the attention of the other students' (who, instead of listening to your presentation, are often busy sweating about their own presentations upcoming in just a few minutes), improve their understanding of the topic, help them remember what your team said (surely this is a one of your instructor's goals!), and also offer proof that your team knows what you're talking about.

Why not come up with a powerful story to make a point? Everyone likes a story, yet so many presentations are just long, seemingly never-ending PowerPoint slides with no way for listeners to connect emotionally and deeply with the material. Stories cause people to connect with ideas. And don't be afraid to use humor, but make sure it is appropriate and that your professor isn't going to wilt or blush when you use it. People relax when they can laugh, so encourage laughter with a well-timed joke or story. You'll all be more at ease.

For any visuals, take the time to make them really stand out. Follow the guidelines shown in the chapter. For example, it's not uncommon to watch a student presentation that includes just about every transition tool in PowerPoint—rather than impress, they often make the viewer cringe in embarrassment.

Don't be afraid to use video. In fact, with new video authoring and editing tools, video can be a real asset to your presentation arsenal. But don't spend more time making the video than you did in researching the topic. Having the proper balance is always important.

Finally, think about using handouts. Sure it costs a little bit to make a few handouts for your fellow students. But do you want them to really remember what you said, or do you want them to scramble to get all the information down on paper before you click to the next slide? Especially for complicated slides or information, a handout can be a real lifesaver. You'll impress your teacher also— a goal I assume you have.

So there you go. Don't forget to review the chapter ideas about how to reduce the jitters. The last one is especially critical, so we'll reiterate it here: PRACTICE!

SUMMARY

Strengthening communication with the buyer is important. It helps focus the buyer's attention, improves the buyer's understanding, helps the buyer remember what was said, and can create a sense of value.

Many methods of strengthening communication are available. These include such items as word pictures, stories, humor, charts, models, samples, gifts, catalogs, brochures, photos, ads, maps, illustrations, testimonials, and test results. Media available include portfolios, video, computers, and visual projectors.

A backbone of many sales presentations is the product demonstration. It allows the buyer to get hands-on experience with the product, something most other communication methods do not offer. Handouts and written proposals can also strengthen presentations.

It is often important to quantify a solution so the buyer can evaluate its costs in relation to the benefits he or she can derive from the proposal. Some of the more common methods of quantifying a solution include simple cost–benefit analysis, comparative cost–benefit analysis, return on investment, payback period, net present value, and calculation of opportunity cost, turnover, and profit margins.

Salespeople should be prepared to present a clear customer value proposition that offers real value to the customer.

All communication tools require skill and practice to be used effectively. Outstanding salespeople follow a number of guidelines to improve their use of visuals, demonstrate their products more effectively, and reduce their nervousness.

KEY TERMS

automatic replenishment (AR)   252
collateral   242
comparative cost–benefit analysis   249
customer value proposition   248
digital collateral management   242
document cameras   243
efficient consumer response (ECR)   252
electronic data interchange (EDI)   253
electronic whiteboard   243
executive briefing center   244
executive summary   247
handouts   245
inventory turnover   252
multiple-sense appeals   234

net present value (NPV)   251
opportunity cost   251
payback period   250
portfolio   241
profit margin   252
quantifying the solution   248
quick response (QR)   252
request for proposal (RFP)   246
return on investment (ROI)   249
sales asset management   242
simple cost–benefit analysis   249
testimonials   241
value analysis   248
visual presenters   243

ETHICS PROBLEMS

1. Men tend to respond more to jokes involving sexual innuendo than women do. Assume this statement is true for a male buyer you are going to call on next Tuesday. You learn that he loves jokes with a sexual bent. Is there any reason you should avoid using a joke with a sexual theme when calling on him?

2. Is encouraging buyers to order a large quantity so they can get a better quantity discount always a good idea? Why or why not?

QUESTIONS AND PROBLEMS

1. In "From the Buyer's Seat 9.1" you learned about a buyer's visit to several supplier production sites. Assume you were the second supplier discussed in that case (one who did not get the business). Is there any way you could have demonstrated to the buyer that you were able to make the number of units required in the time frame allotted? What tools described in this chapter would you use to strengthen your presentation of those facts? Make any assumptions necessary to answer these questions.

2. Assume you plan a demonstration to prove some of the claims you have made for a new hybrid automobile (runs off gasoline as well as electricity). How would the demonstration differ for each of these three individuals: a person who is very concerned about the environment, an economy-minded person, and a safety-minded person?

3. How could you demonstrate the following products?
   a. A textbook with a lay-flat cover (it stays open easily without having to hold it open) to a college professor.
   b. The strength of a new metal stud to an industrial construction contractor.
   c. A highly corrosion-resistant paint for bridges and overpasses to a group of civil engineers.

4. Which communication tools would you use to provide solid proof to address the following concerns expressed by prospects?
   a. I don't think that type of product would do well in a store like ours.
   b. My poorly educated workers would never be able to figure out how to use that feature.
   c. Your competitor has a much more modern, state-of-the-art plant than you do.
   d. You look too young to know what the older customers who shop in my store are looking for.

5. This chapter generally accepts the use of PowerPoint presentations as a positive, useful tool for salespeople. When should PowerPoint not be used in selling? In other words, are there any times when the use of PowerPoint could actually be detrimental to communication effectiveness? Explain.

6. Which communication tools would you use to communicate the following facts?
   a. We have been in business for over 75 years.
   b. As a salesperson, I have been certified by the state to sell this product.
   c. Even though I've been selling this product for only two months, I do possess the necessary product knowledge.
   d. I know our last product was a flop, but this product was developed with extensive test marketing.

e. Unlike our competitors, my company has never been sued by a customer.

7. Assume that you are selling a new video security system to a manufacturing plant in your town. The system will cost $275,000. It is estimated that the new system will reduce theft and pilferage. You expect losses due to theft to drop by $19,500 each year over the next 10 years. At the manufacturing plant's cost of capital, the discounted cash inflows have a value today of $350,000. Use this information to calculate the following:
   a. Return on investment.
   b. Payback period.
   c. Net present value.

8. Are there products for which resellers wouldn't really be that concerned about turnover?

9. Are there any retail situations for which return on space is not a big deal? How about situations where return on space is extremely important?

10. In "Building Partnerships 9.1" you read how the salesperson used entertainment to help generate interest and secure business.
   a. Tell how you would have handled the described situation.
   b. What are some possible ramifications of handling the situation as the seller did?

CASE PROBLEMS

case **9.1**

BrainScope (Part A)

An estimated 1.6 million to 3.8 million sports-related traumatic brain injuries (TBIs) occur each year. Yet all too often, when a person gets hurt in sports, the team doctor asks a few questions and, assuming there are no major concerns, sends the player right back into the game. However, studies show that if a player gets another concussion before the brain has healed, there is a much greater chance of long-term brain damage.

The problem is that there isn't an MRI machine at the sidelines. But that may change if the BrainScope company has its way. It will be introducing a new product that will gauge how serious a concussion is. The tool is small enough and inexpensive enough for all teams to have one on their sidelines.

The feedback from the BrainScope is a meter that shows if brain activity is anywhere near the danger zone. The system does this by picking up brain signals and comparing them to 15,000 scans in its database. The database was created based on scans performed at New York University's Brain Research Lab.

Some doctors claim the technology isn't cutting-edge. Originally developed in the 1930s, the technology uses qEEG (quantitative electroencephalograms). However, the developers of the BrainScope claim that their new device was developed with the advice of 30 leading brain experts.

According to the company's Web site, "BrainScope's novel application of advanced mathematics and miniaturized hardware is designed to bridge the limitations of traditional EEG tools (bulky, expensive, need expert data interpreta-tion) to provide easy-to-use, noninvasive, timely, frontline tools that can assist with an initial assessment of brain function as well as provide adjunctive assessment across the brain care path."

The BrainScope could also be used at hospitals as emergency room testing devices to see if a patient has a real problem and thus needs to have more sophis-ticated testing done. The company is currently focusing its efforts on military settings. For example, the U.S. Army can deploy the device in combat situations. This would be very helpful to assess soldiers who were nearby when a roadside bomb exploded.

In August 2009 BrainScope's ZOOM-100DC brain electrical activity data collec-tion system was cleared for marketing by the U.S. Food and Drug Administration.

Questions

1. Describe how you would use the communication tools described in this chap-ter to sell a BrainScope ZOOM-100DC to a local football or hockey team. Make any assumptions necessary.
2. Develop a short (five-minute) slide show that you can use to introduce Brain-Scope's ZOOM-100DC to potential buyers at a local trade show for sports teams.

Sources: www.brainscope.com; J. Langlois, ScD, MPH, W. Rutland-Brown, MPH, M. Wald, MLS, MPH, "The Epidemiology and Impact of Traumatic Brain Injury: A Brief Overview," *Journal of Head Trauma Rehabilitation* 21, no. 5 (2006), pp. 375–78; Peter Burrows, "Don't Put Me Back In, Coach," *BusinessWeek*, February 11, 2008, p. 61.

case **9.2**

Rough Customers

I was working as an outside sales rep for a restaurant supply company in south-ern California. This was my first job out of college. I was one of the youngest employees in the company and the only female sales rep in my region. My largest client was an upscale seafood chain. I had an arranged face-to-face presentation with the general manager and one of the owners, who flew in from the Bay Area for this meeting. I was promoting a high-end plate that was known for not chip-ping or cracking. Supposedly, it was the most durable plate (and one of the most expensive) on the market.

The manufacturers taught us to demonstrate the plate's durability by dropping it squarely on the base of the plate. If the weight was evenly distributed on the well of the plate, you could drop it on a tile floor and it wouldn't chip or crack. This demo was part of my standard pitch, and the owner had seen it once before. So I set up a lovely table setting of a dozen multicolored plates in an unoccupied room of the restaurant. As soon as I started to drop the first plate, the owner said, "Sit down. I know the drill." He proceeded to toss all 12 plates against the nearest wall, which was covered with leather wallpaper.

Naturally, the plates bounced off the walls and shattered on the tile floor. At first he was trying to make a point. Then he started to amuse himself. By the end, both men were laughing hysterically. The general manager said, "That was fun, what else ya got?"

Questions

1. If you were the salesperson, how would you respond in this situation?
2. What could the seller have done to prevent getting into this situation?

Source: Sarah Gottry, used with permission.

ROLE PLAY CASE

Today you will present to the same person whose needs you identified in Chapter 8. (If you have not done role plays before, you will need to review the information about the various role play customers that can be found at the end of Chapter 3. If you did not do the role play at the end of Chapter 8, choose one of the three companies to sell to.) If you sold to Spear One, you'll do so again; the same goes for McLane Properties and Dart Paper Products. Begin by summarizing the buyer's needs and gaining agreement that these are all the needs. Then make your presentation.

As a buyer, do not offer any objections today. Just listen, add your thoughts on how the product might help if asked, and agree. Ask questions if something seems vague or confusing. Further, ask for proof. For example, if the salesperson says everyone loves it, ask to see a testimonial letter or something of that sort.

When you are the odd person out and observing, look for the following:

- Did the seller tie the features to the buyer's needs? Or did the seller present features that were not needed?
- Did the seller try to gain agreement that the buyer recognized and valued the benefit?
- Did the seller use visual aids as proof sources effectively?
- Did the seller use specific language versus general or ambiguous language (for example, "It's the best")?

Note: For background information about these role plays, please see page 27.

To the instructor: Additional information needed to complete the role play is available in the Instructor's Manual.

ADDITIONAL REFERENCES

Barber, Clifford S., and Brian C. Tietje. "A Research Agenda for Value Stream Mapping the Sales Process." *Journal of Personal Selling & Sales Management* 28, no. 2 (Spring 2008), pp. 155–65.

Bradford, Kevin D., and Barton A. Weitz. "Salespersons' Management of Conflict in Buyer–Seller Relationships." *Journal of Personal Selling & Sales Management* 29, no. 1 (Winter 2008–9), pp. 25–42.

Farber, Barry. "Sales Success: Now Presenting." *Entrepreneur* 35, no. 6 (June 2007), pp. 76–77.

Jalkala, Anne, and Risto T. Salminen. "Communicating Customer References on Industrial Companies' Web Sites." *Industrial Marketing Management* 38, no. 7 (October 2009), pp. 825–37.

Matthyssens, Paul, and Koen Vandenbempt. "Moving from Basic Offerings to Value-Added Solutions: Strategies, Barriers, and Alignment." *Industrial Marketing Management* 37, no. 3 (May 2008), pp. 316–28.

McGaulley, Michael. *Sales Presentations & Demonstrations.* ChamplainHouseMedia, 2010.

Mills, Harry. *Power Points! How to Design and Deliver Presentations That Sizzle and Sell.* AMACOM/American Management Association, 2007.

Theriault, Michel. *Win More Business—Write Better Proposals.* WoodStone Press, 2010.

Williams, Robin. *The Non-Designer's Presentation Book.* Peachpit Press, 2009.

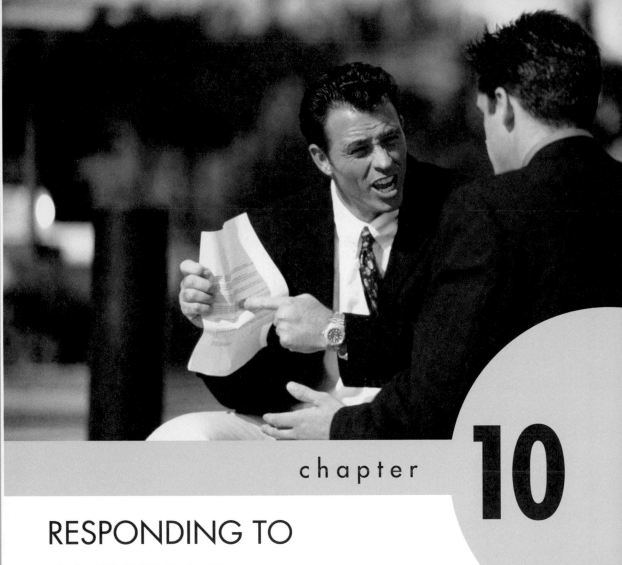

chapter **10**

RESPONDING TO OBJECTIONS

SOME QUESTIONS ANSWERED IN THIS CHAPTER ARE

- How should salespeople sell value and build relationships when responding to objections?
- When do buyers object?
- What objections can be expected?
- Which methods are effective when responding to objections?
- How do you deal with tough customers?

PROFILE

PROFILE My name is Rachel Gober, and I graduated from Texas State University in December 2008 with a bachelor's degree in marketing. I was honored to participate at the National Collegiate Sales Competition in 2007, where our sales team was privileged to be led by the one and only Mrs. Vicki West.

The National Collegiate Sales Competition is actually where I was recruited by Standard Register, a company that specializes in document management systems and services for the health care, industrial manufacturing, financial services, government, retail, and transportation industries.

During my experience here so far, I have found three keys to helpfully respond to objections: (1) anticipate objections and prepare your response, (2) reduce objections from the beginning by helping the buyer to trust you, and (3) ask questions and listen to the answers.

In sales, you are going to get objections from prospects at every stage in the sales cycle, so you might as well be ready for them. When I first started making cold calls, I had a list of typical objections that our reps hear, and wrote out responses to each of them. I kept this sheet in front of me every day when I was on the phone until I felt comfortable with them. It may sound corny, but some buyers use objections just to make you nervous or to get you off the phone or out of their office, so it is better to be prepared than to be left stuttering and mumbling. For example, this is typical: Prospect's objection: "What are you trying to sell me?" My response: "At this point I'm not trying to sell anything. I don't know enough about your current process to recommend a solution, so right now I would just like to set an appointment with you to learn more about it."

Once I set the appointment, I try to find ways to help the buyer trust me. This often reduces objections. For example, buyers will object when they think you are DUMB, which means that the salesperson Doesn't Understand My Business. Many times, at my initial meetings with prospects, I will explain to them the DUMB acronym, and ask them questions about their business so they know I am not trying to sell them something; rather I am trying to learn more about them so that I can put together a custom solution that best fits their needs.

It is important to let buyers know that you are on their side, and you understand where they are coming from. For example, a common objection is "We are happy the way we are currently doing things." By asking simple questions like "How's that working for you?" or "That's great, I'm glad you have a system that works for you, but what could make it better?" you will typically uncover areas for improvement that your product or service might be able to help with.

I think of objections as an opportunity to build relationships with my customers, gain knowledge about their business, and learn how to sell to them.

Visit our Web site at www.standardregister.com.

THE GOAL IS TO BUILD RELATIONSHIPS AND SELL VALUE

An **objection** is a concern or a question raised by the buyer. Salespeople should do everything they can to encourage buyers to voice concerns or questions. The worst type of objection is the one the buyer refuses to disclose because a hidden objection cannot be dealt with. Many sales have been lost because salespeople didn't find out the objections or didn't helpfully respond to them.

Salespeople should keep in mind that the goal with regard to objections is the same as with every other part of the sales call: to sell real value to the buyer. Having a positive attitude about objections is paramount in this regard. Proper attitude is shown by answering sincerely, refraining from arguing or contradicting, and welcoming—even inviting—objections. Objections should be expected and never taken personally.

Simply pretending to be empathetic is useless; buyers can easily see through such pretense. Also, once the buyer gets the idea that the salesperson is talking for effect, regaining that buyer's confidence and respect will be almost impossible. Empathy shows as much in the tone of voice and facial expressions as in the actual words spoken.

The greatest evidence of sincerity comes from the salesperson's actions. One successful advertising agency owner states, "I have always tried to sit on the same side of the table as my clients, to see problems through their eyes." Buyers want valid objections to be treated seriously; they want their ideas to be respected, not belittled. They look for empathetic understanding of their problems. Real objections are logical to the prospect regardless of how irrational they may appear to the salesperson. Salespeople must assume the attitude of helper, counselor, and advisor and act accordingly. To do so, they must treat the prospect as a friend, not a foe. In fact, buyers will feel more comfortable about raising objections and will be much more honest the more they trust the salesperson, the better the rapport, and the stronger the partnering relationship.

The reality is that salespeople run into more rejection in a day than most people have to absorb in weeks or months. Because of the emotional strain, many see selling as a tough way to make a living. However, salespeople must remember that objections present sales opportunities. People who object have at least some level of interest in what the salesperson is saying. Further, objections provide feedback about what is really on the prospect's mind. Only when this openness exists can a true partnering relationship form. To capitalize on these opportunities, salespeople must show that they welcome any and all objections. Salespeople have to make the prospect believe they are sincerely glad the objection has been raised. This attitude shows in remarks such as the following:

I can see just what you mean. I'd probably feel the same way.

That's a great question!

I'm glad you mentioned that, Mr. Atkinson.

If I were purchasing this product, I'd want an answer to that same question.

Maintaining a positive attitude toward objections is paramount. As one international sales consultant put it, "Studies show that prospective clients hate fighting—they don't want you arguing and working to overcome their concerns; they want you to listen to their problems, understand the impact of those issues, and then offer to help, if you are able. That's a world away from the combative old-style approach to selling."[1]

WHEN DO BUYERS RAISE OBJECTIONS?

Salespeople can expect to hear objections at any time during the buyer–seller relationship (see Chapter 3 for a review of the buying process). Objections are raised when the salesperson attempts to secure an appointment, during the approach, during the presentation, when the salesperson attempts to obtain commitment, and during the after-sale follow-up. Objections can also be made during formal negotiation sessions (see Chapter 12).

SETTING UP AN INITIAL APPOINTMENT

Prospects may object to setting the appointment times or dates that salespeople request to introduce the product. This type of objection happens especially when products, services, or concepts are unfamiliar to the buyer. For example, a commercial benefits salesperson for Coast Dental might hear the buyer make the following statement when asked to meet and learn more about a cafeteria-style benefits package: "No, I don't need to see you. I've not heard many good things about the use of cafeteria-style packages for dental products. Most employees just get confused!"

THE PRESENTATION

Buyers can offer objections during the beginning of the presentation (see Chapter 8). They may not like or believe the salesperson's attention-getting opening statement. They may not wish to engage in small talk or may not agree with statements made by the seller attempting to build rapport. Buyers may object to the salesperson's stated goals for the meeting.

Objections often come up to points made in the presentation. For example, a computer disaster recovery salesperson for Rackspace Hosting might hear this objection: "We've never lost a lot of computer data files before! Why should I pay so much money for a service I may never use?"

Such objections usually show the prospect's interest in the topic; thus they can actually be desirable. Compared to a prospect who just says, "No thanks," and never raises his or her concerns, selling is easier when buyers voice their concerns because the salesperson knows where the buyers stand and that they are paying attention.

ATTEMPTING TO OBTAIN COMMITMENT

Objections may be voiced when the salesperson attempts to obtain commitment. For example, an AK Steel salesperson who has just asked the buyer's permission to talk to the buyer's chief engineer may hear this objection: "No, I don't want you talking to our engineers. My job is to keep vendors from bugging our employees."

Skill in uncovering and responding to objections is very important at this stage of the sales call. Also, knowing the objections that are likely to occur helps the salesperson prepare supporting documentation (letters of reference, copies of studies, and so on).

Salespeople who hear many objections at this point in the sales call probably need to further develop their skills. An excessive number of objections while obtaining commitment may indicate a poor job of needs identification and the omission of significant selling points in the presentation. It may also reveal ineffective probing during the presentation to see whether the buyer understands or has any questions about what is being discussed.

AFTER THE SALE

Even buyers who have agreed to purchase the product or service can still raise objections. During the installation, for example, the buyer may raise concerns about the time it is taking to install the equipment, the quality of the product or service, the customer service department's lack of friendliness, or the credit department's refusal to grant the terms the salesperson promised. To develop long-term relationships and partnerships with buyers, salespeople must carefully respond to these objections. After-sale service is more fully discussed in Chapter 14.

COMMON OBJECTIONS

Prospects raise many types of objections. Although listing every objection is impossible, this section attempts to outline the most common buyer objections.[2]

It should be noted that some buyers like to raise objections just to watch salespeople squirm uncomfortably. (Fortunately, most buyers aren't like that!) Seasoned buyers, especially, sometimes like to make life difficult for sellers—particularly for young, nervous sellers. For example, Peggy, a manufacturer's salesperson for Walker Muffler, used to call on a large auto parts store in an attempt to have the store carry her line of mufflers. Jackie, the store's buyer, gave Peggy a tough time on her first two calls. At the end of her second call, Peggy was so frustrated with the way she was being treated that she decided never to call there again. However, as she was walking out of the store, she ran into a Goodyear rep who also called on Jackie to sell belts and hoses. Because the two salespeople were on somewhat friendly terms, Peggy admitted her frustrations to the Goodyear rep. He replied, "Oh, that's just the way Jackie operates. On the third call he is always a nice guy. Just wait and see." Sure enough, Peggy's next call on Jackie was not only pleasant but also productive! Buyers like Jackie usually just want to see the sales rep work hard for the order.

The following sections examine the five major types of objections (objections related to needs, product, source, price, and time), which are summarized in Exhibit 10.1, as well as several other objections that salespeople sometimes hear.

Exhibit 10.1
Five Major Types of Objections

Objections Related to Needs
I do not need the product or service.
I've never done it that way before.

Objections Related to the Product
I don't like the product or service features.
I don't understand.
I need more information.

Objections Related to the Source
I don't like your company.
I don't like you.

Objections Related to the Price
I have no money.
The value does not exceed the cost.

Objections Related to Time
I'm just not interested today.
I need time to think about it.

OBJECTIONS RELATED TO NEEDS

I Do Not Need the Product or Service

A prospect may validly state that the company has no need for what the salesperson is selling. A manufacturer that operates on a small scale, for example, may have no use for expensive machinery designed to handle large volumes of work. Similarly, a salesperson who is selling an accounts receivable collection service will find that a retailer that sells for cash does not require a collection service.

Salespeople may encounter such objections as "My business is different" or "I have no use for your service." These objections, when made by an accurately qualified buyer, show that the buyer is not convinced that a need exists. This problem could have been prevented with better implication and need payoff questions (see Chapter 8).

If the salesperson cannot establish a need in the buyer's mind, that buyer can logically be expected to object. In **pioneer selling**—selling a new and different product, service, or idea—the salesperson has more difficulty establishing a need in the buyer's mind. For example, salespeople for Alken often hear "I don't think we need it" when the buyer is asked to carry a line of biodegradable citrus degreasers.

I've Never Done It That Way Before

Most human beings are creatures of habit. Once they develop a routine or establish a custom, they tend to resist change. Fear or ignorance may be the basis for not wanting to try anything new or different. The buyer's natural tendency to resist buying a new product or changing from a satisfactory brand to a new one can be found behind many objections.

Habits and customs also help to insulate the prospect from certain risks to some degree. For example, suppose you are selling a new line of marine engines to Newton, a newly promoted assistant buyer. If Jane, the previous assistant buyer and now the senior buyer, bought your competitor's product, Newton would appear to take less risk by continuing to buy from your competitor. If Newton buys from you, Jane may think, "I've been doing business with the other firm for 15 years. Now, Newton, you come in here and tell me I've been doing it wrong all these years? I'm not sure you're going to be a good assistant buyer."

OBJECTIONS RELATED TO THE PRODUCT

I Don't Like the Product or Service Features

Often the product or service has features that do not satisfy the buyer. At other times the prospect will request features currently not available. Customers may say things like these: It doesn't taste good to me! I was looking for a lighter shade of red. It took a month for us to receive our last order.

I Don't Understand

Sometimes objections arise because customers do not understand the salesperson's presentation. Because these objections may never be verbalized, the seller must carefully observe the buyer's nonverbal cues. (See Chapter 4 for a discussion of nonverbal communication.) Misunderstandings frequently occur with customers who are unfamiliar with technical terms, unaware of the unique capabilities of a product, or uncertain about benefits arising from services provided with the product, such as warranties. Unfortunately buyers often will not admit that they do not understand something.

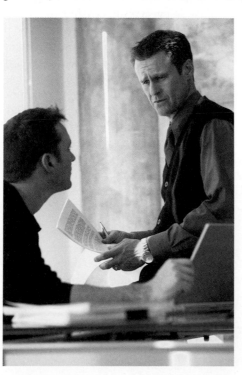

This buyer doesn't understand what the seller is saying.

For example, when desktop publishing programs were introduced for personal computers, a salesperson for an IBM distributor gave a presentation to a very busy plant manager of a consumer products firm. The new software would allow the manager to create and produce the plant's monthly newsletter to plant employees in-house instead of sending the work out to be typeset and printed. The manager, however, did not understand the new product's concept. He thought that the software would create the newsletter but that the firm would still have to send the work out to be typeset and printed. However, he did not want to appear ignorant and simply told the salesperson that he was not interested. The rep never knew that the manager simply had not understood the product until later, when the manager bought a competitor's desktop publishing program.

I Need More Information

Some buyers offer objections in an attempt to get more information. They may have already decided that they want the product or service but wish to fortify themselves with logical reasons they can use to justify the purchase to others. Also, the salesperson may not have provided enough credible proof about a particular benefit.

Conflict may also exist in the buyer's mind. One conflict could be a struggle taking place between the dictates of emotion and reason. Or the buyer may be concerned about the risk, and the seller hasn't sufficiently sold value. The buyer may be trying to decide between two competitive products or between buying and not buying. Whatever the struggle, buyers who object to get more information are usually interested, and the possibility of obtaining commitment is good.

OBJECTIONS RELATED TO THE SOURCE

I Don't Like Your Company

Most buyers, especially industrial buyers, are interested in the sales representative's company because the buyer is put at risk if the seller's firm is not financially sound, cannot continually produce the product, and so forth. These buyers need to be satisfied with the selling company's financial standing, personnel, and business policies. Buyers may ask questions such as these: How do I know you'll be in business next year? Your company isn't very well known, is it? Why does your company have a bad image in the industry?

Of course buyers who don't want to be rude may not actually voice these concerns. But unvoiced questions about the sales rep's company may affect their decisions and the long-term partnerships the sales rep is trying to establish.

I Don't Like You

Sometimes a salesperson's personality clashes with a prospect's. Effective salespeople know they must do everything possible to adjust their manner to please the prospect. At times, however, doing business with some people appears impossible.

Prospects may object to a presentation or an appointment because they have taken a dislike to the salesperson or because they feel they cannot trust the salesperson. Candid prospects may say, "You seem too young to be selling these. You've never worked in my industry, so how can you be trained to know what I need?" More commonly, the prospect shields the real reason and says, "We don't need any."

In some situations, the buyer may honestly have difficulty dealing with a particular salesperson. If the concern is real (not just an excuse), the seller's firm sometimes institutes a **turnover** (**TO**), which simply means the account is given to a different salesperson. Unfortunately, TOs occasionally occur because the buyer has gender, racial, or other prejudices or because the salesperson is failing to practice adaptive selling behaviors.

ethics

thinking **it** through

Assume that you have worked as a salesperson for an industrial chemical firm for six months. You have attended a two-week basic selling skills course but have not yet attended any product knowledge training classes. You are making a sales call with your sales manager. The buyer says, "Gee, you look too young to be selling chemicals. Do you have a chemistry degree?" Before you get a chance to respond, your manager says, "Oh, he [*meaning you*] has already completed our one-month intensive product knowledge course. I guarantee he knows it all!" What would you say or do? What would you do if the buyer later asked you a technical question?

OBJECTIONS RELATED TO THE PRICE

I Have No Money

Companies that lack the resources to buy the product may have been misclassified as prospects. As indicated in Chapter 6, the ability to pay is an important factor in lead qualification. An incomplete or poor job of qualifying may cause this objection to arise.

When leads say they cannot afford a product, they may have a valid objection. If so, the salesperson should not waste time; new prospects should be contacted.

The Value Does Not Exceed the Cost

Most buyers must sacrifice something (called *opportunity costs*—see Chapter 9) to buy a product. The money spent for the product is not available for other things. When we buy as individuals, the choice may be between the down payment on a new car and a vacation trip; for businesses, it may be between expanding the plant and distributing a dividend to stockholders.

Buyers usually object until they are sure that the value of the product or service being acquired more than offsets the sacrifice. Exhibit 10.2 illustrates this concept. The question of value received often underlies customers' objections.

Whatever the price of a product or service, somebody will object that it is too high or out of line with the competition. Here are some other common price objections: I can beat your price on these items. We can't make a reasonable profit if we have to pay that much for the merchandise. I'm going to wait for prices to come down.

Although objections about price occur more often than any other kind of objection, they may be just masks to hide the real reason for the buyer's reluctance. (A more complete discussion of dealing with price objections appears later in this chapter.) Implicit in many price objections is the notion of product or service quality. Thus the buyer who states that your price is too high may actually be thinking, "The quality is too low for such a high price."

Exhibit 10.2

Value: The Relationship between Costs and Benefits

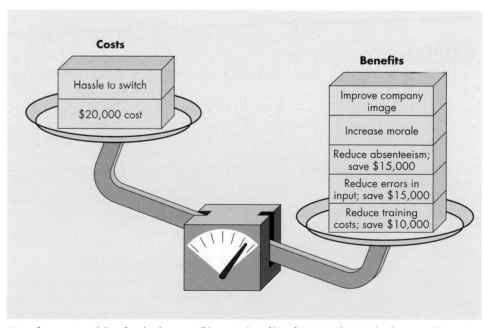

Note: If costs outweigh benefits, the decision will be not to buy. If benefits outweigh costs, the decision will be to buy.

OBJECTIONS RELATED TO TIME

I'm Just Not Interested Today

Some prospects voice objections simply to dismiss the salesperson. The prospect may not have enough time to devote to the interview, may not be interested in the particular product or service, may not be in the mood to listen, or may have decided because of some unhappy experiences not to face further unpleasant interviews.

These objections occur when salespeople are cold calling (see Chapter 6) or trying to make an appointment. Particularly aggressive, rude, impolite, or pesky salespeople can expect prospects to use numerous excuses to keep from listening to a presentation.

I Need Time to Think about It

Buyers often object to making a decision "now." Many, in fact, believe that postponing an action is an effective way to say no. Salespeople can expect to hear objections such as the following, especially from analyticals and amiables (see Chapter 5): I haven't made up my mind. I'd like to talk it over with my partner. Just leave me your literature; I'll study it and then let you know what we decide.

OTHER OBJECTIONS

Listing every possible objection that could occur under any situation would be impossible. However, following are a number of additional objections that salespeople often hear:

> We have no room for your line.
>
> There is no demand for your product.
>
> Sorry, but I just don't do business with people of [your gender or your race or your ethnicity or your sexual preference or your religion, and so forth].
>
> I've heard from my friends that your insurance company isn't the best one to use.
>
> Sure, we can do business. But I need a little kickback to make it worth my time and trouble.
>
> I believe we might be able to do business if you are willing to start seeing me socially.
>
> It's a lot of hassle in paperwork and time to switch suppliers.

Exhibit 10.3

Responding to Objections: Behaviors of Successful Salespeople

They anticipate objections and prepare helpful responses.

They address known problems before the prospect does; that is, they forestall known concerns.

They relax and listen and never interrupt the buyer.

They make sure that the objection is not just an excuse.

They always tell the truth.

BEHAVIORS OF SUCCESSFUL SALESPEOPLE

With regard to objections, successful salespeople anticipate objections and forestall known concerns, listen without interrupting, evaluate objections before answering, and always tell the truth (see Exhibit 10.3).[3] Responding to objections in a helpful manner requires careful thought and preparation. And for what it's worth, "From the Buyer's Seat 10.1" illustrates an ineffective way to handle objections.

ANTICIPATE OBJECTIONS

Salespeople must know that at some time, objections will be made to almost everything concerning their products, their companies, or themselves. Common sense dictates that they prepare helpful,

From the **BUYER'S SEAT**

THIS IS NOT HOW TO HANDLE OBJECTIONS

We've all read about the failures of the mortgage industry and the massive impact that legal and moral lapses there had on the economies of the world. Salespeople, at least some of them, are partly to blame for the mess we are in.

Mortgage wholesalers (who work for banks and other types of money lenders) buy loan applications from independent mortgage brokers and then turn these applications into actual loans. Mortgage wholesalers package a group of such loans into securities and sell the securities in the marketplace. The more loans the mortgage wholesalers could get from brokers, the more the lenders could sell on the marketplace.

Obviously there were many mortgage wholesalers out there, and brokers could easily come up with objections and reasons for going with a different wholesaler. In essence, their objection was "I can get a better deal elsewhere!" The solution? Mortgage wholesalers often hired attractive saleswomen to woo brokers (the brokers were often young and predominantly male) to use the services of their firms.

Evan Stone, the president of a mortgage brokerage company in California, says "minimally trained and minimally dressed" female salespeople would regularly visit his office, wearing unusually short shirts. On these visits the brokers were being encouraged to party at a local steak house with the saleswoman. One mortgage wholesaler even offered to fly Evan to Chicago to "have a good time."

Having the saleswomen attempt to use sexual favors to generate business was a turnoff for Evan. He declined all offers of sexual favors. If the saleswomen were trying to build strong business relationships with Evan in that manner, they failed miserably.

Source: Mara Der Hovanesian, "Sex, Lies, and Mortgage Deals," *BusinessWeek*, November 24, 2008, pp. 71–74.

honest answers to objections that are certain to be raised (probably 80 percent or more can be anticipated) because few salespeople can answer objections effectively on the spur of the moment.

Many companies draw up lists of common objections and helpful answers and encourage salespeople to become familiar with these lists. Most firms also videotape practice role plays to help salespeople become more proficient in anticipating objections and responding effectively in each situation. Successful sales representatives may keep a notebook and record new objections they encounter. For those objections you can't think of an answer to, you might want to use technology, as "Sales Technology 10.1" describes.

FORESTALL KNOWN CONCERNS

Good salespeople, after a period of experience and training, know that certain features of their products or services are vulnerable, are likely to be misunderstood, or are materially different from competitors' products. The salesperson may have products with limited features, may have to quote a price that seems high, may be unable to offer cash discounts, may have no service representatives in the immediate area, or may represent a new company in the field.

In these situations, salespeople often forestall the objection. To **forestall** is to prevent by doing something ahead of time. In selling, this means salespeople raise objections before buyers have a chance to raise them. For example, one salesperson forestalled a concern about the different "feel" of a split computer keyboard

USE TECHNOLOGY TO PREPARE FOR OBJECTIONS

Let's say you're preparing for an upcoming sales call. True to this chapter's suggestion, you decide to list all possible objections that you think can arise. As you do so, you realize that a few of them are tough ones, and you don't know how to answer them. What do you do?

Of course you can talk to your sales manager or other salespeople at your company and see if they have dealt with those issues before. If you're in field selling however, and not physically close to these people on a daily basis, you might use e-mail or texting to get some feedback from them.

But are you constrained to just those people? No. If you have a Twitter account, it's easy to tweet the gist of your objection and ask anyone out there who reads your tweet to supply some feedback. People on Twitter especially like to answer questions instead of just reading what others are doing.

If your question is too long and will take more than the 140 characters that Twitter allows, you can post your question on a blog and then point people on Twitter to that blog. But that raises a new problem: Some blog URLs are just too long to fit on a tweet. Solution? Go to http://tinyurl.com/ to transfer your long URL into a short one that will easily fit on Twitter.

Speaking of blogs, that's another source for finding potential answers to your objection lists. There are many available where you read what others say about objections. On many you can post comments or questions. A few to consider are the following:

http://www.topsalesblog.com/

http://jigsawsworld.typepad.com/garthsworld/

http://heavyhittersales.typepad.com/heavy_hitter_sales_sales_/

http://sellingsherpa.typepad.com/the_selling_sherpas_blog/

www.salessensesolutions.com

http://salesforceone.typepad.com/salesforceone/

No doubt, blogs come and go. You may want to visit http://www.blogs.com/topten/10-popular-sales-blogs/ to find the top 10 blogs for salespeople.

You can also pose a question on your LinkedIn account and have your contacts provide suggestions. Or you can join one of the many sales-related groups on LinkedIn and ask the group the question. There are even several LinkedIn groups by this textbook's authors you may want to use. One is called Selling Partners.

(the ones that are split down the middle to relieve stress and strain on the hands and wrists):

> I know you'll find the feel to be different from your old keyboard. You're going to like that, though, because your hands won't get as tired. In almost every split keyboard I've sold, typists have taken only one day to get accustomed to the new feel, and then they swear that they would never go back to their old-fashioned keyboards again!

A salesperson might bring up a potential price problem by saying, "You know, other buyers have been concerned that this product is expensive. Well, let me show you how little it will really cost you to get the best."

Some salespeople do such a good job of forestalling that buyers change their minds without ever going on record as objecting to the feature and then having to reverse themselves.[4] Buyers are more willing to change their thinking when they do not feel constrained to defend a position they have already stated. Although not all objections can be preempted, the major ones can be spotted and forestalled during the presentation. Forestalling can be even more important in written proposals (see Chapter 9) because immediate feedback between buyer and seller is not possible. Such forestalled objections can be addressed throughout the proposal. For example, on the page describing delivery terms, the seller could insert a paragraph that begins this way: "You may be wondering how we can promise an eight-day delivery even though we have such a small production capacity. Actually, we are able to . . . because. . . ." Another option for forestalling objections in written proposals is to have a separate page or section titled something like "Concerns You May Have with This Proposal." The section could then list the potential concerns and provide responses to them.

This seller is listening carefully.

RELAX AND LISTEN—DO NOT INTERRUPT

When responding to an objection, listen first and then answer the objection. Allow the prospect to state a position completely. A wise man said, "He that answereth a matter before he heareth it, it is folly and shame unto him."[5]

Do not interrupt with an answer, even if the objection to be stated is already apparent to you. Listen as though you have never heard that objection before.

Unfortunately too many salespeople conduct conversations somewhat like the following:

SALESPERSON: Mr. Clark, from a survey of your operations, I'm convinced you're now spending more money repairing your own motors than you would by having us do the job for you—and really do it right!

CUSTOMER: We're probably doing it fine right now. Now, I'm sure your repair service is good, but you don't have to be exactly an electrical genius to be able to . . .

SALESPERSON: Hang on! It isn't a matter of anyone being a genius. It's a matter of having a heavy investment in special motor repair equipment and supplies like vacuum impregnating tanks and lathes for banding armatures, boring bearings, and turning new shafts.

CUSTOMER: Yeah I know all that, but you missed my point. See, what I'm driving at . . .

SALESPERSON: I know what you're driving at, but you're wrong! You forget that even if your own workers are smart cookies, they just can't do high-quality work without a lot of special equipment.

CUSTOMER: But you still don't get my point! The maintenance workers that we now have doing motor repair work . . .

SALESPERSON: Could more profitably spend their time on plant trouble-shooting! Right?

CUSTOMER: That isn't what I was going to say! I was trying to say that between their troubleshooting jobs, instead of just sitting around and shooting the bull . . .

SALESPERSON: Now wait a minute, Mr. Clark. If you think that a good motor rewinding job can be done in someone's spare time, you're wrong!

Obviously attitudes and interruptions like these are likely to bring the interview to a quick end.

Salespeople should plan to relax as buyers offer objections. It's even OK to plan on using humor in your answers to objections. For example, if the buyer objects to the standard payments and asks how low your company could go, you could respond as follows: "Well, if I could get the bank to send you money each month, would you buy it?"

After laughing, the seller could talk about the various payment options. Using humor, as in this example, may help defuse the nervousness that both buyer and seller are feeling during this part of the process. For more insight into the use of humor, see Chapter 4.

What if the buyer asks a question for which you've already covered the material? Don't say, "I've already covered that!" Instead let the buyer finish asking the question and then answer the question with enthusiasm.

EVALUATE OBJECTIONS

To truly sell value and establish a relationship, the seller must evaluate objections before answering. Objections may be classified as unsatisfied needs (that is, real objections) or excuses. **Excuses** are concerns expressed by the buyer that mask the buyer's true objections. Thus the comment "I can't afford it now" would simply be an excuse if the buyer honestly could afford it now but did not want to buy for some other reason.

A buyer seldom says, "I don't have any reason. I just don't want to buy." More commonly the buyer gives a reason that appears at first to be a real objection but is really an excuse: "I don't have the money" or "I can't use your product." The tone of voice or the nature of the reason may provide evidence that the prospect is not offering a sincere objection.

Salespeople need to develop skill in evaluating objections. No exact formula has been devised to separate excuses from real objections. Sometimes it is best to follow up with a question:

> BUYER: I just wish your company sold the full range of insurance products, you know, things like variable annuities.
>
> SELLER: If we did offer variable annuities, would you be interested in having all of your insurance needs met by me?

If the buyer says yes, you know the concern is real. If the buyer says no, you know the buyer is just offering the objection about annuities as an excuse.

Circumstances can also provide a clue to whether an objection is a valid concern. In cold calling, when the prospect says, "I'm sorry, I don't have any money," the salesperson may conclude that the prospect does not want to hear the presentation. However, the same reason offered after a complete presentation has been made and data on the prospect have been gathered through observation and questioning may be valid. Salespeople must rely on observation, questioning, knowledge about why people buy (see Chapter 3), and experience to determine the validity of reasons offered for objections.

One study asked executives how often salespeople offer price discounts when in fact price wasn't the issue. The answer was an astounding 70–100 percent of the time.[6] The moral: Discover the true objection before offering what you think is a solution.

ALWAYS TELL THE TRUTH

In dealing with prospects and customers, truthfulness is an absolute necessity for dignity, confidence, and relationship development. Recall that our purpose is not to manipulate but to persuade, when appropriate, so the buyer can make the most effective decision. Lying and deception are not part of a successful long-term relationship. Over time it will be hard to remember which lie you told to which customer. Salespeople should avoid even white lies and half-truths when they answer objections.

Salespeople who tell lies, even small ones, need to recognize they have a problem and then find ways to change. One way to avoid lies is to spend more time gaining knowledge about their products and the products of their competitors. Sellers who do so aren't as tempted to lie to cover up the fact that they don't know some information requested by the prospect. Sellers also should commit to tell the truth, even if competitors don't follow suit. It is simply the right thing to do.

EFFECTIVE RESPONSE METHODS

Any discussion of specific methods for responding to objections needs to emphasize that no perfect method exists for answering all objections completely. Some prospects, no matter what you do, will never believe their objections have been adequately addressed.

In some instances, spending a lot of time trying to convince the prospect may not be wise. For example, when an industrial recycling salesperson contacts a prospect who says, "I don't believe in recycling," the salesperson may better spend available time calling on some of the vast number of people who do.

This section describes seven common methods for responding to objections. As Exhibit 10.4 indicates, the first two, direct denial and indirect denial, are used only when the prospect makes an untrue statement. The next five methods—compensation, referral, revisiting, acknowledgment, and postponement—are useful when the buyer raises a valid point or offers an opinion.

Before using the methods described in this section, salespeople almost always need to probe to help the prospect clarify concerns and to make sure they understand the objection. This method is often called the **probing method**. If the prospect says, "Your service is not too good," the salesperson can probe by saying, "I'm not sure I understand," or by asking a question. For example, the seller could ask one or more of the following: Not too good? What do you mean by not too good? Exactly what service are you referring to? Is service very important to you? Can you explain what you mean?

Exhibit 10.4
Common Methods
for Responding to
Objections

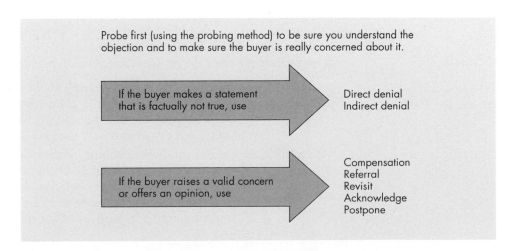

Probe first (using the probing method) to be sure you understand the objection and to make sure the buyer is really concerned about it.

If the buyer makes a statement that is factually not true, use → Direct denial / Indirect denial

If the buyer raises a valid concern or offers an opinion, use → Compensation / Referral / Revisit / Acknowledge / Postpone

While this probing is usually verbal, it can also include nonverbal probing. For example, Professor Donoho at Northern Arizona University teaches a method called the **friendly silent questioning stare (FSQS)** to encourage buyers to elaborate or explain more fully what their concerns are.

Many serious blunders have occurred because a salesperson did not understand a question, answered the wrong question, or failed to answer an objection fully. For example, a sales training manager was listening to a representative for a consulting firm talk about her services. At one point in the conversation, the manager asked, "Has anyone in our industry, the electrical products industry specifically, ever used this training package before?" The consultant answered, "Sure, we have sold this package to several firms. Why, just last week I received a nice letter from Colgate that had nothing but good things to say. . . ." The manager did not buy the training package; he figured that if the consultant did not even know how to listen, the sales training package she was selling could not be very good either. (Chapter 4 provides many helpful suggestions regarding the art of questioning and probing.)

A salesperson who doesn't know the answer to the buyer's objection might say, "I don't know the answer to that question. But I'll find out and get the answer to you." The seller should paraphrase the question, write it down (this step helps jog the seller's memory as well as demonstrate to the buyer that the seller really intends to follow up), gather the information, and follow up quickly and exactly as promised. If you call the customer with the information and he or she is not available, leave the information on voice mail and then call later to verify that the prospect got the information. And don't forget that it is your responsibility to know most facts, so be prepared the next time for similar and additional questions and concerns. You can be sure your competitor is going to try to have complete answers ready.

Remember that sometimes it is in the salesperson's best interest to walk away from a prospect's business. And it is not necessary to resolve all objections in those situations, as "Building Partnerships 10.1" describes.

thinking **it** through | How can the use of technology (such as databases, computers, and communication technology) help prevent a seller from having to answer, "I don't know the answer to that question. But I'll find out and call you with the information as soon as I can get it"?

DIRECT DENIAL

At times salespeople face objections based on incomplete or inaccurate information of the buyer. They should respond by providing information or correcting facts. When using **direct denial**, the salesperson makes a relatively strong statement to indicate the error the prospect has made. For example:

> BUYER: I am not interested in hearing about your guidance systems. Your firm was one of the companies recently indicted for fraud, conspiracy, and price fixing by a federal grand jury. I don't want to do business with such a firm.

> SALESPERSON: I'm not sure where you heard that, but it simply is not true. Our firm has never been involved in such activity, and our record is clean. If you would care to tell me the source of your information, I'm sure we can clear this up. Maybe you're confusing us with another firm.

YES, YOU CAN REFUSE TO DO BUSINESS WITH A PROSPECT

Occasionally, but not often, when an objection arises, it is best for the salesperson to make a decision not to do business with the prospect. That's not because the salesperson doesn't like the question or takes offense at how it was phrased, but because in raising the objection, along with other cues and information, the prospect is revealing that she will not be a good customer.

This is counter to what many salespeople have been taught. As one expert, Jason Compton, noted, "Salespeople are trained to accommodate, entice, and overcome objections, not to raise their own. As organizations take an increasingly long-term view of their sales relationships, however, it is clear that the right decision for some sales opportunities is simply to walk away from the customer who will not be part of a healthy, profitable relationship for years to come." Martha Rogers, cofounder of Peppers & Rogers Group, agrees: "Customers have a right to say, 'This is not a good deal,' and merchants have that same right."

For one property management group, Home America Property Management, the use of "no" when dealing with potential customers is a daily occurrence. The firm has found that refusing to do business with customers who are not going to be profitable is one of the key ways in which it can maintain a strong presence in its marketplace while maximizing long-term profitability.

One small publisher decided not to do business with one of the largest distributors in the country because that distributor kept raising objections and making demands that were not profitable for the publisher to meet. Less than six months later, that distributor called back asking to do business with the publisher; this time it agreed to follow the publisher's methods rather than push for its own demands. Why the change? The distributor realized that the publisher was the only one that could supply the books, and it had no choice other than doing business with the publisher on its terms.

Remember that satisfied customers are going to be one of your best sources of new prospects. Imagine what would happen if you allowed people to be your customers (when you should have said "no" instead) and then they were dissatisfied and gave your company a bad reputation.

Sources: Jason Compton, "The Power of No," *1to1media,* March/April 2008, pp. 40–41; http://creditmanagementassociation.org; personal experience.

No one likes to be told that he or she is wrong, so direct denial must be used with caution. It is appropriate only when the objection is blatantly inaccurate and potentially devastating to the presentation. The salesperson must also possess facts to back up such a denial. Direct denial should never be used if the prospect is merely stating an opinion or if the objection is true. For example, direct denial would be inappropriate to this objection: "I don't like the feel of simulated leather products." Direct denial should be avoided even for a false statement if the objection is of little importance to the buyer. An indirect denial would be more appropriate in that case.

INDIRECT DENIAL

In the **indirect denial method,** the salesperson denies the objection but attempts to soften the response. The salesperson takes the edge off the response by agreeing with the prospect that the objection is an important one. Prospects expect salespeople to disagree; instead, a salesperson who recognizes the sincerity of the objection will carefully respect the prospect's view. This approach avoids a direct contradiction and confrontation. To begin an answer, a salesperson would do well to agree with the prospect, but only to the extent that the agreement does not weaken the validity of the salesperson's later denial. For example:

BUYER: Your machines break down more often than those of most of your major competitors.

SALESPERSON: I can see why you might feel that way. Just 10 years ago that statement would have been right on target. However, things have changed with our new quality assurance program. In fact, just last year Syncos Ratings, a well-respected independent evaluator of quality in our industry, rated us as number one for fewest breakdowns.

The important features of indirect denial are that salespeople recognize the position of the customer who makes the objection and then continue by introducing substantial evidence. The beginning statement should always be true and assure the prospect that the question is a good one. Examples of such statements follow:

With the market the way it is today, I can certainly see why you're concerned about that.

I'll bet 90 percent of the people I call on voice the same concern.

That's really an excellent question, and it allows me to clear up a misconception that perhaps I've given you.

Indirect denial should never be used if the prospect has raised a valid point or is merely expressing an opinion. It can be used for all personality types and is especially effective for amiables and analyticals because they like less assertive salespeople.

COMPENSATION METHOD

Every product has some advantages and some disadvantages compared to competing products. Also, an absolutely perfect product or service has never been developed; the firm always has to make cost–benefit decisions about what features to include.

Buyers note these trade-offs and often object because the salesperson's product is less than perfect. The wise salesperson will admit that such objections are valid and then proceed to show any compensating advantages. This approach is called the **compensation method** of responding to objections. Here is an example:

PROSPECT: This machine has only four filling nozzles. Your competitor's has six nozzles.

SALESPERSON: You're absolutely right. It has only four nozzles, but it costs $4,000 less than the competitor's models, and you said you needed a model that is priced in the lower range. Also, our nozzles are designed for easy maintenance. You have to remove only four screws to get to the filter screens. Most other models have at least 10 screws. Fewer screws will reduce downtime considerably, which is something else you said you were very concerned about.

The compensation method is an explicit use of the multiattribute model discussed in Chapter 3. A low score on one attribute can be compensated for by a high score on another attribute. In fact, the compensation method is often referred to as the **superior benefit method** because the benefit of one attribute overcomes a concern about a less important attribute. The method can be effective for many objections and concerns. It seems most appropriate for analyticals, who are accustomed to conducting trade-off analyses. However, it is useful for all other personality types as well.

Of course the buyer may not value the compensating advantages. The buyer may really need the features at issue (perhaps the machine must have six nozzles to work with another piece of the prospect's equipment). In such cases salespeople can recommend a different product (from their own line, if available, or from a competitor) or search for other prospects.

Another time that the compensation method may be used is when the prospect says, "I'm just going to think about it. I'll be in touch with you later." The seller can show how acting today more than compensates for the "pain" of making a decision today. These reasons usually include explaining the hidden costs of delaying the decision (it will go off sale, you will be saving money over your current system each month that you have our proposed system, our product may be out of stock when you need it, summer is a particularly good time to install a new system, or the like).

A buyer may question the credibility and knowledge of a salesperson. In this situation the salesperson can use the referral method to help resolve those concerns.

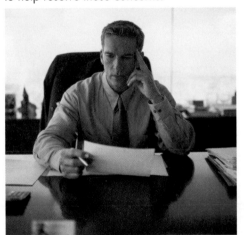

REFERRAL METHOD

When buyers' objections reflect their own attitudes or opinions, the salesperson can show how others held similar views before trying the product or service. In this method, called the **referral method** or the **feel–felt–found method,** the salesperson goes on to relate that others actually found their initial opinions to be unfounded after they tried the product:

> PROSPECT: I don't think my customers will want to buy a DVD player with all these fancy features.
>
> SALESPERSON: I can certainly see how you feel. Bob Scott, down the road in Houston, felt the same way when I first proposed that he sell these. However, after he agreed to display them next to his current DVD line, he found that his customers were very interested. In fact, he called me four days later to order more.

Those who teach this as the feel–felt–found method highlight the importance of the proper sequence, as well as the person or people identified in each stage. The sequence should be as follows: I can see how you feel . . . others felt the same way . . . yet they found. . . . Inexperienced salespeople often mix up the order or the parties identified (for example, by saying ". . . yet you will find").

Proof of the salesperson's assertion in the form of a testimonial letter strengthens the method; in fact, some trainers refer to this approach as the **third-party-testimony method.** If a letter is not available, the salesperson might be able to supply the name and phone number of the third party. The salesperson should always secure the third party's permission first, however. (See Chapter 9 for suggestions about testimonials and references.)

Although the referral method can be used for all personality types, it seems most appropriate for expressives and amiables. Both types tend to care about what other people think and are doing.

REVISIT METHOD

When using the **revisit method** (also called the **boomerang method**) of responding to objections, the salesperson turns the objection into a reason for buying the product or service. This method can be used in many situations (when making an appointment, during the presentation, when attempting to secure commitment, and in postsale situations):

BUYER: I don't think these would sell in my gun shop. They're really drab looking.

SALESPERSON: It's interesting that you mention that. In fact, their drab color is probably their best selling point and the reason you should carry them. You see, when a hunter is in the field, the last thing she wants to do is attract attention to herself. Thanks to the finish we use on this gear . . .

The revisit method requires care. It can appear very pushy and "salesy." This method does have useful applications, however. Often the product or service is actually designed to save the buyer substantial amounts of time or money. If the buyer objects to spending either the time to listen or the money, the revisit method may be a powerful tool to help the buyer see the benefit of investing these resources.

This method works with most personality types. Drivers may require the revisit method more often than other buyers because drivers tend to erect time constraints and other barriers and are less willing to listen to just any salesperson's presentation.

ACKNOWLEDGE METHOD

At times the buyer voices opinions or concerns more to vent frustration than anything else. When this occurs, the best strategy may be to use the **acknowledge method**, also called the **pass-up method**. Simply let the buyer talk, acknowledge that you heard the concern, pause, and then move on to another topic.

BUYER: Hey, you use Tiger Woods in your commercials, don't you? Sure you do. Now I want to tell you that I don't like what he stands for! Kids today need a role model they can look up to. What happened to the kind of role models we used to have?

SALESPERSON: I certainly understand your concern. I remember my dad talking about some of his role models and the respect he had for them. [*Pause*] What were we talking about? Oh, yes, I was telling you about the coupon drop we are planning.

In this example the salesperson used the acknowledge method because the buyer apparently was just blowing off steam. A buyer who really wanted some response from the salesperson would have used the salesperson's pause to ask a direct question (Can't you change your commercials?) or make a statement (I refuse to do business with companies that use stars like Tiger Woods in their commercials!).

In reality a salesperson often can do little about some prospects' opinions. What are the chances that this salesperson's firm will pull a $5 million ad campaign because one buyer objects? It is doubtful that a firm would take such action unless the buyer had tremendous power in the relationship.

Sometimes the salesperson can use the acknowledge method by simply agreeing with the prospect and then moving on, which suggests to the buyer that the concern really should not be much of an issue. For example:

BUYER: You want $25 for this little plastic bottle?!

SELLER: Uh-huh. That's what they cost . . . [*Pause*] Now do you see the switch on this side? It's used if you ever need to . . .

The acknowledge method should not be used if the objection raised is factually false. Also, it should not be used if the salesperson, through probing, could help clarify the buyer's thinking on the topic. Experience is the key to making such a determination. In general, though, the acknowledge method should be used sparingly.

POSTPONE METHOD

In the early part of a sales interview, the prospect may raise objections that the salesperson would prefer to answer later in the presentation, after discovering the prospect's needs. Using the **postpone method**, the salesperson would ask permission to answer the question at a later time:

> BUYER [*very early in the call*]: How much does the brass engraving equipment cost?
>
> SALESPERSON: If you don't mind, I would prefer to answer that question in a few minutes. I really can't tell you how much it will cost until I learn more about your engraving needs and know what kinds of features you are looking for.

The prospect will seldom refuse the request if the sales representative appears to be acting in good faith. The sales representative then proceeds with the presentation until the point at which the objection can best be answered.

Some objections are best answered when they occur; others can be responded to most effectively by delaying the answer. Experience should guide the sales representative. The salesperson should take care not to treat an objection lightly or let it appear that he or she does not want to answer the question. Another danger in postponing is that the buyer will be unable to focus on what the salesperson is saying until the concern is addressed. On the other hand, the salesperson is responsible for helping the buyer to critically evaluate the solution offered, and often the buyer can process information effectively only after learning preliminary facts.

Salespeople make the most use of the postponement method when a price objection occurs early in the presentation. However, this method can be used for almost any type of objection or question. For example, postponing discussions about guarantees, delivery schedules, implementation time frames, and certain unique product features until later in the presentation is often preferable.

What if the buyer is convinced that he or she needs the answer right now? Then the salesperson should answer the objection now. Salespeople usually have more to lose by demanding that the buyer wait for information than by simply providing the answer when the buyer strongly requests it. For example:

> PROSPECT: What are the delivery schedules for this new product?
>
> SALESPERSON: I would really prefer to discuss that after we talk about our unique production process and extensive quality control measures.
>
> PROSPECT: No, I want to know now!
>
> SALESPERSON: Well, keep in mind that my later discussion about the production process will shed new light on the topic. We anticipate a four- to five-month delivery time after the contract reaches our corporate headquarters.

USING THE METHODS

The seven methods just discussed appear in sales training courses across all industries and geographic boundaries. To help you more easily distinguish the

Exhibit 10.5
Responding to
Objections: Using Each
Method

Objection: Your product's quality is too low.

Responses*

Direct denial: That simply is not true. Our product has been rated as the highest in the industry for the last three years.

Indirect denial: I can certainly see why you would be concerned about quality. Actually, though, our product quality has been rated as the highest in the industry for the last three years.

Compensation: I agree that our quality is not as high as that of some of our competitors. However, it was designed that way for consumers who are looking for a lower-priced alternative, perhaps just to use in a weekend cottage. So you see, our somewhat lower quality is actually offset by our much lower price.

Referral: I can certainly understand how you feel. Mortimer Jiggs felt the same way before he bought the product. But after using it, he found that the quality was actually equal to that of other products.

Revisit: The fact that the quality is lower than in other products is probably the very reason you should buy it. You said that some of your customers are looking for a low-priced product to buy for their grandchildren. This product fills that need.

Acknowledge: I understand your concern. You know, one of the things I always look for is how a product's quality stacks up against its cost. [Pause] Now, we were talking about . . .

Postpone: That's an interesting point. Before discussing it fully, I would like to cover just two things that I think will help you better understand the product from a different perspective. OK?

*These are not necessarily good answers to the stated objection. Also, the choice of method would depend on whether the objection is factual. Thus the replies given in this table are designed simply to differentiate the various methods.

differences among the various methods, Exhibit 10.5 provides an example of the use of each method for the objection, "Your product's quality is too low."

Salespeople often combine methods when answering an objection. For example, a price objection may initially be postponed and then be discussed later using the compensation method. At other times several methods can be used in one answer. Here is an example:

> BUYER: I don't think this product will last as long as some of the other, more expensive competitive products.
>
> SALESPERSON: That's probably the very reason you should buy it [*revisit method*]. It may not last quite as long, but it is less than half the cost of competitive products [*compensation method*]. I can certainly understand your concern, though. You know, Mark Hancock felt the way you do. He was concerned about the product's life. But after he used our product for one year, he found that its life expectancy didn't create any problems for his production staff [*referral method*].

Sometimes the buyer will ask multiple questions at once—for example, "How much did you spend on R&D last year, what percentage of your revenue does that represent, and what is your R&D model going forward?" What is a seller to do? Remembering the questions so they don't get lost, the salesperson answers them one by one.

Before moving on with the presentation, the salesperson needs to make sure that the buyer agrees that all objections have been completely answered. Without this commitment, the salesperson does not

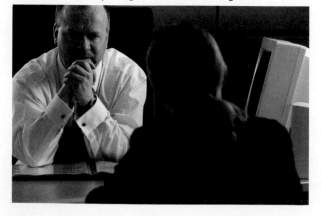

Make sure the buyer agrees before moving on.

know whether the buyer understands the answer or whether the buyer's concerns have been fully addressed. To achieve this commitment, the salesperson can use one or more of the following types of phrases: Did I answer your question? Does that make sense? Do you see why that issue is not as important as you originally thought? Did that resolve your concern?

OBJECTIONS WHEN SELLING TO A GROUP OF BUYERS

Selling to a group of buyers (see Chapter 8) requires some extra care. If one person offers an objection, the seller should try to get a sense of whether other buyers share the concern. At times it may make sense to throw the issue back to the group. For example, if a buyer says that the people in his or her department won't attend the type of training sessions being proposed, the seller might respond as follows: Does anyone else have that same problem in their department? You all know your organizational climate better than I do. Have any of you found a way to deal with that issue that you would like to share with us? Any response from the seller should usually be directed to all buyers, not just the one who asked the question. After responding, the seller needs to make sure that all buyers are satisfied with the answer before moving on.

THE PRICE OBJECTION

Price is the perhaps the most frequently mentioned obstacle to obtaining commitment. In fact, about 20 percent of buyers are thought to buy purely on the basis of price (which means that a full 80 percent buy for reasons other than price). As a result, all salespeople need to prepare for price objections. This section relates the concepts covered in this chapter to this common objection.

Price is still an issue even between partnering firms. One leading firm in its industry has estimated that only 3 percent of its orders are sold at list price; the rest are price-discounted.[7]

Unfortunately the first response of many salespeople to a price objection is to lower the price. Inexperienced salespeople, desiring to gain business, often quote the lowest possible price as quickly as possible. They forget that for a mutually beneficial long-term relationship to exist, their firm must make a fair profit. Also, by cutting prices the firm has to sell more to maintain profit margins, as Exhibit 10.6 clearly illustrates.[8]

When faced with a price objection, salespeople should ensure that they have up-to-date information, establish the value of the product, and use communication tools effectively.

USE UP-TO-DATE INFORMATION

Successful salespeople make sure they have the most current pricing information available to them. They know not only their prices but competitors' prices as well. Firms are helping salespeople in this regard. For example, many firms have developed intranet sites for their salespeople. If a salesperson finds that the company's price points are a little higher than the competition, the salesperson can use the intranet site to look for some sales or trade-in program that she or he can leverage to get the deal. It is important for sellers to have correct pricing facts.

ESTABLISH THE VALUE

The product's value must be established before the salesperson spends time discussing price. The value expected determines the price a prospect is willing to pay. Unless the salesperson can build value to exceed the price asked, a sale will not occur.[9] As a rule, value cannot be established during the early stages of the presentation.

Exhibit 10.6
Look before You Cut
Prices! You Must Sell
More to Break Even

Cut Price	Present Gross Profit					
	5.0%	10.0%	15.0%	20.0%	25.0%	30.0%
1%	25.0	11.1	7.1	5.3	4.2	3.4
2	66.6	25.0	15.4	11.1	8.7	7.1
3	150.0	42.8	25.0	17.6	13.6	11.1
4	400.0	66.6	36.4	25.0	19.0	15.4
5	—	100.0	50.0	33.3	25.0	20.0
6	—	150.0	66.7	42.9	31.6	25.0
7	—	233.3	87.5	53.8	38.9	30.4
8	—	400.0	114.3	66.7	47.1	36.4
9	—	1,000.0	150.0	81.8	56.3	42.9
10	—	—	200.0	100.0	66.7	50.0
11	—	—	275.0	122.2	78.6	57.9
12	—	—	400.0	150.0	92.3	66.7
13	—	—	650.0	185.7	108.3	76.5
14	—	—	1,400.0	233.3	127.3	87.5
15	—	—	—	300.0	150.0	100.0
16	—	—	—	400.0	177.8	114.3
17	—	—	—	566.7	212.5	130.8
18	—	—	—	900.0	257.1	150.0
19	—	—	—	1,900.0	316.7	172.7
20	—	—	—	—	400.0	200.0
21	—	—	—	—	525.0	233.3
22	—	—	—	—	733.3	275.0
23	—	—	—	—	1,115.0	328.6
24	—	—	—	—	2,400.0	400.0
25	—	—	—	—	—	500.0

A business truism says that you can cut, cut, cut until you cut yourself out of business. This can certainly apply to cutting prices in an effort to increase profits. The two don't necessarily go together. For example, select the gross profit being earned at present from those shown at the top of the chart. Follow the left column down until you line up with the proposed price cut. The intersected figure represents the percentage of increase in unit sales required to earn the same gross profit realized before the price cut. Obviously it helps to know this figure so you don't end up with a lot of work for nothing.

See for yourself: Assume that your present gross margin is 25 percent and that you cut your selling price 10 percent. Locate the 25 percent column under Present Gross Profit. Now follow the column down until you line up with the 10 percent cut in selling price in column 1. You will need to sell 66.7 percent more units to earn the same margin dollars as at the previous price.

Price objections are best handled with a two-step approach. First, the salesperson should try to look at the objection from the customer's viewpoint, asking questions to clarify the customer's perspective: "Too high in what respect, Mr. Jones? Could you tell me how much we are out of line? We are usually quite competitive on this model, so I am surprised you find our price high. . . . Are the other quotes you have for the same size engine?"

After learning more about the customer's perspective, the next step is to sell value and quality rather than price (see Chapter 9 for a full discussion of the customer value proposition). Most customers prefer to buy less expensive products if they believe they will receive the same benefits. However, many customers will pay more for higher quality when the quality benefits and features are pointed out to them. Many high-quality products appear similar to lower-quality products; thus salespeople need to emphasize the features that justify a difference.

For example, a Premier Industrial salesperson who sells industrial fasteners and supplies may hear this objection: "That bolt costs $750! I could buy it elsewhere for $75." The salesperson should reply, "Yes, but that bolt is inside your most important piece of production equipment. Let's say you buy that $75 bolt. How much employee time and production downtime would it take to disassemble the machine again and replace that one bolt?" The salesperson can then engage in a complete cost–benefit analysis (see Chapter 9) to solidify the point.

A supplier of integrated circuits (ICs) was competing with another company whose price was 10 cents less. The buyer asked for a price concession, noting that the competitor's product was obviously less expensive. Unbeknownst to the supplier, however, the buyer had already examined the value propositions of the two companies and determined that the higher-priced one was actually worth 12 cents more than the less expensive one, due to services offered. Thus, in reality, the buyer had already realized that the higher-priced one was actually less expensive in terms of value (12 cents more in value minus the 10 cents higher in price = 2 cents higher in value per IC). The higher-priced supplier caved in and gave the buyer a 10 cent reduction in price, costing his firm $500,000 (5 million units at 10 cents each) in potential profits! And the sad fact is that the buyer was already planning on going with the higher-priced supplier.[10]

Intangible features can also provide value that offsets price. Some of these features are services, company reputation, and the salesperson:

- Good service in the form of faster deliveries, technical advice, and field assistance is but one of the many intangibles that can spell value, savings, and profits to a customer. For example, one company cut its prices in response to buyers' demands. However, the company later found that what the customers really wanted was technical support. As the company cut its prices, it had only reinforced its image as low-priced with little technical support.

- For a customer tempted to buy on price alone, salespeople can emphasize the importance of having a thoroughly reliable source of supply: the salesperson's company. It has been demonstrated time and again that quality is measured by the reputation of the company behind it.

- Customers value sales representatives who go out of their way to help with problems and promotions—salespeople who keep their word and follow through when they start something. These services are very valuable to customers.

USE COMMUNICATION TOOLS EFFECTIVELY

One pharmaceutical salesperson often hears that her company's drug for migraines is too expensive. Her response is to paint a word picture:[11]

DOCTOR: How much does this product cost?

SALESPERSON: It costs about $45. . . . There are 15 doses per bottle, so it ends up about $3 per dose.

DOCTOR: That's too much money!

SALESPERSON: Consider your patients who have to lie in the dark because their headaches are so bad they can't see straight, can't think straight, and are nauseated by migraine pain. A price of $3 is really inexpensive to relieve these patients' pain, wouldn't you agree?

Just telling customers about quality and value is not enough; they must be shown. Top salespeople use the communication tools discussed in Chapter 9 to describe more clearly the quality and value of their products. This process includes activities such as demonstrating the product, showing test results and quality control procedures, using case histories, and offering testimonials.

DEALING WITH TOUGH CUSTOMERS

Sellers need to maintain the positive attitude discussed earlier, even with rude, hard-to-get-along-with prospects. It's not easy, and it's not fun.[12]

Salespeople must learn to deal with tough prospects and customers.

Sellers need to realize that we all have bad days. Maybe the buyer is having one. If the rudeness is quite blatant and the seller believes that this behavior is just due to the timing of the visit, the seller might say, "I'm sensing that this might not be the best time to talk. Should we reschedule for another time?"

If the buyer continues to communicate aggressively, being downright rude, you probably need to call attention to the fact.[13] After all, to develop a long-term win–win relationship and partnership, you both need to be on the same footing. Perhaps saying something like this will clear the air: "I'm sorry, Joe. I don't know quite how to say this. But it seems to me that you wish to argue more than learn about my products. I'll gladly continue if you think we can both approach this problem with professionalism and courtesy." By doing so, you are asserting yourself and confronting the issue head-on. At the same time, you are avoiding an emotional reaction of anger. Of course it is important to keep in mind the various personalities that buyers can have (see Chapter 5) and the adjustments suggested for each.

Also remember that the buyer's culture often dictates how he or she will respond to a seller. For example, Germans are known as being thorough, systematic, and well prepared, but they are also rather dogmatic and thus lack flexibility and the desire to compromise. As a result, sellers not accustomed to such a culture could have difficulty dealing with a German prospect who raises a price objection in a strong tone of voice.

Believe it or not, some of the toughest customers aren't those who are noisy and boisterous. Rather, they are often the passive ones, the quiet ones—the ones

Believe it or not, the hardest prospects can be the quiet ones.

who don't object, don't question, and don't buy. What should a seller do? Be open, direct, and honest. Stop talking. Ask questions. Try your best to get the buyer involved. Establish trust so the buyer can feel confident enough to ask questions. If the buyer is still quiet, use a trial close. If this doesn't result in gaining commitment, ask the prospect what he or she would like to do at this point.

SELLING YOURSELF

You will be doing a lot of selling in the next couple of years, from trying to get a job out of college, to getting promotions and raises. You may be selling township leaders on the need to enact new rules that are consistent with your views and may be trying to convince your neighbors to keep their dogs on their own property.

In all of those situations, you can expect that objections are going to arise. The best thing you can do is to prepare for those objections. Make a list of every possible objection or question that someone can raise and then write down what you consider to be a healthy, helpful response. Some responses are going to require you to do more homework, like preparing visuals and graphs, researching what others have done, and analyzing the costs and benefits of going with other approaches. So do your homework well, and give a polished, well-reasoned presentation of your idea.

Sometimes it is best to just forestall known concerns. For example, maybe you've never had a sales job in your life. Don't wait for the interviewer to raise that concern (or worse yet, never raise it, but be thinking it all the time). Instead, raise the issue yourself: "As you can see, I've never held a sales job before. But let me tell you why I think you should still strongly consider me for this sales position. If you look at my résumé you'll see. . . ."

Remember to probe to make sure you know what the other party is objecting to; then provide a clear, unemotional response that addresses those concerns. And don't forget to always probe after you've addressed the objection to make sure your response resolved the concern. In many situations the other party will never tell you that you didn't answer a question unless you ask.

If other parties go off the deep end and start shouting or being overly aggressive, don't go there with them. Bring them back to reasoning and logical discussion. Even if you can't convince them, you will impress others who might be observing the situation. And you will be developing skills in how best to deal with life's toughest situations.

SUMMARY

Responding to objections is a vital part of a salesperson's responsibility. Objections may be offered at any time during the relationship between buyer and salesperson. They are to be expected, even welcomed, and they must be handled with skill and empathy.

Successful salespeople carefully prepare effective responses to buyers' concerns. Salespeople need to develop a positive attitude, commit to always telling the truth, refrain from interrupting, anticipate and forestall known objections, and learn how to evaluate objections.

Buyers object for many reasons. They may have no money, or they may not need the product. They may need more information or misunderstand some information already offered. They may be accustomed to another product, may not think the value exceeds the cost, or may not like the product's features. They may want to get rid of the salesperson or may not trust the salesperson or his or her company. They may want time to think or may object for many other reasons.

Effective methods of responding to objections are available, and their success has been proved. Methods exist both for concerns that are not true and for objections that either are true or are only the buyer's opinion. Sensitivity in choosing the right method is vital. Salespeople need to develop skill in responding to price objections and in dealing with tough customers. Nothing will substitute for developing skill in these areas.

KEY TERMS

ETHICS PROBLEMS

1. A prospect has just raised an objection about the price of your service, which is commercial carpet cleaning. You know that the service you are selling usually goes on sale a couple of times each year, but you're not sure when the next time will be. It could be as soon as a few weeks. Should you tell the buyer about the possible lower price?

2. One student in a selling class once said, "Why are we learning these objection-handling methods? These techniques are just to help us manipulate our buyers!" How would you respond?

QUESTIONS AND PROBLEMS

1. Categorize each of the following responses into the five basic types of objections. Then illustrate one way to handle each:

a. After a sales presentation, the lawyer says, "You've made some good points, but your competitor's product can do just about everything yours can do."

b. After the salesperson answers an objection, the prospect remarks, "I guess your product is all right, but as I told you when you walked in, things are going pretty well for us right now without your product."

c. After a thorough presentation, the prospect answers, "Whew, that's a lot of money!"

d. The customer says, "I can buy that online for a lot less than what you're selling it for."

2. Betty Hadaldo spent considerable time working with a prospective buyer. She thought a good order would be forthcoming on her next call. A portion of her conversation with the buyer went as follows:

BUYER: You know, I like what I hear about your concrete pumping service. But how can I be sure it will be available on the days that we need it for our next project?

BETTY: We've never had any real complaints before. I'm pretty sure they will be easily available.

BUYER: You are sure of that?

BETTY: Well, I've never heard of any problems that I can remember.

BUYER: [appearing unconvinced and looking at some papers on his desk without glancing up]: I'll let you know later what I plan to do. Thanks for dropping by.

How can you improve on Betty's answer to the buyer's concern?

3. Describe the differences between postponing an objection and forestalling an objection. Then provide a clear example of appropriate postponing for this objection: "This iPod is way too expensive. I can buy MP3 players much cheaper than buying your iPod!"

4. Occasionally a buyer will offer several objections at one time. How would you respond if a buyer made the following comments without pausing? "Say, how long does it take your lab to get the results back to us? And what if we need same-day service sometime? Are your technicians certified? That's important, you know!"

5. In "Building Partnerships 10.1" you learned that it is OK to walk away from some prospects and just say "no" to their requests. Make a list of rules you could follow that indicate when it might be appropriate to walk away from a prospect, assuming you are a salesperson.

6. Choose a restaurant in your town. Assume that you work at that restaurant and are planning to make calls to campus club organizations. Assume that the restaurant has a private meeting room available that will seat 25 people. Your objective is to have officers of the clubs schedule their meetings at the restaurant.
  a. Make a list of objections you may expect to encounter.
  b. What can you do to meet these objections effectively? List the answers you would propose, and label the methods used.

7. In "From the Buyer's Seat 10.1" you read about ways that salespeople inappropriately handled the "I can get a better deal somewhere else" objection. How would you respond if you were a salesperson who heard that objection if you knew how other mortgage wholesalers were handling the situation (by offering special favors)?

8. You have been describing to a retail security officer and his boss a new security camera that your firm just introduced. The camera has tracking features that make it easier for security officers to review tapes. The security officer says, "I would really like that!" The boss says, "Well, if it's what you think we need, OK. How much does it cost?" At your reply, "This one is $2,498," the boss exclaims, "For that little thing?" What should you say or do?

9. For each of the following objections, provide answers that clearly demonstrate the direct denial and indirect denial methods. Assume each objection is not true:
  a. My obstetric patients will never need that service.
  b. The cost of replacing the filter will be more than just buying a new unit.
  c. I heard that the paint used in manufacturing your unit can cause cancer.
  d. I can buy this cheaper online.

10. For each of the following objections, provide answers that clearly demonstrate the compensation method and referral method. Assume all the objections are either true or are the prospect's opinion:
  a. Your repossession service costs a lot of money!
  b. I don't think our customers will like the new beverage you're selling.
  c. Your diesel mechanics aren't certified by the ATSG.
  d. My customers have never asked for this brand of dishwasher.

CASE PROBLEMS

case **10.1**

BrainScope (Part B)

An estimated 1.6 million to 3.8 million sports-related traumatic brain injuries (TBIs) occur each year. Yet all too often, when a person gets hurt in sports, the team doctor asks a few questions and, assuming there are no major concerns, sends the player right back into the game. However, studies show that if a player gets another concussion before the brain has healed, there is a much greater chance of long-term brain damage.

The problem is that there isn't an MRI machine at the sidelines. But that may change if the BrainScope company has its way. It will be introducing a new product that will gauge how serious a concussion is. The tool is small enough and inexpensive enough for all teams to have one on their sidelines.

The feedback from the BrainScope is a meter that shows if brain activity is anywhere near the danger zone. The system does this by picking up brain signals and comparing them to 15,000 scans in its database. The database was created based on scans performed at New York University's Brain Research Lab.

Some doctors claim the technology isn't cutting-edge. Originally developed in the 1930s, the technology uses qEEG (quantitative electroencephalograms).

However, the developers of the BrainScope claim that their new device was developed with the advice of 30 leading brain experts.

According to the company's Web site, "BrainScope's novel application of advanced mathematics and miniaturized hardware is designed to bridge the limitations of traditional EEG tools (bulky, expensive, need expert data interpretation) to provide easy-to-use, noninvasive, timely, frontline tools that can assist with an initial assessment of brain function as well as provide adjunctive assessment across the brain care path."

The BrainScope could also be used at hospitals as emergency room testing devices to see if a patient has a real problem and thus needs to have more sophisticated testing done. The company is currently focusing its efforts on military settings. For example, the U.S. Army can deploy the device in combat situations. This would be very helpful to assess soldiers who were nearby when a roadside bomb exploded.

In August 2009 BrainScope's ZOOM-100DC brain electrical activity data collection system was cleared for marketing by the U.S. Food and Drug Administration.

Assume you are selling the new ZOOM-100DC to a team trainer/physician for a local football or hockey team. Assume the tool will sell for $495.00 and comes with a four-year guarantee.

Questions

1. What objections could the buyer raise? (Use any assumptions necessary to develop this list.)
2. Provide a response to each objection you listed in Question 1 (make any assumptions necessary to create your responses). Include the name of the method you recommend for each objection.

case 10.2

Bally Total Fitness
Concepts

Prestwick is a large multinational corporation that manufactures and sells furniture and kitchen and bath fixtures; it also has a group of 20 luxury resort destinations in France and Germany. Thanks to rapid expansion, Prestwick has been able to offer many benefits to its corporate headquarters employees, including a fitness center with a full-size gym. However, over the years, the size of the firm at corporate headquarters has grown tremendously (from 1,500 to over 2,500 employees), resulting in the fitness center becoming more and more crowded. On many days, employees can't get on a treadmill or find room to work out because of the large number of employees trying to use the facility. Currently Prestwick is managing the fitness center itself, staffing it with a small group of employees who oversee the operations there.

Amanda Hightower is a salesperson for Bally Total Fitness Concepts. Bally works with firms like Prestwick and designs and outfits new and remodeled fitness centers. Amanda was called by Jerry Mays, an assistant in the HR department, who told her that Prestwick could really use a larger and more comprehensive facility. However, Jerry asked that his name not be used when Amanda called on the firm.

Amanda made an appointment to meet with Barb Granroth, vice president of human resources for Prestwick, to discuss Prestwick's current fitness center and how Bally could improve it. Specifically, Amanda is planning to discuss creating a larger fitness center with new equipment. Amanda also intends to suggest that the larger and remodeled facility be managed and staffed by Bally personnel.

Questions

1. List objections you think might occur during this first meeting with Barb. Make any assumptions necessary to develop this list.

2. Describe how you would respond to each objection listed in Question 1. Be sure to label the methods. Make any assumptions necessary to create your responses.

ROLE PLAY CASE

Today you will repeat your role play presentation from Chapter 9. (If you have not done role plays before, you will need to review the information about the various role play customers that can be found at the end of Chapter 3. If you didn't do the role play for Chapter 9, you will need to review that material also, which can be found at the end of Chapter 9.) When you act as the observer today, you should identify what objection-handling method the seller used and if it was done effectively. The professor will give you a sheet to use as a buyer, listing objections for you to use during the role play. When you sell, try to use a variety of objection-handling methods.

Note: For background information about these role plays, please see page 27.

To the instructor: Additional information needed to complete the role play is available in the Instructor's Manual.

ADDITIONAL REFERENCES

Bud, Peter Paul. *How to Be a Best Seller: 18 Simple and Proven Steps You Must Know to Succeed.* Lulu, 2009.

Compton, Jason. "The Power of No." *1to1media,* March/April 2008, pp. 40–41.

McGaulley, Michael. *How to Sell Face-to-Face Survival Guide.* ChamplainHouseMedia, 2010.

Mulvey, Richard. *Handling Objections/Closing the Sale.* Perception Business Skills, 2010.

Reilly, Tom. *Crush Price Objections: Sales Tactics for Holding Your Ground and Protecting Your Profit.* McGraw-Hill, 2010.

Shaltz, Gerry. *The DNA of Selling: What You Won't Learn in Business School.* iUniverse, 2009.

Taylor, Charles R., Kyung Hoon Kim, Eunju Ko, Myung Hwan Park, Dong Ryul Kim, and Hak Il Moon. "Does Having a Market Orientation Lead to Higher Levels of Relationship Commitment and Business Performance? Evidence from the Korean Robotics Industry." *Industrial Marketing Management* 37, no. 7 (October 2008), pp. 825–32.

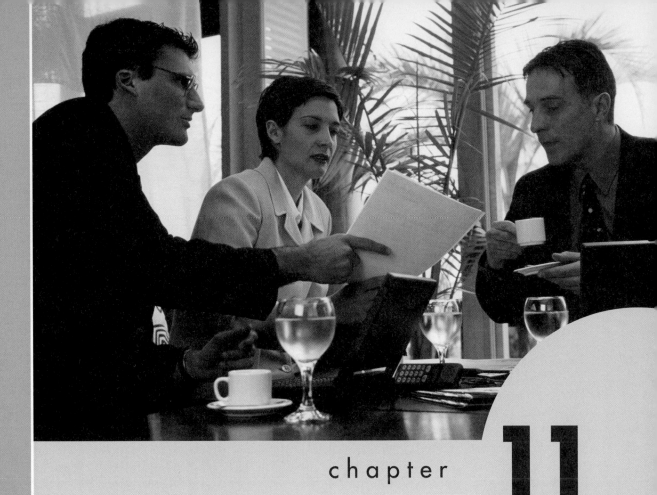

chapter **11**

OBTAINING COMMITMENT

SOME QUESTIONS ANSWERED IN THIS CHAPTER ARE

- How much emphasis should be placed on closing the sale?
- Why is obtaining commitment important?
- When is the best time to obtain commitment?
- Which methods of securing commitment are appropriate for developing partnerships?
- How should pricing be presented?
- What should a salesperson do when the prospect says yes? When the prospect says no?
- What causes difficulties in obtaining commitment, and how can these issues be overcome?

PROFILE

PROFILE All sports fans have experienced a special moment when they look around their team's stadium and see 70,000 fellow supporters passionately cheering on their team. The stadium noise is electrifying. It gives you goose bumps down your arms and raises the hair on the back of your neck. What few people begin to consider is how in the world professional sports teams are able to sell every ticket in the building to create moments like this. Welcome to the wonderful world of closing sales!

I got a taste of inside sales on the first day of my internship. After a brief training session, I was given a telephone and hundreds of people to call. My job was simple: Do whatever it took to sell as many tickets as possible. I found myself selling for boxers I'd never heard of, sports I'd never seen, and venues I'd never been to. I sold boxing, lacrosse, rugby, tennis, hockey, soccer—you name it, I tried to sell it.

After arriving in the City of Angels, my competitive, determined nature led me to strong results within a short period of time. After one month as an intern responsible for selling, hard work and lucky timing enabled me to be promoted to an account executive for the Los Angeles Kings Hockey Club. After another 13 months of more hard work and even luckier timing, I was promoted to the role of manager of ticket sales and service for the Kings.

After only 18 months of hard work, an opportunity knocked 300 miles north of Los Angeles. The five-time Super Bowl Champion San Francisco 49ers were starting a sales and service department, and I quickly jumped at the opportunity to join the National Football League. New town, new city, new sport, but the same goal in mind: Sell tickets.

Working in inside sales is very simple. Your job performance is easily quantifiable, and your peers know what kind of results you're having. Whiteboards are plastered around every office with sales representatives' names and productivity.

Everyone I interview always asks what it takes to be successful in inside sales, and the answer is quite simple: Hard work and going the extra mile. How many times have I been told "No!" and hung up on? Tens of thousands. How you respond will determine your success. Will you take the rejection personally and be fearful for the next 80 calls you need to make in a day? Make no mistake about it—burnout is extremely high in inside sales, but if you can plug away and convert the rejection into a positive learning experience for your calls and sales skills, you will be successful.

Since you'll be working with dozens of other employees in an identical position, you can make yourself stand out with hard work, organization, creativity, and humility. Be prepared to be shot down countless times, but stand back up and be ready to accomplish your goals every single time you pitch a product.

As a manager, my role as a salesperson has not diminished. Sales is a necessary tool for all employees in a sports organization, and everyone is counted on to chip in. While the athletes on the field may be the reason fans show up, the next time you see 70,000 screaming fans in your stadium, remember that it may have taken 170,000 rejections to fill the seats and ignite those goose bumps.

Visit us on the Web at www.49ers.com.

SECURING COMMITMENT TODAY

Asking for the buyer's business, often called **closing,** has always received a great deal of emphasis in sales training. Hundreds of books, DVDs, CDs, and seminar speakers have touted the importance of closing—just Google "close sales" at Amazon, and nearly 300 book titles will appear. Almost all are devoted to a method or methods that will make the decision maker say yes.

Look a little closer at those titles, however, and you'll notice that most of them are old. Some of the books may even be older than your parents! Today's sales professionals recognize that securing a sale is the reason for their existence, but getting that sale should be due to the value created, not the technique used.

Rob Keeney, training director for Frosty Acres Brands, says this about closing:

> I don't see good closers as being "pushy." Assertive, yes. Direct, yes. "Pushy" implies the customer being somehow compelled to do something they really don't want to do. By contrast, a good closer helps a customer make the decision they really want or need to make. And sooner rather than later.

Charles Cohon, president of Prime Devices and an influential speaker in the manufacturer's representation industry, says this about closing:

> Closing an order is not the end of a process, it is the beginning. Concentrate just on closing that order, and it will be the last order you get from that customer. Concentrate instead on developing a relationship with that customer that leads naturally to an order and you will earn not only that order, but also that customer's orders for many years to come.

Others also believe the traditional emphasis on getting the sale no matter what damages trust, insults the buyer's intelligence, and raises the possibility of losing commitment altogether. Customers make a buying decision, rather than the salesperson closing the sale. Buyers want to buy, not to be sold. "From the Buyer's Seat 11.1" illustrates that buyers want transparency from their salespeople and appreciate hard work that pays off with a good exchange for both sides.

Solid research provides strong evidence that questions the value of closing techniques. The research, based on more than 35,000 sales calls over 12 years, has found that in a major sale, reliance on closing techniques actually reduces the chances of making a sale.[1] Further, salespeople who were specifically trained in closing actually closed fewer sales. For very low-priced products (as in door-to-door magazine sales), however, closing techniques may increase the chances of a sale.

So why even cover closing at all? Because there are nonmanipulative and trustworthy ways to gain commitment and because obtaining commitment is critical for the success of salespeople and their firms. Without a buyer's commitment, no sale takes place. Also, buyers rarely volunteer to make a purchase even when that decision is obviously the right thing to do. This chapter covers the topic of obtaining commitment in a manner that is consistent with the theme of the book: developing and building long-term partnerships.

PART OF THE PROCESS

The process of obtaining commitment occurs throughout the natural, logical progression of any sales call. Recall from Chapter 3 that creeping commitment occurs when a customer becomes committed to a particular course of action throughout the buying process. Salespeople actually gain commitment repeatedly: when asking for an appointment, when checking to see whether the customer's entire needs have been identified, and when asking whether the prospect would like to see a

From the BUYER'S SEAT

DID I MISS THE CLOSE?

By Steve Schlesinger, Schlesinger and Associates

Just last week we had a significant purchase to make, not just because it was an expensive or large purchase but because it represented a major change in strategy. Our strategy for information technology has been to build our own. In many ways we were ahead of the market, and off-the-shelf programs did not fit our needs. But last year we needed to make some changes to one of our programs; so we thought, let's explore what's out there off-the-shelf that can be modified. We found a product that we integrated and that worked great with our proprietary software.

When it came time to do the same with our customer management software, our first thought was that it was too expensive. Two years ago we had looked at software for customer management, and it just didn't make sense. But given the success we had with the other program, we decided to take another look.

I called a friend of mine at Salesforce.com, who runs their large account business. We're about a $70 million per year company, so we don't really fit his sales team, but he was able to help us in the process. In addition to the cost, making sure their software integrated well with our custom software and work process was a big concern for us. My friend was able to help assemble a Salesforce team that could address the integration issue.

This time we learned we could accommodate what we needed. The development meeting was excellent, the integration piece was developed, and then they came back with a good cost–benefit analysis. But then the decision got tougher.

With offices across the United States and United Kingdom, we realized we needed everyone who works with clients to have access to the software. This decision increased our license from 10 users to 70 or 80. That raised the costs substantially, and suddenly that cost–benefit analysis wasn't looking so good.

I had forgotten this because I don't deal with salespeople every day. But they had a real sense of urgency to get this done.

Their year ends January 31, so they were very motivated to get the deal done. This deadline spurred more aggressive pricing and help on the integration side, and they really took care of all our needs. And on January 29 we signed the deal.

I never thought about the need to get a deal done from the salesperson's perspective. I'd thought about that when buying a car, but I hadn't really thought about it in this instance. For one thing, it wasn't a hard sell. The beauty is that they were open and honest. They were transparent—they needed to get it done and told us, and they gave me the leeway in the terms that I needed. They were very professional. Would I have gotten different or higher pricing if I had waited past their deadline? I don't know.

But I do know that it is rare to feel like you won in a negotiation. You always wonder if you could have done better. In this case, I needed these guys to win, too. I believe I got a good deal, but since this isn't a one-time purchase and I need these guys to support my integration, I want this relationship to feel good for both sides. So I was happy that we were able to close the deal in their time frame.

Source: Steve Schlesinger, Schlesinger and Associates.

demonstration or receive a proposal. Commitment, of course, is more than just securing an order. As Exhibit 11.1 illustrates, salespeople will attempt to obtain a commitment that is consistent with the objectives of the particular sales call.

Obtaining commitment is also important in moving the account through the relationship process. Once a sale is made, salespeople begin to plan for the next sale or for the next level of commitment that indicates a deepening relationship. At the same time, commitment is a two-way street. Salespeople also make commitments to buyers when the sale is made.

Exhibit 11.1

Examples of
Commitments
Salespeople May
Attempt to Obtain

Examples of Presale Commitments

- To have the prospect agree to come to the Atlanta branch office sometime during the next two weeks for a hands-on demonstration of the copier.
- To set up another appointment for one week from now, at which time the buyer will allow me to do a complete survey of her printing needs.
- To inform the doctor of the revolutionary anticlotting mechanism that has been incorporated into our new drug and have her agree to read the pamphlet I will leave.
- To have the buyer agree to pass my information along to the buying committee with his endorsement of my proposal.
- To have the prospect agree to call several references that I will provide to develop further confidence and trust in my office-cleaning business.
- To have the prospect agree on the first point (of our four-point program) and schedule another meeting in two days to discuss the second point.
- To have the prospect initiate the necessary paperwork to allow us to be considered as a future vendor.

Examples of Commitments That Consummate the Sale

- To have the prospect sign an order for 100 pairs of Levi's jeans.
- To schedule a co-op newspaper advertising program to be implemented in the next month.
- To have the prospect agree to use our brand of computer paper for a trial period of one month.
- To have the retailer agree to allow us space for an end-of-aisle display for the summer presentation of Raid insect repellent.

THE IMPORTANCE OF SECURING COMMITMENT

Overall, gaining commitment tells the salesperson what to do next and defines the status of the client. For example, gaining a needs identification appointment may mean that you have a "suspect"; at the end of that call, gaining commitment for a demonstration means you have a prospect. Gain an order and you gain a customer. Without gaining commitment, the salesperson may waste time doing the wrong things.

Salespeople need to become proficient in obtaining commitment for several other good reasons. First, if they fail to obtain commitment, it will take longer (more sales calls) to obtain a sale, if a sale occurs at all. Taking more time with one sale means fewer sales overall because you lose time for prospecting and other important activities. Second, assuming the product truly satisfies the prospect's needs, the sooner the prospect buys, the sooner she or he can realize the benefits of the product or service. Third, the company's future success depends on goodwill and earning a profit. Finally, securing commitment results in financial rewards for the salesperson; in addition, meeting needs is also intrinsically rewarding for the seller.

One thing to remember is that if you have done your job well and you have a product that the buyer truly needs, then you deserve the sale. The buyer is not doing you a favor by buying, and he or she expects you to ask for the sale if you've done your work professionally. Not only is gaining commitment important for

thinking **it** through

Think for a moment about a major purchase that you or a family member made, such as a new TV or a car. During the shopping process, what were some of the worst closes you experienced? What really angers you when you try to shop for major purchases? What made the difference between those experiences and the ones you found satisfying?

you and your company, it is the professional thing to do. What is not professional is a high-pressure close; typically, high-pressure closing is necessary (and inappropriate) when the salesperson has not done a good job throughout the entire process.[2]

Before we get into how to obtain commitment, some time should be spent on the importance of terms and conditions of the sale and how these influence the total cost. Sometimes terms are an important need and may be presented early in the call. But we present the credit terms here because often a buyer decides what to buy and then explores the financial terms that are available.

FINANCIAL TERMS AND CONDITIONS

Most salespeople try to hold off on presenting price until the end. Yet price is often the first question asked. The final price is really a function of the terms and conditions of the sale and depends on several factors.

Cash flow is an issue for many buyers and can stop a sale. For example, Ram Ramamurthy of RTI needed to buy a $55,000 scanner to complete a job for a customer. But the cash to buy the scanner wouldn't be available until after the customer paid for the job, which was 30 days after the job was completed and 90 days after the scanner was purchased. So Ian Wright, the salesperson selling the scanner, worked out a lease agreement that reduced Ram's cash requirements to only $5,000 up front and $1,500 per month until the job was completed. Ram then paid off the balance when his client paid him.[3]

Factors that affect price are the use of quantity and other discounts, as well as credit and shipping terms. Figuring out the final actual price can be difficult, especially in situations with many options and packages rather than standardized products. Some companies have turned to special software to manage pricing and product complexities, as discussed in "Sales Technology 11.1."

DISCOUNTS

Discounts are given for many reasons and may be based on the type of customer (such as wholesaler or retailer, senior citizen or younger adult), quantity purchased, or some other factor. The most common type of discount is the quantity discount.

Quantity discounts encourage large purchases by passing along savings resulting from reduced processing costs. Businesses offer two types of quantity discounts: (1) the single-order discount and (2) a cumulative discount. An office equipment company offering a 10 percent discount on a single order for five or more facsimile machines is an example of a single-order discount. When offering a **cumulative discount,** that same company might offer the 10 percent discount on all purchases over a one-year period, provided the customer purchases more than five fax machines. The customer may sign an agreement at the beginning of the year promising to buy five or more machines, in which case the customer will be billed for each order at the discounted price (10 percent off). If the customer fails to purchase five fax machines, a single bill will be sent at the end of the year for the amount of the discount (10 percent of the single-unit price times the number of fax machines actually purchased). Another method is to bill the customer at the full price and then rebate the discount at the end of the year, based on the actual number of fax machines purchased.

CREDIT TERMS

Most U.S. sales are made on a credit basis, with **cash discounts** allowed for early payment. These cash discounts are the last discount taken, meaning that if a

NEEDED: KNOWLEDGE TO CLOSE THE DEAL

Knowledge is key to a salesperson's success. One pair of experienced sales consultants, Matt Moore and Keith De La Rue from Australia, say there is a "golden triangle" of knowledge that salespeople have to master: (1) knowledge of sales skills and processes, (2) knowledge of the customer, and (3) knowledge of the offering. Luckily for today's salesperson, there is technology to help manage each leg of the golden triangle.

For example, product configurors help salespeople manage knowledge of offerings. Anritsu, a company that makes highly technical communication devices, uses Configure One's Concept software to allow customers to configure their own products online. Salespeople can use the software, too, and the software frees salespeople to focus on selling, not on product configuration. Katherine van Diepen, Anritsu's marketing communications manager, estimates that this software saves salespeople about 45 minutes per configuration, or the equivalent of adding one sales call per day per salesperson. Increased accuracy in configuration also means more satisfied customers.

CRM systems help manage customer knowledge and knowledge of the process. Typically a CRM system will be designed around a sales process, so simply following the prompts of the system can help keep salespeople on track. But what if the situation calls for specialized customer knowledge—say, knowledge about a particular type of customer or industry?

That's where company-based wikis come in. Just like Wikipedia, companies create Web sites where employees can post information. More sophisticated collaboration systems, like CubeTree, enable salespeople anywhere on the globe to share ideas and information. For example, the Garland Group uses it because its staff often works onsite with customers. Making the most of the company's best employees meant creating a technology solution that enabled fast and easy collaboration. That's where CubeTree comes in. Resembling a Facebook for business, the application is tailored to Garland's needs and is therefore a much more powerful tool.

Knowledge management solutions help salespeople make the most of the knowledge that is available in their organizations without having to learn it all. That's how these technology solutions help close the deal.

Sources: Matt Moore and Keith De La Rue, "Closing the Deal with the Help of Knowledge," *Knowledge Management Review* 11, no. 3 (July/August 2008), pp. 14–19; "Anritsu Case Study," http://www.configureone.com/pdf/ConfigureOnecasestudy-Anritsu.pdf, accessed March 3, 2010; "Enabling the Garland Group's Geographically Distributed Teams to Stay Continuously Connected," case study, http://www.cubetree.com/garland_group_cubetree_case_study.pdf, accessed March 3, 2010.

quantity discount is also offered, the cash discount is calculated after the quantity discount is taken off. A common discount is 2/10, n/30, which means that the buyer can deduct 2 percent from the bill if it is paid within 10 days from the date of invoice. Otherwise the full amount must be paid in 30 days. Another common discount is 2/10, EOM, which means that the 10-day period begins at the end of the month. For example, if the customer receives $1,000 worth of supplies on February 15 with terms of 2/10, EOM and pays the bill on March 5, the customer would pay $980 (that is, $1,000 at 2% = $20 discount for paying cash; $1,000 − $20 = $980). But if the customer pays on March 11, the bill would be the full $1,000.

Credit terms can be very important in capital equipment sales. Capital purchases have long lives and cost more than a buyer can afford to pay all at once. For example, the HVAC (heating, ventilation, and air conditioning) industry relies heavily on financing to sell heating and cooling systems. Johnson Controls offered a six months with no interest plan, called "same as cash." "Most consumers need some type of bridge financing to handle an unplanned $8,000 HVAC expense. That is why we feel we've seen so much business in the same-as-cash programs."[4] Easy credit terms can help salespeople close sales, but sales aren't complete until the buyer takes delivery. One home builder noticed that buyers were willing to put contracts on houses that hadn't been built yet in order to fix their credit during the nine months it took to complete the homes. So many "buyers" were unable to actually get credit and canceled sales that he quit taking orders on prebuilt homes.[5]

SHIPPING COSTS

The terms and conditions of sale include shipping costs. Recall from Chapter 2 that the term *free on board (FOB)* is used to determine the point at which the buyer assumes responsibility for both the goods and the costs of shipping them. Thus FOB destination means the buyer will take responsibility for the goods once they reach the buyer's location, and the seller will pay the freight.

Suppose Hormel quotes an FOB origin price. It will load the truck at its Chicago plant, but the buyer will pay for shipping. If Hormel sold a truckload of pepperoni to Pizza Hut under terms of FOB destination, Hormel would pay for shipping and would have the pepperoni delivered to Pizza Hut's warehouse, where warehouse personnel would unload the truck.

Another form of FOB is *FOB installed,* meaning that title and responsibility do not transfer until the equipment is installed and operating properly. In some instances FOB installed can also mean that operator training must be provided before title transfers. These are important terms because there are significant costs associated with the technical installation and operator training for many pieces of sophisticated equipment. Buyers want to know the total price and what it includes.

The terms and conditions of a sale, including but not limited to price, can often play as important a role as the product itself in determining what is purchased. Creative salespeople understand the terms and conditions they have to work with so they can meet the needs of their buyers while also meeting the profit objectives of their own companies.

If Hormel quotes a price for pepperoni that's FOB origin, then Pizza Hut pays for shipping. If the price is FOB destination, then Hormel pays for shipping.

PRESENTING PRICE

Price is often discussed at the end of the presentation simply because the salesperson may not know what that price will be until the final solution is agreed on. Because price is so important to the buyer, it is worth considering how price should be presented.

Most firms set prices after careful study of competitors' offerings, the value delivered by the product or service, and the cost of providing the product or service. For these reasons the price should represent a reasonable and fair picture of the product's or service's value. Therefore, never apologize for a price or present the price apologetically; rather, present it with confidence.

Bruce Culbert, now chief service officer with the Pedowitz Group, says that salespeople sometimes negotiate against themselves. When he was at IBM,

> I had an account manager who was under pressure to make quota for the quarter. In presenting a proposal to a prospective customer, the salesperson did as was agreed and sent the proposal via e-mail a full two weeks prior to quarter end because the

client said they would be able to make a decision by the end of the month. If this deal closed, the salesperson would hit quota. Several days went by, and there was no response from the prospect. A follow-up e-mail and phone went unanswered. In a panic the salesperson began to submit revised proposals each time, lowering the price in an attempt to get the prospect to respond positively. A week went by with no response. During the week two revised proposals had been submitted, each time lowering the price almost 10 percent. On the Tuesday before the quarter closed the client responded favorably to the original proposal with their apologies that they had not responded sooner but they were on vacation the past week and were just now catching up on e-mail. Needless to say the salesperson was ecstatic to learn of the good fortune just prior to quarter close. About 10 minutes later the salesperson received an additional e-mail from the client informing them to ignore the previous note and that they would like to accept proposal revision 2, which was almost 20 percent less than the original proposal.[6]

As Bruce says, here is a salesperson who panicked and lost the company 20 percent.

In addition to presenting the price with confidence, remember that price is not the focus of your presentation. The real issue is satisfying the needs of the buyer, of which budget is only one. True, a budget limitation can halt progress toward a sale. The real issue, though, is the total cost of ownership, which means the buyer should also factor in the value of the benefits delivered.

WHEN TO ATTEMPT TO OBTAIN COMMITMENT

Novice salespeople frequently ask themselves these questions: Is there a right time to obtain commitment? How will customers let me know they are ready to buy? Should I make more than one attempt? What should I do if my first attempt fails?

The right time to attempt to gain commitment is when the buyer appears ready, as evidenced by buying signals. Some salespeople say that one psychological moment in each sales presentation affords the best opportunity to obtain commitment, and if this opportunity is bypassed, securing commitment will be difficult or impossible. This belief is not true, however. Seldom does one psychological moment govern the complete success or failure of a sales presentation.

Most buyers will commit themselves only when they clearly understand the benefits and costs of such a decision. At times this point occurs early in the call. A commitment to purchase a large system, however, usually will not occur until a complete presentation and several calls have been made and all questions have been answered.

Buying signals, or indications that the buyer is ready to buy, can be evidenced both in the buyer's comments and nonverbally. Buying signals are also called **closing cues.** "Building Partnerships 11.1" presents several salespeople's experience in recognizing buying signals.

BUYER COMMENTS

A customer's comments often are the best indication that he or she is considering commitment. A prospect will seldom say, "All right, I'm ready to endorse this product to our buying committee." Questions about the product or terms of sale and comments in the form of requirements or benefit statements signal readiness to buy, as do responses to trial closes.

Buyer Questions

Here are some examples of questions that signal readiness to buy:

If I agree to go with this cooperative advertising program, do you have any ads already developed that I could use?

WAIT! I'M NOT DONE YET!

Alex Homer, now with Tom James, a custom clothier, sold life insurance while he was in college. As he tells the story, "One day, I met with a prospect to discuss his life insurance. I was fairly new to the business and had just finished training. I was excited with the cache of product knowledge I had accumulated, and I wanted every person I sat down with to know it all. I would explain everything in thorough detail, and most often, it would prove favorable to a potential sale. On this particular appointment, it was very clear that the prospect was considering doing business with me, and rather than ask him to do business, I kept discussing certain features about the policy. The more details I gave him, the more complex his decision-making process became, and I received the ill-fated 'I'll think it over and call you back'."

Alex had talked himself out of the sale by talking through the buyer's closing cues. Despite having a prospect who kept indicating he was ready to buy, Alex kept right on talking.

David Appel, another insurance salesperson, experienced just the opposite situation. Instead of talking his way out of a sale over a two-year period, he couldn't seem to get the buyer to make a decision—any decision. Finally he sent a letter that said, "Dear Bill and Sue, after being in the insurance business for 16 years, I don't know what you want the ending to be—to have life insurance or to not have life insurance. Please give me a call Tuesday so we can get this thing squared away, one way or the other. And if I don't hear from you, I'll call you." David got the call and the sale. He's since used that approach with other procrastinating prospects, and it always works—but for David, what that means is that he gets a decision. Sometimes the decision is "no," but then he can move on.

Sources: Alex Homer, personal correspondence, used with permission; Julie Britt, "Dealing with Procrastinators," *Advisor Today* (December 2008), p. 60.

Do you have any facilities for training our employees in the use of the product?

How soon would you be able to deliver the equipment?

Not all questions signal a readiness to buy. But if the question concerns implementing the purchase and points toward when, not if, the purchase is implemented, the prospect may be getting ready to buy.

Requirements

Requirements are conditions that have to be satisfied before a purchase can take place. For example:

We need a cash discount for a supply order like this.

We need to get this in weekly shipments.

Requirements that are stated near the end of the presentation are need statements that reflect a readiness to buy when they relate to how the purchase will be consummated. As the examples illustrate, requirements relating to financial terms or shipping indicate that the decision to buy the product has been made and now it is time to work out the details.

Benefit Statements

Sometimes prospects offer their own benefit statements, such as these:

Oh, I like the way this equipment is serviced—it will make it much easier on my staff.

Good, that color will match our office decor.

Such positive statements reflect strong feelings in support of the purchase—a sign that the buyer is ready.

Responses to Trial Closes

Salespeople can solicit such comments by continually taking the pulse of the situation with **trial closes,** which are questions regarding the prospect's readiness to buy (first discussed in Chapter 8). Throughout the presentation, the salesperson should be asking questions:

How does this sound to you so far?

Is there anything else you would like to know at this point?

How does this compare with what you have seen of competing products?

Such questions are an important element of any sales process because trial closes serve several purposes, including identifying the customer's proximity to making the decision, gaining agreement on minor points, and creating a true dialogue in which the ultimate close is a natural conclusion. Note that these are more general questions than simply gaining agreement on benefits (discussed in Chapter 8), say as part of a FEBA.

When a seller asks a trial close question, the buyer responds, thus creating a dialogue. Issues can be raised as objections or questions by the buyer, which tell the seller what to cover. Then because the salesperson has been asking closing questions all along, the final close is just a natural part of the ongoing dialogue, as it should be.

NONVERBAL CUES

As in every phase of the presentation, nonverbal cues serve as important indicators of the customer's state of mind, as discussed in Chapter 4. While attempting to gain commitment, the salesperson should use the buyer's nonverbal signals to better identify areas of concern and see whether the buyer is ready to commit. Facial expressions most often indicate how ready the buyer is to make a commitment. Positive signals include eyes that are open and relaxed, face and mouth not covered with hands, a natural smile, and a relaxed forehead. The reverses of these signals indicate that the buyer is not yet ready to commit to the proposal.

Customers' actions also often indicate readiness to buy or make a commitment. For example, the prospective buyer of a fax machine may get a document and operate the machine or place the machine on the table where it will be used. The industrial buyer may refer to a catalog to compare specifications with competing products. A doctor, when told of a new drug, may pick up the pamphlet and begin carefully reading the indications and contraindications. A retailer considering whether to allow an end-of-aisle display may move to the end of an aisle and scan the layout. Any such actions may be signals for obtaining commitment; they should be viewed in the context of all available verbal and nonverbal cues.

Do the two buyers on the right look like they are ready to commit to a purchase?

HOW TO SUCCESSFULLY OBTAIN COMMITMENT

To obtain commitment in a nonmanipulative manner, salespeople need to follow several principles, including maintaining a positive attitude, letting the customer set the pace, being assertive instead of aggressive, and selling the right product in the right amounts.

MAINTAIN A POSITIVE ATTITUDE

Confidence is contagious. Customers like to deal with salespeople who have confidence in themselves, their products, and their companies. On the other hand, unnecessary fear can be a self-fulfilling prophecy. The student who fears essay exams usually does poorly; golfers who believe they will miss short putts usually do. So it is with salespeople: If they fear customers will not accept their proposals, the chances are good they will be right.

One manager related the example of a salesperson selling laundry detergent who unsuccessfully tried to convince a large discount chain to adopt a new liquid version of the product. When the rep's sales manager stopped by the account later in the week to follow up on a recent stockout problem, the buyer related his reasons for refusing the Liquid Tide: "Listen, I know you guys are sharp. You probably wouldn't come out with a new product unless you had tons of data to back up your decision. But honestly, the sales rep who calls on me is always so uptight and apprehensive that I was afraid to adopt the new product! Don't you guys teach them about having confidence?"

LET THE CUSTOMER SET THE PACE

Attempts to gain commitment must be geared to fit the varying reactions, needs, and personalities of each buyer. Thus the sales representative needs to practice adaptive selling. (See Chapter 5 for a complete discussion of adaptive selling.)

Some buyers who react slowly may need plenty of time to assimilate the material presented. They may ask the same question several times or show they do not understand the importance of certain product features. In these circumstances the salesperson must deliver the presentation more slowly and may have to repeat certain parts. Trying to rush buyers is unwise when they show they are not yet ready to commit.

As we discussed earlier in the book, buyers' decision-making styles vary greatly. Japanese and Chinese buyers tend to move more slowly and cautiously when evaluating a proposition. In contrast, buyers working for *Fortune* 500 firms located in the largest U.S. cities often tend to move much more quickly. The successful salesperson recognizes such potential differences and acts accordingly.

BE ASSERTIVE, NOT AGGRESSIVE

Marvin Jolson has identified three types of salespeople: aggressive, submissive, and assertive.[7] Exhibit 11.2 summarizes the differences among assertive, aggressive, and submissive salespeople's handling of the sales interview. **Aggressive** salespeople control the sales interaction but often fail to gain commitment because they prejudge the customer's needs and fail to probe for information. Too busy talking to do much listening, they tend to push the buyer too soon, too often, and too vigorously. They might say, "I can't understand why you are hesitant," but they do not probe for reasons for the hesitancy.

Submissive salespeople often excel as socializers. With customers they spend a lot of time talking about families, restaurants, and movies. They establish rapport quite effectively. They accept the customers' statements of needs and problems but do not probe to uncover any latent needs or opportunities. Submissive salespeople rarely try to obtain commitment, perhaps because they may fear rejection too much.

Assertive salespeople, the third type, are self-confident and positive. They maintain the proper perspective by being responsive to customer needs. Rather than aggressively creating new "needs" in customers through persuasion, they look for buyers who truly need their products and then use questions to acquire information. Their presentations emphasize an exchange of information rather than a one-way presentation.

Selling Activity	Selling Style		
	Aggressive	Submissive	Assertive
Defining customer needs	Believe they are the best judge of customer's needs.	Accept customer's definition of needs.	Probe for need-related information that customer may not have volunteered.
Controlling the presentation	Minimize participation by customer.	Permit customer to control presentation.	Encourage two-way communication and customer participation.
Closing the sale	Overwhelm customer; respond to objections without understanding.	Assume customers will buy when ready.	Respond to objections, leading to somewhat automatic close.

SELL THE RIGHT ITEM IN THE RIGHT AMOUNTS

The chance of obtaining commitment improves when the right product is sold in the right amount. Although this principle sounds obvious, it often is not followed. Sometimes salespeople try to get the biggest order they can. Customers have long memories; they will refuse to do business again with someone who oversells; and they may also lack confidence in someone who undersells.

For example, before attempting to sell two copiers, the office equipment sales representative must be sure that these two copiers, instead of only one copier or perhaps three, best fit the needs of the buyer's office. The chemical company sales representative selling to an industrial firm must know that one tank car of a chemical is more likely to fit the firm's needs than ten 55-gallon drums. The Johnson Wax sales rep who utilizes the firm's Sell to Potential program knows the importance of selling not too few units (the store will run out of stock during the promotion) and not too many units (the store will be stuck with excess inventory after the promotion). The chances to obtain commitment diminish rapidly when the salesperson tries to sell too many or too few units or the wrong grade or style of product.

Also, salespeople should not rely solely on trial orders. A **trial order** is a small order placed by a buyer to see if the product will work, and should not be confused with a trial close. A trial order is no commitment, and all too often a buyer will agree to a trial just to get rid of the salesperson. Further, if any learning curve is necessary, a customer who agrees to a trial might be unwilling to invest the time necessary to fully learn the product and will not fully realize the benefits. The product will be rejected often because customers don't have time to give fair trials. Trial orders can work well when the product is easy to implement (such as selling a new product to a retailer for resale) or when the benefits can be realized only by seeing the product in use.

EFFECTIVE METHODS

"If closing is seen by so many sales experts as manipulative and insulting, are effective methods those that are manipulative but not insulting?" asked one of our students. It is a fair question, and the answer has two elements. First, the salesperson's purpose is to sell the right product in the right amounts. If the prospect does not need what is being sold, the salesperson should walk to the next door and start again. Thus there should never be a need for manipulation (review Chapter 2 for a discussion of manipulation). Second, in addition to selling only what the customer needs, the salesperson should also sell in a fashion consistent with the way the buyer prefers to buy. Therefore, the salesperson should gain commitment in a manner that will help the buyer make the choice, consistent with the principle of persuasion. We use the word *choice* here to mean that the buyer can say no. Salespeople do try to persuade buyers, but with persuasion, the choice remains with the buyer. Manipulative techniques are designed to reduce or eliminate choice; partnering methods are not.

Studying successful methods and techniques enables salespeople to help prospects buy a product or service they want or need. Buyers sometimes have a need or a want but still hesitate to buy the product or service that will satisfy it. For example, an industrial buyer for a candy manufacturer refused to commit to a change in sweeteners, even though she needed better raw material. Why? Because the sweetener rep had met with her on four separate occasions, and the buyer had difficulty remembering all that was said and agreed on. (Apparently this salesperson was not using a software program like NetSuite very effectively.) Had the salesperson used the appropriate method (the benefit summary method, discussed later in this section), commitment might have been obtained. This section describes several of the most important methods for gaining commitment.

DIRECT REQUEST

The most straightforward, effective method of obtaining commitment is simply to ask for it, called the **direct request method.** However, salespeople need to be wary of appearing overly aggressive when using this direct request method. Decisive customers, such as drivers, appreciate getting down to business and not wasting time. Here are some examples:

Can I put you down for 100 pairs of model 63?

Can we meet with your engineer next Thursday to discuss this further?

Will you come to the home office for a hands-on demonstration?

Can you call the meeting next week?

BENEFIT SUMMARY

Early in the interview salespeople discover or reiterate the needs and problems of the prospect. Then, throughout the presentation, they show how their product can meet those needs. They do this by turning product or service features into benefits specifically for that buyer. As they present each benefit, they ask if that benefit meets the need. When using this approach, called the **benefit summary method,** the salesperson simply reminds the prospect of the agreed-on benefits of the proposal. This nonmanipulative method helps the buyer synthesize points covered in the presentation to make a wise decision. For example, a salesperson attempting to obtain a buyer's commitment to recommend a proposal to a buying committee might say this:

> You stated early in my visit that you were looking for a product of the highest quality, a vendor that could provide quick delivery, and adequate engineering support. As I've mentioned, our fasteners have been rated by an independent laboratory as providing 20 percent higher tensile strength than the closest competitor, resulting in a life expectancy of more than four years. We also discussed the fact that my company can deliver fasteners to your location within 3 hours of your request and that this promise holds true 24 hours a day. Finally, I discussed the fact that we have four engineers on staff whose sole responsibility is to provide support and develop specifications for new fasteners for existing customers. Would you be willing to give the information we discussed to the buying committee along with your endorsement of the proposal?

One advantage of the benefit summary method over the direct request method is that the seller can help the buyer remember all the points discussed in the presentation. The summary becomes particularly important in long presentations and in selling situations involving several meetings prior to obtaining commitment. The salesperson cannot assume that the buyer will remember all the major points discussed in the presentation.

BALANCE SHEET METHOD

Sometimes referred to as the *Ben Franklin method* because Franklin described using it to make decisions, the **balance sheet method** aids prospects who cannot make a decision, even though no reason for their behavior is apparent. Such a prospect may be asked to join the salesperson in listing the pros and cons of buying now or buying later, of buying the salesperson's product or that of a competitor, or of buying the product or not buying it at all.

However, like many nonmanipulative sales techniques, this method can insult a buyer's intelligence if used inappropriately. The salesperson may start to obtain commitment with the following type of statement:

The Ben Franklin close is a method of decision making attributed to Franklin. As a closing method, it can seem trite or cheesy.

> You know, Mr. Thacker, Ben Franklin was like you, always determined to reach the right decisions and avoid the wrong ones. I suppose that's how you feel. Well, he suggested taking a piece of paper and writing all the reasons for deciding yes in one column and then listing the reasons for deciding no in a second column. He said that when you make this kind of graphic comparison, the correct decision becomes much more apparent.

That close may seem manipulative; it certainly sounds silly. A more effective start may be to simply draw a T on a plain piece of paper, place captions on each side of the crossbar, and leave space below for the insertion of specific benefits or sales points. Then ask the buyer to list pros and cons of making the purchase. For example, assume the product is National Adhesives' hot-melt adhesive used to attach paper labels to plastic lime-flavored Coke bottles. Coca-Cola is currently using a liquid adhesive made by Ajax Corporation. The top of the T might look like this:

Benefits of Adopting the National Adhesives Hot-Melt Method	Benefits of Staying with the Ajax Liquid Adhesives

The salesperson may say something like, "Making a decision like this is difficult. Let's see how many reasons we can think of for your going with the National Adhesives system." The salesperson would write the benefits (not features) in which the customer has shown interest on the left side of the T. Next the salesperson would ask the customer to list reasons to stay with the Ajax adhesive on the right side. When completed, the T lists should accurately reflect all the pros and cons of each possible decision. At that point the buyer is asked, "Which method do you think is the wisest?"

When used properly, the balance sheet method can help hesitant buyers express their feelings about the decision in a manner similar to the multiattribute matrix (see the appendix of Chapter 3), which gives the salesperson an opportunity to deal with those feelings. It is especially appropriate for a buyer who is an analytical, but would make less sense for an expressive. However, the balance sheet approach takes time and may appear "salesy," particularly if relatively unimportant benefits are considered to be equal to more important reasons not to buy. Also, the list of benefits of the product being sold will not always outnumber the list on the other side of the T.

PROBING METHOD

In the **probing method** sales representatives initially attempt to obtain commitment by another method, perhaps simply asking for it (the direct request method). If unsuccessful, the salesperson uses a series of probing questions designed to discover the reason for the hesitation. Once any reason becomes apparent, the salesperson asks a what-if question. (What if I could successfully resolve this concern? Would you be willing to commit?) An illustrative dialogue follows:

> SALESPERSON: Could we make an appointment for next week, at which time I would come in and do a complete survey of your needs? It shouldn't take more than three hours.
>
> PROSPECT: No, I don't think I am quite ready to take that step yet.
>
> SALESPERSON: There must be some reason why you are hesitating to go ahead now. Do you mind if I ask what it is?
>
> PROSPECT: I'm just not convinced that your firm is large enough to handle a customer of our size.
>
> SALESPERSON: In addition to that, is there any other reason why you would not be willing to go ahead?
>
> PROSPECT: No.
>
> SALESPERSON: If I can resolve the issue of our size, then you would allow me to conduct a survey?
>
> PROSPECT: Well, I wouldn't exactly say that.
>
> SALESPERSON: Then there must be some other reason. May I ask what it is?
>
> PROSPECT: Well, a friend of mine who uses your services told me that often your billing department sends him invoices for material he didn't want and didn't receive.
>
> SALESPERSON: In addition to that, is there any other reason for not going ahead now?
>
> PROSPECT: No, those are my two concerns.
>
> SALESPERSON: If I could resolve those issues right now, would you be willing to set up an appointment for a survey?
>
> PROSPECT: Sure.

This dialogue illustrates the importance of probing in obtaining commitment. The method attempts to bring to the table all issues of concern to the prospect. The salesperson does not claim to be able to resolve the issues but simply attempts to find out what the issues are. When probing has identified all the issues, the salesperson should attempt to resolve them as soon as possible. After successfully dealing with the concerns of the buyer, the salesperson should then ask for a commitment.

There are many modifications of the probing method. Another way to achieve the same results is the following:

> SALESPERSON: Are you willing to buy this product today?
>
> PROSPECT: No, I don't think so.

SALESPERSON: I really would like to get a better feel of where you are. On a scale of 1 to 10, with 1 being absolutely no purchase and 10 being purchase, where would you say you are?

PROSPECT: I would say I'm about a 6.

SALESPERSON: If you don't mind my asking, what would it take to move you from a 6 to a 10?

Also, it is important to always keep cultural differences in mind. For example, if a Japanese businesswoman wants to tell an American salesperson that she is not interested, she might state, "Your proposal would be very difficult," just to be polite. If the seller attempts to use the probing method, the Japanese businesswoman may consider the seller to be pushy or a poor listener. In the same way, an Arab businessperson will never say no directly, a custom that helps both sides avoid losing face.[8]

ALTERNATIVE CHOICE

In many situations a salesperson may have multiple options to present to a buyer. For example, Teo Schaars sells diamonds directly from cutters in the Netherlands to consumers in the United States. When he started in sales, he would display several dozen diamonds on a purple damask–covered table. Sales were few until his father, a Dutch diamond broker, suggested that he limit his customers' choices; there were simply too many diamonds to choose from, overwhelming the buyer. Schaars found his father's comments to be wise advice. Now Schaars spends more time probing about budget and desires and then shows only two diamonds at a time, explaining the key characteristics of each. Then he allows the customer to express a preference. Schaars may have to show half a dozen or more diamonds before a customer makes the final decision, but he rarely shows more than two at a time (www.anschardiamonds.com).

OTHER METHODS

Literally hundreds of techniques and methods to obtain commitment have been tried. Exhibit 11.3 lists a number of traditional methods. Most of them, however, tend to be ineffective with sophisticated customers; nevertheless, many can be used in a nonmanipulative manner if appropriate. For example, the minor-point close can be appropriate if there really is a need to make a choice between two options; the factor that makes the method manipulative is the assumption that the minor choice is the equivalent to making the sale.

No method of obtaining commitment will work if the buyer does not trust the salesperson, the company, and the product. Gaining commitment should not require the use of tricky techniques or methods to force buyers to do something they do not want to do or to manipulate them to buy something they do not need.

IF COMMITMENT IS OBTAINED

The salesperson's job is not over when commitment is obtained. In fact, in many ways the job is just beginning. This section describes the salesperson's responsibilities that accrue after the buyer says yes.

NO SURPRISES

Customers do not like surprises, so now is the time to go over any important information they will need to fully enjoy the benefits of the product or service. For example, if you are selling life insurance and a physical is required, give the customer as much detail as possible to prepare him or her for that experience.

Exhibit 11.3
Some Traditional Closing Methods

Method	How It Works	Remark
Minor-point close	The seller assumes it is easier to get the prospect to decide on a very trivial point than on the whole proposition: What color do you like, blue or red?	This method can upset a prospect who feels he or she is being manipulated or tricked into making a commitment. Even unsophisticated buyers easily spot this technique.
Continuous *yes* close	Throughout the presentation, the seller constantly asks questions for which the prospect most logically would answer yes. By the end of the discussion, the buyer is so accustomed to saying yes that when the order is requested, the natural response is yes.	This method is based on self-perception theory. As the presentation progresses, the buyer begins to perceive himself or herself as being agreeable. At the close, the buyer wants to maintain this self-image and almost unthinkingly says yes. Use of this method can destroy long-term relationships if the buyer later feels manipulated.
Assumptive close	The seller, without asking for the order, simply begins to write it up. A variation is to fill out the order form as the prospect answers questions.	This method does not even give the buyer the courtesy of agreeing. It can be perceived as being very pushy and manipulative.
Standing-room-only close	The seller attempts to obtain commitment by describing the negative consequences of waiting. For example, the seller may state, "If you can't decide now, I'll have to offer it to another customer."	This method can be effective if the statement is true. However, if the prospect really does need to act quickly, this deadline should probably be discussed earlier in the presentation to reduce possible mistrust and the feeling of being pushed.
Benefit-in-reserve close	First the seller attempts to obtain commitment by another method. If unsuccessful, the seller says, "Oh, if you order today I can offer you an additional 5 percent for your trade-in."	This method can backfire easily. The buyer tends to think, "If I had agreed to your first attempt to obtain commitment, I would not have learned about this new enticement. If I wait longer, how much better will your offer be?" The buyer may then seek additional concessions in every future sale attempt.
Emotional close	The seller appeals to the buyer's emotions to close the sale. For example, the seller may say, "This really is a good deal. To be honest with you, I desperately need to secure an order today. As you know, I work on a straight commission basis. My wife is going to have surgery next week, and our insurance just won't cover. . ."	Many obvious problems arise with this method. It is an attempt to move away from focusing entirely on the buyer's personal needs. It does not develop trust or respect. Do not use this close!

Or if a company is going to lease a piece of heavy equipment, let the customer know that delivery will occur after a credit check and how long that credit check will take. John Branton, president of Safe Harbor Financial, requires his salespeople to make sure the client understands how the product works and, if any negative consequences can occur, make sure the client is prepared for it. No customer wants to be surprised with a tax bill later, for example, even if the purchase was still the best choice available.[9]

CONFIRM THE CUSTOMER'S CHOICE

Customers like to believe they have chosen intelligently when they make a decision. After important decisions, they may feel a little insecure about whether the sacrifice is worth it. Such feelings are called **buyer's remorse** or **postpurchase dissonance.** Successful salespeople reassure customers that their choice was the right one. For example:

> I know you will enjoy using your new office machines. You can plan on many months of trouble-free service. I'll call on you in about two weeks to make sure everything is operating smoothly. Be sure to call me if you need any help before then.

Or

Congratulations, Mr. Jacobs. You are going to be glad you decided to use our service. There is no finer service available. Now let's make certain you get off to the right start. Your first bulletin will arrive on Tuesday, March 2.

Or

You've made an excellent choice. Other stores won't have a product like this for at least 30 days.

GET THE SIGNATURE

The buyer's signature often formalizes a commitment. Signing the order is a natural part of a well-planned procedure. The order blank should be accessible, and the signing should be treated as a routine matter. Ordinarily the customer has decided to buy before being asked to sign the order. In other words, the signature on the order blank merely confirms that an agreement has already been reached. The decision to buy or not to buy should not focus on a signature.

The salesperson needs to remember several important points: (1) Make the actual signing an easy, routine procedure; (2) fill out the order blank accurately and promptly; and (3) be careful not to exhibit any excess eagerness or excitement when the prospect is about to sign.

SHOW APPRECIATION

All buyers like to think that their business is appreciated even if they purchase only small quantities. Customers like to do business with salespeople who show that they want the business.

Salespeople may show appreciation by writing the purchaser a letter. This practice especially develops goodwill after large purchases and with new customers. In some situations a small gift, such as a pen with the selling company's name on it, may also be an effective thank-you. Salespeople should always thank the purchaser personally; the thanks should be genuine but not effusive.

Is an e-mail message adequate? Eleanor Brownell doesn't think so. She says, "It (a handwritten note) makes you memorable."[10]

CULTIVATE FOR FUTURE CALLS

In most fields of selling, obtaining commitment is not the end of a business transaction; rather, it is only one part of a mutually profitable business relationship. Obtaining commitment is successful only if it results in goodwill and future commitment. Keep in mind that research shows that it is how the salesperson treats the customer that is the biggest determinant of future sales. How the customer gets treated determines loyalty, which then influences repurchase.[11]

Customers like to do business with salespeople who do not lose interest immediately after securing commitment. What a salesperson does after achieving commitment is called **follow-up.** As Jeffrey Bailey, sales director for Oracle, recognizes, "Making the sale is only the beginning." After making the sale, the salesperson must follow up to make sure the product is delivered when promised, set up appropriately, and so forth. We talk more about follow-up in later chapters. The point here is that the sale does not end with the customer's signature on the order form. Research shows that the quality of follow-up service is an important contributing factor in perceptions of salesperson quality and long-term relationships.[12]

REVIEW THE ACTIONS TO BE TAKEN

An important step, particularly when commitment is next in the buying process, is to review what each party has agreed to do. In the case of a multiple-visit sales cycle, the salesperson must review not only what the client will do but also what the salesperson will do to prepare for the next meeting. To be welcomed on repeat calls, salespeople must be considerate of all the parties involved in buying or using the product. They must pronounce and spell all names correctly, explain and review the terms of the purchase so no misunderstandings will occur, and be sociable and cordial to subordinates as well as those in key positions. In addition, the buyer or user must get the service promised. The importance of this point cannot be overemphasized. Chapter 13 provides detailed information about how to service the account and build a partnership.

IF COMMITMENT IS NOT OBTAINED

Naturally the salesperson does not always obtain the desired commitment. The salesperson should never take this situation personally (which is easier said than done). Doing everything right does not guarantee a sale. Situations change, and customers who may have really needed the product when everything started may find that other priorities make a purchase impossible.

Many times, when a buyer says no, the seller is wise to treat it as "No, not now" rather than "No, never." One salesperson for Factiva, a company that provides research services to businesses, was told no by a prospect. In talking to a gatekeeper, though, he learned of another decision maker in another area of the company who had an interest. That other decision maker bought, and the account is now one of Factiva's largest.[13]

No can mean no forever, though, if the rep isn't listening and isn't sensitive to the buyer's needs. Recall Alex Homer's story at the start of this chapter and how he talked himself out of a sale by providing more information than the buyer wanted. Similarly, Fred Brown, an attorney, had a salesperson who had a service he wanted but didn't have the budget. "When I told her that I couldn't do it now, she kept pushing, and I finally told her to leave. A few months later, when I had the money, I went to someone else because she couldn't listen."[14]

thinking **it** through

> Many students report that asking for the order is the hardest part of selling. Why is it difficult? Does the customer need you to ask for the sale? Have you ever needed a salesperson to ask you to buy? Why or why not?

This section describes some of the common reasons for failing to obtain commitment and offers practical suggestions for salespeople who encounter rejection.

SOME REASONS FOR LOST OPPORTUNITIES

Wrong Attitudes

As discussed earlier in the chapter, salespeople need to have a positive attitude. A fear that obtaining commitment will be difficult may be impossible to hide. Inexperienced salespeople naturally will be concerned about their ability to obtain commitment; most of us have an innate fear of asking someone else to do anything. Some salespeople even fail to ask for the sale because if they never ask, they will never hear no. As a result, they always have more prospects but fewer customers than everyone else. But all salespeople know they need to focus on obtaining commitment to keep their jobs.

Some salespeople display unwarranted excitement when they see that prospects are ready to commit. Research suggests that nonverbals are very important cues and can signal trustworthiness or a lack thereof to buyers. A salesperson who appears excited or overly eager may display nonverbal cues that suggest dishonesty or a lack of empathy.[15] At this point wary buyers may change their minds and refuse to commit.

One of the main reasons for salespeople's improper attitudes toward obtaining commitment is the historical importance placed on closing the sale. Closing has often been viewed as a win–lose situation (if I get the order, I win; if I don't get the order, I lose). Until salespeople see obtaining commitment as a positive occurrence for the buyer, these attitudes will persist.

Poor Presentation

Prospects or customers who do not understand the presentation or see the benefits of the purchase cannot be expected to buy. The salesperson must use trial closes (see Chapter 8) and continually take the pulse of the interview.

A poor presentation can also be caused by haste. The salesperson who tries to deliver a 60-minute presentation in 20 minutes may skim over or omit important sales points. Forgoing the presentation may be better than delivering it hastily. Further, a sales presentation given at the wrong time or under unfavorable conditions is likely to be ineffective.

Another reason for not obtaining commitment is lack of product knowledge. In fact, lack of product knowledge is often cited as an important barrier to obtaining commitment.[16] If the salesperson does not know what the product does, you can be certain the buyer will not be able to figure it out either.

Poor Habits and Skills

Obtaining commitment requires proper habits and some measure of skill. The habit of talking too much rather than listening often causes otherwise good presentations to fail (recall Alex's story). Knowing when to quit talking is just as important as knowing what to say. Some salespeople become so fascinated by the sound of their own voices that they talk themselves out of sales they have already made. A presentation that turns into a monologue is not likely to retain the buyer's interest.

DISCOVERING THE CAUSE

The real reasons for not obtaining commitment must be uncovered. Only then can salespeople proceed intelligently to eliminate the barriers. Some firms have developed sophisticated systems to follow up on lost sales. Sales software, such as NetSuite or salesforce.com, can also identify points in the selling process where a salesperson may be having difficulty. If the sales cycle involves a demonstration, for example, and the salesperson turns fewer leads into demonstrations, the fault may lie in the needs identification skills of that salesperson.

Dave Alexander, account executive for Accenture, says his company does a postsale analysis whether it wins or loses the sale. This discipline causes the sales team to focus on the factors that really lead to success. Dave Stein, author of *How Winners Sell*, says that all too often salespeople will lay the blame for failure on price or the product but will take personal credit for any successes.[17] Both Stein and Alexander agree, however, that an effective win/loss system forces the salesperson to examine the real causes and, if the sale was not won, consider personal strategies for improvement.

SUGGESTIONS FOR DEALING WITH REJECTION

Maintain the Proper Perspective

Probably the inexperienced salesperson's most important lesson is that when a buyer says no, the sales process has not necessarily ended. A no may mean "Not now," "I need more information," "Don't hurry me," or "I don't understand." An answer of no should be a challenge to seek the reason behind the buyer's negative response.

In many fields of selling, most prospects do not buy. The ratio of orders achieved to sales presentations may be 1 to 3, 1 to 5, 1 to 10, or even 1 to 20. Salespeople may tend to eliminate nonbuyers from the prospect list after one unsuccessful call. This practice may be sound in some cases; however, many sales result on the second, third, fourth, or fifth call. Dean Yeck, sales manager with Qwest, says one sale took 15 sales calls.[18] When an earlier visit has not resulted in commitment, careful preparation for succeeding calls becomes more crucial.

Another perspective is that when a buyer says no it is because the buyer is not yet fully informed; otherwise the buyer would have said yes. Consequently, if the buyer has given the salesperson the opportunity to make a presentation, the buyer recognizes that a need exists or is going to exist. What has not happened yet is that match between the offering and the need. At the same time, however, no does not mean "Sell me again right now." It may mean "Sell me again later." Illiki Rai, publisher of *Rising Women* magazine, agrees, noting that when she sells her magazine to prospective advertisers, rejection is often temporary and can lead to referrals as well as future sales opportunities.[19]

The salesperson should have a clear objective for each sales call. When commitment cannot be obtained to meet that objective, the salesperson will often attempt to obtain commitment for a reduced request (a secondary or minimum objective). For example, the salesperson may attempt to gain a trial order instead of an actual order, although, as we discussed earlier, this opportunity should be offered as a last resort.

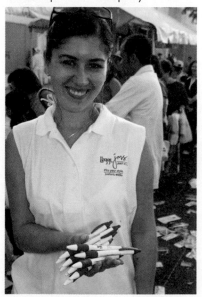

Some companies use promotional products, such as pens with the company's name and phone number on them, as something to leave behind and remind the customer of the salesperson's company.

Recommend Other Sources

A sales representative who uses the consultative selling philosophy (as described in Chapter 5) may recommend a competitor's product to solve the prospect's needs. When recommending other sources, the sales rep should explain why his or her product does not meet the prospect's needs and then provide the name of the competitive product. The goodwill generated by such a gesture should lead to future opportunities when the timing and needs are right.

After recommending other sources, the salesperson usually should ask the prospect for names of people who might be able to buy the seller's product. Also, the salesperson should emphasize the desire to maintain contact with the prospect in the event the seller's firm develops a competitive offering.

Good Manners Are Important

If obtaining commitment fails for any reason, the salesperson should react good-naturedly. Salespeople have to learn to accept no if they expect to call on prospects again. Even if salespeople do not obtain commitment, they should thank prospects for their time. Arguing or showing disappointment gains nothing. The salesperson may plan to keep in contact with these prospects through an occasional phone call, a follow-up letter, or product literature mailings. One salesperson likes to make the following statement at the conclusion of any meeting that does not result in commitment: "I'll never annoy you, but if you don't mind, I'm going to keep in touch."

Many salespeople consider leaving something behind that will let the prospect contact the salesperson in the future. Some firms use promotional products, such as a pen with the company's name and phone number, as a gift after each call to remind the prospect of the salesperson's company. Others may simply use brochures and business cards.

BRINGING THE INTERVIEW TO A CLOSE

Few buyers are interested in a prolonged visit after they commit. Obviously the departure cannot be abrupt; the salesperson should complete the interview smoothly. But goodwill is never built by wasting the buyer's time after the business is concluded.

Remember that most sales take several calls to complete. If an order wasn't signed (and often getting an order isn't even the objective of the call; see Chapter 7) and the prospect wishes to continue considering the proposal, the salesperson should leave with a clear action plan for all parties. An example of the kind of dialogue the salesperson might pursue follows:

> SALESPERSON: When will you have had a chance to look over this proposal?
>
> BUYER: By the end of next week, probably.
>
> SALESPERSON: Great, I'll call on you in about 10 days, OK?
>
> BUYER: Sure, set up something with my secretary.
>
> SALESPERSON: Is there anything else I need to do for you before that next meeting?

The salesperson should always make sure the next step is clear for both parties. Therefore, review what you will do next, what the customer will do next, and when you will meet again.

Follow up promptly with a thank-you and reminder note after the sales call. If you are following up after a sales call in which you gained commitment for the next sales call, an e-mail message is not only sufficient but the best idea. Emily Tanner, of e-Rewards in Dallas, follows up after each sales call with an e-mail message laying out what each person promised to do, including the buyer. If she was told no, the follow-up e-mail message is a simple thank-you with a request to be considered again if the opportunity arises. But if she gets the sale, she sends FairyTale brownies (www.brownies.com) to the buyer's office, along with a personal thank-you.

Similarly, Shirley Hunter, an account executive with Teradata, will also follow up a sale with a handwritten thank-you note. She may also personally present a thank-you gift (her product costs half a million dollars, so a sale is worth celebrating). Her choice of a gift, though, will reflect the situation—a box of Lifesavers for the executive who got behind the purchase, a box of crayons for an architect, or something equally creative.

SELLING YOURSELF

When Carter Simon felt his fraternity needed a stronger recruiting program to attract new members, he had to gain the support of the senior leadership of the chapter. In addition, he had to convince the older members to take on a more active role with the recruiting process. "Getting someone to say they will do something is a lot easier than actually getting them to do it," says Simon.

Laura Carros, marketing manager for JCPenney, had a similar need when she wanted to create a new approach to marketing Penney's own branded products. Her first task was to convince her boss that this new approach was worthwhile. But getting his commitment was insufficient. For the new approach to really work, it would require participation from a broad array of Penney marketing and merchandising professionals—people who would have to volunteer their time and effort to the approach. To secure that participation, she had to get them to buy into her new approach. "It was really a long process. In some instances, I would visit with them personally and we would work out a strategy together. In others, we would hold meetings and I'd have to sell an entire department." The results, though, were worth it. Penney used the new approach to completely rebrand its women's lingerie line. The new product line, Ambrielle, and Carros's new approach became the models for other new product lines and new product launches.[20]

When selling internally, gaining real commitment can mean the difference between a program's success or failure. Just because the choice seems obvious to you—"It's the best decision for our customer and our company!"—doesn't mean that others in the company see it the same way. Nor can someone always order an employee to do something and expect the task to be done well. Commitment skills when selling yourself are critical to a successful career.

As with external customers, though, understanding and selling to others' needs has to come first. If you are interested only in your own needs, no closing skills will carry you.

What's also important to remember is that when selling internally, you have to live with the consequences of the selling process much more intimately than when selling to a customer. Using pushy or cheesy techniques contributes to a reputation that makes future decisions or actions more difficult to secure.

Earlier we noted Shirley Hunter's perspective on thanking a customer for a sale. She also believes, though, that internal celebrations are necessary to say thank you to those who contributed either to a sale or to a successful customer implementation. Cultivating for future calls or decisions is also important. You may not win on this decision, but there will be other opportunities to use your closing skills when selling yourself.

SUMMARY

Commitment cannot be obtained by some magical or miraculous technique if the salesperson has failed to prepare the prospect to make this decision throughout the presentation. Salespeople should always attempt to gain commitment in a way that is consistent with the objectives of the meeting. Obtaining commitment begins with the salesperson's contact with the prospect. It can succeed only when all facets of the selling process fall into their proper place. All sellers need to keep in mind this old saying: "People don't buy products or services; they buy solutions to their problems!"

The process of obtaining commitment is the logical progression of any sales call. Commitment is important for the customer, the seller's firm, and the seller. Commitment should result in a win–win situation for all parties concerned.

Pricing is an important element of any sale and is usually presented at the time of closing. Quantity discounts, payment terms, and shipping terms can affect the final price charged to the buyer as well as influence the decision.

There is no one "right" time to obtain commitment. Salespeople should watch their prospects closely and recognize when to obtain commitment. Successful salespeople carefully monitor customer comments, their buyers' nonverbal cues and actions, and their responses to probes. Comments can be in the form of questions, requirements, benefits, and responses to trial closes.

To successfully obtain commitment, the salesperson needs to maintain a positive attitude, allow the customer to set the pace, be assertive rather than aggressive, and sell the right item in the right amounts. Engaging in these practices will result in a strong long-term relationship between buyer and seller.

No one method of obtaining commitment works best for all buyers. The direct request method is the simplest to use; however, the prospect often needs help in evaluating the proposal. In those instances other methods may be more appropriate, such as the alternative choice, the benefit summary, the balance sheet method, or the probing method. No method of obtaining commitment will work if a buyer does not trust the salesperson.

If commitment is obtained, the salesperson should immediately assure the buyer that the choice was judicious. The salesperson should show genuine appreciation as well as cultivate the relationship for future calls.

If commitment is not obtained, the salesperson should analyze the reasons. Difficulties in obtaining commitment can be directly traced to wrong attitudes, a poor presentation, and/or poor habits and skills. Even if no commitment is obtained, the salesperson should thank the prospect for his or her time.

KEY TERMS

aggressive 301
assertive 301
balance sheet method 304
benefit summary method 303
buyer's remorse 307
buying signals 298
cash discount 295
closing 292
closing cues 298

cumulative discount 295
direct request method 303
follow-up 308
postpurchase dissonance 307
probing method 305
requirements 299
submissive 301
trial close 300
trial order 302

ETHICS PROBLEMS

1. One buyer stated, "All closing methods are devious and self-serving! How can a salesperson use a technique but still keep my needs totally in mind?" Comment. Integrate into your discussion the concepts of persuasion versus manipulation.

2. Reread David Appel's letter in "Building Partnerships 3.1." Do you have any ethical concerns about the letter? Do buyers have an ethical obligation to respond—to make a decision in a timely fashion one way or the other? Why or why not?

QUESTIONS AND PROBLEMS

1. Review the closing methods in Exhibit 11.3, and write a nonmanipulative and a manipulative version of each. What is the difference?

2. "The ABCs of closing are 'Always be closing.'" Another version is "Close early—close often." What is your reaction to these time-honored statements?

3. Harold Bumpurs, a professional purchasing agent, says he has never noticed any tricky closes. His perception is due not to the smooth closing skills of the salespeople who call on him but to the total skill sets they have developed. Prioritize a list of selling skills, from most important to least. How much time should be spent improving commitment-gaining skills as opposed to developing other skills? Why?

4. Reread "Building Partnerships 3.1." Suppose the prospect Alex Homer describes in the opening paragraph said, "What you say sounds interesting, but I want some time to think it over." You answer, "Well, OK. Would next Tuesday be a good day for me to come back?" How can you improve on your answer?

5. One sales manager who worked for a refrigeration equipment company taught his salespeople the following close: Ask questions that allow you to fill out the contract. Assume the sale is made and hand the contract to the buyer, along with a pen. If the buyer doesn't immediately take the pen, drop it and make the buyer pick it up. Once the buyer has the pen in hand, he or she is more likely to use it to sign the contract, so just wait silently until the buyer does.

   a. Would you label this seller as assertive or aggressive?

   b. Is this a trick (manipulative) or merely dramatization (persuasive)?

   c. How would you respond to this behavior if you were the buyer?

6. You've identified a process by which your company could recycle packaging material, saving the company about 10 percent of the packaging costs. But when you talk this over with the person in charge of shipping, he says, "You're just a sales rep! Go sell something and let me do my job!" What do you think is driving his reaction? How would you respond? What would you do next?

7. What makes a Mercedes-Benz worth more than a Volkswagen? How would you convince someone that it is worth more if she or he knew nothing about the various brands of cars? How would the buyer's lack of knowledge influence how you try to gain commitment?

8. Read Todd Pollock's comments at the start of the chapter. How can you handle that much rejection? What is it that people are rejecting? What difference does your answer to that question make?

9. What would you say to a friend to gain his or her commitment to go on a spring break trip? Describe exactly what you would say to your friend using each of the following methods (make any assumptions necessary):

   a. Alternative choice.

   b. Direct request.

   c. Benefit summary.

   d. Balance sheet.

   e. Probing.

10. A customer is willing to order 100 cases listed at $20 per case to get a 15 percent quantity discount. Terms are 2/10, n/30. The customer pays five days after receiving the invoice. How much did the customer pay?

CASE PROBLEMS

case **11.1**

AB Reddy

AB Reddy manufactures handheld scanning devices that are used in inventory management. Used in any environment where tracking inventory is important, these devices scan the UPC bar code and are used to track movement of products within a warehouse or business. Ginger Conlon is calling on Paul Greenberg, senior purchasing director for Advent Systems. Paul has global responsibility for purchasing standardization, and developing a common inventory management system across all of Advent's 32 locations in 12 countries is a task he has to complete this year. Ginger's primary call objective is to have Paul agree to set up an appointment in the next several weeks for Ginger to present to the supply chain committee that will review proposals and narrow the choices down to three systems.

> GINGER: Our scanning systems can support the digital standards of both the United States and Europe, which means that, with some engineering changes in your computer network, your locations can use the same scanners.

> PAUL: Ginger, I've really been thinking that the scanners built by Nortel are industry standard. What has Reddy done differently with these scanners?

> GINGER: Quality is something we take very seriously at Reddy, but having the best-built old product isn't enough, is it? So we've also built

probably the finest engineering staff over the past five years that you'll find anywhere. The result is a product line that was just awarded the Sultan's Engineering Award for Innovation in Egypt last month.

PAUL: That's impressive, and you're right. A well-built product using yesterday's technology is of no benefit to us. But how important is bicontinental use at the scanning level? Can't we just scan and convert the data into a common format later?

GINGER: Yes, you can, but that's really inconsistent with the overall strategy of minimizing the number of vendors and having global suppliers. Plus, you may have seen a report issued by DataMark that indicates some users have had data problems that have been difficult to identify until something goes horribly wrong.

PAUL: I've seen that report from DataMark, as well as an article in the last issue of *Supply Chain Management*. But we've had no plans for such scanners.

GINGER: Why is that?

PAUL: We don't know that it is necessary—we don't think we've got that many locations where scanning is a necessity.

GINGER: What would be considered a significant percentage—of your total sites, I mean?

PAUL: I would guess 50 percent would be acceptable. What are others experiencing?

GINGER: We've got several, maybe four, that have standardized with us globally, and another group of about two dozen that use us in the United States or North America. How does that sound?

PAUL: Intriguing, though we're not the same as others.

GINGER: I know. That's why I'd like to set up a meeting with your supply chain team in the near future. But we'll probably also need someone there from logistics, right?

PAUL: Yes, I suppose we would.

GINGER: Will I have your endorsement at the meeting?

PAUL: We'll have to wait and see. I'll need some documentation on the figures you've given me, and I'd like that before we set up the meeting.

Questions

1. What form of closing did Ginger use to gain Paul's commitment to the idea? Was that appropriate? Why or why not?

2. List how you would attempt to obtain commitment using three other methods of your choice. Write out exactly what you would say for each method (and be sure to identify the method).

3. Although you have been shown only a portion of the conversation, evaluate Ginger's performance in terms of the following:
  a. Selling benefits, not features.
  b. Using trial closes.
  c. Using communication aids to strengthen the presentation.
  d. Responding to objections.
  e. Attempting to gain commitment at the proper time.

Blue Onion is a systems integrator, meaning that it helps companies integrate new software into the old systems and the customer's processes. So when a customer buys SAP software, for example, Blue Onion customizes the software to fit the customer's work processes and to work with the customer's old software.

Sean Thornton just joined the company as an account executive. After five years of systems analysis and sales support for Oracle, a major software provider, he wanted to earn a salesperson's living, so he made the switch. As part of his training he spent some time working with several experienced salespeople. One such salesperson was Mary Kate Danaher.

She filled him in on the client they were about to see as they entered a large office building. "They are buying a system called BOSS," she said. "This is going to be a massive change for them, and it looks like they'll implement in three phases over a two-year period."

"In other words, a big sale for us, right?" replied Sean.

"Yup. And I'm not going to let them get away. They are considering doing the integration on their own, using temporary employees, and that never works well. So I've already filled out a contract and today, when we meet with the CEO, we'll get it signed." The determination in her voice matched the purpose in her step as she strode to the bank of elevators in the center of the lobby.

Once in the CEO's office, sitting around a small conference table with the head of MIS and the CFO, Mary Kate reviewed the key points of the agreement, saying, "Shirley, you know that this is a critical implementation and you can't afford any mistakes. That's why you should rely on Blue Onion," and handed the contract to the CEO.

The head of MIS squirmed uncomfortably. Shirley looked at him, and he said, "Shirley, I really think we can do this ourselves and save a lot of money."

"With all due respect, Jack, my experience would say that you can't. Temporaries just don't care as much as your own people do, nor as much as our people do," said Mary Kate, with conviction.

Silence draped over the table. Sean could hear an antique clock ticking away on the shelf behind Shirley's desk. After what seemed like an hour but was probably only a few seconds, Shirley looked at the CFO, who nodded almost imperceptibly. She took out her pen, signed the contract, and handed it back to Mary Kate.

"Thank you, Shirley. I will personally see this project through to completion, on time and on budget, and at the end, you'll get all you hoped for and more," said Mary Kate.

The MIS director stood, looking at the CEO and then the CFO, then back to the CEO. Then he stuck out his hand, saying, "Congratulations, Mary Kate and good luck." Then he turned, and left the room.

An awkward pause was broken first by Mary Kate. "Shirley, I will set up a meeting with our engineering manager and Jack for next week so that we can lay out the plan for integration. I'm sure that Jack will enjoy meeting her." Small talk ensued, and within five minutes, Mary Kate and Sean were back in the lobby.

"Well, rookie, we got it!" exclaimed Mary Kate. They exchanged high fives and headed to the parking lot.

Questions

1. Assess Mary Kate's style. Is her style something Sean should emulate?

2. Blue Onion's implementation team will need to work very closely with Jack and his people, and it doesn't appear that Jack wants to be helpful. What could Mary Kate have done to avoid this situation? Assume this meeting was called by Shirley. How could Mary Kate have handled it differently?

ROLE PLAY CASE

Once again you will give your presentation to the same buyer (Spear One, McLane Properties, Dart Paper Products) that you did after Chapters 9 and 10 (if you did not do role plays after those chapters, review that material now). This time you will complete your presentation, first summarizing the needs and going all the way to asking for the sale. You will have an opportunity to work on presentation, objection handling, and closing skills.

If two people are involved in the sale (a seller and a buyer) while a third observes, the observer should do the following:

1. Identify any objection-handling methods used.
2. Determine whether the seller is focused on benefits or only features.
3. Note when trial closes are used.
4. Identify the closing method used.

The professor will pass out new buyer sheets.

ADDITIONAL REFERENCES

Aggarwal, Praveen, Stephen B. Castleberry, Rick Ridnour, and C. David Shepherd. "Salesperson Empathy and Listening: Impact on Relationship Outcomes." *Journal of Marketing Theory and Practice* 13 (2005), pp. 16–31.

Agnihotri Raj, Adam Rapp, and Kevin Trainor. "Understanding the Role of Information Communication in the Buyer–Seller Exchange Process: Antecedents and Outcomes." *The Journal of Business & Industrial Marketing* 24, no. 7 (2009), pp. 474–89.

Bradford, Kevin D., J. Michael Crant, and Joan M. Phillips. "How Suppliers Affect Trust with Their Customers: The Role of Salesperson Job Satisfaction and Perceived Customer Importance." *Journal of Marketing Theory & Practice* 17, no. 4 (Fall 2009), pp. 383–94.

Fu, Frank, Willy Bolander, and Eli Jones. "Managing the Drivers of Organizational Commitment and Salesperson Effort: An Application of Meyer and Allen's Three-Component Model." *Journal of Marketing Theory and Practice* 17, no. 4 (Fall 2009), pp. 335–50.

Gough, Orla, and Mohamed Nurullah. "Understanding What Drives the Purchase Decision in Pension and Investment Products." *Journal of Financial Services Marketing* 14, no. 2 (September 2009), pp. 152–72.

Luo, Xueming, and Naveen Donthu. "The Role of Cyber-Intermediaries: A Framework Based on Transaction Cost Analysis, Agency, Relationship Marketing, and Social Exchange Theories." *The Journal of Business & Industrial Marketing* 22, no. 7 (2007), pp. 452–64.

Rutherford, Brian N., James S. Boles, Hiram C. Barksdale Jr., and Julie T. Johnson. "Buyer's Relational Desire and Number of Suppliers Used: The Relationship between Perceived Commitment and Continuance." *Journal of Marketing Theory and Practice* 16, no. 3 (Summer 2008), pp. 247–57.

Turner, Roger, Christophe Lasserre, and Pascal Beauchet. "Marketing Metrics: Innovation in Field Force Bonuses: Enhancing Motivation through a Structured Process-Based Approach." *Journal of Medical Marketing* 7, no. 2 (2007), pp. 126–35.

Weber, John A. "Business Ethics Training: Insights from Learning Theory." *Journal of Business Ethics* 70, no. 1 (2007), pp. 61–85.

Zallocco, Ronald, Ellen Bolman Pullins, and Michael L. Mallin. "A Reexamination of B2B Sales Performance." *The Journal of Business & Industrial Marketing* 24, no. 8 (2009), pp. 598–614.

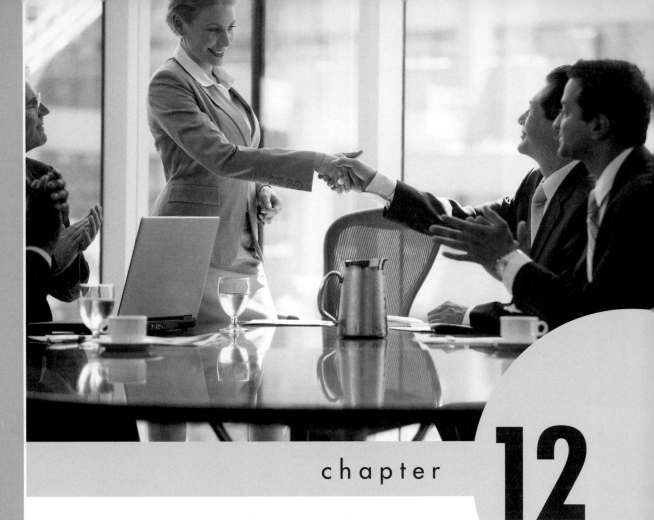

chapter **12**

FORMAL NEGOTIATING

SOME QUESTIONS ANSWERED IN THIS CHAPTER ARE

- What is negotiation selling? How does it differ from nonnegotiation selling?

- What items can be negotiated in selling?

- What type of planning needs to occur prior to a negotiation meeting? How should a seller set objectives?

- How can the negotiation session be effectively opened? What role does friendly conversation play?

- Which negotiation strategies and tactics do buyers use? How should negotiators respond?

- What are the salesperson's guidelines for offering and requesting concessions?

PROFILE

"The earlier in the sales cycle you start uncovering the prospect's needs through strategic questioning techniques, the more you are prepared to complete a successful negotiation. Remember the 5Ps: proper preparation prevents poor performance."

Alex Tagansky

PROFILE

My name is Alex Tagansky, and I graduated from Northern Illinois University with a bachelor of science in marketing and a certificate in professional sales. I took my personal selling class from Dr. Rick Ridnour. I am currently working as a sales executive for Docuforms Inc. (DFI) managing a sales territory and account relationships, and growing my base of business. In the printing industry, negotiations are heavily price-driven, but decisions are usually not made solely based on price. Sales professionals that are successful in negotiations focus on establishing win–win relationships, in which buyers consider price as a portion of the decision criteria but not all of the decision criteria.

The art of negotiation takes years of practice and experience to master. The earlier in the sales cycle you start uncovering the prospect's needs through strategic questioning techniques, the more you are prepared to complete a successful negotiation. Remember the 5Ps: proper preparation prevents poor performance. The more data and information you have regarding the customer's decision criteria, the better you are positioned in the final negotiation table.

In meetings, salespeople ask questions, but negotiators take it one step further by reading the prospect's kinetics (nonverbal body language) and asking follow-up questions to eliminate incorrect perceptions. In doing so, they discover not only what is driving the prospect's decision but also what will enable them to act on that decision. An expert negotiator isn't afraid to hear the word "no" but actually looks to uncover all of the "no" responses early in the negotiation sales cycle because NO really means KNOW. The prospect wants to KNOW more about your value proposition and KNOW he or she is making the right decision.

Responding to objections and concerns is a critical part of the negotiation process. Asking the right questions at the right time will help you uncover concerns (no need, too expensive, we do it internally, happy with current vendor, don't have the authority, not a priority, and so on). In the printing industry, like many other industries, buyers are often fearful of change even if they see cost savings because they have the mentality of "why fix something that isn't broken." Unfortunately many people are content in overpaying for a product or service if they can avoid change. It is the sales professional's job to assure the buyer that her or his decision will add real value to the organization and that the transition will be uneventful.

After the sale, don't boast about your accomplishment; rather, let the buyer take credit for adding value to his or her company because if he or she emerges as a hero in the eyes of that company, you have secured a relationship that can last a lifetime. If you can accomplish this challenge, you have successfully completed a win–win negotiation that can lead to a long-lasting partnership between your organizations.

A successful negotiation usually leads to a contract that binds both parties to be responsible for what was negotiated. A successful partnership is built on mutual trust that you develop both during and after the negotiation by following up and delivering on your promises. Any deviation from this will hinder your opportunity for future successful negotiations.

Visit our Web site at www.dfi-llc.com.

We have all engaged in negotiations of some type. Most of these were informal (such as with your parents about attending a concert) and dealt with relatively minor issues, although they may have been intensely important to you at the time. This chapter discusses formal negotiations that occur between buyers and salespeople. The skills you will learn can also be used in your day-to-day negotiations with friends, parents, and people in authority positions.

THE NATURE OF NEGOTIATION

The bargaining process through which buyers and sellers resolve areas of conflict and arrive at agreements is called **negotiation.** Areas of conflict may include minor issues (like who should attend future meetings) as well as major ones (such as cost per unit or exclusive purchase agreements). The ultimate goal of both parties should be to reduce or resolve the conflict.

Two radically different philosophies can guide negotiations. In **win–lose negotiating** the negotiator attempts to win all the important concessions and thus triumph over the opponent. This process resembles almost every competitive sport you have ever watched. In boxing, for example, one person is the winner, and the other is, by definition, the loser.

In the second negotiating philosophy, **win–win negotiating,** the negotiator attempts to secure an agreement that satisfies both parties.[1] You have probably experienced social situations similar to this. For example, if you want to attend a football game and your friend wants to attend a party, you may negotiate a mutual agreement that you both attend the first half of the game and still make it to the party. If this arrangement satisfies both you and your friend, you have engaged in win–win negotiating.

The discussion in this chapter assumes that your goal as a salesperson is to engage in win–win negotiating. In fact, this entire book has emphasized developing relationships, which is a win–win perspective. Partners attempt to find solutions that benefit both parties because each party is concerned about the other party's welfare. And this is hard work, as "Building Partnerships 12.1" illustrates.

However, the buyer may be using a win–lose strategy, whereby the buyer hopes to win all major concessions and have the seller be the loser. To help you spot and prepare for such situations, we discuss many of these tactics as well.

NEGOTIATION VERSUS NONNEGOTIATION SELLING

How does negotiation differ from the sales presentations we have discussed up to this point? This textbook has already covered many aspects of negotiating an agreement between buyer and seller. For example, in Chapter 10 we discussed the negotiations that occur as the seller is helping the buyer deal with objections. And in Chapter 11 we talked about obtaining commitment, which often requires negotiating on some key points. Importantly, however, we assumed that many, if not most, factors during a regular sales call are constrained, and not open to change or negotiation. For example, the price of Allsteel Energy brand ergonomic seating has been set at $395. The Allsteel salesperson will not lower that price unless, of course, the buyer agrees to purchase large quantities. Even then the buyer will receive just a standard quantity discount as outlined in the seller's price manual. In essence, the salesperson's price book and procedure manual form an inflexible set of rules. If the buyer objects, an attempt to resolve the conflict will occur by using techniques discussed in Chapter 10 (such as the compensation method or the revisit method).

NEGOTIATIONS: THE ROAD TO SUCCESS IS PAVED WITH HARD WORK

As a salesperson for Aprima, I sell software to the medical industry. Our software takes care of medical records, billing, scheduling, and data management. Let me walk you through one negotiation I went through recently with St. Anthony's Hospital so you can see what is involved.

First I met with Jerry, the director of information technology at St. Anthony's, to learn what the hospital system was currently using, what problems they were experiencing, and who the key players were. I then met with Holly, the chief information officer, and later with Erik, the CEO. In these meetings I was also informing them about Aprima and what we had to offer.

The next step was to have the key decision makers and users experience the software remotely. To do this I used GoTo software and allowed Jerry to experience the demo first. After he was pleased with what he saw, I gave the same demo to his staff.

Not surprisingly, Jerry wanted to see the Aprima software live, in action at a hospital, so I arranged a visit to one of our installations. It was important for him to really develop trust in me and our software. During the site visit, I repeatedly stepped out of the room in each meeting with staff and told Jerry to ask anything he wanted to ask. He liked what he saw.

Next I set up a demo for everyone at St. Anthony's Hospital. This was an exhausting 7:00 a.m. to 7:00 p.m. day in which users, decision makers, and administrators came by and played with the software. I had set up the demo in St. Anthony's conference room, and users could simulate many of the tasks they would be doing with the software. I followed up with a meeting of the key decision makers to obtain feedback on what they saw and what questions they had. They were impressed with the software! But we were not through yet.

Next we went through a series of detailed contract negotiations to come to an agreement on price and terms. Finally the decision was made, and they went with us! But it wasn't over. I had to make sure that everything in the postsale went as we had agreed upon.

It was a long road to success, but well worth it. The hospital has a state-of-the-art system, and they are able to better meet the needs of their patients.

Source: Ben Johnson, Aprima, personal correspondence, used with permission; names changed to protect confidentiality.

In contrast, if the Allsteel seller enters formal negotiations with the same buyer, the price and delivery schedules will be subject to modification. The buyer neither expects nor wants the seller to come to the negotiation meeting with any standard price book. Instead the buyer expects most policies, procedures, and prices to be truly negotiable.

Negotiations also differ from regular sales calls in that they generally involve more intensive planning and a larger number of people from the selling firm. Prenegotiation planning may go on for six months or more before the actual meeting takes place. Planning participants usually represent a wide spectrum of functional areas of the firm, such as production, marketing, sales, human resources, accounting, purchasing, and executive officers.

Finally, formal negotiations generally take place only for very large or important prospective buyers. For example, Nestlé Foods might negotiate with some of the largest food chains, such as Walmart Foods and Cub Foods, but would not

Formal negotiations usually involve multiple buyers and multiple sellers.

Exhibit 12.1

Items That Are Often Negotiated between Buyers and Sellers

Inventory levels the buyer must maintain.

Inventory levels the seller must keep on hand to be able to restock the buyer quickly.

Details about the design of the product or service.

Web page development.

How the product will be manufactured.

Display allowances for resellers.

Advertising allowances and the amount of advertising the seller does.

Sales promotion within the channel of distribution.

Delivery terms and conditions.

Retail and wholesale pricing points for resellers.

Prices and pricing allowances for volume purchases.

Amount and location of shelf positioning.

Special packaging and design features.

Service levels after the sale.

Disposing of unsold or obsolete merchandise.

Credit terms.

How complaints will be resolved.

Order entry and ease of monitoring orders.

Type and frequency of communication between the parties.

Performance guarantees and bonds.

engage in a large, formal negotiation session with small local or mom-and-pop grocery stores. Negotiating is an expensive endeavor because it uses so much of so many important people's time. The firm wants to invest the time and costs involved in negotiating only if the long-term nature of the relationship and the importance of the customer justify the expense.

WHAT CAN BE NEGOTIATED?

If the customer is large or important enough, almost anything can be negotiated. Salespeople who have not been involved in negotiations before often find it hard to grasp the fact that so many areas are subject to discussion and change. Exhibit 12.1 lists some items that are often negotiated between buyers and sellers. But in reality, no single negotiation session covers all the areas listed. Each side comes to the bargaining table with a list of prioritized issues; only important points for which disagreement exists are discussed.

ARE YOU A GOOD NEGOTIATOR?

All of us are negotiators; some of us are better than others. We have negotiated with parents, friends, professors, and, yes, sometimes even with opponents. However, the fact that you have engaged in many negotiations in your lifetime does not mean you are good at negotiating.

The traits necessary to successfully negotiate vary somewhat, depending on the situation and the parties involved. Some characteristics, however, are almost universal. For example, a good negotiator must have patience and endurance; after two hours of discussing the same issue, the negotiator needs the stamina and willingness to continue until an agreement is reached. Also, a willingness to take risks and the ability to tolerate ambiguity become especially critical in business negotiations because it is necessary to both accept and offer concessions during the meeting without complete information.

Successful salespeople do not always make great negotiators. In fact, negotiating may be the most difficult skill for any salesperson to develop. Many managers have to coach reps on their negotiating skills because many reps don't want to risk ruining a relationship they worked hard to build. The unconscious reaction of most salespeople in negotiations often ends up being the opposite of the correct thing to do. For example, what if, in preparation for the upcoming negotiation session, the customer asks for detailed specifications about your product? Most salespeople would gladly supply reams of technical data, full glossy pictures, an offer of plant tours, and the like. The problem with that approach lies in the possibility that the customer will pick several features that he or she does not need and then pressure for price concessions. (Look, I don't need that much memory capacity and don't want to pay for something I'm not going to use. So why don't you reduce your price? I shouldn't have to pay for something I'm not planning on ever using!) A salesperson who is a good negotiator would avoid this situation by supplying information to the customer only in exchange for the right to ask the customer more questions and thus gain more information.

People who fear conflict usually are poor negotiators. In fact, some negotiating strategies are actually designed to increase the level of conflict to bring all the issues to the table and reach an equitable settlement. Along the same lines, people

Exhibit 12.2
Negotiation Skills
Self-Inventory

Place a check by each item that accurately reflects your personality and traits on an average, normal day.

_____	1. Helpful	_____	20. Receptive
_____	2. Risk taker	_____	21. Easily influenced
_____	3. Inconsistent	_____	22. Enthusiastic
_____	4. Persistent	_____	23. Planner
_____	5. Factual	_____	24. Stingy
_____	6. Use high pressure	_____	25. Listener
_____	7. Self-confident	_____	26. Controlled
_____	8. Practical	_____	27. Think under pressure
_____	9. Manipulative	_____	28. Passive
_____	10. Analytical	_____	29. Economical
_____	11. Arrogant	_____	30. Gullible
_____	12. Impatient	_____	31. Afraid of conflict
_____	13. Seek new approaches	_____	32. Endurance
_____	14. Tactful	_____	33. Tolerate ambiguity
_____	15. Perfectionist	_____	34. Have strong need to be liked
_____	16. Stubborn	_____	35. Organized
_____	17. Flexible	_____	36. Honest
_____	18. Competitive	_____	37. Belligerent
_____	19. Gambler		

How to score the checklist:

All of the traits listed are positive except for the following negative traits: 3, 6, 9, 11, 12, 15, 16, 19, 21, 24, 28, 30, 31, 34, and 37. To arrive at a total score, give yourself one point for all positive traits and subtract one point for all negative traits. To interpret your total score: 19–22 = excellent; 15–18 = good; 11–14 = fair.

who have a strong need to be liked by all people at all times tend to make very poor negotiators. Other undesirable traits include being closed-minded, unorganized, dishonest, and downright belligerent.

Of course cultural differences do exist. For example, Brazilian managers may believe competitiveness is more important in a negotiator than integrity. Chinese managers in Taiwan may emphasize the negotiator's rational skills less than his or her interpersonal skills.

As this discussion indicates, being a truly excellent negotiator requires a careful balance of traits and skills. Take a moment and complete the questionnaire in Exhibit 12.2 to rate your negotiating skills. Don't be discouraged by a low score. You cannot easily change personality traits, but the rest of this chapter suggests ways to improve your skills.

PLANNING FOR THE NEGOTIATION SESSION

Preparation and planning are the most important parts of negotiation, according to many expert sources.[2] And that planning includes preparing ourselves emotionally for the stress that will occur within a negotiation session.[3] In Chapter 7 we discussed how to gather precall information and plan the sales call. All of that material is equally relevant when planning for an upcoming negotiation session—for example, learning everything possible about the buying team and the buyer's organization. "Sales Technology 12.1" describes software that can be used to plan for a negotiation session.

The meetings the salesperson will have with the buyer before the actual negotiation session facilitate this learning. The buyer may also be, or have been, a

USE SOFTWARE TO BE AN EXPERT NEGOTIATOR

Negotiation can be a frightening and seemingly overwhelming event for salespeople who have not engaged in formal negotiations before. Salespeople look to experts to avoid making mistakes that might cost them and their companies. Although many negotiation books are available, some prefer to use software to help provide structure to their planning process.

ExpertNegotiator® is one such tool. Users of the online software can access the following tools:

- Strategic Planning Tool: Using prebuilt expert planning templates, you can plan out your strategy for the negotiation session.
- Five Golden Rules Method: This component ensures that you get the most out of your session. Using lessons learned from many successful negotiations, it includes such items as how to gain important information from the other team, how to discover and heighten the leverage your team has, how to encourage the other team to engage in fair negotiating and

make sure you do as well, how to determine the your best offer or concession, and how to lay out and keep control of the agenda.

- Counterpart Intelligence Bank: This portion of the software is where you organize the information you have about the other team members, like their reputations, negotiation styles, who can be trusted, and so forth.
- ExpertAdvice Center: Provides you 24/7 online access to negotiation guidance to avoid common negotiation mistakes.
- Negotiation Best Practices Management System: This system helps you manage your and your teams' success rates over time and includes built-in reporting tools.

Readers can access the company's Web site to try the online software free for 30 days. And by searching "negotiation software," salespeople can locate other worthy software to investigate.

Source: http://www.expertnegotiator.com.

customer of the salesperson, with the upcoming negotiation session designed to review contracts or specify a new working relationship. Even in such scenarios, negotiators will want to carefully review the players and learn as many facts about the situation as possible.

LOCATION

Plan to hold the negotiation at a location free from distraction for both teams. A neutral site, one owned by neither party, is usually best; it removes both teams from interruptions by business associates, and no one has a psychological ("home court") advantage. Experienced negotiators find the middle of the workweek best for negotiations and prefer morning to afternoon or evening (because people are more focused on their jobs rather than after-hours and weekend activities).

Some negotiations are now occurring online. Recent research shows that using these new forms can affect the behavior of negotiators.[4] For example, reciprocity doesn't occur as frequently or in the same way. Those who are the first to offer a concession often don't find the other party giving a similar one in return, regardless of the power in the relationship. Furthermore, contrary to face-to-face negotiations, having more power in a relationship doesn't result in the other party giving larger concessions.

TIME ALLOTMENT

As you are probably aware, negotiations can take a tremendous amount of time. Some business negotiations take years. But how much time should be set aside

Sales reps need to set aside time to plan for a negotiation session.

for one negotiation session? The answer depends on the negotiation objectives and the extent to which both sides desire a win–win session. Studies have shown that high time pressure will produce nonagreements and poor outcomes when one or more sides take a win–lose perspective; but if both sides have a win–win perspective, high outcomes are achieved regardless of time pressure.

NEGOTIATION OBJECTIVES

Power is a critical element when developing objectives. The selling team must ask, Do we need them more than they need us? What part of our service is most valuable to them? Can they get similar products elsewhere? Optimally both parties share balanced power, although this situation is rare in practice.

In developing objectives for the session, keep in mind that the seller will almost certainly have to make concessions in the negotiation meeting. Thus setting several objectives, or positions, is extremely important.

The **target position** is what your company hopes to achieve at the negotiation session. Your team should also establish a **minimum position,** which is the absolute minimum level you will accept. Finally, an **opening position**—the initial proposal—should be developed.

For example, for a Fenwal salesperson negotiating the price for a blood collection and transfusion system at a blood bank, the target position could be $2.5 million, with a minimum position of $2 million and an opening position of $3 million. In negotiations over service levels by Gallovidian Fresh Foods in the United Kingdom with Morrisons grocery stores with regard to fresh vegetables, the seller's opening position might be weekly delivery, the target position delivery twice a week, and the minimum position (the most the seller is willing to do) delivery three times a week.

To allow for concessions, the opening position should reflect higher expectations than the target position. However, the buyer team may consider a very high opening position to be unrealistic and may simply walk away. You have probably seen this happen in negotiations between countries that are at war. To avoid this problem, negotiators must be ready to support that opening position with solid information. Suppose the opening position for a Colgate-Palmolive negotiating team is to offer the grocer a display allowance of $1,000 (with a target position of offering $1,500). The team must be ready to prove that $1,000 is reasonable. When developing objectives, negotiators need to sort out all issues that could arise in the meeting, prioritizing them by importance to the firm. Then the negotiators should develop contingency plans to get a good idea, even before the meeting begins, of their planned reactions and responses to the buyer's suggestions.

Talking over these issues beforehand helps the negotiation team avoid "giving away the store" during the heat of the negotiation session. It also allows the team to draw on the expertise of company experts who will not be present during the session.

The buyer team also develops positions for the meeting. Exhibit 12.3 presents a continuum that shows how the two sets of positions relate. With the positions illustrated, the parties can reach an agreement somewhere between the seller's minimum (S_M) and the buyer's maximum (B_M). However, if B_M falls to the left of S_M (has a lower maximum acceptable price), no agreement can be reached; attempts at negotiation will be futile. For example, if the buyer is not willing

Exhibit 12.3
Comparing Buyer and
Seller Price Positions

Note: See Howard Raiffa, *The Art and Science of Negotiation* (Cambridge, MA: Belknap Press, 1982), for a more complex discussion of the mathematical formulations designed to predict negotiation outcomes under various states.

to pay more than \$200 (B_M) and the seller will not accept less than \$250 (S_M), agreement is impossible. In general, the seller desires to move as far to the right of S_M (as high a price) as possible, and the buyer desires to move as far to the left of B_M (as low a price) as possible.

Negotiators need to try to anticipate these positions and evaluate them carefully. The more information collected about what the buyer hopes to accomplish, the better the negotiators will be able to manage the meeting and arrive at a win–win decision.

Negotiators create a plan to achieve their objectives. However, the chance of failure always exists. Thus planners need to consider strategy revisions if the original plan should fail. The development of alternative paths to the same goal is known as **adaptive planning.** For example, a firm may attempt to secure a premium shelf position by using any of the following strategies:

- In return for a 5 percent price discount.
- In return for credit terms of 3/10, n/30.
- In return for a 50–50 co-op ad campaign.

The firm would attempt to secure the premium shelf position by using, for example, the first strategy; if that failed, it would move to the second strategy; and so forth. Fortunately, with laptops and software such as Excel, negotiators can quickly calculate the profitability of various package deals for their firms.

Many firms will engage in a brainstorming session to try to develop strategies that will meet the firm's objectives. A **brainstorming session** is a meeting in which people are allowed to creatively explore various methods of achieving goals. Once again, cultural differences exist. For example, Chinese and Russian businesspeople habitually use extreme initial offers, whereas Swedish businesspeople usually open with a price close to their target position.

TEAM SELECTION AND MANAGEMENT

So far we have discussed negotiation as though it always involves a team of both buyers and sellers. Usually this is the case. However, negotiations do occur with only two people present: the buyer and the salesperson.

Teams offer both pros and cons.[5] Because of team members' different backgrounds, the group as a whole tends to be more creative than one individual could be. Team members can help one another and reduce the chances of making a mistake. However, the more participants, the more time generally required to reach agreement. Also, team members may voice differing opinions among

Exhibit 12.4
People Who May
Serve on the Selling
Negotiation Team

Title	Possible Role
Salesperson	Coordinates all functions.
Field sales manager (district manager, regional manager, etc.)	Provides additional local and regional information. Secures necessary local funding and support for planning and presentations. Offers information about competitors.
National sales manager/ vice president of sales	Serves as a liaison with corporate headquarters. Secures necessary corporate funding and staff support for planning and presentation. Offers competitor information.
National account salesperson/national account sales manager	Provides expertise and support in dealing with issues for important customers. Offers information about competitors.
Marketing department senior executives, product managers, and staff	Provide suggestions for product/service applications. Supply market research information as well as information about packaging, new product development, upcoming promotional campaigns, etc. Offer information about competitors.
Chief executive officer/ president	Serves as an authority figure. Facilitates quicker decisions regarding changes in current policy and procedures. As a peer, can relate well with buyer's senior officers.
Manufacturing executives and staff	Provide information about current scheduled production as well as the possibility/cost of any modifications in the schedule.
Purchasing executives and staff	Provide information about raw materials inflows. Offer suggestions about possible quantity discounts from suppliers.
Accounting and finance executives and staff	Source of cost accounting information. Supply corporate target returns on investment; cost estimates for any needed changes in the firm under various buying scenarios; and information about order entry, billing, and credit systems.
Information technology executives and staff	Provide information about current information systems and anticipated changes needed under various buying scenarios. Help ensure that needed periodic reports for the buyers can be generated in a timely fashion.
Training executives and staff	Provide training for negotiation effectiveness and conduct practice role plays. Also provide information about and suggestions for anticipated necessary buyer training.
Outside consultants	Provide any kind of assistance necessary. Especially helpful if the firm has limited experience in negotiations or has not negotiated with this type of buyer before.

themselves, or one member may address a topic outside his or her expertise. Such things can make the seller's team appear unprepared or disorganized.

In general the seller's team should be the same size as the buyer's team. Otherwise the sellers may appear to be trying to exert more power or influence in the meeting. Whenever possible, strive for the fewest team members possible. Unnecessarily large teams can get bogged down in details; and the larger the team, the more difficult reaching a decision generally becomes.

Each team member should have a defined role in the session. For example, experts are often included to answer technical questions; executives are present as more authoritative speakers on behalf of the selling firm. Exhibit 12.4 lists the types of team members often chosen for negotiations. Many of these people take part in prenegotiation planning but do not actually attend the negotiation session.

Team members should possess the traits of good negotiators, although it often does not work out that way. For example, many technical experts have no

The salesperson's team must prepare for an upcoming negotiation session. Remember that the buyer's team is also planning.

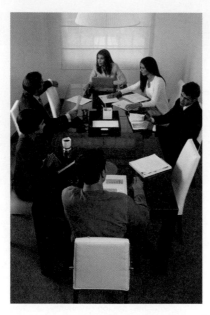

tolerance for ambiguity and may fear conflict. As a result, the team leader needs to help them see clearly what their role is, as well as what they should not get involved in, during the session.

The team leader will manage the actual negotiation session. Because of their intimate knowledge of the buyers and their needs, salespeople, rather than the executives on the team, often fill this post. When selecting a team leader, the seller's management also needs to consider the anticipated leader of the buyer team. It is unwise to choose a leader for the selling team who may be intimidated by the buyer's leader.

The team usually develops rules about who will answer what kinds of questions, who should be the first to respond to a concession offered by the buyers, who will offer concessions from the seller's standpoint, and so on. A set of nonverbal and verbal signals is also developed so team members can communicate with one another. For example, they may agree that when the salesperson takes out a breath mint, all team members are to stop talking and let the salesperson handle all issues; or when the executive places her red book inside her briefcase, the team should move toward its target position, and the salesperson should say, "OK, let's look at some alternatives."

To ensure that team members really understand their respective roles and that all rules and signals arc clearly grasped, the team should practice. This process usually involves a series of videotaped role play situations. Many firms, such as Standard Register, involve their sales training department in this practice. Trainers, using detailed information supplied by the team, realistically play the roles of the buying team members.

The selling team will likely have many meetings before the negotiation session. These will be internal meetings, with members of the selling team, and also meetings with the buyers. Because not every selling team member can be at all meetings, sometimes it is hard for team members to keep abreast of developments.

INDIVIDUAL BEHAVIOR PATTERNS

The team leader needs to consider the personality style of each member of both teams to spot any problems and plan accordingly. Of course one method would be to sort the members into analyticals, amiables, expressives, and drivers based on the dimensions of assertiveness and responsiveness (see Chapter 5 for a full discussion). Some researchers have developed personality profiles specifically for negotiations. This section presents one of the most widely used sets of negotiation profiles.

After studying actual conflict situations, a number of researchers arrived at a set of basic conflict-handling modes based on the dimensions of assertiveness and cooperativeness.[6] Exhibit 12.5 presents these five modes: competing, accommodating, avoiding, compromising, and collaborating. Note that these five styles are different from the social styles (drivers, amiables, expressives, and analyticals) that we have been using throughout the book. Because all negotiations involve some degree of conflict, this typology is appropriate for use by salespeople preparing for a negotiation session.

Exhibit 12.5
Conflict-Handling
Behavior Modes

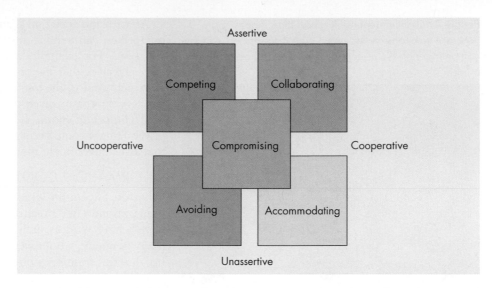

Source: Adapted from Kenneth Thomas, "Conflict and Conflict Management," in *The Handbook of Industrial and Organizational Psychology*, ed. Marvin Dunnette (Skokie, IL: Rand McNally, 1976).

People who resolve conflict in a **competing mode** are assertive and uncooperative. They tend to pursue their own goals and objectives completely at the expense of the other party. Often power oriented, they usually surround themselves with subordinates (often called "yes-men") who go along with their ideas. Team members who use the competing mode look for a win–lose agreement: They win, the other party loses.

Individuals in the **accommodating mode** are the exact opposite of competing people. Unassertive and highly cooperative, accommodators focus on the needs and desires of the other party and seek primarily to satisfy the concerns of the other party.[7] Although they do not necessarily wish to lose, they do want to make sure the other side gets all they want. Accommodators can be spotted by their excessive generosity; their constant, rapid yielding to another's point of view; and their obedience to someone else's order, even if it is obviously not something they desire to do.

Some people operate in the unassertive and uncooperative **avoiding mode.** These people do not attempt to fulfill their own needs or the needs of others. In essence, they simply refuse to address the conflict at all. They do not strive for a win–win agreement; in fact, they do not strive for any agreement.

The **compromising mode** applies to people "in the middle" in terms of cooperativeness and assertiveness. A compromiser attempts to find a quick, mutually acceptable solution that partially satisfies both parties. A compromiser gives up more than a competing person but less than an accommodating person. In many ways the compromiser attempts to arrive at a win–win solution. However, the agreement reached usually does not maximize the satisfaction of the parties. For example, a compromising person might quickly suggest, "Let's just split the difference." Although this sounds fair, a better solution—one that would please both parties more—may be reached with further discussion.

Finally, people in the **collaborating mode** are both assertive and cooperative. They seek to maximize the satisfaction of both parties and hence to reach a truly win–win solution. Collaborators have the motivation, skill, and determination to really dig into an issue or a problem and explore all possible solutions. The best situation, from a negotiation standpoint, would be to have on both teams a number of people who generally use a collaborating mode.

People exhibit different conflict-handling modes. Can you spot someone in this photo who appears to be in the competing mode? The avoiding mode? The collaborating mode?

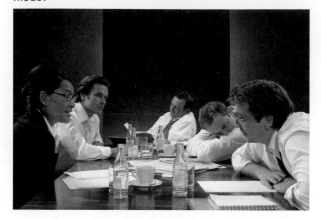

As with the social style matrix described earlier, one person can exhibit different modes in different situations. For example, a buying team negotiator who perceives that his or her position on an issue extremely vital to the long-term welfare of the company is correct may revert from a collaborating mode to a competing mode. Likewise, when potentially heavy damage could occur from confronting an issue, that same buyer might move to an avoiding mode.

INFORMATION CONTROL

What do buyers do while selling teams engage in preparation? They prepare too! Keep in mind that buyers have read as many books and attended as many seminars about negotiation as sellers have because this training is one of their best negotiating tools. Buyers try to learn as much as they can about the seller's team and plans, including the seller's opening, target, and minimum positions. Buyers also are interested in the seller's team membership and decision rules. As a result, the selling team leader needs to emphasize the need for security: Don't give everyone access to all information. In fact, many team members (such as technical support) do not need to have complete and exhaustive knowledge of all the facts surrounding the negotiation.

As an example, one *Fortune* 500 firm was negotiating a $15 million deal with one of its customers. The selling team's leader had to leave the room for a few minutes, and while he was gone, the plant manager for the selling firm came in. The plant manager, though intending to do no harm, bragged about how his company had already invested $2 million in a prototype and retooling just to prepare for the customer's expected commitment. Needless to say, when the seller's team leader returned to the room, the buyer said he had all the information he needed. Two days later the buyer was a very tough negotiator, armed with the knowledge that the seller had already committed to the project. It pays to control the flow of information!

THE NEGOTIATION MEETING

Before discussing what occurs in the negotiation meeting, we should note that some buyers will attempt to engage in a win–lose tactic of beginning to negotiate when the other party does not expect it. This tactic has been called **ambush negotiating** or a **sneak attack.** It can occur during meetings prior to the negotiation meeting or even during installation of the new product. For example, during the first week of installation of a new telecommunications system, the buyer may state, "We're going to have to renegotiate the price of this system. Since we signed that contract, we have learned of a new system being introduced by one of your competitors." The seller should never negotiate in such a situation until prepared to deal with the issue completely.

At the negotiation meeting the buyer team and seller team physically come together and deliberate about topics important to both parties, with the goal of arriving at decisions. As mentioned earlier, this meeting usually has been preceded by one or more smaller buyer–seller meetings designed to uncover needs and explore options. Informal phone conversations probably were used to set some aspects of the agenda, learn about team members who will be present, and so on. Also, the negotiation itself may require a series of sessions to resolve all issues.

PRELIMINARIES

Engaging in friendly conversation to break the ice before getting down to business is usually a good idea. Use this time to learn and use the names of all members on the buyer team. This preliminary activity is especially important in many international negotiation meetings. For example, Japanese businesspeople usually want to spend time developing a personal relationship before beginning negotiations, and alcohol is usually a part of this. Not so in Saudi Arabia, where customs dictate strict abstinence.

Every effort should be made to ensure a comfortable environment for all parties. Arranging ahead of time for refreshments, proper climate control, appropriate size of room, adequate lighting, and correct layout of furniture will go far to establish an environment conducive to negotiating.

Most negotiations occur at a rectangular table. Teams usually sit on opposite sides, with the team leaders at the heads of the table. If possible, try to arrange for a round table or at least a seating arrangement that mixes members from each team together. This seating plan helps the parties feel that they are facing a common task and fosters a win–win atmosphere.

If the buyer team has a win–lose philosophy, expect all kinds of ploys to be used. For example, the furniture may be too large or too small or may be uncomfortable to sit in. The buyers may sit in front of large windows to force you to stare directly into sunlight. You may discover that the sellers' seats are all placed beneath heat ducts and the heat is set too high. You should not continue with the meeting until all unfavorable physical arrangements have been set right.

As far as possible the selling team should establish a win–win environment. This environment can be facilitated by avoiding any verbal or nonverbal threatening gestures, remaining calm and courteous, and adopting an attitude of investigation and experimentation. The leader might even comment,

> I can speak for my team in saying that our goal is to reach agreements today that we can all be proud of. We come to this meeting with open minds and look forward to exploring many avenues toward agreement. I am confident that we will both prosper and be more profitable as a result of this session.

thinking it through

What if you do everything in your power to establish a win–win relationship with the buyer team, but the buyers insist on viewing the negotiation session as a series of win–lose maneuvers? That is to say, your team consists mostly of collaborators who are trying to see that both sides are winners, whereas the buyers are mostly in the competing mode where they hope to win and hope you lose. Since they won't play by win–win "rules," should you?

An **agenda,** a listing of what will be discussed and in what sequence, is important for every negotiation session. It helps set boundaries and keeps everyone on track. Exhibit 12.6 offers an example of a negotiation agenda. The selling team should come to the meeting with a preliminary typed agenda. Don't be surprised when the buyer team also comes with an agenda; in that case the first thing to be negotiated is the agenda itself. In general, putting key issues not at the very first in the agenda is advantageous. This approach allows time for each party to learn the other's bargaining style and concession routines. Moreover, agreement has already been reached on some minor issues, which, in a win–win situation, supports an atmosphere for reaching agreement on the major issues.

Exhibit 12.6

Preliminary Negotiating Session Agenda

Preliminary Agenda

Meeting between FiberCraft and Rome Industrial Inc.

Proposed New Spin Machine for 15 FiberCraft Plants

November 21

1. Introductions by participants.

2. Agree on the meeting agenda.

3. Issues:
   a. Who will design the new machine?
   b. Who will pay the costs of testing the machine?
   c. Who will have ownership rights to the new machine (if it is ever built for someone else)?
   d. Who will be responsible for maintaining and servicing the new machine during trial runs?
   e. Who will pay for any redesign work needed?

4. Coffee break.

5. Issues:
   a. How and when will the machines be set up in the 15 locations? Who will be responsible for installation?
   b. What percentage will be required for a down payment?
   c. What will the price be? Will there be any price escalation provisions? If not, how long is this price protected?

6. Summary of agreement.

GENERAL GUIDELINES

To negotiate effectively, the seller team must put into practice the skills discussed throughout this book. For example, listening carefully is extremely important. Careful listening involves not only being silent when the buyer talks but also asking good probing questions to resolve confusion and misunderstanding.

The team leader must keep track of issues discussed or resolved. During complicated negotiations many items may be discussed simultaneously. Also, some issues may be raised but not fully addressed before someone raises a separate issue. The leader can provide great assistance by giving periodic status reports, including what has been resolved and the issues being discussed. More important, he or she can map out what still needs to be discussed. In essence this mapping establishes a new agenda for the remainder of the negotiation session.

Once again, cultural differences are important in negotiations. For example, most Canadians and Americans are uncomfortable with silence; most Japanese, on the other hand, are much more comfortable with extended periods of silence. North Americans negotiating with Japanese businesspeople usually find this silence stressful. Negotiators must prepare themselves for such probabilities and learn ways to reduce stress and cope in this situation.

If negotiations require an interpreter, carefully select someone well qualified for the job. And don't expect everything you say to be translated correctly. Here are some items that have been translated into English from another language (so you can get a sense of the problem of translation errors):[8]

- In a family-style restaurant in Hong Kong: Come broil yourself at your own table.

- From an Italian hotel in the mountains: Standing among the savage scenery, the hotel offers stupendous revelations. There is a French window in every room. We offer commodious chambers, with balcony imminent to a romantic gorge. We hope you want to drop in. In the close village you can buy jolly memorials for when you pass away.

- In a Moscow newspaper under the heading "INTERPRETING": Let us you letter of business translation do. Every people in our staffing know English like the hand of their back. Up to the minute wise-street phrases, don't you know, old boy!

- In a Sarajevo hotel: Guests should announce abandonment of their rooms before 12 o'clock, emptying the rooms at the latest until 14 o'clock for the use of the room before 5 at the arrival or after the 16 o'clock at the departure will be billed as one more night.

Finally, keep in mind that during negotiations, people need to save **face**, which is the desire for a positive identity or self-concept. Of course not all people strive for the same face (some want to appear "cool," some "macho," some "crass," and so on). Negotiators will at least try to maintain face and may even use the negotiation session to improve or strengthen this identity.

From the BUYER'S SEAT

NEGOTIATIONS TAKE HONESTY AND TACT

By Angela Gilley, City of Milwaukee

You may not think about it, but there are buyers in almost every organization, even not-for-profits and government entities. I'm a senior buyer for the city of Milwaukee, Wisconsin. I've had a lot of experience with sellers as we negotiate agreements, both good and bad.

I was negotiating with one company to buy structural steel, which included beams and angles (that are used to connect the beams). I was actually looking at several suppliers at the time, some local and some out of the area. The low-cost negotiated supplier was from out of the area. The local guy, Eric, who wasn't going to get my business, called and asked me, "Why aren't you using a local supplier? Don't you want to give jobs to local industry?" My response was, "The out-of-town company is selling us their steel for 20 percent less, and that price includes delivery to our docks. It looks like you are either trying to increase your profits by selling your steel at such a high price, or you just aren't able to source steel as cheaply as this other company can."

Eric didn't like that answer. He decided to play politics with the situation and talked to some of the city officials, trying to convince them to pressure me to accept his bid.

Sure enough, they did come to me. When those politicians talked with me, complaining about me not using a local supplier, I simply opened my books to them and let them see for themselves. When they saw the numbers, they agreed with me. The local company was not the best deal for the city.

What I really hate is when companies negotiate with us by lowballing. The city was putting in a new gas line, and we negotiated with several suppliers. One salesperson, George, came in with a price much lower than the rest. But George's proposed contract included a rider, or clause, stating that he could add in the costs of any mats that might be needed when working in wetland areas. George knew that the project called for some work in wetland areas. The other companies who negotiated for our business included the cost of working in wetland areas in their proposals. I got so ticked by this that I sat down with the mayor and told him what George had done. The mayor, also upset, disqualified the bid. We didn't then, and wouldn't in the future, work with George or his company.

Source: Angela Gilley, City of Milwaukee, personal correspondence; used with permission; names changed to protect confidentiality.

DEALING WITH WIN–LOSE NEGOTIATORS

Many books have been written and many consultants have grown rich teaching both buyers and sellers strategies for effective negotiating. Unfortunately many of these techniques are designed to achieve a win–lose situation. We describe several to illustrate the types of tactics buyers might engage in during negotiations. This knowledge will help the negotiating team defend its position under such attacks. "From the Buyer's Seat 12.1" illustrates how one salesperson engaged in such a maneuver.

Both buyers and sellers occasionally engage in the win–lose strategies described here. However, because we are assuming that sellers will adopt a win–win perspective, this section focuses on how to handle buyers who engage in these techniques. Exhibit 12.7 presents an effective overall strategy for dealing with win–lose negotiators.

Good Guy–Bad Guy Routine

You have probably seen the **good guy–bad guy routine** if you watch police movies or TV shows.[9] A tough police detective interrogating the suspect gets a little rough. The detective uses bright lights and intimidation. After a few minutes a

Exhibit 12.7
What to Do When the
Buyer Turns to Win–Lose
Strategies

Detach yourself.	Don't respond right away. Instead give yourself time to think about the issue. Say something like "Hold on, I'm not sure I follow you. Let's go back over what you just said again." Use the time you have gained to rethink your positions and what would be in the best interests of both parties.
Acknowledge their position and then respond.	In using this tool, you are trying to create a favorable climate for your response. You would start off by mentioning that you agree with them by saying something like "Yes, you have a good point there when you said . . ." After agreeing, you then make your point. For example, you might conclude by saying, "and I would like to make sure you continue to have minimal downtime. And for that to happen, you know, we really need to have someone from your firm attend the training." This tool is somewhat similar to the indirect denial and revisit techniques discussed in Chapter 10.
Build them a bridge.	Come up with a solution that incorporates the buyer's suggestion. For example, "building on your idea, what if we . . ." or "I got this idea from something really neat you said at our meeting last Friday." This approach helps the buyer save face.
Warn, but don't threaten.	Sometimes you may have to help a buyer understand the consequences of his or her position. For example, if the buyer indicates that she or he must have a cheaper fabric for the furniture in an office building, you can say, "I know how important the choice of fabric is to your firm's image, but if you choose that fabric, you won't achieve the image you're really looking for. How much will that cost you in lost clients who might not get a sense that you are very successful?" A warning is not the same thing as a threat. A threat is what will happen if you don't get *your way;* a warning is what will happen if they do get *their* way.

second officer (who has been watching) asks his companion to "go out and get some fresh air." While the tough detective (the "bad guy") is outside, the other detective (the "good guy") apologizes for his partner's actions. The good guy goes on to advise the crook to confess now and receive better treatment rather than wait and have the bad guy harass him or her some more. The routine works on the "hurt and rescue" principle: The bad guy offers discomfort and tension, and then the good guy offers escape and a way to bring closure to the situation.

Negotiators often try the same routine. One member of the buyer team (the bad guy) makes all sorts of outlandish statements and requests:

Look, we've got to buy these for no more than $15 each, and we must have credit terms of 2/10, net 60. After all the business we've given you in the past, I can't believe you won't agree to those terms!

Then another member of the buyer team (the good guy) takes over and appears to offer a win–win solution by presenting a lower demand:

Hang on, Jack. These are our friends. Sure, we've given them a lot of business, but remember they've been good to us as well! I believe we should let them make a decent profit, so $15.50 would be more reasonable.

According to theory, the sellers are so relieved to find a friend that they jump on the good guy's suggestion.

As an effective defense against such tactics, the selling team must know its position clearly and not let the buyer's strategy weaken it. Obviously the selling team needs the ability to spot a good guy–bad guy tactic. A good response might be

We understand your concern. But based on all the facts of the situation, we still feel our proposal is a fair one for all parties involved.

Lowballing

You may also have experienced **lowballing,** which occurs when one party intentionally underestimates or understates a cost.[10] Car dealers have used it for years. The salesperson says, "This car sells for $19,613." After you agree to purchase it, what happens? "Oh, I forgot to tell you that we have to charge you for dealer prep and destination charges, as well as an undercoating already applied to the car. So let's see, the total comes to $20,947. Gee, I'm sorry I didn't mention those expenses before!" Most people go ahead and buy. Why? They have already verbally committed themselves and do not want to go against their agreement. Also, they do not want to start the search process again.

The technique is also used in buyer–seller negotiations in industrial situations. For example, after the sellers have signed a final agreement with the buyer team, one of the buyer team members says, "Oh, I forgot to mention that all of our new contracts must specify FOB destination, and the seller must assume all shipping insurance expenses."

The best response to lowballing is just to say no. Remind the buyer team that the agreement has been finalized. The threat of lowballing underscores the importance of getting signatures on contracts and agreements as soon as possible. If the buyers insist on the new items, the selling team will simply be forced to reopen the negotiations. (Try this tactic on car dealers too!)

A variation of lowballing, **nibbling,** is a small extra, or add-on, the buyer requests after the deal has been closed. Compared to lowballing, a nibble is a much smaller request. For example, one of the buyers may state, "Say, could you give us a one-time 5 percent discount on our first order? That would sure make our boss happy and make us look like we negotiated hard for her." Nibbling often works because the request is so small compared to the entire agreement.

The selling team's response to the nibble depends on the situation. It may be advantageous to go ahead and grant a truly small request that could be easily met. On the other hand, if the buyer team uses nibbling often, granting these requests may need to be restricted. Again, the best strategy is to agree on the seller's position before the meeting begins and set guidelines for potential nibbles. Often the seller grants a nibble only if the buyer agrees to some small concession in return.

Emotional Outbursts

How do you react when a close friend suddenly starts crying, gets angry, or looks very sad? Most of us think, What have I done to cause this? We tend to feel guilty, become uneasy, and try to find a way to make the person stop crying. That is simply human nature.

Occasionally buyer teams will appeal to your human nature by engaging in an **emotional outburst tactic.** For example, one of the buyers may look directly at you, shake his or her head sadly, slowly look down, and say softly,

If a member of the buying team engages in an emotional outburst tactic, the seller should never respond in like fashion.

> I can't believe it's come to this. You know we can't afford that price. And we've been good partners all these years. I don't know what to say.

This statement is followed by complete silence among the entire buyer team. Members hope you will feel uncomfortable and give in to their demands. In an extreme case one or more buyers would actually walk out of the room or begin to shout or cry.

The selling team, once again, needs to recognize this behavior as the technique it is. Assuming no logical reason exists for the outburst, the negotiators should respond with a gentle but firm reminder of the merits of the offer and attempt to move the buyer group back into a win–win negotiating frame of mind.

Budget Limitation Tactic

In the **budget limitation tactic,** also called a **budget bogey,** the buyer team states something like the following:

> The proposal looks great. We need every facet of the program you are proposing in order for it to work in our business. But our budget allows us only $250,000 total, including all costs. You'll have to come down from $300,000 to that number, or I'm afraid we can't afford it.

This statement may be absolutely true. If so, at least you know what you have to work with. Of course claims of budget ceilings are sometimes just a ploy to try to get a lower price.

The best defense against budget limitations is to do your homework before going into the negotiation session. Learn as much as you can about budgets and maximums allowed. Have alternative programs or proposals ready that incorporate cost reduction measures. After being told of a budget limitation during the negotiation session, probe to make sure that the claim is valid. Check the possibility of splitting the cost of the proposal over several fiscal years. Probe to find out whether the buyer would be willing to accept more risk for a lower price or to have some of the installation work done by the buyer's staff. You can also help forestall this tactic by working closely with the buyer before the negotiation meeting, providing reasonable ballpark estimates of the cost of the proposal.

Browbeating

Sometimes buyers will attempt to alter the selling team's enthusiasm and self-respect by **browbeating** them. One buyer might make a comment like the following:

> Say, I've been reading some pretty unflattering things about your company in *The Wall Street Journal* lately. Seems like you can't keep your unions happy or your nonunion employees from organizing. It must be tough to get out of bed and go to work every day, huh?

If the selling team feels less secure and slightly inferior after such a comment, the tactic was successful.

You should not let browbeating comments influence you or your proposal. That's easier said than done, of course. Presumably you were able to identify in prenegotiation meetings that this buyer had this type of personality. If so, you could prepare by simply telling yourself that browbeating will occur but you will not let it affect your decisions. If you can make it through one such comment, buyers usually will not offer any more because they can see that browbeating will not help them achieve their goals.

One response to such a statement would be to practice **negotiation jujitsu.**[11] In negotiation jujitsu the salesperson steps away from the opponent's attack, rather than attacking his or her position, and then directs the opponent back to the issues being discussed. Instead of striking back, the seller breaks the win–lose attempt by not reacting negatively. The seller may even ask for clarification, advice, or criticism, but will not try to defend her ideas. The goal in all of this is to calm the buyer, giving the person a chance to release anger or frustration and make his or her position more clear while helping the seller maintain control of her own emotions. For example, the salesperson may say,

> I hear what you're saying. We're concerned about our employees and are working to resolve all problems as quickly as we can. If you have any ideas that would help us in this regard, we'd sure like to hear them. . . . Now, we were discussing price . . .

Other Win–Lose Tactics

Of course many other tactics are used, and it is beyond the purpose of this book to list them all. However, here are a few more:

- Limited authority: "Sorry, but we don't have the authority to make that decision here today." Solution: Verify the truth of that statement. If true, get the person with authority to the table.

- **Red herring** (bringing up a minor point first to distract the other side from considering the main issue): "We're going to have to have Saturday delivery in our agreement." Solution: Ask to set it aside temporarily until more substantive issues are dealt with.

- **Trial balloons** (floating an idea without really offering it as a concession or agreement; the goal is just to get information): "So have you considered going to a deferred shipping plan?" Solution: Don't just supply the information; ask "Well, if we did, what would your offer be?"

- Total silence by the buyer after you make an offer (most salespeople are uncomfortable with silence and will start offering some solution to break the buyer's silence): [Buyers just sit there and stare at the sellers.] Solution: Restate your offer, but don't offer new suggestions until they have acted on what you suggested. Just repeat your terms.

MAKING CONCESSIONS

One of the most important activities in any negotiation is the granting and receiving of concessions from the other party. One party makes a **concession** when it agrees to change a position in some fashion. For example, if your opening price position was $500, you would be granting a concession if you agreed to lower the price to $450.

Based on many successful negotiations in a wide range of situations, a number of guidelines have been formulated to make concessions effectively:[12]

1. Never make concessions until you know all of the buyer's demands and opening position. Use probing to help reveal these.

2. Never make a concession unless you get one in return and don't feel guilty about receiving a concession.

3. Concessions should gradually decrease in size. At first you may be willing to offer "normal size" concessions. As time goes on, however, you should make much smaller ones; for example, use a pattern like the following: 300–245–220–205–201–200. This approach helps the prospect see that you are approaching your target position and are becoming much less willing to concede.

4. If a requested concession does not meet your objectives, don't be afraid to simply say, "No. I'm sorry, but I just can't do that."

5. All concessions you offer are tentative until the final agreement is reached and signed. Remember that you may have to take back one of your concessions if the situation changes.

6. Be confident and secure in your position, and don't give concessions carelessly. If you don't follow this advice, your buyers may lose respect for your negotiating and business skills. Everyone wants to conduct business with someone who is sharp and who will be in business in the future. Don't give the impression that you are not and will not.

7. Don't accept the buyer's first attempt at a concession. Chances are the buyer has built in some leeway and is simply testing the water.

8. Help the buyer to see the value of any concessions you agree to. Don't assume the buyer will understand the total magnitude of your "generosity."

9. Start the negotiation without preconceived notions. Even though the buyers may have demanded certain concessions in the past, they may not do so in this negotiation meeting.

10. If, after making a concession, you realize you made some sort of mistake, tell the buyer and begin negotiating that issue again. For example, if you made a concession of delivery every two weeks instead of every four weeks but then realize that your fleet of trucks cannot make that route every two weeks, put the issue back on the table for renegotiation.

11. Don't automatically agree to a "let's just split the difference" offer by the buyers. Check out the offer to see how it compares to your target position.

12. If the customer says, "Tell us what your best price is, and we'll tell you whether we are interested," remain noncommittal. Respond, "In most cases, a price of $X is the best we can do. However, if you want to make a proposal, we'll see what we can do."

13. Know when to stop. Don't keep trying to get more, even if you can.

14. Use silence effectively. Studies have shown cultural differences in the negotiator's ability to use silence. For example, Brazilians make more initial concessions (use less silence early) than North Americans, who make more than the Japanese.

15. Plan the session well. In one study of successful negotiators, Neil Rackham found that "80 percent of the concessions obtained during negotiation resulted from things done before the negotiation started."[13]

The granting and receiving of concessions is often very complex and can result in the negotiations taking months or years to complete. Setting the proper environment early in the meeting puts you well on the way to a successful negotiation. Remember to develop an agenda and be aware of win–lose strategies that buyers may use. Offer concessions strategically.

RECAP OF A SUCCESSFUL NEGOTIATION MEETING

This chapter discussed win–win and win–lose negotiation sessions. Seasoned veterans will note that in some situations, the session could more accurately be classified as **win–win not yet negotiating**. In win–win not yet, the buying team achieves its goals while the selling team doesn't. However, the sellers expect to achieve their goals in the near future, thanks to the results of that negotiation session. For example, Antonio Willars in Monterrey, Mexico, relates the following:

I was working for the magazine *Revista Motor y Volante* and negotiating with Gonher, a lubricating oil company. At that time, no oil companies advertised in my magazine. So I negotiated an agreement with Gonher with a lower price than I had hoped to achieve, based on the belief that that sale would result in increased business over the long term. Although I didn't achieve my pricing goals in that session, I took a longer-term view. It paid off. That was the first of many, consistent sales to

Gonher, all at our regular rates. Plus, many oil companies, such as Quaker State, now advertise in the magazine. So although I had a "win not yet" outcome in that first meeting, we have now achieved a complete win–win situation.

When the session is over, be sure to get any negotiated agreements in writing. If no formal contract is possible, at least summarize the agreements reached. And don't forget to do postnegotiation evaluation and learn from your mistakes.

thinking **it** through

How can the use of information technology help keep track of issues during a negotiation session and ensure that all agreements reached during a negotiation session are included in the final written agreement?

Studies have shown that more cooperation exists if both sides expect future interactions. Keep in mind that your goal is to develop a long-term partnership with your buyer. This process can be aided by being levelheaded, courteous, and, above all, honest. Also, do not try to get every concession possible out of your buyer. If you push too hard or too long, the buyer will get irritated and may even walk out. Never lose out on an agreement by being too greedy. Remember your goal: to reach a win–win settlement. As CEO Nicholson at Enterprise states, "There's definitely some negotiation involved to make sure we get the best transaction possible, but we make certain we're always amicable partners at the end. We find ways to come to an agreement based on their needs, what works for us, and taking into account any current and expected future incentives."[14]

SELLING YOURSELF

It may be hard to imagine that you will ever engage in a formal negotiation. But it may happen in your life sooner than you think. For example, you may decide to build a house and thus negotiate with the builder on the price, details of the construction, and timing. A club you belong to may negotiate with a local venue for an upcoming event, and the negotiation may involve costs, catering, security details, and so forth. You may buy a new car or a home and negotiate the price and other terms in the agreement. Someone else may approach you and attempt to negotiate for something you own, or to contract for the use of your skills and talents.

Let's assume your club is going to host a fund-raising event called "The Battle of the Bands." Your club will bring in five of the top bands in your area to a local venue, and you will charge a cover price to all attending. The money you raise will be donated to a charity, like Habitat for Humanity.

Assume that many aspects of the event are negotiable, like the cost of the venue, the types of service offered by the venue, the promotion provided by the venue, the number and type of security officers on hand, the number of stage hands to build and break down the bands' sets, food and drink specials offered to patrons, and so forth. The first thing you want to do is to sit down with your club and plan for the negotiation session. Who should attend the negotiation session from your club? Certainly the person responsible for the activity should attend, as well as a club executive officer, and probably someone like the club treasurer. Your team needs to work out your target, minimum, and opening positions on all of the important issues. For example, on the issue of security, you positions might be these: opening—restaurant agrees to have three security guards present at all times; minimum – restaurant agrees to have one security guard present for the first two-thirds of the evening; target—restaurant agrees to have two security guards on duty at all times. The group needs to practice adaptive planning, deciding how obtaining the opening position on one issue, for example, might impact the requested amount of another issue.

Your team should practice, preferably with your club's faculty advisor or another mentor, to get a feel for how the negotiation session might occur as well as to work out any signals that will be passed during the meeting by your group. Your group also needs to be honest about the conflict-handling modes of the various team members and be prepared to resolve issues that arise, for example, if one of your team members is an accommodator.

For the meeting itself, make sure both sides agree on an agenda, keep track of agreements reached, and avoid falling into win–lose tactics. All concessions should be offered as tentative until the final agreement is reached and should be reciprocal. If you follow the suggestions outlined in this chapter, you should arrive at an agreement that is beneficial both to your group and to the venue.

SUMMARY

This chapter described how to engage in win–win negotiating. It also described how buyers may engage in win–lose negotiating.

Almost anything can be negotiated. The areas of negotiation will depend on the needs of both parties and the extent of disagreement on major issues.

A successful salesperson is not necessarily a good negotiator. Important negotiator traits include patience and endurance, willingness to take risks, a tolerance for ambiguity, the ability to deal with conflict, and the ability to engage in negotiation without worrying that every person present will not be on one's side.

As in regular sales calls, careful planning counts. This step involves choosing the location, setting objectives, and developing and managing the negotiating team. The salesperson does not act alone in these tasks, but instead draws on the full resources of the firm.

Preliminaries are important in sales negotiation sessions. Friendly conversation and small talk can help to reduce tensions and establish rapport. Agendas help to set boundaries and keep the negotiation on track. Win–lose strategies that buyers use include a good guy–bad guy routine, lowballing, emotional outbursts, budget limitation, browbeating, and other tactics. As much as possible, the salesperson should respond to any win–lose maneuvers calmly and with the intent of bringing the other side back to a win–win stance.

Concessions, by definition, will occur in every negotiation. Many guidelines have been established to help negotiators avoid obvious problems. For example, no concession should be given unless the buyer gives a concession of equal value. Also, any concessions given are not formalized until the written agreement is signed; thus all concessions are subject to removal if appropriate.

KEY TERMS

accommodating mode   331
adaptive planning   328
agenda   333
ambush negotiating   332
avoiding mode   331
brainstorming session   328
browbeating   338

budget bogey   338
budget limitation tactic   338
collaborating mode   331
competing mode   331
compromising mode   331
concession   339
emotional outburst tactic   337

ETHICS PROBLEMS

1. "Try to get a big concession from your opponent by giving away a small, insignificant concession yourself." Comment.

2. "If your opponent begins to use an unethical tactic, walk out of the room." Comment on this statement.

QUESTIONS AND PROBLEMS

1. In "From the Buyer's Seat 12.1" you read about a salesperson, Eric, whose bid wasn't well received, so he engaged in politics to try and secure the deal. If you were Eric, how would you have proceeded when you learned that your bid wasn't going to get accepted?

2. Suppose you're a salesperson with a local milk producer, and you're negotiating with a regional grocer over the number of deliveries you will make to its stores in a given week. Your maximum is nine times a week, your opening is four times a week, and your target is six times a week. After negotiating for some time, the grocer states, "Look, we're not willing to accept anything less than 14 times a week." What do you do now?

3. Assume you're a salesperson who is known for your excellent negotiating skills. You're a true collaborator in every sense of the word. Today you're supposed to engage in a negotiation with an important client. It's taken three months to set up this meeting, and your team of five, including your vice president, is assembled and ready to walk into the meeting. You are your team's designated leader. Your cell phone rings, and it's a relative, telling you that a close loved one has passed away unexpectedly. With the news comes a desire to just quit everything. What do you do now?

4. In "Sales Technology 12.1" you read about ExpertNegotiator software. Get on the Web and locate one other negotiation software tool. Then compare the two types of software.

5. According to the text, engaging in friendly conversation to break the ice before getting down to business is usually a good idea. When would it not be a good idea?

6. Assume you are going to have your fourth and final job interview with Sherwin Williams, a manufacturer of paints and other coatings, next Friday. Knowledgeable friends have told you that because you passed the first three interviews, you will be offered the job during the fourth interview. Also, you know that Sherwin Williams likes to negotiate with its new hires.
   a. Think about your own needs and desires for your first job (such as salary, expense reimbursement, benefits, geographic location, and promotion cycle).
   b. For each need and desire listed, establish your target position, opening position, and minimum position.
   c. Sherwin Williams has probably also developed positions that might meet each of your needs and desires. Describe how you could discover these positions before next Friday's meeting.

7. Susie Campbell, a salesperson for Proctor & Gamble, is preparing for an important negotiation session with Kroger, a large national food chain, regarding an upcoming promotional campaign. Her boss has strongly suggested that he attend the meeting with her. The problem is that her boss is not a good negotiator; he tends to get angry, is unorganized, and tries to resolve conflict by talking nonstop and thus wearing down the buyer team with fatigue. Her boss definitely has a win–lose negotiating philosophy. What should Susie do?

8. "You are the worst possible person to have to negotiate for yourself. You care too much about the outcome. Always let someone else negotiate for you." State your reaction to this statement. What implications does it have in industrial sales negotiations?

9. During negotiation, buyers make all kinds of statements. What would be your response to the following, assuming each occurred early in the meeting?

a. We refuse to pay more than $809.00 each. That's our bottom line—take it or leave it!

b. Come on, you've got to do better than that!

c. You know, we're going to have to get anything we decide here today approved by our corporate management before we can sign any kind of a contract.

d. One of our buyers can't make it here for another hour. But let's go ahead and get started and see what progress we can make.

e. Tell you what, we need to see a detailed cost breakdown for each individual item in your proposal.

10. "As a salesperson negotiator, my buyer's problem becomes my problem." Comment.

CASE PROBLEMS

case **12.1**

Gulfstream G150

Thanks to fuel-efficient Honeywell engines, combined with numerous aerodynamic improvements, the Gulfstream G150 is the fastest midsized business aircraft in the world today. In the award-winning Gulfstream PlaneView® cockpit, Gulfstream has some of the most advanced technology available. The result is a system that enhances flight crew performance and improves the overall level of flight safety.

With a longer, wider, more oval-shaped cabin, the G150 offers users a choice of three seating configurations accommodating up to eight passengers. It also provides more seated shoulder room, headroom, and legroom than any competing aircraft in the midsized category.

On the financial side, the G150 has the lowest operating costs in the industry. And the warranty is one of the most coveted also, covering its primary structures, engines, and all production components for five years. This is combined with Gulfstream's award-winning worldwide product support, aided by a network of 3,000 fully trained professionals found on six continents.

Satisfied clients of Gulfstream include a wide range of commercial users, the military, and law enforcement agencies. For each market segment, Gulfstream manufactures a wide range of jets to meet individual needs and budgets.

Today Jeannette Longly, a salesperson for Gulfstream, and her team of five engaged in a negotiation session with IBM. The session began pleasantly enough, and Jeannette was convinced that an agreement was going to be reached soon in the meeting. In prenegotiation meetings, Jeannette had discovered exactly what IBM wanted and had developed the negotiation session around the exact model that would fit IBM's needs.

Everything was going great until Jeannette was startled to hear Emery Jones, the key negotiator for IBM, say,

> The proposal looks great, Jeannette. We need every bell and whistle on the G150 that you are proposing. That's a fact. But there's something you don't know. We've just been given mandated budget cuts from our home office. Unless you can lower the price by 35 percent, I'm afraid we're going to have to give more serious consideration to your competitors. That's too bad, because we really like your jet the best!

Jeannette didn't know what to say. The price cut being requested by Emery was 5 percent less than Gulfstream's minimum price objective.

Questions

1. Evaluate the negotiation meeting to this point. How could Jeanette have better planned for the meeting?
2. What should Jeannette do now? Be explicit and give reasons for your answers. Make any necessary assumptions.

Source: This is a fictitious scenario. Information about Gulfstream came from its Web site, www.gulfstream.com.

case **12.2**

Identifying Conflict-Handling Modes

This chapter described a number of basic conflict-handling modes that people use in negotiation. These include competing, collaborating, compromising, avoiding, and accommodating.

Carefully reread the section that describes these modes. For each mode, identify someone you know who falls into the mode and answer the following questions. It will probably help to think of a specific situation that you have observed or have experienced with the person.

Questions

1. How do you know this person has this conflict-handling mode? Identify specific behaviors that you have observed or heard about to support your assertion about this person.
2. How do you (and others) interact with this person during a conflict situation? In other words, what do you do? How do you respond to this person's behavior? Is your approach effective?
3. Would you like to have this person on your team during an important negotiation session? Why or why not?

ROLE PLAY CASE

Break up into pairs; one person will serve as a buyer and the other as a NetSuite salesperson. The buyer is the VP of sales for the Atlanta regional office of UPS shipping. UPS is an international carrier that does overnight express package delivery, package delivery, and international shipping. It can ship anything anywhere. There are 54 salespeople employed, with six sales managers reporting to the VP. The salespeople use a card system, whereby they get the buyer's business card and staple it to an index card on which they can keep their notes. The company plans to add five salespeople per year until it doubles in size, with a new sales manager every other year. Sales force turnover is 15 percent per year, and often the cards are not turned over or are incomplete. One other problem is that growth is not meeting targets. Managers train their sales teams, but reps complain that it isn't what they need. Managers don't know what they need because they don't know where in the sales process the reps are not effective. NetSuite can provide pipeline analysis as well as better reporting of activity and results, a key need. Each rep generates about $1 million in shipping revenue per year.

About half the reps are not particularly computer literate and don't use computers to keep track of their accounts now. About half the reps have software they use to record call information, but that information is not tied to the company's computers or database. All salespeople have laptops, which they can use to access shipping records via a wireless Internet connection.

As a rep or as a buyer, take a few minutes to determine your opening and target positions on such factors as price, training, service, and anything else you can think of. Both of you can use information about NetSuite found in the role play section at the end of the book or on the NetSuite Web site to determine your positions and negotiating strategies. In your planning, include the use of a win–lose tactic, but be willing to move back to win–win if the other person responds appropriately. No additional information will be provided by the instructor.

Note: For background information about these role plays, please see page 27.

To the instructor: Additional information that will help you with this exercise is available in the Instructor's Manual.

ADDITIONAL REFERENCES

Batt, Peter J. "Building Social Capital in Networks." *Industrial Marketing Management* 37, no. 5 (July 2008), pp. 487–91.

Brooks, Bradley W., and Randall L. Rose, "The Influences of Matched versus Mismatched Negotiation Orientations on Negotiating Processes and Outcomes." *Journal of Marketing Theory and Practice* 16, no. 3 (Summer 2008), pp. 199–218.

Challagalla, Goutam, R. Venkatesh, and Ajay K. Kohli. "Proactive Postsales Service: When and Why Does It Pay Off?" *Journal of Marketing* 73, no. 2 (2009), pp. 70–87.

Diener, Marc. "Real Deal." *Entrepreneur* 35, no. 8 (August 2007), p. 68.

Donaldson, Michael C. *Fearless Negotiating.* McGraw-Hill, 2007.

Elfenbein, Hillary Anger, Maw Der Foo, Judith White, Hwee Hoon Tan, and Voon Chuan Aik. "Reading Your Counterpart: The Benefit of Emotion Recognition Accuracy for Effectiveness in Negotiation." *Journal of Nonverbal Behavior* 31, no. 4 (December 2007), pp. 205–24.

Gorin, Eli. "Latin America Is about Relationships." *Successful Meetings* 56, no. 7 (June 2007), p. 88.

Gosselin. Tom. *Practical Negotiating: Tools, Tactics & Techniques.* Wiley, 2007.

Heath, Chip, and Dan Heath. *Made to Stick.* Random House, 2007.

Heyden, Bill. "Negotiating versus Selling." *Electrical Wholesaling* 88, no. 9 (September 2007), pp. 62–63.

Lages, Luis Filipe, Andrew Lancastre, and Carmen Lages. "The B2B-RELPERF Scale and Scorecard: Bringing Relationship Marketing Theory into Business-to-Business Practice." *Industrial Marketing Management* 37, no. 6 (August 2008), pp. 686–97.

Lammers, Frauke. "Fairness in Delegated Bargaining." *Journal of Economics & Management Strategy* 19, no. 1 (2010), pp. 169–85.

Latz, Marty. "The Golden Rules of Negotiation." *Sales & Marketing Management,* January/February 2009, p. 24.

Lee, Micheal Soon. "10 Common Negotiating Mistakes That Cost You Thousands." *American Salesman* 52, no. 9 (September 2007), pp. 25–28.

Malhotra, Deepak, and Max H. Bazerman. "Pitch Your Offer—and Close the Deal." *Negotiation,* August 2007, pp. 1–4.

Muir, Clive. "Tapping the Subjective Values Present in Negotiations: Face, Feelings, and Friendships." *Academy of Management Perspectives* 21, no. 1 (February 2007), pp. 72–74.

"No: The Only Negotiating Strategy You Need for Work and Home." *Publishers Weekly* 254, no. 7 (February 12, 2007), p. 74.

Nyden, Jeanette. *Negotiation Rules: A Practical Guide to Big Deal Negotiation.* Sales Gravy Press (2009).

Rudd, Jill E., and Diana R. Lawson. *Communicating in Global Business Negotiations: A Geocentric Approach.* Sage Publications, 2007.

Strelecky, John. "Take 3 Simple Steps to Mastering Negotiations." *Selling,* September 2004, p. 8.

Thorn, Jeremy G. *How to Negotiate Better Deals.* Global Management Enterprises, 2009.

Wang, Jingguo, and Stanley Zionts. "Negotiating Wisely: Considerations Based on MCDM/MAUT." *European Journal of Operational Research* 188, no. 1 (July 1, 2008), pp. 191–205.

Wood, John Andy, James S. Boles, Wesley Johnston, and Danny Bellenger. "Buyers' Trust of the Salesperson: An Item-Level Meta-Analysis." *Journal of Personal Selling & Sales Management* 28, no. 3 (Summer 2008), pp. 263–84.

chapter **13**

BUILDING PARTNERING RELATIONSHIPS

SOME QUESTIONS ANSWERED IN THIS CHAPTER ARE

- What different types of relationships exist between buyers and sellers?
- When is each type of relationship appropriate?
- What are the characteristics of successful partnerships?
- What are the benefits and risks in partnering relationships?
- How do relationships develop over time?
- What are the responsibilities of salespeople in partnerships?

PROFILE

Before attending the University of Tennessee for undergraduate school, I thought the term "logistics" was some sort of foreign language. Little did I know that four short years later I would be starting a career with an up-and-coming company such as Total Quality Logistics (TQL). I had always wanted to go into some sort of sales while in college because no two sales are alike and it is such a fast-paced environment. Let's also be honest—the earning potential in a sales environment can also be limitless. Therefore, when I met Ken Oaks, TQL's CEO, at a career fair in 2003, it felt like the perfect storm.

When I took this career path, I will have to admit I was kind of skeptical because it was a 100 percent commission-based job, but there was no cap on earning potential that a logistics account executive could earn. The job was also designed with the entrepreneur at heart because you make all the decisions on the industries that you want to cold call and how you want to run your own personal business within their organization.

I have worked at TQL for seven years and was one of the original 35 employees that were started in the bottom floor of an office high-rise in Cincinnati. Today TQL has grown into a third-party logistics powerhouse, rising all the way to number 6 in the industry with over 1,000 employees. Total Quality Logistics moves over 7,000 loads a week and enjoyed over $500 million in revenue last year.

After going through an extensive training program that shows you exactly what this foreign language "logistics" is all about, I was given a phone and an unlimited database of companies that I could cold call to build my own book of business. What separates this industry and type of cold calls from other industries is that the customers on the other end of the line actually need your services as much as you need their business. The reason Ken Oaks started TQL traces back to his prior job in the produce industry. He found reliable transportation extremely difficult to find. Once TQL was started, he knew exactly what would separate us from the other companies in the industry, and that was after-sales service. Service and relationships are the keys to any successful sales job. While price might also be a determinant, especially in this economy, if you can show the value and go above and beyond on service, then the customers will always return. I always explain to my customers that you can't have champagne service with Coca-Cola prices though. They usually get a good laugh out of that one, but it generally holds pretty true, especially in transportation. Generally you are going to get what you pay for, and that is where TQL shines.

When going into cold calling for new potential clients, I always believed that I am selling more than what TQL has to offer—I am selling myself because I will be their daily point of contact, and if they don't like me first, then they won't like TQL no matter what I have to offer. Customers are always going to agree to a person first and then the product or service second. I have seen many salespeople come and go at TQL because of the difficulty level and stress of a fast-paced sales job. One thing that has always held true, though, is that the most successful people always knew that they were selling themselves first and foremost and steered clear of gimmicks or quick fixes that resulted in quick sales numbers that don't hold up. If there is anything that you cannot fake or have a gimmick for in sales, it is your personality and integrity. The most successful salespeople in any industry have a glowing personality and a rock-solid integrity level, and can adapt and change to any situation that may come up around them.

After initially gaining a new customer, the next step is taking care of them. Transportation makes customers extremely anxious because there are so many things that can go wrong, from pickup to delivery. So many aspects are out of the customer's control, such as weather, truck breakdown, theft, accidents, and in some cases temperature control throughout a shipment's travel. Communication keeps customers feeling secure; my main service component is letting the customer know at any moment if something goes wrong. We are available literally 24/7/365 and occasionally deal with issues at 2:00 a.m. or even on Christmas day. This level of service, though, is necessary because we always say that doing the right thing is better than trying to cover up a mistake that actually makes it worse. Our commitment and communication also give the customer peace of mind that whenever they tender a load with TQL, it will be done the right way all the time. That goes a long way if we can eliminate stress from their lives. By following these simple steps I have built long-lasting customer relationships, but I can honestly call many of my customers very good friends due to the relationships that we have built throughout the years.

Total Quality Logistics has been the only job that I have had out of college, and I don't think that I could have made a better decision than to take a chance on this up-and-coming company. What I have learned here so far will last me a lifetime, and as I continue to get my MBA at the University of Cincinnati, I eventually hope to move up into upper management within the organization. Then I can show the newer account executives where going above and beyond with your service level can actually take you.

Visit our Web site at www.tql.com.

THE VALUE OF CUSTOMERS

Many people believe the emphasis in selling is on getting the initial sale. For most salespeople, however, sales increases from one year to the next are due to increasing the revenue from existing accounts, not just from getting new accounts. Even in industries where purchase decisions are made infrequently, salespeople gain a competitive advantage by maintaining strong relationships with their customers. Eventually, when buying decisions need to be made, those customers look to people they know and trust. Kevin Clonch, for example, discussed in the opening profile the importance of being trustworthy because people want to buy from people they know and trust.

Customers are, of course, the primary revenue source for companies. Some customers are worth more in terms of revenue than some salespeople recognize. For example, a car salesperson may think only of the immediate sale, but each customer is potentially worth hundreds of thousands of dollars in revenue over the salesperson's lifetime. Exhibit 13.1 illustrates the value of a small attorney's office over a 20-year period for just a few salespeople. For example, if an office equipment/supply salesperson sold all the copiers and office supplies needed during that 20-year period, total revenue would be almost $100,000! This is an example of **customer lifetime value (CLV)**, which is the combined total of all future

Exhibit 13.1
Selected Expenses for a Small Law Firm over a 20-Year Period

Item	Cost	Total
Computers	7 @ $2,000	$14,000
Copiers	5 @ $5,000	25,000
Copying supplies	$50 per month	12,000
Printer/scanner/fax	5 @ $2,000	10,000
Fax supplies	$20 per month	4,800
Telephone systems	3 @ $1,000	3,000
Other office supplies	$100 per month	24,000
Office furniture	$5,000	5,000
Total over 20 years		$97,800

sales (typically discounted back into current dollars). If the salesperson thinks in terms of just one sale, however, the customer is worth no more than $5,000.

Research shows that successfully retaining customers is important to all companies. Using a consultative customer-oriented sales approach has been shown to improve both customer retention and firm profitability, even with commodity products.[1] Yet another study finds that the average company loses 20–50 percent of its customer base every year, and the rate is increasing.[2] Salespeople are critical to the process of keeping customers: Another study finds that the relationship quality between the salesperson and the buyer is one driver of financial performance. The better the relationship, the better the firm's performance.[3]

In tough times, such as the economy has recently experienced, keeping customers and avoiding competition based solely on price is difficult. In "Building Partnerships 13.1" two sales professionals offer their advice on how to thrive in tough times.

We have already discussed the importance of good service in generating referrals and of becoming a trusted member of the community in which your buyers operate so you can acquire more customers (see Chapter 6). The value of satisfied customers is so high that it makes good business sense to build the strongest possible relationships. In this chapter we discuss the nature of relationships and the types of relationships that can be built, and we begin to explore how to build those relationships over time. In the next chapter we focus on strategies to build longer-term relationships.

Buyers who are attitudinally loyal to Apple and its computers may also be behaviorally loyal, buying products like the iPad when they are introduced.

RELATIONSHIPS AND SELLING

Many students may have heard of relationship marketing or customer relationship management (CRM) and wonder how these compare with building partnerships. *Relationship marketing* is a term with several meanings, but all reflect companies' attempts to develop stronger relationships with their customers. The premise is that loyal customers buy more, are willing to pay more, influence friends to also buy, and are willing to help develop new products.[4] Building a stronger relationship is accomplished through building loyalty. For example, American Airlines may think of its Advantage frequent flyer program as the heart of relationship marketing; loyalty is rewarded with air miles that can be redeemed for free flights. But in professional selling, **relationship marketing** refers to creating the type of relationship that best suits the customer's need, which may or may not require a partnership.

There are two types of loyalty: behavioral and attitudinal.[5] **Behavioral loyalty** refers to the purchase of the same product from the same vendor over time. When someone purchases out of habit, for example, that pattern is behavioral loyalty. Recall that earlier we pointed

IN TOUGH TIMES, CAN WE AFFORD PARTNERSHIPS?

When the economy goes down, all aspects of business are affected. Just as a rising tide lifts all boats, so a sinking tide casts many boats ashore. But if you listen carefully to what sales professionals say about how to sell in tough times, it's clear that correct actions remain correct, even when the tide comes back up.

Cathie Black, president of Hearst Magazines, got her start in sales. Now she manages over $1.5 billion in sales per year, running a company that includes O, The Oprah Magazine; Cosmo; Esquire; and numerous others. Listed by Forbes as one of the 100 most powerful women, she offers these tips for salespeople who are faced with tough times:

1. Get, and stay, in front of your customers as much as possible. "Everyone is searching for ideas right now, and even if your client is trying to dodge you...get in there and look that client in the eye...(and the client) will eventually think, 'Maybe this person does have some ideas that could work for me.'

2. Be essential. Essentially Black says you have to find ways to add value, both for your customer and your company.

3. Use this time to innovate, brainstorming solutions for clients. What are new ways to add value for clients? Use the downturn as a chance to try new solutions.

Neil Rackham, inventor of SPIN, agrees that down economic periods are great times to break out of old habits and find new ways to add value. He also suggests that continued skills improvement is more important than ever, and it's easier to see the need for stronger skills when times are tough.

Neil Watson, sales director for the United Kingdom–based company Viatel, urges salespeople to resist the urge to sell on price alone. Watson, as does Black, emphasizes that decisions are still made based on value. He claims, "Those who compete on price alone will win fewer deals with less margin—often the result of a lack of confidence in selling more complex products."

And in tough times, nothing may be more important than maintaining one's reputation. Watson says that maintaining a reputation as being customer-first and providing specialized knowledge that gives real value to customers is what will win the day.

There's an old saying that tough times come and go, but tough people last. What works when times are tough will work when times are good—and the reverse is not always true.

Sources: Neil Watson, "Channel Challenge," Computer Reseller News, (January 11, 2010), p. 18; Kim Wright Wiley, "Make Things Happen," Selling Power (November/December 2009), pp. 46–49, Neil Rackham, "Selling in a Down Economy," Training & Development 63, no. 6 (June 11, 2009), p. 16.

out that buyers calculate profit by subtracting both price and shopping costs from the benefits received. Buying out of habit can reduce shopping costs and increase profit when past experience can indicate future satisfaction. **Attitudinal loyalty** is an emotional attachment to a brand, company, or salesperson. For example, some computer users develop an emotional attachment to Apple; they may also exhibit behavioral loyalty by buying only Apple products whenever possible or even buying a new iPad just because it is an Apple product.

Companies prefer buyers who are both attitudinally and behaviorally loyal; moreover, companies want loyal customers who stay customers forever. Companies want to receive as much of a buyer's lifetime value, or CLV, as possible. Further, not every customer's CLV is the same. Recall the attorney firm in Exhibit 13.1—not every firm of that size will spend money on equipment the same way. Some firms will need more, others less. Thus companies want loyal customers who are also bigger spenders. Lower lifetime value customers may not be as important to the company.

Customer lifetime value is influenced by more than just that customer's purchases, though. How much more might that attorney be worth as a customer to an office equipment dealer in terms of referrals, sales to the associates who leave and open their own offices, and additional repeat business if the dealership really kept the attorney as a customer for life? What about the value of a new product idea generated by the attorney? All these elements can add value to the company.

There are entire books written about loyalty; the important element to recognize here is that the emphasis in this book is on building long-term relationships, in part to capture as much CLV as possible. Salespeople with the longer-term view recognize the power of CLV and consider both behavioral and attitudinal loyalty as an objective sell in a different way than if focused only on making the next sale. There are, however, different types of relationships, as we discuss next.

TYPES OF RELATIONSHIPS

Each time a transaction occurs between a buyer and a seller, the buyer and the seller have a relationship. Some relationships may involve many transactions and last for years; others may exist only for the few minutes during which money is exchanged for goods.

This section describes two basic relationship types: market exchanges and partnerships.[6] There are two types of each, summarized in Exhibit 13.2.

MARKET EXCHANGES

A **market exchange** is a transaction between a buyer and a seller in which each party is concerned only about its own benefit. The seller is concerned only with making the sale, the buyer with getting the product at the lowest possible price. Most business transactions are market exchanges, and there are two types: solo exchanges and functional relationships.

Solo Exchanges

Suppose you are driving to the beach for spring break. A warning light on your car's dashboard comes on. You stop at the next gas station, and the service attendant says your car needs a new alternator. The alternator will cost $650, including installation. At this point you might pay the quoted price, bargain with the service attendant for a lower price, or drive to another service station a block away and get a second opinion. After you select a service station, agree on a price, have the alternator replaced, and pay for the service, you have completed a

Exhibit 13.2
Types of Relationships between Buyers and Sellers

Factors Involved in the Relationship	Type of Relationship			
	Solo Market Transaction	Functional Relationship	Relational Partnership	Strategic Partnership
Time horizon	Short term	Long term	Long term	Long term
Concern for other party	Low	Low	Medium	High
Trust	Low	Low	High	High
Investments in the relationship	Low	Low	Low	High
Nature of the relationship	Conflict, bargaining	Cooperation	Accommodation	Coordination
Risk in relationship	Low	Medium	High	High
Potential benefits	Low	Medium	High	High

one-shot market exchange. Neither you nor the service station attendant expects to engage in future transactions.

Because the parties in the transaction do not plan on doing business together again, both the buyer and the seller in a **solo exchange** pursue their own self-interests. In this example, you try to pay the lowest price for the alternator, and the service station tries to charge the highest price for it. The service station is not concerned about your welfare, just as you are not concerned about the service station's welfare. Or perhaps more accurately, the service station calculates profit from the relationship immediately after the transaction. The issue is not an ethical one; there is no intent to maliciously hurt the other party. At the same time, however, there is no future consideration to worry about in terms of whether the transaction was worthwhile.

Functional Relationships

Functional relationships are long-term market exchanges characterized by behavioral loyalty; the buyer purchases the same product out of habit or routine. Buyers in this type of relationship tend to have the same orientation as they do in solo exchanges, but the previous purchase influences the next purchase. As long as the buyer is satisfied and the product is available at a reasonable price and does what it is supposed to do, the buyer will continue to buy.

Sometimes firms buy from the same supplier for a long time because it is easier than searching for a new supplier every time they need an item. In functional relationships (as in any long-term buyer–seller relationship), customer satisfaction is very important. Without customer satisfaction, behavioral loyalty cannot develop. **Customer satisfaction** occurs when the buyer's expectations are met and needs are fulfilled (we discuss this in detail later in this chapter).[7] When satisfied, a buyer is less likely to shop around for the next purchase because less hassle means more buyer profit.

For example, a buyer for your school purchases janitorial supplies—paper towels, soap, cleanser, and mops—for the cleaning crew. However, the buyer and the janitorial supply distributor have little interest in working closely together. The relationship between the buyer and the distributor's salesperson is not critical to the school's success as an educational institution. The buyer can decide to deal with another distributor if service is poor, the product fails to perform, or another distributor works harder to get the business—in other words, if the buyer becomes dissatisfied.

Even in these long-term market exchanges, both parties are interested primarily in their own profits and are unconcerned about the welfare of the other party. In market exchanges price may be the critical decision factor. It serves as a rapid means of communicating the bases for the exchange. Basically the buyer and the salesperson in a market exchange are always negotiating over how to "split up the pie," or how to make more in the transaction. Each calculates profit at the end of each transaction or at least on a frequent basis, usually reflective of the billing cycle. If the janitorial supply company invoices the university monthly, for example, then each side will calculate profit monthly. If the school's buyer gets an invoice that seems too large, it may cause the buyer to shop around next time because there was insufficient "profit" or value for the buyer.

On the positive side, market exchanges offer buyers and sellers a lot of flexibility. Buyers and sellers are not locked into a continuing relationship, and thus buyers can switch from one supplier to another to make the best possible deal. However, these minimal relationships do not work well when buyers and sellers have an opportunity to increase the size of the pie by developing products and services tailored to their needs. These more complex transactions cannot be conducted solely on the basis of price. High levels of trust and commitment are needed to manage these types of relationships because buyers and sellers need to share sensitive information.[8]

PARTNERSHIPS

There are two types of partnerships: relational and strategic. In a partnership both parties are concerned about each other's welfare and about developing a **win–win relationship.** By working together, both parties benefit because the size of the pie increases.

Relational Partnerships

Many times the buyer and the salesperson have a close personal relationship that allows them to communicate effectively. These friendships create a cooperative climate between the salesperson and the customer. When both partners feel safe and stable in the relationship, open and honest communication takes place. Salesperson and buyer work together to solve important problems. The partners are not concerned about small details because they trust each other enough to know these will be worked out. These types of partnerships are not necessarily strategic to either organization, although they may be to the individuals involved, and are called **relational partnerships.**

The benefits of a relational partnership go beyond simple increased short-term profits. Although both partners are striving to make money in the relationship, they are also trying to build a working relationship that will last a long time. Recall Kevin Clonch's statement in the opening profile: "I have built long-lasting customer relationships, but I can honestly call many of my customers very good friends due to the relationships that we have built throughout the years."

Relational partnerships can occur between a buyer and seller not only because of personal ties but also because each is important to the other professionally. For example, a trade show program may not be important enough to the organization to demand a strategic partner but is very important to the trade show manager. That manager may seek a relational partnership with a supplier, complete with personal investment of time and departmental resources, rather than a strategic organizational investment and commitment.

In Asian countries, the personal relationship is an important precursor to strategic partnerships. Several studies have found that social bonding and interpersonal commitment are necessary ingredients to any long-term partnership between Asian organizations.[9] In several studies examining relationships between buyers and sellers in China, interpersonal commitment was a precursor to organizational relationships; so without friendship, there was no partnership.[10]

In this chapter we talk about relationships between buyers and sellers, but these concepts also apply to personal relationships. A relational partnership is like a close friendship. In a close friendship you are not concerned with how the pie is split up each day because you are confident that, over the long run, each of you will get a fair share; further, the pie will be bigger because of your friendship. You trust your friend to care about you, and she or he trusts you in return. The founder of the country's largest department store chain, James Cash Penney, once said, "All great businesses are built on friendship."

Strategic Partnerships

Strategic partnerships are long-term business relationships in which the partner organizations make significant investments to improve the profitability of both parties. In these relationships the partners have gone beyond trusting each other to "putting their money where their mouths are." They take risks to expand the pie and to give the partnership a strategic advantage over other companies.

Strategic partnerships are created for the purpose of uncovering and exploiting joint opportunities. Members of strategic partnerships have a high level of dependence on and trust in each other; share goals and agree on how to accomplish those goals; and show a willingness to take risks, share confidential information, and make significant investments for the sake of the relationship. An example is the partnership between Simmons Mattress and Westin Hotels. Simmons manufactures a special mattress for Westin, called the Heavenly Bed. This special product can be purchased through Westin Hotels or through other channels, but Westin is the only hotel to which Simmons will sell the Heavenly Bed mattress.

Similarly, Levi Strauss teams worked with JCPenney to create a specially designed area in its stores to display Dockers merchandise. Then teams from each company developed sophisticated inventory control systems to make sure the stores were always stocked with the styles and sizes that were selling well. As a result, JCPenney is now Levi Strauss's largest customer worldwide. JCPenney also increased its own profits because it was able to offer merchandise to its customers that was not available from its competitors.

Many students wonder about the exclusivity of strategic partnerships. Does a strategic partnership mean, for example, that JCPenney cannot carry Wranglers or that Westin can't use Sealy? In the Westin situation the agreement was for an exclusive arrangement that tied the two companies together. But Penney also sells Wrangler jeans as well as a private-label brand. Strategic partnerships do not necessarily mean exclusivity for either buyer or seller—Levi can still sell to customers that compete with JCPenney.

Many salespeople are involved in both solo exchanges and functional relationships. Some customers buy once and are never heard from again. Others become loyal as long as everything goes smoothly. A few become friends, but strategic partnerships are rare. Exhibit 13.3 illustrates the differences in the nature of selling in market exchanges and long-term relationships.

Westin Hotels' partnership with Simmons created the Heavenly Bed, a mattress and bed linens product line that is popular with business travelers. You can even buy the mattress and linens through Westin's Web site.

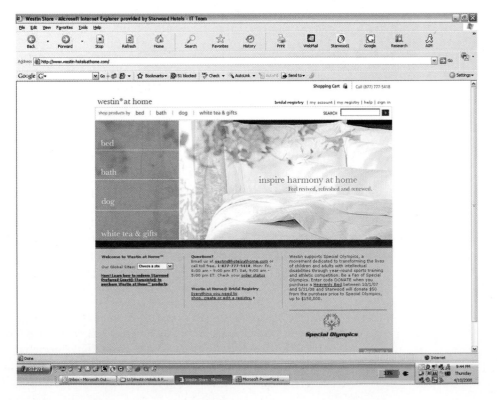

Exhibit 13.3
Selling in Market Exchanges and Long-Term Relationships

Market Exchange Selling Goal: Making a Sale	Long-Term Relationship Selling Goal: Building Trust

Making Contact
• Find someone to listen.
• Make small talk.
• Ingratiate and build rapport.
 	
Closing the Sale
• Deliver a sales pitch to
  • Get the prospect's attention.
  • Create interest.
  • Build desire.
  • Get the prospect to take action.
• Stay alert for closing signals.
• Use trial closes.
• Overcome objections.
• Close early and often.
 	
Following Through
• Reestablish contact.
• Resell self, company, and products.
	Initiating the Relationship
	• Engage in strategic prospecting and qualifying.
	• Gather and study precall information.
	• Identify buying influences.
	• Plan the initial sales call.
	• Demonstrate an understanding of the customer's needs.
	• Identify opportunities to build a relationship.
	• Illustrate the value of a relationship with the customer.
	
	Developing the Relationship
	• Select an appropriate offering.
	• Customize the relationship.
	• Link the solution to the customer's needs.
	• Discuss customer concerns.
	• Summarize the solution to confirm benefits.
	• Secure commitment.
	
	Enhancing the Relationship
	• Assess customer satisfaction.
	• Take actions to ensure satisfaction.
	• Maintain open, two-way communication.
	• Expand collaborative involvement.
	• Work to add value and enhance mutual opportunities.

Source: Adapted from Thomas Ingram, "Relationship Selling: Moving from Rhetoric to Reality," *Mid-American Journal of Business* 11 (1996), p. 6.

Each type of relationship has its pluses and minuses. Companies cannot develop a strategic advantage from a market exchange, but they do get the flexibility to buy products from the supplier with the lowest cost when the order is placed. On the other hand, strategic partnerships create a win–win situation, but the companies are committed to each other and flexibility can be reduced. In the next section we talk about the characteristics of successful relationships—relationships that have the potential to develop into strategic partnerships.

thinking it through

Think about how you are treated when you walk into a clothing store. How much do you spend on average per month for clothing? How much would that be during your time in school? Does the store treat you on the basis of your value as a solo exchange? How would your treatment change if the store considered your lifetime value as a customer? What form of relationship would be needed for it to capture your CLV?

MANAGING RELATIONSHIPS AND PARTNERING

Salespeople are usually responsible for determining the appropriate form of relationship and for making sure that their companies develop the appropriate types of relationships with customers. In other words, some customers want, and need, a market exchange; others need a functional relationship; and still others

Size matters! Most strategic partnerships involve larger customers like JCPenney rather than Jordans because their size makes the investment in the partnership worthwhile.

need a strategic partnership. As salespeople identify customer needs for product benefits, they also identify needs for relationship benefits and select the appropriate strategy as a result. Salespeople are likely to manage a portfolio of relationships.[11] With some accounts, a strategic partnership may be called for. With others, it may be a relational partnership or functional relationship. The salesperson must determine which relationship type is appropriate for optimizing the customer's lifetime value.

CHOOSING THE RIGHT RELATIONSHIP

As you can see from the discussion about what makes for a strategic relationship, at least one factor that influences a salesperson's choice of relationship is the type of relationship the customer desires. Becoming a strategic partner requires investment by both parties, and if the customer isn't willing to make that investment, then another type of relationship is called for. Even then, not every customer who wants a strategic partnership should become your strategic partner. Some of the factors to consider are size of the account, access and image in the market, and access to technology.

Size

JCPenney has a strategic partnership with Levi Strauss. Would Levi Strauss have a similar partnership with Jordans, a single store? Probably not. The return could not be great enough to justify the investment. The thought is that by partnering with large accounts, the accounts invest in the supplier and become locked in. Economies of scale can often justify lower prices and higher investments. Size of the account, then, is one aspect to consider. But that doesn't mean that one should partner only with the largest accounts. In some cases larger accounts are not necessarily the most profitable, particularly when the seller's investments are factored in.[12] In other cases smaller accounts provide important benefits that larger accounts cannot, as we will discuss.

Access and Image

A strategic partnership may be called for if an account can provide access to a specific, desired market or can enhance the image of the seller. For example, SRI is a software company that has carefully selected initial customers in each market it serves. By first selling to customers with strong reputations, SRI is likely to gain other customers.

Access to Innovation

Some companies are called **lead users** because they face and resolve needs months or years ahead of the rest of the marketplace. These companies often develop innovations that the supplier can copy, either in the way it uses a product or by altering a product. Stonewood Dental, for example, wanted to develop a new patient relationship management program based on CRM principles.

The initiative required its patient records software provider, EagleSoft, to make some changes to the software; but when Eaglesoft saw what Stonewood wanted, it quickly realized that the result would be a new product that could be sold to other dentists. In this situation Stonewood was a lead user.

Note that one important function salespeople provide is the ability to listen to customers and deliver that knowledge back to the company so better products can be developed.[13] That function is important in new product development, but does not necessarily require deep relationships. What lead users provide is more than information; they provide the opportunity to co-create innovations that can then be converted into products. Note also that this contributes to the customer lifetime value of such customers.

Other lead users may develop innovations in other areas of the business, such as logistics, that suppliers can copy. For example, HEB is a grocery chain covering Texas and Mexico that has led the development of radio frequency identification (RFID), a technology used in logistics. Several suppliers such as Campbells have spent time with HEB logistics engineers to learn how RFID can make logistics more efficient. Astute salespeople can identify such companies and develop strategic partnerships that lead to joint development of new products or technologies— important outcomes regardless of the size of the account.

USING TECHNOLOGY TO INCREASE EFFICIENCY

Companies are using technology to drive two key areas of salesperson performance. The first is the use of technology to help salespeople manage all the information required to be effective, a type of **knowledge management technology.** Such knowledge management technology might include product catalogs and all the detailed specifications of those products, but knowledge management technology also includes customer records and transaction/service histories.

The second is relational management technology, which can build on customer knowledge management systems to create models that can be used to develop strategy.

Companies are also creating direct links with their customers and suppliers. Xerox and Baxter have developed electronic ordering mechanisms with their customers, and IBM uses private Web sites and Lotus Notes to enable suppliers to communicate with each other and with IBM buyers. "Sales Technology 13.1" describes how two companies use CRM software to manage relationships in order to improve customer service and salesperson efficiency.

PHASES OF RELATIONSHIP DEVELOPMENT

Although not all relationships should become partnerships, strategic partnerships tend to go through several phases: (1) awareness, (2) exploration, (3) expansion, (4) commitment, and sometimes (5) dissolution.[14] Recent research indicates that the middle three stages are most important.[15] Cultural differences may alter the way buyers and sellers move through these phases, but strategic partnerships go through these stages in most situations.

AWARENESS

In the **awareness** stage it is likely that no transaction has taken place. During the awareness phase salespeople locate and qualify prospects, while buyers identify various sources of supply. Buyers may see a booth at a trade show, an ad in a magazine, or some other form of marketing communication and seek additional information. Reputation and image in the marketplace can be very important for sellers at this point. One important trend is toward **supplier relationship management (SRM),** which is the use of technology and statistics to identify important

SALES 2.0

Sales force automation and customer relationship management software offerings have a long way to go. In a recent study of 170 CEOs and chief sales officers, 85 percent gave their software a grade of C or less, and 55 percent gave it a low F. So what's the problem?

Like most business situations, there isn't just one problem. Poor data entry by salespeople (often due to a poor data plan), a lack of understanding of how to use the data, and a separation of responsibilities between sales and marketing are three of the primary causes, but are by no means all of the problems, according to a study by Baylor University sales professor Jeff Tanner. But despite these challenges, many businesses are finding greater sales success by incorporating CRM technology into their sales processes.

For example, BNY Mellon (formerly Bank of New York) has found success with its technology. "There was a need at our company to better coordinate and understand what our clients were thinking and doing across our multiple products with multiple sales forces, and internally there was a need to cross-sell better," says Erik R. Beck, managing director of global strategic sales at BNY Mellon. Analytics available in the software, according to Beck, include sales rep performance versus goals, customer activities versus sales, why opportunities were lost or won and the impact of those results on revenue, and success rates/market share. The data that drive these analytics are input by salespeople, but because of how executives use the data, BNY Mellon has overcome the salesperson data entry problem. Executives review the data with salespeople to understand whom the firm is competing against, what's in the pipeline, why it won or lost particular client sales, and trends over months, quarters, or years, so not inputting the data just isn't tolerated.

Isuzu's commercial vehicle fleet sales division is another organization benefiting from the use of technology. "We had some old-time people who would maintain accounts on the back of an envelope, but with NetSuite's ease of use and a little internal competition, we were able to load hundreds of our most important customer contacts in the first month," says Todd Bloom, VP of marketing and fleet operations at ICTA. Because the system has increased time with customers, thereby increasing sales performance, getting salespeople to buy into using the system and putting in good data have taken some time. Recognizing the benefits didn't come right away. But like BNY Mellon, top executives used the system daily to manage the business, so it didn't take long for salespeople to recognize the importance of using the system.

Sources: Anonymous, "Sales Lead Management Association Study Finds 64.9% of B2B Marketers Cannot Track ROI," *Marketing Weekly News*, March 6, 2010, p. 14; Penny Crosman, "Intelligent Enterprise, BNY Mellon Taps BI for Customer Insight," *Wall Street & Technology* 28, no. 1 (January/February 2010), p. 10; Anonymous, "Customer Success Story: Isuzu Commercial Truck of America," http://www.netsuite.com/portal/home.shtml, accessed March 22, 2010.

suppliers and opportunities for cost reduction, greater efficiency, and other benefits. Thus awareness may result from analyzing current suppliers to identify those with whom a partnership may be possible.

Recognize, though, that relationships do not necessarily move from solo exchange to functional relationship to relational partnership to strategic partnership. Customers may actively seek partnerships for key areas of the firm's purchases, which may mean working to develop a strategic partnership with a new vendor. Or the relationship may develop over time and may involve one or more of the other forms of relationship. There is no requirement, however, that a partnership must start out as a solo exchange.

EXPLORATION

The **exploration** stage is a search and trial phase for both buyer and seller. Both parties may explore the potential benefits and costs of a partnership. At this point the buyer may make purchases, but these are likely in the form of market exchanges because neither side has committed to the relationship. Each purchase can be thought of as a test of the supplier's capability.

Satisfaction is key for the relationship to move beyond exploration. We focus on satisfaction in Chapter 14; however, several points about satisfaction should be understood in the context of relationships. First, keep in mind that satisfaction with the salesperson and satisfaction with the company and its products and services both influence the development of the relationship.[16] Such salesperson characteristics as dependability and competence are tested in the exploration phase and improve satisfaction. Second, buyers will object during the exploration phase to characteristics of the salesperson's offer. How those objections are handled (the topic of Chapter 10) is an important factor in successfully negotiating the exploration stage.[17]

EXPANSION

At this point the supplier has passed enough tests to be considered for additional business. The **expansion** stage involves efforts by both parties to investigate the benefits of a long-term relationship. The relationship can still devolve into a functional relationship rather than a strategic partnership, but the intention of both parties is to develop the appropriate type of relationship. The buyer's dependence on the seller as a primary source of supply grows and may lead to the purchase of additional products. Further, both sides begin to probe regarding interest in a partnership; such probing is both internal and external. Remember that the decision for a strategic partnership requires credible commitments, so many in the selling organization may need to review the opportunity.

COMMITMENT

In the **commitment** stage the customer and seller have implicitly or explicitly pledged to continue the relationship for a period of time. Commitment represents the most advanced stage of the relationship. Investments are made in the relationship, especially in the form of sharing proprietary information, plans, goals, and the like.

In Chapter 11 we discussed obtaining commitment as a stage in the sales process. In that sense we are talking about asking the buyer to make a decision—a decision either to buy the product or to take the next step in the decision process. The commitment stage in a relationship involves promises by both buyer and seller to work together over many transactions, not just a single decision.

DISSOLUTION

Dissolution can occur at any time in the relationship process, though it doesn't necessarily have to occur at all. Dissolution is the process of terminating the relationship and can occur because of poor performance, clash in culture, change in needs, and other factors. When dissolution occurs in latter stages of the relationship, the loss of investments made in the relationship can be significant and have an impact throughout both organizations.

CHARACTERISTICS OF SUCCESSFUL PARTNERSHIPS

Successful relationships involve cultivating mutual benefits as the partners learn to trust and depend on each other more and more. As trust develops, buyer and salesperson can resolve conflicts as they arise, settle differences, and compromise when necessary. Without trust there is no loyalty, and unhappy customers leave. While trust is important, other elements also characterize successful long-term relationships. The five foundational elements of strategic partnerships are

Exhibit 13.4
Foundations of
Successful Relationships

(1) mutual trust, (2) open communication, (3) common goals, (4) commitment to mutual gain, and (5) organizational support (see Exhibit 13.4).

MUTUAL TRUST

The most important element in the development of successful long-term customer relationships is trust. **Trust** is a belief by one party that the other party will fulfill its obligations in a relationship. That trust has to be mutual, however. When salespeople and buyers trust each other, they are more willing to share relevant ideas, clarify goals and problems, and communicate more efficiently. Information shared between the parties becomes increasingly comprehensive, accurate, and timely. There is less need for salesperson and buyer to constantly monitor each other's actions because both believe the other party would not take advantage of them if given the opportunity.

Trust is an important building block for long-term relationships. A study of partnerships in both Latin America and Europe found trust to be the most important variable that contributes to the success of the relationship.[18] Trust is a combination of five factors: dependability, competence, customer orientation, honesty, and likability. In this section we discuss these factors and how salespeople demonstrate their own trustworthiness.

Dependability

Dependability, the buyer's perception that the salesperson, and the product and company he or she represents, will live up to promises made, is not something a salesperson can demonstrate immediately. Promises must be made and then kept. Early in the selling process, a salesperson can demonstrate dependability by calling at times agreed to, showing up a few minutes early for appointments, and providing information as promised.

Third-party references can be useful in proving dependability, especially if the salesperson has not yet had an opportunity to prove it personally. If the seller can point to a similar situation and illustrate, through the words of another customer, how the situation was resolved, the buyer can verify the seller's dependability. Some companies also prepare case studies of how they solved a particular customer's problem to aid salespeople in proving the company's dependability.

Product demonstrations, plant tours, and other special types of presentations can also illustrate dependability. A product demonstration can show how the product will work, even under difficult conditions. A buyer for appliance component parts was concerned about one company's ability to produce the large volumes required. The salesperson offered a plant tour to prove that the company could live up to its promises of on-time delivery. When the buyer saw the size of the plant and the employees' dedication to making quality products, she was convinced.

The salesperson's prior experience and training can also be used to prove dependability. For a company (and a salesperson) to remain in business, there must be some level of dependability. Length of experience, however, is a weak substitute for proving dependability with action.

As time goes on and the relationship grows, the buyer assumes dependability. For example, a buyer may say, "Well, let's call Sue at Mega. We know we can depend on her." At this point the salesperson has developed a reputation within the account as dependable. But reputations can spread beyond that account through the buyer's community. A reputation for dependability, however, can be quickly lost if the salesperson fails to continue to deliver as promised.

Competence

Salespeople demonstrate **competence** when they can show that they know what they are talking about. Knowledge of the customer, the product, the industry, and the competition are all necessary to the success of the salesperson; in fact, recent research suggests that competence is a key component in developing trust.[19] Through the use of this knowledge, a salesperson demonstrates competence. For example, when a pharmaceutical representative can discuss the treatment of a disease in medical terms, the physician is more likely to believe that the rep is medically competent.

Salespeople recognize the need to appear competent. Unfortunately their recognition of the importance of competence may lead them to try to fake knowledge. Because buyers test the trustworthiness of a seller early in the relationship, they may ask questions just to see the salesperson's response. Salespeople should never make up a response to a tough question; if you don't know, say so but promise to get the answer quickly and then do it. At the same time, salespeople should try to present information objectively. Buyers can tell when salespeople are exaggerating the performance of their products.

Product knowledge is the minimum; customers expect salespeople to know everything about their own products and their company. That's why company training is so important. Johnson and Johnson's Vistakon division, which serves the contact lens market, provides eight weeks of training to new salespeople as you can see in Exhibit 13.5. One-fourth of that training is devoted to products, but a significant amount of additional training covers competitors, customers, and other market factors that salespeople need to know to be competent members of the industry. In addition to product competence, though, selling competence is also important. Much of the training focuses on increasing salespersons' selling competence so they can deliver the appropriate solutions to meet customers' needs. The result is a highly competent sales force that works in partnership with customers, helping them to run their businesses more successfully.[20]

Customer Orientation

Customer orientation is the degree to which the salesperson puts the customer's needs first. Salespeople who think only of making sales are sales-oriented rather than customer-oriented. Buyers perceive salespeople as customer-oriented when sellers stress benefits and solutions to problems over features. Buyers who perceive that a product is tailored to their unique requirements are likely to infer

Exhibit 13.5

Vistakon New Hire
Training and
Development

- On-boarding: 4 weeks
  - Week 1: District manager orientation and home study.
  - Week 2: Work with peer coach and home study.
  - Week 3: Work with field sales trainer in trainer's territory.
  - Week 4: Attend preceptorship and work with district manager to get certification.
- Primary sales school
  - Weeks 5 and 6: Attend primary sales school.
- Sales development
  - Week 7: Work with district manager in own territory.
  - Week 8: Field sales trainer works with rep in the rep's territory.
- Advanced sales development seminar
  - 2 weeks.

a customer orientation. Stating pros and cons can also be perceived as being customer-oriented because understanding the cons also indicates that the salesperson understands the buyer's needs.

Emphasizing the salesperson's availability and desire to provide service also indicates a customer orientation. For example, the statement "Call me anytime for anything that you need" indicates availability. Offering the numbers for toll-free hot lines, voice mail, and similar concrete information indicates a desire to respond promptly to the buyer and can serve as proof of a customer orientation. Most of Raymond James representative Jeff Pope's customers, for example, have his home phone and his cell phone numbers.

Several studies show that customer orientation is vital to achieving sales performance and customer satisfaction. One survey of salespeople showed customer orientation as a critical variable in predicting sales success;[21] similarly, a study of buyers found that buyers are more loyal and more willing to tell others when their salesperson is customer-oriented.[22]

Honesty

Honesty is both truthfulness and sincerity. While honesty is highly related to dependability ("We can count on you and your word because you are honest"), it is also related to how candid a salesperson is. For example, giving pros and cons can increase perceptions of honesty as well as a customer orientation.

Honesty is also related to competence. As we said earlier, salespeople must be willing to admit that they do not know something rather than trying to fake it; buyers consider salespeople who bluff to be dishonest.

The opposite, of course, is lying. Buyers figure out pretty quickly when they've been lied to; one salesperson lied to his customer about the expected response to the marketing program he sold. When it failed, not only did the customer refuse to purchase again, he threatened to blow up the salesperson's house![23] Although not every customer who has been lied to will threaten physical harm, without honesty, a customer cannot trust a salesperson. As discussed in Chapter 2, lying will not just cost a salesperson business in the short term; the long-term damage can be quite serious to the success of the business and may bring on lawsuits or criminal charges.

Likability

According to research, likability may be the least important component of trust because most people can be nice, although in some countries other than the United States, likability is much more important.[24] **Likability** refers to behaving in a friendly manner and finding a common ground between buyer and seller. Although likability is not as important as other dimensions, salespeople should still attempt to find a common ground or interest with all buyers. Buyers resent any attempts, though, of insincere rapport building. Do not feign interest if you truly aren't interested.

Likability can also be influenced with personal communications such as birthday cards, handwritten notes, and so forth. Many businesses send holiday cards and gifts to all customers, but personal touches make these gestures meaningful.

As you have probably noticed, the five dimensions of trust are tightly interrelated. Honesty affects customer orientation, which also influences dependability, for example. Salespeople should recognize the interdependence among these factors rather than simply focusing on one or two. For example, at one time many salespeople emphasized only likability. In today's market, professional salespeople must also be competent, dependable, honest, and customer-oriented.

OPEN COMMUNICATION

Open and honest communication is a key building block for developing successful relationships. Buyers and salespeople in a relationship need to understand what is driving each other's business, their roles in the relationship, each firm's strategies, and any problems that arise over the course of the relationship. (Chapter 4 focuses on approaches for improving communication.) Such understanding comes through listening carefully to buyers. In fact, research shows that listening is important for building both trust and customer satisfaction.[25]

Open communication should lead to stronger relationships, though Suzanne Morgan, president of Print Buyers Online (a buying group for commercial printers), worries that concern for the other party may make customers reluctant to share their opinions when something goes wrong. Buyers, perhaps more so than sellers, may worry about hurting the salesperson's feelings, and thus not be as open as the situation requires. She recommends, as does David Dennis of SBC Advertising, that salespeople make it as easy as possible for the buyer to speak up.[26]

One difference between a relational partnership and a strategic partnership is the strength and number of lines of communication. In a relational partnership, most communication between the buyer and the selling organization goes through the salesperson. In a strategic partnership, there will be more direct communication ties between the buying organization and the selling organization. For example, the selling company's shipping department may talk directly with the buying organization's receiving department when a problem arises with a shipment.

Cultural differences in communication style can be easily misunderstood and thus hinder open and honest communication. For example, all cultures have ways to avoid saying no when they really mean no. In Japan maintaining long-lasting, stable relationships is very important. To avoid damaging a relationship, customers rarely say no directly. Some phrases used in Japan to say no indirectly are "It's very difficult," "We'll think about it," and "I'm not sure"; alternatively, customers may leave the room with an apology. In general, when Japanese customers do not say yes or no directly, it means they want to say no.

COMMON GOALS

Salespeople and customers must have common goals for a successful relationship to develop. Shared goals give both members of the relationship a strong incentive to pool their strengths and abilities. When goals are shared, the partners can focus on exploiting opportunities rather than arguing about who will benefit the most from the relationship.

Shirley Hunter is an account executive for Teradata (a division of NCR) and has only one account, EDS. Her primary job is to help EDS sell Teradata as a part of the solutions EDS offers its clients. Hunter spends most of her time coordinating the efforts of Teradata and EDS salespeople selling to end users, but it is important that she understands EDS's goals and that she makes sure that everyone in Teradata understands and shares those goals.

Shared goals also help sustain the partnership when the expected benefit flows are not realized. If one Teradata shipment fails to reach an EDS customer on time because of an uncontrollable event, such as misrouting by a trucking firm, EDS will not suddenly call off the whole arrangement. Instead EDS is likely to view the incident as a simple mistake and will remain in the relationship. EDS knows that it and Teradata are committed to the same goal in the long run.

Clearly defined, measurable goals are also very important. Hunter has a sales budget she has to meet; but more important, the two organizations set joint goals such as sales revenue, on-time delivery, service response time, and others. Performance is assessed monthly to determine if these goals are being met so the two organizations can work together to rectify any problems quickly.

Effective measuring of performance is particularly critical in the early stages of the partnership. The achievement of explicitly stated goals lays the groundwork for a history of shared success, which serves as a powerful motivation for continuing the relationship and working closely together into the future.

COMMITMENT TO MUTUAL GAIN

Members of successful partnerships actively work to create win–win relationships by making commitments to the relationship. For example, SRI provides scanning services to GRM, one of the largest box storage companies in the world. GRM then sells these services to its customers. SRI arranged free training for the GRM salespeople. While this training would increase sales of all of GRM's services, SRI also knew that more scanning services would get sold, too.

In a partnership, commitment to mutual gain means that one does not take advantage of the other. One party is always more powerful than the other party, but in a partnership, it does not exercise that power over the other. Mutual dependence creates a cooperative spirit. Both parties search for ways to expand the pie and minimize time spent on resolving conflicts over how to split it.

Mutual Investment

As a successful relationship develops, both parties make investments in the relationship. **Mutual investments** are tangible investments in the relationship by both parties. They go beyond merely making the hollow statement "I want to be a partner." Mutual investment may involve spending money to improve the products and services sold to the other party, though research says that sellers tend to invest more in relationships than buyers.[27] For example, a firm may hire or train employees, invest in equipment, and develop computer and communication systems to meet the needs of a specific customer. These investments signal the partner's commitment to the relationship in the long run and are important to securing loyalty.[28]

Thus it is not enough to say that you are committed to the relationship; actions of commitment must follow to signal that the commitment is real. These actions make the commitment believable. Mutual investments are also called **relationship-specific assets;** in other words, these are resources specific to the relationship and cannot be easily transferred to another relationship.

ORGANIZATIONAL SUPPORT

Another critical element in fostering good relationships is giving **boundary-spanning employees**—those employees who cross the organizational boundary and interact with customers or vendors—the necessary support. Some areas of support are training, rewards that support partnering behavior, and structure and culture. We start with structure and culture because these elements foster the others.

Structure and Culture

The organizational structure and management provide the necessary support for the salespeople and buyers in a partnering relationship. All employees in the firm need to "buy in"—in other words, accept the salesperson's and buyer's roles in developing the partnership. Partnerships created at headquarters should be recognized and treated as such by local offices, and vice versa. Without the support of the respective companies, the partnership is destined to fail.

The issue isn't just creating a culture among salespeople, however. The entire firm must have an orientation to building partnerships. Recall that strategic partnerships are characterized by direct, open communication between multiple members of both firms. If those nonselling members of the selling firm do not have a customer orientation, then the partnership may be doomed.

Training

Special training is required to sell effectively in a relationship-building environment. Salespeople need to be taught how to identify customer needs and work with customers to achieve better performance.

Steve Trerotola, of Alfa Color Imaging Inc., constantly trains his salespeople in relationship skills, needs identification skills, and other sales skills. In fact, he regularly puts salespeople in situations where he knows customers might need services the company can't offer and then waits to see if the rep overpromises or exaggerates company capabilities. These opportunities are used to train the rep how to respond in ways that improve, not damage, the relationship.[29]

Training is vital in helping salespeople identify ways to make it easier for customers to do business with them. At Alcoa Aluminum sales representatives are trained to look at what their customers do to a product that Alcoa could make for them. For example, one salesperson noticed that customers stack materials in skids in various size stacks, sometimes 10 feet tall. When an order is pulled from inventory, a forklift driver must go into the stacks and pull a particular skid. Sometimes the skids are not stacked with a packing ticket on the outside, so the driver has a hard time identifying the right skid. Alcoa began to put packing tickets on both ends of skids so drivers can always see the package numbers, no matter how the skids are stacked.

Rewards

Reward systems on both sides of the relationship should be coordinated to encourage supportive behaviors. In market exchanges buyers are rewarded for wringing out concessions from the salespeople, and salespeople are rewarded on the basis of sales volume. In a partnering relationship, rewarding short-term behaviors can be detrimental. For example, recent research regarding sales contests indicates that these short-term compensation events lead to short-term behaviors, such as getting sales at the expense of relationships.[30]

SELLING YOURSELF

Relationships are important in every area of life. As your faculty can tell you, some students want a transactional relationship (just come to class and get the grade) while others want a deeper relationship. If you use the Selling Partners mentor group on LinkedIn, you'll meet many sales professionals, many of whom are former students of instructors who use this book. These sales professionals developed deeper relationships with their sales instructors.

Faculty, though, are like customers in the sense that not all faculty want to develop deeper relationships with students. When they do want deeper relationships, it is likely to be with students who show an interest in the class and who are worthy of the professor's trust. That means students who are dependable, competent, honest, and likable. A professor with a deeper relationship will understand your job interests more completely, putting you in line for positions not directly available, providing access to job markets in the same way a customer may provide a salesperson with access to markets. While the concepts of this chapter are derived directly from research into business relationships, you can see how these concepts can apply now in your relationships with others.

SUMMARY

As we discussed in Chapter 1, many businesses are moving toward partnering strategies. A key premise is that long-term relationships can enable sellers to capture much, if not all, of a customer's lifetime value. Loyal buyers buy more and are willing to work more closely with sellers in mutually beneficial ways. However, most transactions between buyers and sellers will not be strategic partnerships. Many exchanges will continue to be market transactions and functional relationships.

Functional relationships and strategic partnerships are characterized by a mutual concern of each party for the long-run welfare of the other party. Both types of long-term relationships are based on mutual trust. However, strategic partnerships involve the greatest commitment because the parties are willing to make significant investments in the relationship.

Mutual trust, open communication, common goals, a commitment to mutual gain, and organizational support are key ingredients in successful relationships. These five factors form the foundation for win–win relationships between customers and salespeople.

Customers trust salespeople who are dependable, capable, and concerned about the customers' welfare. To build trust, salespeople need to be consistent in meeting the commitments they make to customers. Salespeople also need to demonstrate their concern for the well-being of customers.

KEY TERMS

attitudinal loyalty   352
awareness   359
behavioral loyalty   351
boundary-spanning employees   366
commitment   361
competence   363
customer lifetime value (CLV)   350
customer orientation   363
customer satisfaction   354
dependability   362
dissolution   361
expansion   361
exploration   360
functional relationship   354

honesty   364
knowledge management technology   359
lead user   358
likability   364
market exchange   353
mutual investment   366
relational partnership   355
relationship marketing   351
relationship-specific assets   366
solo exchange   354
strategic partnership   355
supplier relationship management (SRM)   359
trust   362
win–win relationship   355

ETHICS PROBLEMS

1. If partnerships are win–win, does that mean that market exchanges are win–lose? Is there an ethical difference between win–win and win–lose? Does the customer's value equation [recall from Chapter 1 that Value = Benefits − (Selling price + Time and effort)] have to be equal in profit to the seller's profit equation for a transaction to be ethical?

2. A customer is loyal to one of your competitors, but the contract is expiring soon. A request for proposals (RFP) has been written and issued; but the way it is written, only that competitor can win the contract renewal. You know that your product and service could satisfy the needs of the company better. Is there an ethics problem here? If so, what is it and why? If not, why not?

QUESTIONS AND PROBLEMS

1. When might relational partnerships become potentially dangerous for selling companies? Or should companies encourage salespeople to develop relational partnerships with all accounts? Why or why not?

2. Which is more important to the seller: attitudinal or behavioral loyalty? Why? What can a salesperson do to increase loyalty in buyers? How does loyalty relate to customer lifetime value?

3. Why do customers make relationships more difficult in tough economic times? In "Building Partnerships 13.1" some ideas are presented to help salespeople when times are tough. But the author of the article says that these ideas are useful in good times, too. Why or how?

4. How can a company use technology to strengthen a relationship with a buying organization? With consumers? (Be sure to review "Sales Technology 13.1.")

5. Which factors should a salesperson consider when deciding the type of relationship formed with a customer? How would these factors change when considering functional relationships versus strategic partnerships? What factors should the customer consider?

6. How do buyers calculate profit, or value? What is the role of the relationship type in increasing buyer profit? What role does satisfaction play in calculating profit?

7. Kevin Clonch, in the opening profile, describes several factors in his business that seem to make deeper relationships between customers and vendors more important. What are they?

8. Assume you have a functional relationship with a buyer. You have been informed that the next order placed by the buyer is going to be shipped late. The buyer has already told you that the order must be delivered on time. You contact the factory and cannot do anything to speed up delivery. What should you do next? Does relationship type matter in your decision, and if so, how? If not, why not?

9. There are five foundational elements to strategic partnerships. How do these differ for relational partnerships? Functional relationships? What if four of the five are strong—what type of relationship is that?

CASE PROBLEMS

case **13.1**

How to Lose an Account

Robert Lawrence was aghast. Despite practicing the sales call four times, despite being told before the sales call exactly what to say when the question arose, and despite being directed by the account manager how to respond while in the sales call, the regional director of service still blew it—and away walked a $5.5 million customer.

Robert, branch manager for Mobile Connections, knew that the customer, Health Resources of Texas (HRT), was having problems with two of the copiers provided by Mobile. Further, these were reoccurring problems that should be resolved by replacing the equipment. To make matters worse, one of the problem copiers was used by Sharon Collins, one of the decision makers. He knew that Sharon was going to raise the issue of how Mobile would handle "lemons" and whether Mobile would honor its replacement promise. The service director was also aware of the problems but had not processed the request to replace them yet, so he didn't know with certainty whether the free replacement copiers would be approved. But Robert had rehearsed with Tony Lagera, the service director, to say that the company was reviewing the request and the copiers would either be replaced in the week or shifted to areas with less volume.

Sharon raised the question, just as Robert expected. And Tony flubbed it. He hemmed. He hawed. He did everything but answer the question directly. Unfortunately Robert couldn't just answer for Tony—the service area was Tony's responsibility, not Robert's. Robert and the account manager sat in stunned silence.

After the call, Robert asked, "So, Tony, how do you think it went?"

"Fine, Robert!" he replied with a smile. "You were right on target about Sharon's question."

"And you think you handled it?"

"Oh yes—I think she really liked my response!"

Robert didn't respond, though he thought about asking Tony why she repeated the question four times. Two weeks later, Robert got a copy of the letter that went to his salesperson, thanking Mobile for the presentation but informing them that Mobile would not be allowed to bid on the job. After serving HRT for three years without any hitch other than those two machines (and there were over 100 machines), Mobile wasn't even going to get a chance to bid.

Questions

1. Things had gone well with this account overall. What, though, were the critical issues in determining the customer's satisfaction that led to the loss of the customer? Was the problem simply a lack of satisfaction with the product? Using concepts from the chapter, describe how the customer's value equation was influenced by the experiences both before the call and during the call.

2. Was there anything the sales rep or his boss, Robert Lawrence, could have done after the sales call to save the business?

3. Not only were there no other problems during the previous three-year contract, but Mobile had originally won the business away from a competitor and significantly improved HRT's situation. Why didn't that enter the picture?

Source: This really happened, but the names have been changed to protect privacy. Used with permission.

case **13.2**

Pilgrim Plumbing

Frank Pilgrim returned from the Korean war and started a commercial plumbing company that provided subcontractor services for companies building commercial buildings. Frank and his crew traveled all over Florida, Georgia, and Alabama while based in a small central Florida town called Orlando. Of course Disney came along, Orlando exploded, and Pilgrim found he could stay home and have plenty of work. In 1994 Pilgrim retired, turning the company over to his son and daughter, twins that had grown up in the business. John handled installations and service, while Jackie took care of the books and sales.

One of the mainstays in Pilgrim's customer portfolio has always been Pledger Construction. The company was a major player in the construction boom in Orlando and has continued to grow with construction projects across the Southeast. Pledger once accounted for about 60 percent of Pilgrim's business, but other customers have grown in size. Now, with 8 percent of Pilgrim's total sales volume, Pledger is the sixth largest account (the top five ranging from 9 percent to 12 percent). Recently, though, Pledger has experienced significant growth and has been pressing Pilgrim for price concessions to continue its growth. Growth for the account could be as much as 25 percent over the next year, but Pledger's strategy seems to be entirely based on being the lowest cost.

"Jackie, look, we've grown up together. You know we're growing like wildfire," said Chris Pledger, grandson of the founder of Pledger Construction and a lifelong friend, "and I'd hate to have to go to someone new after all these years. You've got to do better on this bid for the new Marriott resort."

"Chris, I'd like to, but if I cut that any more, I'm likely to take a loss," she said. The conversation dragged to an end after Chris reiterated his threat to take his plumbing business elsewhere.

After that phone call came another, this one from Southern Prime Contractors (SPC). SPC was a brand new company six short years ago and now is half the size of Pledger. "Jackie, I'd like to bid on the new Marriott resort. Can I count on you to provide us with a bid similar to the Gaylord job?" asked Mario Medrano, a project manager at SPC. The Gaylord job was a large, world-class resort that was the jewel in the crown of SPC's brief history. Pilgrim's margin on that job was a full 50 percent more than Pledger was offering Jackie on this new project.

"Can I get back to you on that, Mario?" asked Jackie. "I've got to talk that over with John first." She glanced up as John entered the room. "Let me call you back—shouldn't take but about 10 minutes." She hung up the phone as John sat down.

Questions

1. Should Jackie prepare one bid and give it to both Pledger and SPC? Or should she prepare a separate bid for each, or go with only one company? Why? If only one company is chosen, which one should it be, and why?
2. What information would you like to know before you make that decision?

ROLE PLAY CASE

As with other role plays, you are a salesperson for Netsuite software. For additional information about Netsuite, you may want to review the information in the Netsuite role play at the end of Chapter 1; additional information can also be found at the end of the text.

ConsumerTel is a manufacturer and distributor of cell phone accessories, such as cell phone cases, hands-free sets, extra power cords, and other products. The company has 24 salespeople who call on retailers, which then sell the accessories to consumers. There are two sales managers and one national sales vice president.

Seller: You are calling on the national sales vice president, and you would like to understand that person's interest in relationship type. Take a few minutes and prepare some questions that you think will help you determine which relationship will be appropriate. After you are finished, tell the buyer what relationship type (choose only one) you thought you were dealing with and why. See if you were right!

Buyer: As you role-play the buyer, pick one of the relationship types. Before the role play starts, think about how you would answer the questions you developed. Also consider what your expectations would be in terms of after-sale service, pricing, and the like based on the relationship type you select.

Note: There is no additional information provided in the Instructor's Manual for this assignment. However, teaching notes are provided.

ADDITIONAL REFERENCES

Backstrom, Lars, "Trusting Relationships: How Salespeople View the Quality of Relationships with Friends and Customers," *Management Dynamics* 17, no. 3 (2008), pp. 20–27.

Belonax Jr., Joseph J., Stephen J. Newell, and Richard J. Plank. "The Role of Purchase Importance on Buyer Perceptions of the Trust and Expertise Components of Supplier and Salesperson Credibility in Business-to-Business Relationships." *Journal of Personal Selling & Sales Management* 27, no. 3 (2007), pp. 247–61.

Camarero, Carmen. "Relationship Orientation or Service Quality? What Is the Trigger of Performance in Financial and Insurance Services?" *The International Journal of Bank Marketing* 25, no. 6 (2007), pp. 406–19.

Carr, Jon C., and Tará Burnthorne Lopez. "Examining Market Orientation as Both Culture and Conduct: Modeling the Relationships between Market Orientation and Employee Responses." *Journal of Marketing Theory and Practice* 15, no. 2 (2007), pp. 113–24.

Clark, Paul, Richard A. Rocco, and Alan J. Bush. "Perceiving Emotion in the Buyer–Seller Interchange: The Moderated Impact on Performance." *Journal of Personal Selling & Sales Management* 27, no. 2 (2007), pp. 119–32.

Doney, Patricia M., James M. Barry, and Russell Abratt. "Trust Determinants and Outcomes in Global B2B Services." *European Journal of Marketing* 41, no. 9–10 (2007), pp. 1096–110.

Feng-Cheng Tung. "Using the E-CRM Information System in the Hi-Tech Industry: Predicting Salesperson Intentions." *Journal of American Academy of Business* 11, no. 2 (2007), pp. 131–45.

Gee, Robert, Graham Coates, and Mike Nicholson. "Understanding and Profitably Managing Customer Loyalty." *Marketing Intelligence & Planning* 26, no. 4 (2008), pp. 359–73.

Hulten, Bertil. "Customer Segmentation: The Concepts of Trust, Commitment, and Relationships." *Journal of Targeting, Measurement and Analysis for Marketing* 15, no. 4 (2007), pp. 256–71.

Kidwell, Blair, Richard G. McFarland, and Ramon A. Avila. "Perceiving Emotion in the Buyer–Seller Interchange: The Moderated Impact on Performance." *The Journal of Personal Selling & Sales Management* 27, no. 2 (2007), pp. 119–30.

Kilic, Ceyhan, and Turkan Dursun. "Antecedences and Consequences of Customer Orientation: Do Individual Factors Affect Customer Orientation?" *The Business Review* 7, no. 1 (2007), pp. 19–32.

Kilic, Ceyhan, and Turkan Dursun. "The Effect of Organizational Culture on Customer Orientation." *Journal of the Academy of Business* 15, no. 2 (2010), pp. 1–7.

Liu, Sandra S., and Lucette B. Comer. "Salespeople as Information Gatherers: Associated Success Factors." *Industrial Marketing Management* 36, no. 5 (2007), pp. 565–81.

Long, Mary M., Thomas Tellefsen, and J. David Lichtenthal. "Internet Integration into the Industrial Selling Process: A Step-by-Step Approach." *Industrial Marketing Management* 36, no. 5 (2007), pp. 676–89.

Muir, Clive. "Relationship-Building and Sales Success: Are Climate and Leadership Key?" *Academy of Management Perspectives* 21, no. 1 (2007), pp. 71–90.

Musalem, Andrés, and Yogesh V. Joshi. "How Much Should You Invest in Each Customer Relationship? A Competitive Strategic Approach." *Marketing Science* 28, no. 3 (May/June 2009), pp. 555–67.

Palmatier, Robert W., Lisa K. Scheer, Jan Benedict, and E. M. Steenkamp. "Customer Loyalty to Whom? Managing the Benefits and Risks of Salesperson-Owned Loyalty." *Journal of Marketing* 44, no. 2 (2007), pp. 185–99.

Piercy, Nigel F., David W. Cravens, and Nikala Lane. "Enhancing Salespeople's Effectiveness." *Marketing Management* 16, no. 9–10 (2007), pp. 18–29.

Rauyruen, Papassapa, and Kenneth E. Miller. "Relationship Quality as a Predictor of B2B Customer Loyalty." *Journal of Business Research* 60, no. 1 (2007), pp. 21–38.

Sanzo, Maria José, Maria Leticia Santos, Luis I. Alvarez, and Rodolfo Vazquez. "The Effect of a Buyer's Marketing Orientation on Attitudinal Loyalty toward a Supplier: Is Dependence a Moderator?" *Supply Chain Management* 12, no. 4 (2007), pp. 267–78.

Schwepker Jr., Charles H., and David J. Good. "Exploring the Relationships among Sales Manager Goals, Ethical Behavior and Professional Commitment in the Salesforce: Implications for Forging Customer Relationships." *Journal of Relationship Marketing* 6, no. 1 (2007), pp. 3–14.

Sharma, Arun. "The Shift in Sales Organizations in Business-to-Business Services Markets." *Journal of Services Marketing* 21, no. 5 (2007), pp. 326–39.

van Triest, Sander, Maurice J. G. Bun, Erik M. van Raaij, and Maarten J. A. Vernooij. "The Impact of Customer-Specific Marketing Expenses on Customer Retention and Customer Profitability." *Marketing Letters* 20, no. 2 (June 2009), pp. 125–38.

chapter

14

BUILDING LONG-TERM PARTNERSHIPS

SOME QUESTIONS ANSWERED IN THIS CHAPTER ARE

- How important is service after the sale?
- How should salespeople stay in contact with customers?
- Which sales strategies stimulate repeat sales and new business in current accounts?
- Which techniques are important to use when handling complaints?

PROFILE

PROFILE I'm a strong believer that "You can have everything you want in life if you can help enough others get what they want out of life." This saying is especially true when trying to create successful long-term relationships.

I love everything about sales, and I knew early in my career that I wanted to be in sales. To do great things you must go above average and do what the average person won't. This belief has led me on a fast track to reach my career goals sooner than I anticipated. I joined Kennesaw State's sales team in the National Collegiate Sales Competition, then graduated with a professional sales degree. During this time I was very fortunate to really see what every day was like in the life of a sales rep through an internship with ADP, the world's number one payroll and human resources (HR) company. After shadowing a few very successful reps and seeing a day in the life of an ADP rep, I was so excited that I was even more driven and could hardly wait to start my own sales career. I was ready!

I quickly realized that my client relationships are the most important factor in determining my success. I spend about 50 percent of my time nurturing these relationships. Although selling payroll and HR services may seem like a transactional relationship, I try to make most customer relationships long-term. Strong relationships are important because I grow my business from referrals.

These relationships differentiate me from my competitors. Unlike most sales reps in my industry, who try to get in, close the sale, and get out, I try to create a long-lasting relationship. My strategy works because many of my clients have been shocked that unlike many of their payroll reps that win their business they claim they never see ever again, mine see me regularly. I value my relationships, knowing this is what my clients want and appreciate. However, I always determine what kind of relationship the client will be before I spend too much time on certain relationships. Some clients are in fact just transactional if I know that there is no value to either party and they simply need payroll. Others, such as franchise owners, investors, or restaurant owners, can gain value from a long-term relationship.

Once I've gained my clients' trust and I feel like I have their loyalty, I can go to them for business just like I would ask a friend for referrals. In fact, some of my clients know me so well and we have such a great relationship that they ask me to randomly stop by, and if they haven't seen me stop by for weeks, they will call to see where I've been. These are the kind of relationships that help me get to where I need to be. In fact, I'm so close to these clients that they always know when I'm trying to hit a goal or win a trip, and when they see me running through the door they laugh and know I'm expecting referrals. . .and they always pull through for me. In fact, I was short by two deals and I had only 24 hours left in order to qualify to win my very first trip, so I went to one of my clients. We had such a great relationship that he called another one of his friends in the restaurant industry using my competitor and booked the appointment for me. Needless to say, the owner not only gave me his business but referred me to one of his friends who also signed up for me, all within 24 hours. I won my very first company trip. . .all because of the relationship I had created with my client!

I often determine immediately after meeting with a prospect if I will make it a long-term or short-term relationship depending on the value of the relationship and if it will be beneficial. Because my sales are a short cycle, many of my clients that I have long-term relationships with all became more personal after the sale. For instance, I signed up a restaurant owner on a one-call close, and throughout the sales call I determined that I wanted to make this new client of mine a long-term relationship because of his value. Throughout the call I built rapport and found out that he was an investor with many other small businesses that I could potentially win over after he gained my trust. I also try to build long-term relationships with clients I know will be growing, opening more locations, or work in an industry selling to other small business. These are all great partnerships for me.

Because I work from referrals, I know that I must create trust and likability. Most of my clients know me on a personal level. Your clients must like you or they won't refer you. I always let them know that I have their best interest at heart, and I go out of my way to bring them business. After signing up a new client I always send out a mass e-mail to my clients I've signed up with my new client's business info and their contact. For example, one client had just opened up a tanning salon, so I send out a mass e-mail with his coupon to all my clients in the area and asked two of my clients to have his flyers on their counter (one being a new restaurant, another being a day care), and in return my new client put those two clients' info on his counter. My clients love to see me working for them. I send out monthly e-mails with all my clients' contacts for one another with coupons to generate business for one another. I make it a point to know that I appreciate their business and I want to help them out. Any opportunities I get to take a prospect or client out, I always make sure it is at one of my long-term clients' locations. I also send out coupons and grand openings for new clients to all of my partners.

I get to really know my clients. I'd like to believe that all my long-term clients are friends. It's important for me to know that they feel as though they aren't just another sale. I make a huge effort to keep my clients satisfied. I take notes on their personal lives and follow up. For example, my client's father was ill, so I made a reminder to call him over the next couple of weeks to find out how he was doing because that's what you do with friends. These foundations have allowed me to hit a lot of my goals over the short amount of time I've been with my company—goals I didn't even know I was capable of reaching.

Visit our Web site at www.adp.com.

As we discussed in the previous chapter, relationships go through several stages, beginning with awareness and ending in dissolution. In this chapter we focus on the three stages between awareness and dissolution—exploration, expansion, and commitment—as illustrated in Exhibit 14.1. As you read the rest of the chapter, you will see how trust is built and maintained throughout the life of the partnership.

EXPLORATION

In the exploration stage, the relationship is defined through the development of expectations for each party. The buyer tests the seller's product, how the seller responds to requests, and other similar actions after the initial sale is made.

Exhibit 14.1
Stages of Partnerships

A small percentage of the buyer's business is given to minimize the risk in case the vendor cannot perform. When the vendor performs well, trust is developed, as is a personal relationship.

Beginning the relationship properly is important if the relationship is going to last a long time. Keep in mind that the customer is excited about receiving the benefits of the product as promised by the salesperson. An unfavorable initial experience with the product or with the company may be extremely difficult to overcome. Beginning the relationship properly requires that the salesperson set the right expectations, monitor order processing, ensure proper use of the product, and assist in servicing the product.

SET THE RIGHT EXPECTATIONS

The best way to begin a relationship is for each party to be aware of what the other expects. To a large degree, customers base their expectations on sales presentations.

Salespeople should make sure customers have reasonable expectations of product performance. If the salesperson exaggerates the capabilities of the product or the company, the customer will be disappointed. Admitting there has been a misunderstanding will not satisfy a customer who has registered a complaint. Avoiding complaints by setting proper expectations is best. Long-term relationships are begun by making an honest presentation of the product's capabilities and eliminating any misconceptions before the order is placed. In "From the Buyer's Seat 14.1" Steve Hinsch, fleet manager for Clarke County in Athens, Georgia, shares his expectations when buying equipment for the county.

MONITOR ORDER PROCESSING

Although many people may work on an order before it is shipped, the salesperson is ultimately responsible, at least in the eyes of the customer, for seeing that the product is shipped when promised. Salespeople should keep track of impending orders and inform buyers when the paperwork is delayed in the customer's plant. Orders placed directly with a salesperson should be transmitted to the factory immediately. Also, progress on orders in process should be closely monitored. If problems arise in filling the order, the customer should be informed promptly; on the other hand, if the order can be filled sooner than promised, the customer should be notified so the proper arrangements can be made.

Fortunately computers have made the sales representative's job easier. Salespeople can use handheld terminals and notebook PCs to check inventory and order status. Progressive firms have introduced automated order systems that allow the customer to sign a pad on the computer; the signature is sent to the company electronically, avoiding delays that might result if the contract were mailed.

Many firms, such as GE and Baxter Healthcare, facilitate the automatic placement of orders by having their own computers talk to customers' computers. This technology, called **electronic data interchange,** boosts the productivity of both the salespeople and the purchasing managers they call on. As a result, salespeople spend less time writing orders and more time solving problems; buyers save on ordering and inventory costs. Computerized communication for order placement is particularly useful when managing a customer's needs worldwide. Problems arising from elements such as time zones and language barriers are minimized.

Monitoring order processing and other after-sale activities is critical to developing a partnership. Studies continually show that buyers are most often displeased with salespeople in this respect (recall Steve Hinch's comments in "From the Buyer's Seat 14.1"). Rossignol, the French ski and snowboard company, uses its CRM system to monitor order processing, ski shop inventories, and other data so salespeople can provide better after-sale service. Because skiing is a seasonal

From the BUYER'S SEAT

ROLL ON! GREAT SERVICE IN FLEET MANAGEMENT IS A MUST

By Steve Hinsch

As a fleet management superintendent for a small, semirural local government, I have found great success in the adoption of some commonsense philosophies when it comes to buying. When I first began my career with government, I was told that things always evolve at a snail's pace. I was determined to change that conception, at least in my division.

Because our customers are other government employees who utilize a variety of vehicles, equipment, and motor fuels, it is incumbent upon me to know their needs. To best provide for our customers, it is imperative that I receive products and services that are delivered on time and as described. Such high-level service is typically achieved by a vendor's provision of a Web site, product brochures, and product demonstrations. While checking some vendors is more time-consuming than others, all require some research and a possible reference. *Service after the sale* (along with my other points of criteria, *quality of product* and *price*) is essential. Sometimes references don't really pan out to an acceptable level because we stay in heavy pursuit of service after the sale. The quickest way to our blacklist is to become readily *unavailable* postsale.

I look to vendors to provide me with a kind of checklist of attributes, typically separating the novice from the veteran. I want and expect eye contact, a clear product description, performance measures, and service and warranty information along with ballpark pricing and a service after the sale agreement up front. . . .all of this hinging on an appointment. Cold calls tell me that they want to see me at all costs, but not necessarily on my timetable. If this does not scare them off and I "feel" a sincerity about the vendor, then I ask for a committed response about the need for service after the sale. I explain that postsale service is what will keep their business card in my file and their service agreement valid. And I *always* make it crystal clear that if I provide unremarkable service to my customers due to their ability to provide products or service to us, the relationship ends. I do not say these things with malicious intent, and find that the vast majority or vendors not only respect this approach but appreciate my candor.

As a brief example, I have one specific tire vendor that has provided retreads as well as new tires to us for 20 plus years. This man knows how serious I am about being frugal with taxpayer dollars and appreciates it as a local citizen. He knows that there are many vendors in this field that court our business, so he remains highly competitive. He comes to our shop once a week, and if he will be unavailable for any reason, gives us notice of an alternate contact. He provides a stellar product at a competitive price while always standing behind his product. If there is ever a problem such as a retread separating or failing prematurely, he is quick to provide a replacement product. He is the kind of vendor that will work late to provide whatever level of service we as his customer may need.

Source: Contributed by Steve Hinsch.

activity, sales are seasonal too. The company takes orders six months before shipping in order to plan ahead for the ski sale season, which is the early part of winter. But stores don't pay for the skis and snowboards until six months after shipping, or when orders are taken for the next year. Although it sounds like there is a lot of time to make sure things go smoothly, what is ordered for next year is a function of what is sold this year. The CRM system helps salespeople stay on top of how well their customers are doing in selling current inventory, so they can help sell that inventory out and make room for more. Thus the partnership is created by helping both parties achieve their goals.[1]

ENSURE PROPER INITIAL USE OF THE PRODUCT OR SERVICE

Customer dissatisfaction can occur just after delivery of a new product, especially if the product is technical or requires special installation. Customers unfamiliar with

This salesperson is training the customer in how to use the product properly. Getting customers off to the right start is essential to building long and satisfying relationships.

the product may have problems installing or using it. They may even damage the product through improper use. Many salespeople visit new customers right after initial deliveries to ensure correct use of the product. In this way they can also help the customer realize the full potential benefits of the product.

Some buyers may be knowledgeable about how to use the basic features of a product or service, but if it is not operating at maximum efficiency, the wise salesperson will show the buyer how to get more profitable use out of it. Many firms have staffed a customer service department to aid salespeople in this task. The salesperson is still responsible, however, to make sure the customer service department takes proper care of each new customer.

To be most effective, the salesperson should not wait until the user has trouble with the product. The fewer the difficulties allowed to occur, the greater will be the customer's confidence in the salesperson and the product.

FOLLOW UP

The first follow-up a salesperson should perform after the sale is a call to say thank you and to check to see that the product is working appropriately. Some salespeople use specialty advertising, or gifts imprinted with their company's name, to say thanks. These items are generally small enough to avoid concerns about bribery and can include desk clocks, pens, and the like. Chuck Gallagher, COO for American Funeral Financial, says the choice of a thank-you method is dependent on the buyer's social style. An analytical may prefer a concise e-mail message, whereas an expressive may enjoy a small gift. Rob Truss at DMG Construction also adds that the type and stage of relationship affect the choice of how thank you is said. Because his company builds buildings, the thank you may involve a big opening ceremony.[2]

Follow-up, though, doesn't stop with thank you. Salespeople should also follow up regularly with their accounts to identify any changing needs or possible problems. In fact, failing to follow up is a major complaint that buyers have about salespeople. One recent study indicated that 80 percent of sales executives believed their company provides great service, but only 8 percent of their customers agreed.[3] Why the mismatch in perceptions? Because salespeople all too often fail to follow up.

Recall, too, that different functional areas and members of the buying center had different needs to start with. Follow-up with only the users or those most directly involved with the product may result in other members of the buying center becoming dissatisfied. The nature of the follow-up should reflect their needs, which means, for example, that for a purchasing agent, follow-up should reflect the agent's concerns with the financial aspects and return on investment.[4]

Personal visits can be the most expensive form of follow-up because of the time it takes to travel and because the sales call will last longer than one conducted through other means. A personal visit, though, can be extremely productive because the salesperson can check on inventories or the performance of the machine or other aspects that can be accomplished only at the customer's site.

Plus, a customer may be more likely to disclose more information, such as a minor complaint or compliment, in a personal setting than over the phone. Regular personal visits can also build trust, a key component needed to move the relationship forward.

Between personal visits, it is often a good idea to make contact via telephone. A salesperson can make 12 or more such calls within an hour, efficiently checking on clients. Telephone calls are two-way communication, giving the customer an opportunity to voice any concerns and minimizing intrusion. Contact management software, such as NetSuite, can help salespeople schedule telephone follow-ups.

Many companies provide form letters or thank-you cards to encourage their salespeople to follow up on new sales. Salespeople can also create their own form letters and use their contact management software to generate the most appropriate mailing list. The problem, though, is that these are still form letters. Creative use of certain fields in contact management software like NetSuite, however, enables salespeople to add a personalized paragraph, creating that special touch that can dramatically increase the impact of such a letter. E-mail is also becoming a common form of customer contact, with customers appreciating the opportunity to choose when to read and respond to the salesperson's contact.

Following up with customers signals that the salesperson is dependable and customer-oriented. Although the objective may be to create a functional relationship rather than a strategic partnership, such follow-up is still necessary to remind the customer that you are the salesperson with whom they want to do business.

HANDLE CUSTOMER COMPLAINTS

Handling complaints is critical to developing goodwill and maintaining partnerships. Complaints can occur at any time in the partnering process, not just during the exploration stage; but they may be more important in the early stages of a partnership. Attempts to establish partnerships often collapse because of short-sightedness in handling customer complaints. Some firms spend thousands of dollars on advertising but make the mistake of insulting customers who attempt to secure a satisfactory adjustment.

Complaints normally arise when the company and its products do not live up to the customer's expectations. Assuming the proper expectations were set, customers can be disappointed for any of the following reasons: (1) the product performs poorly, (2) it is being used improperly, or (3) the terms of the sales contract were not met. Although salespeople usually cannot change the product or terms, they can affect these sources of complaints, minimizing them by setting proper expectations and ensuring proper use.

We've long known that people tell more friends about bad experiences than they do good experiences. Studies repeatedly show that when a company fails in its dealings with a complaint, the latter will tell twice as many people as when the experience is good. For every dissatisfied person who complains, an estimated 50 more simply stop buying the product; but handle the situation well, and repurchase intentions increase.[5] One study found that half of those told about a bad experience refused to ever consider the offending vendor.[6] Companies that can improve customer satisfaction will see positive financial results.[7]

Most progressive companies have learned that an excellent way to handle customer complaints is through personal visits by sales representatives. Thus the salesperson may have total responsibility for this portion of the company's public relations. Salespeople who carry this burden must be prepared to do an effective job.

Complaints cannot be eliminated; they can only be reduced in frequency. The salesperson who knows complaints are inevitable can learn to handle them as a

Exhibit 14.2
Responding to Complaints

normal part of the job. The following discussion presents some techniques for responding to complaints; Exhibit 14.2 provides an overview.

- Encourage buyers to tell their story.
- Determine the facts.
- Offer a solution.
- Follow through with action.

Encourage Buyers to Tell Their Story

Some customers can become angry over real or imaginary grievances. They welcome the salesperson's visit as an opportunity to voice complaints. Other buyers are less emotional in expressing complaints and give little evidence of irritation or anger, but the complaint is no less important. In either case customers need to tell their stories without interruption. Interruptions add to the irritation of emotionally upset buyers, making it almost impossible to arrive at a settlement that is fair to all parties.

Customers want a sympathetic reaction to their problems, whether real or imagined. They want their feelings to be acknowledged, their business to be recognized as important, and their grievances handled in a friendly manner. An antagonistic attitude or an attitude that implies the customer is trying to cheat the company seldom paves the way for a satisfactory adjustment. You can probably relate to this feeling if you have ever had to return a defective product or get some kind of adjustment made on a bill. Exhibit 14.3 suggests ways to handle irate customers.

Good salespeople show they are happy the grievance has been brought to their attention. After the customer describes the problem, the salesperson may express regret for any inconvenience. An attempt should then be made to talk about points of agreement. Agreeing with the customer as far as possible gets the process off to the right start.

Determine the Facts

It is easy to be influenced by a customer who is honestly making a claim for an adjustment. An inexperienced salesperson might forget that many customers make their case for a claim as strong as possible. Emphasizing the points most likely to strengthen one's case is human nature. But the salesperson has a responsibility to his or her company too. A satisfactory adjustment cannot be made until all the facts are known.

Whenever possible, the salesperson should examine, in the presence of the customer, the product claimed to be defective. Encouraging the customer to pinpoint the exact problem is a good idea. If the defect is evident, this step may be unnecessary. In other instances, make certain the complaint is understood. The purpose of getting the facts is to determine the cause of the problem so the proper solution can be provided.

Experienced salespeople soon learn that products may appear defective when actually nothing is wrong with them. For example, a buyer may complain that paint was applied exactly as directed but repainting became necessary in a short

Exhibit 14.3
Handling Rude or Irate Customers

1. Follow the Golden Rule—treat your customer the way you would like to be treated, no matter how difficult the client becomes.
2. Prove you listened—paraphrase the customer's concern, recognizing the customer's feelings along with the facts.
3. Don't justify, excuse, or blame others—be positive and thank the customer for bringing the problem to your attention so that you can resolve it.
4. Do the hard things first—the faster they get done, the more your customer will appreciate you and your efforts.
5. Call back if the customer hangs up.
6. Give the customer someone else to call, but only in case you are not available—don't pass the buck!

time; therefore, the paint was no good. However, the paint may have been spread too thin. Any good paint will cover just so much area. If the manufacturer recommends using a gallon of paint to cover 400 square feet with two coats and the user covers 600 square feet with two coats, the product is not at fault.

On the other hand, salespeople should not assume product or service failure is always the user's fault. They need an open mind to search for the facts in each case. In one instance, the paint spilled out of the bucket all over the buyer's truck while the customer took it back to Home Depot to register a complaint that the paint was too thin—like painting with milk. The Home Depot customer service representative refused to believe the buyer that the paint had spilled (even though the paint-covered truck was in the Home Depot parking lot), assuming the buyer used it and was trying to get it for free. The buyer agreed that it was reasonable to require him to take the claim up with the manufacturer, but the Home Depot clerk's assumption that the buyer lied about the missing paint cost Home Depot a $10,000 per year customer. Some companies have the policy that the customer is always right, in which case there is no need to establish responsibility. While there is still a need to determine what the cause was so the right solution can be offered, do not assume the customer is to blame.

In this phase of making an adjustment, salespeople must avoid giving the impression of stalling. The customer should know that the purpose of determining the facts is to permit a fair adjustment—that the inquiry is not being made to delay action or avoid resolution.

Offer a Solution

After the customer tells his or her story and the facts are determined, the next step is to offer a solution. At this time the company representative describes the process by which the company will resolve the complaint, and the rep should then gain agreement that the proposed solution is satisfactory. Recent research suggests that offering several solutions and allowing a customer to choose one is far more effective than telling the customer what the solution will be. Giving the customer a choice puts the customer in control, which increases satisfaction with how the compliant was handled.[8]

Company policies vary, but many assign the responsibility for settling claims to the salesperson. Other companies require the salesperson to investigate claims and recommend a settlement to the home office. Salespeople are in the best position to make adjustments fairly, promptly, and satisfactorily, especially if the customer and salesperson are geographically distant from the home office. Permitting salespeople to only recommend a course of action, though, assures the customer of attention from a higher level of management, increasing the likelihood that the customer will accept the action taken.

Whatever the company policy, the customer desires quick action and fair treatment and wants to know the reasons for the action. Most customers are satisfied if they quickly receive fair treatment. Customers are seldom convinced of the fairness of a solution that isn't exactly what they wanted unless the reasoning behind the decision is explained to them. Nothing discourages a customer more than having action postponed indefinitely or being offered vague promises. Although some decisions may take time, the salesperson should try to expedite action. The opportunity to develop a partnership may be lost if the time lapse is too great, even though action is taken in the customer's favor.

Some salespeople make disparaging remarks about their own companies or managers in an effort to shift the blame. Blaming someone else in the company is a poor practice because this behavior can cause the customer to lose faith in both the salesperson and the company. Moreover, if the customer does not like the proposed solution, the salesperson trusted to make an adjustment or recommendation should shoulder the responsibility. Any disagreement on the action taken should be ironed out between the salesperson and the home office staff. When reported to the customer, the action must be stated in a sound, convincing manner.

The action taken may vary with the circumstances. Some possible settlements when a product is unsatisfactory are

1. Replace the product without cost to the customer.
2. Replace the product and share the costs with the customer.
3. Instruct the customer on how to proceed with a claim against a third party (for example, the paint manufacturer in the Home Depot situation).
4. Send the product to the factory for a decision.

Occasionally customers make claims they know are unfair. Although they realize the company is not at fault, they still try to get a settlement. Fortunately, relatively few customers do this.

To assume that a customer is willfully trying to cheat the company would be unwise. He or she may honestly see a claim as legitimate even though the salesperson can clearly tell that the company is not at fault. The salesperson does well, then, to proceed cautiously and, if any doubt exists, to treat the claim as legitimate.

A salesperson convinced that a claim is dishonest has two ways to take action. First, he or she can give the buyer an opportunity to save face by suggesting that a third party may be to blame. For example, if a machine appears not to have been oiled for a long time, a salesperson may suggest, "Is it possible that your maintenance crew neglected to oil this machine?" Second, the salesperson can unmask the fraudulent claim and appeal to the customer's sense of fair play. This procedure may cause the loss of a customer. In some cases, however, the company may be better off without that customer.

Answers to the following questions often affect the action to be taken:

- What is the dollar value of the claim? Many firms have established standard procedures for what they classify as small claims. For example, one moving and storage firm considers any claim under $200 to be too insignificant to investigate fully; thus a refund check is issued automatically for a claim under this amount. Firms may also have a complete set of procedures and policies developed for every size of claim.

- How often has this customer made claims? If the buyer has instituted many claims in the past, the company may need to not only resolve the specific complaint but also conduct a more comprehensive investigation of all prior claims. Such a probe may reveal systematic flaws in the salesperson's company, product, or procedures. For example, Agria (a Swedish commercial insurance company) routinely examines customer complaints to determine if new services should be developed. One result is that Agria is one of the fastest-growing insurance companies in Europe.[9]

- How will the action taken affect other customers? The salesperson should assume that the action taken will be communicated to other prospects and customers. If the complaining customer is part of a buying community (discussed in Chapter 6), chances are good that others will learn about the resolution of the claim. Thus the salesperson must take actions necessary to maintain a positive presence in that community, possibly even providing a more generous solution than the merits of the case dictate.

The solution that will be provided must be clearly communicated to the customer. The customer must perceive the settlement as being fair. When describing the settlement, the salesperson should carefully monitor all verbal and nonverbal cues to determine the customer's level of satisfaction. If the customer does not agree with the proposed course of action, the salesperson should seek ways to change the settlement or provide additional information about why the settlement is fair to all parties.

Follow Through with Action

A fair settlement made in the customer's favor helps to resell the company and its products or services. The salesperson has the chance to prove what the customer has been told for a long time: that the company will devote time and effort to keeping customers satisfied.

The salesperson who has authority only to recommend an adjustment must take care to report the facts of the case promptly and accurately to the home or branch office. The salesperson has the responsibility to act as a buffer between the customer and the company. After the claim is filed, contact must be maintained with the customer to see that the customer secures the promised settlement.

The salesperson also has a responsibility to educate the customer to forestall future claims. After a claim has been settled to the customer's satisfaction is a fine time to make some suggestions. For example, the industrial sales representative may provide a new set of directions on how to oil and clean a machine.

Achieve Customer Satisfaction

Although complaints always signal customer dissatisfaction, their absence does not necessarily mean customers are happy. Customers probably voice only 1 in 20 of their concerns. They may speak out only when highly dissatisfied, or a big corporation's buyer may not be aware of problems until the product's users vent their frustration. Lower levels of dissatisfaction still hurt sales especially in today's high tech environment when a tweeted complaint can reach hundreds of followers. Salespeople should continuously monitor customers' levels of satisfaction and perceptions of product performance because customer satisfaction is the most important reason for reordering at this stage in the relationship. Some companies also monitor Twitter, as you can see in Selling Technology 14.1.

When the customer is satisfied, an opportunity for further business exists. Complaints and dissatisfaction can occur at any time during the relationship, but handling complaints well during the exploration stage is one way to prove that the salesperson is committed to keeping the customer's business. When customers sense such commitment, whether through the handling of a complaint or through other forms of special attention, they may be ready to move to the expansion stage.

EXPANSION

The next phase of the buyer–seller relationship is expansion. When a salesperson does a good job of identifying and satisfying needs and the beginnings of a partnership are in place, the opportunity is ripe for additional sales. For example, Craig Murchison, account manager for ABCO, a printing company, was given a small job as his first sale to Acclivus. When he proved that ABCO could save Acclivus money by reducing waste, he was given bigger jobs. Over time, greater trust developed, and he was ultimately awarded all of Acclivus's business.[10] With greater trust, the salesperson can focus on identifying additional needs and providing solutions. In this section we discuss how to increase sales from current customers to expand the relationship. Keep in mind, however, that the activities

TWEET! SERVICE FOUL!

OK, an old-school professor probably thought that "tweet" in this box's title meant a referee blowing a whistle and calling a foul. In today's world, however, it means a customer put out a message on Twitter complaining about an experience or a product. For example, the European company Carphone Warehouse monitors Twitter to quickly identify when a customer tweets a complaint. Then a customer service representative will respond directly to the customer, either through Twitter or by e-mail, depending on what will be quickest.

Twitter is not the only online method for identifying customer service issues. Other microblogging sites, like Yammer.com, are also gaining ground as a place where customers can post comments about a company's performance. Phone Works founder Anneke Seley says, "Fundamentally, it's important to understand whether your customers are using social media or not. . .if you're in sales and trying to be of service to other people, it's about understanding what's going to help them. If they want to use Twitter, then let them communicate with you via Twitter."

Dell recognized this early. With over a million followers through various Dell Twitter accounts, Dell used the Twitter channel as a way to sell off excess inventory and low-volume inventory. The result was over $3 million in sales last year.

Individual salespeople can also benefit from staying in touch with customers via social media. Dan Harding, a regional sales director, uses LinkedIn to find out what's important to his customers. If a service issue arises through a posting on LinkedIn or Twitter or in a customer's blog, Dan finds it quickly and responds quickly. Additionally, though, he has a better sense of what's important to each customer now, and he can identify sales opportunities too.

Sources: James M. Curran and Matthew L. Meuter, "Encouraging Existing Customers to Switch to Self-Service Technologies: Put a Little Fun in Their Lives," *Journal of Marketing Theory & Practice* 15, no. 4 (Fall 2007), pp. 283–98; Lisa Gschwandtner, "It's All about Strategy," *Selling Power* (January/February 2010), pp. 32–36; Natalie Petouhoff, "The Social Customer Economy," *Customer Relationship Management* (March 2010), p. 14.

of the exploration stage (monitoring order processing, handling complaints, and so on) still apply.

There are several ways to maximize the selling opportunity each account represents. These include generating reorders, upgrading, full-line selling, and cross-selling.

GENERATING REPEAT ORDERS

In some situations the most appropriate strategy is to generate repeat orders. For example, Cargill provides salt and other cooking ingredients to Kellogg's. The best strategy for the Cargill salesperson may be to ensure that Kellogg's continues to buy those ingredients from Cargill. Several methods can be used to improve the likelihood of reorders. We discuss each method in turn.

Be Present at Buying Time

One important method of ensuring reorders is to know how often and when the company makes decisions. NetSuite and other CRM software can provide order histories for accounts and give you a customer's buying cycle. For example, if you know that a particular customer reorders every 90 days, you can call on the 80th day with an offer and increase reorders.

Buyers do not always have regular buying cycles, which can make it difficult for salespeople to be present at buying time. In these situations the seller still

Contractor David Richardson, owner of Richardson Heating and Air Conditioning in Louisville, Kentucky, is measuring wet bulb and dry bulb temperatures from a supply register as part of making sure that a new installation is meeting customer requirements.

wants to be present in the buyer's mind. Two items that can help keep the seller present are catalogs and specialty advertising items. Catalogs are useful for buyers, who will usually refer to them when ready to buy. Specialty advertising items, such as pens or desk calendars, also aid buyers in reordering, especially if the toll-free number is easy to find. Florida Furniture Industries has used desk calendars for more than 70 years to remind furniture store buyers of whom to call when inventories are low.

Help to Service the Product

Most products need periodic maintenance and repair, and some mechanical and electronic products require routine adjustments. Such service requirements offer salespeople a chance to show buyers that the seller's interest did not end with the delivery of the product. Salespeople should be able to make minor adjustments or take care of minor repairs. If they cannot put the product back into working order, they must notify the proper company representative. They should then check to see that the repairs have been completed in a timely manner and to the customer's complete satisfaction.

As we discuss in Chapter 16, part of the salesperson's job is getting to know the company's maintenance and repair people. These repair people can act as the salesperson's eyes and ears when they make service calls. When a good relationship is established with service personnel, salespeople can learn of pending decisions or concerns and take the necessary action.

Sometimes service is about making sure the customer gets the most out of a product, even when things don't go as planned. In "Building Partnerships 14.1" the plight of two different customers in the same industry illustrates the importance of being willing to do what it takes to make sure the customer's needs are met.

thinking **it** through

Some customers take advantage of salespeople by trying to have them perform almost all the routine maintenance on a product for free. What can you as a salesperson do to curb such requests? How do you know where to draw the line?

Provide Expert Guidance

An industrial buyer or purchasing agent may need help in choosing a proper grade of oil or in selecting a suitable floor cleaner. A buyer for a retail store may want help developing sales promotion ideas. Whether the buyer needs help in advertising, selling, or managing, good salespeople are prepared to offer worthwhile suggestions or services.

The salesperson usually prospers only if the buyer prospers. Obviously, unless buyers can use a product or service profitably or resell it at a profit, they have no need to continue buying from that product's seller. One expert suggests finding non-selling-related ideas to offer your customers. When you use your industry expertise to solve problems or develop opportunities for your clients that do not involve the sale of your product, you add value to the relationship, which can ultimately help you expand your business within the account.

Many firms have developed a team approach to providing guidance and suggestions. For example, Verizon uses a systems approach to help develop and

BUILDING Partnerships

DO WE HAVE A PLAN B?

The trade show business is one of the toughest professions there is. An exhibit manager is responsible for taking a slab of concrete in the middle of a large warehouse-like building and turning it into a beautiful, professional showcase for a company. Not only must this showcase grab the attention of potential customers, it also has to impress the exhibit manager's own executives who paid for it. You can imagine, then, why making sure everything is exactly perfect is so important to an exhibit manager. But things don't always go right.

Rusty Taphous, exhibit and marketing coordinator for Vita-Mix Corp. in Cleveland, found this out when his audiovisual equipment failed to complete the trip from a show in Chicago to a show in Atlanta. While he suspected foul play, what was disappointing was the lack of assistance his vendor, GES, provided. It had no help to offer, at least not until the missing crate was found and not without some significant pressure. Then, and only then, did it offer to help, shipping the missing crate to Atlanta overnight in time for the show. Taphous didn't say whether he still does business with GES, but this story went out to thousands of others in the same job and with the same needs as Taphous. This is not the type of PR you want to generate!

Betsy Andrews, medical conferences supervisor for UCB Inc. in Smyrna, Georgia, had a different experience with her exhibit house. It wasn't that her crates were missing—they were stuck in a blizzard in Amarillo when they were supposed to be in Las Vegas. But unlike GES, this exhibit house had a sales rep who jumped right in, organizing resources from his own company, from a graphics company, and from an audiovisual company. After hearing that the booth was stuck in Amarillo, her staff showed up surprised to see a fully functional and professional eye-catching booth. When asked if they managed to free the shipment, she just smiled and said, "In the face of a freak snowstorm in Texas, you don't need a miracle. You just need a great team to dig you out of trouble." And that team included her salesperson. Unfortunately she didn't name either the vendor or the salesperson in her article. And that's too bad because all too often customers feel more like Taphous than like Andrews.

Sources: Betsy Andrews, "Fixing Snafus: Snow Show," *Exhibitor Magazine* (December 2009), p. 48; Rusty Taphous, "Fixing Snafus: The Old Switcheroo," *Exhibitor Magazine* (January 2010), pp. 43–44.

maintain the communication systems of its major accounts. The major account service team (MAST) is composed of marketing (as chairperson), engineering, service, supply, and traffic representatives. This interdepartmental approach brings together all skills required to provide expert guidance and suggestions to meet the expanding, sophisticated needs of large customers.

Standard Register's philosophy for success in the highly competitive field of selling business forms includes expert advice. Its forms management program makes the company a business partner with, rather than merely a supplier to, its major accounts. Customers are shown how to control the costs of buying and using forms by such practices as redesigning existing forms, grouping forms for more economical ordering, keeping records of quantities on hand and on order, and keeping track of the dollar value of the inventory. Standard Register's customers welcome such advice, and the result is a high reorder rate.

Provide Special Assistance

Salespeople are in a unique position to offer many types of assistance to the buyer. This section briefly mentions a few of the types of assistance salespeople can give their customers.

Salespeople engage in many activities to provide special assistance. For example, salespeople for Cott Beverages, a Canadian maker of private-label soft drinks for companies like Walmart, work as consultants, offering advice on product design and store layout. Salespeople at Simmons help set up mattress displays in furniture stores. Makita power tool salespeople provide free demonstrations for customers of hardware stores. Most salespeople who sell to resellers will tidy up the shelves and physically restock them from the stockroom supplies. Salespeople also help train the reseller's employees in how to sell the products to the final consumers.

Gail Walker of Marquis Communications, a trade show and special events service agency, worked in the customer's booth at a trade show when one of the customer's salespeople got sick. She worked as hard as if she were one of the firm's employees. Providing such special assistance is one hallmark of excellence in selling. Good relationships are built faster and made more solid by the salesperson who does a little something extra for a customer, performing services beyond his or her normal responsibilities.

UPGRADING

Similar to generating reorders is the concept of upgrading. **Upgrading,** also called *upselling,* is convincing the customer to use a higher-quality product or a newer product. The salesperson seeks the upgrade because the new or better product serves the needs of the buyer more effectively than the old product did.

Upgrading is crucial to companies like Konica-Minolta. For this office equipment manufacturer, over 70 percent of equipment sold this year will be replacements, not new installations. As a result, postsale service is more important than ever, and service reps work closely with salespeople so that opportunities for upgrading can be identified.[11]

When you upgrade, it is a good idea to emphasize during the needs identification phase that the initial decision was a good one. Now, however, technology or needs have changed, and the newer product fits the customer's requirements better. Otherwise the buyer may believe that the seller is trying to take advantage of the relationship to foist a higher-priced product.

FULL-LINE SELLING

Full-line selling is selling an entire line of associated products. For example, a Xerox copier salesperson may sell the copier but also wants to sell the dry ink and paper the copier uses and a service contract. Or a Campbell Soup Company salesperson will ask a store to carry cream of potato soup as well as tomato soup.

The emphasis in full-line selling is on helping the buyer realize the synergy of owning or carrying all the products in that line. For example, the Xerox salesperson may emphasize the security in using Xerox supplies, whereas the Campbell rep will point out that sales for all soups will increase if the assortment is broader.

CROSS-SELLING

Cross-selling is similar to full-line selling except the additional products sold are not directly associated with the initial products. For example, cross-selling occurs when the Xerox salesperson attempts to sell a fax machine to a copier customer or when a Campbell Soup Company rep sells spaghetti sauce to a soup buyer. Cross-selling involves leveraging the relationship with a buyer to identify needs for additional products; one reason is that it can cost much less to cross-sell to an existing client than to acquire a new client.[12] Again, trust in the selling organization and the salesperson already exists; therefore, the sale should not be as difficult as it would be with a new customer, provided the needs exist. Cypress Care sells health care plans and services to companies and has two distinct sales forces. The products differ, and often the buyers are different. But in some instances, the same buyer buys

Convincing a retailer to carry all Stubbs barbecue sauce flavors is full-line selling; convincing the retailer to also carry Stubbs marinades and rubs is cross-selling. Cross-selling leverages existing relationships to increase account share, or the percentage of a customer's business that you can earn.

plans and services. In these instances, Cypress Care salespeople work across team lines to jointly serve the client and cross-sell the other offerings.[13]

Cross-selling (and full-line selling) requires additional training, as illustrated in Exhibit 14.4. Some attempts at cross-selling, though, can resemble the initial sale because the buying center may change. For example, the spaghetti sauce buyer may not be the same person who buys soups. If that is the case, the salesperson will have to begin a relationship with the new buyer, building trust and credibility.

COMMITMENT

When the buyer–seller relationship has reached the commitment stage, there is a stated or implied pledge to continue the relationship, as we discussed in the last chapter. Formally this pledge may begin with the seller becoming a **preferred supplier,** which is a much greater level of commitment than the levels discussed in Chapter 11. Although preferred-supplier status may mean different things in different companies, in general it means that the supplier is assured of a large percentage of the buyer's business and will get the first opportunity to earn new business. For example, at John Deere, only preferred suppliers are eligible to bid on new product programs. Thus preferred supplier is one term used for "partnership."

DaimlerChrysler classifies its relationships with suppliers into four categories. The first is transactional, or what we called *solo exchange* in the previous chapter. The second is coordinative, in which DaimlerChrysler may sign an annual contract. These two types of relationships are market exchanges. The next two are more strategic, with selective partnership being the first level. Suppliers are integrated into product development processes and work closely with DaimlerChrysler to develop effective interfaces. Alliances, or strategic partnerships, go even further,

Exhibit 14.4
Seven Tips for Effective Cross-Selling

1. *Product knowledge:* Salespeople have to know all their company's products. When companies introduce new cross-selling opportunities, training is needed to learn the new product lines.
2. *Cross-selling skills:* Salespeople must know how to identify the appropriate decision maker, how to leverage current relationships, and how to use other cross-selling skills. Cross-selling often requires additional training.
3. *Incentives:* Many salespeople are afraid of losing the first piece of business by asking for too much, so incentives can help make it worthwhile to ask.
4. *Reasonable quotas or goals:* The first goal when implementing a cross-selling strategy is to get salespeople to simply ask for the opportunity. Goals that are too tough encourage salespeople to force the cross-sale.
5. *Results tracking:* Effective organizations track results by individual and by sales team to identify cross-selling success. Many companies use contact management software like NetSuite or salesforce.com for results tracking.
6. *Timing:* Creating a promotion campaign to support cross-selling efforts, particularly when seasonality is an issue, can make a cross-selling strategy successful. Timing also refers to making sure training occurs before the program starts.
7. *Performance appraisals:* Salespeople need feedback to identify where and how in the process to improve.

Source: Vicki West, PhD, and Jan Minifie, PhD. Used with permission.

with integration of departments across the two companies, investment in joint assets, and joint concept development taking place. Such commitment is rare; few companies are strategic partners.

What does it take to become a preferred supplier? PPG, as part of its Supplier Added Value Effort (SAVE) program, uses several criteria (listed in Exhibit 14.5). In some cases a PPG preferred supplier is a distributor, not a manufacturer. In these situations the supplier and PPG work in tandem to find the best manufacturers at the lowest prices, with the result being increased sales volume and better volume discounts. PPG gets the lowest price possible at the required service level, and the distributor makes more profit. Clearly this is a win–win opportunity.

Note that upgrading, full-line selling, cross-selling, and handling complaints will continue to occur during the commitment stage. Because a commitment has been made by both parties to the partnership, however, expectations are greater. Handling complaints properly, appropriately upgrading or cross-selling, and fulfilling new needs are even more important because of the high level of commitment made to the partner.

Many buyers evaluate suppliers on criteria similar to those used by PPG (see Exhibit 14.5). Although the salesperson may not be able to influence corporate culture, she or he plays an important role in managing the relationship and leading both sides into commitment.

SECURING COMMITMENT TO A PARTNERSHIP

When firms reach the commitment stage, elements in addition to trust become important. Trust may be made operational in the form of shared risk, such as

Exhibit 14.5
Examples of Supplier Criteria to Sell to PPG

Hard Savings
- Payment terms, such as cash discounts.
- Improve process:
    Cycle time reduction (shorter order/delivery cycles, for example).
- Inventory management:
    Vendor inventory management.
- Quality and innovation:
    Variability reduction—no defects and no adjustments needed to make products fit our applications.
- Supply chain management:
    Optimum packaging—light packaging that reduces shipping costs while still protecting the product.

Soft Savings
- Commercial:
    Minority-owned vendors.
- Global initiatives:
    New markets—provide access to new markets, either by partnering into new markets or by adjusting products to fit needs of new markets.
- Improve process:
    Improve safety or environmental procedures.
- Quality and innovation:
    Training.
- Supply chain management:
    Bar coding—can reduce the time our employees take to process a shipment.

Source: www.ppg.com/crp_purchasing/$ave/measurement_grid.htm (accessed March 1, 2008).

Baxter International's agreements with some customers to share savings or expenses for joint programs. Along with the dimensions of trust such as competence and dependability and honesty (or ethics), there must be commitment to the partnership from the entire supplying organization, a culture that fits with the buyer's organizational culture, and channels of communication so open that the seller and buyer appear to be part of the same company.

COMMITMENT MUST BE COMPLETE

Commitment to the relationship should permeate both organizations, from top management to the secretary who answers the phone. This level of commitment means devoting the resources necessary to satisfy the customer's needs and even anticipating needs before the buyer does.

The salesperson owns the responsibility to secure commitment from his or her own company. Senior management must be convinced of the benefits of partnering with a specific account and must be willing to allow the salesperson to direct the resources necessary to sustain the partnership. (Chapter 16 explores the process of building the internal partnerships the salesperson needs to coordinate those resources.)

Commitment also requires that all employees be empowered to handle the needs of the customer. For example, if the customer has a problem with a billing process, administration should be willing to work with the partner to develop a more satisfactory process. In a partnership the customer should not have to rely on only the salesperson to satisfy its needs. For Mike Power, sales manager for Lovejoy Inc., a big part of the equation is making sure that someone in the organization is always accessible to provide an answer or solve an opportunity. "Accessibility means that we can respond quickly to customer or distributor emergencies. For example, recently we received a call about a coupling breakdown at a steel mill at 1 a.m. From the time the mill's maintenance supervisor called the distributor's sales representative to the time we loaded the coupling on the truck for delivery, less than four hours had passed."[14] Accomplishing this feat took many more employees than just a salesperson.

COMMUNICATION

In the exploration stage, availability must be demonstrated (we already discussed the example of toll-free hot lines and voice mail to allow the seller's organization to respond quickly to customer calls). But in the commitment phase of a partnership, the seller must take a proactive communication stance. This approach means actively seeking opportunities to communicate at times other than when the salesperson has something to sell or the customer has a problem to resolve.

Partners are usually the first to learn about each other's new products, many times even codeveloping those products.[15] Part of the commitment between suppliers and their customer partners is the trust that such early knowledge will be kept confidential. Partners want to know what is coming out soon so they can make appropriate plans. But what happens if the new product is delayed or needs to have some bugs worked out? That happened to Jeff Meisner, president of Skyline DFW, a distributor of Skyline trade show displays. Skyline introduced a new product, but Meisner added a few weeks to the launch date just in case the product wasn't ready. He then did an e-mail campaign to let customers know about the new product. Several were interested and placed orders. A manufacturing delay pushed back the delivery date by several months, which could have caused Meisner significant problems with customers who had ordered the new product. Fortunately he had warned them about the possibility of a delay when each customer placed an order, and he had a "Plan B" in place to take care of them. The result was that all these partners were taken care of in the manner they've come to expect from Meisner.[16]

Salespeople should also encourage direct communication among similar functional areas. In previous stages the two firms communicated through the buyer and the salesperson. If multilevel selling occurred, it occurred at even levels— that is, vice presidents talking to one another. But when two firms commit to a partnership, the boundaries between them, at least in terms of communication, should blur, as illustrated in Exhibit 14.6.

The buyer's production department, for example, should be able to communicate directly with the seller's engineering department rather than going through the salesperson, if production needs to work on a change in the product design.

Exhibit 14.6

Direct Communication between Partners

In traditional settings, companies communicate through a single buyer or purchasing agent and the salesperson. Partners, though, allow direct communication between members of the selling and buying companies.

Buyer–supplier interface: traditional

Supplier   Buyer

Buyer–supplier interface team

Supplier   Buyer

Although the salesperson would want to be aware of a product design change and ensure that engineering responded promptly to the customer's concern, direct communication means more accurate communication and a better understanding of the customer's needs. A better solution is more likely to result when there is direct communication.

CORPORATE CULTURE

Corporate culture is the values and beliefs held by senior management. A company's culture shapes the attitudes and actions of employees and influences the development of policies and programs.[17] For example, consider the following scene. In a large room with concrete floors are a number of cubicles built from plywood. Each cubicle has a card table, two folding chairs, and a poster that says, "How low can you go?" Such is the scene in Bentonville, Arkansas, the corporate headquarters of Walmart, where salespeople meet their buyers for Sam's Club and Walmart. That room reflects Walmart's culture of the lowest possible price.

A similar culture of constantly seeking ways to drive down costs is necessary for a seller to develop a partnership with Walmart. A single salesperson will not change a company's corporate culture to secure a partnership with a buyer, but the salesperson must identify the type of culture both organizations hold and make an assessment of fit. Although a perfect match is not necessary, the salesperson must be ready to demonstrate that there is a fit. Offering lavish entertainment to a Walmart buyer, for example, would not demonstrate a fit. Telling the buyer that you are staying at a Circle 6 Motel might.

Companies have often sought international partners as a way to enter foreign markets. Walmart partnered with Cifra when the U.S. retailer entered the Mexican market. Cifra provides distribution services and products to Walmart for Sam's Club and Walmart stores located in Mexico City, Monterrey, and Guadalajara. When partnering with companies from other countries, country culture differences as well as corporate culture differences can cause difficulties.

Though not attempting to change a company's culture, the salesperson who seeks a partnering relationship seeks change for both organizations. In the next section we discuss what types of changes salespeople manage and how they manage those changes.

THE SALESPERSON AS CHANGE AGENT

To achieve increasing revenue in an account over time, the salesperson acts as a **change agent,** or a cause of change in the organization. Each sale may involve some type of change—perhaps a change from a competitive product or simply a new version of the old one. Partnering, though, often requires changes in both the buying and selling organizations.

For example, American Distribution Systems (ADS), a pharmaceutical distributor, and Ciba-Geigy, a pharmaceutical manufacturer, took six months to implement a joint operating plan that integrated systems of both companies. ADS created a cross-functional team that recreated ADS systems to function as part of Ciba-Geigy. At the same time Ciba-Geigy had to share information and other resources to take full advantage of the benefits of the relationship. In this instance both buyer and seller had to change significantly for the partnership to work.

Change is not easy, even when it is obviously beneficial. The objective is to manage change, such as changing from steel to iron pipe, in the buyer's organization while giving the appearance of stability. Two critical elements to consider about change are its rate and scope. The **rate of change** refers to how quickly the change is made; the **scope of change** refers to the degree to which the change affects the organization. Broad changes affect many areas of the company, whereas narrow

Exhibit 14.7

Change and Resistance

Resistance to change is
greatest when the scope
is broad and the rate of
change is fast.

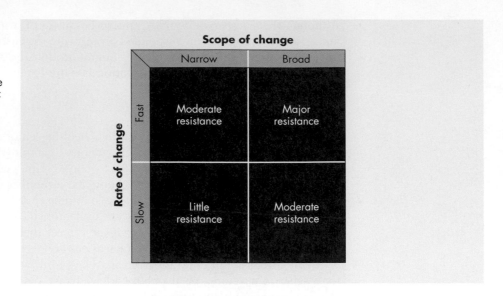

changes affect small areas. In general, the faster and broader the change, the more likely it will meet with resistance, as illustrated in Exhibit 14.7.[18]

To overcome resistance to change, the salesperson should consider several decisions. The first decision involves finding help in the buying organization for selling the proposal. Other important decisions are positioning the proposal, determining the necessary resources, and developing a time-based strategy.

Champions

First, the choice of one or more champions must be made. **Champions,** also called advocates or internal salespeople, work for the buying firm in the areas most affected by the proposed change and work with the salesperson to make the proposal successful. These champions can build momentum for the proposal by selling in arenas or during times that are off limits to the salesperson. For example, a champion may sell for the salesperson during a company picnic in a casual conversation with a coworker.

It is also important to recognize that the change in status from preferred supplier to strategic partner may also require a champion. Champions not only help persuade the firm to change but also help implement the change once the decision has been made. Such was the case at Tyco when the company wanted to revamp how it purchased services and maintenance products. Not only did the situation call for a complete review of vendors, it also required changing how these products and services were purchased. Getting the changes through to all the departments required identifying champions who would lead the change.[19] Thus champions are important to salespeople.

Salespeople can help potential champions by providing them with all the knowledge they will need. Knowledge builds confidence; champions will have the courage to speak up when they are certain they know what they are talking about. Salespeople can also motivate champions to participate fully in the decision process by showing how the decision meets their needs as well as the overall needs of the company.

Positioning the Change

Positioning a change is similar to positioning a product in mass marketing, as you may have learned in your principles of marketing course. In this case, however, the salesperson examines the specific needs and wants of the various constituencies in the account to position the change for the greatest likelihood of success.

Because salespeople are highly proactive in finding areas for improvement (or change) in their partners' organizations, positioning a change may determine who is involved in the decision. For example, suppose the Dell representative who calls on your school recognizes that the student computer labs are getting out of date. Is a proposal for new equipment primarily the domain of the computer services department, or is it the domain of faculty who teach computing classes? If the computer services department favors Dell but the users favor Apple, the Dell rep will be better served by positioning the change as the responsibility of the computer services department. Positioning the proposed change appropriately may spell success or failure for the proposal.

Determining the Necessary Resources

The customer's needs may be beyond the salesperson's expertise. For example, Fram, a maker of auto parts, may be working with CarQuest, an auto parts retailer, to develop a major advertising program that will highlight their growing partnership. Such a change may require some selling to the advertising department at CarQuest. The Fram account representative will use the expert advice of Fram's own advertising department, its marketing research department, and probably its marketing management as well. These experts may visit CarQuest with the account rep and aid in securing that change in CarQuest's advertising focus.

The salesperson must assess the situation and determine what resources are needed to secure the buyer's commitment. Although the preceding example discusses allocation of personnel, salespeople must manage other resources as well, such as travel and entertainment budgets or sample supplies. (We discuss how to build internal partnerships to effectively coordinate company resources in Chapter 16.)

Developing a Time-Based Strategy

The salesperson must determine a strategy for the proposed change and set that strategy against a time line. This action accomplishes several objectives. First, the strategy is an outline of planned sales calls, with primary and minimum call objectives determined for each call. Second, the time line estimates when each call should occur. Of course objectives and planned times will change depending on the results of each call; but this type of planning is necessary to give the salesperson guidance for each call, determine when resources are to be used, and make sure each call contributes to strategic account objectives.

For example, the Fram salesperson may determine that calls need to be made on five individuals at CarQuest. A time-based strategy would indicate which person should be visited first and what should be accomplished during that visit, as well as the order of visits to the remaining four members of the buying center. The strategy would also alert the salesperson as to when the advertising personnel were needed. Exhibit 14.8 illustrates such a time line.

DISSOLUTION

Too often salespeople believe that once a customer has committed to a partnership, less work is needed to maintain that relationship. That belief is untrue. Moreover, the recognition that everyone who touches the account has to continue to strengthen the account is important. Those who fail to strengthen the

Exhibit 14.8
Time Line for Fram/CarQuest

Month 1	Month 2	Month 3	Month 4	Month 5	Month 6
Visit director of marketing.	Visit merchandising manager and director of advertising.	Visit director of marketing.	Arrange tour of Fram facilities for VP of retail, director of marketing, and advertising and merchandising managers.	Submit plan to director of marketing.	Implement advertising program.
Primary objective: Determine marketing needs.	Primary objective: Secure support in principle.	Primary objective: Specify objectives for new advertising plan and secure commitment in principle.	Primary objective: Obtain commitment for review of plan.		
Minimum objective: Secure permission to see merchandising and advertising.					

relationship may inadvertently weaken it.[20] Salespeople who subscribe to the belief that partnerships require less work fall victim to one or more common problems. As discussed in the previous chapter, the final stage for partnerships is dissolution, or breakup, but this stage can occur at any point, not just after commitment. Several potential problems, including maintaining few personal relationships, failing to monitor competitor actions or the industry, and falling into complacency, can lead to dissolution.

LIMITED PERSONAL RELATIONSHIPS

Salespeople tend to call on buyers they like; it is natural to want to spend time with friends. The result is that relationships are cultivated with only a few individuals in the account. Unfortunately for such salespeople, buyers may leave the organization, transfer to an unrelated area, or simply not participate in some decisions. Truly effective salespeople attempt to develop multiple relationships within an account.

Darryl Lehnus, noted sales professional in the sports sales profession, advocates a *3-by-3 strategy*. What he means is make sure you have three personal relationships at three levels of the organization (at least nine relationships total). When you maintain a 3-by-3 strategy, the chances of getting surprised and losing an account are substantially reduced.[21]

FAILING TO MONITOR COMPETITOR ACTIONS

No matter how strong the partnership is, the competition will want a piece of the business. And no matter how good the salesperson is, there will still be times when the account is vulnerable to competitor action. Accounts are most vulnerable when a personnel change occurs (especially if the rep has developed relationships with a limited number of people in the account), when technology changes, or when major directional changes occur, such as a company starting a new division or entering a new market.

The successful salesperson, however, monitors competitor action even when the account seems invulnerable. For example, an insurance agency had all the insurance business at a state university in Texas for more than 10 years but failed to monitor competitor action at the state capital and lost the account when another insurance agency found a sympathetic buyer in Austin. The loss of this one account cut annual earnings by more than 70 percent.

Monitoring competitor action can be as simple as checking the visitor's log at the front desk to see who has dropped by or keeping up with competitor actions and asking buyers for their opinions. Frequently, developing relationships with the many potential influencers in an account will also keep salespeople informed about competitor actions. As each person is visited, questions and comments about competitors will arise, indicating the activity level of competition.

Monitoring competition also means thinking about the benefits competitors offer, what their products do, and what their selling strategies are. When salespeople understand what the competition offers, they can position their own company's unique capabilities more effectively. It is not enough to know where competitors have made calls; good salespeople also know what the competition is saying.

FAILING TO MONITOR THE INDUSTRY

Similar to failing to monitor competition is a failure to monitor the industry in which either the salesperson or the customer operates. Salespeople often assume that the responsibility of monitoring the industry lies with someone else—either higher-ups in their own company or the customer. But salespeople who fail to monitor both industries may miss opportunities that change creates. As an extreme example, what would happen to an advertising agency's account executive if the Internet were ignored?

How does a professional salesperson monitor the industry? By reading trade magazines, blogs, and e-newsletters, and by attending trade shows and conferences. The NetSuite sales representative who handles the John Deere account not only has to read Paul Greenberg's blog to know what's going on in the CRM industry, but also Beauchamp McSpadden's blog on agribusiness and farm insurance. It's not enough to know your company's industry; with strategic partners, you must also know their industry.

FALLING INTO COMPLACENCY

Perhaps the most common thief of good accounts is complacency. In sales terms, **complacency** is assuming that the business is yours and will always be yours. It is failing to continue to work as hard to keep the business as you did initially to earn the business. For example, Coca-Cola was the sole supplier to El Volcan, the stadium for the professional soccer team Los Tigres in Monterrey, Mexico. After many years the stadium's concessions manager began to become annoyed with Coca-Cola because service seemed lackadaisical. As a result, the contract was put out to bid; Pepsi responded with a significantly better offer and won the business.

Monty Covington, vice president of sales for Grocery Supply Co. (GSC), schedules annual account reviews with key accounts. In these reviews, he and the account manager ask the customer to evaluate GSC's performance and to identify strategies that can help both companies continue to grow. These annual reviews do not allow GSC to become complacent.

To avoid complacency, salespeople should regularly audit their own customer service. Some of the questions a salesperson may want to consider are these:

- Do I understand each individual's personal characteristics? Do I have these characteristics in my computer file on each account?
- Do I maintain a written or computerized record of promises made?
- Do I follow up on every customer request promptly, no matter how insignificant it may seem?
- Do I follow up on deliveries, make sure initial experiences are positive, and ensure that all paperwork is done correctly and quickly?
- Have I recently found something new that I can do better than the competition?

CONFLICT

Not all dissolution is the result of conflict, as you can see from the types of reasons that most often lead to dissolution. But conflict between buyer and seller can occur, and when it does, the issues can be much more complex than the "usual" complaint.

Customer–supplier conflict is sometimes the result of conflicting policies within the customer's organization and even conflict between parts of the organization. For example, members of a buying center may not agree on what is best; whoever doesn't get his or her way may then take it out on the salesperson. Or the conflict may be a long-standing dispute unrelated to the salesperson that results in poor purchasing policies. A salesperson can moderate such conflict by helping the customer develop appropriate policies; one salesperson even brought in her own purchasing VP to consult with one of her clients so the client could get some ideas on better purchasing policies.

Trust-destroying conflicts can be avoided with several steps. First, start with a clear product description. If the product is a component part or critical for other reasons, and the potential for ambiguity exists, write out a clear description. Services providers are especially vulnerable to ambiguity in the sales process because services are intangible. Specifying those services as completely as possible helps avoid later conflict. Another important element is to define who has authority to do what—both for the customer and for the selling organization. For example, it has to be clearly understood who can authorize change orders if the product specs have to be modified. Both these ideas require clear documentation, but good documentation is critical should such a dispute reach the courts.

Recognize that complaints can be the beginning of major conflict. Pathology Associates Medical Laboratories (PAML) lost a million-dollar client simply because small complaints added up over time. There was no major problem, at least at the start: an error on a bill, a late shipment, or a lost product. But these escalated into major conflict and the loss of the account, in part because

Failing to monitor industry trends and changes is often a cause for losing a customer. One way to monitor the industry is to visit trade shows and see what the competition is offering.

PAML was unable to track the complaints. It now uses Microsoft Dynamics (CRM software like NetSuite) to track complaints so it can both attack and solve any problems while also maintaining stronger customer relationships.[22] We discussed complaint handling as part of the exploration stage, but keep in mind that poor handling of complaints leads to the dissolution stage! Complaints in later stages are likely to lead to full-blown conflict if trust is not carefully salvaged. To repair damage to trust in a conflict, one consultant recommends the following seven steps (compare to the complaint-handling process discussed earlier):

1. Observe and acknowledge what has happened to lead to the loss of trust.
2. Allow your feelings to surface, but take responsibility for your actions.
3. Gain support—offer your peer a chance to save face and gain agreement on any mitigating circumstances.
4. Put the experience in the larger context to affirm your commitment to the relationship.
5. Shift the focus from assigning blame to problem solving.
6. Implement the solution.
7. Let go and move on.

Keep in mind that while the relationship may be between two organizations, even the deepest strategic partnership is ultimately the responsibility of two people.

Whatever the reason for dissolution, all is not necessarily lost. Customers who defect, or buy from other vendors, sometimes return. In fact, seeking to woo customers back is an important strategy for many companies. Trevose, a Philadelphia-based weight loss management clinic, has a salesperson whose job is devoted to winning back clients. While dieters may be notorious as on-again off-again customers, every company has business potential among former customers, and that potential can be great.

SELLING YOURSELF

In the previous chapter we discussed how the concept of different types of relationships can also be applied to the relationships between students and professors, and why you might want to work toward different relationships with different instructors. The focus is on how to build strong partnerships, which will apply to only certain situations.

One such situation is when you are involved in an organization on campus. Your organization will need to work with other organizations, both on campus and off. If you have big ideas you want to sell to others, the changes those will necessitate may also be big. That means identifying potential champions for change—people who will represent your ideas well to members in their own organizations or their departments of the school. Further, documenting decisions as part of the follow-up process will help avoid any conflict later, as well as demonstrate your professionalism and competence. Such follow-up will certainly set you apart!

Similarly, your organization may organize a fund-raising project or have T-shirt sales or some other sales transaction. How will you monitor orders (in the case of a T-shirt sale), how will you handle delivery, and will you engage in any postsale follow-up? If so, how?

In many different chapters in this book, you'll find references to the competitive advantage gained by having a personal reputation for integrity and competence. When opportunities for on-campus awards, scholarships, and postgraduation jobs arrive, your personal reputation will influence your ability to capitalize on those opportunities. In this chapter you've learned ways to demonstrate integrity and competence to satisfy and retain customers; apply those to your school environment and you'll enjoy the type of personal reputation that leads to success.

SUMMARY

Developing partnerships has become increasingly important for salespeople and their firms. Salespeople can develop partnerships and generate goodwill by servicing accounts properly and by strategically building relationships. Both salespeople and buyers benefit from partnering.

Many specific activities are necessary to ensure customer satisfaction and to develop a partnering relationship. The salesperson must maintain the proper perspective, remember the customer between calls, build perceptions of trust, monitor order processing, ensure the proper initial use of the product or service, help to service the product, provide expert guidance and suggestions, and provide any necessary special assistance.

The best opportunities to develop goodwill are usually provided by the proper handling of customer complaints. Sales representatives should encourage unhappy customers to tell their stories completely, fully, and without interruption. A sympathetic attitude to a real or an imaginary product or service failure cannot be overemphasized. After determining the facts, the salesperson should implement the solution promptly and monitor it to ensure that proper action is taken.

The appropriate solution will depend on many factors, such as the seriousness of the problem, the dollar amount involved, and the value of the account. A routine should be developed to handle all complaints fairly and equitably.

In the expansion phase of the relationship, key sales activities are generating repeat orders, upgrading, cross-selling, and full-line selling. The goal is to achieve a partnership, in which case the seller is often designated a preferred supplier.

At this level of relationship, it is important that both organizations commit to the relationship from top to bottom and open communication directly between appropriate personnel in both organizations. At this point, salespeople become change agents as they work in both organizations to seamlessly integrate the partnership.

Sometimes relationships break up. When partnerships dissolve, usually there are multiple reasons for the breakup. For example, when a salesperson leans too heavily on a few personal relationships and those people leave, or when the salesperson fails to monitor competitive actions, then the buying organization may feel less commitment to the relationship. Other reasons for dissolution include failing to monitor changes in the industry and becoming complacent. Winning a customer back is still a possibility and should be pursued when appropriate.

KEY TERMS

champion   394
change agent   393
complacency   397
corporate culture   393
cross-selling   388
electronic data interchange   377

full-line selling   388
preferred supplier   389
rate of change   393
scope of change   393
upgrading   388

ETHICS PROBLEMS

1. A customer is claiming you misrepresented a product in order to get the sale, so the contract should be voided. You know from other sources that the customer is in dire financial straits. You did not, at least in your mind, misrepresent the product. If your company agrees to cancel the contract, it is the same as saying you did misrepresent the product, and you could face termination or less drastic negative consequences. What should be done? (This is based on an actual event.)

2. The fairest solution to a customer's complaint is one that turns out to be against company policy, though certainly not against the law or unethical in any way. If you tried to do it, the chances are you could get away with it; but if caught, you would be terminated. What would you do?

QUESTIONS AND PROBLEMS

1. Your company sells manufacturing equipment, and a new machine had a control problem that affected about 20 percent of customers. The problem was written about in several magazines before your company fixed it. The problem turned out be a software glitch that could be fixed by downloading a patch from your company Web site, which could be done by customers. How would you deal with this problem if a customer brought it up? How would you respond if a prospect brought it up? Once the patch was written, what would you do?

2. Explain how active listening can be applied to a situation in which a customer makes a complaint. What can applying this art accomplish? What forms of active listening might actually cause *more* problems?

3. Read through Stephanie Meagher's opening profile. What is the foundation of her sales strategy? What makes her approach appropriate, and what would make it inappropriate?

4. The Miami Heat, like lots of sports teams, has a sales force that sells season tickets. Once someone is sold a season ticket package, the customer becomes someone else's responsibility. Every person in the office, no matter his or her regular job, has responsibility for a group of current customers; management believes this makes everyone more responsive to customer needs. But some customers complain; they would rather have the same salesperson who sold the tickets fix any problems. When should salespeople handle all complaints? When is it better to have everyone in the company take on some customer responsibility? When is it best to have one customer service department? Justify each response.

5. Some research suggests that how salespeople handle complaints is more important than whether there are problems. In fact, handling complaints well is one way to win loyalty. So should a company not fix a problem that it knows will lead to some minor complaints, thus giving its reps a chance to satisfy those complaints?

6. What is your reaction to the statement "The customer is always right"? Is it a sound basis for making adjustments and satisfying complaints? Can it be followed literally? Why or why not?

7. Review both "Building Partnerships 14.1" and "From the Buyer's Seat 14.1." What is the common thread? How can you, as a salesperson, gain a competitive advantage in the marketplace from these stories? What would these themes mean for you as a student or as a professional in a nonselling field?

8. How do you know when full-line selling, upgrading, or cross-selling strategies are appropriate?

9. What are the various ways a salesperson can provide a potential champion with knowledge to build confidence? What types of knowledge will the champion need?

Digital Test & Equipment (DTE) is a distributor of test equipment used in mining and oil applications. When Mark Polonsky, of Albany Manufacturing, got the call from Amy Sheppard at DTE, he was excited. For over a year he worked to get DTE to carry Albany's geothermal test equipment, but there was no progress—until today, when Amy asked if the Albany Geo-Core Xcel would handle conditions in the North Sea oil fields.

"I don't know," Mark replied. "I've personally not had any customers drilling in that area, but I will ask our senior engineer and find out. What's the situation?"

"We've got a really good shot at landing some business from British Petroleum, but we've got some holes in our product line," she replied. "I'm really thinking of making this an all-Albany pitch, which would be about a $400,000 contract. Or I may give them two solutions, one all Albany and one a mix of other products." She went on into detail about the conditions in which the Geo-Core would have to work so Mark would know what questions to ask.

After the call, Mark called the senior engineer and asked if the product would work. Assured that it would, he went to work on a great proposal. Not only would a $400,000 sale represent a month's quota, he knew that DTE was good for five times that in its other accounts. This opportunity was huge!

Amy called Mark immediately when she got his e-mail with the proposal attached. "This looks great, Mark! I think the all-Albany approach is best, so that's what we'll go with. I'll submit this to BP tomorrow."

Two months later the first Geo-Cores were installed and operational. But within a week it was obvious that they weren't up to the demanding weather conditions of the North Sea. The machines were breaking down on average about every four hours. Allison called Mark, quite upset with the results, particularly because BP now wanted to cancel the entire agreement.

Questions

1. Assume you are Mark. What should you do?
2. Does the stage of the buyer–seller relationship matter? Which buyer is most important, British Petroleum or DTE?
3. Your first call after hanging up with Allison is with the senior engineer who gave you the wrong information. He claims there is a simple fix, but a DTE engineer will have to make the trip there to do it, and that will be about a $5,000 trip. First, what would you say to your manager who has to sign off on that expense? Second, how do you handle Allison?

Soho Software began by selling accounting software in the single office–home office (SOHO) market. Growth led the company to expand its offerings, and the company now sells hosted (SaaS) software applications through resellers to companies of all sizes. Ian Weingarten heads up reseller relationships and wants to encourage resellers to go through a certification process that includes an online training program. He called Training by Professionals (TBP), a company that specializes in creating e-learning programs, and asked it to create a training program to teach resellers how to use and sell Soho software. Lindsey Howell, TBP account rep, was surprised when Ian called and essentially bought an e-learning service in one phone call. But she was happy to take the order, and her company began working on the project.

One month later she e-mailed a pilot version of the new e-learning course to Ian. Her phone rang almost immediately. "I can't believe this is what I'm spending all this money for," he shouted into the phone. "This looks terrible! It is barely more than PowerPoint slides with a voice reading what's on the slide!"

"I'm sorry, Ian, but I don't understand. The samples I e-mailed you when we were talking on the phone were just like this," replied Lindsey.

"But these are terrible—it's boring as can be! There should be animation! Maybe some video!"

"But Ian, when we discussed your budget, I mentioned that those were beyond what you were willing to spend." The call continued, but it was pretty clear that Ian was not going to be satisfied. He closed the call by saying he wouldn't pay anything for this and slammed the phone down.

Questions

1. What caused this situation to turn so negative? Who is at fault, and why?
2. What should Lindsey do? What additional information would you like to know and why?

Source: This is based on an actual situation, but the names have been changed.

ROLE PLAY CASE

Today you will receive a telephone call from one of your accounts. The account is Fournier Equipment, a company that manufactures small construction equipment sold worldwide. There is one plant in St. Albans, Vermont, one in Montpellier, France, and one in Canberra, Australia. With 12 salespeople in the United States, 6 in Latin America, 4 in Australia/Asia, and 6 in Europe, the company does about $450 million a year in gross revenue. Fournier bought 40 licenses from you, which it began using about two weeks ago. Training was done through four different independent certified NetSuite trainers, one in each country. The vice president of sales was the decision maker and the only person you met. The primary needs were to get better forecasting so the plant would not fall behind or schedule things wrong, leading to stockouts or overruns; to get more customer information so it can market directly to customers and get them to prefer Fournier for all of their needs; and to reduce the amount of time spent on paperwork by salespeople.

Each of you will take turns being the buyer and the seller. If divided into teams of three, the third person will observe. Your professor will give you a sheet to use when you are the buyer.

ADDITIONAL REFERENCES

Bendixen, Michael, and Russell Abratt. "Corporate Identity, Ethics, and Reputation in Supplier–Buyer Relationships." *Journal of Business Ethics* 76, no. 1 (2007), pp. 69–82.

Caceres, Ruben C., and Nicholas G. Paparoidamis. "Service Quality, Relationship Satisfaction, Trust, Commitment and Business-to-Business Loyalty." *European Journal of Marketing* 41, no. 7–8 (2007), pp. 836–50.

Forman, Howard, Susan K. Lippert, and Prabakar Kothandaraman. "Understanding Users' Performance Evaluation of IT Solutions." *Industrial Marketing Management* 36, no. 6 (2007), pp. 745–61.

Haytko, Diana L. "Firm-to-Firm and Interpersonal Relationships: Perspectives from Advertising Agency Account Managers." *Journal of the Academy of Marketing Science* 32 (Summer 2004)), pp. 312–29.

Morgan, Felicia, Dawn Deeter-Schmelz, and Christopher R. Moberg. "Branding Implications of Partner Firm–Focal Firm Relationships in Business-to-Business Service Networks." *Journal of Business & Industrial Marketing* 22, no. 6 (2007), pp. 372–82.

Zhang, Lida L., Long W Lam, and Clement S F Chow. "Segmenting the Customer Base in a CRM Program According to Customer Tolerance to Inferiority: A Moderator of the Service Failure–Customer Dissatisfaction Link." *Journal of Consumer Satisfaction, Dissatisfaction and Complaining Behavior* 22, (2009), pp. 68–87.

Zolkiewski, Judy, Barbara Lewis, Fang Yuan, and Jing Yuan. "An Assessment of Customer Service in Business-to-Business Relationships." *Journal of Services Marketing* 21, no. 5 (2007), pp. 313–24.

chapter 15

MANAGING YOUR TIME AND TERRITORY

SOME QUESTIONS ANSWERED IN THIS CHAPTER ARE

- Why is time so valuable for salespeople?
- What can you do to "create" more selling time?
- What should you consider when devising a territory strategy?
- How does territory strategy relate to account strategy and building partnerships?
- How should you analyze your daily activities and sales calls?
- How can you evaluate your own performance so you can improve?

PROFILE

PROFILE Just five short weeks after graduating from Elon University in May 2008, I began my own personal sales journey. ConvaTec, a market leader in medical devices, was brave enough to appoint me into its Sales Select Program. This program has been the most invaluable experience in my short career and has opened many doors that would typically be considered unreachable for a person of my tenure and level of experience in the medical device industry.

Headquartered just 10 miles away from my childhood hometown, ConvaTec was part of Bristol-Myers Squibb Co. when I began. The Sales Select Program is a highly competitive "fast track" into the world of medical sales with six months of exclusive product/clinical training in all of our core business units, the opportunity to work with both global and U.S. marketing on brand management projects, and most importantly, the development of priceless relationships acquired both in-house and in the field. By the commencement of the program, numerous changes were occurring within the company and within me. ConvaTec divested from Bristol-Myers Squibb Co. and became a stand-alone company composed of three business units while I was fired up, hungry to get into the field, to start banging down doors and making sales. I was creating and making hour-long sales presentations about ConvaTec's products and services meant for an audience of chief surgeons, residents, and executive suite financial decision makers, interviewing for positions in the sales force, and learning the most complex nature of sales in the acute hospital setting: pricing and contracting.

I accepted the territory manager position in the Boston area for our Wound Therapeutics Division, calling on hospitals and outpatient clinics in southeastern Massachusetts. Because I was completely unfamiliar with the area, initially creating my business plan and zoning my key accounts were beyond a challenge. I found it helpful to use a combination of resources in order to make my "strategic plan" in my first territory: sales tracking numbers from the previous year, gathering information from territory managers in the other business units that share a few of the same call points within the facilities, working closely with my manager, and the most helpful contributor—asking the right questions of my customers.

Every account is different in any area of sales; but within clinical settings, not only are the policies on vendor access within each individual hospital dissimilar, but so are the most important things to the salesperson—the decision-making processes. Questions like "How are you involved in the decision-making process?" or "What is the procedure here for evaluating new product technologies?" are absolutely imperative when trying to figure out how to, where to, and with whom to spend the most of your time in each account. At times it is relatively easy to hit a roadblock when you are spending time with customers who believe that their opinions are key in the decision-making process, but over time you may come to realize that their involvement is minimal or even nonexistent. Approaching each account from multiple angles is something I try to practice. I develop relationships within several settings in the hospital: the nursing staff, critical care, hospitalists, surgeons, wound care, purchasing, storeroom, central supply, and so on in order to make sure I don't pigeonhole myself into a specific area of the account and potentially hit a dead end that I would not be able to recover from. The worst thing that happens is that I realize this person is not going to be able to make a decision, but he or she may be able to lead me to the person who does; and having his or her support will only help me in the future.

Selling in the medical device industry can be a complicated, long process. Close, trusting relationships with my customers are crucial. Not only do I create solutions to save them time and increase positive patient outcomes in their practice, but I am in charge of coordinating the education for these solutions to their entire staff. Allocating resources and acquiring the proper tools to service my customers can take up a lot of time, and subsequently this is time I cannot recreate to call on my other customers. This is one of the many reasons why time management and analyzing how you spend your time are vital. In order to prioritize your efforts and measure your performance, it is important to track and constantly alter your weekly, monthly, and quarterly goals. At ConvaTec we have a tool to assist in tracking and update this information for each call. At the end of each week you can see where you spent your time, whom you spoke with, what you intended to accomplish in the meeting, and then what actually happened. By working hard all week to hit this goal and to set up the next week, it feels like an accomplishment to sit down on Friday and enter the outcome of each presentation to see where you stand. If there is a week where you spent a large amount of your time taking care of matters that did not move the sales process forward, which happens from time to time, it is almost refreshing to start the new week off with a clean slate.

In my Boston territory, I had nearly 40 accounts, which subsequently produced a large amount of windshield time driving from hospital to hospital. By using that time to catch up on voice mail, check in with my manager, make sure my distributors are able to fill orders, and prepare for the rest of my

weekly presentations, I reduced stress and workload for when I would get home that evening. Not only is managing your sales time important, but managing your work–life balance let you successfully coexist with your career rather than let it define you.

With countless competitors in the market that know your products almost as well as you do, barriers of access to key decision makers due to hospital vendor policies, and around-the-clock needs of customers caring for patients, the thing that sets ConvaTec ahead of the competition are not only our evidence-based products and solutions for clinicians and physicians, but also our clinical and educational support team teeming with renowned and respected consultants who are geared to help our customers achieve their goals.

In January ConvaTec relocated me from Boston to New York to be a territory manager for its new Critical Care Division. My role, territory, and account sizes are extremely different, but I am finding that the same lessons I learned in my first territory apply to a larger scale: Have a business plan, use it as an ever-evolving and changing blueprint, and manage your time effective and efficiently. In sales, each move you make must be deliberate, as it is for your competitor. I always assume if I am not in an account that my competition is; that's what makes me jump out of bed in the morning.

Visit our Web site at www.convatec.com.

THE VALUE OF TIME

The old axiom "Time is money" certainly applies to selling. If you work 8 hours a day for 240 days of a year, you will work 1,920 hours that year. If you earn $50,000, each of those hours will be worth $26.05. An hour of time would be worth $31.25 if your earnings climb to $60,000. Looking at your time another way, you would have to sell $260 worth of product per hour to earn $50,000 if you earned a 10 percent commission!

The typical salesperson spends only 920 hours a year in front of customers. The other 1,000 hours are spent waiting, traveling, doing paperwork, or attending sales meetings. Thus, as a typical salesperson, you really have to be twice as good, selling $520 worth of products every hour to earn that $50,000 commission.

The lesson from this analysis is clear: Salespeople must make every hour count to be successful. Time is a resource that cannot be replaced if wasted. But time is just one resource, albeit a critical resource, at the salesperson's disposal.

Managing time and territory is often a question of how to allocate resources. Allocating resources such as time is a difficult management process, but when done well, it often spells the difference between stellar and average performance. Many times it is difficult to know what is really important and what only seems

Salespeople have to carefully allocate resources such as time. Although every job will occasionally require burning the midnight oil, carefully planning one's time can make for a more balanced and enjoyable life.

important. In this chapter we discuss how to manage your time. Building on what you have learned about the many activities of salespeople, we also provide strategies for allocating resources among accounts—that is, managing your territory.

THE SELF-MANAGEMENT PROCESS

The self-management process in selling has four stages. The first stage is setting goals, or determining what is to be accomplished. The second stage is allocating resources and determining strategies to meet those goals. In the third stage the salesperson implements the time management strategies by making sales calls, sending e-mail or direct mail pieces, or executing whatever action the strategy calls for. In the fourth and final stage, the salesperson evaluates performance to determine whether the goals will be reached and the strategies are effective or whether the goals cannot be reached and the strategies must change. This process is illustrated in Exhibit 15.1 and will serve as an outline for this chapter.

SETTING GOALS

THE NEED FOR GOALS

The first step in managing any worthwhile endeavor is to consider what makes it worthwhile and what you want to accomplish. Salespeople need to examine their careers in the same way. Career goals and objectives should reflect personal ambitions and desires so the individual can create the desired lifestyle, as illustrated in Exhibit 15.2. When career goals reflect personal ambitions, the salesperson is more committed to achieving those goals.

Exhibit 15.1
The Self-Management Process

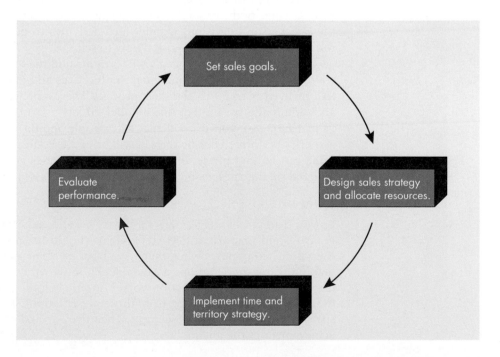

Exhibit 15.2

The Relationship of Goals

Career goals are devised from lifestyle objectives. Sales goals should reflect career goals. Although activities lead to sales, performance goals are usually set first. Then, using conversion goals, activity goals are set.

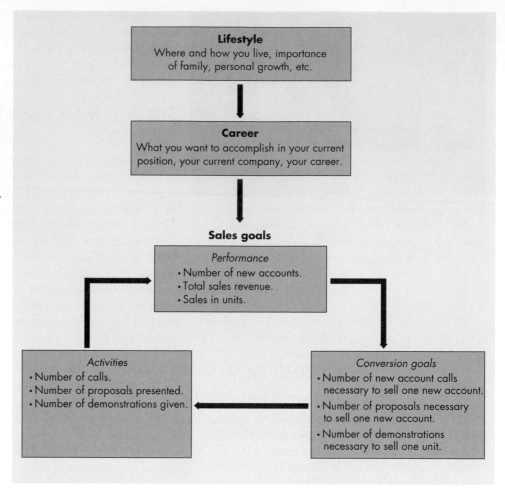

To achieve career objectives, salespeople must set sales goals. These sales goals provide some of the means for reaching personal objectives. Sales goals also guide the salesperson's decisions about which activities to perform, when to perform those activities, whom to see, and how to sell.

The salesperson lacking goals will drift around the territory, wasting time and energy. Sales calls will be unrelated to objectives and may be minimally productive or even harmful to the sales process. The result will be poor performance and, eventually, the need to find another job.

In Chapter 7 you learned that salespeople should set call objectives so the activities performed during the call will bring them closer to those objectives. The same can be said for setting sales goals: When sales goals are set properly and adhered to, the salesperson has a guide to direct his or her activities.

THE NATURE OF GOALS

As you read in Chapter 7, goals should be specific and measurable, achievable yet realistic, and time-based (SMART). Goals should be specific and measurable so the salesperson knows when they have been met. For example, setting a goal of making better presentations is laudable, but how would the salesperson know if the presentations were better or worse? A more helpful goal would be to increase the number of sales resulting from those presentations. The best goal would be a specific increase, such as 10 percent. Then there would be no question about the achievement of the goal.

Some salespeople keep a reminder, like a photo of a new house, of their personal goals in front of them to help motivate themselves.

Goals should also be reachable yet challenging. One purpose of setting personal goals is to motivate oneself. If goals are reached too easily, little has been accomplished. Challenging goals, then, are more motivating. But if the goals are too challenging, or if they are unreachable, the salesperson may give up.

Goals should be time-based; that is, goals should have deadlines. Putting a deadline on a goal provides more guidance for the salesperson and creates a sense of urgency that can be motivating. Without a deadline, the goal is not specific enough, and the salesperson may be able to drag on forever, never reaching the goal but thinking progress is being made. Imagine the motivational difference between setting a goal of a 10 percent increase in sales with no deadline and setting a goal of a 10 percent increase for the next month. The first instance lacks a sense of urgency, of needing to work toward that goal now. Without a deadline, the goal has little motivational value.

One problem some people have is periodically creating goals and then forgetting them. Goals should be written down and then posted. For example, each month Will Pinkham has a goal for selling five new accounts (Will sells office equipment for Ikon Office Solutions). At the start of each month, he puts a new list on the wall over his desk, and as he sells each new account, he adds it to the list starting at the bottom. He starts the list at the bottom to remind him that his goal is to sell five, so when he sells one, his goal becomes four, and so forth. Probably not all goals should be posted in highly public areas, but the idea is to keep the goal in front of you so it continues to direct your activities.

thinking **it** through

What types of goals have you set for yourself in your college career? For specific classes? How would these goals meet the criteria of specific and measurable, reachable yet challenging, and time-based? How do you keep these goals in front of you? What would you do differently now?

TYPES OF SALES GOALS

Salespeople need to set three types of sales goals: performance, activity, and conversions (refer back to Exhibit 15.2). Although many salespeople focus only on how many sales they get, setting all three types of goals is necessary to achieve the highest possible success.

Performance Goals

Goals relating to outcomes are **performance goals.** In sales, outcomes such as the size of a commission or bonus check, the amount of sales revenue generated or number of sales generated, and the number of prospects identified are common performance goals. For example, the salesperson in Exhibit 15.3 set a performance goal of $6,000 in commissions and another performance goal of eight sales. Revenue quotas are an example of goals set by the company, but each salesperson should also consider setting personally relevant goals. For example, you may want to set higher goals so you can achieve higher earnings. People are more committed to achieving goals they set themselves; that commitment makes

Exhibit 15.3
Goal Calculations

Monthly earnings goal (performance goal):	$6,000
Commission per sale:	$750
$6,000 earnings ÷ $750 per sale = 8 sales	
Monthly sales goal (performance goal):	8
Closings goal (conversion goal):	10%
8 sales × 10 prospects per sale = 80 prospects	
Monthly prospects goal (performance goal):	80
Prospects per calls goal (conversion goal):	1 in 3
80 prospects × 3 calls per prospect = 240 calls	
Monthly sales calls goal (activity goal):	240
240 calls × 20 working days per month = 12 calls	
Daily sales calls goal (activity goal):	12

achieving them more likely. Performance goals should be set first because attaining certain performance levels is of primary importance to both the organization and the salesperson.

Personal development goals, such as improving presentation skills, are important to long-term professional growth and are a form of performance goals. Every person, whether in sales or other fields, should have some personal development goals. Reaching those goals will not only improve overall job performance but also increase personal satisfaction. Like all performance goals, however, these goals should meet the criteria of being specific, challenging, and time-based. Further, it helps to make these goals measurable. For example, if you set improving presentation skills as a performance goal, some outcome such as increased sales or fewer objections should occur that you can measure to determine if your skills are truly improving.

Activity Goals

Salespeople also set activity goals. **Activity goals** are behavioral objectives: the number of calls made in a day, the number of demonstrations performed, and so on. Activity goals reflect how hard the salesperson wants to work. The company may set some activity goals for salespeople, such as a quota of sales calls to be made each week. Exhibit 15.3 lists two activity goals: 240 sales calls per month and 12 calls per day.

All activity goals are intermediate goals; that is, achieving them should ultimately translate into achievement of performance goals. As Teradata discovered by auditing sales performance, activity goals such as a specific number of telephone calls per day are needed for the salespeople to achieve the overall performance goals.[1] Activity goals help salespeople decide what to do each day, but those goals must ultimately be related to making sales.

However, activity goals and performance goals are not enough. For example, a salesperson may have goals of achieving 10 sales and making 150 calls in one month. The salesperson may get 10 sales but make 220 calls. That salesperson had to work much harder than someone who managed to get 10 sales in only 150 calls. What caused the difference? Answer that question and you, too, can work smarter rather than harder; but the answer presupposes that you first measured conversions and then set goals based on what should be achieved.

Conversion Goals

Conversion goals are measures of a salesperson's efficiency. Conversion goals reflect how efficiently the salesperson would like to work, or work smarter. Unlike performance goals, conversion goals express relative accomplishments, such as the number of sales relative to the number of calls made or the number of customers divided by the number of prospects. The higher the ratio, the more efficient the salesperson. Exhibit 15.3 lists two conversion goals: closing 10 percent of all prospects and finding one prospect for every three calls. In the preceding example, a rep earning 10 sales while making 150 calls could close 4 or 5 more sales by making 220 calls because that rep gains a sale every 15 calls.

Conversion goals are important because they reflect how efficiently the salesperson uses resources, such as time, to accomplish performance goals. For example, Freeman Exhibit Company builds custom trade show exhibits. Customers often ask for booth designs (called speculative designs) before making the purchase to evaluate the offerings of various competitors. Creating a custom booth design is a lot of work for a designer, and the cost can be high, but it does not guarantee a sale. If a salesperson has a low conversion rate for speculative designs, overall profits will be lower because the cost for the unsold designs must still be covered. If the rep can increase the conversion rate, the overall costs for unsold designs will be lower, hence increasing profits.

Working harder would show up as an increase in activity; working smarter should be reflected in conversion goals. For example, a salesperson may be performing at a conversion rate of 10 percent. Reaching a conversion goal of 12 percent (closing 1 out of 8 instead of 1 out of 10) would reflect some improvement in the way the salesperson operates—some method of working smarter.

Measuring conversions tells salespeople which activities work best. For example, suppose a salesperson has two sales strategies. If A generates 10 sales and B generates 8 sales, the salesperson may think A is the better strategy. But if A requires 30 sales calls and B only 20, the salesperson would be better off using strategy B. Thirty sales calls would have generated 12 sales with strategy B.

Comparing your performance with the best in your organization is a form of **benchmarking**.[2] Benchmarking can help you see where you are falling short. For example, if your conversion ratio of leads to appointments (the number of leads needed to get one appointment) is the same as that of the top seller but you are closing only half of your spec designs and that person is closing 80 percent, you know you are losing sales at the spec design stage. You can then examine what that person does to achieve the higher conversion ratio.

SETTING SALES GOALS

Performance and conversion goals are the basis for activity goals. Suppose a sale is worth $500 in commission. A person who wants to earn $4,000 per month (a performance goal) needs to make eight sales each month. If the salesperson sees closing 1 out of 10 prospects as a realistic conversion goal, a second performance goal results: The rep must identify 80 prospects to yield eight closings. If the rep can identify one prospect for every three sales calls (another conversion goal), 240 sales calls (an activity goal) must be made. Assuming 20 working days in a month, the rep must make 12 sales calls each day (another activity goal). Thus activity goals need to be the last type of goals set because they will be determined by the desired level of performance at a certain rate of conversion.

Even though the conversion analysis results in a goal of 12 calls each day, that conversion rate is affected by the strategy the salesperson employs. A better strategy results in a higher conversion rate and better allocation of time, one of many important resources that must be allocated properly to achieve sales goals. We discuss how to allocate resources in the next section.

ALLOCATING RESOURCES

The second stage of the time and territory management process is to develop a strategy that allocates resources properly. These resources are allocated to different sales strategies used with different types of accounts with the purpose of achieving sales goals in the most effective and efficient manner possible.

RESOURCES TO BE ALLOCATED

Salespeople manage many resources. Some of these are physical resources, such as free samples, demonstration products, trial products, brochures, direct mail budgets, and other marketing resources. Each of these physical resources represents a cost to the company, but to the salesperson they are investments. Salespeople consider physical resources as investments because resources must be managed wisely to generate the best possible return. Whereas financial investments may return dividends or price increases, the salesperson's investments should yield sales.

A key resource that salespeople manage is time. Time is limited, and not all of a salesperson's work time can be spent making sales calls. Some time must be spent attending meetings, learning new products, preparing reports for management, traveling to sales calls, and handling other nonselling duties; in fact, nonselling activities can take up to 70 percent of a salesperson's time. Thus being able to manage time wisely is important. As we discuss in the next chapter, salespeople also coordinate many of the company's other departments to serve customers well. Salespeople must learn how to allocate these resources in ways that generate the greatest level of sales.

WHERE TO ALLOCATE RESOURCES

For salespeople the allocation of resources is often a question of finding the customers or companies that are most likely to buy and then allocating selling resources to maximize the opportunities they offer. As you may have learned in your principles of marketing course, some market segments are more profitable than others. And just as the company's marketing executive tries to determine which segments are most profitable so that marketing plans can be directed toward those segments, salespeople examine their markets to allocate their selling resources.

Maximizing the opportunity means finding profitable ways to satisfy the greatest number of customers, but not necessarily everybody.[3] One study of services customers found that only 44 percent were profitable; the rest cost the company money.[4] In the following section we discuss how to analyze the market to identify potential customers that are most likely to buy so resources will be allocated properly.

ACCOUNT CLASSIFICATION AND RESOURCE ALLOCATION

Not all customers have the same buying potential, just as not all sales activities produce the same results. The salesperson has to concentrate on the most profitable customers and minimize effort spent with customers that offer little opportunity for profitable sales. The proportion of unprofitable accounts is usually greater than one would think. As a rule, 80 percent of the sales in a territory come from only 20 percent of the customers. Therefore, salespeople should classify customers on the basis of their sales potential to avoid spending too much time and other resources with low-potential accounts, thus helping to achieve sales goals.

Customer management is not just a time management issue. Managing customers includes allocating all the resources at the salesperson's disposal in the most productive manner. Time may be the most important of these resources, but salespeople also manage sample and demonstration inventories, entertainment and travel budgets, printed materials, and other resources.

ABC Analysis

The simplest classification scheme, called **ABC analysis,** ranks accounts by sales potential. The idea is that the accounts with the greatest sales potential deserve the most attention. Using the 80/20 rule, the salesperson identifies the 20 percent of accounts that (could) buy the most and calls those A accounts. The other

80 percent are B accounts, and noncustomers (or accounts with low potential for sales) are C accounts. Eli Lilly (a pharmaceuticals company) classifies physicians and SC Johnson Wax classifies retail stores this way. One use is planning sales calls; so for example, A accounts could be seen every two weeks, B accounts every six weeks, and C accounts only if there is nothing else to do. An example of an account analysis appears in Exhibit 15.4. As you can see, Sam Thompson has used estimated potential to classify accounts so he can allocate sales calls to accounts with the greatest potential.

ABC classification schemes work well only in industries that require regular contact with the same accounts, such as consumer packaged goods and pharmaceuticals. Some industries (plant equipment, medical equipment, and other capital products) may require numerous sales calls until the product is sold. After that sale, another sale may be unlikely for several years, and the number of sales calls may diminish. Then the A, B, and C classification may not be helpful.

Salespeople in some industries find grid and customer relationship analysis methods more useful than ABC analysis. They have learned that simply allocating sales activities on the basis of sales potential may lead to inefficiencies. For example, to maximize great potential, satisfied customers may need fewer calls than accounts of equal potential that are loyal to a competitor.

Exhibit 15.4
Account Classification

Salesperson: Sam Thompson A. Analysis of Call Pattern: 2011

Customer Type	Number of Customers Contacted	Number of Calls	Average Calls per Customer	Sales Volume	Average Sales per Call
A	15	121	8.1	$212,515	$1,756
B	21	154	7.3	115,451	756
C	32	226	7.0	78,010	345
D	59	320	5.4	53,882	168
Total	127	821		$460,859	561

B. Annual Territory Sales Plan (dollars in thousands)

Account	Actual Sales 2009	2010	2011	2012 Estimated Potential Sales	Forecast	Number of Calls Allocated	Classification
Allied Foods	$100	$110	$150	$250	$150	48	A
Pic N-Save	75	75	90	300	115	48	A
Wright Grocers	40	50	60	175	90	24	B
H.E.B.	20	30	30	150	30	24	B
Piggly Wiggly	10	10	25	100	55	18	C
Sal's Superstore	0	0	30	100	80	18	C
Buy-Rite	0	0	0	80	75	18	C
Tom Thumb	0	10	20	75	70	18	C
Apple Tree	0	5	12	60	60	12	D
Buy Lo	0	0	10	60	50	12	D
Whyte's Family Foods	10	8	9	50	40	12	D

Although Dr. Liu's practice may appear smaller than that of the clinic on the right, the astute salesperson would determine each business's sales potential before classifying either as an A, B, or C account.

Grid Analysis

The **sales call allocation grid** classifies accounts on the basis of the company's competitive position with an account, along with the account's sales potential. As with ABC analysis, the purpose of classifying accounts through grid analysis is to determine which accounts should receive more resources. By this method, each account in a salesperson's territory falls into one of the four segments shown in Exhibit 15.5. The classification is determined by the salesperson's evaluation of the account on the following two dimensions.

First, the **account opportunity** dimension indicates how much the customer needs the product and whether the customer is able to buy the product. Some factors the salesperson can consider when determining account opportunity are the account's sales potential, growth rate, and financial condition. This rating is similar to the ABC analysis and is a measure of total sales potential. Again, the idea is that accounts with the greatest opportunity deserve the greatest resources.

Second, the **strength of position** dimension indicates how strong the salesperson and company are in selling the account. Some factors that determine strength of position are the present share of the account's purchases of the product, the attitude of the account toward the company and the salesperson, and the relationship between the salesperson and the key decision makers in the account. The strength of position helps the salesperson understand what level of sales is likely in the account. The account opportunity may be tremendous—say, $1 million. But if the account has always purchased another brand, the salesperson's strength of position is weak, and his or her real potential is something much less than $1 million.

Global accounts represent a difficult challenge in terms of determining potential and position. Position may be strong in one location and weak in another; potential may also vary. Marvin Wagner, an engineer with John Deere, has been working with Deere engineers and suppliers to Deere to standardize products globally. He's had to help suppliers negotiate buying centers involving engineers in as many as four different countries, all with different expectations and preferences for different vendors. What may be preferred by engineers at the Arc-les-Gray plant in France may not even be considered by engineers in Ottumwa, Iowa.

Exhibit 15.5
Sales Call Allocation
Grid

	Strength of Position	
	Strong	**Weak**
High	*Segment 1* Attractiveness: Accounts are very attractive because they offer high opportunity, and the sales organization has a strong position. Sales call strategy: Accounts should receive a high level of sales calls because they are the sales organization's most attractive accounts.	*Segment 2* Attractiveness: Accounts are potentially attractive because they offer high opportunity, but the sales organization currently has a weak position with accounts. Sales call strategy: Accounts should receive a high level of sales calls to strengthen the sales organization's position.
Low	*Segment 3* Attractiveness: Accounts are somewhat attractive because the sales organization has a strong position, but future opportunity is limited. Sales call strategy: Accounts should receive a moderate level of sales calls to maintain the current strength of the sales organization's position.	*Segment 4* Attractiveness: Accounts are very unattractive because they offer low opportunity, and the sales organization has a weak position. Sales call strategy: Accounts should receive a minimal level of sales calls, and efforts should be made to selectively eliminate or replace personal sales calls with telephone sales calls, direct mail, etc.

Account Opportunity (vertical axis label)

Source: Raymond W. LaForge, Clifford E. Young, and B. Curtis Hamm, "Increasing Sales Productivity through Improved Sales Call Allocation Strategies," *Journal of Personal Selling and Sales Management*, November 1983, pp. 53–59.

The appropriate sales call strategy depends on the grid segment into which the account falls. Accounts with high potential and a strong position are very attractive because the salesperson should be able to sell large amounts relatively easily. Thus these attractive accounts should receive the highest level of sales calls. For example, if you have an account that likes your product and has established a budget for it, and you know that the customer needs 300 units per year, you may consider that customer to be a segment 1 account (assuming 300 units is a high number) and plan to allocate more calls to that account. But if a competitor has a three-year contract with the account, you might be better off spending less time there. The account may buy 3,000 units per year, but you have little chance of getting any of that business. By classifying the account as a segment 2, you would recognize that the most appropriate strategy is to strengthen your position in the account. The sales call allocation grid, then, aids salespeople in determining where, by account, to spend time in order to meet sales goals.

THE GRID AND CURRENT CUSTOMERS The sales call allocation grid is a great tool for analyzing current customers. Recall the value of a customer that was discussed in Chapter 13; many businesses experience little or no profit in the first year of a customer's life. But over time profit grows if the salesperson can increase sales in the account, find ways to reduce the cost to serve the account (for example, shipping more can lower shipping costs), and so on.

From the BUYER'S SEAT

15.1

THE VALUE OF JUST SHOWING UP

John Ragsdale is vice president of the Service and Support Professionals Association, and he helps companies make technology purchases. In this position, he has the rare opportunity to observe what happens in buying decisions from both sides.

> I don't think developers and marketers at high-tech companies have any idea how many deals they are losing based on the personality of the sales rep. What is really shocking is how many times the obvious "best fit" vendor is dismissed from the deal because
>
> - The sales rep was arrogant (I've heard this a dozen times about one vendor in particular).
> - The sales rep was late to multiple meetings and conference calls, and the company felt the vendor didn't want the business.
> - The sales rep didn't know bubkes (sic) about the product functionality and tried to BS his or her way through.

These reasons are simply inexcusable. Reagan Ramsower, chief technology officer for Baylor University, recalls a similar frustration in dealing with a company that sells sales force automation. "We arranged a meeting to look at their software to manage our fund-raising officers. The rep called 15 minutes after the scheduled start time of the meeting to say that it was raining and he couldn't come." Raining? Really? Does that mean his customers can get service only on sunny days?

Helene Kennedy purchased a $30,000 annuity from an insurance salesperson. Gave him the check and everything, then didn't hear from him for nearly 30 days. "I found out he hadn't completed all of the paperwork when I called the company." After another week of delays, she rescinded the sale and got her money back. "I asked the company how much commission he would get, and it was over $1,000. I guess he didn't need the money badly enough to complete the job."

Ragsdale says he's actually called some of the vendors to get their side, but all he gets are excuses. He suggests that someone outside of sales conduct a win/loss review so companies have more accurate information about problems stemming from lack of salesperson effort and other problems.

Rob Keeney, director of training for the food distributor Frosty Acres Brands, wonders if sales managers are just getting lazy. "Too many are going to phone call reviews with their salespeople instead of riding with them in the field and coaching them based on actual observation." Ragsdale asks the same question, but the root of the question is simply based on laziness that starts with the sales manager and flows to the rep.

Woody Allen says, "80 percent of success is just showing up." If that's the case, then opportunities abound in sales simply by just working a full workweek.

Sources: Ragsdale quotes are from Marshall Lager, "The Psychology of the Sale," *Customer Relationship Management* 13, no. 5 (May 2009), pp. 34–37; all other quotes are from personal interviews.

In a landmark study of the paper and plastics industry, the key to a company's profit was found to be customer share, not market share. **Customer share,** also called **account share,** is the average percentage of business received from a company's accounts in a particular category. A similar term is **share of wallet,** which is the same thing but usually for an individual consumer. Over 15 years ago, an analysis of companies in that industry indicated that even if a company was the dominant supplier to a group of buyers, another company could be more profitable if it served fewer customers but had all their business.[5] Since that study, numerous studies have found similar insights. As a result, many companies are looking for how to increase account share, rather than the number of accounts.[6]

LEAD SCORING AND PREDICTIVE MODELING IN SALES

For finding opportunities for new sales, there are two broad types of sales situations. The first is a finite and known customer universe. For example, if you sell to hospitals, there is a known and finite list of hospitals in the world. New hospitals don't suddenly spring up; salespeople don't drive around hoping to spot a new hospital. The other situation, though, is a customer universe that is broad, not known, and seemingly limitless. But no matter the situation, salespeople are limited in their time and have to make good decisions about how to use that time, including choosing accounts to call.

IBM's Software Group has the first situation. Although it sells to all types of companies, and companies can come and go, the universe of companies it would sell to is small enough to be finite and known. The group developed a set of analytical models designed to predict revenue based on current customers' purchase history. Factors such as market segment, economic leading indicators, and other variables were added to models to increase predictive accuracy. The models were then applied to existing customers and noncustomers, predicting future sales. The models predict future sales for each account individually. The accounts are ranked, and salespeople can focus on accounts with the greatest probability of sales. The process has been extended to serve over 13,000 IBM salespeople.

Profiles International falls into the second group. It sells hiring services, such as testing, to companies of any size all over the world. This potential customer universe is too large and too rapidly changing to be known. As a result, Profiles engages in marketing designed to create some initial interest on the part of a human resources or other hiring manager working for potential customers. If the person responds, say to an e-mail message or a direct mail piece, by visiting the Web site, Eloqua software tracks the person's behavior on the Web site. Eloqua recognizes the visitor if he or she clicked through an e-mail message or logs into the site, and Eloqua has predictive models built in to consider that person's behavior. Eloqua calls the buyer's online activity "digital body language." If the digital body language appears to show enough interest, based on the predictive model, the person is designated as a lead. In addition, based on that digital body language, the model can determine exactly what the prospect is interested in. A salesperson is then given a lead that not only says who the buyer is and how to contact the buyer, but also what the buyer is interested in. This system enabled Profiles to grow by over 20 percent in 2009—a year when most companies were experiencing falling sales.

Sources: Dario Parolo, interview February 4, 2010; Rick Lawrence, Claudia Perlich; Saharon Rosset, and Ildar Khabibrakhmanov, "Operations Research Improves Sales Force Productivity at IBM," *Interfaces* 40, no. 1 (2010), pp. 33–53.

INVESTING IN ACCOUNTS

Planning based on customer analysis should result in more effective use of the opportunities presented by accounts. This improvement relates to better use of time, which is allocated to the appropriate accounts. But developing good strategies entails more than developing good time use plans; strategies require the use of other resources as well.

Salespeople invest time, free samples or trials, customer training, displays, and other resources in their customers. As you can see in "Sales Technology 15.1," companies such as IBM use predictive modeling to determine which accounts are likely to be more productive. This knowledge helps salespeople determine where to invest resources—time, samples, displays, and so forth. Sales costs, or costs associated with the use of such resources, are not always costs in the traditional sense, but rather are investments in the asset called customers. This asset generates nearly all of a firm's revenue. Viewed from this perspective, formulating a strategy to allocate resources to maintaining or developing customers becomes vitally important.

Salespeople must determine not only which customers require sales effort, but also what activities should occur. CRM software can assist through **pipeline analysis:** a process for identifying and managing sales opportunities, also known as *opportunity management*. Recall that in Chapter 6 we discussed how accounts can move through stages from lead to prospect to customer. NetSuite, for example, can complete a pipeline analysis, telling the salesperson how well she is moving accounts from one stage to the next. In addition to being useful in determining conversion ratios and ensuring that a salesperson is creating enough opportunities to reach sales goals, pipeline analysis requires identifying which stage an account is in. Recognizing the account's stage in the pipeline is useful to determine what steps are appropriate. You don't want to try to do a spec design with a prospect for whom you haven't finished identifying needs, for example.

IMPLEMENTING THE TIME MANAGEMENT STRATEGY

Time is a limited resource. Once spent, it cannot be regained. How salespeople choose to use their time often means the difference between superstar success and average performance. Susan Flaviano, a sales manager for Lonseal, offers the following tips for managing your time as a salesperson; keep these in mind as you read through this section:

- Start early. Get a jump start to the day before anyone else. Then you control the day without the day controlling you.
- Manage responsiveness. Although responsiveness is key to being successful, you cannot let customer calls, e-mail messages, and voice mail consume your day. We now have the ability to respond immediately, but it is important to choose specific times during the day to reply to correspondence.
- Schedule in advance. I set most of my appointments one week in advance, which helps me stay on target. Usually, if there is not a set commitment, it is easy to justify staying in the office to get caught up on paperwork.
- Use downtime wisely. If you have a canceled appointment or extra time over lunch, or you arrive to an appointment early, use this time to plan or follow up. With our laptops and sophisticated project tracking tools, you can use this time anywhere and reduce the amount of time spent in your office or at home on Saturday catching up on paperwork![7]

Remember that your time is worth $30 to $40 an hour, but only if you use it to sell. Use it to hone a golf game or spruce up the yard, and opportunities to sell disappear. Although no manager really knows how a salesperson uses time, when the results are posted, accurate conclusions can be drawn.

thinking **it** through

How do you plan your time now? Do you use a computer to help you manage your time? How much of your time is planned by others, and how much of it are you free to allocate? What do you do to make sure you use your time wisely?

DAILY ACTIVITY PLANNING

To be effective time planners, salespeople must have a good understanding of their own work habits. For example, some people tend to procrastinate in getting the day started, whereas others may want to knock off early. If you are a late riser, you may want to schedule early appointments to force yourself to get started.

On the other hand, if your problem is heading for home too early, schedule late appointments so you work a full day.

Many salespeople have the opposite problem—they never seem to stop working. One study found that 81 percent of salespeople felt like they had to be available to their customers 24/7.[8] The BlackBerry, iPhone, and other similar products make the Internet and phone ubiquitous, but that is no excuse for failing to plan adequately. Susan Flaviano, now a sales manager for Lonseal, believed quantity of calls was the most important thing. But after a while, she realized she had no personal life and, more importantly, no more success than anyone else. She backed off the quantity of calls and began to spend more time planning her activities; the result was an increase in both sales and personal time.[9]

GUIDELINES

Salespeople need to include time for prospecting and customer care in their daily activities. Some minimize the time for such activities because they think sales do not occur on such calls, but prospects and happy customers feed future sales. Ikon, an office equipment dealer, requires salespeople to handle customer care calls before 9 a.m. and after 4 p.m. and to schedule prospecting activities between 10 a.m. and noon and between 2 p.m. and 3 p.m. Scheduled appointments are worked in when customers require them. The company bases these guidelines on its experience with buyers and when they are available.

Such planning guides are designed to maximize **prime selling time**—the time of day at which a salesperson is most likely to see a buyer. One salesperson, Lee Brubaker with Sandler Systems, calls this "pay time."[10] Prime selling time depends on the buyer's industry. For example, a good time to call on bankers is late afternoon, after the bank has closed to customers. However, late afternoon is a bad time to call on physicians, who are then making rounds at the hospital or trying to catch up on a full day's schedule of patients. Prime selling time should be devoted to sales calls, with the rest of the day used for nonselling activities such as servicing accounts, doing paperwork, or getting information from the home office.

Prime selling time varies from country to country. In the United States prime selling time is usually 9 a.m. to 4 p.m. with the noon hour off for lunch. In Mexico lunch starts and ends later, generally from 12:30 to 2:00 p.m.; offices may not close until 7 p.m. or later. In Great Britain prime selling time starts later; a British Telecom rep may not begin making calls until 10 a.m.

PLANNING PROCESS

A process exists to help you plan your daily activities, with or without the aid of planning guides. This process can even help you now, as a student, take more control of your time and use it effectively.

As Exhibit 15.6 shows, you begin by making a to-do list. Then you determine the priority of each activity on your list. Many executives rank activities as A, B, or C, with A activities requiring immediate action, B activities being of secondary importance, and C activities being done only if time allows. You can correlate these A, B, and C activities with the A, B, and C accounts discussed earlier, as well as activities such as paperwork and training. Prioritizing activities helps you choose which activities to perform first.

Note the difference between activities that seem urgent and activities that truly are important. For example, when the phone rings, most people stop whatever they are doing to answer it. The ringing phone seems urgent. Activities such as requests from managers or even customers may have that same sense of urgency; the desire to drop everything else to handle the request is called the "tyranny of the urgent." And the "urgent" can get overwhelming: The average businessperson

Exhibit 15.6
Activities Planning
Process

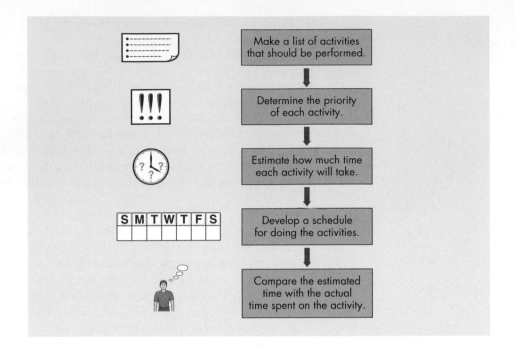

receives 274 personal e-mail messages and 304 business e-mail messages weekly, and according to another study, that number will grow as marketers increase their use of e-mail marketing.[11] Of course these statistics do not include telephone requests from customers. Yet, like most phone calls, even requests from customers may be less important than other tasks. Successful businesspeople learn to recognize what is truly urgent and prioritize those activities first.

The next step in the planning process is to estimate the time required for each activity. In sales, as we mentioned earlier, time must be set aside for customer care and prospecting. The amount of time depends on the activity goals set earlier and on how long each call should take. However, salespeople often have unique activities, such as special sales calls, demonstrations, customer training, and sales meetings, to plan for as well. Time must also be set aside for planning and paperwork.

The next step, developing an effective schedule, requires estimating the amount of time such activities will require. As follow-up, be sure to compare how long an activity actually took with how long you thought it would take. Comparing actual time to planned time with the aid of planning devices such as a DayRunner or DayTimer (paper-based calendars and planners) or computer software like NetSuite can help you plan more accurately in the future.

Using the Computer for Planning

Many of the same customer management programs that salespeople use to identify and analyze accounts incorporate time-planning elements. This software can generate to-do lists and calendars through a tickler file or by listing certain customer types. A **tickler file** is a file or calendar that salespeople use to remember when to call specific accounts. For example, if customer A says to call back in 90 days, the computer will remind ("tickle") the salesperson in 90 days to call that customer. Or if the company just introduced a product that can knock out competitor B, the computer can generate a list of prospects with products from competitor B; the salesperson then has a list of prospects for the new product.

Need for Flexibility

Although working out a daily plan is important, occasions will arise when the plan should be laid aside. You cannot accurately judge the time needed for each sales call, and hastily concluding a sales presentation just to stick to a schedule would be foolish. If more time at one account will mean better sales results, the schedule should be revised.

To plan for the unexpected, your first visit of the day should be to a prime prospect (in the terms discussed earlier, this would be an A account or activity); then the next best potential customer should be visited (provided the travel time is reasonable); and so forth. If an emergency causes a change of plans, at least the calls most likely to result in sales will have been made.

MAKING MORE CALLS

Making daily plans and developing efficient routes are important steps toward better time use. But suppose you could make just one more call per day. Using our analysis from the beginning of this chapter and Exhibit 15.3, this change would mean 240 more calls per year, which is like adding one month to the year!

Some salespeople develop an "out Tuesday, back Friday" complex. They can offer many reasons why they need to be back in the office or at home on Monday and Friday afternoons. Such a behavior pattern means the salesperson makes 20 to 30 percent fewer calls than a salesperson who works a full week. John Plott, with DG Vault, got one large sale by working the full week. He was making cold calls on a Friday afternoon, trying to set up appointments for the following week, when he reached an attorney whose current vendor was unable to meet a deadline. The attorney said if he could get the software set up that afternoon, he could have the business. The result was a $30,000 account and $4,500 in commission.[12]

To get the most out of a territory, the sales representative must make full use of all available days. For example, the days before or after holidays are often seen as bad selling days. Hence, while the competition takes those extra days off, the salesperson can be working and making sales calls he or she would otherwise miss. The same reasoning applies to bad weather: Bad weather reduces competition and makes things easier for the salesperson who doesn't find excuses to take it easy. On the other hand, good weather can tempt the salesperson to the golf course, doing yard work, or otherwise avoiding the job. No matter the weather, the professional salesperson continues to work.

Salespeople who make calls in bad weather often find that their competition has taken the day off, leaving the field wide open for those who want to succeed.

Salespeople can use certain techniques to increase the time they spend in front of customers selling instead of traveling. We mentioned Susan Flaviano's (Lonseal sales manager) challenges in managing her time earlier. One of her solutions, in addition to planning her time more effectively, was to use GPS routing software to help her plan her travel time more efficiently. Using routing techniques means she spends less time in the car and more time in front of customers.[13]

Routing

Routing is a method of planning sales calls in a specific order to minimize travel time. Two types of sales call patterns, routine and variable, can be more efficient with effective routing. Using **routine call patterns,** a salesperson sees the same customers regularly. For example, Eli Lilly pharmaceutical salespeople's call plans enable them to see all important doctors in their territory at least once every six weeks. Some doctors (those who see large numbers of certain types of patients) are visited every two weeks. The salesperson repeats the pattern every six weeks, ensuring the proper call level.

Variable call patterns occur when the salesperson must call on accounts in an irregular order. In this situation the salesperson would not routinely call on each account within a specified period. Routing techniques are useful, but the salesperson may not repeat the call plan on a cyclical basis.

The four types of routing plans, **circular routing, leapfrog routing, straight-line routing,** and **cloverleaf routing,** are illustrated in Exhibit 15.7. If an Eli Lilly salesperson used the cloverleaf method (with six leaves instead of four) for a routine call pattern, every sixth Tuesday would find that salesperson in the same spot. But

Exhibit 15.7
Types of Routing Plans

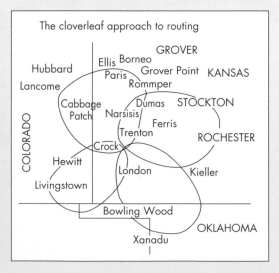

Exhibit 15.8

Zoning a Sales
Territory
A salesperson may work
in zone 1 on Monday,
zone 2 on Tuesday, and
so forth.

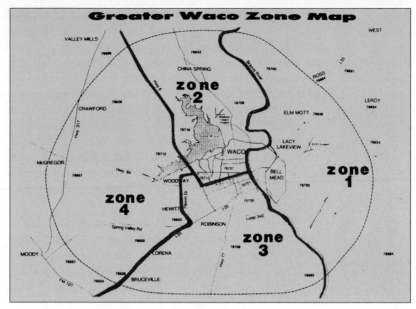

Source: *Waco Tribune Herald.*

a salesperson with variable call patterns could use the cloverleaf method to plan
sales calls for an upcoming week and then use the straight-line method the next
week. The pattern would vary depending on the demands of the customers and
the salesperson's ability to schedule calls at convenient times.

Zoning

Zoning means dividing the territory into zones, based on ease of travel and concentration of customers, to minimize travel time. First the salesperson locates
concentrations of accounts on a map. For example, an office supply salesperson
may find that many accounts are located downtown, with other concentrations
around the airport, in an industrial park, and in a part of town where two highways cross near a rail line. Each area is the center of a zone. The salesperson
then plans to spend a day, for example, in each zone. In a territory zoned like the
one in Exhibit 15.8, the salesperson might spend Monday in zone 1, Tuesday in
zone 2, and so forth.

Zoning works best for compact territories or for situations in which salespeople do not call regularly on the same accounts. (In a large territory, such as the
entire Midwest, a salesperson is more likely to use leapfrog routes, but the principle is similar.) Calling on customers that are in a relatively small area minimizes
travel time between calls.

Salespeople can also combine zoning with routing, using a circular approach
within a zone, for example. When zones are designed properly, travel time
between accounts should be minimal.

Using E-Mail and Telephone

Customer contacts should not always be in-person sales calls—the phone or
e-mail can be effective. For example, some customer care calls can be handled
by simply sending the customer an e-mail message asking whether everything is
OK. The customer may appreciate the e-mail more than a personal visit because
it can be read and responded to when the customer has time and doesn't interfere
with other pressing responsibilities. The salesperson may be able to make more
customer care calls by e-mail, increasing the number of contacts with customers.

Keep in mind, though, that not all customer care activities should be handled by e-mail or phone. Recall from Chapter 14 that there are many reasons, such as reorders and cross-selling, to continue to make sales calls in person to current customers. For example, Jenifer Rutter serves a number of nonprofit agencies as a consultant. One client kept calling with lots of little problems. "I realized I just needed to jump in the car and drive the 200-mile round trip to see them, or they would continue to have questions, make mistakes, and grow frustrated." But she also adds that because most of her clients are even farther away, "I've got to use phone and e-mail as well, or I can't handle the volume of business I need to do."[14]

Similarly, the telephone and direct mail can be used profitably for prospecting, as we discussed in Chapter 6. More calls, or customer contacts, can be made equally effectively with judicious use of e-mail and the telephone.

HANDLING PAPERWORK AND REPORTS

Every sales job requires preparing reports for management. All salespeople complain about such paperwork, but it is important. As we discuss later, paperwork can provide information that helps a salesperson determine what should be improved. The information also helps management decide what types of marketing plans work and should be used again. Therefore, every salesperson should learn to handle paperwork efficiently.

Paperwork time is less productive than time spent selling to customers, so completing it quickly is important. Salespeople can do several things to minimize the impact of paperwork on their prime selling time.

First, salespeople should think positively about paperwork. Although less productive than selling, it can increase their productivity and the productivity of the company's marketing programs by facilitating a detailed review of selling activities and marketing programs.

Second, salespeople should not let paperwork accumulate. We once knew of a salesperson who never did expense reports. He finally offered a summer intern 10 percent if she would complete his expense reports for the previous 12 months. This deal cost him $600; in addition, he was essentially lending the company $500 per month, interest free.

Routine reports should be completed daily. Nonproductive time (like time spent waiting for a customer) can be used for paperwork. Call reports and account records should be updated immediately after the calls so that important points are remembered and any follow-up actions can be planned.

Finally, salespeople should set aside a block of nonselling time for paperwork. The quickest way to do this job is to concentrate on it and avoid interruptions. Setting aside a small amount of time at the beginning or end of each day for writing thank-you and follow-up notes and completing reports saves prime selling time for selling activities while ensuring that the salesperson keeps up with paperwork.

Using the Computer to Handle Paperwork and Communications

Many companies, such as McGraw-Hill, give their salespeople laptop or notebook computers. These computers can be hooked up to the company's network to access customer information and process other paperwork automatically. Salespeople who travel can thus complete their paperwork while in a hotel, an airport waiting area, and other places. Voice recognition systems enable salespeople to do paperwork without any paper. Companies such as Giant Eagle, a grocery distributor, use such systems to enable salespeople to call orders in and handle other paperwork from their cell phones.[15]

Many companies now provide their salespeople with wireless notebook or pad computers so they can access customer information and complete paperwork in the field, sometimes even in the car.

Salespeople calling on overseas accounts can also file reports or check the status of orders, even though the home office in another time zone may be closed for the night. Computers can help international selling organizations operate smoothly by reducing communication barriers between the field and the home office. Computers and fax machines enable salespeople to communicate with colleagues and customers all around the world, despite significant time differences.

Some customer relationship management packages, like NetSuite, include territory management capabilities. These packages allow salespeople to track their performance by calculating conversion rates, commissions, expenses, and other important figures. Such technology enables salespeople to file reports quickly. Salespeople for J&K Sales Associates (Manchester, New Hampshire) input detailed call information into a simple Outlook file. The detail includes the buyer's stage in the buying cycle (J&K uses five stages, from introduction to postsale follow-up) based on the purpose of the sales call. The company has seen greater than 20 percent productivity improvement throughout the organization simply because all company members, from the purchasing department to customer billing, have the information they need at their computers.[16]

To manage your time wisely, you must exploit a scarce resource in the most effective manner possible. Your objective is to make as many quality calls as possible by reserving prime selling time for selling activities. Routing, zoning, goal setting, and other methods of planning and scheduling time will help you maximize your prime selling time.

EVALUATING PERFORMANCE

Success in sales is a result of how hard and how smart a salesperson works. Unlike many other workers, salespeople have a great deal of control over both how hard and how smart they work. Evaluating performance is the component of self-management that provides direction for how hard the salesperson should be working as well as an opportunity to determine which strategies work best. Salespeople should evaluate each sales call individually but also look at which activity leads to desired outcomes and at what rate. Let's examine each component in more detail.

POSTCALL ANALYSIS

At the end of each call, many salespeople take a moment to write down what occurred and what needs to be done, perhaps using a printed form or entering the information into a territory management program such as NetSuite. Information such as the customer's purchase volume, key people in the decision process, and current vendors is important to have, but so is personal information such as the fact that the buyer's three children play soccer. The salesperson can use that information when preparing for the next call.

Remember the plan you made for each sales call? That plan included one or more objectives. Postcall analysis should include reflecting on whether those objectives were reached. The professional salesperson not only looks for specific areas to improve but also evaluates the success of the overall sales call.

ACTIVITY ANALYSIS

When planning their time, salespeople set certain activity goals. They use these goals not only as guidelines but also to evaluate their own performance. At the end of each day, week, and month, salespeople should review their activities in relation to the goals they set. Goals are written down or entered into NetSuite when they are set—say, Sunday evening when planning the following week. Then, on Friday evening, the actual activities from each day would be tallied and totaled for the week and compared to the goals. The salesperson could then evaluate whether more calls of a certain type are needed in the following week.

Merrill Lynch, for example, recommends that new brokers make 100 telephone calls each day (calls count even if no one answers). Frank Baugh, a new broker in central Texas, made 7,544 calls in his first 92 working days, or 82 calls per day. His goal is now 120 calls per day to bring his average up to 100 in the next quarter.

PERFORMANCE ANALYSIS

Salespeople also need to evaluate performance relative to performance goals set earlier. For example, they often evaluate sales performance in terms of percentage of quota achieved. Of course a commission or a bonus check also tells the salesperson if the earnings goal was met.

An earnings goal can be an effective check for overall performance, but salespeople also need to evaluate sales by product type, as outlined in Exhibit 15.9.

Exhibit 15.9
Sales Evaluation Measures

Evaluation Measure	Calculation	How to Use It

Conversion rate
  For total performance
  By customer type
  By product type
	$\dfrac{\text{Number of sales}}{\text{Number of calls}}$	Are your strategies effective? Do you need to improve by working smarter (i.e., a better strategy to improve your hit rate)? Compare yours to your company and/or industry average.

Sales achievement	$\dfrac{\$ \text{ Actual sales}}{\$ \text{ Sales goal}}$	Is your overall performance where you believe it should be? Are you meeting your goals? Your company's goals?
Commission	$\dfrac{\$ \text{ Actual commission}}{\$ \text{ Earnings goal}}$	
Sales volume (in dollars) By customer type		Where are you most effective? Do you need help with a customer type?
By product category		Are you selling the whole line?
By market share		How are you doing relative to your competition?
By new customers		Are you building new business?
By old customers		Are you servicing your accounts properly?

Sales calls
  Prospecting calls
  Account calls
  Sales presentations
  Call frequency by
  customer type
		Are your efforts in the right place?

RELEVANCE AND THE SALES TEAM

Lydia Pearce, account executive for Teradata, believes relevance is the foundation of her success. "At a high level relevance means knowing your customer's business, aligning its business drivers to your products and services, and articulating this to each and every person from a perspective that is meaningful to him or her," says Pearce.

Teradata is the leading provider of data warehouses—special computers created specifically to store massive amounts of data and to make those data available on demand as quickly as they are entered into the system. Companies like Continental Airlines and Bank of America use Teradata systems to manage all their data.

While the average sales cycle is 18 months, the initial Teradata sale is simply the start of a long relationship. Account executives manage only one to three customers and/or prospects. The core sales team consists of an account executive who owns the account (and quota!) and drives all activities—"in this case, me," laughs Pearce. "The other two core members of the team include a solution architect and an industry consultant. Solution architects are technologists well versed in how our technology works and where it fits within various IT environments. They can articulate our value proposition and key differentiators to a variety of audiences. From business users who are concerned about query complexity to IT executives concerned about leveraging their existing infrastructure, the solution architect's expertise is leveraged throughout the sales cycle."

Industry consultants bring industry-specific experience to the team to address the particular various business challenges that can be overcome with Teradata's technology. They are often called upon to conduct business discovery and build business cases that include revenue and cost impact models and deployment roadmaps based on the customer's financial metrics and business processes,

respectively. In addition, there is the rich pool of subject domain experts that Teradata has assembled to augment the core sales team. These folks routinely share best practices with customers on a wide range of specialized subject areas including customer relationship management, finance and performance management, data mining for predictive analytics, and industry-specific logical data models.

Each new sales effort begins with an opportunity plan. Here the team plans how to create demand through careful execution of effective and highly tailored messaging to a targeted group of people high, wide, and deep. Once executed, the opportunity plan becomes the foundation from which the account executive begins to map the customer's organizational structure. As initial points of contacts are made, account executives begin building their network of intelligence that links specific people to specific business functions, business functions to business challenges, and the alignment of these functions to products and service offers. When initial points of contact give way to genuine interest, more frequent and narrowly focused meetings begin to take place. At this point Pearce, along with her team, develops a strategic plan for winning the business. The strategy encompasses what the first solution will include, the specific business challenges it will address along with a means to quantify its value, and how it will be sold. The "how" includes a time line of meetings, critical messaging, technology benchmarks, and proof of concepts and/or pilots, along with the objectives and the essential "close" for each. Strategic plans need to be continuously modified based on the outcome of each activity. Because the exact composition of the sales team changes throughout the sales process, the strategic plan also keeps everyone who will be interacting with the customer apprised of the previous and planned activities.

Source: Contributed by Lydia Pearce; used with permission.

Salespeople who sell only part of the product line may be missing opportunities for cross-selling or full-line selling, which means they have to work harder to achieve the same level of sales as the salesperson who successfully integrates cross-selling and full-line selling in the sales strategy.

PRODUCTIVITY ANALYSIS

Salespeople also need to identify which strategies work. For example, if using a certain strategy improved the ratio of appointments to cold calls made, that approach should be continued. Otherwise the salesperson should change it or go back to a previous approach. Frank Baugh, the Merrill Lynch broker, tried several approaches before settling on one that works well for him. Of course Baugh keeps good records so he knows what works and what does not.

The **conversion ratio,** or number of sales per calls, is an important measure of effectiveness. Conversion ratios should also be calculated by account type; for example, a conversion ratio for type A accounts should be determined. Other conversion ratios can also pinpoint effective strategies and areas that need improvement.

Conversion ratios can also be calculated for each step of the sales cycle. Profiles International, for example, calculates the conversion ratio of leads to prospects to determine which marketing activities generate the highest number of qualified sales leads. These leads can be tracked all the way to the close, too, telling Dario Parolo, vice president of marketing, where to invest his marketing activities.

SELLING YOURSELF

A theme for this chapter is self-analysis to improve performance. As a student, engaging in self-analysis is important so you repeat activities that are successful (lead to good grades) and avoid those that are not. Did pulling an all-nighter improve your exam performance? Or did you do better when you studied for shorter periods each day beginning a week ahead?

Similarly, if you are in an organization and examine the organization's recruiting practices, you'll find that some methods work better than others. What method of finding leads worked best—posting a flyer in the dorms or posting an e-vite on Facebook? What events attracted the largest crowds, and which events provided the best prospective members? By applying what you've learned in this chapter to organizational recruiting (or fund-raising or other activities that mimic the sales process), you'll be able to improve your organization's performance.

But what about you? Do you set goals for your academic performance each semester? Do you track your progress toward those goals and keep the goals visible as a way to motivate yourself? One sales trainer said, "I have to know myself—what makes me work, when I want to slack, and even what tricks I can pull on myself to do what I need to do to reach my goals because there is no one else who will do it for me." Although his comments were aimed at salespeople, they apply to students as well.

SUMMARY

A sales territory can be viewed as a small business. Territory salespeople have the freedom to establish programs and strategies. They manage a number of resources, including physical resources such as sample inventory, displays, demonstration equipment, and perhaps a company vehicle. More important, they manage their time, their customers, and their skills.

Managing a territory involves setting performance, activity, and conversion goals. Salespeople use these goals to allocate time to various activities and to manage customers.

To manage customers well, the salesperson must analyze their potential. Accounts can be classified using the ABC method or the sales call allocation grid. These analyses tell how much effort should be put into each account. Some organizations use CRM software to conduct these analyses on the entire customer database, which helps identify patterns within a territory. Salespeople can use these patterns to develop account sales strategies.

More calls (working harder) can be accomplished by moving nonselling activities, such as paperwork, to nonselling time. Also, selling time can be used more efficiently (working smarter). For example, routing and zoning techniques enable the salesperson to spend more prime selling time in front of customers instead of behind the steering wheel of a car.

Effective planning of the salesperson's day requires setting aside time for important activities such as prospecting and still making the appropriate number of sales appointments. Using the full workweek and employing technology such as telephones, computers, and fax machines can help the salesperson stay ahead of the competition.

Finally, salespeople must manage their skills. Managing skills involves choosing how to make sales calls and improving the way one sells. Improvement requires that salespeople first understand what they do well and what needs improvement. Evaluating their performance can provide them with that insight.

KEY TERMS

ABC analysis   412
account opportunity   414
account share   416
activity goals   410
benchmarking   411
circular routing   422
cloverleaf routing   422
conversion goals   410
conversion ratio   428
customer share   416
leapfrog routing   422
performance goals   409

pipeline analysis   418
prime selling time   419
routine call patterns   422
routing   421
sales call allocation grid   414
share of wallet   416
straight-line routing   422
strength of position   414
tickler file   420
variable call patterns   422
zoning   423

ETHICS PROBLEMS

1. A sales manager schedules all sales training and sales meetings on the weekend so salespeople lose no selling time. Is this ethical? Does your answer depend on how they get paid—straight salary, salary plus commission, or straight commission?
2. One company's culture is "flashy," meaning salespeople are expected to wear custom-tailored clothing, flaunt expensive jewelry and watches, and drive expensive cars. Assume you are about to graduate and go to work for this company. Consider this culture, and relate it to your goals—how might this culture influence your goals? Is that influence healthy? Why or why not?

QUESTIONS AND PROBLEMS

1. Look over "Building Partnerships 15.1." How does the concept of relevance apply to understanding where an account is on the sales call allocation grid?

2. Lydia Pearce, Susan Flaviano, and many other salespeople work out of their homes. Pearce and Flaviano both recognize how tempting it is to work longer and to put off paperwork until

the weekends because it is so convenient. What problems might succumbing to such temptation cause? What safeguards can they put into place?

3. Compare and contrast the special problems of self-management for a computer salesperson who works in a computer store with those of a computer salesperson who calls on customers in their offices.

4. Shakespeare wrote, "To thine own self be true." How would you apply this statement to your planning and development activities?

5. Which factors are important for classifying customers? Why? How would these factors change depending on the industry?

6. Distinguish between routing and scheduling and between routing and zoning. Explain how routing and scheduling can interact to complement the planning of an efficient day's work.

7. How might a pharmaceutical salesperson increase the number of calls made per day? A financial services representative selling pension plans to companies? A financial services representative selling retirement plans to consumers? A representative who sells golf clubs to retailers and pro shops?

8. One sales manager said, "Sales is a numbers game. To make more sales, make more sales calls." Should sales managers encourage salespeople to continually increase the number of calls made each week? Explain your answer. Reread "From the Buyer's Seat 15.1." How does this essay relate to your answer?

9. One recruiter told a class that students are used to getting feedback on how they are doing every couple of months, but salespeople do not get a "final grade" until a year has gone by. He claims that students have a hard time making that adjustment when they enter the work world. What do salespeople do to know where they stand at any given time? What do you do now that helps you know where you stand in your classes? Why is such knowledge important?

10. How would you use the sales call allocation grid to determine a prospecting plan? Be specific, and number each step of the process you would use.

11. How does predictive modeling improve salesperson performance? You may want to review "Sales Technology 15.1" as you develop your answer.

CASE PROBLEMS

case **15.1**

MicroDyne

When Bill Maguire saw the headline that Micro-Automation and Dynamic Tools merged, he almost passed out. MicroDyne, the new company, would be his account, but what kind of account would it be?

Two years ago Bill landed the Dynamic Tools business after a hard-fought negotiation and sales process. First, the company had been using Bill's strongest competitor, Target Supply, for almost 10 years. Although some minor issues had arisen, overall Dynamic Tools was pretty satisfied. The director of manufacturing, Jack Reilly, really liked the Target Supply rep and fought hard against Bill. In one meeting Jack not only shouted at Bill, he told the head of purchasing that he resented Bill's company even getting a chance to bid! But in the end Bill's lower price and several customer testimonials, including one from a good friend of the CFO, won the business.

Over the two years since, Bill made a lot of progress in strengthening the relationship, except with Jack. But then, six months ago, Jack left Dynamic to take a position with Micro-Automation, also one of Bill's accounts. The first thing he did was call Bill. "Well, guess what, Bill. I'm canceling all outstanding orders with your company as of now. And that pallet of sweepers you sent yesterday? You can come get it. I switched all our business to Target."

Micro-Automation's business for Bill was much smaller than that of Dynamic, so the loss wasn't so bad. But Micro-Automation is bigger overall, and Dynamic Tool was acquired by Micro. Jack was back, as the movie promos say, "bigger and badder than ever."

Suddenly Bill's cell phone rang. The caller ID showed Micro-Dyne. Was Jack calling to cancel already?

Questions

1. Assess the new Micro-Dyne account in terms of the sales call allocation grid.

2. Assume the call is not from Jack but from the former Dynamic Tool CFO. She tells you that she is the new CFO, and they will be reviewing all vendors. You ask about Jack's responsibility and job title, and she laughs. "I know what you're thinking. But don't worry. You've done a great job for us. We just want to consolidate all purchases so we know we're getting the best deal." How should Bill respond? What should he do?

case **15.2**

McGraw-Hill

Pierce Totten is a salesperson for McGraw-Hill, the company that publishes this textbook. Pierce works from Minneapolis–St. Paul; his territory includes northern Minnesota and the following accounts:

Bemidji State, Bemidji: This school has 12 faculty members in the business administration program. It offers five majors: finance, generalist, management, marketing, and small business. It is a small school with approximately 400 undergraduate business students.

Central Lakes College, Brainerd: There are 11 faculty members at the Brainerd campus of Central Lakes in the business department. The school offers eight majors: finance, management, marketing, accounting, information systems, insurance, economics, and entrepreneurship in a two-year associate program. This pre-BBA program can be combined with programs at schools such as St. Scholastica. The school has 350 students at the Brainerd campus and another 100 taking courses online.

Lake Superior College, Duluth: There are approximately 8,500 students at Lake Superior. The business department has 10 full-time faculty members and offers 19 majors in the bachelor's program. There are approximately 30 adjunct professors who teach one class each, but in almost all cases the full-time faculty decides what books to use.

University of Minnesota Duluth: There are over 9,000 students total at UMD. The school of business and economics has over 40 faculty members (full-time) in four departments, and approximately 60 percent of all undergraduates are business majors.

St. Cloud University, St. Cloud: There are five departments offering 10 majors at St. Cloud. Over 70 faculty members teach in the undergraduate program, serving approximately 3,500 students.

Source: Based on information and a scenario suggested by Dr. Jeff Totten, Southeastern Louisiana University, and a sales representative from another textbook publisher.

Questions

1. Plan an appropriate schedule for Pierce.

2. What are the three most important issues Pierce needs to consider in scheduling his time? Why are these issues so important?

ROLE PLAY CASE

Six months ago, you went through your accounts and determined that how you've allocated your effort is not consistent with the potential of each account and your relative position. In one instance, National Barns, you've got a great relationship with the CIO (chief information officer or head of information technology) and have called on National Barns once or twice a month. There are, however, only 24 salespeople there, and the company isn't growing, so there isn't much opportunity. You decided that this is an account you no longer plan to visit in person but will check by phone.

Another account, Maguire Manufacturing, merited more calling. It had 34 salespeople six months ago and has 44 now. Because it continues to grow and has indicated that it may grow through acquisition of other companies, you've decided to visit it once or twice a month.

Grafton Gifts, a distributor of gifts and greeting cards, has been a tough account to understand. Its 120 salespeople who call on retailers around the country use a paper-based system to keep track of their accounts. Orders are placed on special handheld computers that are downloaded at night. The VP of sales says that's all the company needs, but the VP of marketing wants more information so a CRM marketing strategy can be used. Today you will visit the VP of marketing to determine whether you want to continue with this account.

Your professor will give you buyer sheets for your turn as a buyer.

ADDITIONAL REFERENCES

Berry, Julian. "How Should Goals for 'Contact Optimisation' Be Set, and How Should Contact Optimisation Be Managed in a Multi-Channel Inbound and Outbound Environment?" *Journal of Database Marketing & Customer Strategy Management* 16, no. 4 (2009), pp. 241–46.

Eggert, Andreas, Wolfgang Ulaga, and Sabine Hollmann. "Benchmarking the Impact of Customer Share in Key Supplier Relationships." *Journal of Business & Industrial Marketing* 24, no. 3–4 (2009), pp. 154–69.

Fleischer, Mark. "Key Account Management in the Managed Markets: Visibility and Collaboration for Greater Effectiveness." *Journal of Medical Marketing* 10, no. 1 (January 2010), pp. 53–60.

Helm, Sabrina, Ludger Rolfes, and Bernd Gunter. "Suppliers' Willingness to End Unprofitable Customer Relationships: An Exploratory Investigation in the German Mechanical Engineering Sector." *European Journal of Marketing* 40, no. 3–4 (2006), pp. 366–83.

Koller, Monika, and Thomas Salzberger. "Benchmarking in Service Marketing: A Longitudinal Analysis of the Customer." *Benchmarking* 16, no. 3 (2009), pp. 401–20.

Lambert, Douglas M. "Customer Relationship Management as a Business Process." *Journal of Business & Industrial Marketing* 25 no. 1 (2010), pp. 4–17.

Sweet, Catherine, Tim Sweet, Beth Rogers, Valerie Heritage, and Mike Turner. "Developing a Benchmark for Company-wide Sales Capability." *Industrial and Commercial Training* 39, no. 1 (2007), pp. 18–28.

Zallacco, Ronald, Ellen Bolman Pullins, and Michael L. Mallin. "A Reexamination of B2B Sales Performance." *Journal of Business & Industrial Marketing* 24, no. 8 (2009), pp. 598–611.

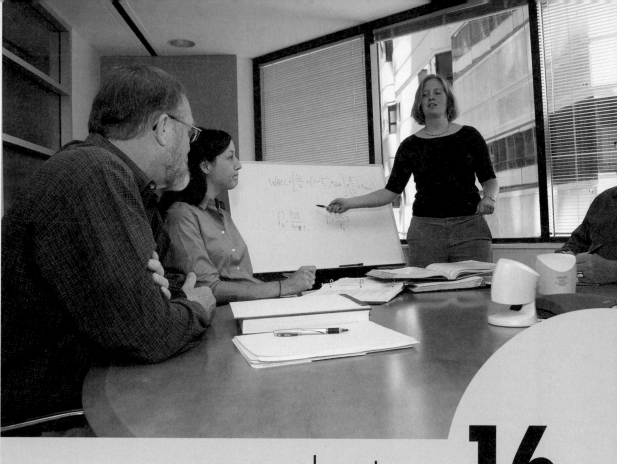

chapter **16**

MANAGING WITHIN YOUR COMPANY

SOME QUESTIONS ANSWERED IN THIS CHAPTER ARE

- Which areas of the company work with salespeople to satisfy customer needs?
- How do salespeople coordinate the efforts of various functional areas of the company?
- How do salespeople work with sales managers and sales executives?
- How do company policies, such as compensation plans, influence salespeople?
- How do salespeople work within the company to resolve ethical issues?
- What is the organizational structure, and how does it influence salesperson activities?

PROFILE International logistics is a $3 trillion a year industry that is highly regulated and changing on a routine basis. Phoenix International is a privately owned freight forwarder and customs broker that supports companies involved in international trade. As a sales executive at Phoenix International my role extends beyond selling new business. On a daily basis my focus is to ensure that my client's needs and wants are met. This may seem like an easy task, but it takes a solid relationship and strong management to be successful. Each client, commodity, and country I work with is a new canvas. Through active listening, research, and building a relationship with my clients, I am able to learn their business processes, specific requirements, frustrations, and wants. This knowledge allows me to create customized solutions that improve my customers' supply chains.

Once I have earned the trust of my clients and they choose to enter a partnership with Phoenix International, it is my responsibility to act as their advocate. Before working with a new client, I ensure that all departments have an understanding of the company, the client's needs, and any specific handling instructions. I develop standard operating procedures with the operational staff to make the customer's needs transparent. I work with the credit department and account receivables to establish appropriate credit levels and payments terms. My information systems team and I work together to provide the customer real-time visibility and reporting capabilities. Internally we all know sales can bring the first shipment in the door, but it is operations that play a vital role in maintaining and growing the business. The relationship between the operational coordinator and the customer is extremely significant, but more important is that the relationship is well managed.

Specifically here is an example of how I work with the operational coordinator: Today I received a phone call from one of my clients, Jon. He was upset because his shipment was not going to arrive on the original estimated day due to a number of events. As his representative I knew how critical this deadline was for him, and I wanted to assure him that we would use all possibilities to meet his deadline. I called his coordinator at Phoenix International to discuss various scenarios we could take to overcome the obstacle. The solution was simple and didn't take much time to resolve; with teamwork we were able to meet the customer's demands and make him happy.

Had I not worked with the operations coordinator and let the customer take a late delivery, how would my reaction have affected the business relationship between the client and Phoenix International? In my industry one small mistake, even if it was made by the customer, can cost you the account. In a company that prides itself on customer service, it is important for the sales executive to act in the best interest of the client and ensure that the coordinator is doing everything possible to make the shipment happen as smoothly as possible.

Typically when a problem arises the operational staff are the first to be made aware of it, and then the customer finds out. It is critical for the person in operations to notify me of what is going on because the next phone call I receive is going to be an upset customer. International trade is a complex business arena full of pitfalls and potential problems. My job in supporting my clients is to help the clients navigate through those pitfalls. When customers call with a concern and you have a logical explanation along with a solution, you save their day.

As a sales executive I have a number of individuals I report to. My sales manager, general manager, and all the way to the CEO of the company have a vested interest in how I am performing. Our internal systems allow management to easily track my productivity through the number of client visits and scheduled appointments, as well as my gross profit.

This visibility gives them the transparency to track my progress and determine where there may be room for improvement. This tool is very useful for my superiors to manage me; it also helps me manage myself.

Managing yourself is one of the most important roles for a sales executive. In sales you don't punch a time clock and receive a "to do" list when you walk through the door. Managing your priorities is the number one task where most people fail. There are several duties that consume your day, taking away from your core responsibilities: to sell new business and retain current customers. Once you have developed the skills to manage yourself, you are on the road to success!

Finally, no matter what position you are in or what company you work for, remember that your clients, no matter how big or small, deserve to be treated with respect and dignity and to be your number one concern. In addition the people you work with deserve the same treatment because without their support and hard work the company and you will not succeed.

Visit our Web site at http://www.phoenixintl.com.

BUILDING INTERNAL PARTNERSHIPS

To effectively coordinate the efforts of various areas of a company, a salesperson must develop partnerships with the individuals in those areas. **Internal partnerships** are partnering relationships between a salesperson and another member of the same company. These partnerships should be dedicated to satisfying customer needs.

THE IMPORTANCE OF INTERNAL PARTNERSHIPS

By definition, a sales representative represents something. Students often think the title means that the salesperson represents only a company or a product, but at times the salesperson must represent the customer to the company. For example, the salesperson may have to convince the warehouse manager to ship a customer's product next to meet a special deadline. The salesperson does not have the authority to order the manager to ship the product, but he or she must use persuasion. Or the rep may have to negotiate with production to get a product manufactured to a customer's specifications. Sometimes success in landing a sale may depend on the salesperson's ability to manage such company efforts.

This ability to work with groups inside the company can directly affect the rep's pocketbook. One of the authors, while selling for a major corporation, had an opportunity to earn a large bonus by making 30 sales. He had 31 orders, but a sale didn't count until the product was delivered. Unfortunately two orders were delivered after the deadline, and he did not get the bonus. In tracking down the slow deliveries, the hapless salesperson learned that the order entry clerk had delayed processing the orders. A little probing uncovered the reason: She was upset with the way he prepared his paperwork! Her performance was evaluated on how quickly an order was delivered, but his sloppy paperwork always slowed her down and got her into trouble. Delaying work on his orders was her way of getting his attention.

It worked! For several months after that, he enlisted her help in filling out the paperwork properly before he turned it in. After that, she never had a problem with his orders. And when necessary to meet a customer's requirements, she would prioritize his orders.

THE ROLE OF SALES

Salespeople not only sell a company, its products, and its services to customers but also sell their customers' needs to their companies. Carrying the customer's voice across the organization is one of the most important functions of the sales force. Although many companies work to increase the customer contact time for support personnel so they will understand customers, often the only person who really understands what the customer needs and why is the salesperson. The salesperson's ability to carry the voice of the customer across the organization is key to any firm.

Nucor Fastener uses its CRM system to capture the voice of the customer. Salespeople's notes, along with a deep analysis of data from other systems, helped the company identify specific customer needs that required special treatment. For example, 50 percent of all rush orders were generated by only 12 customers. The account executives for those accounts were able to identify customer requirements that led to new service offerings, greater revenue, and higher customer satisfaction.[1]

But when companies do not have a formal voice of the customer process, salespeople still have a responsibility to their customers to ensure that the company is responsive to their changing needs. In "Building Partnerships 16.1" Dave Brock describes an experience he had with a salesperson for a marketing agency who had not taken the time and effort to make sure his company was meeting customers' needs.

SELLING INTERNALLY

To service customers well, salespeople must often rely on personnel in other areas of the firm to do their respective jobs properly. But how well those other employees assist salespeople may be a function of the relationship the salesperson has already established with them. That relationship should be a partnership, just like the one the salesperson wants to establish with appropriate customers. To establish the appropriate partnership, the salesperson must invest time in understanding the customer's needs and then work to satisfy those needs.

thinking **it** through

Consider the impact electronic forms of communication have had on your life so far. How do such forms of communication help build internal partnerships, particularly when a salesperson is stationed far from company headquarters? How can such forms of communication hinder a salesperson's efforts to build internal partnerships?

As summarized in Exhibit 16.1, the first step of selling laterally is to recognize that it is the salesperson's responsibility to develop relationships with other departments. Rarely do other departments have an incentive to take the initiative. Salespeople who expect other workers to serve them are frustrated by the lack of support they receive. The better perspective is, How can I serve them so we can serve the customer better?

Use questioning skills such as SPIN to understand the personal and professional needs of personnel in other departments. Salespeople should have excellent communication skills but sometimes fail to use these skills when dealing with internal customers and support groups. SPIN and active listening are just as important to understanding the needs of colleagues as they are to satisfying customer needs. For example:

SALESPERSON: What do you do with these credit applications? (*Situation*)

CREDIT REP: We key the information into the computer system, and then it is processed by a credit company each night. The next morning we get a report that shows who has been approved and who hasn't. That's why it is so important to have a clean copy.

SOMETIMES I'M ASHAMED TO BE A SALESPERSON

I like talking to salespeople trying to sell me something. It's always interesting to be on the customer side and to be able to look at how I am being sold to. Often I talk to really great salespeople. They are professional, they listen well, they execute their sales process well. Even though I may not buy, I'll find a way to point those people to an opportunity, or at least thank them for their professionalism. Then I get the calls like I got today.

The phone call actually started well because it was short. The salesperson was trying to sell me some marketing services. Like every company, we are interested in opportunities to extend our reach and attract interest. The sales guy told me about his company's great capability to create content, interesting designs, powerful graphics, and compelling messages. He further talked about getting that content into multiple channels in a cohesive way.

I was interested in what he had to say. I asked him to send information and some references I could talk to. We set a follow-up for next week. Within a few minutes I got the e-mail—things were going well. He was meeting my expectations, though I did set the bar pretty low.

I received a series of Word documents. I opened the first one. It was poorly written and confusing and had major formatting problems and even a few spelling errors. Hmm.

I opened the second; it was no better; same with the third. I was beginning to wonder. Here is a company that presented itself as creating compelling content, powerful messages, and high-impact materials. If its own marketing materials represented the firm so poorly, would it represent my company any better?

I was curious, so I opened the list of references. The salesperson, in the e-mail, had told me to feel free to contact any directly. The references were four pages of testimonials—but by only four people. Three pages were two testimonials from the same person. The formatting and flow were terrible. It looked like exactly what it was: a cut-and-paste job. There were people's names, but no contact information—I guess the salesperson wanted me to work for the information.

I clicked on the first link, hoping to be taken to the reference's Web site. The site I was taken to was one that declared the company's offerings a scam! It had many testimonials about how the salesperson's company took your money but either failed to deliver the service or delivered the poorest quality of service.

This was an interesting approach; never saw this one before; I thought I'd seen just about everything! I read the dismal reviews. What they said about the company's marketing programs was actually reinforced by the poor-quality marketing materials the company had developed for itself. The other reference that I could link to took me not to the reference's Web site but to a completely different company, having nothing to do with the reference. 0 for 2, so far. I decided to stop wasting my time.

I wonder if the salesperson ever looked at the materials he sent. I wonder if he ever bothered to click on the links. He clearly did not take my request for references seriously because there were no portfolio examples, the collateral he had sent was garbage, and I had no means of finding a legitimate reference.

The company was a legitimate company. I actually pulled its D&B (a financial report available from Dunn & Bradstreet). It wasn't big, but nothing stood out as saying it wasn't real. The story wasn't good when I went to the Better Business Bureau site; there were a number of complaints there.

You might ask, Why are you blaming the salesperson, the company is bad? After all, it's providing him with bad materials and poor references. Absolutely, I agree, this company is terrible! But the salesperson bears responsibility as well. He had so little pride in what he was doing that he did not bother to look at the documents and fix them. He never bothered to look at the references and where the links went. He was simply going through the motions but not paying attention to what he was doing.

Doing your homework includes knowing your own materials, proposals, and other collateral. Make sure they respond to what the customer has requested. Make sure they present the image of the company that you want to present. If they don't, take the time to fix it.

Salespeople cannot just go through the motions! True professionals take pride in what they do, execute with precision, and always present themselves and their companies professionally. I like being around professionals—they make me want to be better. Every encounter with companies and salespeople that aren't discourages me. If they are salespeople, it makes me ashamed to be called a salesperson.

Source: Dave Brock is president and CEO of Partners in EXCELLENCE, a global consulting company focused on helping its clients achieve profound improvements in the performance of their sales organizations. Used with permission.

Exhibit 16.1

Seven Principles of Selling Internally

1. Understand that it's your problem. **Accept responsibility** for gaining the support of the internal staff.

2. **Appeal to a higher objective.** For example, show how what you are asking for meets an important company objective.

3. Probe to find out and **understand the personal and professional needs** of the internal customer. Use SPIN and active listening techniques.

4. Use arguments for support that adequately **address the internal customer's needs** as well as your own. Use your presentation skills.

5. Do not spend time or energy resenting the internal customers' inability to understand or accept your sense of urgency. Rather, spend this time fruitfully by trying to figure out how you can better communicate your needs in a manner that will **increase the internal customer's sense of urgency** to the level you need.

6. **Never personalize** any issues. Don't call names, blame the person in public, or hold a grudge.

7. Be prepared to **negotiate**.

SALESPERSON: So the quality of the copy we give you is a problem? (*Problem*)

CREDIT REP: That's right.

SALESPERSON: What happens when you can't read the copy we give you? (*Implication*)

CREDIT REP: We put in incorrect information, which can result in a customer's credit application being rejected when it should have been accepted.

SALESPERSON: What happens when that happens? (*Implication*)

CREDIT REP: That's when we call you. Then we get the right information and reenter it. But we get in trouble because the approval cycle was made longer, and you know that the goal is to have a customer's order shipped in three days. We can't meet that goal if we're still working on its credit application.

SALESPERSON: So you need legible applications—and probably e-mail would be better than handwritten, right? (*Needs payoff*)

CREDIT REP: Yes, that would help a lot.

Keep in mind too that the salesperson cannot simply order a colleague to do what the salesperson wants, such as approving a customer's credit application. But if a salesperson can show that doing what he or she wants will also meet the needs of the colleague, the salesperson is more likely to receive the desired aid. Just as when selling to an external customer, persuasion requires the salesperson to meet the other person's needs as well. For example, if a salesperson can show a plant manager how an expedited order will result in a higher profit margin, thereby more than covering the plant manager's higher costs and helping that manager make production targets, both the plant manager's needs and the customer's needs will be met.

People from other departments, except for billing and customer service, do not have direct contact with the customer. Therefore, they do not feel the same sense of urgency the customer or the salesperson feels. Successful internal sellers can communicate that sense of urgency by relating to the needs of the internal customer. Just as they do with external customers, salespeople need to communicate the need to act now when they sell internally. They need to secure commitment to the desired course of action. Also, just as with external customers, the salesperson should be sure to say thank you when someone agrees to provide the support requested.

Selling to internal customers also means keeping issues professional. Personal relationships can and should be developed. But when conflicts arise, focus on the issue, not the person. Personalizing conflict makes it seem bigger and harder to resolve. For example, rather than saying, "Why won't you do this?" ask, "If you can't do this, how can we resolve the customer's concern?" This type of statement focuses the other individual on resolving the real problem rather than arguing about company policy or personal competence.

Be prepared to negotiate. Remember from Chapter 12 that negotiation is a set of techniques to resolve conflict. Conflicts between salespeople and members of the firm representing other areas will occur, and negotiation skills can be used to respond to conflicts professionally.

Salespeople must work with many elements of their organization. In fact, few jobs require the boundary-spanning coordination and management skill that the sales job needs. In the next section we examine the many areas of the company with which the salesperson works, what their needs are, and how they partner with the salesperson to deliver customer satisfaction.

COMPANY AREAS IMPORTANT TO SALESPEOPLE

The sales force interacts with many areas of the firm. Salespeople work with manufacturing, sales administration, customer service, and personnel. In some industries requiring customization of products, engineering is an important department for salespeople. Finance can get into the picture as well when that department determines which customers receive credit and what price is charged. In addition, salespeople work with members of their own department and the marketing department.

MANUFACTURING

In general, manufacturing is concerned with producing product at the lowest possible cost. Thus in most cases manufacturing wants long production runs, little customization, and low inventories. Customers, however, want their purchases shipped immediately and custom-made to their exact specifications. Salespeople may have to negotiate compromises between manufacturing and the customer. Salespeople should also develop relationships with manufacturing so they can make accurate promises and guarantees to customers.

In addition, we've already discussed the importance of the salesperson in ensuring that customers' needs are heard and products designed that fit their needs. Research shows that close, collaborative relationships between salespeople and manufacturing yield better new product designs—better in the sense of greater market acceptance and sales volume.[2] Hose Master Inc., a manufacturer of industrial hoses, actually brings salespeople and customers together with manufacturing for training on products. Frank Caprio, major market specialist for Hose Master, says these training sessions always yield new ideas for products or product enhancements that manufacturing can implement quickly.[3]

Salespeople who develop internal partnerships with people in areas such as manufacturing and service can count on their internal partners for support.

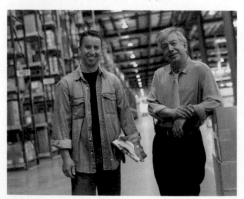

ADMINISTRATION

The functions of order entry, billing, credit, and employee compensation require each company to have an administrative department. This department processes orders and sees that the salesperson gets paid for them. Employees in this area (as discussed earlier) are often evaluated on how quickly they process orders and how quickly the company receives customer payment. Salespeople can greatly influence both processes and realize substantial personal benefit for themselves.

The credit department is an important part of administration. Understanding the needs of the credit department and assisting it in collecting payments can better position the salesperson to help customers receive credit later. A credit representative who knows that you will help collect a payment when a problem arises is more likely to grant credit to one of your customers. Some companies do not pay commission until after the customer has paid to ensure that salespeople sell to creditworthy accounts. These companies, such as Ruhrpumpen Inc. (an industrial pump manufacturer) and General Electric, believe a close working relationship between sales and credit is critical to the financial health of the company. In fact, GE has a "Walk a Mile" program where salespeople spend a day in credit, and credit personnel spend a day in the field with salespeople. This program leads to greater understanding and communication that last long after the day of walking a mile in someone's shoes.[4]

SHIPPING

The scheduling of product shipments may be part of sales administration or manufacturing, or it may stand alone. In any case salespeople need the help of the shipping department. When salespeople make special promises to expedite a delivery, they actually must depend on shipping to carry out the promise. Shipping managers focus on costs, and they often keep their costs under control by planning efficient shipping routes and moving products quickly through warehouses. Expedited or special-handling deliveries can interfere with plans for efficient shipping. Salespeople who make promises that shipping cannot or will not fulfill are left with egg on their faces. That's why Andrea Kinnard, sales representative for Konica-Minolta in Fort Worth, has been known to help load a delivery truck so a customer could get a much-needed copier.

CUSTOMER SERVICE

Salespeople also need to interact with customer service. The need for this relationship should be obvious, but many salespeople arrogantly ignore the information obtained by customer service representatives. A technician who fixes the company's products often goes into more customers' offices or plants than the salesperson does. The technician often has early warning concerning a customer's switch to a competitor, a change in customer needs, or failure of a product to satisfy. For example, if an IBM technician spies a competitor's computer in the customer's office, the technician can ask whether the unit is on trial. If a good working relationship exists between the technician and the salesperson, the technician will warn the salesperson that the account is considering a competitive product. Close relationships and support of customer or technical service representatives mean not only better customer service but faster and more direct information flow to the salesperson. This information will help the salesperson gain and keep customers.

Salespeople, in turn, can help customer service by setting reasonable expectations for product performance with customers, training customers in the proper use of the product, and handling complaints promptly. Technicians are evaluated on the number of service calls they make each day and how long the product works between service calls, among other things. Salespeople can reduce some service calls by setting the right expectations for product performance. Salespeople can also extend the amount of time between calls by training customers in the proper use of the product and in preventive maintenance. An important by-product of such actions should be higher customer satisfaction.

MARKETING

Sales is part of marketing in some firms and separate from marketing in others. Marketing and sales should be highly coordinated because their functions are closely related. Both are concerned with providing the right product to the customer in the most efficient and effective manner. Sales acts as the eyes and ears of marketing, while marketing develops the promotions and products that salespeople sell. Salespeople act as eyes and ears by informing the marketing department of competitor actions, customer trends, and other important market information. Marketing serves salespeople by using that information to create promotional programs or design new products. Marketing is also responsible for generating leads through trade show exhibiting, direct mail programs, advertising, and public relations.

Unfortunately not all marketing and sales departments just naturally get along. A study of Dutch firms found one reason to be simply that no one is responsible for interfacing between the departments.[5] Several other studies have shown that sales and marketing departments fail to communicate, don't trust each other, and even sabotage each other.[6] One study suggested that the biggest problem seems to be a lack of communication.[7] Other studies, however, suggest that the differences run deeper than communication; the differences are driven by beliefs about what should be done and by whom, the perceived value of marketing versus sales, and other basic differences.[8] Proactive salespeople won't wait for marketing managers to make the first move. Rather than complain about poor marketing programs, proactive salespeople and sales managers prefer to participate in marketing decisions and keep communication lines open. When sales and marketing work together, salespeople have better programs with which to sell.[9]

SALES

Within any sales force, there may be several types of salespeople. As you learned in earlier chapters, global account managers may work with the largest accounts while other representatives handle the rest of the customers, and the salesperson must interact with certain sales executives and sales managers. How these people work together is the subject of the next section.

PARTNERS IN THE SALES ORGANIZATION

The sales function may be organized in many different ways, but no matter how it is organized, it is rarely perfect. Usually some customer overlap exists among salespeople, meaning several salespeople have to work together to serve the needs of one account. Customer needs may require direct customer contact with the sales executive as well as the salesperson. At the same time, the salesperson must operate in an environment that is influenced by the policies and procedures created by that same sales executive and executed by the salesperson's immediate manager. In this section we examine how the activities of sales management affect salespeople.

SALES MANAGEMENT

Salespeople should understand the roles of both sales executives and field sales managers. Salespeople who are able to develop partnerships with their managers will have more resources available to perform at a higher level.

The Sales Executive

The sales executive is the manager at the top of the sales force hierarchy. This person is a policy maker, making decisions about how the sales force will accomplish corporate objectives. Sales executives play a vital role in determining the company's strategies with respect to new products, new markets, sales forecasts, prices, and competition. The executives determine the size and organization of the sales force, develop annual and long-range plans, and monitor and control sales efforts. Sales executives also strive, or should strive, to create a corporate culture that supports appropriate behaviors by their sales managers and salespeople—behaviors that are both ethical and customer-oriented.[10] Duties of the sales executive include forecasting overall sales, budgeting, setting sales quotas, and designing compensation programs.

Size and Organization of the Sales Force

The sales executive determines how many salespeople are needed to achieve the company's sales and customer satisfaction targets. In addition, the sales executive must determine what types of salespeople are needed. For example, the sales executive determines whether global account management is needed. Many other types of salespeople can be selected, which we discuss later in this chapter. For now, keep in mind that the sales executive determines the level of customer satisfaction necessary to achieve sales objectives and then designs a sales force to achieve those goals. How that sales force is put together is important because salespeople often have to work together to deliver appropriate customer service and successfully accomplish sales goals.

Forecasting

Sales executives use a number of techniques to arrive at sales forecasts. One of the most widely used techniques is **bottom-up forecasting,** or simply adding each salesperson's own forecast into a forecast for total company sales. At each level of management, the forecast would normally be adjusted based on the manager's experience and broader perspective. This technique allows the information to come from the people closest to the market: the salespeople. Also, the forecast comes from the people with the responsibility for making those sales. But salespeople tend to be optimistic and may overestimate sales, or they may underestimate future sales if they know their bonuses depend on exceeding forecasts or if they think their quotas will be raised. Wise managers should quickly realize when salespeople are underestimating forecasts, though the salespeople may be able to obtain significant earnings the first time. Such behavior, though, not only is unethical but also creates many problems for the organization.[11]

Salespeople are especially important to the forecasting process when the executive is attempting to forecast international sales. Statistics used in the United States to forecast sales are often not available in other countries or, if available, may be unreliable. Companies in Europe operate in so many different countries that the only consistent numbers available may come from the sales force. One candy company found that its salespeople provided the best forecast possible, in part because they were closest to the customer but also because each country's data were collected and compiled in different ways, making comparisons impossible.[12] But even companies in the United States are pushing forecasting to the field. Coty Fragrance, makers of such fragrance brands as Jennifer Lopez, Vera Wang, and Kenneth Cole, began requiring salespeople to develop forecasts based on the data in their CRM system. Coty's forecasting improved, leading to a significant reduction in stockouts, which also accounted for an increase in sales when the industry was hit by the recession.[13]

Expense Budgets

Managers sometimes use expense budgets to control costs. An expense budget may be expressed in dollars (for example, the salesperson may be allowed to spend up to $500) or as a percentage of sales volume (such as expenses cannot exceed 10 percent of sales). A regional manager or salesperson may be awarded a bonus for spending less than the budget allocates. However, such a bonus may encourage the salesperson to underspend, which could hurt sales performance. For example, if a salesperson refuses to give out samples, customers may not be able to visualize how a product will work; thus some may not buy. The salesperson has reduced expenses but hurt sales.

Although salespeople may have limited input into a budget, they do spend the money. Ultimately it is the salesperson's responsibility to manage the territorial budget. The salesperson not only has control over how much is spent and whether expenditures are over or under budget but also, and more important, decides where to place resources. Recall from Chapter 15 that these resources, such as samples and trial units or trips to the customers' location, are investments in future sales. If they are used unwisely, the salesperson may still meet the expense budget but fail to meet his or her sales quota.

Control and Quota Setting

The sales executive faces the challenge of setting up a balanced control system that will encourage each sales manager and salesperson to maximize his or her individual results through effective self-control. As we have pointed out throughout this text, salespeople operate somewhat independently. However, the control system management can help salespeople manage themselves more effectively.

Quotas are a useful technique for controlling the sales force. A **quota** represents a quantitative minimum level of acceptable performance for a specific period. A **sales quota** is the minimum number of sales in units, and a **revenue quota** is the minimum sales revenue necessary for acceptable performance. Often sales quotas are simple breakdowns of the company's total sales forecast. Thus the total of all sales quotas equals the sales forecast. Other types of quotas can also be used. Understanding quotas is important to the salesperson because performance relative to quota is evaluated by management.

Profit quotas or **gross margin quotas** are minimum levels of acceptable profit or gross margin performance. These quotas motivate the sales force to sell more profitable products or to sell to more profitable customers. Some companies assign points to each product based on the product's gross margin. More points are assigned to higher-margin products. The salesperson can then meet a point quota by selling either a lot of low-margin products or fewer high-margin products. For example, assume an office equipment company sells fax machines and copiers. The profit margin (not including salesperson compensation) is 30 percent on copiers but only 20 percent on fax machines. Copiers may be worth three points each, whereas faxes are worth two. If the salesperson's quota is 12 points, the quota can be reached by selling four copiers, or six faxes, or some combination of both.

One challenge sales managers face is recognizing that performance quotas can negatively influence a customer orientation as salespeople put the need to make quota ahead of their customers' needs.[14] One type of quota that can avoid this dilemma is an activity quota. **Activity quotas,** similar to the activity goals we discussed in the preceding chapter, are minimal expectations of activities for each salesperson. The company sets these quotas to control the activities of the sales force. This type of quota is important in situations where the sales cycle is long and sales are few because activities can be observed more frequently than sales. For example, for some medical equipment, the sales cycle is longer than one year, and a salesperson may sell only one or two units each quarter. Having a monthly sales target in this case would be inappropriate, but requiring a certain minimum number of calls to be made is reasonable. The assumption made by management is that if the salesperson is performing the proper activities, sales will follow with the customer's needs in mind. Activities for which quotas may be established include number of demonstrations, total customer calls, number of calls on prospects, or number of displays set up.

Compensation and Evaluation

An important task of the sales executive is to establish the company's basic compensation and evaluation system. The compensation system must satisfy the needs of both the salespeople and the company. You, as a salesperson, need an equitable, stable, understandable system that motivates you to meet your objectives. The company needs a system that encourages you to sell products at a profitable price and in the right amounts.

Salespeople want a system that bases rewards on effort and results. Compensation must also be uniform within the company and in line with what competitors' salespeople receive. If competitors' salespeople earn more, you will want to leave and work for that competitor. But your company expects the compensation system to attract and keep good salespeople and to encourage you to do specific things. The system should reward outstanding performance while achieving the proper balance between sales results and costs.

Compensation often relates to quotas. As with quotas, salespeople who perceive the system as unfair may give up or leave the firm. A stable compensation system ensures that salespeople can reap the benefits of their efforts, whereas a constantly changing system may lead them to constantly change their activities but never make any money. A system that is not understandable will be ignored.

The sales executive decides how much income will be based on salary or incentive pay. The salesperson may receive a **salary,** which is a regular payment regardless of performance, or **incentive pay,** which is tied to some level of performance. There are two types of incentives: commission and bonus. A **commission** is incentive pay for an individual sale, whereas a **bonus** is incentive pay for overall performance in one or more areas. For example, a bonus may be paid for acquiring a certain number of new customers, reaching a specified level of total sales in units, or selling a certain amount of a new product.

Many companies offer incentives, such as special awards, bonuses, and other rewards, for outstanding sales performance.

Sales executives can choose to pay salespeople a straight salary, a straight commission, or some combination of salary, commission, and/or bonus. Most firms opt for some combination of salary and bonus or salary and commission. Fewer than 4 percent pay only commission, and slightly fewer than 5 percent pay only salary. Exhibit 16.2 illustrates how various types of compensation plans work.

Under the **straight salary** method, a salesperson receives a fixed amount of money for work during a specified time. The salesperson is assured of a steady income and can develop a sense of loyalty to customers. The company also has more control over the salesperson. Because income does not depend directly on results, the company can ask the salesperson to do things in the best interest of the company, even if those activities may not lead to immediate sales. Straight salary, however, provides little financial incentive for salespeople to sell more. For example, in Exhibit 16.2, the salesperson receives $3,500 per month no matter how much is sold.

Straight salary plans are used when sales require long periods of negotiation, when a team of salespeople is involved and individual results cannot be measured, or when other aspects of the marketing mix (such as advertising) are more important than the salesperson's efforts in generating sales (as in trade selling of consumer products). Most sales trainees also receive a straight salary.

A **straight commission** plan pays a certain amount per sale and includes a base and a rate but not a salary. The **commission base,** the item from which commission is determined, is often unit sales, dollar sales, or gross margin.

Exhibit 16.2
How Different Types of Compensation Plans Pay

		Amount Paid to Salesperson			
Month	Sales Revenue	Straight Salary	Straight Commission*	Combination†	Point Plan‡
January	$50,000	$3,500	$5,000	$1,500 (salary)	$3,800
	6 copiers			3,000 (commission)	
	10 faxes			4,500 (total)	
February	$60,000	3,500	6,000	1,500 (salary)	4,800
	6 copiers			3,600 (commission)	
	15 faxes			5,100 (total)	
March	$20,000	3,500	2,000	1,500 (salary)	1,600
	2 copiers			1,200 (commission)	
	5 faxes			2,700 (total)	

*Commission plan pays 10 percent of sales revenue.
†Commission portion pays 6 percent of sales revenue.
‡Copiers are worth three points, faxes are worth two, and each point is worth $100 in commission.
Note: These commission rates are used only to illustrate how compensation schemes work. Point plans, for example, do not necessarily always yield the lowest compensation.

Exhibit 16.3
An Example of a Draw Compensation Plan

Month	Draw	Commission Earned	Payment to Salesperson	Balance Owed to Company
January	$3,000	$0	$3,000	$3,000
February	3,000	5,000	3,000	1,000
March	3,000	4,500	3,500	

The **commission rate,** which determines the amount paid, is expressed as a percentage of the base (such as 10 percent of sales or 8 percent of gross margin) or as a dollar amount (like $100 per sale). Exhibit 16.2 illustrates two straight commission plans: One pays 10 percent of sales revenue, and the other is a point plan that pays $100 per point (using the copier and fax example we discussed previously).

Commission plans often include a draw. A **draw** is money paid to the salesperson against future commissions—in essence a loan that guarantees a stable cash flow. For example, in Exhibit 16.3 the salesperson receives a draw of $3,000 per month. No commissions were earned during January, but the salesperson still received $3,000. In February the rep earned $5,000, but $2,000 went to pay back some of the draw from January, and the rep received only $3,000. In March the rep earned $4,500, of which $1,000 finished paying off the balance from January. Thus the rep was given $1,500 in March.

Straight commission plans have the advantage of tying the salesperson's compensation directly to performance, thus providing more financial incentive for the salesperson to work hard. However, salespeople on straight commission have little company loyalty and certainly are less willing to perform activities, such as paperwork, that do not directly lead to sales. Xerox experimented with such a plan but found that customer service suffered, as did company loyalty among salespeople.

Companies that do not emphasize service to customers or do not anticipate long-term customer relationships (like a company selling kitchen appliances directly to consumers) typically use commission plans. Such plans are also used when the sales force includes many part-timers because part-timers can earn more when their pay is tied to their performance. Also, part-timers may need the extra motivation straight commission can provide.

Under a bonus plan, salespeople receive a lump-sum payment for a certain level of performance over a specified time. Bonuses resemble commissions, but the amount paid depends on total performance, not on each individual sale. Bonuses, awarded monthly, quarterly, or annually, are always used with salary and/or commissions in **combination plans.** Combination plans, also called salary-plus-commission plans, provide salary and commission and offer the greatest flexibility for motivating and controlling the activities of salespeople. The plans can incorporate the advantages and avoid the disadvantages of using any of the basic plans alone.

The main disadvantage of combination plans lies in their complexity. Salespeople confused by this complexity could unknowingly perform the wrong activities, or sales managers could unintentionally design a program that rewards the wrong activities. Using the earlier office equipment example, if faxes and copiers were worth the same commission (for example, $100 per sale), the salesperson would sell whatever was easiest to sell. If faxes were easier to sell than copiers, the firm may make less money because salespeople would expend all of their effort selling a lower-profit product unless the volume sold made up for the lower margin. Even then, however, the firm may be stuck with a warehouse of unsold copiers.

thinking **it** through   As a buyer, under which plan would you prefer your salesperson to work? Which would you prefer if you were a salesperson? What conflicts might occur between buyer and seller because of the type of compensation plan?

FIELD SALES MANAGERS

Salespeople report directly not to a sales executive but to a **field sales manager.** Field sales managers hire salespeople, evaluate their performance, train them, and perform other important tasks. Salespeople find it useful to partner with their managers because the managers often represent the salespeople to other parts of the organization. Also, the salesperson often has to sell the manager first on any new idea before the idea can be pitched to others in management. Building a partnering relationship with managers can go a long way toward getting ideas accepted.[15]

Evaluating Performance

Field sales managers are responsible for evaluating the performance of their salespeople. The easiest method of evaluating performance is to simply add up the amount of sales that the salesperson makes. But sales managers must also rate their salespeople's customer service level, product knowledge, and other, less tangible qualities. Some companies, such as Federal Express, use customer satisfaction surveys to evaluate salespeople. In other companies the manager rates each salesperson, using evaluation forms that list the desired aspects. (An example of an evaluation form appears in Exhibit 16.4.) Such evaluations help managers determine training needs, promotions, and pay raises.

The records and reports salespeople submit also play an important role in communicating their activities to the sales manager. The manager uses these reports to evaluate performance in a manner similar to the way the salesperson would. But these written reports are not enough; sales managers should also make calls with salespeople to directly observe their performance. These observations can be

Exhibit 16.4
Behavioral Observation
Scale (BOS)

	Almost Never						Almost Always
1. Checks deliveries to see whether they have arrived on time.	1	2	3	4	5	6	7
2. Files sales reports on time.	1	2	3	4	5	6	7
3. Uses promotional brochures and correspondence with potential accounts.	1	2	3	4	5	6	7
4. Monitors competitors' activities.	1	2	3	4	5	6	7
5. Brushes up on selling techniques.	1	2	3	4	5	6	7
6. Reads marketing research reports.	1	2	3	4	5	6	7
7. Prospects for new accounts.	1	2	3	4	5	6	7
8. Makes service calls.	1	2	3	4	5	6	7
9. Answers customer inquiries when they occur.	1	2	3	4	5	6	7

the basis for recommendations for improving individual performance or for commending outstanding performance. Other information, such as customer response to a new strategy, can be gained by making calls. This information should be shared with upper management to improve strategies.

Training

The sales manager trains new hires and provides refresher training for experienced salespeople. To determine what refresher training they need, managers often use information gathered while observing salespeople making sales calls. Content of training for new salespeople may be determined by a sales executive, but the field sales manager is often responsible for carrying out the training.

Most experienced salespeople welcome training when they perceive that it will improve their sales. Unfortunately salespeople often view training as an inconvenience that takes away from precious selling time. Dave Stein argues, though, that basic sales training is just that—basic—and if you want to sell to higher levels of the organization, if you want to work on bigger deals, and if you want to make more money, advanced skills are needed. Unfortunately he cites one study showing that less than half of companies surveyed offer any training, and of those, only half offer sales training. Thus, in some organizations, salespeople have to find advanced training on their own.[16] You should continue to welcome training, no matter how successful you are. It always offers the opportunity to improve your performance, or at least achieve the same level with less effort. Also, as you will see in Chapter 17, continuing to learn is important to the salesperson who is part of a learning organization.

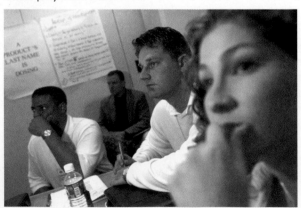

Professional salespeople constantly need to upgrade their skills; here a group at InFocus Systems is reviewing a role play sales call.

MANAGING ETHICS IN SALES

Salespeople, particularly those within certain industries, have earned a reputation that is unfavorable. Most salespeople, though, want to act ethically. Because we have emphasized throughout this book methods of selling that help people solve problems and satisfy needs, we believe it is important to understand what companies do to encourage ethical behavior and how salespeople should work with their sales management partners to choose ethical options. First we discuss the sales executive's role in making ethics policy. Then we cover the roles of the field sales manager and the salesperson in implementing that policy.

ETHICS AND THE SALES EXECUTIVE

As mentioned earlier, sales executives should strive to create an ethical culture. While part of a sales executive's job is to determine corporate policy concerning what is considered ethical and what is not and how unethical behavior will be investigated and punished, it is also important that the sales executive support positive behaviors.[17] In addition, the sales executive must ensure that other policies, such as the performance measurement and compensation policies, support the ethics of the organization. Performance measurement and compensation policies that reward only outcomes may inadvertently encourage salespeople to act unethically because of pressure to achieve and a culture supporting the credo "the end justifies the means." But when behavioral performance measurement systems are in place, the compensation system can reward those who do things the right way. In addition, research shows that closer relationships with ethical managers support ethical behavior.[18] Although unethical behaviors may result in short-term gain (and therefore may accidentally be rewarded in an outcome-only compensation scheme), they can have serious long-term effects, such as loss of customers, unhappy salespeople who quit, and other negative outcomes.[19]

Sales executives must therefore develop a culture that creates behavioral norms regarding how things should be done and what behaviors will not be tolerated. Such a culture can be enhanced through the development of formal policy, training courses in ethics, ethics review boards, and an open-door policy. **Open-door policies** are general management techniques that allow subordinates to bypass immediate managers and take concerns straight to upper management when the subordinates perceive a lack of support from the immediate manager. Open-door policies enhance an ethical culture because salespeople can feel free to discuss troublesome issues that involve their managers with someone in a position to respond. Two versions are **ethics review boards** and ethics officers, both providing expert advice to salespeople who are unsure of the ethical consequences of an action. Ethics review boards may consist of experts inside and outside the company who are responsible for reviewing ethics policies, investigating allegations of unethical behavior, and acting as a sounding board for employees.

Salespeople also have the right to expect ethical treatment from their company. Fair treatment concerning compensation, promotion policies, territory allocation, and other actions should be delivered. Compensation is probably the area with the most common concerns, although problems can arise in all areas. Compensation problems can include slow payment, hidden caps, or compensation plan changes after the sale.

For example, IBM published a brochure for its salespeople that said that there was no **cap,** or limit, on earnings. Yet the brochure also had, in bold letters, the statement that IBM had the right to modify the program—even after the sale—until the commission was paid. When a salesperson sold one major account $24 million worth of software, the company changed his commission plan so he received less than $500,000 instead of the $2.6 million he expected. The salesperson filed suit, but IBM won in part because of the modification statement in the letter.[20] IBM had every legal right to take the action it did, and caps are not unethical; what was questionable was that the salesperson was not made aware of the cap prior to making the sale.

ETHICS AND THE FIELD SALES MANAGER

Salespeople often ask managers for direction on how to handle ethical problems, and the sales manager is usually the first person to investigate complaints of unethical behavior. Field sales managers can provide a role model for salespeople by demonstrating ethical behavior in role plays during training or when conducting sales calls in the field. Sales managers should also avoid teaching high-pressure techniques and manipulative methods of selling.

RESPONDING TO UNETHICAL REQUESTS

Salespeople may find themselves facing a sales manager who encourages them to engage in unethical behavior. When that situation occurs, a salesperson has several ways to avoid engaging in such behavior. Perhaps the most obvious option is to find another job, but that is not always the best solution. If the organizational culture supports the unethical request, however, finding another job may be the only choice. Exhibit 16.5 lists choices available to the salesperson.

Another way to handle unethical requests is to blow the whistle, or report the behavior, if the salesperson has adequate evidence (if adequate evidence is not available, sometimes simply threatening to blow the whistle may work). If this course of action is followed, the salesperson must be ready to accept a perception of disloyalty, retaliation by the manager, or other consequences. However, if senior management is sincere in efforts to promote ethical behavior, steps should be taken to minimize those negative outcomes. If an open-door policy or an ethics review board exists, the salesperson can take the concern to higher levels for review. For example, the salesperson could say, "I'm not sure that is appropriate. I'd like to get the opinion of the ethics review board." If the action is unethical, the sales manager may back down at that point. It is also possible that the manager will try to coerce the salesperson into not applying to the ethics review board; if that is the case, another course of action may prove to be a better choice.

Another strategy is to negotiate an alternative. This response requires the salesperson to identify an alternative course of action with a high probability of success. For example, if a sales manager tells the salesperson to offer a prospect a bribe, the salesperson should be prepared to prove that a price reduction would be just as effective. A similar tactic is simply to ignore the request. The salesperson may say to the manager that the request was carried out, when in fact it was not; the potential problem with this approach is that the salesperson has admitted to carrying out an unethical act (even though she or he did not), which can lead to future problems. Finally, the salesperson can simply deny the request. Denial can be a dangerous action in that it opens the salesperson to possible retaliation, particularly retaliation that is not obviously linked to the denial, such as denying access to training or reducing the size of the salesperson's territory.

Exhibit 16.5
Strategies for Handling Unethical Requests from a Manager

- Leave the organization or ask for a transfer.
- Negotiate an alternative course of action.
- Blow the whistle, internally or externally.
- Threaten to blow the whistle.
- Appeal to a higher authority, such as an ethics officer or ethics review board or a senior executive if ethics offices do not exist.
- Agree to the demand but fail to carry it out.
- Refuse to comply with the request.
- Ignore the request.

thinking **it** through

Is it ethical to lie to your manager and say that you will engage in the unethical behavior that your manager demanded when you know you won't? Is all fair when you are combating a request to engage in unethical behavior?

The salesperson's choice of action will depend on how much proof is available, what alternative actions to the unethical action exist, and the type of relationship with the manager. Other factors to consider include the ethical climate of the organization and whether an open-door policy exists. The salesperson is always in control of his or her behavior and should never rationalize a behavior by placing responsibility on the sales manager.

SALESPEOPLE AS PARTNERS

Many types of salespeople exist, including telemarketing representatives, field salespeople, product specialists, and account specialists. Often there is some overlap in responsibilities; when overlap occurs, companies should have policies that facilitate serving the customer.

GEOGRAPHIC SALESPEOPLE

Most sales departments are organized geographically. A **geographic salesperson** is assigned a specific geographic territory in which to sell the company's products and services. Companies often combine geographic territories into larger branches, zones, or regions. For example, Eli Lilly has geographic regions that include 50 or more salespeople. Each Lilly salesperson has responsibility for a specific geographic area. For example, one rep may call on physicians in a portion of Dallas, using zip code boundaries to determine the territory; that rep may have all physicians in zip codes 75212, 75213, 75218, 75239, 75240, and 75252. Geographic salespeople may also work with account managers, product specialists, inside salespeople, and other members of the company's sales team.

ACCOUNT SALESPEOPLE

Companies may organize salespeople by account in several ways. The most extreme example is to give a salesperson the responsibility to sell to only one company but at every location of that company in the country or the world. In another common form of specialization, some salespeople develop new accounts while others maintain existing accounts. Developing new accounts requires skills different from maintaining an already sold account. For example, Holland 1916 recently reorganized around these lines. The decision was based on a desire to focus on larger accounts that could grow, recognizing that growing these accounts might require a different skill set than was needed to acquire the accounts. As a result of this thinking, Jim Humrichouse, CEO, developed a list of larger accounts with potential for more growth (recall the sales effort allocation grid from the last chapter—these would be high opportunity/strong position current accounts), then assigned these to reps with a track record of success in growing current customers. He then hired new salespeople to take over those reps' geographic territories and tasked them with new account acquisition.[21]

Similar customers often have similar needs, whereas different types of customers may have very different needs for the same product. In such cases salespeople may specialize in calling on only one or a few customer types, although they sell the same products. NCR has different sales forces for calling on manufacturing companies, retailers, and financial companies. Andritz, an international heavy machinery company, has salespeople who sell only to paper producers and other salespeople who sell only to wastewater treatment plants, even though the same product is being sold. Some Procter & Gamble salespeople call on central buying offices for grocery store chains; others call on food wholesalers.

Companies also divide their customers on the basis of size. Large customers, sometimes called **key accounts,** may have a salesperson assigned only to that account; in some cases a small sales force is assigned to one large account. In some firms one company executive coordinates all the salespeople who call on an account throughout the nation or the world. These executives are called **national account managers (NAMs)** or **strategic account managers (SAMs).** These account managers are more than salespeople; they are business executives.

Strategic account managers sometimes manage large teams of salespeople. Account strategy for a global account may be determined by this strategic account manager, who has to rely on local salespeople to implement the strategy at the local level. For example, Hershey's has an account rep that calls on Walmart in Bentonville, Arkansas, but local salespeople work with individual stores and store managers. The local geographic rep's responsibility may involve coordinating delivery with the local customer. This coordination may also require customer training on the product (if the product is a machine or some other system) or working with a local store manager to set up displays, plan inventories, and so on. Local reps should also look for sales opportunities in the customer's location and provide this information to the SAM. They often become the eyes and ears of the SAM and provide early notice of opportunities or threats in the account, just as a service rep does for the geographic rep. SAMs often report directly to the vice president of sales or to a director of global sales, as illustrated in Exhibit 16.6, but work with geographic reps.

As described in Chapter 6, a **house account** is handled by a sales or marketing executive in addition to that executive's regular duties, and no commission is paid on any sales from that account. House accounts are often key accounts, but not all key accounts are house accounts. The main difference is that house accounts have no "true" salesperson. Walmart has negotiated to be a house account with some suppliers with the expectation that those suppliers will pass on to Walmart what they do not have to pay in commission or salary. General Dynamics attempted the same strategy when buying, but abandoned the plan upon realizing that lower costs also meant reduced service.

Somewhat different is the mega-account strategy used at Motorola. The top 20 international accounts are actually managed by Motorola's CEO, who

Exhibit 16.6
SAMs in the Sales Force

Although SAMs and geographic salespeople have different immediate managers, they still work together. SAMs coordinate the efforts of geographic reps within local buying offices of global accounts.

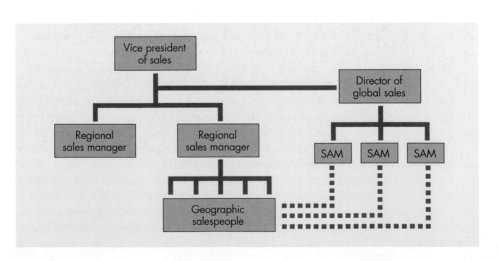

From the BUYER'S SEAT

SELLING IN MY COMPANY

By Anonymous

As marketing manager of a *Fortune* 500 company, I'm tasked with analyzing customer data to find new markets and new ways to generate revenue. I have to think about how to generate new sales from existing customers, and that means I need the right tools to understand my market and convince them to make additional purchases.

At the same time, however, I have to convince my management to spend the money to get the right tools. Currently we're in the midst of some major changes in how we seek to understand our customers, and these changes will require an investment of a million dollars or more for the right set of tools.

The process of selling my management on the need for these tools has been a long process, and it's not over yet. Among some of the leadership, the belief is that marketing doesn't influence demand—if people want our service, they will purchase it whether we market to them or not. So if I sell my new tools on the premise that these tools will help us convince people to buy more, I'll lose the sale based on my premise. Although I have a solid understanding of how these tools will help, not all of the leadership team does. Part of my job, then, is educating within the people I report to on how this will all work.

The primary tool we need is called Speed-Trap, a software product that provides detailed data about our customers' Web site activities. To complicate matters, we would also need to enhance our services from Teradata, the company that provides us with data warehousing services.

Most of the time, a presales group from a company like Teradata or Speed-Trap is responsible for teaching someone how to change the business. They have to create internal champions by selling them on the vision and educating them on the need and process for change. Usually they look for a vice president, not just a marketing manager. But Speed-Trap recognized that I already knew what they could do, that I didn't need their education as much as I needed their support, and they supported me in my internal selling. We had biweekly calls to discuss how to move this along, some pricing and configuration conversations, and some presentation conversations; and we jointly planned a presentation to the leadership team. I gave Speed-Trap cases to configure their presentation within the context of our business problems. The day before the big presentation, we met and made sure that everything was aligned properly.

In addition, while we needed Teradata people there to answer any questions about interfaces and implementation, this wasn't their sale. True, they have a product and services that we will need to buy in order to make this work, but the big decision for my management team is the Speed-Trap purchase. I had to make sure that Teradata understood their role and participated appropriately.

The big meeting lasted all day. At the end of it, not only did my company's leadership team understand and appreciate the need for Speed-Trap, they also recognized that they needed someone who understood the business model around the Speed-Trap implementation. That led to a promotion for me.

Still, I'm not done yet. The next question is how will we pay for this? Remember, it costs more than a million dollars. So now I'm working on the business case, documenting how Speed-Trap will save money as well as generate new revenue. Saving money is a little easier to document; increasing revenue requires some things to happen that I don't have complete control over. But I'm working on it!

Source: Personal interview; anonymous by request.

works directly with the CEO in each account. These accounts are a form of house account, but the CEO has sales responsibility and sales goals to achieve.

PRODUCT SPECIALISTS

When companies have diverse products, their salespeople often specialize by types of products. Johnson & Johnson, which sells baby products, has two specialized sales forces: the disposable products sales force and the toiletries sales force. Hewlett-Packard has separate sales forces that specialize in selling computers, electronic test instruments, electronic components, medical test equipment, or analytical test equipment. Each sales force has its own regional, district, and area sales managers. Insuror's of Texas has salespeople who specialize in auto insurance, others who specialize in homeowner's insurance, and still others who specialize in medical and disability insurance. However, all of Insuror's salespeople operate under the same sales management structure. Regardless of the management structure, sometimes the technical knowledge requirements are so great that organizing territories by product makes sense.

In addition to having management responsibilities similar to those for geographic reps, product salespeople must coordinate their activities with those of salespeople from other divisions. Success can be greater for all involved when leads and customer information are shared. For example, a Hewlett-Packard test instrument salesperson may have a customer who is also a prospect for electronic components. Sharing that information with the electronic components rep can help build a relationship that can pay off with leads for test instruments.

INSIDE VERSUS OUTSIDE

Our discussion to this point has focused on outside salespeople, called **field salespeople**—that is, salespeople who sell at the customer's location. **Inside salespeople** (first identified in Chapter 1) sell at their own company's location. Inside salespeople may handle walk-in customers or work entirely over the telephone and Internet, or they may handle both duties. For example, a plumbing supply distributor may sell entirely to plumbers and employ inside salespeople who sell to those plumbers who come into the distributorship to buy products.

As we discussed in Chapter 6, the job of some inside salespeople is to provide leads for field salespeople. Other types of inside salespeople include account managers, field support reps, and customer service reps. An inside salesperson who is an account manager has the same responsibilities and duties as a field salesperson except that all business is conducted over the phone. Jean Heger, vice president of business development for Rail Europe, began her career in inside sales, where she managed relationships with tour and travel organizers.

A **field support rep** is a telemarketer who works with field salespeople and does more than prospect for leads. For example, field support reps at e-Rewards (you will meet one of the salespeople for this marketing research company in the next chapter) write proposals and price jobs, work directly with vendors to ensure satisfactory project completion, and interact with clients when needed. We discuss these representatives further when we address team selling strategies shortly.

Customer service reps (CSRs) are inbound salespeople who handle customer concerns. **Inbound** means they respond to telephone calls placed by customers, rather than **outbound**, which means the telemarketer makes the phone call (prospectors, account managers, and field support telemarketers are outbound reps). For example, if you call the 800 telephone number on the back of a tube of Crest toothpaste, you will speak with an inbound customer service rep. Many companies are now using customer service reps to identify cross-selling and up-selling opportunities, either by sending leads to field salespeople or closing the sales themselves. SuddenLink Communications, for example, has implemented a predictive model system that uses data from the CRM system to identify potential offers for customers who call about service. The customer service reps then make the sales pitch. Because the offers are more likely to be relevant to the buyer than a generic offer, customers don't seem to mind. In fact, they seem to like the approach—sales have increased over 20 percent since the launch of this system.[22]

Many companies use teams to work with large accounts. There may be members of management, finance, manufacturing, and engineering on the account team.

SALES TEAMS

A growing number of companies are adopting a team approach to sales.[23] This concept is being used by companies that recognize they can best build partnerships by empowering one person, the account manager, to represent the organization. In **team selling** a group of salespeople support a single account. Each person on the team brings a different area of expertise or handles different responsibilities. As you see in Exhibit 16.7, each specialist can be called on to team up with the account managers.

Before adopting team selling, companies may have had one salesperson for each product line. Xerox, for example, once had separate copier, supplies, fax machine, printer, computer workstation, and communication network salespeople all calling on the same buyer. These reps would pass in customers' lobbies without recognizing one another. Customers grew tired of seeing as many as six salespeople from Xerox. Now one account manager calls on the buyer and brings in product specialists as needed.

Xerox uses permanent teams, whereas Teradata forms teams as needed. The data warehousing company will create a team that might include an expert in the vertical market in which the customer operates, a group of finance experts who can help develop the right financial measures for the decision, software engineers who make sure the Teradata product will work with the systems the customer already has in place, and the account manager.

In an extension of team selling, **multilevel selling,** members at various levels of the sales organization call on their counterparts in the buying organization. (As charted in Exhibit 16.8, for example, the vice president of sales calls on the vice president of purchasing.) Multilevel selling can take place without a formal multilevel sales team if the account representative requests upper-level

Exhibit 16.7
Team Selling Organization

In team selling, product specialists work with account managers, who have total account responsibility. Product specialists are responsible for sales and service of only a limited portion of the product line and may work with several account managers.

management's involvement in the sale. For example, you may ask your company's vice president of sales to call on the vice president of operations at a prospect's company to secure top-level support for your proposal.

Another type of sales team is made up of the field rep and the field support rep (see Exhibit 16.9). Some companies use one telemarketer for each field salesperson, whereas other companies have several salespeople working with a telemarketer. The telemarketer performs as many selling tasks as possible over the telephone. But when a sales call is needed at the customer's location, the field support rep makes the appointment for the field rep. Such is the case with IBM.com, a division of IBM that provides software and technology consulting. Good communication and joint planning are necessary to avoid overbooking the field rep, as well as to prevent duplication of effort.

Technology has played a key role in promoting good communication and joint planning. Companies can use CRM systems, for example, to give every member of the sales team access to all of the same customer records. This access means everyone knows what sales calls are planned and what happens as a function of the call. Another form of technology, represented by services like WebEx, enables someone to deliver a PowerPoint presentation to people scattered all over the world. Using WebEx, an account manager could present the account strategy, for example, to the sales team no matter where the members are located or present a proposal to a customer on another continent. See "Sales Technology 16.1" for additional insight into the use of technology to promote good communication and joint planning.

SELLING YOURSELF

Many times students have to engage in team projects, sometimes without much instruction in what makes an effective team. Yet the quality of the team is much more than just the sum of the individuals who are team members. Just as in team

MAKING THE MOST OF SALES TECHNOLOGY

A common response when times get tough is to try to make the most of what you have. Companies aren't likely to spend a lot on new technologies, particularly if they think there are gains to be had with what's already on hand. And sometimes what you have on hand is what you sell.

Cisco, for example, manufactures and sells Internet technology. Susan Denny, sales manager for Cisco, says the recession forced Cisco to look for ways to improve salesperson productivity. "We immediately implemented a hiring freeze and a travel freeze, so we had to find ways to do more with less." Cisco turned to its own products and services, and began implementing virtual training and virtual meetings. Cisco, for example, owns WebEx, a service that enables online meetings. Combining voice with visual presentation, participants around the world can log in and participate in a meeting that includes telephone conversations, instant messaging, PowerPoint, and other visual media.

Jeffrey Bailey, sales manager for Oracle, says his organization is similar. Oracle provides CRM software among its many offerings. Making the most of that software was one of its strategies. "We knew we had great solutions that our customers were using, and it was time we used them, too. A key factor for us was the need to collaborate across sales teams. We have so many products that require sales specialists—no one account manager can know or do it all. So using our technology enabled identification of more sales opportunities, as well as better collaboration once an opportunity was identified."

Mac MacIntosh, a noted B2B marketing consultant, agrees and suggests that salespeople can make these systems significantly more powerful simply by entering the right data. Here are some of the questions he recommends:

- When customers buy, are they solving technical problems or business problems?
- Who drives the decision? Who else is involved? Who should be involved but isn't?

MacIntosh says that the answers are already known to most salespeople, but the data aren't in the CRM database. As a result, marketing programs that could drive more leads to the salespeople are less effective.

Coca-Cola Bottling Co. Consolidated couldn't turn to its own products to improve sales force efficiency, so it turned to Microsoft. Using collaboration tools like Microsoft SharePoint, the company rolled out mobile devices that equip salespeople to take orders, conduct surveys, and communicate with the distribution sales team. "The biggest efficiency the technology has brought is more time out in the field doing core selling," says Onyeka Nchege, vice president of information systems. Bill Elmore, president and chief operating officer, also believes that the collaboration across distribution and sales was another major point of efficiency.

In each of these situations, the key has been to increase sales productivity through collaborative technology. Now that the recession seems to be easing, though, there's no going back. Says Nchege, "The organization is ready to take advantage and leverage some of the technologies that are coming ahead."

Sources: Susan Denny and Jeffrey Bailey, personal interview; M.H. "Mac" MacIntosh, "For the Win," *Print Professional* 48, no. 3 (March 2010), p. 18; Elizabeth Fuhrman, "Bottler of the Year: Coca-Cola Bottling Co. Consolidated," *Beverage Industry* 101, no. 1 (January 2010), pp. 30–35.

selling, each member of the team has to understand what the overall objective is, what each individual's role is, and what activities have to be undertaken when. But simply understanding what to do is a small part of making the team successful. More importantly, each individual has to perform and complete each task on time.

In addition, each class has a compensation plan—how grades are distributed. Sometimes the grades are team-based, just as in sales. Sometimes grades are entirely individual, and sometimes the overall grade is a function of both team and individual evaluations. But other motivations can entice students to learn. Recognition, the opportunity to work on real business problems, recognition of the relevance of the material being covered, and even monetary awards in competitions such as the National Collegiate Sales Competition can motivate different students to different levels of effort.

As you think about the courses you are taking, consider how you are compensated. Does the official compensation plan (grades, recognition, or the like) meet your motivational needs? In a group project, are your group members' needs being met? And are they living up to their responsibilities? These are real questions that plague professionals, whether they be salespeople or sales managers. Understanding how these questions apply to you now will help you select the right job later, as well as help you perform to your goals now.

SUMMARY

Successful salespeople manage resources and build internal partnerships with people in order entry, credit, billing, and shipping, as well as sales and marketing. These partnerships allow salespeople to keep the promises they make to customers when someone else must carry out those promises.

Salespeople in learning organizations also have a responsibility to carry the voice of the customer to other areas of the organization. Successful learning organizations are more adept at adapting to changing customer needs and developing successful products when salespeople fulfill their role of speaking for the customer.

In the sales organization salespeople work with and for a sales executive and a field sales manager. The sales executive determines policy and maintains financial control over the sales organization. Salespeople participate in the development of forecasts that the sales executive uses in the planning process.

Another policy decision involves the method of compensation for the sales force. The four basic methods are straight salary, straight commission, bonus, and a combination plan. Straight commission plans provide strong financial incentives for salespeople but give the company little control over their activities. Salary plans give greater control to the company but offer less incentive for salespeople to work hard.

Sales executives are also responsible for creating a culture that supports ethical activities. Policies (such as open-door policies) can encourage salespeople to act ethically. Ethical review boards are also useful in reviewing ethics policies, investigating potential ethics violations, and counseling salespeople who have concerns about the ethics of possible actions. Sometimes, however, salespeople face unethical requests from their managers. If that occurs, salespeople can choose from several courses of actions, such as blowing the whistle or appealing to an ethics review board.

Partnerships must be built within the sales force too. Some examples include team selling with product specialists, inside and outside teams, and multilevel selling.

KEY TERMS

activity quota 444
bonus 445
bottom-up forecasting 443
cap 449
combination plans 447
commission 445
commission base 445
commission rate 446

customer service rep (CSR) 454
draw 446
ethics review board 449
field sales manager 447
field salespeople 454
field support rep 454
geographic salesperson 451
gross margin quota 444

ETHICS PROBLEMS

1. It took you four months to find a job, and you were almost out of money, when you finally landed your position. Today your boss asked you to do something you think is unethical, but she assures you that it is normal for this industry. You aren't sure what the corporate culture is yet because you are new at the company. How do you respond?

2. Your company pays straight commission based on gross margin, and you have some ability to determine the price, thereby influencing gross margin. The product is standard, and changes are not made to it when it is sold. What should determine how much you charge someone?

QUESTIONS AND PROBLEMS

1. In Dave Brock's essay, "Building Partnerships 16.1," he describes a very poor sales effort. What was the problem? What should the rep have done? Who has the responsibility for creating the materials you use as a salesperson? If you are in a company with poor support materials, what should you do?

2. A company that rents office equipment to businesses pays its salespeople a commission equal to the first month's rent. However, if the customer cancels or fails to pay its bills, the commission is taken back, even if the customer cancels 10 months later. Is this policy fair? Why or why not? Why would the company have this plan?

3. Look at the opening profile (Lillie Sanchez) and "From the Buyer's Seat 16.1" (Teradata and Speed-Trap). Draw or describe the relationships that each must develop in their business, and discuss how they are similar or different, and why.

4. What is the role of the geographic salesperson in a national or strategic account? Assume that you are a NAM. What would you do to ensure the support of geographic reps? How would that support differ if you were a product specialist and worked in a team situation, with different NAMs on different accounts? As a product specialist, how would you get the support of the account manager?

5. Consider your own experience in group work at school. What makes groups effective? How can you translate what you have learned about group work into working as part of a sales team? Reread "Sales Technology 16.1." What do you think are the characteristics of effective sales teams that have to operate virtually? Could you use any technology tools to collaborate in school work groups more effectively?

6. Some companies are using contact management software to observe salespeople's activities and to supervise salespeople more closely. Some salespeople, though, are not supervised closely—as long as they close enough sales, the company is satisfied. To what extent should salespeople be allowed to manage themselves? What risks do you take as a sales manager when you allow self-management among salespeople? How can you minimize those risks?

7. A sales manager gets one too many complaints about pushy salespeople, poor follow-up after the sale, and a lack of customer care and wonders if the compensation plan is to blame. What can a manager do with compensation to promote greater customer service? Are there other ways to motivate good customer service?

8. Many wise people say to worry about the things you can control and not to worry about the things you can't control. What does that mean for a salesperson, when so many promises a salesperson makes are actually fulfilled by someone else?

9. An experienced salesperson argues against salaries: "I don't like subsidizing poor performers. If you paid us straight commission, we'd know who could make it and who couldn't. Sure, it may take a while to get rid of the deadwood; but after that, sales would skyrocket!" Explain why you agree or disagree with this statement.

10. In "From the Buyer's Seat 16.1" a former student describes the situation and the people involved in one purchase. Create a flowchart based on the information provided, and determine who was involved when, from both sides. Could this process have been managed more efficiently? If you were the Speed-Trap representative, what would you do now? How would your answer differ if you were the account manager for Teradata with sales responsibility for this customer?

CASE PROBLEMS

case **16.1**

Flow Master Controls

Flow Master Controls, a manufacturer of heating and air conditioning control systems, has the following compensation program. Reps are paid a $2,500 draw per month, with straight commission paid on a point system and a bonus based on quota performance. The Digital Master, Flow Master's newest product, does much the same thing as the older Flow Master but is 30 percent faster and has greater accuracy. The point system is shown in Table 1.

Table 1

Product	Points/Sale	Quota
Digital Master	50	4 (units per month)
Flow Master	40	5
Hydrameter	35	6
Quadrameter	25	8
Triplex Scanner	5	45

Reps are paid $5 per point, or $5,165 plus a bonus of $500, if they sell quota for each product, for a total of $5,675. The total number of points to reach each month is 1,035, but reps have to reach quota for each product to get the bonus. Tables 2–4 show the performance of the district.

Table 2

Product	Quota	Number Sold
Digital Master	40	22
Flow Master	50	78
Hydrameter	60	63
Quadrameter	80	82
Triplex Scanner	450	479

Table 3

Name	Digital Master	Flow Master	Hydrameter	Quadrameter	Triplex Scanner	Total Points
McMahon	3	11	7	9	52	1,320
Davis	5	6	7	9	53	1,255
Foreman	2	9	7	11	46	1,210
Wu	4	8	6	8	48	1,160
Sanchez	3	8	7	6	48	1,105
Gruber	2	8	6	7	48	1,045
Sakamoto	1	8	6	8	48	1,020
Flora	1	7	7	8	47	1,010
Ricks	1	7	5	8	45	930
Dixon	0	6	5	8	44	835
Total	22	78	63	82	479	

Table 4
Total Sales Calls

Sales Call	Digital Master	Flow Master	Hydrameter	Quadrameter	Triplex Scanner	Total Calls
Quota	20	20	10	10	10	70
Foreman	28	16	11	9	10	75
Gruber	24	24	8	8	7	71
District average	27.2	18.6	9.5	10.4	9.7	75.4

Questions

1. Evaluate the district's sales performance. Draw conclusions ("Where are we doing well? Doing poorly?"), but don't fix anything yet. Justify your conclusions.
2. Compare the performance of Foreman and Gruber. What are some possible explanations for the poor Digital Master sales?
3. The VP of sales says the problem is the compensation plan. How would you fix it?
4. The company is planning to create a new position called product specialist. This salesperson will work with territory salespeople and will have a sales quota for Digital Master only. The product specialist salesperson will work with one sales team (8 to 12 salespeople), and once a territory rep has identified a Digital Master prospect, the rep will bring in the product specialist. How should the compensation plan be adjusted? Why?
5. The VP of sales managed to get the product specialist idea approved by the CEO, even though the CEO argued that the salespeople were just too lazy to make the effort to sell the Digital Master. "Lower the compensation on it to the territory reps, and everyone will sell the Flow Master at its lower price," the CEO says. "The best way to get more Digital Master sales is to cut compensation on the Flow Master to 20 points." What do you think should be done? Why?

Karen Kennedy looked up, surprised to see her manager standing next to her. She had just hung up the phone after talking with Miranda in the Credit Department. "Um, did I get a little too loud, Rick?" she asked her manager.

"Why don't you come in my office and let's talk over what just happened," he replied, grimly.

"Great," she thought to herself. "First, the Kansas Hospital Resources order gets delayed to the point where they want to cancel it, then Credit wants me to get another form filled out, and now, the boss wants to talk over what just happened. Well, what just happened was I lost my temper, but they deserved it!" She sat down across the desk from Rick in his office, as he looked at her expectantly.

"I got a call this morning from Kansas Hospital Resources; you know, that's the 10-machine order I took two weeks ago." Rick nodded, so Karen continued. "They were upset because nothing has been delivered yet, but I had told them lead times were only a week. Which is what I was told."

"Yes, they are a week. Why hasn't this shipped?" he asked.

"That's what I wanted to know. So I called Frank and asked him." Frank Mangione is head of the warehouse in St. Louis that serves all of Kansas, Missouri, and a few other areas. "Frank said the order was a credit hold. What you heard was my conversation with Miranda in Credit. She tells me that it's on hold because a signature is missing on one of the forms. What gets me is no one called or e-mailed me about it. They let it sit, and I had to call and ask them. Rick, I'm tired of our Credit Department being a Sales Prevention Department. It's as if they do everything they can to screw us up. Now KHR is threatening to cancel the order if I can't get them a machine by Friday, but I've got to call them and say we missed a signature line and it will be a week after that before I can get them their first machine! Does IKOH want me to sell or what?"

Rick sat silently for a moment, then began to speak in a lower voice, trying to lower the tension in the room. But he knew she wouldn't like what he had to say. "Sounds like you have a problem to me."

Karen protested, "I have a problem? No, IKOH has a problem. It's just like trying to get paid. I can't get them to pay the right commission. And service. Don't get me started on our so-called service department! They never seem to want to fix my customers' machines!"

Rick said quietly, "Listen, we have 12 reps here in the Kansas City office. Of the 12, I have only one that keeps having problems with people in corporate or at the distribution center or with the service department. So I've got two questions for you. How are you going to handle KHR? And how are you going to fix your problems with everyone else?"

Questions

1. Answer Rick's questions as if you were Karen. To help you with your answer, consider that she and the service reps are in Kansas City, distribution is in St. Louis, and the corporate office (where credit, payroll, and other such functions are located) is in San Francisco. Regarding KHR, would it matter to your answer if this were a new customer versus a long-time customer? Why or why not, and if so, how?

2. What should or could Rick do to help Karen? Assume her sales performance is good, and he doesn't consider firing her an option.

ROLE PLAY CASE

You've just gotten back from KB Homes, one of the fastest-growing home builders in the United States. The KB Homes sales leadership team is considering NetSuite for all of their salespeople, and they've raised a number of questions that you need to get answered. If successful, this sale could be as big as 1,000 units. But they want to know several things:

1. Can you create a kiosk that will allow customers who visit KB's model homes to input their own data directly into a file that will load with NetSuite?

2. The buying center wants a license that includes all upgrades for three years.

3. They want permission to send a rep to your corporate headquarters to make a presentation to all the NetSuite employees about KB Homes. Employees who work in the field will be mailed a DVD presentation about KB Homes.

Each student will take turns playing the salesperson. The first question has to be addressed by the chief engineer. The second has to be addressed by the legal department. The final question has to be solved by the chief operations officer. If there are three people in a group, take turns observing. Your instructor will provide you with sheets for your role as one of the other NetSuite managers.

ADDITIONAL REFERENCES

Avlonitis, George J., and Nikolas G. Panagopoulos. "Exploring the Influence of Sales Management Practices on the Industrial Salesperson: A Multisource Hierarchical Linear Modeling Approach." *Journal of Business Research* 60, no. 7 (2007), pp. 765–77.

Brehmer, Per-Olof, and Jakob Rehme. "Proactive and Reactive: Drivers for Key Account Management Programmes." *European Journal of Marketing* 43, no. 7–8 (2009), pp. 961–84.

Guenzi, Paolo, Catherine Pardo, and Laurent Georges. "Relational Selling Strategy and Key Account Managers Relational Behaviors: An Exploratory Study." *Industrial Marketing Management* 36, no. 1 (2007), pp. 121–34.

Guenzi, Paolo, Laurent Georges, and Catherine Pardo. "The Impact of Strategic Account Managers' Behaviors on Relational Outcomes: An Empirical Study." *Industrial Marketing Management* 38, no. (2009), pp. 300–12.

Jones, Eli, Lawrence B. Chonko, Deva Rangarajan, and James Roberts. "The Role of Overload on Job Attitudes, Turnover Intentions, and Salesperson Performance." *Journal of Business Research* 60, no. 7 (2007), pp. 663–78.

Joshi, Ashwin W. "Salesperson Influence on Product Development: Insights from a Study of Small Manufacturing Organizations." *Journal of Marketing* 74, no. 1 (January 2010), pp. 94–108.

Judson, Kimberly, Denise D. Schoenbachler, Geoffrey L. Gordon, Rick E. Ridnour, and Dan C. Weilbaker. "The New Product Development Process: Let the Voice of the Salesperson Be Heard." *Journal of Product and Brand Management* 15, no. 3 (2007), pp. 194–210.

Liu, Sandra S., and Lucette B. Comer. "Salespeople as Information Gatherers: Associated Success Factors." *Industrial Marketing Management* 36, no. 5 (2007), pp. 565–80.

Paparoidamis, Nicholas G., and Paolo Guenzi. "An Empirical Investigation into the Impact of Relationship Selling and LMX on Salespeople's Behaviours and Sales Effectiveness." *European Journal of Marketing* 43, no. 7–8 (2009), p. 1053.

Pappas, James M., Karen E. Flaherty, and C. Shane Hunt. "The Joint Influence of Control Strategies and Market Turbulence on Strategic Performance in Sales-Driven Organizations." *Journal of Behavior and Applied Management* 8, no. 2 (2007), pp. 141–64.

Rouziès, Dominique, Anne T. Coughlan, Erin Anderson, and Dawn Iacobucci. "Determinants of Pay Levels and Structures in Sales Organizations." *Journal of Marketing* 73, no. 6 (November 2009), pp. 92–104.

Smith, Brent, Trina Larsen, and Bert Rosenbloom. "Understanding Cultural Frames in the Multicultural Sales Organization: Prospects and Problems for the Sales Manager." *Journal of Transnational Management* 14, no. 4 (October 2009), pp. 277–92.

Steward, Michelle D., Michael D. Hutt, Beth A. Walker, and Ajith Kumar. "Role Identity and Attributions of High-Performing Salespeople." *The Journal of Business & Industrial Marketing* 24, no. 7, pp. 463–76.

Vilela, Belen Bande, Jose Antonio Varela Gonzalez, Pilar Fernandez Ferrin, and M. Luisa del Rio Araujo. "Impression Management Tactics and Affective Context: Influence on Sales Performance Appraisal." *European Journal of Marketing* 41, no. 5–6 (2007), pp. 624–39.

chapter **17**

MANAGING YOUR CAREER

SOME QUESTIONS ANSWERED IN THIS CHAPTER ARE

- Which entry-level jobs are available to new college graduates?
- Where do I find these jobs?
- How should I go about getting interviews, and what should I do when I have an interview?
- What selection procedures besides interviews might I go through?
- Which career paths are available in sales?
- How can I prepare myself for a promotion into management?

PROFILE

PROFILE When I took Business Marketing at TCU my junior year, I really had no idea what I would do after I graduated. I just hoped my first job would be fun and exciting and present opportunities to develop a set of skills to use throughout my career. I got more than I could have ever hoped for. In the past five years since I graduated, I've been able to touch a number of different aspects of my company's marketing and sales initiatives, and have been able to really control my career path. The following is a look back at how I have arrived at where I am today.

The summer after I graduated, I obtained an internship at eRewards Inc., an online market research company. The company was relatively small and growing, and due to that growth, the summer position presented me with many unique opportunities, including assisting the EVP of sales in developing sales performance tracking and forecasting. Upon completion of the internship, e-Rewards offered me a full-time position to support some of the day-to-day sales and marketing tasks of the organization. In this role, I expanded my knowledge of the company and the overall market research industry by supporting the sales team in helping to develop marketing brochures and advertising campaigns, as well as coordinating trade shows.

The company continued to grow rapidly, and after a year, we had hired seven people to support the sales and marketing function, creating a role known as sales support, which I managed as the team leader. In addition to coordinating marketing initiatives, we also wrote sales proposals and assisted sales managers and directors in calculating pricing for quote requests.

After a year and a half in my role leading the sales support team, I decided to pursue a role as a sales manager on the health care sales team. I had developed a strong interest in the area and felt there was a lot of opportunity within the group. Health care market research was a new division in the company, and as e-Rewards had previously focused on other markets, I felt there was great growth potential in this niche market. In the first six months with the division, we had grown the team to four people and grown our customer base substantially. In this new role, I have also been presented with opportunities to represent the company at various conferences and trade shows, both domestically and internationally.

So far, things have gone pretty well in the health care market. Even with the down economy, my business has done pretty well. One result is that just last week, I was promoted to sales director. This position will give me more authority to carry out what I need to do to serve my customers more effectively.

Looking back on the time since graduation, I can't imagine any other opportunity that could have been better. Business marketing companies may not be household words, but we do everything the consumer companies do and more. By choosing to start my career with an emerging organization like e-Rewards, I have been presented with the opportunity to contribute more to an organization in a shorter time than I would have anywhere else.

Visit our Web site at www.erewards.com.

Landing that first career position is an exciting moment! However, the job search is just the first task in managing your career. Like the chess player who is thinking two or three moves ahead, you too must think about subsequent opportunities. Also like the chess player, you must maintain some flexibility so you do not checkmate your career if one strategy does not work.

Sales is a great place to begin a career. Just ask Mark Hurd, CEO of Hewlett-Packard. Hurd came into a Hewlett-Packard that had slipped badly, and its sales force was in total disarray. Hurd's sales background at NCR was a primary reason for his choice as HP's leader. Because salespeople must represent the entire company, they learn about many aspects of the business and get to know people in various parts of the industry. All this knowledge can be put to use later in a career—and was critical for Hurd to lead HP's turnaround.[1]

OPPORTUNITIES IN SELLING

Selling offers many opportunities.

Corporate executives clearly recognize the importance of selling experience in any marketing career, as evidenced by people like Mark Hurd and Emily Tanner (profiled at the start of this chapter). Many people, though, have also found career satisfaction by staying in sales throughout their working lives.

Whether the career is sales or any other field, similar questions apply when searching for a job. In this chapter the focus is on the search for a sales position and how to land the first job. We examine how companies make hiring decisions and offer tips on how to build selling and management skills while managing a career.

MAKING A GOOD MATCH

The keys to being successful and happy lie in finding a good match between what you need and desire in a position and the positions companies offer.[2] The first step, then, is to understand yourself, what you need, and what you have to offer. Then you must consider what each company needs and what each has to offer. As Exhibit 17.1 illustrates, a good match means your needs are satisfied by what the company offers and what you offer satisfies the company's needs.

Exhibit 17.1
A Good Match between Salesperson and Company

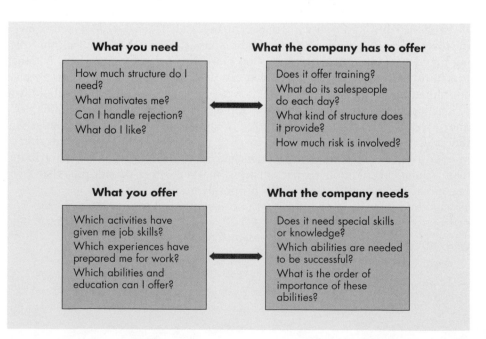

What you need
How much structure do I need?
What motivates me?
Can I handle rejection?
What do I like?

What the company has to offer
Does it offer training?
What do its salespeople do each day?
What kind of structure does it provide?
How much risk is involved?

What you offer
Which activities have given me job skills?
Which experiences have prepared me for work?
Which abilities and education can I offer?

What the company needs
Does it need special skills or knowledge?
Which abilities are needed to be successful?
What is the order of importance of these abilities?

Many companies, such as Konica-Minolta, Oracle, IBM, and others, use exotic trips as a reward for top performers.

UNDERSTANDING YOURSELF

Shakespeare said, "To thine own self be true"; but to be true to yourself, you must know who you are, what you need, and what you can offer others.[3] Knowing these things about yourself requires substantial self-examination. We will pose some questions that can help you follow Shakespeare's suggestion.

Understanding Your Needs

The first step in making a good match between what you have to offer and a company's position is to determine what you need. Important questions to consider include the following:

1. *Structure:* Can you work well when assignments are ambiguous, or do you need a lot of instruction? Do you need deadlines that others set, or do you set your own deadlines? If you are uncomfortable when left on your own, you may need structure in your work life. Many sales positions, such as missionary and trade sales, are in a structured environment with well-defined procedures and routines. Other positions require the salesperson to operate with little guidance or structure.

2. *Motivation:* Will financial incentives, personal recognition, or simply job satisfaction get you going? Probably it will be some combination of the three, but try to determine the relative value of each to you. Then you can weigh compensation plans, recognition programs, and other factors when considering which sales position is right for you. You may want to review the section on compensation plan types in Chapter 16 to aid in determining which plan best suits your needs.

3. *Stress and rejection:* How much stress can you handle? Are you a risk taker, or do you prefer more secure activities? What do you do when faced with stress? With rejection? These are important questions in understanding what you need from a sales position. For example, capital equipment sales jobs can be high-stress positions because sales are few and far between. Other jobs may require you to wade through many rejections before landing a sale. If you thrive on that kind of challenge, the rewards can be gratifying. Some sales positions, though, involve working only with current customers, and salespeople incur little outright rejection. Every grocery store, for example, will carry at least some Procter & Gamble products.

4. *Interest:* What do you find interesting? Mechanical or technical topics? Merchandising? Art or fashion? You cannot sell something that bores you. You would just bore and annoy the customer.

Understanding What You Have to Offer

Other resources that can help you understand the person you are may be available through your college's placement center. You must also take inventory of what you bring to the job:

1. *Skills:* What activities and experiences taught you certain skills? What did you learn from those experiences and your education that you can apply to a career? Keep in mind that it is not the activities in which you participated that matter to hiring companies; it is what you learned by participating that counts.

2. *Knowledge:* College has provided you with many areas of knowledge, but you have also probably learned much by participating in hobbies and other interests. For example, you may have special computer knowledge that would be useful in selling software, or you may have participated in a particular sport that makes you well suited to sell equipment to sporting goods stores. Kristen Scott found that her course in CRM and her experience in selling NetSuite at the National Collegiate Sales Competition enabled her to compete against other salespeople with years of experience and win a sales position with Oracle straight out of college.[4]

3. *Qualities and traits:* Every person has a unique personality. What parts of your personality add value for your potential employer? Are you detail-oriented and systematic? Are you highly creative? In other words, what can you bring to the job that is uniquely you? Exhibit 17.2 lists traits of top salespeople, according to a study conducted for *Sales & Marketing Management* magazine.

Your answers to these questions will generate a list of what you have to offer companies. Then when you are in an interview, you can present features that make you a desirable candidate.

When to Ask These Questions

Unfortunately many students wait until just before graduation before seriously considering the type of career they desire. According to one career services director, students who start a search while in school will find a job three times faster than those who start after graduation. Although it is not always realistic to expect every student to map out a life plan prior to senior year, asking questions such as these as early as possible can guide a student to better course selection, better use of learning opportunities, and ultimately a better career decision. Then the student can begin actively searching for the job at the beginning of the senior year so that graduation signals the beginning of a career, not a career search.

UNDERSTANDING THE COMPANY

While developing a good feel for who you are and what you have to offer companies, you should also explore what is available and which companies offer positions that appeal to you. As you can see in Exhibit 17.3, numerous sources provide information about positions and growth opportunities in various industries and specific companies. Don't forget, though, that the best sources are personal; be sure to talk over job opportunities with your friends, friends of your parents, and your professors. Use term papers as an excuse to call professionals in a field that interests you. Join trade and professional associations now because these offer great networking opportunities. As someone who has studied sales, you should use your prospecting skills too. Next let's discuss how to evaluate what you learn about the companies and their positions.

What the Company Has to Offer

When you meet a salesperson or sales manager, you should ask about compensation and recognition programs, training, career opportunities, and other information to determine whether the company truly

Exhibit 17.2

Traits of Top Salespeople

1. Strong ego: able to handle rejection with healthy self-esteem.
2. Sense of urgency: getting it done now.
3. Ego driven: obsessive about being successful.
4. Assertive: being firm without being aggressive (see the discussion in Chapter 11).
5. Willing to take risks: willing to innovate.
6. Sociable: good at building relationships.
7. Abstract reasoner: able to handle complex selling situations and ideas.
8. Skeptical: a healthy bit of suspicion, not counting on commission until the sale is really a sale.
9. Creative: able to set oneself apart from the competition.
10. Empathic: able to place oneself in the buyer's shoes.

Source: Adapted from Erika Rasmusson, "The Ten Traits of Top Salespeople," *Sales & Marketing Management*, August 1999, pp. 34–37.

Exhibit 17.3
Sources of Job
Information

Source	Example
Government	U.S. Industrial Outlook
Research services	Standard & Poor's Industry Surveys
Industry associations	Christian Booksellers' Association
Professional organizations	Sales and Marketing Executives International
General magazines	*BusinessWeek, Money*
Trade magazines	*Sales & Marketing Management, Selling Power*
Placement services	University placement office; nonfee private agencies such as Personnel One
Personal sources	Friends, relatives, industry association executives at trade shows, recruiters at career fairs
Web sites	marketingjobs.com

offers benefits to satisfy your needs. You should also explore daily activities of the salesperson, likes and dislikes about the job, and what that person thinks it takes to succeed. This information will help you determine whether a match exists.

For example, if you need structure, you should look for a sales position in which your day is structured for you. Any industry that relies on repeated sales calls to the same accounts is likely to be highly structured. Industries with a structured sales day include consumer packaged goods sales (Procter & Gamble, Quaker Oats, and the like) and pharmaceutical sales (Novartis, Eli Lilly Company, and so forth). Even these sales positions offer some flexibility and independence. Office and industrial equipment sales provide much less structure when the emphasis is on getting new accounts.

Knowing your comfort level with risk and your need for incentives should help you pick a company with a compensation program that is right for you. If you need the security of a salary, look for companies in trade sales, equipment sales, pharmaceuticals, or consumer packaged goods. But if you like the risk of straight commission, which can often be matched with greater financial rewards for success, explore careers in areas such as convention sales, financial services, and other straight commission jobs.

Other factors to consider include the size of the company and its promotion policies, particularly if the company is foreign. Many companies have a "promote from within" policy, which means that whenever possible they fill positions with people who already are employees. One example is Worldwide Express, a company that sells for DHL in the United States (DHL is a shipping and overnight express company based in Belgium). Alex BeMent was promoted after working at Worldwide Express for only six months to managing three salespeople, with responsibility for increasing the office to five or more.[5] Such policies are very attractive if you seek career growth into management. A company that is foreign-owned, however, may prefer to staff certain positions with people from its home country.

Take advantage of interests you already have. If you are intrigued by medical science, seek a medical sales position. If merchandising excites you, a position selling to the trade would be appropriate. A bar of soap by itself is not exciting, but helping customers find ways to market that bar of soap is.

What the Company Needs

At this point in your job search, you may have narrowed your selection to a group of industries or companies. At a minimum you have a good picture of what

WHAT THE RECRUITER SAYS!

By Dawn Loehr

Because sales drive a company's revenues and play the important part of representing its image, it is no surprise that these key positions often are the most challenging to fill. As a recruiter visiting college campuses to hire graduates into sales positions, my responsibility is to find candidates who best fit these critical roles. Although I look for many things when sourcing qualified sales candidates, there are a few behaviors that often make individuals stand out early in the process.

While growing our sales team when I was with Savvis, I came across Brian Davis. Brian didn't have any direct sales experience, but what he lacked in experience he made up for in persistence. Ideally this sales position required a minimum of two years of industry sales experience; however, I was impressed by Brian's ease in overcoming objections while maintaining his professionalism. Clearly, handling rejections is an essential function of any sales role.

Along with Brian's persistence, he did a great job at preparation. Prior to our interview, he had already had an informational meeting with one of our sales leaders, had done extensive research on the company, and began learning more about our products. Brian made an impression because he interviewed me. His enthusiasm and interest in the job were clear because he was planning his success in the position before ever being offered the job.

Finally, Brian was able to demonstrate his achievements. While he did not have sales experience, Brian had many other accomplishments in life through his involvement in sports, community events, and fund-raising projects. His past achievements demonstrated his ability to interact effectively with people and groups as well as his willingness to approach and ask customers to participate in a promotion.

Whether you come to the table with years of experience or none at all, as a human resources professional, I am going to be looking for certain basic qualities when filling sales positions. Make sure you demonstrate your value. Be persistent, always prepare, and be ready to discuss how your past wins will make you a star in sales.

Source: Contributed by Dawn Loehr; used with permission.

---

a company should offer to land you as a salesperson. The next step is to find a company that needs you. Finding out what a company needs will require some research, but you will find this step fun and rewarding. Dawn Loehr, a human resources professional who has recruited college students and others for sales positions with several companies, provides her perspective on how to impress recruiters in "From the Buyer's Seat 17.1."

In general, companies look for three qualities in salespeople: good communication skills, self-motivation, and a positive and enthusiastic attitude. Recall from Exhibit 17.2 that other characteristics are important, such as a sense of urgency.

Companies in certain industries may also desire related technical skills or knowledge, such as medical knowledge for the field of pharmaceutical sales or insurance knowledge to enter that field. All companies need salespeople with computer skills because computers are increasingly being used to track and manage accounts, communicate internally, and perform other important activities. If you want to enter a field requiring specialized knowledge or skills, now is the time to begin acquiring that knowledge. Not only will you already have the knowledge when you begin to search for a position; you will also have demonstrated self-motivation and the right kind of attitude by taking on the task of acquiring that knowledge and skill.

Career fairs, such as this one at a hotel during spring break, can be a great opportunity to find internships or permanent sales positions.

THE RECRUITING PROCESS

Early in this book we discussed the buying process so you would understand the purchase decision buyers make. Now we will look at the recruiting process so you will understand how companies will view you as a candidate for a sales job or any other position.

SELECTING SALESPEOPLE

In recent years companies have made considerable progress in screening and selecting salespeople. Most have discarded the myth that there is a "sales type" who will be successful selling anything to anybody. Instead they seek people who match the requirements of a specific position, using various methods to gain information and determine whether a good match will be made.

APPLICANT INFORMATION SOURCES

To determine whether a match exists between the job requirements and the applicant's abilities, information about the applicant must be collected. Companies use five important sources of information: application forms, references, tests, personal interviews, and assessment centers. We describe these five sources from the perspective of the company so you can understand how they are used to make hiring decisions. We also explain how you should use these sources of information so you can present yourself accurately and positively.

The **application form** is a preprinted form that the candidate completes. You have probably already filled these out for part-time jobs you have had. The form should include factual questions concerning the profile the company established for the position. Responses on the form are also useful for structuring the personal interview. Résumés provide much of the same information application forms do but are often too individualized for easy comparison. For this and other reasons, companies must supplement résumés with an application form (we discuss résumés in greater detail later in this chapter).

Contacting **references,** or people who know the applicant, is a good way to validate information on the application form. References can also supplement the information with personal observations. The most frequently contacted references are former employers. Other references are coworkers, leaders of social or religious organizations, and professors. You should be aware that some organizations try to develop relationships with faculty so they can receive leads on excellent candidates before visiting the placement office. Professors recommend students who have demonstrated the qualities the recruiting companies desire.

When you select references, keep in mind that companies want references that can validate information about you. Choose references that provide different information, such as one character reference, one educational reference, and one work-related reference.

Experienced sales managers expect to hear favorable comments from an applicant's references. More useful information may be contained in unusual comments, gestures, faint praise, or hesitant responses that may indicate a problem. Before you offer someone's name as a reference, ask that person for permission. At that time you should be able to tell whether the person is willing to give you a good recommendation.

Intelligence, ability, personality, and interest **tests** provide information about a potential salesperson that cannot be obtained readily from other sources. Tests can also correct misjudgments made by sales managers who tend to act on "gut feelings." Although tests were widely criticized in the early 1980s for failing to predict success better than other sources did, recent studies indicate that assessment tests are growing in popularity once more, in part because of their improved predictive power.[6] The new assessment tests, however, are more accurate when they are specifically related to sales and the situations potential salespeople may encounter.

Several types of tests may be given. H. R. Challey Inc. designs tests to determine a person's psychological aptitude for different sales situations. BSRP offers a test that measures a salesperson's call reluctance, or fear of initiating contact. IBM requires sales candidates to demonstrate technical aptitude through a test, while Skyline requires a test that indicates the individual's ability to handle details. Like many companies, KB Homes requires candidates to pass a math test because of the importance of calculating price correctly. Still other tests indicate a candidate's ethical nature. Companies may require candidates to take tests in all these categories.

The important point to remember about tests is to remain relaxed. If the test is a valid selection tool, you should be happy with the outcome no matter what it is. If you believe the test is not valid—that is, does not predict your ability to succeed in that job—you may want to present your feelings to the recruiter. Be prepared to back up your line of reasoning with facts and experiences that illustrate why you are a good candidate for the position.

Interviews, or personal interaction between recruiter and candidate, are an important source of information for recruiters. Companies now give more attention to conducting multiple interviews in the selection process because sometimes candidates show only slight differences. Multiple interviews can improve a recruiter's chances of observing the differences and selecting the best candidate. We cover interviews in more detail later in the chapter.

Companies sometimes evaluate candidates at centrally located **assessment centers.** In addition to being used for testing and personal interviews, these locations may simulate portions of the job. Simulating the job serves two purposes. First, the simulation lets managers see candidates respond to a joblike situation. Second, candidates can experience the job and determine whether it fits them.

For example, Merrill Lynch sometimes places broker candidates in an office and simulates two hours of customer telephone calls. As many as half the candidates may then decide that being a stockbroker is not right for them, and Merrill Lynch can also evaluate the candidates' abilities in a lifelike setting.

Companies use many sources of information in making a hiring decision, perhaps even asking for a copy of a videotaped presentation you may make for this class. These sources are actually selling opportunities for you. You can present yourself and learn about the job at the same time, continuing your evaluation of the match.

SELLING YOUR CAPABILITIES

With an understanding of the recruiting process from the company's point of view, you can create a presentation that sells your capabilities and proves you have the skills and knowledge the company wants. Preparing the résumé, gaining an interview, and presenting your capabilities in the interview are important activities that require sound planning to present yourself effectively.

PREPARING THE RÉSUMÉ

The résumé is the brochure in your marketing plan. As such, it needs to tell the recruiter why you should be hired. Tom Day, sales manager for Hormel, says he literally gets hundreds of résumés for sales positions, whether he has a position available or not. His company prefers to hire inexperienced salespeople right out of college, as do many companies, so don't let a lack of experience create anxiety or lead to misrepresentation on your résumé.[7] Whether you choose the conventional style or the functional style of résumé, the purpose is to sell your skills and experience.

Conventional Résumés

Conventional résumés are a form of life history, organized by type of experience. The three categories of experience most often used are education, work, and activities/hobbies (see the example in Exhibit 17.4). Although it is easy to create conventional résumés, it is also easy to fail to emphasize important points. To avoid making this mistake, follow this simple procedure:

- List education, work experience, and activities.
- Write out what you gained in each experience that will help you prove you have the desired qualities.
- Emphasize what you learned and that you have the desired qualities under each heading.

For example, the résumé in Exhibit 17.4 is designed for a student interested in a sales career. Note how skills gained in this class are emphasized in addition to GPA and major. The candidate has also chosen to focus on customer service skills gained as a camp counselor, a job that a recruiter would otherwise overlook. Rather than just listing herself as a member of the soccer team, the candidate highlights the leadership skills she gained as captain.

Functional Résumés

Functional résumés reverse the content and titles of the conventional résumé, organizing by what the candidate can do or has learned rather than by types of experience. As you can see in Exhibit 17.5, an advantage of this type of résumé is that it highlights more forcefully what the candidate can do.

When preparing a functional résumé, begin by listing the qualities you have that you think will help you get the job. Narrow this list to three or four

Exhibit 17.4
Conventional Résumé
Example

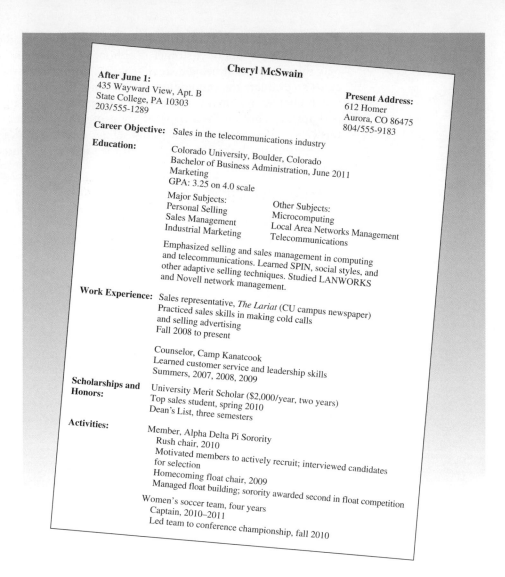

Cheryl McSwain

After June 1:
435 Wayward View, Apt. B
State College, PA 10303
203/555-1289

Present Address:
612 Homer
Aurora, CO 86475
804/555-9183

Career Objective: Sales in the telecommunications industry

Education:
Colorado University, Boulder, Colorado
Bachelor of Business Administration, June 2011
Marketing
GPA: 3.25 on 4.0 scale

Major Subjects:
Personal Selling
Sales Management
Industrial Marketing

Other Subjects:
Microcomputing
Local Area Networks Management
Telecommunications

Emphasized selling and sales management in computing and telecommunications. Learned SPIN, social styles, and other adaptive selling techniques. Studied LANWORKS and Novell network management.

Work Experience:
Sales representative, *The Lariat* (CU campus newspaper)
Practiced sales skills in making cold calls and selling advertising
Fall 2008 to present

Counselor, Camp Kanatcook
Learned customer service and leadership skills
Summers, 2007, 2008, 2009

Scholarships and Honors:
University Merit Scholar ($2,000/year, two years)
Top sales student, spring 2010
Dean's List, three semesters

Activities:
Member, Alpha Delta Pi Sorority
Rush chair, 2010
Motivated members to actively recruit; interviewed candidates for selection
Homecoming float chair, 2009
Managed float building; sorority awarded second in float competition
Women's soccer team, four years
Captain, 2010–2011
Led team to conference championship, fall 2010

qualities, and then list activities and experiences to prove that you have those skills and abilities. The qualities are the headings for the résumé; the activities and experiences show that you have those qualities. One difficulty with this type of résumé is that one past job may relate to several qualities. If that is the case, emphasize the activity within the job that gave you the experience for each specific quality.

GAINING THE INTERVIEW

Students should begin examining different industries as early as possible, as we suggested earlier. As graduation looms closer and the time for serious job hunting arrives, your knowledge of the industries and companies that interest you will put you a step ahead. You will also understand the process the company will go through in searching for a new salesperson.

Using Personal Contacts

More important, you have already begun to make personal contacts in those fields—contacts you can now use to gain interviews. The same salespeople and

Exhibit 17.5
Functional Résumé
Example

Cheryl McSwain

After June 1:
435 Wayward View, Apt. B
State College, PA 10303
203/555-1289

Present Address:
612 Homer
Aurora, CO 86475
804/555-9183

Career Objective: Sales in the telecommunications industry

Sales and Customer Service Experience:

Studied SPIN and adaptive selling techniques in personal selling.
Sold advertising in *The Lariat*, campus newspaper. Responsibilities included making cold calls, presenting advertising strategies, and closing sales.
Performed customer service tasks as camp counselor at Camp Kanatcook.
Served as the primary parent contact during drop-off and pick-up periods, answering parent queries, resolving parental concerns, and handling similar responsibilities.

Management and Leadership Experience:

Studied situational management in sales management.
Served as rush chair for sorority. Responsible for motivating members to recruit new members and developed and implemented a sales training seminar so members would present the sorority favorably within university guidelines.
Managed homecoming-float project. Sorority awarded second place in float competition.
Captained the women's varsity soccer team to a conference championship.

Telecommunications Skills and Experience:

Studied LANWORKS and Novell network management in telecommunications.
Designed, as a term project, a Novell-based LAN for a small manufacturing business.
Purchased and installed a six-computer network in a family-owned wholesaling business.

Scholarships and Honors:

University Merit Scholar ($2,000/year, two years)
Top sales student, spring 2010
Dean's List, three semesters

sales managers who gave you information before to help you with term projects will usually be happy to introduce you to the person in charge of recruiting. Contacts you made at job fairs and trade shows can also be helpful.

thinking **it** through

Many students feel uncomfortable asking for favors from people they barely know, such as asking an acquaintance to forward a résumé to a decision maker or set up an interview. How can you overcome such feelings of discomfort? Why would someone want to help you find places to interview? What obligations do you have to people who give you the names of job contacts?

Using Employment Postings

Responding to Web postings or newspaper advertisements can also lead to job interviews. You will need to carefully interpret employment postings and then respond effectively to them.

All ads are designed to sell, and employment ads are no exception. But what sounds great may not be wonderful in reality. Here are some phrases often found in such ads and interpretations of them:

Independent contractor: You will work on straight commission with no employee benefits. You will probably receive no training and little, if any, support. Some experienced salespeople prefer this type of position, but it is probably not the best place to start.

Earn up to $ (or *unlimited income* or *our top rep made $500,000 last year*): You need to know what the average person makes and what the average first-year earnings are, not what the top rep made or the upper limit. The job could still be desirable, but you need to find out what reality is before accepting a position.

Sales manager trainee: This is another title for sales representative. Don't be put off or overly encouraged by high-sounding titles.

Bonuses paid weekly, daily commissions, or *weekly commissions:* These are high-pressure jobs and probably involve high-pressure sales.

Ten salespeople needed now! That's because everyone has quit. This company uses salespeople and then discards them.

You should look for two things in an ad: what the company needs and what it has to offer. The company should provide concrete information about training, compensation plan (although not necessarily the amount), amount of travel to expect, and type of product or service you will sell. You should also expect to find the qualifications the company desires, including experience and education. If this is a job you really want but you do not have the experience now, call and ask how to get it. Be specific: "What companies should I pursue that will give me the experience you are looking for?" If the ad requires e-mail response only, send an e-mail message and mention that you are a student. Many people are willing to help someone get started.

Responding to Postings

Many postings and ads will ask you to write or e-mail and may not list the company's name. A blind box number is given when the company name is not included in a newspaper ad; the box number is usually at the address of the newspaper. For example, the ad may say to send a résumé to Job Posting 943 at Monster.com. Don't be put off by the lack of company name; the posting or ad may be placed by a company such as IBM that would otherwise receive a large number of unqualified applicants. Companies use blind postings and blind box numbers for many legitimate reasons.

Writing the Cover Letter

When you write in response to a posting, you are writing a sales letter—even if you send it by e-mail. Like any sales letter, it should focus on what you can do for the company, not what you expect from it. The letter should start with an attention getter. Here is one example:

In today's economy, you need someone who can become productive quickly as a territory representative. Based on your posting at Monster.com, I believe that I am that person.

This attention getter is direct, focuses on a probable need, and refers to the posting. The attention getter tells why you should be considered. The probability of getting a response to this e-mail is far greater than if you simply said,

The Internet is a great source of leads for jobs; however, recruiters report receiving hundreds, and sometimes thousands, of résumés for every job they post. If you really want a job with a particular company, approach it like a sales opportunity and use your prospecting and relationship building skills.

Please consider me for the territory representative position you posted at Monster.com.

The body of the letter should center on two or three reasons why you should be hired. For example, if you have the qualities of self-motivation and leadership, devote two paragraphs relating each to the position. Use your résumé as proof. For example:

A territory representative position often requires self-motivation. As you can see from the attached résumé, I demonstrated self-motivation as a sales representative for the campus newspaper, as a volunteer for the local food bank, and as a member of the Dean's Honor Roll during two of the last four semesters.

The letter should close with a request for action. Ask for an interview and suggest times you are available. For example:

Please call me to arrange an interview. My schedule allows me to meet with you on Tuesday or Thursday afternoon.

An alternative is to state that you will call:

I will call you early next week to discuss my potential as a salesperson for XYZ Corporation.

No response does not necessarily mean you have been rejected; follow up with a phone call if you do not hear anything within a week. One former student got a job because he called to verify that the sales manager had received his résumé. She had never seen it but was impressed enough with the student's phone call to arrange an appointment. Sometimes e-mail is lost or delayed, goes to a junk mail file and gets deleted, or simply is deleted accidentally—and you would not want a company to miss out on the opportunity to hire you because of a computer glitch!

THE INTERVIEW

Many students do not realize how much competition exists for the best entry-level sales positions, or perhaps they do not know what companies look for in new employees. Students often act as though they are shopping for a job. Job shoppers, however, are not seriously considered by recruiters, who are usually astute enough to quickly pick up on the student's lack of interest. If the job shopper does become interested, it is probably too late because the recruiter has already discounted this applicant. Like it or not, you are really competing for a job. As in any competition, success requires preparation and practice.

Preparing for the Interview

Students who know something about the company and its industry lead the competition. You have already looked for company and industry information in the library, in business reference books, and in periodicals. You visited its Web site. You have also interviewed the company's customers, salespeople, and sales managers. You can use this knowledge to demonstrate your self-motivation and positive attitude—two of the top three characteristics sales managers look for in sales candidates. You will find it easier to demonstrate the third top characteristic, communication skills, with the confidence you gain from proper preparation.

In addition to building knowledge of the "customer," you must plan your responses to the questions you will be asked. Exhibit 17.6 lists standard interview questions.

Scenario questions are popular with recruiters. These questions ask what the candidate would do in a certain situation involving actions of competitors. (For example, what would you do if a customer told you something negative about your product that you knew to be untrue, and the customer's source of information was your competitor?) Such questions test ethics regarding competitors and the ability to handle a delicate situation. Scenario questions also test the candidate's response to rejection, ability to plan, and other characteristics. You can best prepare for these types of questions with this class and by placing yourself in the situations described in the cases and exercises in this book. You may also want to review the questions at the ends of the chapters.

The sales field has several unusual characteristics, such as travel, that influence the type of questions asked. For example, if significant travel is part of the position, you may be asked, "Travel is an important part of this job, and you may be away from home about three nights per week. Would you be able and willing to travel as the job requires?" However, some questions are illegal, and you do not have to answer them—such as "What is your marital status? Do you plan to have a family? Will that affect your ability to travel?" Exhibit 17.7 lists some questions that are illegal, as well as legal questions that you may have to answer.

Exhibit 17.6
Frequently Asked Interview Questions

1. What are your long-range and short-range goals and objectives? When and why did you establish these goals, and how are you preparing yourself to achieve them?
2. What do you consider to be your greatest strengths and weaknesses?
3. Why did you choose the career for which you are preparing?
4. How do you think a friend or professor who knows you well would describe you?
5. Why should I hire you?
6. In what ways do you think you can make a contribution to our company?
7. Do you think your grades are a good indication of your academic achievement?
8. What major problem have you encountered, and how did you deal with it?
9. What do you know about our company? Why are you seeking a position with us?
10. If you were hiring a graduate for this position, what qualities would you look for?

Exhibit 17.7
Examples of Legal and
Illegal Questions

Subject	Legal Questions	Illegal Questions
Name	Have you ever used another name?	What is your maiden name?
Residence	Where do you live?	Do you own or rent your home?
Birthplace or national origin	Can you, after employment, verify your right to work In the United States?	Where were you born? Where were your parents born?
Marital or family status	Statement of company policy regarding assignment of work of employees who are related. Statement of company policy concerning travel: Can you accept this policy?	With whom do you reside? Are you married? Do you plan a family?
Arrest or criminal record	Have you ever been convicted of a felony? (Such a question must be accompanied by a statement that a conviction will not necessarily disqualify the applicant.)	Have you ever been arrested?

Source: Baylor University Career Services Center.

So what do you do when you are asked an illegal question? One thing you should do is report the incident to your school's career services personnel if the interview is taking place on campus or as a result of the campus career services center. But when actually faced with the question, you have several choices. One is to ask, "Why do you ask? Is that important?" You may find that it is a question asked by an interviewer out of personal curiosity, and the interviewer may not have realized the question was inappropriate. Another response is to simply reply, "I'm sorry, I would prefer not to answer that question." If probed, you can state that you believe the question is not legal, but you will check with career services later; if the question is legal, you will answer it later. If the interviewer is simply ignorant, you will probably get an apology, and then the interview will move on. Otherwise you've identified a company where you may not wish to work. Your final option is, of course, to go ahead and answer the question.

At some point during the interview, the recruiter will ask whether you have any questions. In addition to using the standard questions concerning pay, training, and benefits, you should prepare questions that are unlikely to have been answered already. For example, suppose your research has uncovered the fact that the company was recently awarded the Malcolm Baldrige Award for Quality; you might plan to ask what the company did to win that award.

You may also want to plan questions about the interviewer's career, how it got started, and what positions he or she has held. These questions work best when you are truly interested in the response; otherwise you might sound insincere. Answers to these questions can give you a personal insight into the company. Also, you may often find yourself working for the interviewer, so the answers to your questions may help you decide whether you like and can work with this person.

Other important subjects to ask about are career advancement opportunities, typical first-year responsibilities, and corporate personality. You also need to know how financially stable the company is, but you can find this information for public firms in the library. If the firm is privately owned, ask about its financial stability.

Finally, it may seem trivial, but shine your shoes! You are interviewing for a professional position, so look professional. Recruiters have told us about students showing up for interviews dressed in cut-off shorts and a T-shirt or looking hung over. Those interviews were over before they began. One interviewer even described how a student took a phone call from her mother during the interview. She told her mom that the interview was going great! Well, it was until she took the phone call. If you do not look the part now, an interviewer will not see you in the part.

During the Interview

The job interview is much like any other sales call. It includes an approach, needs identification, presentation, and gaining commitment. There are, however, several important differences because both parties are identifying needs and making presentations.

THE APPROACH Social amenities will begin the interview. You will not need the same type of attention getter that you would on a cold call. However, you may want to include an attention getter in your greeting. For example, use a compliment approach, such as "It must be very exciting to work for a Malcolm Baldrige award winner."

NEEDS IDENTIFICATION One difference between sales calls and job interviews is that both parties have needs they have individually defined before the meeting (in a sales call, SPIN helps you assist the buyer in defining needs). A question such as "Are you willing to relocate?" is used not to define needs so much as to determine whether the company's needs will be met. You should prepare questions that will help you learn whether the company's offer will meet your needs.

Take notes during the interview, especially when asking about the company, so you can evaluate whether your needs will be met. Carry a portfolio with extra résumés and blank paper and pens for note taking. You may want to ask, "Do you mind if I take notes? This information is important to me, and I don't want to forget anything."

Try to determine early whether your interviewer is a sales manager or a personnel manager. Personnel managers may have a difficult time telling you about the job itself, its daily activities, and so forth; they may be able to outline only things such as training and employee benefits. Sales managers can tell you a lot about the job, perhaps to the point of describing the actual territory you will work in.

Personnel managers do not like being asked about salary; you will find that many people will advise you not to ask about money on the first interview. On the other hand, you are making an important decision. Why waste your time or theirs if the salary is much lower than your other alternatives? Sales managers are less likely to object; but just in case, you may want to preface a question about earnings by saying, "Compensation is as important a consideration for me as training and other benefits when making a decision. Can you tell me the approximate earnings of a first-year salesperson?" You will probably get a range rather than a specific figure. You could also wait until a later meeting to ask about earnings.

People who prefer security desire compensation plans with an emphasis on salary. Other people like the potential rewards of straight commission. If either is important to you, ask about the type of compensation plan in the first meeting. For example, you should ask, "What type of compensation plan do you offer: salary, straight commission, or a combination of salary plus commission or bonus?"

PRESENTATION Features alone are not persuasive in interviews, just as features alone do not persuade buyers to purchase products. Recall the FEBA technique presented in Chapter 8, which stands for feature, evidence, benefit, agreement. Cheryl McSwain (see Exhibit 17.4) might say, "I was a camp counselor for two summers at Camp Kanatcook (*feature*), as you can see on my résumé (*evidence*). This experience taught me customer service skills that you will appreciate when I sell for you (*benefit*), don't you agree?"

If asked to describe yourself, use features to prove benefits. Recruiters will appreciate specific evidence that can back up your claims. For example, if you say you like people and that is why you think you would be a good salesperson, be prepared to demonstrate how your love of people has translated into action.

Many students carry portfolios into interviews. A **portfolio** is an organized collection of evidence of one's career.[8] For example, a portfolio might contain letters of reference, a résumé, thank-you letters from customers, a paper about an internship, a strategic plan created for a business policy class, or even photographs of the homecoming float for which you were chairperson. Some of our students offer videos of their sales calls from this class as part of their portfolios. Portfolios are one method of offering proof that you can deliver benefits.

thinking **it** through

How would you describe yourself in terms of features? What needs would be satisfied by those features so they could become benefits? What would go on your Web site or in your portfolio to prove your features? How could you use a Web site to market yourself?

Keep in mind that the interviewer also will be taking notes. Writing down answers takes the interviewer longer than it takes for you to speak. Once a question is answered sufficiently, stop and allow the interviewer time to write. Many applicants believe they should continue talking; the silence of waiting is too much to bear. Stay silent; otherwise, you may talk yourself out of a job.

GAINING COMMITMENT Because sales positions usually require skill at gaining commitment, sales managers will want to see whether the candidate has that skill. Be prepared to close the interview with some form of gaining commitment: "I'm very excited about this opportunity. What is our next step?"

Be sure to learn when you can expect to hear from the company, confirm that deadline, and write it down. You may want to say, "So I'll receive a call or a letter within the next two weeks. Let's see, that would be the 21st, right?"

Asking for commitment and confirming the information signal your professionalism and your organizational and selling skills.

SPECIAL TYPES OF INTERVIEWS

You can face many types of interviews: disguised interviews, stress interviews, and panel interviews, among others. **Disguised interviews,** or interviews in which the candidate is unaware that the interviewer is evaluating the candidate, are common at college placement offices. In the lobby you may meet a **greeter,** probably a recent graduate of your college, who will try to help you relax before a scheduled interview and offer you an opportunity to ask questions about the job and the company. Although you can obtain a lot of good information from a greeter, you may want to save some questions for the real interview. You may also want to repeat some questions in the interview to check for consistency. Keep in mind that the greeter is also interviewing you, even though the meeting seems like friendly conversation. Keep your enthusiasm high and your nerves low.

A **stress interview** is designed to place the candidate under severe stress to see how the candidate reacts. Stress interviews have been criticized as being unfair because the type of stress one experiences on a job interview often differs from the type of stress one would actually face on the job. Still, many reputable companies believe it is appropriate to try to determine how a candidate reacts to stress because stress is a real part of just about every sales position. One tactic is to ask three questions at once and see how the candidate answers; another is to ask, "How are you going to lose money for me?" (*translation:* What mistakes have you made in the past and what might you do in the future?) or other reversed versions of appropriate questions. Another strategy is to ask questions such as "What is 36 cubed?" or "What will the interest rates be on such and such a date (two years from now), to the exact one-hundredth please?"[9] While questionable in terms of measuring the appropriate form of stress, these methods are less questionable than the following: The interviewer asks the applicant to reveal something personal, such as a time when the person felt emotionally hurt. Once the situation has been described, the interviewer may mock the applicant, saying the situation wasn't that personal or that hurtful and surely the applicant can dig deeper. Another stress tactic is to ask the interviewee to sell something such as a pencil or a table; while this question is reasonable when used to observe selling style, being an unreasonable "customer" can turn the call into a stress interview.

You probably will not see stress interviews at a college placement office, but you could face one at some point in the job-hunting process. You may find it helpful to deal with a stress interview by treating it as a game (say to yourself, "She's just trying to stress me out; I wonder how far she will go if I don't react?"). Of course you may simply refuse to play the game, either by terminating the interview or by changing the subject. If you terminate the interview, you will probably not get the job.

In **panel interviews** you will encounter multiple interviewers. During a panel interview try to make eye contact with each interviewer. Focus on each person for at least three seconds at a time; anything less than that and you are simply sweeping the room. When asked a question, begin your answer by directing it to the questioner but then shift your attention to the group. By speaking to the group, you will keep all interviewers involved and avoid a two-person conversation. You may want to review how to sell to a group, described in Chapter 8.

Group interviews are similar to panel interviews, but they include several candidates as well as several interviewers. Group interviews may take place in a conference room or around a dinner table. If you find yourself in a group interview, avoid trying to top the stories of the other candidates. Distinguish yourself by asking interviewers about their careers and what they find it takes to be successful.

Panel interviews require special tactics by the candidate to keep all interviewers involved. A focus on only the older gentleman may cost this young man a position.

Treat social occasions during office or plant visits as interviews, and avoid alcohol or overeating. As with stress interviews, the key is to maintain your cool while being yourself. You cannot do that if you overindulge. Remember that companies are still evaluating you during these "social" events.

FOLLOW-UP

Regardless of the type of interview, you should send a thank-you note shortly afterward. Send one to the greeter, if possible (thus you will probably want to get this person's business card). If you had a panel interview, find out who the contact person is and write to that person. After thanking the person in the first paragraph, write a paragraph that summarizes the interview. Focus your summary on the reasons why you should be hired. In the final paragraph reiterate your thanks and end with an assumptive statement, such as "I look forward to seeing you again."

If you do not hear by the target date, contact the person. Call if the interviewer was a sales manager; write if a personnel manager spoke with you. Sales managers will appreciate the saleslike perseverance; personnel managers may not. Within another week, call the personnel manager also. Simply ask for the status of your application rather than whether you got the job. The process of deciding may have taken longer than expected, or other situations may have caused delays. You need to know where you stand, however, so you can take advantage of alternatives, if possible.

INTERVIEWING NEVER ENDS

Even if you spend your entire career with one company, your job interviewing days are not over after you land that first job; you will interview for promotions as well. Some companies even interview candidates for admission to management development programs. The same techniques apply in all these cases. You will still need to prepare properly, conduct the interview professionally, close for some level of commitment, and follow up.

MANAGING YOUR CAREER GOALS

An important aspect of career management is to set life-based objectives and then use them to determine your career objectives. Balance between family and work goals is necessary, or one of several negative consequences could occur, such as divorce or success without fulfillment. One survey reported that a lack of work–life balance was one of the top reasons that managers resigned, were terminated, or were poorly evaluated.[10] Another study indicated that the recession of the late 2000s significantly impacted work–life balance for the worse. Nearly 50 percent of workers reported significant increases in stress due to work–life conflict.[11]

Balance, then, is important when setting career goals. Career decisions must be compatible with family and personal objectives. Keeping life goals in mind and remembering your reasons for setting those goals will help you map out a career with which you can be happy.

MAKING THE TRANSITION FROM COLLEGE TO CAREER

That first year after college is a unique and important time in anyone's life. How this transition is handled can have a big influence in whether you reach success or experience disappointment. Although a life's work is not created or ruined in the first months, a poor start can take years to overcome. It is not just a matter of giving up student attitudes and behaviors; making the transition also requires taking the time to understand and earn the rights, responsibilities, and credibility of being a sales professional. You will make mistakes during that transition; everyone does. But as many successful salespeople have learned, it isn't whether you make mistakes, but rather whether you learn from them.

Many new hires want to make a great first impression, so they charge ahead and fail to recognize that the organization was there long before they were and has already developed its own way of doing things. The first thing to do is learn the organization's culture, its values, and the way things are done there.

Another important aspect of the first year is that you are under a microscope. Your activities are watched closely as management and your peers try to decide

INSIDE SALES: IT'S NOT WHAT YOU THINK!

Many students approach their first job as if it is their entire career; they put too much pressure on themselves to make the right choice. As a result, they may overlook, avoid, or turn down inside sales jobs as a place to start. That's probably a mistake.

Todd Pollock of the Forty-Niners (profiled in Chapter 11) would certainly agree. Inside sales is where he got his start. So did Jeff Moss with IBM. Both are now in account management positions but credit their fast career start to their time in inside sales.

"At IBM," says Moss, "some sales professionals actually entered inside sales later in their career and plan to stay in inside sales. Our inside sales team does visit each major customer at the customer's location once or twice a year, sometimes more, but most of their work is on the phone. Each rep in that inside sales position handles only a few major accounts and supports account executives from other parts of our business, too."

Inside sales is not calling people during dinner to sell them something they don't want. Professional salespeople like Moss and Pollock have an established list of clients that they visit with regularly. These salespeople engage in the same needs identification and presentations that you might expect in a business setting; it's just over the phone.

"Now with WebEx and other online tools," says Bruce Culbert, noted sales technology expert, "inside salespeople can actually sell more and build stronger customer relationships because they can talk to their customers more often by phone and through e-mail that they could face-to-face."

"There's also that sense that you're not in it by yourself," notes Ashley Harrell, now an account executive with D Magazine who got her start in inside sales. "When you run into tough situations, there's someone right there to talk you through it and help you out."

Culbert agrees. "Inside sales is a great place to start out because the learning curve is so fast. Not only do you have supporters right there, you also make more contacts, learning more quickly as a result." He also points out that the lower cost per contact and buyers' increasing needs for efficient interactions will drive increased use of inside sales positions. "It's not what your parents may think of as telemarketers. Today's inside sales professionals are product experts with strong career opportunities. Inside sales is a great place to start."

whether you are someone they can depend on. Demonstrate a mature willingness to learn, plus respect for those with experience. Part of this mature willingness to learn means you hold your expectations in check and keep your promotion hopes realistic. Remember that recruiters tend to engage in puffery when presenting the opportunities and benefits of a company. Although the recruiter said it may be possible to earn a promotion in six months, the average may be much longer.

Seek a partnership with your manager. Although partnership implies a peer-level relationship and you do not have the experience to be a true peer with your manager, use the same partnering skills with him or her that you would use with customers. Find out what your manager needs and wants and then do it. Every workday is a test day except that you sometimes write the questions. Just like your professor, your manager wants the answers, not the problems. Give your boss solutions, and you will be well on the way to a partnership.

DUAL CAREER PATH

When you start out in sales, many career options are open. Career paths can alternate between sales and marketing or follow a route entirely within sales or entirely within marketing. You may even wind up as chief executive officer of a major global corporation, like Mark Hurd at HP. Exemplifying how you

Exhibit 17.8
Sales Advancement at Schneider Electric

might pursue various positions, Exhibit 17.8 depicts the various career paths for salespeople at Schneider Electric. In addition to sales management opportunities, many companies also have opportunities in marketing and product development that begin in sales.

CONTINUE TO DEVELOP YOUR KSAS

Knowledge, skills, and abilities, or **KSAs,** are the package that you offer your employer. You just spent four or five years and a lot of money developing a set of KSAs, but like any asset, your KSAs will begin to decay if you do not continue to invest in them. Because you are the person in your company to whom your career means the most, many companies, such as Cisco, have recognized that ownership of development belongs to the person, not to the company, and have turned training into self-directed development programs. In addition to self-directed training, much of the company's training has also gone virtual, meaning salespeople can access it online at any time.[12] Even if your company has not formalized development into a self-directed program or if the development program does not provide many options, take the time and effort to invest in yourself so you can grow in your career. As the philosopher Eric Hoffer said, "In times of change, the learners inherit the earth, while the learned find themselves beautifully equipped to handle a world that no longer exists."[13]

Research indicates that career development opportunities vary widely among companies, especially for salespeople. Look for programs that involve assessment of your skills, as well as direction and development of those skills. In Exhibit 17.9 Jeffrey Bailey summarizes soft KSAs developed in salespeople at Oracle. As he says, "We expect the reps to be able to spot challenges that our solutions can address, and then be able to explain the value our solutions can deliver. We really don't try to train them on the products, only on understanding business issues and then being able to highlight the value we can bring. It is our sales consultants who get the real deep product training. There are just too many products to expect the reps to be deep in any of them."

Exhibit 17.9

Soft Skills Developed at Oracle

-Negotiation
-Value messaging
-Competitive positioning
-Reference selling
-Working with partners
-Prospecting skills
-Best practices for how to lead a good sales cycle

Lifelong learning is important in today's learning organization. Although many companies have downsized, it is the versatile, well-educated employee who not only keeps a job but also develops a career.

Lifelong learning can be an important factor in not only improving your position but also enjoying what you do. Once you have a position within an organization, your objective will be to develop yourself to get a promotion and then to be successful in that promotion. (To get the promotion after that, you will need to do well in the job you are seeking.) You should take several significant actions in each position along the way. The first action is to understand your options because sales can often lead to various positions.

Sources of Improvement

Most companies continue to train their salespeople after basic sales training, but most training of experienced salespeople is product-related rather than sales skills–related. If you want to improve your selling skills, you may have to actively seek assistance.

The first place to start is with the field sales manager. When that person works with you in your territory, solicit feedback after each call. During these curbside conferences, you can learn a great deal about what you are doing from an objective observer. One warning, however: Make sure your manager only observes during the sales call and does not try to get into the act! As we discussed in the previous chapter, many sales managers are former salespeople who get excited in the heat of battle and may try to take over the sales call.

Peers provide another source. Who is successful in the company? When gathered together for a sales meeting, many successful salespeople pick one another's brains for new ideas and strategies. Offer to work with them in their territories for a day or so in order to learn from them. In most situations they will be flattered and helpful. Noncompeting salespeople in professional organizations such as Sales and Marketing Executives, an international organization of salespeople and marketing managers, will also be flattered to share their tips with you.

Bookstores offer a wealth of material for developing sales skills. Many good books remind salespeople of the basics of selling and present advanced methods of selling and negotiating. Be sure to keep this book, too, because you will want to refer to it when you are in the field.

Sales seminars—in-person, online, or on DVDs and CDs—are also available. Seminars, such as those offered by Zig Ziglar, Dale Carnegie, Wilson Learning, and Tom Hopkins, can be very motivating. However, many experienced salespeople desire more than just motivation; they look for seminars that also teach new ways to present and gain commitment, as well as other sales skills. Some even learn to play golf because that's what their customers do.[14]

Another source of improvement is an industry association. Many industries and professions offer certification programs, which not only require that you improve and update your knowledge and skills but also offer proof to your customers that you have made that effort. Francisco Limas, sales representative with National Restaurant Supply in El Paso, sought certification in food safety and is now pursuing certification as a Foodservice Equipment Distributors Association Certified Salesperson. Though he's been recognized by the industry's top salespeople, he realizes that the certification provides both education and an assurance

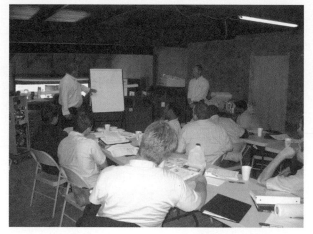

Learning doesn't end at graduation. This team of salespeople at Mechanical Service Company is learning about a new product.

of quality to customers.[15] Certification was one measure of service quality that these buyers used when comparing suppliers.

Industry associations, though, can and do provide many training opportunities that may not lead to certification. For example, the National Association of Insurance and Financial Advisors (NAIFA) offers a number of professional development courses, including one called the NAIFA Sales System. The program is primarily delivered online, though it also includes a book and access to NAIFA mentors who will coach students through challenges that arise in their regular sales calls.[16]

In this course you have begun to develop your interpersonal persuasion, or selling, skills. Whether or not you plan a career in sales, you owe it to yourself to continue to develop these skills.

Learn Your Current Job

Learn all you can about the job you have now. Many people want promotions as fast as they can get them, regardless of their readiness. But consider that you will probably be managing the people who will be holding your current job. To be truly effective as their manager, you should learn all you can about the job of the people you hope to manage while in the best position to do so: while you are one of them.

Learn the Job You Want Next

A manager once said, "In order to become a manager, you must first be a manager." He meant that promoting someone is easier when that person already has the characteristics the position requires—that is, already acts like a manager—rather than having only potential.

Several ways exist for you to learn about the job you desire. First, solicit the help of people who hold the job now. Many companies expect managers to develop their people. Take advantage of that fact; ask for the help of such managers. Find out what they did to prepare themselves and what you should do.

Second, volunteer to take on special projects that will demonstrate your leadership and organizational abilities. Taking projects off the hands of your manager can also let you see the manager's responsibilities. Look for ways you can contribute to the overall sales team to show your commitment to the organization, your ability to lead and develop others, and your management skills.

In addition to improving your skills, many sales professionals also recommend building a personal brand—a professional reputation that is not only strong and positive, but also widely recognized. Social media offer one outlet for building that brand, as discussed in "Sales Technology 17.1."

MANAGING STRESS

Selling can be a stressful career. For example, with three days left in the month, Richard Langlotz, a sales manager at Konica-Minolta, faced a sales team that lost $100,000 in business. One sale alone, worth $60,000, would have made the team's quota, but that account delayed its order for a few months. The other prospects decided to go with the competition. Suddenly it looked as though Langlotz

PERSONAL BRANDING

Ever since the concept of branding was developed, people have applied the concept to their own professional identity. Marketers talk about a brand promise as being what the consumer expects from the brand—in terms of performance on key dimensions, how the product is marketed, and how the consumer is taken care of in the event of a problem. While an interesting discussion could be had about whether a personal brand is any more than a professional reputation, the reality is that every salesperson should consider building a personal brand, and today's social media can help do that.

Jim Stradinger is a partner of Holland 1916, a company that manufactures labels and other identification products that go onto other companies' products. For example, Holland 1916 aids companies in the design and implementation of RFID by creating RFID tags embedded into the casing of a product. Humrichouse recently tasked his sales staff with developing a personal brand by using social media. He challenged his salespeople to blog regularly and taught them to use Twitter effectively and integrate social media into a comprehensive campaign that also involves speaking at trade conferences and other traditional forms of branding. "Ours could be a commodity business. But when a company has an unusual problem, we want our salesperson to be the *go-to* for the solution," says Stradinger.

Recently Jeffrey Bailey, sales manager for Oracle, stated that the company wouldn't even consider hiring a salesperson who hasn't used social media personally. "If a prospective salesperson isn't using Facebook and LinkedIn professionally already, then they can't sell in today's environment," believes Bailey. Dan Harding, regional sales director for ConnectandSell, agrees. Not only does he monitor job changes and other important information via LinkedIn, he also stays abreast of his customers by reading their blogs or key industry blogs. These blogs tell him what is on his customers' minds now; occasionally he can respond, but only when he really has

something to contribute to the dialogue that lets his customers know that he is aware. These comments also help Harding build that personal brand.

Perhaps one of the most extreme examples of personal branding was created by Dave Schrader, an analyst for Teradata. Schrader's job is to promote Teradata by educating the market on what data warehousing, Teradata's product category, can do. He changed his name to eDave during the dot-com boom, when it seemed that every company was also adding *dot com* or *e-* to its name, just as Apple seems to be inserting *i* before everything now. While he did so with tongue firmly planted in his cheek, he ultimately changed it back to just plain Dave when the dot-com bubble burst. He seems a little embarrassed by it all now, but he's also much better known now.

Several factors are important when using social media to build a personal brand. The first factor is that the brand is personal; as Lisa Gschwandtner writes, "Greater personal transparency—sharing thoughts, feelings, and even insecurities—is what wins friends and followers." Another factor is to be strategic. Being strategic means choosing media and opportunities that fit the brand you are trying to build. Don't comment on every blog your customer writes; comment only when you really have something to say and what you have to say contributes to both your brand and the conversation. (Keep in mind that the first factor of being personal does allow, and even encourages, you to comment on that fine pitching performance in the Yankees/Red Sox game—your comments don't have to always be on the brand mark. But commenting on how long it took to recover from the party at the trade show is probably not a good idea.) Finally, be where your customers are. If they are using Twitter, you need to be there.

Sources: Gschwandtner quote and Harding material are from Lisa Gschwandtner, "It's all about Strategy," *Selling Power* (January–February 2010), pp. 32–36; the rest of the material is from personal interviews.

was going to finish the month well below quota. To top it off, one of his salespeople quit. What did he do? "I took my sales team to a pizza place," Langlotz says. He thought about calling a meeting and getting tough with his team, but he realized they already had enough stress and didn't need any more from him.

At the pizza parlor, without any prompting from him, each salesperson examined his or her prospect lists and determined how the team was going to move sales forecast for the next month into the current month. The team was successful, and Langlotz says he learned a valuable lesson. "When you have good people doing their best, they don't need more stress from their manager." Many salespeople liken sales to a roller-coaster ride, with great emotional highs when sales are good but emotional lows when sales are poor. Research shows that support from the sales manager, such as that offered by Langlotz, can go a long way to reduce stress among salespeople.[17]

For some people, coping with stress results in changing jobs. Changing jobs may be the right thing for some people to do. Others turn to less healthful releases, such as absenteeism, drugs, alcohol, and so forth.[18] All jobs have some stress; managing that stress is important to leading a happy and healthy life. However, managing stress does not always mean removing the cause of stress. Sometimes, as with the loss of a loved one, most people find they must manage stress because they cannot remove or change its cause. Two types of stress common to salespeople because of the unique nature of sales positions are situational stress and felt stress.

SITUATIONAL STRESS

Situational stress is short-term anxiety caused by a situational factor.[19] You may face situational stress when waiting to make a sales presentation for your class, for example. The best strategy to deal with situational stress is to leave the situation or remove the situational factor causing the stress, but that approach is not always possible. You cannot, for example, simply tell your instructor that you are too stressed to sell in class today, so you are leaving! One technique for managing situational stress is to imagine that the situational factor has been removed (see Exhibit 17.10 for more ideas). In class, imagine that you have already finished your role play. Mentally consider that feeling of relief you get when you know you have done a job well. Sometimes imaging success can reduce feelings of stress.

In sales situational stress may be caused by impending presentations, deadlines for closing orders (as in Richard Langlotz's case), and similar situations. Situational stress can cause stage fright in even the most experienced salespeople. One price of success is that situational stress will continue to occur, but successful salespeople learn to control their feelings of situational stress.

Exhibit 17.10
Coping with Situational Stress

Use imaging: Close your eyes and imagine yourself past the source of stress. Try to feel the actual sensation of what it will be like when the stress is gone.

Exercise: Exercise can moderate feelings of stress. When situational stress occurs over a period of time, set time aside for exercise breaks.

Take breaks: Take a walk, phone a friend, do something. If working on a stressful project, take regular stress breaks. Combine imaging techniques with breaks to increase the stress-reducing power of breaks.

Rest: In addition to breaks, be well rested when the situation arises. If you have a major presentation, get a good night's rest beforehand.

Prepare: If the situation involves future performance, prepare and practice. Prepare for every contingency, but don't let the tension build by thinking only of things going wrong.

Recover: Plan time for postsituation recovery before you charge into the next high-stress situation. Doing two major presentations in one day, for example, may not provide you with the recovery time you need to do well in the second presentation.

FELT STRESS

Felt stress lasts longer than situational stress because the causes are more enduring. **Felt stress** is psychological distress or anxiety brought about by job demands or constraints encountered in the work environment. For example, one study showed that when salespeople felt obliged to use coercive sales tactics, their levels of felt stress increased because they knew they were engaging in ethically questionable techniques.[20] Perhaps the most common form of felt stress is role stress, or feelings of stress caused by the salesperson's role.

Role stress is brought about by role conflict, role overload, and/or role ambiguity. **Role conflict** occurs when two partners demand incompatible actions of the salesperson. A common such occurrence is when the customer wants something that seems reasonable but the company won't allow it. Ted Howell represents a training company and was selling an e-learning training program. A customer wanted to see previous work, especially because he didn't like the demo version the company offered. Ted knew that the demo version didn't represent the client's solution, but his manager kept telling him that the demo should be sufficient. Ted's frustration level hit the boiling point in one call, to the point where his manager asked what was wrong. How do you tell your manager that he's the problem? Ted didn't, but he also gave the client another demo that was more in line with his needs. Seeing the right demo was all the client needed, and Ted got the sale.[21] Conflict occurred with the salesperson caught in the middle. **Role ambiguity** occurs when the salesperson is not sure what actions are required. The salesperson may not be sure what is expected, how to achieve it, or how performance will be evaluated and rewarded. **Role overload** is what happens when the role demands more than the person can perform. Asking a new salesperson to make the same types of presentations to high-level accounts that a veteran would make could cause role overload.

In general, the best way to handle role stress is to increase role accuracy (see Exhibit 17.11 for specific ideas). When the problem is role ambiguity, simply asking for further instruction or reviewing training materials may be helpful. Coaching and other management support can also be requested. Role conflict and role ambiguity require prioritizing activities. In the example of the salesperson who feels stress due to conflict between the customer's and the manager's demands, the salesperson must decide whose needs will be met. Once that decision is made, further stress can be avoided by refusing to dwell on the conflict. Note that the conflict is still there (both parties have conflicting demands), but the effect on the salesperson is minimized.

In either case a strong partnership with the sales manager can greatly aid in reducing stress. When a partnership is formed between a sales manager and a salesperson, the salesperson has a better understanding of the demands of the job, which activities should receive priority, and how the job should be

Exhibit 17.11
Reducing Role Stress

Prioritize: Set your own priorities so that when different people place conflicting expectations on you, your preset priorities determine where your actions will go.

Seek support: Enlist support of your priorities from your spouse, your manager, and other key people. By focusing on goals and priorities, you can reduce conflict over specific activities.

Reset expectations: By prioritizing and seeking support, you can reset expectations of various constituencies so that they are in harmony. Communicate and gain agreement on what you are capable of doing so that others' expectations of you are realistic.

Act and move on: Once you have made a decision to act, don't dwell on the conflict. Act and move on.

performed. Partners also have access to more resources and more information, which can help remove some of the organizational constraints that can bring about stress.[22]

Strong sales skills can also reduce feelings of stress. Mastery of the job will reduce feelings of stress because the salesperson is in control of the situation.

SELLING YOURSELF

This entire chapter is about selling yourself throughout your career. Here we focus on some aspects specific to college students looking for a career.

College students may not realize the competition they face. That company is interviewing not only at your school, but also probably at three or four others. At each school it may talk to 15 students, or about 75 total, all for one position. In addition, recruiters get hundreds and sometimes thousand of résumés if they also post the job on the Internet. The key is to make yourself stand out and still be truthful.

Keeping the résumé simple is one way to get noticed. According to Eric Ruiz, CEO of SalesJobs.com, one mistake college students make is to put in too much detail. "All they want to know is if you can sell and what kind of numbers you've produced. For recent graduates, that's just a matter of putting the right spin on your part-time job at the local burger shack; instead of saying you 'worked the order window,' write that your shift had the highest sales numbers of any shift, or that you increased ice cream sales by 6 percent by suggesting a weekly 'buy one get one half-off' day."[23]

When responding to a posting on the Internet, don't just cut and paste your résumé into an online form. Special formatting may not come across properly when the recruiter looks at it online unless the file is saved as rich text. Similarly, don't use an uncommon software format that few recruiters may have. Your résumé may come across as dots, blocks, and zeroes.

Ruiz also suggests that you don't write a cover letter for each online posting. "Writing a cover letter does not help you in the sales industry. The people reading your résumé are HR professionals and sales recruiters; they're generally overworked, and find cover letters superfluous. Again, they're only interested in seeing hard data regarding what you've sold, whom you sold it to, and what numbers you produced. They are focused on your previous performance because being successful in sales requires such a specialized skill set," says Ruiz.

He suggests creating an individually tailored version of your résumé for each industry in which you're seeking employment, emphasizing knowledge and experience that would transfer to different industries. For example, if you're working in food and beverage sales but you want to get into medical equipment sales, write that you "have a large percentage of hospital accounts" and are "familiar with the purchasing staff at all the local hospitals" and that you've "sold to doctors before."

E-mail addresses like *myvixen* and *partystupid* may be fine in college but not when you're looking for a job. "E-mail addresses should be professional—first name, last name, and a number is fine," notes Ruiz. While Ruiz recognizes that many people apply for sales jobs, "It's the little things, like a follow-up e-mail address, that can help you get that dream job." Once you create a professional address, be sure to check it often, don't change it again (some companies report being unable to track down a good candidate), and don't let the mailbox fill up.

And clean up your Myspace and Facebook pages. Many companies regularly review these pages before making a hiring decision. Similarly, create a professional voice mail message. It's time to get professional!

SUMMARY

A sales career offers many opportunities for growth and personal development, but that career has to start somewhere. That is the purpose of the job search: to find a good match between what you need and have to offer and what a company needs and has to offer.

To achieve a match that results in mutual satisfaction, you must first understand who you are—specifically what you need and what you have to offer. You can ask yourself a number of questions to stimulate your thinking about the type of person you are and what you will need from a sales position. In addition, as you review your experiences in school, work, and other activities, you can identify the skills and characteristics that you have to offer.

Finding industries and companies with the characteristics you desire will require you to apply your marketing research skills. The library contains many sources of information that will help you. Personal sources can also be useful in providing information as well as leads for interviews, as can the Internet.

Sources for job interviews include the campus placement office, personal contacts, and advertisements. Résumés are personal brochures that help sell a candidate. Writing effective cover letters will help you get interviews off campus, while the interview itself is similar to a sales call. Plan questions that demonstrate your knowledge of and interest in the company. Also, plan to ask for information that will help you make your decision. Follow up after the interview to demonstrate your desire and perseverance.

You are the person in the company to whom your career means the most. Therefore, you must actively manage your own career. Set career goals that are compatible with family and personal objectives. Keeping the reasons for these career goals in front of you will enable you to make better decisions.

Learn the job you have now. You may someday manage people who have this job; the better you know it, the better you will be at managing it. To become a manager, you must first be a manager. Learn the manager's job as well, and volunteer for activities and projects that will let you demonstrate your management ability.

Stress can occur in any job. Situational stress is short term, whereas felt stress is longer term. For many people, the key to managing stress is to reduce the influence of stressors because the causes of stress often cannot be eliminated.

Sales offers a challenging and exciting career. The opportunities are so varied that almost anyone can probably fit into some sales position. Even if you choose a career in another field, take advantage of the material in this chapter. You should find these job search and career management tips helpful in any field. Good luck!

KEY TERMS

application form 471
assessment center 472
conventional résumé 473
disguised interview 481
felt stress 490
functional résumé 473
greeter 481
group interview 482
interview 472
KSAs 485

panel interview 482
portfolio 481
references 472
role ambiguity 490
role conflict 490
role overload 490
role stress 490
situational stress 489
stress interview 482
tests 472

ETHICS PROBLEMS

1. You are interviewing for your dream job. Suddenly the interviewer notices your wedding ring and compliments you on it. But then he says, "You know, this job requires a lot of travel. What is your spouse going to say to that?" You answer the question, and he replies, "That's great, now, when you don't have kids. You don't have kids, do you? Because it is tough to be successful if you don't get the travel done." What do you do? What would you do if the interviewer said, "You know, handling conflict is an important part of this job. Describe a conflict you've had with your spouse and how you handled it."

2. Some people recommend signing up for as many interviews as possible, reasoning that the experience will be helpful when you find a company with a job you really want. (And who knows? You might find a job you like.) Is this practice ethical? Why or why not? If you answer that it depends, what does it depend on?

QUESTIONS AND PROBLEMS

1. What would you do differently if you were being interviewed by an amiable, a driver, an analytical, or an expressive? What about a panel interview with one driver and one amiable? One analytical and one expressive?

2. Emily Tanner began her career in a small but rapidly growing company (look back at the opening profile). What were the advantages to her start? What do you think she may have missed out on by not working for a big, well-known company?

3. Analyze yourself against the traits of a successful salesperson in Exhibit 17.2. What type of sales would best suit you? Why? Are you qualified for that job? If not, what do you need, and how would you go about getting it? That list was created in 1999. Do you think it should be revised for today? If so, how?

4. Some interviews are conducted over the phone or by videoconference. What do you think is important and different about these types of interviews compared to face-to-face interviews? Do you think these difference carry over into selling by phone versus in person? Reread "Building Partnerships 17.1." Would you consider an inside sales position? Why or why not?

5. Reread "Sales Technology 17.1." What changes do you need to make to your social media presence to prepare for transitioning to a professional career or to build your personal brand?

6. Answer the questions in Exhibit 17.6 as you would in a sales job interview.

7. Your summer internship in a sales job was a bad experience. Your biggest complaint was that the sales manager seemed incompetent. Despite this negative experience, you like sales, so you are interviewing for a sales position. What would you say if asked why you do not seek full-time employment with the summer internship firm?

8. One recruiter called a professor to check on a student that the professor referred. The recruiter said, "You gave this student my name last Wednesday and now it is Tuesday. Does this delay signal a lack of interest?" How would you answer that if the recruiter was asking you the question and you were the student? Why would a recruiter comment on the time it took to call?

9. You are in an interview, and you think this is your dream job. How would you secure commitment? What would you say different in the first interview if it is a screening interview on campus versus the fourth interview at company headquarters? Is securing commitment more or less important for sales positions than for other types of positions?

10. What stresses do you have now? How do you deal with stress? What healthy ways to handle stress do you use? What are some ways you respond to stress that may not be so healthy?

case **17.1**

Choices, Choices!

While studying for the final exam for the sales class, a group of students began talking about jobs. "I just don't think I could do sales," said Amanda. "I just don't think I could either go cold calling or try to call people on the phone I don't know and try to sell them something. But I like working with people."

"I think I could," replied Bill. "I just don't know what I want to sell. It has to be something I believe in." Murmurs of agreement followed. "And I want to have something different every day—I don't think I could sit behind a desk with the same old routine."

"I'm more like Amanda," said Emily. "I don't think I could do a lot of cold calling, but I'd like to be in sales anyway. Maybe something where they come to me or I see the same people. I'm good with people once I get to know them."

"I heard a lot of companies start you out on the phones first," Roger noted. "Like IBM. You start out on the phones, and if you're good, then you get to go out into the field."

Questions

1. What kinds of jobs would Bill be suited for? Emily? Can Emily's fears be overcome, or should she just find a job that doesn't involve cold calling?
2. Using the Web, find a position for each student to apply for. Print the ad, and then on the same sheet (write on the back if you need to), justify your choice.
3. Pick one of the four positions you used in Question 2 for yourself. Why is that a good fit for you?

case **17.2**

It's Not My Fault!

I graduated from a fairly well-known university in the Midwest knowing I wanted to go into sales. I worked two summer internships in sales actually selling for companies (one was a minor league baseball team where I was the leading salesperson when I returned to school for the fall), and I knew it was for me. So when I got the job with a company to move to the Northeast and begin to sell, I was thrilled! Graduation was made all the more exciting by knowing that I was packing up and moving the next day to the big city.

Now it's been three months and I've made one sale. And the company lost that one by not delivering on time. Then today I got a call from my manager, who told me that we both nearly got fired for lack of production. I'm making my calls—he's not! I know I can document my activity because I'm entering it into the software system. My boss told me that his boss, the one who nearly fired both of us, said I wasn't to know about our near-death experience. What should I do? I'm so stressed out, I can barely function!

Source: This case is based on a real situation.

ROLE PLAY CASE

Congratulations, you just got promoted! Now you have to replace yourself by hiring a college graduate to take over your sales territory. Given everything you've learned about NetSuite this semester and what you know about sales, take a few minutes to identify the three most important features a salesperson should bring to the job and the questions you'd ask to determine if the candidate had those features. Then take turns interviewing each other in your group. There is no candidate information to be provided—each student will portray himself or herself when playing the candidate role.

ADDITIONAL REFERENCES

Avlonitis, George J., and Nikolaos Panagopoulos. "Exploring the Influence of Sales Management Practices on Industrial Salesperson: A Multisource Hierarchical Linear Modeling Approach." *Journal of Business Research* 60, no. 7 (2007), pp. 765–87.

Fan, Chiang Ku, and Chen-Liang Cheng. "Gender Differences in Burnout among Life Insurance Sales Representatives in Taiwan." *Journal of the American Academy of Business* 11, no. 1 (2007), pp. 214–22.

Knight, Dee K., Hae-Jung Kim, and Christy Crutsinger. "Examining the Effects of Role Stress on Customer Orientation and Job Performance of Retail Salespeople." *International Journal of Retail & Distribution* Management 35, no. 5 (2007), pp. 381–403.

Lewin, Jeffrey E., and Jeffrey K Sager. "An Investigation of the Influence of Coping Resources in Salespersons' Emotional Exhaustion." *Industrial Marketing Management* 38, no. 7 (October 2009), pp. 796–811.

Mallin, Michael L., Edward O'Donnell, and Michael Y. Hu. "The Role of Uncertainty and Sales Control in the Development of Sales Manager Trust.," *Journal of Business & Industrial Marketing* 25, no. 1 (2010), pp. 30–42.

Onvernah, Vincent. "The Effects of Coaching on Salespeople's Attitudes and Behaviors: A Contingency Approach." *European Journal of Marketing* 43, no. 7–8 (2009), pp. 938–51.

Smith, J. Brock, and Mark Colgate. "Customer Value Creation: A Practical Framework." *Journal of Marketing Theory and Practice* 15, no. 1 (2007), pp. 7–23.

Srivastava, Rajesh, and Deva Rangarajan. "Understanding the Salespeople's 'Feedback–Satisfaction' Linkage: What Role Do Job Perceptions Play?" *Journal of Business & Industrial Marketing* 23, no. 3 (2008), pp. 151–64.

Valenzuela, Leslier M., Jay P. Mulki, and J. Fernando Jaramillo. "Impact of Customer Orientation, Inducements, and Ethics on Loyalty to the Firm: Customers' Perspective." *Journal of Business Ethics* 93, no. 2 (May 2010), pp. 277–93.

Weinrauch, J. Donald, Meral Anitsal, and Ismet Anitsal. "Manufacturers' Representative Profession: A Model about the Impact of Agency Success and Marketing Methods on Willingness to Hire Recent College Graduates." *Academy of Marketing Studies Journal* 11, no. 2 (2007), pp. 69–86.

ROLE PLAY CASE 1

STUBB'S BAR-B-Q

Stubb's Bar-B-Q is an Austin, Texas, manufacturer of barbecue sauces and marinades. Founder C. B. Stubblefield states on the Web site, "My recipes are known throughout Texas and the world as the best in barbecue, and I've put my heart and soul into each one. With my picture on the label and my recipe inside, you can be sure you're getting the finest quality available. Simply put, my life is in these bottles."

Stubb's offers a wide variety of products (see its Web site for the most up-to-date list of products and prices):

Product	Suggested Retail Price	Reseller Case Prices (When Buying Fewer Than 20 Cases in a Single Order)
Stubb's Bar-B-Q Sauce	$3.89	6 for $21
Stubb's Marinades (come in Pork, Beef, Teriyaki, and Chicken varieties)	$4.29	6 for $23
Stubb's Rubs (come in Bar-B-Q, Burger, Rosemary Ginger, Chili Lime, and Herbal Mustard varieties)	$3.79	12 for $38
Stubb's Liquid Smokes (come in Hickory and Mesquite flavors)	$2.19	12 for $19
Stubb's Chicken Wing Sauces (come in Original and Inferno varieties)	$4.29	6 for $23

Marinade is usually used for about an hour, or a bit longer for more intense flavor, before cooking. Then the chef can baste the meat with fresh marinade as it cooks and serve it with one of the Stubb's Bar-B-Q Sauces. Rubs are spice mixtures applied to meat before it is grilled or smoked. Rubs are just like a marinade except that they add a layer of crust to the meat. The Liquid Smokes are offered for customers who want to add a natural hickory or mesquite smoky flavor to meats.

Stubb's offers noncumulative quantity discounts for resellers (the total number of cases can be based on mixed items; thus a reseller that buys 10 cases of Spice Rubs in any varieties and 11 cases of Moppin' Sauce in any varieties would get the additional 5 percent discount):

Quantity Purchased	Discount
Fewer than 20 cases	Standard reseller case prices
21–100 cases	An additional 5 percent off reseller case prices
Over 100 cases	An additional 10 percent off reseller case prices

Stubb's also offers a number of promotions for resellers. Resellers that set up an end-of-aisle display of at least 50 cases of a mix of sizes and flavors earn an extra $1 per case discount on all cases purchased. For resellers that advertise Stubb's products in the newspaper, there is a 50 percent co-op payment for the actual portion of the page cost of the advertisement. Thus if a grocery store runs a newspaper ad that includes one-eighth of a page for Stubb's products, Stubb's will reimburse the grocery store for 50 percent of the cost of the ad.

There are many competitive barbecue sauces, including such brands as K.C. Masterpiece, Porky's Gourmet, Cattlemen's Barbecue Sauce, Ukuva iAfrica, and various flavors offered by Hunt's, Heinz, and Kraft.

Sources: http://stubbsbbq.elsstore.com; http://www.stubbsbbq.com. For more up-to-date information, please visit the Web sites. Information about discounts and promotions for retailers is fictitious but reflects the types of promotions allowed by manufacturers to retailers.

Situation 1: Target—Corporate Headquarters (Resell Situation)

The first Target store opened in Roseville, Minnesota, in 1962. Its trendy merchandise at affordable prices launched a new era in discount retailing. This "T-1" store was easy to shop, attractive, and always clean. It served as the prototype for every Target store opened since then, and it changed how consumers think about discount shopping.

Today Target operates nearly 1,750 stores in 49 states, including more than 240 SuperTarget® stores that include an upscale grocery shopping experience. In addition to the photo processing centers, pharmacies, and Food Avenue® restaurants found in almost every Target, SuperTarget stores include in-store bakery, deli, meat and produce sections. (Source: www.target.com)

You are a salesperson for Stubb's. You are calling on a corporate headquarters grocery buyer of Target. Assume Target has not carried Stubb's products in the past. Your goal is to have Target's corporate headquarters approve the offering of at least some Stubb's products in its stores and stock them in Target's distribution warehouses. Assume the final decisions about which products will be offered in individual stores are up to the local store managers.

Situation 2: Target—Local Supermarket (Resell Situation)

The first Target store opened in Roseville, Minnesota, in 1962. Its trendy merchandise at affordable prices launched a new era in discount retailing. This "T-1" store was easy to shop, attractive, and always clean. It served as the prototype for every Target store opened since then, and it changed how consumers think about discount shopping.

Today Target operates nearly 1,750 stores in 49 states, including more than 240 SuperTarget® stores that include an upscale grocery shopping experience. In addition to the photo processing centers, pharmacies, and Food Avenue® restaurants found in almost every Target, SuperTarget stores include in-store bakery, deli, meat and produce sections. (Source: www.target.com)

You are a salesperson for Stubb's. You are calling on the grocery manager of a local SuperTarget. Assume that Target's corporate headquarters has approved the offering of Stubb's products and that Target carries them in its distribution centers. However, this SuperTarget has never carried Stubb's products in the past. Your goal is to have this store manager approve the offering of at least some Stubb's products in her or his store. Note: If the store manager agrees to offer Stubb's, he or she will simply order the products from the Target distribution center.

Situation 3: Mount Royal Fine Foods Grocery Store (Resell Situation)

Mount Royal Fine Foods is a family-run grocery store with that hometown appeal and where customer service is top priority. The store includes homemade deli salads and entrees, gourmet cheese, sushi bar, salad bar, fresh meats and produce, full-line grocery, dairy and frozen, and an in-store bakery. (Source: adapted from www.mountroyalfinefoods.com)

You are a salesperson for Stubb's. Your goal is to introduce Stubb's products to the grocery store manager and secure a sale of at least some of the products. The store carries several brands of barbecue sauce but has never carried Stubb's.

Situation 4: Hasty Market Convenience Stores (Resell Situation)

Hasty Market is a successful chain of food stores with over 250 locations throughout Ontario, Canada. As a company recognized for variety, quality, and convenience, Hasty Market has been serving local communities with efficiency and effectiveness since 1981. With locations spanning across Ontario and stores ranging from 1,500 to 5,000 square feet, Hasty Market is committed to serving each community with many products and services.

Hasty Market is a Canadian owned and operated corporation, with the head office situated in Oakville, Ontario. This central location enables the company to contribute to and be a part of the various communities as well as maintain a close relationship with the stores and their clients.

At Hasty Market, customer service and convenience are the top priority. It is essential for each of its stores to be community oriented, with the customer's interest in mind. With this initiative, the needs of the local customer are met with a unique combination of products and services at each individual store. (Source: adapted from www.hastymarketcorp.com/)

You are a salesperson for Stubb's. Your goal is to introduce Stubb's Legendary Bar-B-Q sauce to a grocery buyer of Hasty Market and to secure at least a trial order.

Situation 5: Menard's—Corporate Headquarters (Resell Situation)

Menard's is the third largest home improvement retailer in the United States, behind Lowes and Home Depot. Menards has 252 stores in 12 states: Ohio, Michigan, Indiana, Illinois, Wisconsin, Minnesota, Iowa, Missouri, Nebraska, South Dakota, North Dakota, and Wyoming. In addition to selling many items for do-it-yourselfers like building materials, hardware, electrical, millwork, wall coverings, plumbing, housewares, floor coverings, cabinets, and appliances, it also sells a limited number of outdoor living products that include items such as barbecue grills, grill accessories, and grill cleaning and cooking tools. During grilling season it carries a few of the best-selling brands of barbecue sauce next to the grills. (Source: www.menards.com)

You are a salesperson for Stubb's. You are calling on the corporate headquarters buyer for outdoors products at Menard's. Menard's has not carried Stubb's products in the past. Your goal is to have Menard's corporate headquarters approve the offering of at least some of Stubb's products in its stores, and carry the products in the Menard's distribution warehouse. Assume the final decisions about which products will be offered in individual stores are up to the local store managers.

Situation 6: Menard's—Individual Store (Resell Situation)

Menard's is the third largest home improvement retailer in the United States, behind Lowes and Home Depot. Menards has 252 stores in 12 states: Ohio, Michigan, Indiana, Illinois, Wisconsin, Minnesota, Iowa, Missouri, Nebraska, South Dakota, North Dakota, and Wyoming. In addition to selling many items for do-it-yourselfers like building materials, hardware, electrical, millwork, wall coverings, plumbing, housewares, floor coverings, cabinets, and appliances, it also sells a limited number of outdoor living products that include items such as barbecue grills, grill accessories, and grill cleaning and cooking tools. During grilling season it carries a few of the best-selling brands of barbecue sauce next to the grills. (Source: www.menards.com)

You are a salesperson for Stubb's. You are calling on the outdoors department manager for one Menard's store. Assume that the Menard's corporate headquarters has approved the offering of Stubb's products and carries them in the Menard's distribution center. However, this Menard's has never carried Stubb's products in the past. Your goal is to have this outdoors department manager approve the offering of at least some Stubb's products in her or his store. Note: If the store manager agrees to offer Stubb's, he or she will simply order the products from the Menard's distribution center.

Situation 7: Trader Joe's—Corporate Headquarters (Resell Situation)

Trader Joe's is a grocery store chain of 339 stores located in 24 states, with a heavy concentration in California. The stores are stocked with foods and beverages from the basics like milk, bread, and butter to more exotic fare like imported cheeses, organic produce, and hand-tossed pizza from Italy. Every product sold is tasted before the store decides to sell it. Trader Joe's keeps its costs low, cuts out the middleman whenever possible, and passes its savings on to the customer. The stores carry unconventional and interesting products in the Trader Joe's label as well as everyday basics. They buy products they think are winners and that will find a following among their customers. (Source: adapted from www.traderjoes.com)

You are a salesperson for Stubb's. Your goal is to introduce Stubb's products to the grocery buyer of Trader Joe's at corporate headquarters and secure an agreement that allows the offering of at least some Stubb's products in the stores. Assume the final decisions about which products will be offered in individual Trader Joe's stores are up to the local store managers. Also assume the local store manager, if interested, would buy the products directly from Stubb's.

Situation 8: Trader Joe's—Local Store (Resell Situation)

Trader Joe's is a grocery store chain of 339 stores located in 24 states, with a heavy concentration in California. The stores are stocked with foods and beverages from the basics like milk, bread, and butter to more exotic fare like imported cheeses, organic produce, and hand-tossed pizza from Italy. Every product sold is tasted before the store decides to sell it. Trader Joe's keeps its costs low, cuts out the middleman whenever possible, and passes its savings on to the customer. The stores carry unconventional and interesting products in the Trader Joe's label as well as everyday basics. They buy products they think are winners and that will find a following among their customers. (Source: adapted from www.traderjoes.com)

You are a salesperson for Stubb's. You are calling on the store manager of a local Trader Joe's. Assume that the corporate headquarters of Trader Joe's has approved the offering of Stubb's products. However, this Trader Joe's has never carried Stubb's products in the past. Your goal is to have this local manager approve the offering of at least some Stubb's products in her or his store. Note: If the store manager agrees to offer Stubb's, he or she will need to purchase the products directly from Stubb's because the Trader Joe's distribution center does not stock Stubb's products.

Situation 9: Chili's Grill & Bar

Chili's Grill & Bar is a restaurant chain founded by Larry Lavine. The chain has over 1,400 casual dining restaurants, mostly located in the United States and Canada, and a full menu. Chili's now has locations in all 50 U.S. states and 28 international locations. From fresh, hand-prepared salads to mouth-watering burgers, Chili's kicks up the flavor with food that is anything but ordinary. (Source: adapted from www.chilis.com)

You are a salesperson for Stubb's calling on the corporate headquarters of Chili's. Chili's restaurants have never carried your sauce, and you have not called on the chain before. Your goal is to have Chili's make Stubb's sauce available for customers to use with their meals, either as a standard item placed on dining tables or available on request. Note: You are not requesting that Chili's sell Stubb's products to customers.

Situation 10: The Joint

The Joint is a New Orleans restaurant that serves up the juiciest of slow-cooked pulled pork and beef brisket, chicken, and ribs as well as a host of sides and fixings. The Joint made the list of Bon Appetit's Top 10 New Barbecue Restaurants. *Hemispheres* magazine has written, 'The Joint . . . serves some of the most powerful barbecue in the South." *Offbeat* magazine says, "For consistent excellence, coupled with value and a welcoming ambience, the Joint has no equal among local barbecue purveyors." (Source: adapted from www.alwayssmokin.com)

You are a salesperson for Stubb's calling on the chef of The Joint. Your goal is to have the chef consider using Stubb's barbecue products as she prepares meals that use barbecue sauce and marinades. You would also like Stubb's products to be available if patrons request them during a meal. Note: You are not requesting that The Joint sell Stubb's products to customers.

ROLE PLAY CASE 2

NETSUITE

NetSuite is an award-winning contact management software package that integrates personal databases on accounts with calendar management, word processing, and other computer software applications. From the salesperson's perspective, NetSuite serves as a combination of a card file and calendar, and it enables salespeople to quickly identify prospects for new products, search for prospects in a given area, and perform other similar operations. In addition, all call records are maintained in a manner that enables salespeople to instantly recall personal information about any individual inside any account.

From the sales manager's perspective, the software's reporting features enable closer supervision of salespeople. The manager can observe who has made what calls on which prospects, intervene with helpful suggestions based on call notes provided by the salesperson, and create sales forecasts. Further, if a salesperson leaves, all of the territory information remains with the company because it is stored in NetSuite. Visit www.netsuite.com and click on the CRM button for more information.

The product sells for a suggested retail price of $129 per month per user or $1,548 per year per user. The minimum contract length is one year, and the price can be locked in for three years (with no more than a 5 percent increase) if a client wants to sign a three-year agreement. There is no installation cost. The software is a hosted product, meaning it resides on NetSuite servers and is maintained fully by NetSuite. No IT department is required! To use it, though, users must be able to access the Internet to download the account information and update it. Further, any customization has to be done by the user (or through a reseller).

NetSuite wins a lot of awards for its ease of use and functionality (check out its home page for a complete listing at www.netsuite.com—click on CRM). The home page also has many reviews of NetSuite and other packages, so read it to understand the features and benefits more fully. In addition, you can watch several online demos to learn more about how salespeople use the software (click on the "Role-Based Demo" button).

NetSuite CRM + Pricing	Base Package		
Features	Monthly	Annual	Included Units
Each full user	$129	$1,548	1 User
Customer self-service portal	—	—	Included
Partner relationship management module	—	—	Included
Technical support: Silver*	—	—	Included
Expense reporting + intranet + employee SS	—	—	For full users
Offline sales client	—	—	Included
Mail merge/e-mail communications	—	—	30,000 per month
E-mail marketing campaigns	—	—	10,000 per month

Netsuite's major competitors are GoldMine (www.frontrange.com), ACT! (www.symantec.com), Siebel (www.siebel.com), and Salesforce.com (www.salesforce.com). Spend some time at each of these Web sites not only to learn what they do differently or better, but to learn in general how CRM/SFA software works.

Resellers are also called value-added resellers, or VARs. To be a NetSuite VAR, the VAR has to agree to take a 16-hour training course to learn how to customize the software, which costs $495 per person. VARs can sell their customization services, though, at any price they want, which is how they can really make big money. They also get 15 percent commissions on anything they sell. Some VARs also package consulting on e-mail campaigns and similar services.

Reseller Situations

XLR8 WORKFLOW Today you are calling on the owner of XLR8 (Accelerate) Workflow. The company is a small VAR that specializes in software systems for hospitals and health clinics. You had a mutual friend set up a meeting with the owner. Your friend says that XLR8 has primarily been a custom software provider. The owner of XLR8 is a talented businessperson and is known for being tough on everybody.

PROFIT FROM TRAINING (PFT) PFT is a sales training organization. You looked at its Web page after getting a phone call from the president, and you know that the company has offices across a five-state area. It specializes in sales training for the hospital supply industry. When you spoke with the president on the phone to set up the appointment, this person told you that the company has to expand its offerings in order to grow its business—training has reached saturation. It has already looked at Sage (makers of both Act! and SalesLogix) and liked it.

CULBERT TECHNOLOGIES Today you are calling on the owner of Culbert Technologies, a new CRM consultancy. The company was founded only a month ago by three former Accenture partners. They are well known in the industry, and one wrote a best-selling book about CRM and sales force automation. Another member of the firm held a similar position at another VAR for NetSuite before joining Accenture.

TOTAL OFFICE Today you are calling on the owner of Total Office. Total Office provides a range of office supplies for small businesses (furniture, paper, pens, and so on) You met the owner because he went to high school with your father. There are three locations, one each in a different suburb of the metropolitan area. The owner has about 15 outside salespeople and 30 inside salespeople, divided equally among the locations. Most of their sales are delivered from the company's central warehouse. Out of courtesy for your dad's friend, you made an appointment to see this person.

DIXON AND FROST Today you are calling on the information technology manager for Dixon and Frost, a national sales consultancy. Dixon and Frost is already a VAR for Act! and provides training on how to use Act!. It also sells several personality profile tests to companies for use in selecting new salespeople, as well as other sales consulting services. You cold-called the information technology manager last week, and although the person seemed genuinely interested in meeting you and discussing this software package, time wasn't available then, so you made an appointment for today.

Industrial User Situations

SHIPP BELTING This company provides custom belts, hoses, and other products to manufacturers, farmers, and large plant (like a university) maintenance departments. The company serves a three-state area with 16 salespeople. The company was just taken over by the third generation of the Shipp family, and the new president wants to grow the business aggressively. You found this out at your Lion's Club meeting last Wednesday.

PARSONS ROOFING Today you are calling on the president of Parsons Roofing. Parsons Roofing has about 25 estimators (work a lot like salespeople) and 20 project managers. The company deals with commercial buildings, plus hospitals, schools, and other buildings with large roofs. The primary product is the Dura-Last roof, and Parsons is the only licensee for Dura-Last in a five-state area. Approximately 30 projects are "live" at any particular time. These projects generally last between 2 weeks and 3 months. The projects require several meetings with clients, suppliers, and municipal building inspectors. The buyer wishes to increase the number of projects that the company can handle without additional personnel. You met the buyer at a charity golf tournament about three weeks ago.

GREENBRIAR Today you are calling on the sales supervisor for the local region of Greenbriar. The buyer has about 30 outside salespeople and 15 inside salespeople for the region. Greenbriar imports machinery used in poultry and fish processing. The sales supervisor called you after being told about your product by a friend of his.

COMMUNITY BANK Today you are calling on the founding CEO for Community Bank. This young bank has been in business for about four years and only recently moved into its own building. You saw the new building open up and thought it would be a good idea to drop in. When you dropped in, you were told that there were two managers with seven loan officers each. Each officer was assigned about 200 clients. You were able to meet the CEO but scheduled an appointment for today because the CEO was quite busy when you dropped in.

M2 AEROSPACE Today you are calling on the engineering manager for M2 Aerospace, a company that refurbishes and retrofits aircraft for corporate and military clients. Work can include updating the avionics, replacing the cabin furnishings, and even replacing engines or wing structures. The buyer has over 200 engineers employed. Each of these engineers, to varying degrees, has meetings with management, clients, and suppliers. M2 Aerospace recently adopted the notion that "everyone is a salesperson" at M2. You met the prospect at a conference in Las Vegas about two months ago, and you scheduled an appointment to discuss your product.

PHOTO CREDITS

CHAPTER 1

Page 2, © Comstock/PunchStock/DAL; page 3, Courtesy of Lauren Bearden; page 4, © Business Cartoons by UK Cartoonist Morris/Visual Humour; page 9, © Custom Medical Stock Photo/Alamy/RF; page 11, © Royalty-Free/Corbis/DAL; page 16, © Richard Lord Enterprises, Inc./The Image Works; page 19, © Keith Brofsky/Getty Images/DAL.

CHAPTER 2

Page 22, © Jupiterimages/Comstock Premium/DAL; page 30, © Rubberball/Corbis/RF; page 31, Courtesy of Patricia Gietl; page 41, © moodboard/Corbis/RF; page 44, © Royalty-Free/Corbis; page 49, © David Silverman/Getty Images; page 52, © Keith Brofsky/Getty Images/DAL; page 53, © Jupiterimages/Creatas/Alamy/RF.

CHAPTER 3

Page 62, © Andersen Ross/Getty Images/DAL; page 63, Courtesy of Jenna Weber; page 66, Courtesy of STUBB's Legendary Kitchen; page 69, Courtesy of Deere & Company; page 75 top left, © Phototake Inc./ Alamy; page 75 top right, © Jupiterimages/Thinkstock/Alamy/RF; page 75 bottom left, © Imagemore Co. Ltd./Getty Images/RF; page 85, © Jean-Marc Charles/Sygma/Corbis.

CHAPTER 4

Page 98, © Digital Vision/PunchStock/DAL; page 99, Courtesy of Azure Barbeau; page 101, © S. Pearce/PhotoLink/DAL; page 103, © Digital Vision/Getty Images/RF; page 106, © Keith Brofsky/Getty Images/DAL; page 109 top, © Gary Ombler/ Getty Images; page 109 bottom, © Betsie Van Der Meer/Getty Images; page 110 left, © Michael J. Hruby; page 110 middle, © Michael J. Hruby; page 110 right, © Michael J. Hruby; page 113, © Creatas Images/PictureQuest/DAL; page 117, © Royalty-Free/Corbis; page 120, © Pankaj Insy Shah/Getty Images.

CHAPTER 5

Page 126, © Ryan McVay/Getty Images/DAL; page 127, Courtesy of Meggie Dominguez; page 130, © William Taufic/ Corbis; page 132, © Keith Brofsky/Getty Images/DAL; page 136 top left, © AP Photo/Elizabeth Dalziel; page 136 top right, © AP Photo/Frank Franklin II; page 136 bottom left, © Peter Macdiamid/Getty Images; page 136 bottom right, © Eric Thayer/Getty Images; page 142, Courtesy of Business Resource Software, Inc.

CHAPTER 6

Page 148, © Masterfile/DAL; page 149 Courtesy of Kevin Johnson; page 156, © Corbis—All Rights Reserved; page 160, Courtesy of Deere & Company; page 163, © AP Photo/Wally Santana; page 166, © BananaStock Ltd./DAL; page 169, © Dennis MacDonald/PhotoEdit; page 171; © Jose Luis Pelaez/ Getty Images.

CHAPTER 7

Page 178, © Getty Images/Blend Images/DAL; page 179, Courtesy of Marcel Dalby; page 180, © Walter Hodges/Getty Images; page 185, Courtesy of Hoover's, Inc.; page 189, © Kim Steele/Getty Images/DAL; page 191, © Michael Keller/Corbis; page 195 top, © Royalty-Free/Corbis; page 195 middle, © Paul Redman/Getty Images.

CHAPTER 8

Page 202, © Royalty-Free/Corbis; page 203, Courtesy of Jennifer VanWinkle; page 205, © Andersen Ross/Getty Images/ RF; page 208, © John Cummings/Getty Images/RF; page 212, © Kaz Mori/Getty Images; page 219, Courtesy of Huron Window Corp. Manitoba, Canada; page 221, © Eric Audras/ Getty Images/RF; page 225, © Royalty-Free/Corbis.

CHAPTER 9

Page 232, © Royalty-Free/Corbis; page 233, Courtesy of Andrew Gaffka; page 238, © Doug Menuez/Photodisc/Alamy; page 240, Photo Courtesy of JELD-WEN Windows & Doors; page 243, © The McGraw-Hill Companies, Inc./Jill Braaten, photographer; page 244 top, © Digital Vision/PunchStock/DAL; page 244 bottom, © Digital Vision/Getty Images/RF; page 246, © Creatas Images/PictureQuest/DAL; page 250, © 2007 Getty Images/DAL.

CHAPTER 10

Page 260, © Dynamic Graphics/PictureQuest/DAL; page 261, Courtesy of Rachel Gober; page 265, © LWA-Dann Tardif/Corbis; page 271, © Royalty-Free/Corbis; page 277, © Stockbyte/PunchStock Images/DAL; page 280, © Jupiterimages/ Brand X/Alamy/RF; page 284 top, © Getty Images/ Stockbyte/ DAL; 284 bottom, © Keith Brofsky/Getty Images/DAL.

CHAPTER 11

Page 290, © Javier Pierini/Getty Images/DAL; page 291, Courtesy of Todd Pollock; page 297, © Cathy Melloan Resources/ PhotoEdit; page 300, © Royalty-Free/Corbis/DAL; page 304, © Bettmann/Corbis; page 311, © Jeff Goldberg/PhotoEdit.

CHAPTER 12

Page 320, © Rob Melnychuk/Getty Images/DAL; page 321, Courtesy of Alex Tagansky; page 323, © Frank Herholdt/ Getty Image; page 327, © Brand X Pictures/Jupiterimages/DAL; page 330, © Javier Pierini/Getty Images/DAL; page 332, © Image Source Black/Alamy; page 337, © Stockbyte/PunchStock Images/DAL.

CHAPTER 13

Page 348, © Digital Vision/Getty Images/DAL; page 349, Courtesy of Kevin Cloch; page 351 top, © David Paul Morris/Getty Images; page 351 bottom, Courtesy of Apple; page 356, Courtesy of Starwood Hotels & Resorts; page 358 top, © AP Photo/LM Otero; page 358 bottom, © Dennis Macdonald/PhotoEdit.

CHAPTER 14

Page 374, © Ronnie Kaufman/Larry Hirshowitz/Getty Images/DAL; page 375, Courtesy of Stephanie Meagher; page 379, © Bonnie Kamin/PhotoEdit; page 386, Courtesy of David Richardson Heating and Air Conditioning, Frankfort, KY; page 389, Courtesy of Eddy Patterson, STUBB's Legendary Kitchen, Austin, TX; page 398, Courtesy of Keith Reznick, Creative Training Solutions.

CHAPTER 15

Page 404, © Royalty-Free/Corbis/DAL; page 405, Courtesy of Tony Fiorello; page 407, © Digital Vision/DAL; page 409, © Patti McConville/Getty Images; page 414 left, © Ryan McVay/Getty Images/DAL; page 414 right, © Stockbyte/Punch Stock/DAL; page 421, © Ablestock/Alamy/RF; page 425, © Tetra Images/Getty Images/RF.

CHAPTER 16

Page 434, © The McGraw-Hill Companies, Inc./Christopher Kerrigan, photographer; page 435, Courtesy of Lillie Sanchez; page 440, © Walter Hodges/Photodisc/Getty Images/RF; page 445, © Digital Vision/Getty Images/DAL; page 448, © Najlah Feanny/Corbis; page 455, © Warren Morgan/Corbis.

CHAPTER 17

Page 464, © Digital Vision/Getty Images/DAL; page 465, Courtesy of Emily Tanner; page 467, © Art Directors & Trip/Alamy; page 471, © Robert Nickelsberg/Getty Images; page 477, Courtesy of Sales Jobs Inc.; page 482, © Upper Cut Images/SuperStock/RF; page 487, Courtesy of Mechanical Service Company Inc., Virginia Beach, VA.

ENDNOTES

CHAPTER 1

1. Wendell Berry, *The Unsettling of America*, 3rd ed. (San Francisco: Sierra Club Books, 1996).
2. See "Customer Analytics: Becoming Customer-Centric," *CRM Magazine* 11, no. 9 (September 2007); Loofie Gutterman, "The Benefits of Being Customer-Centric," *EE-Evaluation Engineering,* May 2007, p. 12; Eric Krell, "The DNA of a Customer-Centric Culture," *1to1 Magazine,* July–August 2007, pp. 26–30; Fernando Jaramillo and Douglas B. Grisaffe, "Does Customer Orientation Impact Objective Sales Performance? Insights from a Longitudinal Model in Direct Selling," *Journal of Personal Selling & Sales Management* 29, no. 2 (Spring 2009), pp. 167–78; "Customer-Centric Communication," *Multichannel Merchant* 25 (May 1, 2008), p. 5.
3. Mark W. Johnson, Clayton M. Christensen, and Henning Kagermann, "Reinventing Your Business Model." *Harvard Business Review* 86, no. 12 (2008), pp. 50–59.
4. See Jeff Lehman, *The Sales Manager's Mentor,* 2nd ed. (Mentor Press LLC, 2006, ISBN: 0-9768999-1-4). (Jeff Lehman may be reached at jjlehman@earthlink.net.)
5. See Paul Greenberg, "Managing Social Customers for Profit: A New Paradigm Calls for a Reassessment of an Industry Metric," *CRM Magazine* 13, no. 8 (2009), p. 48; Nicolas Glady, Bart Baesens, and Christophe Croux, "Modeling Churn Using Customer Lifetime Value," *European Journal of Operational Research* 197, no. 1 (2009), p. 402–11; V. Kumar and Bharath Rajan, "Profitable Customer Management: Measuring and Maximizing Customer Lifetime Value," *Management Accounting Quarterly* 10, no. 3 (2009), p. 1.
6. For more insight into marketing communication programs, see Simone Barratt and Steve Davis, "Connected Commerce: The Intersection of E-Commerce and E-Communication," *Journal of Direct, Data and Digital Marketing Practice* 10, no. 3 (2009), p. 249–61.
7. Mike McCue, "Lessons from the Master," *Sales and Marketing Management,* March/April 2008, p. 22.
8. Gabriele Troilo, Luigi M. De Luca, and Paolo Guenzi, "Dispersion of Influence between Marketing and Sales: Its Effects on Superior Customer Value and Market Performance," *Industrial Marketing Management* 38, no. 8 (November 2009), pp. 872–82.
9. Karen E. Flaherty and James M. Pappas, "Expanding the Sales Professional's Role: A Strategic Re-Orientation?" *Industrial Marketing Management* 38, no. 7 (October 2009), pp. 806–13.
10. The Alexander Group, Inc., SalesTime Maker, Software Services, February 8, 2002, tools.saleslobby.com/-perfMgmt/2001_STM_Presentation.pdf. See also Mark Ellwood, "How Sales Reps Spend Their Time," www.getmoredone.com/How Sales Reps Spend Their Time. pdf, accessed February 15, 2010.
11. See, for example, Paul C. S. Lian and Angus W. Laing, "Relationships in the Purchasing of Business to Business Professional Services: The Role of Personal Relationships," *Industrial Marketing Management* 36, no. 6 (August 2007), pp. 709–18; Esko Penttinen and Jonathan Palmer, "Improving Firm Positioning through Enhanced Offerings and Buyer–Seller Relationships," *Industrial Marketing Management* 36, no. 5 (July 2007), pp. 552–64.
12. Dave Rich, "New Routes to New Customers: A Customer-Centric Approach for Emerging Markets," *CRM Magazine* 13, no. 7 (2009), p. 14.
13. See Ram Charan, "What the Customer Wants You to Know: How Everybody Needs to Think Differently about Sales," *Portfolio,* 2007.
14. Jay Prakash Mulki, Fernando Jaramillo, and Greg W. Marshall, "Lone Wolf Tendencies and Salesperson Performance," *Journal of Personal Selling & Sales Management* 27, no. 1 (Winter 2007), pp. 25–38.
15. Excerpts from communication by Glenn R. Price; used by permission.
16. See for example, Ken Le Meunier-FitzHugh and Nigel F. Piercy, "Does Collaboration between Sales and Marketing Affect Business Performance?" *Journal of Personal Selling and Sales Management* 27, no. 3 (Summer 2007), pp. 207–20; Graham R. Massey and Philip L. Dawes, "The Antecedents and Consequences of Functional and Dysfunctional Conflict between Marketing Managers and Sales Managers," *Industrial Marketing Management* 36, no. 8 (November 2007), pp. 1118–29.
17. Sandra S. Liu and Lucette B. Comer, "Salespeople as Information Gatherers: Associated Success Factors," *Industrial Marketing Management* 36, no. 5 (July 2007), pp. 565–74.
18. This is important because salespeople can be instrumental in breaking down functional silos. See for example, Avinash Malshe and Ravipreet S. Sohi, "Sales Buy-In of Marketing Strategies: Exploration of Its Nuances, Antecedents, and Contextual Conditions," *Journal of Personal Selling & Sales Management* 29, no. 3 (Summer 2009), pp. 207–26.
19. For example, see George Zimmer, "What Qualities and Backgrounds Should You Look For When Hiring Salespeople?" *Inc. Magazine,* July 2007, p. 57.
20. Risto Seppanen, Kirsimarja Blomqvist, and Sanna Sundqvist, "Measuring Interorganizational Trust: A Critical Review of the Empirical Research in 1990–2003," *Industrial Marketing Management* 36, no. 2 (February 2007), pp. 249–65; Sara Denize and Louise Young, "Concerning Trust and Information," *Industrial Marketing Management* 36, no. 7 (October 2007), pp. 968–82.
21. See, for example, John D. Hansen and Robert J. Riggle, "Ethical Salesperson Behavior in Sales Relationships," *Journal of Personal Selling & Sales Management* 29, no. 2 (Spring 2009), pp. 151–66.
22. Technical skills are important. See, for example, Peter A. Reday, Roger Marshall, and A. Parasuraman, "An

Interdisciplinary Approach to Assessing the Characteristics and Sales Potential of Modern Salespeople," *Industrial Marketing Management* 38, no. 7 (October 2009), pp. 838–44.

23. M. Port, "The Human Approach," *Entrepreneur* 37, no. 9 (September 2009), p. 30; Guijun Zhuang, Youmin Xi, and Alex S. L. Tsang, "Power, Conflict, and Cooperation: The Impact of Guanxi in Chinese Marketing Channels," *Industrial Marketing Management* 39, no. 1 (January 2010), pp. 137–49; Blair Kidwell, Richard G. McFarland, and Ramon A. Avila, "Perceiving Emotion in the Buyer–Seller Interchange: The Moderated Impact on Performance," *Journal of Personal Selling & Sales Management* 27, no. 2 (Spring 2007), pp. 119–32; Osman Yildirim, "Discriminating Emotional Intelligence–Based Competencies of IT Employees and Salespeople," *Journal of European Industrial Training* 31, no. 4 (April 2007), pp. 274–82.

24. The most widely use test of emotional intelligence is the EQ-i® Emotional Quotient-Inventory. See http://www.mhs.com/product.aspx?gr=IO&prod=eqi&id=overview for details. See also Harvey Deutschendorf, "EQ Boost," *T+D* 63, no. 10 (2009), p. 92–93.

25. Menninger Clinic, www.menningerclinic.com/resources/emotional_maturity.htm, accessed February 15, 2010.

26. Nick Tasler and Lac D. Su, "The Emotional Ignorance Trap," *BusinessWeek Online*, January 19, 2009.

27. Tasler and Su, "The Emotional Ignorance Trap."

28. Manpower, Inc., "Talent Shortage Survey 2007 Global Results," *Confronting the Talent Crunch 2007: A Manpower White Paper.*

29. Rebecca Aronauer, "Trends," *Sales and Marketing Management Magazine* 159, no. 4 (May 2007), pp. 38–39.

CHAPTER 2

1. Lauren Etter, "Plenty of Spilled Milk to Cry Over for Dairymen Lured to US," and Mark Maremont and Leslie Scism, "Investors Recruit Terminally Ill to Outwit Insurers on Annuities," *The Wall Street Journal*, February 16, 2010, pp. A1, A4, and A16.

2. Douglas B. Grisaffe and Fernando Jaramillo, "Toward Higher Levels of Ethics: Preliminary Evidence of Positive Outcomes," *Journal of Personal Selling & Sales Management* 27, no. 4 (2007), pp. 355–71; F. Juliet Poujol and John F. Tanner Jr. (2010), "The Impact of Sales Contests on Salesperson Customer Orientation," *Journal of Personal Selling & Sales Management* 30 (1), 33–46.

3. J. Tsalikis and Walfried Lassar, "Measuring Consumer Perceptions of Business Ethical Behavior in Two Muslim Countries," *Journal of Business Ethics* 89 (2009), pp. 91–98.

4. Anne Underwood, "Thanks But No Thanks," *Newsweek*, October 2007, accessed at http://www.newsweek.com/id/57342, February 15, 2010.

5. Thomas Wotruba, "The Evolution of Personal Selling," *Journal of Personal Selling & Sales Management* (Summer 1991), pp. 1–12; William C. Moncrief and Greg W. Marshall, "The Evolution of the Seven Steps of Selling," *Industrial Marketing Management* 34 (January 2005), pp. 13–22.

6. George W. Dudley and John F. Tanner Jr., *The Hard Truth about Soft Selling* (Dallas: Behavioral Science Research Press, 2005).

7. Sergio Roman and Salvador Ruiz, "Relationship Outcomes of Perceived Ethical Sales Behavior: The Customer's Perspective," *Journal of Business Research* 58 (April 2005), pp. 439–51.

8. John D. Hansen and Robert J. Riggle, "Ethical Salesperson Behavior in Sales Relationships," *Journal of Personal Selling & Sales Management* 29, no. 2 (2009), pp. 151–66.

9. Steve L. Grover and Cathy A. Enz, "The Influence of Company Rules, Ethical Climate, and Individual Characteristics," *Journal of Australian and New Zealand Academy of Management* 11, no. 2 (2005), pp. 27–36; Jay P. Mulki, Jorge Fernando Jaramillo, and William B. Locander, "Critical Role of Leadership on Ethical Climate and Salesperson Behaviors," *Journal of Business Ethics* 86 (2009), pp. 125–41; John W. Cadogan, Nick Lee, Anssi Tarkainen, and Sanna Sundqvist, "Sales Manager and Sales Team Determinants of Salesperson Ethical Behaviour," *European Journal of Marketing* 43 (2009), pp. 907–37.

10. Christophe Fournier, John F. Tanner Jr., Lawrence B. Chonko, and Chris Manolis, "Revisiting Antecedents of Salesperson Propensity to Leave: The Moderating Role of Ethical Climate," *Journal of Personal Selling & Sales Management* (2009), pp. 7–22.

11. Eberhard Schnebel and Marge Bienert, "Implementing Ethics in Business Organizations," *Journal of Business Ethics* 53 (2004), pp. 203–11; Jay Prakash Mulki, Fernando Jaramillo, and William B. Locander, "Effects of Ethical Climate and Supervisory Trust on Salesperson's Job Attitudes and Intentions to Quit," *Journal of Personal Selling & Sales Management* 26, no. 1 (2006), pp. 19–37.

12. Dennis N. Bristow, Rajesh Gulati, Douglas Amyx, and Jennifer Slack, "An Empirical Look at Professional Selling from a Student Perspective," *Journal of Education for Business* 81, no. 5 (May–June 2006), pp. 242–49.

13. Dudley and Tanner, *The Hard Truth about Soft Selling.*

14. Paul Milgrom, "What the Seller Won't Tell You: Persuasion and Disclosure in Markets," *Journal of Economic Perspectives* 22, no. 2 (2008), pp. 115–31.

15. Shirley Hunter, personal correspondence. Used with permission.

16. William Bearden, Thomas Ingram, and Raymond LaForge, *Marketing: Principles and Perspectives* (New York: McGraw-Hill/Irwin, 2004).

17. "Exclusive IOMA Survey: How Employers Address Sexual Harassment," *HR Focus* 78, no. 12 (2007), pp. 3–5.

18. Rich Kraus, personal correspondence. Used with permission.

19. Tara J. Radin and Carolyn E. Predmore, "The Myth of the Salesperson: Intended and Unintended Consequences of Product-Specific Sales Incentives," *Journal of Business Ethics* 36 (2002), pp. 79–92.

20. Halliburton, "Sensitive Transactions," www.halliburton.com/about/sensitive-transactions.jsp (accessed February 8, 2005).

21. Meryl Davids, "Global Standards, Local Problems," *Journal of Business Strategy,* January–February 1999, pp. 22–35; Sak Onkvisit and John Shaw, "International Corporate Bribery: Some Legal, Cultural, Economic, and Ethical–Philosophical and Marketing Considerations," *Journal of Global Marketing* 42 (1991), pp. 5–20.

22. O.C. Ferrell, Thomas N. Ingram, and Raymond W. LaForge, "Initiating Structure for Legal and Ethical Decisions

in a Global Sales Organization," *Industrial Marketing Management* 29 (2000), pp. 555–64.

23. Evan Perez and Brent Kendall, "Twenty-Two Arrested in U.S. Bribery Probe," *The Wall Street Journal* (Eastern Edition), January 20, 2010, p. A3.

24. Edmund W. Searby and George P. Farragher, "Foreign Corrupt Practices Act Poses Risk for Middle Market Companies," *Marketing Weekly News,* January 2, 2010, p. 146.

25. Paulina Diosdado de la Pena and Presha Neidermeyer, "U.S. Businesses' Code of Ethics as an Instrument to Comply with the Federal Corrupt Practices Act," *International Business & Economics Research Journal* 8, no. 12, December 2009, pp. 67–73.

CHAPTER 3

1. Eddy Patterson, personal correspondence. Used with permission.

2. Scot Case and Dana Arnold, "Greening Federal Purchasing," *Government Procurement* 13, no. 4 (2005), pp. 18–22.

3. Susan W. Solovic, "Federal Procurement Opportunities for Women Business Owners: Good News–Bad News Scenario," *Women in Business* 56, no. 4 (2004), pp. 11–12.

4. Marvin Wagner, personal correspondence. Used with permission.

5. Nick Zubko, "Strategies for Strategic Sourcing," *Industry Week* 257, no. 1 (2008), pp. 28–29.

6. Aaron Back, Jung-Ah Lee, and Charmian Kok, "Analysts Expect iPad to Give Lift to Asian Manufacturers," *The Wall Street Journal (online)*, January 29, 2010, http://online.wsj.com/article/SB10001424052748704878904575030633950504718.html, accessed February 26, 2010.

7. Robert Dwyer and John F. Tanner Jr., *Business Marketing: Connecting Strategy, Relationships, and Learning,* 4th ed. (New York: McGraw-Hill/Irwin, 2009).

8. Stephen J. Bistritz, "Selling to the C-Suite," *BtoB* 95 (February 8, 2010), p. 7.

9. Alan Earls, "BASF Procurement Gets Deep into R&D," *Purchasing* 138 (June 18, 2009), p. 31.

10. Dwyer and Tanner, *Business Marketing.*

11. For an interesting look at satisfaction by role in the buying center and by buy class, see Jeanne Rossomme, "Customer Satisfaction Measurement in a Business-to-Business Context: A Conceptual Framework," *Journal of Business & Industrial Marketing* 18 (February 3, 2003), pp. 179–96.

12. Carol C. Bienstock and Marla B. Royne, "The Differential Value of Information in Industrial Purchasing Decisions: Applying an Economics of Information Framework," *International Journal of Physical Distribution and Logistics* 37 (2007), pp. 389–402; M. José Garrido Samaniego, Ana M. Gutiérrez-Arranz, and Rebeca San José-Cabezudo, "Determinants of Internet Use in the Purchasing Process," *Journal of Business & Industrial Marketing* 21 (2006), pp. 164–78.

13. Dwyer and Tanner, *Business Marketing.*

14. Ron Swift, personal correspondence. Used with permission.

15. Goutam Chakraborty, Prashant Srivastava, and Fred Marshall, "Are Drivers of Customer Satisfaction Different for Buyers/Users from Different Functional Areas?" *Journal of Business & Industrial Marketing* 22, no. 1 (2007), pp. 20–39.

16. Robert B. Miller and Stephen E. Heiman, with Tad Tuleja, *Strategic Selling* (New York: Warner Books, 1985).

17. Alicia Young, "Lean, Mean, and Keen," *Supply Management* 12, no. 25 (2007), p. 38.

18. Ming Haw Leong and Jane Dunnett, "Customer Perceptions of Attribute Importance in Business-to-Business Environment," *The Business Review* 8, no. 1 (2007), pp. 40–45.

19. Lionel Dace, personal interview.

20. Robert T. Yoki, "If You Can Measure It, Then You Can Improve It," *Hospital Materials Management* 32, no. 12 (2007), pp. 10–11.

21. David Lenling, personal correspondence, used with permission.

22. M. José Garrido-Samaniego, A. María Gutiérrez-Arranz, and Rebeca San José-Cabezudo, Assessing the Impact of E-Procurement on the Structure of the Buying Centre, *International Journal of Information Management* 30 (April 2010), 135–51; Margy Conchar, George Zinkhan, Cara Peters, and Sergio Olavarrieta, "An Integrated Framework for the Conceptualization of Consumers' Perceived-Risk Processing," *Journal of the Academy of Marketing Science* 32, no. 4 (2004), pp. 418–37.

23. Susan Avery, "Procurement's Good Fortune Continues," *Purchasing* 138 (December), p. 43.

24. Tobias Mettler and Peter Rohner, Supplier Relationship Management: A Case Study in the Context of Health Care," *Journal of Theoretical and Applied Electronic Commerce Research* 4 (December 2009), pp. 58–61; Hank Darlington, "How to Pick the Best Vendor Partners for Your Business," *Supply House Times* 46 (February 2004), pp. 52–53.

25. Tom Stundza, "One Way to Get a Raise: Take a Course," *Purchasing* 138 (December 2009), p. 50.

26. Susan Avery, "Bell Thinks outside the Box," *Purchasing* 136, no. 15 (2007), p. 60.

27. Timothy G. Hawkins, Wesley S. Randall, and C. Michael Wittmann, "An Empirical Examination of Reverse Auction Appropriateness in B2B Source Selection," *Journal of Supply Chain Management* 45 (October 2009) pp. 55–71.

28. Christopher A. Sawyer, "Teaching Tata," *Automotive Design & Production,* 120, no. 2 (2008), p. 19.

29. Timothy G. Hawkins, Michael J. Gravier, and C. Michael Wittmann, " Enhancing Reverse Auction Use Theory: An Exploratory Study," *Supply Chain Management* 15 (2010), pp. 21–38; John Geraint, "Smart Saucing," *Supply Management* 23 no. 9 (2004), p. 40.

30. William Ho, Xiaowei Xu, and Prasanta Dey, "Multi-Criteria Decision Making Approaches for Supplier Evaluation and Selection: A Literature Review," *European Journal of Operational Research* 202 (April 2010), pp. 16–31.

CHAPTER 4

1. Jim Blythe, "Trade Fairs as Communication: A New Model," *Journal of Business and Industrial Marketing* 25, no. 1 (2010), pp. 57–62.

2. Frank Luntz, "Words That Pack Power," *BusinessWeek,* November 3, 2008, p. 106.

3. Kitty O. Locker and Donna Kienzler, *Business and Administrative Communication* (New York: McGraw-Hill, 2008), p. 93.

4. See Katherine I. Miller, "Compassionate Communication in the Workplace: Exploring Processes of Noticing,

Connecting, and Responding," *Journal of Applied Communication Research* 35, no. 3 (August 2007), pp. 223–45.

5. See "Hear Ye! Hear Ye!" *Selling Power*, April 2007, pp. 44–46; Lorraine Ukens, "How Can We Train You Today?" *T+D* 61, no. 8 (August 2007), pp. 24–26; Karen E. Klein, "Building Customer Relations by Listening," *BusinessWeek*, June 5, 2007, p. 7.

6. Robert D. Ramsey, "The Most Important Skills for Today's Supervisors." *Supervision* 68, no. 11 (2007), pp. 3–6.

7. Erika Rasmusson Janes, "The Upside of Anger," *1 to 1 Magazine*, July–August 2007, pp. 41–42.

8. Diane F. Wyzga, "What Do You Hear When You Listen? Principles and Tips for Developing Critical Listening Skills: Honing Your Listening Skills Can Help You Hear the Meaning behind the Messages, Leading to Personal and Professional Success," *Government Finance Review* 24, no. 3 (2008), pp. 68–71.

9. For pertinent research on listening, see Lucette Comer and Tanya Drollinger, "Active Empathetic Listening and Selling Success: A Conceptual Framework," *Journal of Personal Selling & Sales Management* 9 (Winter 1999), pp. 15–29; C. David Shepherd, Stephen Castleberry, and Rick Ridnour, "Linking Effective Listening with Salesperson Performance: An Exploratory Study," *Journal of Business & Industrial Marketing* 12 (1997), pp. 315–32; Stephen Castleberry and C. David Shepherd, "Effective Interpersonal Listening and Personal Selling," *Journal of Personal Selling & Sales Management*, Winter 1993, pp. 35–50; Stephen B. Castleberry, C. David Shepherd, and Rick E. Ridnour, "Effective Interpersonal Listening in the Personal Selling Environment: Conceptualization, Measurement, and Nomological Validity," *Journal of Marketing Theory and Practice*, Winter 1999, pp. 30–38.

10. See for example, Julie Andersen, "Developing Active Listening Skills: Can You Hear Me Now? How Effective Communication Will Enhance Your Career," *IDEA Fitness Journal* 5, no. 5 (2008), pp. 85–87; Debra Stein, "Reducing Audience Aggression by Reflecting Back," *Public Management* 91, no. 1 (2009), p. 34.

11. See for example, Dale Klamfoth, "Socrates Makes a Call," *Sales & Marketing Management*, November/December 2008, p. 8.

12. See "Take the Time to Listen," *U.S. News & World Report* 31 (December 2007), p. 61.

13. See Anita Raghavan, "Watch Your Body Language," *Forbes*, March 16, 2009, p. 92; Shari Alexander, "Networking and Selling Using Body Language Secrets," *Sales & Marketing Management* (2009), p. 82; Rebecca Aronauer, "Express Yourself: Your Body Language Speaks Volumes," *Sales & Marketing Management* 159, no. 1 (January–February 2007), p. 15.

14. Dave Zielinski, "Body Language Myths," *Presentations*, April 2001, p. 39.

15. Owen Hargie, *The Handbook of Communication Skills*, 2nd ed. (London: Routledge, 1997).

16. Mark McCrum, "Some Helpful Pointers," *New Statesman* 137, no. 4859 (August 27, 2007), p. 45.

17. John Perry, "Palm Power in the Workplace," *The American Salesman* 46 (October 2001), p. 22.

18. A source to learn how to control facial nonverbals is Malcolm Gladwell, *Blink: The Power of Thinking without Thinking* (Boston: Back Bay Books, 2007). In his book he claims that Bill Clinton has "got this way of rolling his eyes with a certain expression, and what it conveys is 'I'm a bad boy.' . . . I could teach him how not to do that in two or three hours. And he [Clinton staffer] said, 'Well, we can't take the risk that he's [Bill's] known to be seeing an expert on lying,'" pp. 205–6.

19. See M. Bond, "Come-to-Work Eyes," *New Scientist* 204, no. 2731 (October 24, 2009), pp. 6–7.

20. See Linda Talley, "Louder Than Words: You've Got Plenty of Great Things to Say. Make Sure That Your Body Language Doesn't Betray Your Message," *T + D* 63, no. 11 (2009), pp. 30–32.

21. Mark Bowden, *Winning Body Language* (New York: McGraw-Hill, 2010).

22. Dale Carnegie, a noted sales training consultant, would disagree with this advice. He suggests that not offering a handshake shows a lack of assertiveness.

23. Brian Johnston, "Body of Work: Greetings around the World Can Take Many Forms: Should You Shake Hands, Bow, or Hug the Next Time You Do Business Abroad?" *Business Traveller Middle East*, May–June 2007, pp. 43–47.

24. "Britons Waving Goodbye to Humble Handshake," http://www.indianexpress.com/news/britons-waving-goodbye-to-humble-handshake/572050/, accessed February 5, 2010.

25. For an interesting read on the meaning of where you sit in a meeting, see Aili McConnon, "You Are Where You Sit," *BusinessWeek*, July 23, 2007, pp. 66–67.

26. See Rebecca Aronauer, "You're Wearing That?" *Sales & Marketing Management*, March 2007, p. 7.

27. All material presented in the five principles was written by Vicki L. West; used by permission.

28. See Terry Flynn, "Work with—and around—Voicemail," *Multichannel Merchant*, June 1, 2009, p. 26.

29. See Locker and Kienzler, *Business and Administrative Communication*, pp. 306–7.

30. Keith Wiedenkeller, "Communicating for Success: Some Simple Rules for Effective Interaction," *Film Journal International* 110, no. 10 (October 2007), p. 41.

31. Bob Popyk, "Why Snail Mail Still Works! Email Is Great, But Customers Still React to a Piece of Paper in the Mail, and Retailers Find That Direct Mail Really Pulls," *Music Trades* 157, no. 10 (2009), p. 56.

32. "There's a Message in Every Email," *Fast Company*, September 2007, p. 43.

33. Rebecca Aronauer, "Are You Taking E-mail Seriously?" *Sales & Marketing Management*, September 2007, p. 9.

34. "Open Sesame," *Marketing News*, September 1, 2007, p. 5.

35. Definition is adapted from about.com. http://weblogs.about.com/od/bloggingglossary/g/SocialNetwork.htm, accessed February 23, 2010.

36. See, for example, Natalia Maldonado, "Connect and Promote: Social Media Is Changing the Face of Online Marketing," *Career World*, February–March 2010, pp. 26–30; Meryl K. Evans, "32 Ways to Use Facebook for Business," July 21, 2009, http://webworkerdaily.com/2009/07/21/32-ways-to-use-facebook-for-business/, accessed February 12, 2010.

37. See Chris Brogan, "50 Ideas on Using Twitter for Business," August 20, 2008, http://www.chrisbrogan.com/

50-ideas-on-using-twitter-for-business/, accessed February 12, 2010; Frank Eliason, "So Should a Business Be On Twitter?" February 13, 2009, http://www.eliasonfamily. info/blog/?p=327, accessed February 12, 2010; Jennifer Lai, "5 Twitter Tips for Your Company," July 22, 2009, CNN Money.com, http://brainstormtech.blogs.fortune. cnn.com/2009/07/22/5-twitter-tips-for-your-company/, accessed February 12, 2010; Twitter 101, "A Special Guide," http://business.twitter.com/twitter101/, accessed February 12, 2010; "Twitter 101—Best Practices," http:// business.twitter.com/twitter 101/best practices, accessed February 12, 2010.

38. See www.transperfect.com for important differences to consider when translating into other languages.

39. See Locker and Kienzler, *Business and Administrative Communication*, pp. 440–41.

40. From Dean Foust, "Starting Time: The Etiquette Course," *BusinessWeek*, May 28, 2007, p. 76.

CHAPTER 5

1. William F. Kendy, "One Size Doesn't Fit All," *Selling Power*, March 2007, pp. 44–46.

2. Fernando Jaramillo, William B. Locander, Paul E. Spector, and Eric G. Harris, "Getting the Job Done: The Moderating Role of Initiative on the Relationship between Intrinsic Motivation and Adaptive Selling," *Journal of Personal Selling & Sales Management* 27, no. 1 (Winter 2007), pp. 59–74.

3. Blair Kidwell, Richard G. McFarland, and Ramon A. Avila, "Perceiving Emotion in the Buyer–Seller Interchange: The Moderated Impact on Performance," *Journal of Personal Selling & Sales Management* 27, no. 2 (Spring 2007), pp. 119–32.

4. Izabella Iizuka, "If You Want to Improve, Train Your Brain," *Sales & Marketing Management*, January/February 2008, pp. 22–23.

5. See Richard A. Lancioni and Rajan Chandran, "Managing Knowledge in Industrial Markets: New Dimensions and Challenges," *Industrial Marketing Management* 38, no. 2 (February 2009), pp. 148–51.

6. Brian C. Williams and Christopher R. Plouffe, "Assessing the Evolution of Sales Knowledge: A 20-Year Content Analysis," *Industrial Marketing Management* 36, no. 4 (May 2007), pp. 408–19.

7. See Arun Sharma, Michael Levy, and Heiner Evanschitzky, "The Variance in Sales Performance Explained by the Knowledge Structures of Salespeople," *Journal of Personal Selling & Sales Management* 27, no. 2 (Spring 2007), pp. 169–81.

8. See "SAVO: Sales Enablement on Demand," *KM World* 16, no. 8 (September 2007), p. 29.

9. Adam Rapp, Raj Agnihotri, and Lukas P. Forbes, " The Sales Force Technology–Performance Chain: The Role of Adaptive Selling and Effort," *Journal of Personal Selling & Sales Management* 28, no. 4 (Fall 2008), pp. 335–50.

10. "Knowledge Management 2.0," *CRM Magazine* 12, no. 11 (2008), pp. S11–S13.

11. Dorit Nevo, Izak Benbasat, and Yair Wand, "Who Knows What?" *The Wall Street Journal Eastern Edition*, October 26, 2009, p. R4.

12. David Merrill and Roger Reid, *Personal Styles and Effective Performance* (Radnor, PA: Chilton, 1981); "Wilson Learning to Release Revised, Versatility-Based Module This Month," *Corporate Training & Development Advisor* 11, no. 8 (April 14, 2006), pp. 1–6.

13. See http://wilsonlearning.com/capabilities/social_styles1/ for details.

14. See L. Romdhane, N. Fadhel, and B. Ayeb, "An Efficient Approach for Building Customer Profiles from Business Data," *Expert Systems with Applications* 37, no. 2 (March 2010), pp. 1573–85.

15. Adapted from Kerry J. Sulkowicz, "One Snarls, the Other Doesn't," *BusinessWeek*, June 18, 2007, p. 16.

CHAPTER 6

1. It is even important for nonprofit organizations.

2. "Best-in-Class Lead Prioritization and Lead Scoring Techniques," *Research Brief* (white paper), Aberdeen Group, March 2008, p. 1.

3. See also "Determine If Your Lead Is Worth Your Time," *Sales Leader*, August 2007, p. 1.

4. See Elisabeth A. Sullivan, "Take the (Qualified Lead)," *Marketing News*, May 15, 2008, p. 8.

5. Don Peppers and Martha Rogers, "Making Word-of-Mouth Work," *Sales & Marketing Management*, January/February 2008, p. 11.

6. See "Look for Referrals in Your Own Backyard," *Sales Leader* 12, no. 23 (January 15, 2007), p. 3.

7. Jeffrey Meshel, "Building a Network," *Sales & Marketing Management* 158, no. 1 (January–February 2006), p. 15.

8. Michael Krause, "20 Ways to Recognize Your Star Clients," www.salessensesolutions.com, accessed March 1, 2010.

9. It is essential that salespeople avoid negative referrals.

10. Phil Birt, personal correspondence; used by permission.

11. Al Slavin, "Network News: Agent Survey Shows a Growing Role for Online Sales Leads," *Best's Review* 110, no.1 (2009), pp. 84–85.

12. See, for example, William Baldwin, "Making Connections," *Forbes* 179, no. 10 (May 7, 2007), p. 22; Jack Hubbard, "'Networthing': The Fine Art of Giving It Away," *RMA Journal* 89, no. 9 (June 2007), pp. 78–79; Marcia Hales, "Lessons from a Compulsive Networker," *Franchising World* 39, no. 9 (September 2007), p. 31–32; Chuck Hester, "Hello, My Name Is…: Networking Is an Art That Can Be (Painlessly) Learned," *Public Relations Tactics* 14, no. 4 (April 2007), p. 21; Michael Dulworth, "Peer Networks," *Leadership Excellence* 24, no. 4 (April 2007), p. 15.

13. See Jessica Werb, "Instigate," *BC Business* 35, no. 5 (May 2007), p. 19.

14. Tim Sanders, "The Gift That Keeps On Giving: Networking Your Way to Personal Gold," *Success* (2008), pp. 84–85; Jessica Werb, "Don't Be Desperate," *BC Business* 35, no. 5 (May 2007), p. 19.

15. See bni.com for more information.

16. For the roster, see http://www.businessconnectionnj.com.

17. Thanks to Karl Sooder for introducing this concept to the author.

18. See the following blog postings by Mike Krause for more information: "How to Connect with a CEO: 12 Easy Social Media Steps Part II," December 30, 2009; "How to Connect with a CEO: 12 Easy Social Media Steps (and Why It's Faster Than Cold Calling)," December 22,

2009; "Social Media: 5 Reasons It Will Increase Your Sales," December 16, 2009. All are on the Web site www.salessensesolutions.com, accessed March 1, 2010.

19. See, for example, Lynne Noella, "Ten Tips to Raise Your Business Visibility through Social Networks," *Financial Executive* 25, no. 9 (2009), p. 17; Karen Schuele and Roland Madison, "Navigating the 21st Century Job Search," *Strategic Finance* 91, no.7 (2010), pp. 49–53.

20. See Mike Krause, "3 Succinct Steps to Get Sales through Social Media," www.salessensesolutions.com, January 6, 2010, accessed March 1, 2010.

21. See "5 Twitter Trips for your Company," Jennifer Lai, CNN Money.com, July 22, 2009, http://brainstormtech.blogs .fortune.cnn.com/2009/07/22/5-twitter-tips-for-your-company/, accessed February 12, 2010.

22. See www.deere.com.

23. "Lead Generator," *Sales and Marketing Management* 156 (January 2004), p. 16.

24. See Alex Salkever, "Turning Sales into Science," *Inc.* 28, no. 12 (December 2006), pp. 112.

25. Linda Armstrong, "Demo Day Camp," *Exhibitor Magazine,* October 2009, pp. 32–37.

26. See "Delivering Quality Leads, Not Just Quantity: The Interactive Value of Webinars," *CRM Magazine* 13, no. 3 (March 2009), pp. 3–6.

27. For information about SIC and NAICS codes, see the excellent listing of Web resources available at www.d.umn .edu/~jvileta/naics.html.

28. See "Sales Sagging? Try Curing Your Need for Leads with These Web sites," *Bank of America 2007 Sales Newsletter.*

29. "How to Identify Your Best Prospects (Hint: It Starts with Your Best Customers)," *Go-to-Market Strategies,* April 13, 2007; Jessica Sebor, "Too Much Pork for Just One Fork: Shiny, Clean Data and Solid Lead Qualification Will Help Satisfy All by Closing the Nutritional Sales-and-Marketing Info Loop," *CRM Magazine* 11, no. 5 (May 2007), pp. 28–31.

30. Ted Sperides, personal correspondence; used with permission.

31. Mike Krause, "4 Telemarketing Questions Every Business Owner Needs to Ask," www.salessensesolutions.com, February 11, 2010, accessed March 1, 2010.

32. "Prospecting Tips," *Sell!ng,* October 2005, p. 12.

33. See Daniel B. Honigman, "Make a Statement," *Marketing News,* May 1, 2008, p. 8.

34. See, for example, Sandra Beckwith, "Going Deeper," *Deliver Magazine,* December 2009, pp. 13–17.

35. This is found in many places on the Web, including http:// www.answerology.com/index.aspx/question/2674611_i-cdnuolt-blveiee-taht-I-cluod-aulaclty-uesdnatnrd-waht-I-was-rdanieg-The-phaonmneal-pweor-of-the-.html, accessed March 5, 2010.

36. This poem is found in many places, including http://www. quoteland.com/topic.asp?CATEGORY_ID=23, accessed March 5, 2010.

37. Betsy Cummings, "Prospecting at the Multiplex," *Sales & Marketing Management* 159, no. 2 (March 2007), p. 8.

38. Pete Millard, "Networking While Pedaling a Bicycle," *The Business Journal,* March 23, 2007, pp. A25–A29.

39. For the classic treatment of the funneling process, see Robert B. Miller, Stephen E. Heiman, and Tad Tuleja, *The New Strategic Selling* (New York: Warner Business, 2005).

40. "Pop Quiz: A Quick Test of Your Managerial Skills," *Sales & Marketing Management* 157, no. 11 (November 2005), p. 21.

41. Christopher Hosford, "Lead Management Far from Easy Task: Identify Prospects and Know What to Do with Them," *B to B* 92, no. 10 (August 13, 2007), p. 15.

42. See, for example, V. Kumar, J. Andrew Peterson, and Robert P. Leone, "How Valuable Is Word of Mouth?" *Harvard Business Review* 85, no. 10 (October 2007), pp. 139–46; Bob Donath, "Tap Full Potential of Sales Leads for Growth," *Marketing News* 41, no. 8 (May 1, 2007), pp. 7–8; Christopher Hosford, "Watkins Soaks Up Better Lead Tracking," *B to B* 92, no. 10 (August 13, 2007), p. 15; Christopher Hosford, "Lead Management Far from Easy Task," *B to B* 92, no. 10 (August 13, 2007), p. 15.

43. See Mike McCue, "Lessons from the Master," *Sales & Marketing Management,* March/April 2008, p. 23.

44. See http://www.salesleadmgmtassn.com.

45. For another example, see "Unlock your Prospect Database with Lead Management," *CRM Magazine* 13, no. 3 (March 2009), p. 10.

46. Betsy Cummings, "Is It a Hot or Cold Pursuit?" *Sales & Marketing Management* 159, no. 6 (July–August 2007), p. 10.

47. See Lynn Vincent, "Overcoming Your Fear of Prospecting," *Advisor Today* 102, no. 2 (February 2007), pp. 28–32.

48. See also Maureen Hrehocik, "Why Prospecting Gets No Respect," *Sales & Marketing Management* 159, no. 8 (October 2007), p. 7.

49. Alison Stein Wellner, "Are You Sales Phobic? Alas, the Cure Is to Sell More Often," *Inc.* 29, no. 3 (March 2007), pp. 52–56.

CHAPTER 7

1. See Alex Stein and Michael Smith, "CRM Systems and Organizational Learning: An Exploration of the Relationship between CRM Effectiveness and the Customer Information Orientation of the Firm in Industrial Markets," *Industrial Marketing Management* 38, no. 2 (2009), pp. 198–206.

2. Jeremy Nedelka, "Putting an End to Cold Leads," *1to1 Magazine,* November/December 2008, pp. 41–42.

3. Dawn Hedges, personal correspondence; names changed to protect confidentiality.

4. Neil Rackham, *Major Account Sales Strategy* (New York: McGraw-Hill, 1989), p. 39.

5. For their latest book on the topic, see Robert B. Miller, Stephen E. Heiman, Diane Sanchez, and Tad Tuleja, *The New Conceptual Selling: The Most Effective and Proven Method for Face-to-Face Sales Planning* (New York: Warner Business, 2005).

6. See Anne Stuart, "Create Order from Chaos," *delivermagazine,* July 2009, pp. 22–25.

7. Jim Hersma, personal correspondence; used with permission.

8. See Tara Lorigan, "Your Value Proposition," *NZ Business* 21, no. 3 (April 2007), p. 9; Nirmalya Kumar, James C. Anderson, and James A. Narus, *Value Merchants: Demonstrating and Documenting Superior Value in Business Markets* (Harvard Business School Press Books, 2007);

Heather Clancy, "Time for Next-Gen Demand Generation," *CRN* 1235 (April 9, 2007), p. 14.

9. Special thanks to Karl Sooder for sharing this information.

10. Neil Rackham, *Major Account Sales Strategy* (New York: McGraw-Hill, 1989).

11. Rackham, *Major Account Sales Strategy,* p. 30.

12. Stanley Reed, Emily Thornton, and Eamon Javers, "A Queue in the Sand," *BusinessWeek,* December 17, 2007, pp. 24–26.

13. For some stories about the best time to call on prospects, see Susan Greco, "The Need for Speed: How to Rev Up Your Sales Cycle," *Inc.,* April 2007, pp. 38–40.

14. See Judy A. Wagner and Noreen M. Klein, "Who Wants to Go First? Order Effects within a Series of Competitive Sales Presentations," *Journal of Personal Selling & Sales Management* 27, no. 3 (Summer 2007), pp. 259–76.

15. For hints on how to do this, see Leah Hoffman, "Beyond YouTube: New Uses for Video, Online and Off," *Inc.* 29, no. 10 (October 2007), pp. 53–54.

16. See Erin Biba, "Webcasting Is on the Upswing: Webinar Industry Pegged at $83.3 Million In '07 and Ready to Grow More Than 28.2%," *BtoB* 93, no. 14 (2008), p. 14; Jan Ozer, "Webcasting for the Masses: Between Live Streaming Service Providers and Rich Media Communications Solutions, There Have Never Been More Options for Webcasting Live Events," *Streaming Media,* 2009, pp. 24–32. And salespeople should ensure quality sound, as this source suggests: Carmine Gallo, "Record Voice for Your Next Presentation," *BusinessWeek Online,* January 7, 2010.

CHAPTER 8

1. Building partnerships and strong relationships is a process that starts when a lead is identified and continues throughout all postsale service and future calls.

2. Based on personal correspondence with Karl Sooder; used with permission.

3. Of course many aspects of first impressions, such as race and gender, are outside the control of the salesperson.

4. Matt Leaf, personal correspondence; used with permission.

5. William T. Brooks, *Perfect Phrases for the Sales Call* (McGraw-Hill, 2006), p. 64.

6. See Christine Comaford-Lynch, "Education-Based Marketing Sells," *BusinessWeek,* October 9, 2007, p. 11; Myles Murchison and Sue Dritmanis, "The Death of Spin, Sleaze, and the Cold Call: Five Sales Strategies for the New Millennium," *BC Business* 35, no. 7 (July 2007), pp. 163–74.

7. For more examples and tips on how to engage in small talk, see "How to Make Small Talk," http://www.ehow.com/how_10812_make-small-talk.html, accessed March 13, 2010.

8. See Ken Dooley, "Conversation Topics That Kill Sales," March 9, 2010, http://www.businessbrief.com/conversations-topics-that-kill-sales-pass-this-list-on-to-your-newbies/, accessed March 13, 2010.

9. R. Peterson and Limbu Y. "The Convergence of Mirroring and Empathy: Communications Training in Business-to-Business Personal Selling Persuasion Efforts." *Journal of Business-to-Business Marketing* 16, no. 3 (July 2009), pp.193–219.

10. This classic example can be found, along with other humorous ones, in Ken Delmar, *Winning Moves* (New York: Warner, 1984), p. 4.

11. Dan Seidman, "Hilarious Selling Mistakes," http://www.sellingpower.com/content/video, accessed March 16, 2010.

12. Neil Rackham, *SPIN Selling* (New York: McGraw-Hill, 1988).

13. Angie Main; used with permission.

14. Rackham, *SPIN Selling.*

15. Anita Sirianni, "Talking Trash on 'Feature Dumping,'" *Proofs,* September 2004, p. 70.

16. Michael Port. "Take Out The Garbage." *Entrepreneur.* Aug. 2009. pp. 26.

17. Kevin Zimmerman, "What's in It for Me?" *1to1 Magazine,* October 2007, pp. 32–36.

18. Neil Rackham, "Sales Strategies to Capture Market Share in a Down Economy: Selling Is Tough Business in the Current Economic Climate," *Today's Manager,* 2009, pp. 38–40.

19. Ray Hanson, personal correspondence; used by permission.

20. This can be found at many places on the Web, including http://www.puzzle.dse.nl/tests/index_us.html, accessed March 13, 2010.

21. Credibility can obviously be strengthened in other ways. See, for example, Joseph J. Belonax Jr., Stephen J. Newell, and Richard E. Plank, "The Role of Purchase Importance on Buyer Perceptions of the Trust and Expertise Components of Supplier and Salesperson Credibility in Business-to-Business Relationships," *Journal of Personal Selling & Sales Management* 27, no. 3 (Summer 2007), p. 247–58.

22. Jim Hersma, personal correspondence; used with permission.

23. See, for example, "Increasing Sales with a Credibility Statement," April 9, 2009, http://silverbulletselling.com/increasing-sales-with-a-credibility-statement, accessed March 16, 2010.

24. Todd Graf, personal correspondence; used with permission.

25. Tracey Brill, personal correspondence; used with permission.

CHAPTER 9

1. See Marie Swift, "Great Communicators," *Financial Planning* 37, no. 6 (June 2007), pp. 119–24.

2. A. Herasimchuk, "PowerPoint Is Not an Excuse," *DESK-TOP* 64, no. 1 (February 2010), pp. 74–77.

3. Izabella Iizuka, "Not Your Father's Presentation," *Sales & Marketing Management* (March/April 2008), pp. 33–35.

4. Iizuka, "Not Your Father's Presentation," p. 33.

5. Personal correspondence.

6. See, for example, www.kadient.com.

7. "Perfect Proposals," *Sales & Marketing Management* 159, no. 1 (January 2007), p. 9.

8. For more information about creating value, see Bob Donath, "Value Is Not Always Apparent—So Spell It Out," *Marketing News* 41, no. 2 (February 1, 2007), pp. 8–10; "Cost, Performance, and Value," *Marketing Management* 16, no. 3 (May–June 2007), p. 7.

9. Karl Sooder, "The Value Presentation," used with permission; James C. Anderson, Nirmalya Kumar, and James

A. Narus, "Become a Value Merchant," *Sales & Marketing Management,* May/June 2008, pp. 21–23; Nicholas A. C. Read and Stephen Bistritz, *Selling to the C-Suite* (McGraw-Hill, 2010).

10. The first example is adapted from an example from Read and Bistritz, *Selling to the C-Suite,* p. 135. The second example is provided by Karl Sooder.

11. See Jill Konrath, "How to Write a Value Proposition," http://www.sideroad.com/Sales/value_proposition.html, accessed March 3, 2010.

CHAPTER 10

1. Lenann Gardner, "Selling Isn't What You Might Think It Is," *American Salesman* 52, no. 2 (February 2007), p. 4.

2. See also "The 8 Objections," http://www.justsell.com/the-8-objections, accessed March 24, 2010.

3. See also "The Key to Eliminating Objections and Increasing Sales," http://www.powerhomebiz.com/vol147/sales.htm, accessed March 10, 2010.

4. Salespeople can forestall known concerns but shouldn't bring up issues that aren't even a problem with a particular prospect. Thus the need for good precall information gathering becomes obvious.

5. Prov. 18:13.

6. Richard Hodge and Lou Schachter, *The Mind of the Customer* (McGraw-Hill, 2006), p. 61.

7. Personal correspondence; name of firm and industry withheld by request.

8. Dr. Reed K. Holden, "End the Discounting Habit," *Sales & Marketing Management,* March/April 2008, p. 48.

9. Gwen Moran, "Adapt to Survive," *Deliver Magazine,* July 2009, pp. 16–18.

10. James C. Anderson, Normalya Kumar, and James A. Narus (2008), "Become a Value Merchant," *Sales & Marketing Management,* May/June 2008, p. 21.

11. Tracey Brill, personal correspondence; used with permission.

12. Connie Podesta, "Dealing with Difficult People," *Success,* April/May 2008, pp. 104–5.

13. See also "Dealing with Angry Customers," http://www.callcentrehelper.com/dealing-angry-customer.htm, accessed March 13, 2010; Carmine Gallo, "Dealing with Angry Customers: How You Handle Mistakes and Improve Service Could Mean the Difference between Losing Customers and Keeping Their Business," *BusinessWeek Online,* June 20, 2007, http://www.businessweek.com/smallbiz/content/jun2007/sb20070620_974061.htm, accessed March 19, 2010.

CHAPTER 11

1. Neil Rackham, *SPIN Selling* (New York: McGraw-Hill, 1988), pp. 19–51.

2. Mark Skaer, "Having Sales Awareness and Effectiveness," *Air Conditioning, Heating & Refrigeration News* 227, no. 1 (2006), pp. 50–52.

3. Ram Ramamurthy, personal correspondence, February 20, 2008; used with permission.

4. Joanna R. Turpin, "Financing Those Dream Systems," *Air Conditioning, Heating, & Refrigeration News* 237 (June 22, 2009), pp. 1–3.

5. Bill Lurz, "Qualifying Buyers a Big Problem," *Giants* 4 (September 2008), p. 14.

6. Bruce Culbert, personal correspondence, February 20, 2008; used with permission.

7. Marvin A. Jolson, "Selling Assertively," *Business Horizons,* September–October 1984, pp. 71–77.

8. Albert Chan and David Choo, "Not Saying No Doesn't Mean Yes," *The Conference Board Review* 43, no. 3 (2006), pp. 13–15.

9. John Branton, "Closing Sales the Right Way," *National Underwriter, Life & Health* 113, no. 5 (March 2, 2009), p. 31.

10. Eleanor Brownell, "How to Make Yourself Memorable," *American Salesman* 55, no. 3 (March 2010), pp. 24–28.

11. Paolo Guenzi and Laurent Georges, "Interpersonal Trust in Commercial Relationships: Antecedents and Consequences of Customer Trust in the Salesperson," *European Journal of Marketing* 44, no. 1–2 (2010), pp. 114–29.

12. Stefanos Mousas, Stephan Henneberg, and Peter Naudé, "Trust and Reliance in Business Relationships," *European Journal of Marketing* 41, no. 9–10 (2007), pp. 1016–32; Nelson Oly Ndubisi and Christian N. Madu, "The Association of Gender to Firm–Customer Relationship," *The International Journal of Quality & Reliability Management* 26, no. 3 (2009), pp. 283–301.

13. Betsy Cummings, "Done Deal: How One Sales Pro Closed a Big Customer," *Sales and Marketing Management* 158, no. 9 (2006), p. 13.

14. Fred Brown, personal correspondence, February 21, 2008; used with permission.

15. Jasmin Bergeron and Michel Laroche, "The Effects of Perceived Salesperson Listening Effectiveness in the Financial Industry," *Journal of Financial Services Marketing* 14, no. 1 (June 2009), pp. 6–25.

16. Raj Agnihotri, Adam Rapp, and Kevin Trainor, "Understanding the Role of Information Communication in the Buyer–Seller Exchange Process: Antecedents and Outcomes," *Journal of Business & Industrial Marketing* 24, no. 7 (2009), pp. 474–99.

17. Dave Stein, "Smart Sales: Let's Role the Videotape," *Sales and Marketing Management* 160, no. 3 (May–June 2008), p. 8.

18. Dean Yeck, personal correspondence; used with permission.

19. Illiki Rai, "Embracing Rejection: Six Strategies to Successful Sales," *Rising Women,* www.risingwomen.com, accessed March 7, 2005.

20. Interview, October 19, 2008.

CHAPTER 12

1. See Johna Till Johnson, "Telecom Negotiations: The Sales Side of the Story," *Network World,* January 11, 2007; Tom Reilly, "Negotiate for the Customer," *Industrial Distribution* 96, no. 9 (September 2007), p. 19; "Negotiating Success," *Sales & Marketing Management* 159, no. 6 (July–August 2007), p. 46.

2. Ken Dooley, "6 Tips for Negotiating in a Tough Economy," *Sales & Marketing Business Brief,* March 9, 2010, http://www.businessbrief.com/6-tips-for-negotiating-in-a-tough-economy, accessed March 25, 2010; "Are You Really Ready to Negotiate?" *Negotiation,* September 2007, pp. 1–4.

3. Jim Mullen, "Negotiation Checklist Revisited," *Inside Supply Management,* January 2007, pp. 10–11.

4. Norman A. Johnson and Randolph B. Cooper, "Power and Concession in Computer-Mediated Negotiations: An Examination of First Offers," *MIS Quarterly* 33, no. 1 (2009), pp. 147–70.

5. Christopher R. Plouffe and Donald W. Barclay, "Salesperson Navigation: The Intraorganizational Dimension of the Sales Role," *Industrial Marketing Management* 36, no. 4 (May 2007), pp. 528–39.

6. The information in this section was developed from Kenneth Thomas, "Conflict and Conflict Management," in *The Handbook of Industrial and Organizational Psychology,* ed. Marvin Dunnette (Skokie, IL: Rand McNally, 1976).

7. Roy Lewicki, Bruce Barry, and David Saunders, *Essentials of Negotiation* (McGraw-Hill, 2010).

8. "Fractured English," *Have a Good Day,* January 1997, pp. 1–2.

9. See "Good Guy/Bad Guy," http://changingminds.org/disciplines/negotiation/tactics/good-bad_guy.htm, accessed March 25, 2010.

10. John Patrick Dolan, "How to Overcome the Top Ten Negotiating Tactics," http://www.myarticlearchive.com/articles/5/025.htm, accessed March 25, 2010.

11. See Roger Fisher and William Ury, *Getting to Yes: Negotiating Agreement without Giving In,* 2nd ed. (Boston: Houghton Mifflin, 1991).

12. See Roger Dawson, "Power Negotiating: Skills for Today's Tough Times," *Success,* 2009, pp. 90–91; Jim Thomas, "Setting the Envelope: In the Second of a Series of Articles, Negotiating Pundit Jim Thomas Explains Rule Three of the Seven Rules of Negotiating," *American Executive* 6, no. 8 (2008), pp. 32–35.

13. Neil Rackham, "Winning the Price War," *Sales and Marketing Management,* November 2001, p. 26.

14. Kirk Kazanjian, *Exceeding Customer Expectations* (New York: Currency Doubleday, 2006), p. 144.

CHAPTER 13

1. Alfred Pelham, "Do Consulting-Oriented Sales Management Programs Impact Salesforce Performance and Profit?" *Journal of Business & Industrial Marketing* 21, no. 3 (2006), pp. 175–86; Zhen Zhu and Cheryl Nakata, "Reexamining the Link between Customer Orientation and Business Performance: The Role of Information Systems," *Journal of Marketing Theory & Practice* 15, no. 3 (2007), pp. 187–203; Mojtaba P. Salami, "Impact of Customer Relationship Management (CRM) in the Iran Banking Sector," *International Journal of Organizational Innovation* 2, no. 1 (Summer 2009), pp. 225–53; Alfred Pelham, "The Impact of Industry and Training Influences on Salesforce Consulting Time and Consulting Effectiveness," *Journal of Business & Industrial Marketing* 24, no. 8 (2009), pp. 575–89.

2. "Can Mobile Firms Ring the Changes and Slash Churn?" *Precision Marketing,* January 11, 2008, p. 12.

3. Robert W. Palmatier, Lisa K. Scheer, Mark B. Houston, Kenneth R. Evans, and Srinath Gopalakrishna, "Use of Relationship Marketing Programs in Building Customer–Salesperson and Customer–Firm Relationships: Differential Influences on Financial Outcomes," *International Journal of Research in Marketing* 24, no. 3 (2007), pp. 210–24.

4. Werner J. Reinartz and V. Kumar, "The Impact of Customer Relationship Characteristics on Profitable Lifetime Duration," *Journal of Marketing* 67, no. 1 (2003), pp. 77–99; Rajkumar Venkatesean and V. Kumar, "A Customer Lifetime Value Framework for Customer Selection and Resource Allocation Strategy," *Journal of Marketing* 68, no. 4 (2004), pp. 106–25; Sofie Hansen, "The Global Diffusion of Relationship Marketing," *European Journal of Marketing* 42, no. 11–12 (2008), pp. 1156–70.

5. Rebekah Russell-Bennett, Janet McColl-Kennedy, and Leonard V. Coote, "Involvement, Satisfaction, and Brand Loyalty in a Small Business Services Setting," *Journal of Business Research* 60, no. 12 (2007), pp. 1253–64.

6. Robert Dwyer, Paul Schurr, and Sejo Oh, "Developing Buyer–Seller Relationships," *Journal of Marketing,* April 1987, pp. 11–27; Sandy Jap and Barton Weitz, "A Taxonomy of Long-Term Relationships" (working paper, College of Business Administration, University of Florida, 1996); Lloyd M. Rinehart, James A. Eckert, Thomas J. Page Jr., and Thomas Atkin, "An Assessment of Supplier–Customer Relationships," *Journal of Business Logistics* 25, no. 1 (2004), pp. 25–63; Aurelia Lefaix-Durand, Robert Kozak, Robert Beauregard, and Diane Poulin, "Extending Relationship Value: Observations from a Case Study of the Canadian Structural Wood Products Industry," *The Journal of Business & Industrial Marketing* 24, no. 5/6 (2009), pp. 389–401.

7. Sunmee Choi and Anne S. Mattila, "Perceived Controllability and Service Expectations: Influences on Customer Reactions Following Service Failure," *Journal of Business Research* 61, no. 1 (2008), pp. 24–41.

8. Vishal Kashyap, Aurea H. P. Ribeiro, Anthony Asare, and Thomas G. Brashear, "Developing Sales Force Relationalism: The Role of Distributive and Procedural Justice," *Journal of Personal Selling & Sales Management* 27, no. 3 (2007), pp. 235–51.

9. Robert W. Armstrong and Siew Min Yee, "Do Chinese Trust Chinese? A Study of Chinese Buyers and Sellers in Malaysia," *Journal of International Marketing* 9, no. 3 (2001), pp. 63–86; Y. H. Wong, Humphry Hung, and Wing-ki Chow, "Mediating Effects of Relationship Quality on Customer Relationships: An Empirical Study in Hong Kong," *Marketing Intelligence & Planning* 25, no. 6 (2007), pp. 581–99.

10. Felix T. Mavondo and Elaine M. Rodrigo, "The Effect of Relationship Dimensions on Interpersonal and Interorganizational Commitment in Organizations Conducting Business between Australia and China," *Journal of Business Research* 52 (2001), pp. 111–21; Wen-Hung Wang, Chiung-Ju Liang, and Yung-De Wu, "Relationship Bonding Tactics, Relationship Quality, and Customer Behavioral Loyalty–Behavioral Sequence in Taiwan's Information Services Industry," *Journal of Services Research* 6, no. 1 (2006), pp. 31–57.

11. Michael D. Johnson and Fred Selnes, "Customer Portfolio Management: Toward a Dynamic Theory of Relationships," *Journal of Marketing* 68, no. 2 (2004), pp. 1–17; Robert C. Dudley and Das Narayandas, "A Portfolio Approach to Sales," *Harvard Business Review* 84 (July–August 2006),

pp. 16–24; Leff Bonney and Brian C. Williams, "From Products to Solutions: The Role of Salesperson Opportunity Recognition," *European Journal of Marketing* 43, no. 7/8 (2009), pp. 1032–45.

12. Dennis Campbell and Frances Frei, "The Persistence of Customer Profitability: Empirical Evidence and Implications from a Financial Services Firm," *Journal of Service Research* 7, no. 2 (2004), pp. 107–124.

13. Glen L. Urban and John R. Hauser, "Listening In to Find and Explore New Combinations of Customer Needs," *Journal of Marketing* 68, no. 2 (2004), pp. 72–87; Xuan Lorna Wang and David Bowie, "Revenue Management: The Impact on Business-to-Business Relationships," *Journal of Services Marketing* 23, no. 1 (2009), pp. 31–44.

14. Dwyer, Schurr, and Oh, "Developing Buyer–Seller Relationships."

15. Reinartz and Kumar, "The Impact of Customer Relationship Characteristics."

16. Brian N. Rutherford, James S. Boles, Hiram C. Barksdale Jr., and Julie T. Johnson, "Single Source Supply versus Multiple Source Supply: A Study into the Relationship between Satisfaction and Propensity to Stay within a Service Setting," *Journal of Personal Selling & Sales Management* 26, no. 4 (2006), pp. 371–84; Paolo Guenzi and Laurent Georges, "Interpersonal Trust in Commercial Relationships: Antecedents and Consequences of Customer Trust in the Salesperson," *European Journal of Marketing* 44, no. 1–2 (2010), pp. 114–28.

17. Kim Sydow Campbell, Lenita Davis, and Lauren Skinner, "Rapport Management during the Exploration Phase of the Salesperson–Customer Relationship," *Journal of Personal Selling & Sales Management* 26, no. 4 (2006), pp. 359–70.

18. Constanza Bianchi and Abu Saleh, "On Importer Trust and Commitment: A Comparative Study of Two Developing Countries," *International Marketing Review* 27, no. 1 (2010), pp. 55–70.

19. Guenzi and Georges, "Interpersonal Trust in Commercial Relationships."

20. Joseph Matton, Vistakon; used with permission.

21. Mark E. Cross, Thomas G. Brashear, Edward E. Rigdon, and Danny N. Bellenger, "Customer Orientation and Salesperson Performance," *European Journal of Marketing* 33, 41, no. 7–8 (2007), pp. 821–39.

22. Gerrard Macintosh, "Customer Orientation, Relationship Quality, and Relational Benefits to the Firm," *Journal of Services Marketing* 21, no. 3 (2007), pp. 150–68; Jon C. Carr and Tara B. Lopez, "Examining Market Orientation as Both Culture and Conduct: Modeling the Relationship between Market Orientation and Employee Responses," *Journal of Marketing Theory & Practice* 15, no. 2 (2007), pp. 113–27.

23. Erin Strouth, "To Tell the Truth," *Sales & Marketing Management* 154, no. 7 (2002), pp. 40–48.

24. John M. Hawes, Kenneth Mast, and John E. Swan, "Trust Earning Perceptions of Sellers and Buyers," *Journal of Personal Selling & Sales Management* (Spring 1989), pp. 1–8; J. Tsalikis and Walfried Lassar, "Measuring Consumer Perceptions of Business Ethical Behavior in Two Muslim Countries," *Journal of Business Ethics* 89 (2009), pp. 91–98.

25. Jasmin Bergeron and Michel Laroche, "The Effects of Perceived Salesperson Listening Effectiveness in the Financial Industry," *Journal of Financial Services Marketing* 14, no. 8 (June 2009), pp. 6–25.

26. Lisa Cross, "Establishing Customer Loyalty," *Graphic Arts Monthly* 76, no. 9 (2004), pp. 39–42; Kimberly Scher, "Breaking Up Is Hard to Do: Knowing When a Customer Relationship Is Worth Keeping," *Catalyst,* September–October 2008, pp. 26–29.

27. Gilbert N. Nyaga, Judith M. Whipple, and Daniel F. Lynch, "Examining Supply Chain Relationships: Do Buyer and Supplier Perspectives on Collaborative Relationships Differ?" *Journal of Operations Management* 28, no. 2 (March 2010), pp. 101–15.

28. Constanza Bianchi and Abu Saleh, "On Importer Trust and Commitment: A Comparative Study of Two Developing Countries," *International Marketing Review* 27, no. 1 (2010), pp. 55–70.

29. Betsy Cummings, "Dodging Dishonesty," *Sales & Marketing Management* 157, no. 2 (2005), p. 10.

30. F. Juliet Poujol and John F. Tanner Jr., "The Impact of Contests on Salespeople's Customer Orientation: An Application of Tournament Theory," *Journal of Personal Selling & Sales Management* 30 no. 1 (Winter 2010), pp. 33–46.

CHAPTER 14

1. Dough Henschen, "SaaS-Based BI Tracks Rossignol Ski and Snowboard Sales," *Intelligent Enterprise Online,* January 5, 2010, http://intelligent-enterprise.informationweek.com/showArticle.jhtml;jsessionid=14FHIGTREQRNLQE1GHRSKH4ATMY32JVN?articleID=222200361, accessed March 24, 2010.

2. Chuck Gallagher and Rob Truss, personal correspondence; used with permission.

3. Samuel Greengard, "Keeping the Customer Satisfied," *CIO Insight* 109 (November 2009), pp. 32–35.

4. Goutam Chakraborty, Prashant Srivastava, and Fred Marshall, "Are Drivers of Customer Satisfaction Different for Buyers/Users from Different Functional Areas?" *Journal of Business & Industrial Marketing* 22, no. 1 (2007), pp. 20–32.

5. Celso Augusto de Matos, Carlos A.V. Rossi, Ricardo T. Veiga, and Valter A. Vieira, "Consumer Reaction to Service Failure and Recovery: The Moderating Role of Attitude toward Complaining," *Journal of Services Marketing* 23, no. 7 (2009), pp. 462–75; Constantine Lymperopoulos and Ioannis E. Chaniotakis, "Price Satisfaction and Personnel Efficiency as Antecedents of Overall Satisfaction from Consumer Credit Products and Positive Word of Mouth," *Journal of Financial Services* 13, no. 1 (2008), pp. 63–71.

6. Rob Gerlsbeck, "Bad Reputation Can't Be Beat," *Marketing* 111, no. 14 (2006), p. 6.

7. Rajiv D Banker and Raj Mashruwala, "Simultaneity in the Relationship between Sales Performance and Customer Satisfaction," *Journal of Consumer Satisfaction, Dissatisfaction and Complaining Behavior* 22 (2009), pp. 88–104.

8. Chia-Chi Chang, "When Service Fails: The Role of the Salesperson and the Customer," *Psychology & Marketing* 23, no. 3 (2006), pp. 203–14.

9. "Ikea: Not Sweden's Only Quality Company," *Strategic Direction* 22, no. 5 (2006), pp. 5–7.

10. Craig Murchison, personal correspondence; used with permission.

11. Richard Langlotz, personal correspondence, March 24, 2010.
12. Christopher Hosford, "Nurturing Possibilities in a Tough Economy," *B to B* 94, no. 7, p. 4.
13. Robert Dwyer and John F. Tanner Jr., *Business Marketing: Connecting Strategy, Relationships, and Learning,* 4th ed. (Burr Ridge, IL: McGraw-Hill/Irwin, 2009).
14. Mike Power, "Accessibility Is Top Priority," *Industrial Distribution* 94, no. 10 (2005), p. 56.
15. Dwyer and Tanner, *Business Marketing.*
16. Jeff Meisner, personal correspondence; used with permission.
17. John W. Barnes, Donald W. Jackson Jr., Michael D. Hutt, and Ajith Kumar, "The Role of Culture Strength in Shaping Sales Force Outcomes," *Journal of Personal Selling & Sales Management* 26, no. 3 (2006), pp. 255–70.
18. John F. Tanner Jr., Jorge Wise, Christophe Fournier, and Sandrine Hollet, "Executives' Perspectives of the Changing Role of the Sales Profession: Views from France, the United States, and Mexico," *Journal of Business and Industrial Marketing* 23, no. 3 (2008), pp. 193–202.
19. Paul Teague, "Congratulations to Tyco International," *Purchasing* 138, no. 9 (September 17, 2009), p. 11.
20. Jim Baston, "Leveraging Techs' Customer Relationships," *Air Conditioning, Heating, and Refrigeration News* 230, no. 10 (2007), pp. 36–37.
21. Darryl Lehnus, personal correspondence; used with permission.
22. Jessica Sebor, "CRM Gets Serious," *Customer Relationship Management,* February 2008, pp. 23–26.

CHAPTER 15

1. Leigh Ann Pearson, "Teradata Research Project," May 15, 2009.
2. Jussi Hätönen and Mika Ruokonen, "Revising Marketing Strategies for Supplier Selection Criteria: Small Firm Approach from the Information and Communications Industry," *Journal of Business & Industrial Marketing* 25, no. 2 (2010), pp. 159–73; Tim Lukes and Jennifer Stanley, "Bringing Science to Sales," *Marketing Management* 13 (October 2004), pp. 36–42; Catherine Sweet, Tim Sweet, Beth Rogers, Valerie Heritage, and Mike Turner, "Developing a Benchmark for Companywide Sales Capability," *Industrial and Commercial Training* 39, no. 1 (2007), pp. 18–28.
3. Oyvind Helgesen, "Customer Segments Based on Customer Account Profitability," *Journal of Targeting, Measurement, and Analysis for Marketing* 14, no. 3 (2006), pp. 225–37.
4. Lawrence Ang and Ben Taylor, "Managing Customer Profitability Using Portfolio Matrices," *Journal of Database Marketing & Customer Strategy Management* 12, no. 4 (2005), pp. 298–304.
5. Adel El-Ansary and Waleed A. El-Ansary, *Winning Customers, Building Accounts: Some Do It Better Than Others* (Jacksonville, FL: Paper and Plastics Education and Research Foundation, 1994).
6. Wagner Kamakura, "Cross-Selling: Offering the Right Product to the Right Customer at the Right Time," *Journal of Relationship Marketing* 6, no. 3–4 (January 2008), pp. 41–54.
7. Susan Flaviano, personal correspondence; used with permission.

8. "Survey Says Employees Feel Obligated 24/7," *Manufacturing Business Technology* 24, no. 9 (2006), p. 9.
9. Flaviano, personal correspondence.
10. Lee Brubaker, "Make Sure Pay Time Pays," *American Salesman* 51, no. 8 (2006), pp. 27–29.
11. E-mail receipt statistics are from Datran Media's "Marketing & Media Survey" (2008), and the increase in e-mail estimate is based on David Daniels (December 2007), Jupiter Research, with both sources available at www.emailstatcenter.com/Usage.html, accessed March 1, 2008.
12. John Plott, personal correspondence, March 1, 2008; used with permission.
13. Flaviano, personal correspondence.
14. Jenifer Rutter, personal correspondence, March 5, 2008; used with permission.
15. Adam Boretz, "Freedom in the Field," *Speech Technology* 14, no. 3 (May 2009), pp. 15–19.
16. Jim Olsztynski, "Making Money by Mining Technology," *Supply House Times* 52, no. 4 (June 2009), pp. 34–36.

CHAPTER 16

1. Neville May, "Communication Breakdown," *Sales & Marketing Management* 160, no. 4 (July–August 2009), pp. 12–13.
2. Ashwin W. Joshi, "Salesperson Influence on Product Development: Insights from a Study of Small Manufacturing Organizations," *Journal of Marketing* 74, no. 1 (January 2010), pp. 94–108.
3. Frank Caprio, "There Is Power in a Self-Assured Salesperson," *Industrial Distribution* 98, no. 6 (November 2009), p. 55.
4. Matthew Carr, "Stepping in Time: Unifying Cross-functional Relationships to Mitigate Risk and Improve Cash Flow," *Business Credit* 111, no. 5 (May 2009), pp. 56–58.
5. Wim G. Biemans and Maja Makovec Brencic, "Designing the Marketing–Sales Interface in B2B Firms," *European Journal of Marketing* 41, no. 3–4 (2007), pp. 257–71.
6. Robert Dwyer and John F. Tanner Jr., *Business Marketing: Connecting Strategy, Relationships, and Learning,* 4th ed. (Burr Ridge, IL: McGraw-Hill/Irwin, 2009).
7. "Selling Events Internally and to Customers," *Folio* 33 (November 2004), pp. 35–37.
8. Avish Malshe, "How Is Marketers' Credibility Construed within the Sales–Marketing Interface?" *Journal of Business Research* 63 (January 2010), pp. 13–19; Michael Beverland, Marion Steel, and G. Peter Dapiran, "Cultural Frames That Drive Sales and Marketing Apart: An Exploratory Study," *The Journal of Business & Industrial Marketing* 21, no. 6 (2006), pp. 386–402.
9. Philip L. Dawes and Graham R. Massey, "A Study of Relationship Effectiveness between Marketing and Sales Managers in Business Markets," *Journal of Business and Industrial Marketing* 21, no. 6 (2006), pp. 346–67; Paolo Guenzi and Gabriele Troilo, "The Joint Contribution of Marketing and Sales to the Creation of Superior Customer Value," *Journal of Business Research* 60, no. 2 (2007), pp. 98–113.
10. Christophe Fournier, John F. Tanner Jr., Lawrence B. Chonko, and Chris Manolis, "The Moderating Role of Ethical Climate on Salesperson Propensity to Leave," *Journal of Personal Selling & Sales Management* 30,

no. 1 (2010), pp. 7–22; John W. Barnes, Donald W. Jackson Jr., Michael D. Hutt, and Aith Kumar, "The Role of Culture Strength in Shaping Sales Force Outcomes," *Journal of Personal Selling & Sales Management* 26, no. 3 (2006), pp. 255–70; Craig A. Martin and Alan J. Bush, "Psychological Climate, Empowerment, Leadership Style, and Customer-Oriented Selling: An Analysis of the Sales Manager–Salesperson Dyad," *Journal of the Academy of Marketing Science* 34, no. 3 (2006), pp. 419–38.

11. Richard Herrin, "The Politics of Forecasting," *The Journal of Business Forecasting* 29, no. 1, pp. 18–19.

12. Johanna Smaros and Markus Hellstrom, "Using the Assortment Forecasting Method to Enable Sales Force Involvement in Forecasting: A Case Study," *International Journal of Physical Distribution & Logistics Management* 34 (2004), pp. 140–57.

13. Doug Henschen, "A Matter of Survival," *InformationWeek* 1222, pp. 29–35.

14. F. Juliet Poujol and John F. Tanner Jr., "The Impact of Sales Contests on Salespeople's Customer Orientation: An Application of Tournament Theory," *The Journal of Personal Selling & Sales Management* 30 (Winter 2010), pp. 33–46.

15. Michael L. Mallin, Edward O'Donnell, and Michael Y. Hu, "The Role of Uncertainty and Sales Control in the Development of Sales Manager Trust," *The Journal of Business & Industrial Marketing* 25, no. 1 (2010), pp. 30–44; Thomas G. Brashear, Chris Manolis, and Charles M. Brooks, "The Effects of Control, Trust, and Justice on Salesperson Turnover," *Journal of Business Research* 58 (March 2005), pp. 241–57.

16. Dave Stein, "When Sales 101 Isn't Enough," *Sales and Marketing Management* 160, no. 6, p. 7.

17. Jay P. Mulki, Jorge Fernando Jaramillo, and William B Locander, "Critical Role of Leadership on Ethical Climate and Salesperson Behaviors," *Journal of Business Ethics* 86, no. 2 (May 2009), pp. 126–51; Nigel F. Percy, David W. Cravens, Nikala Lane, and Douglas W. Vorhies, "Driving Organizational Citizenship Behaviors and Salesperson In-Role Behavior Performance: The Role of Management Control and Perceived Organizational Support," *Journal of the Academy of Marketing Science* 34, no. 2 (2006), pp. 244–52.

18. Mulki, Jaramillo and Locander, "Critical Role of Leadership on Ethical Climate and Salesperson Behaviors,"; William H. Murphy, "In Pursuit of Short-Term Goals: Anticipating the Unintended Consequences of Using Special Incentives to Motivation the Sales Force," *Journal of Business Research* 57 (November 2004), pp. 1265–77.

19. Poujol and Tanner, "The Impact of Sales Contests on Salespeople's Customer Orientation"; Sean Valentine and Gary Fleischman, "Ethics Training and Businesspersons' Perceptions of Organizational Ethics," *Journal of Business Ethics* 52 (July 2004), pp. 391–409.

20. Norman L. Tolle, "Brochure Setting Forth Sales Incentive Plan Did Not Create Binding Contract," *Employee Benefit Plan Review* 61, no. 5 (2006), pp. 26–27.

21. Jim Humrichouse, personal interview.

22. Heather Fletcher, "Suddenlink Calls for Change," *Target Marketing* 33, no. 2 (February 2010), p. 10.

23. Eli Jones, Andrea L. Dixon, Lawrence B. Chonko, and Joseph P. Cannon, "Key Accounts and Team Selling: A Review, Framework, and Research Agenda," *Journal of Personal Selling & Sales Management* 25, no. 2 (2005), pp. 181–98.

CHAPTER 17

1. Mark Veverka, "It's Too Early to Hit Restart on Dell Shares," *Barron's* 88, no. 16 (April 21, 2008), p. 28; "HP Expects to Pass IBM as IT Revenue Leader This Year," *CRN*, November 27, 2006, p. 68.

2. John Graham, "Ask the Right Questions before Taking Any Sales Job," *American Salesman* 53, no. 2 (2008), pp. 20–25.

3. Graham, "Ask the Right Questions."

4. Kristen Scott, personal correspondence.

5. Alex Bement, personal correspondence.

6. George W. Dudley and Shannon L. Goodson, *Earning What You're Worth? The Psychology of Sales Call Reluctance*, 2nd ed. (Dallas: Behavioral Science Research Press, 2008).

7. Tom Day, personal interview.

8. Lucy Aitken, "Me and My Portfolio," *Campaign*, May 14, 2004, pp. 36–37; Denny E. McCorkle, Joe E. Alexander, James Reardon, and Nathan D. Kling, "Developing Self-Marketing Skills: Are Marketing Students Prepared for the Job Search?" *Journal of Marketing Education* 25 (December 2003), pp. 196–207.

9. Laura Huag, "Intimidation and Stress: All in a Day's Interview," *Financial Times*, November 28, 2005, p. 14.

10. Julia Chang, "Beating Burnout," *Sales and Marketing Management* 156, no. 3 (2004), pp. 47–48.

11. "Employee Satisfaction: Key to Recovery Success?" *HR Focus* 87, no. 4 (April 2010), pp. 1–5.

12. Susan Denny, personal interview.

13. Diane McGrath, "Continuous Learning," *Update*, Fourth Quarter 1998, p. 8.

14. Stefanie L. Boyer and Brian Lambert, "Take the Handcuffs off Sales Team Development with Self-Directed Learning," *T&D* 62, no. 11 (November 2008), pp. 62–67.

15. Lisa White, "Francisco Limas," *Foodservice Equipment & Supplies* 60, no. 7 (2007), p. 49.

16. Diane Powers, "Achieving Professional Sales Growth," *Advisor Today* 104, no. 5 (May 2009), pp. 53.

17. Jeffrey E. Lewin and Jeffrey K. Sager, "Salesperson Burnout: A Test of the Coping–Mediational Model of Social Support," *The Journal of Personal Selling & Sales Management* 28, no. 3 (Summer 2008), pp. 233–46.

18. Songqi Liu, Mo Wang, Yujie Zhan, and Junqi Shi, "Daily Work Stress and Alcohol Use: Testing Cross-Level Moderation Effects of Neuroticism and Job Involvement," *Personnel Psychology* 62, no. 3 (Autumn 2009), pp. 575–97; Anthony Urbaniak, "Managing Stress," *SuperVision* 67, no. 8 (2006), pp. 7–9.

19. Neil McAdam, "Situational Stress and Restriction of Stylistic Repertoire in High Potential Managerial Aspirants: Implications for the Implementation of the 'New Organization,'" *Journal of Management and Organization* 12, no. 1 (2006), pp. 40–67.

20. Richard G. McFarland, "Crisis of Conscience: The Use of Coercive Sales Tactics and Resultant Felt Stress in the

Salesperson," *Journal of Personal Selling & Sales Management* 23, no. 4 (2003), pp. 311–31.

21. Ted Howell, personal correspondence, March 4, 2008; used with permission.

22. Lewin and Sager, "Salesperson Burnout"; Praveen Aggarwal, John F. Tanner Jr., and Stephen B. Castleberry, "Factors Associated with Propensity to Leave the Organization: A Study of Salespeople," *Marketing Management Journal* 14, no. 1 (2004), pp. 90–102.

23. Eric Ruiz, personal interview; used with permission.

GLOSSARY

ABC analysis Evaluating the importance of an account. The most important is an A account, the second most important is a B account, and the least important is a C account.

accommodating mode Resolving conflict by being unassertive and highly cooperative. When using this approach, people often neglect their own needs and desires to satisfy the concerns of the other party.

account opportunity Another term for the sales potential dimensions of the *sales call allocation grid*.

account share See *customer share*.

acknowledge method Responding to an objection by letting the buyer talk, acknowledging that you heard the concern, and then moving on to another topic without trying to resolve the concern.

active listening Process in which the listener attempts to draw out as much information as possible by actively processing information received and stimulating the communication of additional information.

activity goals Behavioral objectives, such as the number of calls made in a day.

activity quota A type of quota that sets minimal behavioral expectations for a salesperson's activities. Used when the sales cycle is long and sales are few. Controls activities of salespeople.

adaptive planning The development of alternative paths to the same goal in a negotiation session.

adaptive selling Approach to personal selling in which selling behaviors and approaches are altered during a sales interaction or across customer interactions, based on information about the nature of the selling situation.

administrative law Laws established by local, state, or federal regulatory agencies, such as the Federal Trade Commission or the Food and Drug Administration.

advantages Reasons why a feature would be important to someone.

agenda List of what will be discussed, and in what sequence, in a negotiation session.

agent Person who acts in place of his or her company. See also *manufacturers' agents*.

aggressive Sales style that controls the sales interaction but often does not gain commitment because it ignores the customer's needs and fails to probe for information.

always a share A buyer who will always allocate only a share to each vendor, never giving one vendor all of the business. See also *lost for good*.

ambush negotiating A win-lose tactic used by a buyer at the beginning of, or prior to, negotiations when the seller does not expect this approach.

amiable Category in the social style matrix; describes people who like cooperation and close relationships. Amiables are low on assertiveness and high on responsiveness.

analogy Drawing a parallel between one thing and another.

analysis paralysis When a salesperson prefers to spend practically all his or her time analyzing the situation and gathering information instead of making sales calls.

analytical Category in the social style matrix; describes people who emphasize facts and logic. Analyticals are low on assertiveness and responsiveness.

annual spend The amount that is spent with each vendor and for what products.

application form Preprinted form completed by a job applicant.

articulation The production of recognizable speech.

assertive Sales manner that stresses responding to customer needs while being self-confident and positive.

assertiveness Dimension of the social style matrix that assesses the degree to which people have opinions on issues and publicly make their positions clear to others.

assessment center Central location for evaluating job candidates.

attitudinal loyalty An emotional attachment to a brand, company, or salesperson.

automatic replenishment (AR) A form of just-in-time inventory management where the vendor manages the customer's inventory, and automatically ships and stocks products at the customer's location based on mutually agreed-upon standards.

avoiding mode Resolving conflict in an unassertive and uncooperative manner. In this mode people make no attempt to resolve their own needs or the needs of others.

awareness The first phase in the development of a buyer–seller relationship, in which salespeople locate and qualify prospects and buyers consider various sources of supply.

backdoor selling Actions by one salesperson that go behind the back of a purchaser to directly contact other members of the buying center.

balance sheet method Attempts to obtain commitment by asking the buyer to think of the pros and cons of the various alternatives; often referred to as the Ben Franklin method.

balanced presentation Occurs when the salesperson shows all sides of the situation—that is, is totally honest.

banner advertising Ads placed at the top, sides, or bottom of a Web page, encouraging the viewer to visit a different Web site.

barriers Buyer's subordinates who plan and schedule interviews for their superiors; also called screens.

behavioral loyalty The purchase of the same product from the same vendor over time.

benchmarking A process of comparing your activities and performance with those of the best organization or individual in order to improve.

benefit How a particular feature will help a particular buyer.

benefit opening Approach in which the salesperson focuses on the prospect's needs by stating a benefit of the product or service.

benefit summary method Obtaining commitment by simply reminding the prospect of the agreed-on benefits of the proposal.

bird dog Individual who, for a fee, will provide the names of leads for the salesperson; also called a spotter.

blitz Canvassing method in which a large group of salespeople attempt to make calls on all prospective businesses in a given geographic territory on a specified day.

body language Nonverbal signals communicated through facial expressions, arms, hands, and legs.

bonus Lump-sum incentive payment based on performance.

boomerang method A method of objection handling where the reason for objecting is turned into a reason to buy or move to the next phase.

bottom-up forecasting Forecast compiled by adding up each salesperson's forecast for total company sales.

bounce-back card Card returned from a lead that requests additional information.

boundary-spanning employees Employees who cross the organizational boundary and interact with customers or vendors.

brainstorming session Meeting in which people are allowed to creatively explore different methods of achieving goals.

bribes Payments made to buyers to influence their purchase decisions.

browbeating Negotiation strategy in which buyers attempt to alter the selling team's enthusiasm and self-respect by making unflattering comments.

budget bogey Negotiation strategy in which one side claims that the budget does not allow for the solution proposed; also called budget limitation tactic.

budget limitation tactic See *budget bogey*.

business defamation Making unfair or untrue statements to customers about a competitor, its products, or its salespeople.

buyer's remorse The insecurity a buyer feels about whether the choice was a wise one; also called postpurchase dissonance.

buying center Informal, cross-department group of people involved in a purchase decision.

buying community Small, informal group of people in similar positions who communicate regularly, often both socially and professionally.

buying signals Nonverbal cues given by the buyer that indicate the buyer may be ready to commit; also called closing cues.

canned sales pitch A scripted sales pitch to follow without deviation.

cap A limit placed on a salesperson's earnings.

capital equipment Major purchases made by a business, such as computer systems, that are used by the business for several years in its operations or production process.

cash discount Price discount given for early payment in cash.

center-of-influence method Prospecting method wherein the salesperson cultivates well-known, influential people in the territory who are willing to supply lead information.

champion Person who works for the buying firm in the areas most affected by the proposed change and works with the salesperson for the success of the proposal; also called advocate or internal salesperson.

change agent Person who is a cause of change in an organization.

circular routing Method of scheduling sales calls that includes using circular patterns from the home base in order to cover the territory.

closed questions Questions that can be answered with a word or short phrase.

closing Common term for obtaining commitment, which usually refers only to asking for the buyer's business.

closing cues See *buying signals*.

cloverleaf routing Method of scheduling sales calls that involves using loops to cover different portions of the territory on different days or weeks; on a map it should resemble a cloverleaf.

coach Someone in a buying organization who can advise a salesperson.

cold call See *cold canvass method.*

cold canvass method Prospecting method in which a sales representative tries to generate leads for new business by calling on totally unfamiliar organizations; also called cold calls.

collaborating mode Resolving conflict by seeking to maximize the satisfaction of both parties and hence truly reach a win–win solution.

collateral Collection of documents that are designed to generate sales, and include such items as brochures, sales flyers and fact sheets, and short success stories.

collusion Agreement among competitors, made after contacting customers, concerning their relationships with customers.

combination plan Compensation plan that provides salary and commission; offers the greatest flexibility for motivating and controlling the activities of salespeople.

commission Incentive payment for an individual sale; often a percentage of the sale price.

commission base Unit of analysis used to determine commissions—for example, unit sales, dollar sales, or gross margin.

commission rate Percentage of base paid or the amount per base unit paid in a commission compensation plan—for example, a percentage of dollar sales or an amount per unit sold.

commitment The fourth stage in the development of a buyer–seller relationship in which the buyer and seller have implicitly or explicitly pledged to continue the relationship for an extended period.

common law Legal precedents that arise out of court decisions.

comparative cost–benefit analysis A comparison of the buyer's current situation's costs with the value of the seller's proposed solution. Can also be a comparison of the seller's product with a competitor's product.

compensation method Method used to respond helpfully to objections by agreeing that the objection is valid, but then proceeding to show any compensating advantages.

competence Whether the salesperson knows what he or she is talking about.

competing mode Resolving conflict in an assertive and noncooperative manner.

complacency The assumption that the business is yours and will always be yours.

compliment opening Approach in which the salesperson begins the sales call by complimenting the buyer in some fashion.

compromising mode Resolving conflict by being somewhat cooperative and somewhat assertive. People using this approach attempt to find a quick, mutually acceptable solution that partially satisfies both parties.

concession Agreement of one party in a negotiation meeting to change his or her position in some fashion.

conspiracy Agreement among competitors, made prior to contacting customers, concerning their relationships with customers.

contract to sell Offer made by a salesperson that received an unqualified acceptance by a buyer.

conventional résumé Form of life history organized by type of work experience.

conversion goals Measures of salesperson efficiency.

conversion ratio Similar to a batting average; calculated by dividing performance results by activity results (for example, dividing the number of sales by the number of calls).

corporate culture The values and beliefs held by a company and expressed by senior management.

creativity The trait of having imagination and inventiveness and using it to come up with new solutions and ideas.

credibility The characteristic of being perceived by the buyer as believable and reliable.

credibility statement A description of the seller and his or her company, offered to buyers to show that the seller can meet their needs.

credulous person standard Canadian law stating that a company is liable to pay damages if advertising and sale presentation claims and statements about comparisons with competitive products could be misunderstood by a reasonable person.

creeping commitment Purchase decision process that arises when decisions made early in the process have significant influence on decisions made later in the process.

cross-selling Similar to full-line selling except that the additional products sold are not directly associated with the initial products.

cultural relativism A view that no culture's ethics are superior to those of another culture's.

cumulative discount Quantity discount for purchases over a period of time; the buyer is allowed to add up all the purchases to determine the total quantity and the total quantity discount.

customer benefit proposition Statement showing how a product addresses the buyer's specific needs.

customer lifetime value (CLV) The sum of the customer's purchases over its entire life.

customer orientation Selling approach based on keeping the customer's interests paramount.

customer relationship management (CRM) A system to organize information about customers, their needs, company information, and sales information.

customer satisfaction Fulfillment of the buyer's expectations and needs.

customer service rep (CRP) Inbound salesperson who handles customer concerns.

customer share The percentage of business received from a company's accounts. Also called account share or share of wallet.

customer-centric Process of making the customer the center of everything that the selling firm does. See also *customer orientation*.

customer value proposition (also called value proposition) The way in which a salesperson's product or service will meet the prospect's needs and how that is different from the offerings of competitors, especially the next-best-alternative.

customized presentation Presentation developed from a detailed and comprehensive analysis or survey of the prospect's needs that is not canned or memorized in any fashion.

data mining The use of artificial intelligence and statistical tools to discover hidden insights in the volumes of data in a database.

databases Information about leads, prospects, and customers.

deception Unethical practice of withholding information or telling white lies.

deciders Buying center members who make the final selection of the product to purchase.

decoding Communication activity undertaken by a receiver interpreting the meaning of the received message.

dependability The act of the salesperson living up to promises made; is not something a salesperson can demonstrate immediately.

derived demand Situation in which the demand for a producer's goods is based on what its customers sell.

diagnostic feedback Information given to a salesperson indicating how he or she is performing.

digital collateral management Systems that archive, catalog, and retrieve digital media and text. Used by sales people to create presentation.

direct denial Method of answering objections in which the salesperson makes a relatively strong statement indicating the error the prospect has made.

direct request method Act of attaining commitment by simply asking for it in a straightforward statement.

disguised interview Discussion between an applicant and an interviewer in which the applicant is unaware that the interviewer is evaluating the applicant for the position.

dissolution The process of terminating the relationship; can occur because of poor performance, clash in culture, change in needs, and other factors.

distribution channel Set of people and organizations responsible for the flow of products and services from the producer to the ultimate user.

document cameras Cameras similar to traditional overhead projectors in their ability to display transparencies. However, because they are essentially cameras, document cameras are also capable of displaying any three-dimensional object without the use of a transparency. Also called *visual presenters*.

draw Advance from the company to a salesperson made against future commissions.

driver Category in the social style matrix; describes task-oriented people who are high on assertiveness and low on responsiveness.

economic influencer Someone who is concerned about the financial aspects of a purchase decision.

efficient consumer response (ECR) Distribution system that drives inventory to the lowest possible levels, increases the frequency of shipping, and automates ordering and inventory control processes without the problems of stockouts and higher costs.

80–20 listening rule A guideline that suggests salespeople should listen 80 percent of the time and talk 20 percent of the time.

electronic data interchange (EDI) Computer-to-computer linkages between suppliers and buyers for information sharing about sales, production, shipment, and receipt of products.

electronic whiteboard A digital version of an easel.

e-missives Timely, useful information that a seller provides to a buyer. This information might have nothing to do with the seller or the seller's product. The goal is to help make friends with the buyer and cement the relationship.

emotional intelligence The ability to effectively understand and use your own emotions and those of people with whom you interact. Includes four aspects: (1) knowing your own feelings and emotions as they are happening, (2) controlling your emotions so you do not act impulsively, (3) recognizing your customer's emotions (called empathy), and (4) using your emotions to interact effectively with customers.

emotional needs Organizational and/or personal needs that are associated with some type of personal reward and gratification for the person buying the product.

emotional outburst tactic Negotiation strategy in which one party attempts to gain concessions by resorting to a display of strong emotion.

encoding Communication activity undertaken by a sender translating his or her thought into a message.

end users Businesses that purchase goods and services to support their own production and operations.

endless-chain method Prospecting method whereby a sales representative attempts to get at least one additional lead from each person he or she interviews.

e-selling Utilizing e-mail to generate leads.

ethical imperialism The view that the ethical standards that apply locally or in one's home country should be applied to everyone's behavior around the world.

ethics Principles governing the behavior of an individual or a group.

ethics review board A group of experts inside and outside the company who are responsible for reviewing ethics policies, investigating allegations of unethical behavior, and acting as a sounding board for employees.

exclusive sales territories Method that uses a prospect's geographic location to determine whether a salesperson can sell to that prospect.

excuses Concerns expressed by the buyer that are intended to mask the buyer's true objections.

executive briefing center Presentation rooms set aside to highlight a company's products and capabilities.

executive summary In a written proposal, a summary of one page or less that briefly describes the total cost minus total savings, the problem to be solved, and the proposed solution.

expansion The third phase in the development of a relationship, in which it takes a significant effort to share information and further investigate the potential relationship benefits.

expert system Computer program that mimics a human expert.

exploration The second phase in the development of a relationship, in which both buyers and sellers explore the potential benefits and costs associated with the relationship.

expressed warranty Warranty specified through oral or written communications.

expressive Category in the social style matrix; describes people who are both competitive and approachable. They are high on assertiveness and responsiveness.

extranet Secure Internet-based network connecting buyers and suppliers.

FAB When salespeople describe the features, advantages (why that feature is important), and benefits of their product or service.

face A person's desire for a positive identity or self-concept.

False Claims Act An 1863 law encouraging citizens to press claims against vendors that sell fraudulently.

feature (1) Quality or characteristic of the product or service. (2) Putting a product on sale with a special display and featuring the product in advertising.

feature dumping Talking about lots of features of little interest to the customer and wasting the buyer's time.

FEBA A method of describing a product or service where salespeople mention the feature, provide evidence that the feature actually does exist, explain the benefit (why that feature is important to the buyer), and then ask whether the buyer agrees with the value of the feature and benefit.

feedback See *diagnostic feedback.*

feel–felt–found method A method of objection handling where the salesperson acknowledges how the buyer feels, then relates how someone else felt the same but found that the objection was misguided.

felt stress Persistent and enduring psychological distress brought about by job demands or constraints encountered in the work environment.

field sales manager First-level manager.

field salespeople Salespeople who spend considerable time in the customer's place of business, communicating with the customer face-to-face.

field support rep Telemarketer who works with field salespeople and does more than prospect for leads.

FOB destination The seller has title until the goods are received at the destination.

FOB factory The buyer has title when the goods leave the seller's facility.

focus of dissatisfaction The person in the organization who is most likely to perceive problems and dissatisfactions; leads to the focus of power.

focus of power The person in the organization who can approve, prevent, or influence action.

focus of receptivity The person in the organization who will listen receptively and provide a seller with valuable information; leads to the focus of dissatisfaction.

follow-up Activity that a salesperson performs after commitment is achieved.

Foreign Corrupt Practices Act Law that governs the behavior of U.S. business in foreign countries; restricts the bribing of foreign officials.

forestall To resolve objections before buyers have a chance to raise them.

free on board (FOB) See *FOB destination* and *FOB factory.*

friendly silent questioning stare (FSQS) The act of silently waiting to encourage buyers to elaborate or explain more fully what their concern is.

full-line selling Selling the entire line of associated products.

functional relationship Series of market exchanges between a buyer and a seller, linked together over time. These relationships are characterized as win–lose relationships.

functional résumé Life history that reverses the content and titles of a conventional résumé and is organized by what a candidate can do or has learned rather than by types of experience.

gatekeepers Buying center members who influence the buying process by controlling the flow of information and/or limiting the alternatives considered. Sometimes called barriers or screens.

geographic salesperson Salesperson assigned a specific geographic territory in which to sell all the company's products and services.

good guy–bad guy routine Negotiation strategy in which one team member acts as the "good guy" while another team member acts as the "bad guy." The goal of the strategy is to have the opposing team accept the good guy's proposal to avoid the consequences of the bad guy's proposal.

go-to-market strategies The various options that firms have to sell their products. Examples include the Internet, franchises, telemarketers, agents, value added resellers, field salespeople, and so on.

greeter Interviewer who greets the applicant and may conduct a disguised interview.

gross margin quota Minimum levels of acceptable profit or gross margin performance.

group interview Similar to panel interview but includes several candidates as well as several interviewers.

halo effect How one does in one thing changes a person's perceptions about other things one does.

handouts Written documents provided to buyers before, during, or after a meeting to help them remember what was said.

honesty Combination of truthfulness and sincerity; highly related to dependability.

house accounts Accounts assigned to a sales executive rather than to the specific salesperson responsible for the territory containing the account.

implication questions Questions that logically follow one or more problem questions (in SPIN); designed to help the prospect recognize the true ramifications of the problem.

implied warranty Warranty that is not expressly stated through oral or written communication but is still an obligation defined by law.

impression management Activities in which salespeople engage to affect and manage the buyer's impression of them.

inbound Salespeople or customer service reps who respond to calls placed to the firm by customers rather than placing calls out to customers.

inbound telemarketing Use of the telephone, usually with a toll-free number, that allows leads and/or customers to call for additional information or to place an order.

incentive pay Compensation based on performance.

indirect denial method Method used to respond to objections in which the salesperson denies the objection but attempts to soften the response by first agreeing with the prospect that the objection is an important one.

inflection Tone of voice.

influencers Buying center members inside or outside an organization who directly or indirectly influence the buying process.

influential adversaries Individuals in the buyer's organization who carry great influence and are opposed to the salesperson's product or service.

initiator The person who starts the buying process.

inside salespeople Salespeople who work at their employer's location and interact with customers by telephone or letter.

integrated marketing communications Coordinated communications programs that exploit the strengths of various communication vehicles to maximize the total impact on customers.

internal partnerships Partnering relationships between a salesperson and another member of the same company for the purpose of satisfying customer needs.

interview Personal interactions between candidates and job recruiters for the purpose of evaluating job candidates.

intimate zone That physical space around a buyer that is reserved primarily for a person's closest relationships. See also *social zone, public zone,* and *personal zone.*

introduction opening Approach method in which salespeople simply state their names and the names of their companies.

inventory turnover Measure of how efficiently a retailer manages inventory; calculated by dividing net sales by inventory.

invitation to negotiate The initiation of an interaction, usually a sales presentation, that results in an offer.

just-in-time (JIT) inventory control Planning system for reducing inventory by having frequent deliveries planned just in time for the delivered products to be assembled into the final product.

key accounts Large accounts, usually generating more than a specified amount in revenue per year, that receive special treatment.

kickbacks Payments made to buyers based on the amount of orders they place for a salesperson's products or services.

knowledge management technology Information technology that captures knowledge from people, organizes that knowledge, and makes it available to others.

KSAs Acronym for knowledge, skills, and abilities; the package that a candidate offers an employer.

lead A potential prospect; a person or organization that may have the characteristics of a true prospect.

lead management system The part of the lead process in which salespeople carefully analyze the relative value of each lead.

lead qualification system A process for qualifying leads.

lead user Company that faces and resolves needs months or years ahead of the rest of the marketplace.

leapfrog routing Method of scheduling calls that requires the identification of clusters of customers; visiting these clusters and "leaping" over single, sparsely located accounts should minimize travel time from the sales office to customers.

life-cycle costing Method for determining the cost of equipment or supplies over their useful life.

likability Behaving in a friendly manner and finding a common ground between the buyer and seller.

lost for good A buyer who gives all business to one vendor is considered lost for good for all of the out-suppliers because the buyer has cemented this relationship for a long period of time. See also *always a share*.

loudness Speech characterized by high volume and intensity.

lowballing Negotiation strategy in which one party voices agreement and then raises the cost of that agreement in some way.

lubrication Small sums of money or gifts, typically paid to officials in foreign countries, to get the officials to do their jobs more rapidly.

major sale Sale that involves a long selling cycle, a large customer commitment, an ongoing relationship, and large risks for the buyer if a bad decision is made.

manipulation Practice by a salesperson to eliminate or reduce the buyer's choice unfairly.

manufacturers' agents Independent businesspeople who are paid a commission by a manufacturer for all products and services the agents sell.

market exchange Relationship that involves a short-term transaction between a buyer and a seller that do not expect to be involved in future transactions with each other.

material requirements planning (MRP) Planning system for reducing inventory levels by forecasting sales, developing a production schedule, and ordering parts and raw materials with specific delivery dates.

merchandise market A form of exhibition or trade show used in fashion industries for manufacturers to sell products to retailers.

minimum call objective The minimum that a salesperson hopes to accomplish in an upcoming sales call.

minimum position Negotiation objective that states the absolute minimum level the team is willing to accept.

missionary salespeople Salespeople who work for a manufacturer and promote the manufacturer's products to other firms. Those firms buy products from distributors or other manufacturers, not directly from the salesperson's firm.

modified rebuy Purchase decision process associated with a customer who has purchased the product or service in the past but is interested in obtaining additional information.

MRO supplies Minor purchases made by businesses for maintenance and repairs, such as towels and pencils.

multichannel strategy The process of a firm using various go-to-market strategies at the same time.

multilevel selling Strategy that involves using multiple levels of company employees to call on similar levels in an account; for example, the VP of sales might call on the VP of purchasing.

multiple-sense appeals Method of attracting as many of the senses (hearing, sight, touch, taste, and smell) as possible.

mutual investment Tangible investments in the relationship by both parties (seller and buyer).

national account manager (NAM) Sales executive responsible for managing and coordinating sales efforts on a single account nationwide.

need payoff questions Questions that ask about the usefulness of solving the problem.

negative referral A customer who tells others about how poorly you or your product performed.

negotiation Decision-making process through which buyers and sellers resolve areas of conflict and arrive at agreements.

negotiation jujitsu Negotiation response in which the attacked person or team steps away from the opponent's attack and then directs the opponent back to the issues being discussed.

net present value (NPV) The investment minus the net value today of future cash inflows (discounted back to their present value today at the firm's cost of capital).

networking Establishing connections to other people and then using those networks to generate leads, gather information, generate sales, and so on.

new task Purchase decision process associated with the initial purchase of a product or service.

nibbling Negotiation strategy in which the buyer requests a small extra or add-on after the deal has been closed. Compared with *lowballing*, a nibble is a much smaller request.

noises Sounds unrelated to the message being exchanged between a salesperson and a customer.

nonverbal communication Nonspoken forms of expression—body language, space, and appearance—that communicate thoughts and emotions.

North America industry classification system (NAICS) A uniform classification system for all businesses for all countries in North America.

objection Concern or question raised by the buyer.

offer Specific statement by a seller outlining what the seller will provide and what is expected from the buyer.

office scanning Activity in which the salesperson looks around the prospect's environment for relevant topics to talk about.

open questions Questions for which there are no simple yes–no answers.

open-door policy General management technique that allows subordinates to bypass immediate managers and take concerns straight to upper management when the subordinates feel a lack of support from the immediate manager.

opening A method designed to get the prospect's attention and interest quickly and make a smooth transition into the next part of the presentation. Examples include introduction, product, question, referral, and so on.

opening position The initial proposal of a negotiating session.

opportunity cost The return a buyer would have earned from a different use of the same investment capital.

optimistic call objective The most optimistic outcome the salesperson thinks could occur in a given sales call.

orders Written orders that become contracts when they are signed by an authorized representative of a salesperson's company.

original equipment manufacturer (OEM) Business that purchases goods (components, subassemblies, raw and processed materials) to incorporate into products it manufactures.

outbound Salespeople, customer service reps, prospectors, account managers, and field support telemarketers who place phone calls out to customers.

outbound telemarketing Using the telephone to generate and qualify leads to determine whether they are truly prospects; also used to secure orders and provide customer contact.

outlined presentation Systematically arranged presentation that outlines the most important sales points. Often includes the necessary steps for determining the prospect's needs and for building goodwill at the close of the sale.

panel interview Job interview conducted by more than one person.

pass-up method A method of handling objections that essentially entails not handling the objection but ignoring it.

payback period Length of time it takes for the investment cash outflows to be returned in the form of cash inflows or savings.

performance feedback A type of feedback that salespeople often get from their supervisors that focuses on the seller's actual performance during a sales call.

performance goals Goals relating to outcomes, such as revenue.

personal selling Interpersonal communication process in which a seller uncovers and satisfies the needs of a buyer to the mutual, long-term benefit of both parties.

personal zone That physical space around a buyer that is reserved for close friends and those who share special interests. See also *public zone, social zone,* and *intimate zone.*

persuasion Practice by a salesperson designed to influence the buyer's decision, not manipulate it. See also *manipulation.*

pioneer selling Selling a new and different product, service, or idea. In these situations the salesperson usually has difficulty establishing a need in the buyer's mind.

pipeline analysis A process for identifying and managing sales opportunities; also called opportunity management.

portfolio Collection of visual aids that can be used to enhance communication during a sales call.

postcard pack Cards that provide targeted information from a number of firms; this pack is mailed to prospective buyers.

postpone method Objection response technique in which the salesperson asks permission to answer the question at a later time.

postpurchase dissonance See *buyer's remorse.*

preferred supplier Supplier that is assured a large percentage of the buyer's business and will get the first opportunity to earn new business.

prequalification Determination by firms whether leads are qualified before turning them over to the field sales force.

price discrimination Situation in which a seller gives unjustified special prices, discounts, or special services to some customers and not to others.

primary call objective Actual goal the salesperson hopes to achieve in an upcoming sales call.

prime selling time Time of day at which a salesperson is most likely to be able to see a customer.

privacy laws Laws that limit the amount of information that a firm can obtain about a consumer and specify how that information can be used or shared.

probing method Method to obtain commitment in which the salesperson initially uses the direct request method and, if unsuccessful, uses a series of probing questions designed to discover the reason for the hesitation.

problem questions Questions about specific difficulties, problems, or dissatisfactions that the prospect has.

producer Firm that buys goods and services to manufacture and sell other goods and services to its customers.

product opening Approach in which the salesperson actually demonstrates the product features and benefits as soon as he or she walks up to the prospect.

profit margin The net profit the reseller makes, expressed as a percentage of sales.

profit quota Minimum levels of acceptable profit or gross margin performance.

promoters Your most loyal customers who not only keep buying from you but also urge their friends and associates to do the same.

prospect A lead that is a good candidate for buying what the salesperson is selling.

prospecting The process of locating potential customers for a product or service.

public zone That physical space around a person in which listening to speeches and interacting with passersby is comfortable for that person. See also *personal zone, intimate zone,* and *social zone.*

push money See *spiffs.*

qualifying a lead The process of determining whether a lead is in fact a prospect.

quantifying the solution Showing the prospect that the cost of the proposal is offset by added value.

question opening Beginning the conversation with a question or stating an interesting fact in the form of a question.

quick response (QR) system System of minimizing order quantities to the lowest level possible while increasing the speed of delivery to drive inventory turnover; accomplished by prepackaging certain combinations of products.

quota Quantitative level of performance for a specific time period.

rapport Close, harmonious relationship founded on mutual trust.

rate of change The speed at which change is occurring; a critical element to consider about change.

rational needs Organizational and/or personal needs that are directly related to product performance.

reciprocity Special relationship in which two companies agree to buy products from each other.

red herring A minor point brought up to distract the other side from the main issue being negotiated.

references People who know an applicant for a position and can provide information about that applicant to the hiring company.

referral event Gatherings designed to allow current customers to introduce prospects to the salesperson in order to generate leads.

referral method Method of helpfully responding to objections in which the salesperson shows how others held similar views before trying the product or service.

referral opening Approach in which the name of a satisfied customer or friend of the prospect is used at the beginning of a sales call.

referred lead Name of a lead provided by either a customer or a prospect of the salesperson.

relational partnership Long-term business relationship in which the buyer and seller have a close, trusting relationship but have not made significant investments in the relationship. These relationships are characterized as win–win relationships.

relationship marketing Marketing that seeks to win customers by building the right type of relationship desired by those customers.

relationship-specific assets Resources that are specific to a relationship and cannot easily be transferred to another one.

request for proposal (RFP) Statement issued by a potential buyer desiring bids from several potential vendors for a product. RFPs often include specifications for the product, desired payment terms, and other information helpful to the bidder. Also called request for bids or request for quotes.

requirements Conditions that must be satisfied before a purchase can take place.

resale price maintenance Contractual term in which a producer establishes a minimum price below which distributors or retailers cannot sell their products.

resellers Businesses, typically distributors or retailers, that purchase products for resale.

response time The time between sending a message and getting a response to it.

responsiveness The degree to which people react emotionally when they are in social situations. One of the two dimensions in the social style matrix.

return on investment (ROI) Net profits (or savings) expected from a given investment, expressed as a percentage of the investment.

revenue quota The minimum amount of sales revenue necessary for acceptable performance.

reverse auction An auction, but instead of a seller offering a product and buyers bidding, a buyer offers a contract and sellers bid; prices fall as sellers compete to win the sale.

revisit method Process of responding to objections by turning the objection into a reason for acting now.

role ambiguity The degree to which a salesperson is not sure about the actions required in the sales role.

role conflict The extent to which the salesperson faces incompatible demands from two or more constituencies that he or she serves.

role overload A role (or job) demanding more than the person can perform.

role stress The psychological distress that may be a consequence of a salesperson's lack of role accuracy.

routine call patterns Method of scheduling calls used when the same customers are seen regularly.

routing Method of scheduling sales calls to minimize travel time.

salary Compensation paid periodically to an employee independently of performance.

sale The transfer of title to goods and services by the seller to the buyer in exchange for money.

sales asset management A system used to archive, catalog, and retrieve digital media and text.

sales call allocation grid Grid used to determine account strategy; the dimensions are the strength of the company's position with the account and the account's sales potential.

sales force–intensive organization Firms whose go-to-market strategy relies heavily on salespeople.

sales portals Online databases that include in one place many sources of information that the salesperson might need. Include items such as account data, competitor intelligence, and news about the industry, the company, and the economy.

sales puffery Exaggerated statements about the performance of products or services.

sales quota The minimum number of sales in units.

scope of change The extent or degree to which change affects an organization; a critical element to consider about change.

screens See *barriers.*

search engines The tools that individuals use to locate information on the Internet or on a specific Web site.

secondary call objectives Goals a salesperson hopes to achieve during a sales call that have somewhat less priority than the primary call objective.

seeding Sending the customer important and useful items or information prior to the meeting.

selective perception The act of hearing what we want to hear, not necessarily what the other person is saying.

selling center A team that consists of all people in the selling organization who participate in a selling opportunity.

selling deeper Selling more to existing customers.

services End-user purchases such as Internet and telephone connections, employment agencies, consultants, and transportation.

sexual harassment Unwelcome sexual advances, requests for sexual favors, and other, similar verbal (such as jokes) and nonverbal (such as graffiti) behaviors.

share of wallet See *customer share.*

simple cost–benefit analysis Simple listing of the costs and savings that a buyer can expect from an investment.

situation questions General data-gathering questions about background and current facts that are very broad in nature.

situational stress Short-term anxiety caused by a situational factor.

six sigma selling programs Programs designed to reduce errors introduced by the selling system.

small talk Talk about current news, hobbies, and the like that usually breaks the ice for the actual presentation.

sneak attack See *ambush negotiating.*

social networking Using Web sites to interact.

social style matrix Method for classifying customers based on their preferred communication style. The two dimensions used to classify customers are assertiveness and responsiveness.

social zone The physical space around a person in which business transactions and other impersonal relationships are comfortable for the person. See also *public zone, intimate zone,* and *personal zone.*

solo exchange Both the buyer and the seller pursue their own self-interests because they do not plan on doing business together again.

speaking–listening differential The difference between the 120-to-160-words-per-minute rate of speaking versus the 800-words-per-minute rate of listening.

spiffs (push money) Payments made by a producer to a reseller's salespeople to motivate the salespeople to sell the producer's products or services.

SPIN Logical sequence of questions in which a prospect's needs are identified. The sequence is situation questions, problem questions, implication questions, and need payoff questions.

spotter See *bird dog.*

standard industrial classification (SIC) A uniform classification system for an industry. The SIC system is being replaced by the new *North America industry classification system (NAICS).*

standard memorized presentation Carefully prepared sales story that includes all the key selling points arranged in the most effective order; often called a canned sales presentation.

statutory law Laws based on legislation passed by either state legislatures or Congress.

straight commission Compensation method of a certain amount per sale; plan includes a base and a rate but not a salary.

straight rebuy Purchase decision process involving a customer with considerable knowledge gained from having purchased the product or service a number of times.

straight salary Compensation method that pays a fixed amount of money for working a specified amount of time.

straight-line routing Method of scheduling sales calls involving straight-line patterns from the home base in order to cover the sales territory.

strategic account manager (SAM) A company executive who coordinates all the salespeople who call on an account throughout the nation or the world. Also called national account manager (NAM).

strategic partnership Long-term business relationship in which the buyer and seller have made significant investments to improve the profitability of both parties in the relationship. These relationships are characterized as win–win relationships.

strength of position Dimension of the sales call allocation grid that considers the seller's strength in landing sales at an account.

stress interview Any interview that subjects an applicant to significant stress; the purpose is to determine how the applicant handles stress.

submissive Selling style of salespeople who are often excellent socializers and like to spend a lot of time talking about nonbusiness activities. These people are usually reluctant to attempt to obtain commitment.

subordination Payment of large sums of money to officials to get them to do something that is illegal.

superior benefit method Type of compensation method of responding to an objection during a sales presentation that uses a high score on one attribute to compensate for a low score on another attribute.

supplier relationship management (SRM) The use of technology and statistics to identify important suppliers and opportunities for cost reduction, greater efficiency, and other benefits.

supply chain management (SCM) Set of programs undertaken to increase the efficiency of the distribution system that moves products from the producer's facilities to the end user.

systems integrator Outside vendor who has been delegated the responsibility for purchasing; has the authority to buy products and services from others.

target position Negotiation objective that states what the team hopes to achieve by the time the session is completed.

team selling Type of selling in which employees with varying areas of expertise within the firm work together to sell to the same account(s).

technical influencer A person who makes sure that a purchase meets technical requirements.

telemarketing Systematic and continuous program of communicating with customers and prospects via telephone and/or other person-to-person electronic media.

testimonial Statement, usually in the form of a letter, written by a satisfied customer about a product or service.

tests Personality or skills assessments used in assessing the match between a position's requirements and an applicant's personality or skills.

third-party-testimony method Method of responding to an objection during a sales presentation that uses a testimonial letter from a third party to corroborate a salesperson's assertions.

tickler file File or calendar used by salespeople to remind them when to call on specific accounts.

trade fair The European term for *trade show.*

trade salespeople Salespeople who sell to firms that resell the products rather than using them within their own firms.

trade secrets Information owned by a company that gives it a competitive advantage.

trade show Short exhibition of products by manufacturers and distributors.

trial balloon An idea floated without being actually offered.

trial close Questions the salesperson asks to take the pulse of the situation throughout a presentation.

trial order A small order placed by a buyer in order to test the product or the vendor. Not to be confused with trial close.

trust Firm belief or confidence in the honesty, integrity, and reliability of another person.

turnover (TO) An account is given to another salesperson because the buyer refuses to deal with the current salesperson.

24/7 service A phrase that highlights the fact that customers expect a selling firm to be available 24 hours a day, 7 days a week.

two-way communication Interpersonal communication in which both parties act as senders and receivers. Salespeople send messages to customers and receive feedback from them; customers send messages to salespeople and receive responses.

tying agreement Agreement between a buyer and a seller in which the buyer is required to purchase one product to get another.

Uniform Commercial Code (UCC) Legal guide to commercial practice in the United States.

upgrading Convincing the customer to use a higher-quality product or a newer product.

users Members of a buying center that ultimately will use the product purchased.

value The total benefit that the seller's products and services provide to the buyer. Also, the customer's perceived benefit received minus the selling price and minus the costs and hassles of buying.

value analysis Problem-solving approach for reducing the cost of a product while providing the same level of performance. See *quantifying the solution.*

variable call patterns A nonsystematic method that a salesperson occasionally uses for calling on accounts.

vendor analysis A formal method used by organizational buyers to summarize the benefits and needs satisfied by a supplier.

vendor loyalty Commitment of a buyer to a specific supplier because of the supplier's superior performance.

versatility A characteristic, associated with the social style matrix, of people who increase the productivity of social relationships by adjusting to the needs of the other party.

videoconferencing Meetings in which people are not physically present in one location but are connected via voice and video.

virtual sales call See *Webcasting.*

visual presenters See *document cameras.*

voice characteristics The rate of speech, loudness, pitch, quality, and articulation of a person's voice.

warranty Assurance by the seller that the goods will perform as represented.

Webcasting Videoconferencing in which the meeting is broadcast over the Internet.

Webiner Online seminar.

win–lose negotiating Negotiating philosophy in which the negotiator attempts to win all the important concessions and thus triumph over his or her opponent.

win–win negotiating Negotiating philosophy in which the negotiator attempts to secure an agreement that completely satisfies both parties.

win–win not yet negotiating A negotiation session in which the buying team achieves its goals while the selling team does not. However, the sellers expect to achieve their goals in the near future, thanks to the results of that negotiation session.

win–win relationship Type of relationship in which firms make significant investments that can improve profitability for both partners because their partnership has given them some strategic advantage over their competitors.

word picture Story or scenario designed to help the buyer visualize a point.

zoning Method of scheduling calls that divides a territory into zones. Calls are made in a zone for a specified length of time and then made in another zone for the same amount of time.

COMPANY INDEX

SUBJECT INDEX

impression management and, 205
legs and, 110
patterns in, 110–111
sending messages with, 111–113
space and physical contact and, 113–114
Nonverbal cues
explanation of, 108
indicating commitment readiness, 300
message delivery and, 98, 108
during sales presentations, 221–222
types of, 109–113
Nordstrom, Alfred, 145
North American industry classification system (NAICS), 164
Nurullah, Mohamed, 318
Nussbaum, Ken, 209
Nyaga, Gilbert N., EN-10
Nyden, Jeanette, 346

Oaks, Ken, 349
Obama, Barack, 136
Obama, Michelle, 89
Obermayer, James, 176
Objection response methods
acknowledgment as, 278–279
compensation as, 276–277
direct denial as, 274–275
explanation of, 273–274
indirect denial as, 275–276
postponement as, 279
referral as, 277
revisit as, 277–278
use of, 279–281
Objections
anticipation of, 268–269
evaluation of, 272
explanation of, 262
forestalling known concerns about, 269–271
listening to, 271–272
price, 281–283
related to needs, 264–265
related to price, 267, 281–284
related to product, 265–266
related to source, 266
related to time, 268
from tough customers, 284
truthfulness in dealing with, 272–273
when buyers raise, 263–264
when selling to group of buyers, 281
Obligations, 50
O'Donnell, Edward, 495, EN-12
Offer, 49
Office scanning, 208
Oh, Sejo, EN-9, EN-10
Olavarrieta, Sergio, EN-3
Olsztynski, Jim, EN-11
Onkvist, Sak, EN-2
Onvernah, Vincent, 495
Open communication, 103–104, 365
Open-door policies, 449
Opening position, 327
Openings, sales presentation, 207–208
Open questions, 212–213
Opportunity costs, 251, 267

Opportunity management, 418
Optimism, 19
Optimistic call objectives, 189
Oral agreements, 49
Orders
explanation of, 49
generating repeat, 385–387
Orem, Tina, 125
Organizational buying decisions. See also Purchasing
complexities of, 68–69
creeping commitment in, 71
individual needs of buying center members for, 80–82
individuals responsible for, 74–76
process of, 69–71
purchasing trends and, 82–87
supplier evaluation and choice and, 76–80
types of, 71–74
Organizational conflict of interest (OCI), 32
Organizational needs
economic criteria and, 77
quality criteria and, 78–79
service criteria and, 79–80
Organizations
codes of ethics of, 38
as information source, 184
knowledge of, 468–469
needs of, 469–470
precall information about, 181–183
relationships with salesperson's, 44–47
structure and culture of, 367
Original equipment manufacturers (OEMs)
buying decisions and, 73, 74
explanation of, 64–65
function of, 66
Orning, Russ, 192
Outbound salespeople, 454
Outbound telemarketing, 166
Outlined presentations, 128, 129
Ozer, Jan, EN-7

Page, Thomas J., Jr., EN-9
Pajunen, Kalle, 231
Palmatier, Robert W., 372, EN-9
Palmer, Jonathan, EN-1
Panagopoulos, Nikolas G., 463, 495
Panel interviews, 482
Paparoidamis, Nicholas G., 403, 463
Paperwork, 424–425
Pappas, James M., 463, EN-1
Parasuraman, A., EN-1
Pardo, Catherine, 147, 201, 463
Parinello, Anthony, 201
Park, Myung Hwan, 289
Parker, Shirley, 91
Parolo, Dario, 417
Partnership phases
commitment, 389–395
dissolution, 395–399
expansion, 384–389
exploration, 376–384
Partnerships. See also Relationships
characteristics of successful, 361–362
commitment to mutual gain in, 366

common goals in, 365–366
ethics in, 34–36
internal, 436–440
long-term, 376–399
management of, 357–359
model of building, 22–23
open communication in, 365
organizational support for, 366–367
relational, 355
with sales managers, 490–491
in sales organization, 15, 442–448
securing commitment in, 390–391
strategic, 355–357
technology for efficiency in, 359
trust in, 42, 362–365
Pass-up method, 278
Patterson, Eddy, EN-3
Paulraj, Antony, 97
Paulssen, Marcel, 97
Pavlovich, Tim, 64
Payback period, 250–251
Pearce, Lydia, 427, 429
Pearson, Leigh Ann, EN-11
Pederson, Evan, 124
Pelham, Alfred, EN-9
Pels, Jaqueline, 97
Penney, James Cash, 355
Penttinen, Esko, EN-1
Peppers, Don, EN-5
Perez, Evan, EN-3
Performance
feedback for, 132
goals for, 409–410
Performance evaluation
activity analysis for, 426
field sales managers' role in, 447–448
performance goals and, 426–427
postcall analysis for, 425–426
productivity and, 428
Performance quotas, 444–445
Perkins, Caroline, 42
Perlich, Claudia, 417
Permeh, Amir, 235
Perreault, William D., 147
Perry, John, EN-4
Personal attire, 114–116
Personal branding, 488
Personal development, 410
Personal selling. See also Adaptive selling; Selling
effects of, 128
ethics and, 33–40
explanation of, 5
flexibility of, 8
principles of, 5–7
reasons to learn about, 4–5
Personal space, 113–114
Personal zone, 113
Persuasion, 36
Petauhoff, Natalie, 385
Peters, Cara, EN-3
Peterson, J. Andrew, EN-6
Peterson, R., EN-7
Pettijohn, Charles E., 28, 61
Pettijohn, Linda S., 28, 61
Phillips, Joan M., 318

Photographs, 239, 241
Physical appearance
    first impressions and, 205
    as nonverbal communication, 114–115
    of salespeople, 115–116
Physical contact, 113–114
Piercy, Nigel F., 28, 97, 372, EN-1, EN-12
Pilgrim, Frank, 370
Pilgrim, Jackie, 370–371
Pilgrim, John, 370–371
Pinkard, Diane Marie, 125
Pinkham, Will, 409
Pioneer selling, 264
Pipeline analysis, 418
Pitt, Leyland, 125
Plank, Richard E., 28, 231, 372, EN-7
Pledger, Chris, 371
Plott, John, 421, EN-11
Plouffe, Christopher R., 147, EN-5, EN-9
Podesta, Connie, EN-8
Pollock, Todd, 291, 315, 484
Polonsky, Mark, 402
Pope, Jeff, 364
Popyk, Bob, EN-4
Porkka, Pasi, 147
Port, Michael, EN-2, EN-7
Porter, Constance Elise, 147
Portfolios, 241–242
Postcard pack, 162
Postpone method, 279
Postpurchase dissonance, 307
Posture, 113. See also Nonverbal
        communication
Poujol, F. Juliet, 28, EN 2, EN-10, EN-12
Poulin, Diane, EN-9
Power, Mike, 391, EN-11
PowerPoint (Microsoft), 243
Powers, Diane, EN-12
Powers, Thomas L., 147
Predmore, Carolyn E., EN-2
Preferred suppliers, 389
Prequalification, of leads, 169
Presentations. See Sales presentations
Price
    credit terms and, 295–297
    discounts and, 295–297
    objections related to, 267, 281–283
    presentation of, 297–298
    shipping costs and, 297
Price, Glenn R., 10, EN-1
Price discrimination, 53–54
Primary call objectives, 188–189
Prime selling time, 419
Pritchett, Lou, 14
Privacy laws, 54
Probing method
    to obtain commitment, 305–306
    to respond to objections, 273–274
Problem questions, 215
Problem/solution model, 220
Procurement Integrity Act, 32
Producers, 64
Productivity, 428, 457
Product opening, 207
Products
    buying decisions for, 70
    demonstration of, 244–245

evaluating performance of, 71
insuring proper use of, 378–379
knowledge of, 18, 131, 223–224
nature of selling, 16
objections related to, 265–266
servicing of, 386
upgrading, 388
vulnerable features of, 269–270
Product specialists, 453–454
Professional associations, 486–487
Profit, 9
Profit margin, 65, 252
Profit quotas, 444
Prohibition, 235
Promoters, 156
Proposals
    acquisition and analysis of, 70
    evaluation of, 70
    presentation of, 247
    request for, 246–247
    written, 237
Prospecting
    allocating time for, 419
    explanation of, 150
    importance of, 150
    overcoming reluctance for, 171–172
Prospecting directories, 164
Prospects. See also Customers
    ads and direct mail to obtain, 162
    appointments with, 204–210
    characteristics of good, 150–155
    cold calling to obtain, 165
    data mining and CRM systems to
        obtain, 164–165
    developing lists of, 164
    endless-chain method to obtain,
        157, 158
    expertise in methods to obtain,
        166–167
    identifying needs of, 210–218
    information sources about, 183–186
    Internet sources to obtain, 161–162
    leads to obtain, 169–171
    lists and directories to obtain, 164
    networking to obtain, 157–160
    offering value to, 218–222
    precall information about, 181–183
    sales letters to obtain, 167–168
    satisfied customers as leads to obtain,
        156–157
    seminars to obtain, 164
    shows, fairs and merchandise markets to
        obtain, 162–163
    social networking to obtain, 160–161
    sources for, 155
    spotters to obtain, 165
    telemarketing to obtain, 166
    use of proposals by, 247
    webinars to obtain, 164
Publicity, 8
Public sector
    as customers, 66–67
    selling to, 31–32, 51
Public speaking, 253
Public zone, 113
Pugatch, Courtney Beth, 176
Pullins, Ellen Bolman, 318, 433

Purchasing. See also Buying centers;
        Organizational buying decisions
    decisions regarding, 14–15
    diversity in, 78
    supplier relationship management
        and, 3–85
    supply chain management and, 82–83
    trends in, 82–87
Purchasing agents, as gatekeepers, 75–76
Push money, 53
Pyropoulou, Stavroula, 97

Quaddus, Mohammed, 177
Qualify the lead, 151–155. See also Leads
Quality, buying decisions based on, 78–79
Quantifying the solution, 248. See also
        Value analysis
Question opening, 207
Questions
    about buyer's needs, 211–217
    employment interview, 478, 479
    need payoff, 216
    open and closed, 212–213
    problem, 215
    situation, 214–215
    that signal readiness for commitment,
        298–299
Quick response (QR), 82, 252
Quintilion, 101
Quotas, 444–445

Rackham, Neil, 187, 192, 220, 352, EN-6,
        EN-7, EN-8, EN-9
Radin, Tara J., EN-2
Radio frequency identification (RFID), 259
Raghavan, Anita, 125, EN-4
Ragsdale, John, 416
Rai, Illiki, 311, EN-8
Raiffa, Howard, 328
Rajan, Bharath, 28, EN-1
Ramamurthy, Ram, 295, EN-8
Ramani, Girish, 231
Ramsey, Robert D., EN-4
Ramsower, Reagan, 416
Randall, Wesley S., EN-3
Rangarajan, Deva, 463, 495
Rapp, Adam, 318, EN-5, EN-8
Rapport, 208–210
Rasmusson, Erika, 468
Rate of change, 393
Rational needs, 77
Rauyruen, Papassapa, 372
Rawls, Margaret, 78
Read, Nicholas A. C., 231, EN-8
Reagan, William R., 147
Reardon, James, EN-12
Receptionists, 185–186
Reciprocity, 52
Recruitment
    challenges of, 470
    interviews for, 472–483
    process for, 471–473
Reday, Peter Alan, 97, EN-1
Reed, Eric, 174
Reed, Stanley, EN-7
References, employment, 472
Referral events, 156